To Harley: Give Lori the strength.
To Beluga: I'll always be sorry, Blue.
To Lori: You are the reason, Little Bird.

About the Author

Brian Schwab has officially been in the game industry since 1993. He got his first "Out of Memory" error two days after he bought his first computer, a Mattel Aquarius (which cost him 6 months of his allowance), when he was 10 years old. This allows him to truthfully state that he has been optimizing game code for over 25 years.

He spent almost a year living in Austin, Texas as a homeless man trying to get his first game job. Since then, he has worked at everything from a three-man studio to his current job at Sony Computer Entertainment of America, where he works as an AI/Gameplay Lead Programmer. He has also worked as a game designer for several products, including Lead Designer on two titles.

Over the years, he has created almost every type of game: educational, role playing, flight sim, a squad-based real-time strategy game, an arcade game, a fighter, a first-person shooter, and a sports franchise. He has found that no matter what the genre, there is always the challenge of creating good AI-controlled characters.

In addition to this book, he has also been the AI editor for *Game Gems* 6 and 7. He is a member of the AI Game Programmer's Guild, the AI Interface Standards Committee, and is active in the planning of the AIIDE conference.

Contents

Preface

There are not many books on general game programming, and even fewer on game artificial intelligence (AI) programming. This text will provide the reader with four principal elements that will extend the current library.

1. *A clear definition of "game AI."* Many books use a general or far too wide-sweeping meaning for the term *AI,* and as such, the reader never feels completely satisfied with the solutions provided. This lack of satisfaction may further the "mystical" nature of AI that pervades the common knowledge of both the general public and industry people.
2. *Genre-by-genre breakdown of AI elements and solutions.* Too many books rely on one type of game, or one narrow demonstration program. This text breaks apart the majority of the modern game genres and gives concrete examples of AI usage in actual released titles. By seeing the reasoning behind the different genre choices of AI paradigms, the reader will gain greater understanding of the paradigms themselves.
3. *Implemented code for the majority of commonly-used AI paradigms.* In the latter parts of the book, real code is given for each AI technique, both in skeletal form, and as part of a real-world example application. The code is broken down and fully discussed to help show the actual handling of the system.
4. *A discussion of future directions for improvement.* With each genre and AI technique, the text gives examples of ways the system could be extended. This is done by pointing out common AI failings in current and classic games, as well as by detailing ways in which systems could be optimized for space, speed, or some other limitation.

Introduction

The book is divided into a few major areas: theory and background, major genre divisions, AI techniques with code, and AI engine development concerns. Readers of the book should note that there might be some confusion if read from start to finish, since the genre chapters make mention of some of the AI techniques discussed later in the book. However, discussion of the AI techniques first would have made mention of game genre issues, so the current ordering was thought to be best.

Content Overview

Chapters 1–3 provides an overall look at game AI, covers the basic terminology that will be used throughout the book, looks at some of the underlying concepts of game AI, and dissects the parts of a game AI engine. Chapters 4–14 cover specific game genres and how they use the differing AI paradigms. Although the book cannot be all-inclusive (by detailing how each and every game "did it"), it does discuss the more common solutions to the problems posed by games of each genre. Chapters 15–21 provides the actual code implementations for the basic AI techniques, and Chapters 22–24 covers the more advanced ones. In the last four chapters, a variety of concepts and concerns are broken down, dealing with real game AI development: general design and development issues, distributed AI as an overall paradigm that can help with the organization of almost any AI engine, debugging AI systems, and the future of AI.

Audience

This book was written to provide game developers with the tools necessary to create modern game artificial intelligence (AI) engines, and to survey the capabilities of the differing techniques used in some current AI engines. AI programming is a very challenging aspect of game production, and although many books have been written on generic game-related data structures and coding styles, very few have been written specifically for this important and tech-heavy subject.

This book is specifically written for the professional game AI programmer, or the programmer interested in expanding his area of interest into AI. If you are having difficulties determining which techniques to use, have questions about, or need working code for the engine best suited for a particular game, this is the book for you. This book provides a clean, usable interface for a variety of useful game AI techniques. The book emphasizes primary decision-making paradigms, and as such does not delve into the important areas of pathfinding (at least, not directly; many of the techniques presented could be used to run a pathfinder) or perception, although they are discussed.

This book assumes a working knowledge of C++, the classical data structures, and a basic knowledge of object-oriented programming. The demonstration programs are written in Microsoft Visual C++® under the Windows® platform, but only the rendering is platform specific, and the rendering API used is the GLUT extension to OpenGL, so that you could easily port to another system if necessary. See the CD-ROM for information on GLUT and OpenGL.

After reading this book, you will be familiar with a good portion of the huge landscape of knowledge that a game AI programmer has to master. The genre discussions will supply the programmer with insights into how to build an AI system from start to finish, given the realities of the product and the schedule. The code in the book is generic enough to build almost any type of AI system and it provides clear ways to combine techniques into much more complex and usable game-specific AI engines.

1 Basic Definitions and Concepts

In This Chapter

- What Is Intelligence?
- What Is "Game AI"?
- What Game AI Is Not
- How this Definition Differs from that of Academic AI
- Applicable Mind Science and Psychology Theory
- Lessons from Robotics
- Summary

Welcome to *AI Game Engine Programming*. This book is meant to give the game artificial intelligence (AI) programmer the knowledge and tools needed to create AI engines for modern commercial games. What exactly do we mean by "game AI"? It turns out this isn't as straightforward a question as you would think.

First, the term "game" is somewhat hazy itself. A "game" could refer to a spoken ritual that a class full of kids might play or to a complex technological undertaking by our government for training purposes. For this book, we'll be referring to electronic video games exclusively, although some of the concepts that we'll cover would probably be applicable to board games, or other strategic competitive game-like activities.

Second, we come to the term "AI." Seeing as its foundations were created in the 1950s, the science of AI is relatively young. The usage of AI techniques within games is even more contemporary, because of the computation and storage-space limitations of earlier game machines (not to mention the simplistic nature of many early games). The field's immaturity means that the definition of game AI is not clear for most people, even those who practice game production. This chapter will define the term *game AI*, identify practices and techniques that are commonly mistaken for game AI, and discuss areas of future expansion. Later in the chapter, relevant concepts from other fields, including mind science, psychology, and robotics, will be discussed regarding game AI systems.

WHAT IS INTELLIGENCE?

The word intelligence is fairly nebulous. The dictionary will tell you it is the capacity to acquire and apply knowledge, but this is far too general. This definition, interpreted literally, could mean that your thermostat is intelligent. It acquires the knowledge that the room is too cold and applies what it learned by turning on the heater. The dictionary goes on to suggest that intelligence demonstrates the faculty of thought and reason. Although this is a little better (and more limiting; the thermostat has been left behind), it really just expands our definition problem by introducing two even more unclear terms, thought and reason. In fact, the feat of providing a true definition of intelligence is an old and harried debate that is far beyond the scope of this text. Thankfully, making good games does not require this definition.

Actually, this text will agree with our first dictionary definition, as it fits nicely with what we expect game systems to exhibit to be considered intelligent. For our purposes, an intelligent game agent is one that acquires knowledge about the world, and then acts on that knowledge. This is not to say that our notion of intelligence is completely reactive, since the "action" we might take is to build a complex plan for solving the game scenario. The quality and effectiveness of these actions then become a question of game balance and design.

WHAT IS "GAME AI"?

Let us start with a rigorous, academic definition of AI. In their seminal AI Bible, *Artificial Intelligence: A Modern Approach*, Russel and Norvig [Russel 95] say that AI is the creation of computer programs that emulate acting and thinking like a human, as well as acting and thinking rationally. This definition encompasses both the cognitive and the behavioral views of intelligence (by requiring emulation of both actions and thinking). It also includes, yet separates, the notions of rationality and "humanity" (because being human is sometimes far from rational, but is still considered intelligent; like running into a burning building to save your child).

In contrast, games don't require such a broad, all-encompassing notion of AI. Game AI is specifically the code in a game that makes the computer-controlled elements appear to make smart decisions when the game has multiple choices for a given situation, resulting in behaviors that are relevant, effective, and useful. Note the word "appear" in the last sentence. The AI-spawned behaviors in games are very *results*-oriented, and thus, we can say that the game world is primarily concerned with the behavioralist wing of AI science. We're really only interested with the responses that the system will generate, and don't really care how the system arrived at it. We care about how the system acts, not how it thinks. People playing the game don't care if the game is using a huge database of scripted decisions, is making directed searches of a decision tree, or is building an accurate knowledge base of its surroundings and making inferred choices based on logical rules. The proof is in the pudding as far as game AI goes.

Modern game developers also use the term AI in other ways. For instance:

- Some people refer to the behavioral mechanics of the game as AI. These elements should actually be thought of as *gameplay*, but any time the AI controlled agents do something, people tend to think of it as AI, even if it's using the exact mechanism that the human players use.
- Many people think of game AI primarily as animation selection. Once a game entity makes a decision as to *what* to do, animation selection then makes a lower level decision as to *how* (on a visual level) to perform the move. Say that your AI controlled baseball pitcher has decided to throw a curveball. The exact animation that he goes through performing that decision is animation selection. How does the windup go, where does he look, does he tip his hat, etc.? Perceptions are polled, and an intelligent contextual decision is made. But this kind of low-level decision making is much more short range than the kind of intelligence we are talking about. People that think of animation selection as AI tend to be working on games with very simple AI requirements, games that don't require heavily strategic solutions.
- Even the algorithms that govern movement and collision can sometimes fall under this label (if the game uses animation-driven movement, rather than physics-based methods).

In fact, the term "AI" is a broadly-used moniker in the game-development world. When discussing AI with someone else in the industry (or even within the company at which you work), it's important to know that you both agree on the meaning and scope of the term; miscommunication can occur if your notion of AI is vastly different from the other person's (be it simpler or more complex, or just at opposite ends of the responsibility spectrum). So, let's be clear. When this book refers to AI, it will use the rather narrow definition of character-based behavioral intelligence. We care only about the behavioral smarts exhibited by some character within the game (the main character, a camera, an overseeing "god," or any other agent within a game world).

In the old days, AI programming was more commonly referred to as "gameplay programming," because there really wasn't anything intelligent about the behaviors exhibited by the CPU-controlled characters. See Figure 1.1 for an overall game AI timeline.

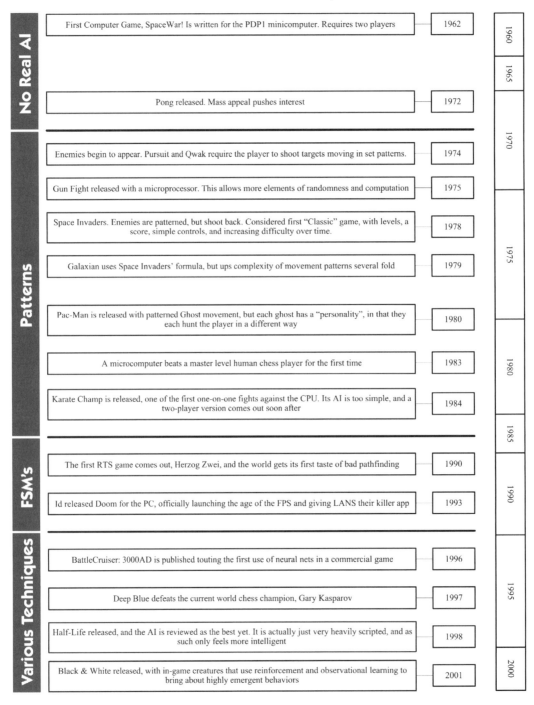

FIGURE 1.1 Game AI timeline.

In the early days of video gaming, most coders relied on patterns or some repetitive motions for their enemies (for example, *Galaga* or *Donkey Kong*), or they used enemies that barely moved at all but were vulnerable to attack only in certain "weak points" (like *R-Type*). The whole point of many of these early games was for the player to find the predetermined behavior patterns so that the player could easily beat that opponent (or wave of opponents) and move on to another. The extreme restraints of early processor speed and memory storage lead naturally to this type of game. Patterns could be stored easily, requiring minimal code to drive them, and required no calculation; the game simply moved the enemies around in the prescribed patterns, with whatever other behavior they exhibited layered on top (for instance, the *Galaga* enemies shoot while moving in a pattern when a player is beneath them).

In fact, some games that used supposed "random" movement could sometimes lead to a pattern. The random number generator in many early games used a hard-coded table of pseudo-random numbers, eventually exposing a discernable sequence of overall game behavior.

Another commonly used technique in the past (and sadly, the present) to make games appear smarter was to allow the computer opponents to cheat; that is, to have additional information about the game world that the human player does not have. The computer reads that a player pushed the punch button (before the player has even started the punch animation) and responds with a perfectly timed blocking move. A real-time strategy (RTS) game employing AI cheating might have its workers heading toward valuable resource sites early in the game, before they had explored the terrain to legitimately find those resources. AI cheating is also achieved when the game grants *gifts* to the computer opponent, by providing the opponent additional (and strategically timed) abilities, resources, and so forth that the opponent uses outright, instead of planning ahead and seeing the need for these resources on its own. These tactics lead to more challenging but ultimately less satisfying opponents because a human player can almost always pick up on the notion that the computer is accomplishing things that are impossible for the human player to accomplish, because the "cheats" are not available or given to the human player.

One of the easier-to-notice and most frustrating examples of this impossible behavior is the use of what is called *rubber banding* in racing games. Toward the end of a race, if a player is beating the AI-controlled cars by too much, some games simply speed up the other cars until they've caught up with the human player, after which the AI-controlled cars return to normal. Sure, it makes the race more of a battle, but for a human player, watching a previously clueless race car suddenly perform miracles to catch up to him or her borders on ridiculous. The opposite case can be equally frustrating. The AI-controlled cars are so far ahead of the player that the game reacts by having the leaders suddenly crash, screw up, or just slow down until the human catches up. Most players realize they're being coddled; they don't feel as much of a sense of accomplishment when the computer gives up.

In modern games, the old techniques are being abandoned. The primary selling point of games is slowly but surely evolving into the realm of AI accomplishments and abilities, instead of the graphical look of the game as it was during the last big phase of game development. This emphasis on visuals is actually somewhat causal in this new expansion of AI importance and quality; the early emphasis on graphics eventually led to specialized graphics processors on almost every platform, and the main CPU is increasingly being left open for more and more sophisticated AI routines. Now that the norm for game graphics is so high, the "wow" factor of game graphics is finally wearing thin, and people are increasingly concentrating on other elements of the game itself.

So, the fact that we now have more CPU time is very advantageous, considering that the current consumer push is now for games that contain much better AI-controlled enemies. In the 8-bit days of gaming or before, 1 to 2 percent of total CPU time was the norm, if not an overestimation, for a game's AI elements to run in. Now, games are routinely budgeting 10 to 35 percent of the CPU time to the AI system [Woodcock 01], with some games going even higher.

Today's game opponents can find better game solutions without cheating and can use more adaptive and emergent means—if for no reason other than that they have access to faster and more powerful processors driving them. Modern game AI is increasingly leading towards "real" intelligence techniques (as defined by academic AI), instead of the old standby of pre-scripted patterns or behaviors that only mimic intelligent behavior. As games (and gamers' tastes) become more complex, game AI work will continue to be infused with more complex AI techniques (heuristic search, learning, planning, etc.).

WHAT GAME AI IS NOT

The term game AI can be used as quite the broad label, often loosely used when referring to all sorts of areas within a game: the collision avoidance (or pathfinding) system, the player controls, the user interface, and sometimes the entire animation system. To some extent, these elements do have something to add to the AI world and are elements that, if done poorly, will make the game seem "stupider," but they are not the primary AI system in a game. An exception to this might be a game in which the gameplay is simple enough that the entire smarts of the enemies are in moving around or choosing the right animations to play.

The difference is this: Game AI makes intelligent decisions when there are multiple options or directions for play. The above-mentioned secondary-support systems, while making decisions from a pool of options/animations/paths, are more "find the optimal" (read: singular) solution for any particular input. The main AI in contrast might have many equally good solutions, but needs to consider planning, resources, player attributes (including esoteric attributes like personality type or things like character flaws), and so on to make decisions for the game's bigger picture.

An alternative way of thinking about this differentiation is that these support systems are much more low-level intelligence, whereas this book will focus mostly on the high-level decisions that an AI system needs to make. For example, you get out of your chair and walk across the room to the refrigerator. The thought in your mind was, "I want a soda out of the fridge." But look at all the low-level intelligence you used to accomplish the task: your mind determined the right sequence of muscle contractions to get you out of the chair (animation picking), and then started you moving toward the fridge (behavior selection), threading you through all the things on the floor (pathfinding). In addition, you slightly lost your balance but regained it quickly (physics simulation) and scratched your head on the way there (secondary behavior layering), in addition to a myriad of other minor actions. None of these secondary concerns changed the fact that your entire plan was to go get a soda, which you eventually accomplished. Most games split up the various levels of decision making into separate systems that barely communicate. The point is that these low-level systems do support the intelligence of the agent but, for this book's purposes, do not define the intelligence of an AI-controlled agent.

A completely separate point to consider is that creating better game AI is not necessarily a result of writing better code. This is what puts the "A" in AI. Many programmers believe that AI creation is a technical problem that can be solved purely with programming skill, but there's much more to it than that. When building game AI, a good software designer must consider balancing issues from such disparate areas as gameplay, aesthetics, animation, audio, and behavior of both the AI and the game interface. It is true that a vast number of highly technical challenges must be overcome by the AI system. However, the ultimate goal of the AI is to provide the player with an entertaining experience, not to be a demonstration for your clever code. Gamers will not care about your shiny new algorithm if it doesn't feel smart and fun.

Game AI is not the best code; it is the best *use* of code and a large dollop of "whatever works." Some of the smartest-looking games have used very questionable methods to achieve their solutions, and although this book is not advocating poorly written code, nothing should be thrown away if it helps to give the illusion of intelligence and enhances the fun factor of the game. Plus, some of the most elegant game code in the world started out as a mindless hack, which blossomed into a clever algorithm later, upon retrospection and cleanup.

On a less serious note, game AI is also not some kind of new life form—a disconnected brain that will eventually take over your PlayStation® and command you to feed it regularly. Hollywood routinely tells us that something sinister is probably what AI has in store for us, but the truth is likely far less dramatic. In the future, we will most likely have access to a truly generic AI paradigm that will learn to competently play any game, but for now this is not the case. Right now, game AI is still very game-specific and very much in the hands of the coders who work on it. The field is still widely misunderstood by the non-programming public, however, and even by those people working in game development who don't regularly work with AI systems.

HOW THIS DEFINITION DIFFERS FROM THAT OF ACADEMIC AI

The world of academic AI has two main goals. First is to help us understand intelligent entities, which will, in turn, help us to understand ourselves. Second is to build intelligent entities, for fun and profit, you might say, because it turns out that these intelligent entities can be useful in our everyday lives.

The first goal is also the goal of more esoteric fields, such as philosophy and psychology, but in a much more functional way. Rather than the philosophical, "Why are we intelligent?," or the psychological, "Where in the brain does intelligence come from?," AI is more concerned with the question, "How is that guy finding the smart-sounding answer?" The second goal mirrors the nature of the practical economy (especially in the western world), in that the research that is most likely to result in the largest profits is also the most likely to win the largest funding.

As stated earlier, Russel and Norvig [Russel 95] define AI as the creation of computer programs that emulate four things:

1. thinking humanly
2. thinking rationally
3. acting humanly
4. acting rationally

In academic study, all four parts of this definition have been the basis for building intelligent programs. The Turing test is a prime example of a program specifically created for acting humanly—the test states that if you cannot tell the difference between the actions of the program and the actions of a person, that program is intelligent. Some cognitive theorists, who are helping to blend traditional human mind science into AI creation, hope to lead towards human-level intelligence by actually getting a computer to think humanly. Sheer logic systems try to solve problems without personal bias or emotion, purely by thinking rationally. Lastly, many AI systems are concerned with acting rationally—always trying to come up with the correct answer that, in turn, directs the system to behave correctly.

But, the vast majority of academic AI study is heavily biased towards the rationality side. If you think about it, rationality lends itself much more cleanly to a computing environment, since it is algorithmic in nature. If you start with a true statement, you can apply standard logical operators to it and retain a true statement. In contrast, game AI focuses on acting "human," with much less dependence on total rationality. This is because game AI needs to model the highs and lows of human task performance, instead of a rigorous search toward the best decision at all times. Games are played for entertainment, of course, and nobody wants to be soundly beaten every time.

Say you're making a chess game. If you're making this chess game as part of an academic study, you probably want it to play the best game possible, given time and memory constraints. You are going to try to achieve perfect rationality, using highly-tuned AI techniques to help you navigate the sea of possible actions. If instead, you are building your chess game to give a human player an entertaining opponent to play against, then your goal shifts dramatically. Now you want a game that provides the person with a suitable challenge, but doesn't overwhelm the human by always making the best move. Yes, the techniques used to achieve these two programs might parallel in some ways, but because the primary goal of each program is different, the coding of the two systems will dramatically diverge. The people who coded Big Blue did not care if Kasparov was having fun when playing against it. But the people behind the very popular Chessmaster games surely spend a lot of time thinking about the fun factor, especially at the default difficulty setting.

Chess is an odd example because humans playing a chess program usually expect it to perform pretty well (unless they're just learning and have specifically set the difficulty rating of the program to a low level). But imagine an AI-controlled Quake "bot" deathmatch opponent. If the bot came into the room, dodged perfectly, aimed perfectly, and knew exactly where and when powerups spawned in the map, it wouldn't be very fun to play against (not for very long, anyway). Instead, we want a much more human level of performance from a game AI opponent. We want to play against an enemy that occasionally misses, runs out of ammo in the middle of a fight, jumps wrong and falls, and everything else that makes an opponent appear human. We still want competent opponents, but because our measure of competence, as humans, involves a measure of error, we expect shortcomings and quirks when determining how intelligent, as well as how real, something is. Anything that is too perfect isn't seen as more intelligent; it is usually seen as either cheating, or alien (some might say "like a computer").

Academic AI systems are generally not trying to model humanity (although there is the odd rare case). They are mostly trying to model intelligence—the ability to produce the most rational decision given all the possible decisions and the rules. This is usually their one and only requirement and, as such, the reason why all our limitations in games (such as time or memory) are not given thought. Also, by distancing themselves from the issues of humanity, they don't run into the sticky problems in dealing with questions about what constitutes human intelligence and proper problem solving. They just happily chug along, searching vast seas of agreed-upon possibility for the maximum total value.

Eventually, computing power, memory capacity, and software engineering will become so great that these two separate fields of AI research may no longer be dissociated. AI systems may achieve the kind of performance necessary to solve even the most complex of problems in real time, and as such, programming them might be more like simply communicating the problem to the system. Game programmers would then use the same general intelligence systems that any programmer would.

APPLICABLE MIND SCIENCE AND PSYCHOLOGY THEORY

Thinking about the way that the human mind works is a great way to flavor your AI programming with structural and procedural lessons from reality. Try to take this section with a grain of salt, and note that different theories exist on the workings and organization of the brain. This section is meant to give you ideas and notions of how to break down intelligence tasks in the same ways that the human mind does.

BRAIN ORGANIZATION

Classically, the brain is divided up into three main subsections: the hindbrain (or brain stem), the midbrain, and the forebrain. Most people may have heard these divisions somewhat wrongly referred to as the reptilian brain, the mammalian brain, and the human brain, but recent research has shown this sort of clear-cut, species-related division to be false. Almost all animal brains have all three parts, just in different sizes and, in some cases, in dramatically different locations (thus, snakes have a mammalian brain region).

These brain regions can be divided into smaller working structures, each of which operate independently by using local working memory areas and accessing neighboring synaptic connections to do specific tasks for the organism (fear conditioning in humans is mostly centered in a brain structure called the amygdala, for example). But these regions are also interconnected, some areas heavily so, to perform global-level tasking as well (the above-mentioned amygdala, through the thalamus and some cortical regions, is also a primary first-step collection spot for emotional data, which will then be sent to another brain structure called the hippocampus for blending with other sensory input and eventual storage into long-term memory). If you think of the brain as being an object-oriented class, the amygdala would be a small class, with its own internal functions and data members. But it would also be an internal structure within other classes, like Long-Term Memory, or Forebrain. This object-oriented, hierarchical organizational model of the brain has merit when setting up an AI engine, as seen in Figure 1.2, which shows a nice mirroring between brain and game systems.

By breaking down your AI tasks into atomic modules that require little knowledge of each other (like the brain's small, independent structures), you'll find it much easier to follow good object-oriented programming principles. Combinations of the atomic modules can be blended into more complex representations as needed, without replicating code. This also represents the kind of efficiency we should be trying to achieve in our AI systems. Avoid single-use calculations and code whenever possible, or input conditions that are so rare as to be practically hard-coded. Alas, inefficiency cannot be completely overcome, but most inefficiencies can be eliminated with clever thinking and programming.

KNOWLEDGE BASE AND LEARNING

Although the inner workings of the human memory system are not fully understood, the common idea is that information is stored in the form of small changes in brain nerve cells at the synapse level. These changes cause differences in the electrical conductivity of different routes through the network and, as such, affect the firing potential of specific nerve cells as well as whole sub-networks. If you use a particular neural pathway, it gets stronger. The reverse is also true. Thus, memory systems use a technique that game designers could learn a lot from (no pun intended), that of plasticity. Instead of creating a set-in-stone list of AI behaviors and reactions to human actions, we can keep the behavior mix exhibited by the AI malleable through plasticity. The AI system could keep track of its actions and make note of whether or not the human consistently chooses certain behaviors in response. It could then recognize trends and bias its behaviors (or the requisite counter measures, as a defense) to plastically change the overall behavior mix that the AI uses.

Of course, an AI memory system would require a dependable way of determining what is "good" to learn. We humans rely on teaching conventions and retrospection to gain insight into which information to value, and which to discard. Without these aids, the human brain would just store everything, leading to misconception, miscommunication, and even delusion. Although very contextually complex, a filter on AI learning would keep the human player from exploiting a learning system by teaching it misleading behaviors, knowing that the system will respond in kind. Does the AI always use a low block to stop the next incoming punch after the player has punched three times in a row? An advanced player would perceive that and punch three times followed by a high punch to get a free

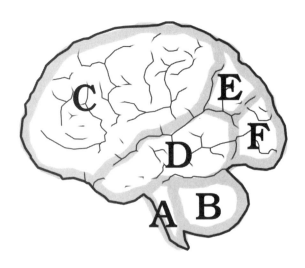

Organization of:		
	The Brain	A Game AI System
A	Brain Stem - Reflex - Lower Functions/Survival	- Collision - Animation Selection
B	Cerebellum - Motor Center/Sensory Mixing and Coordination	- Physics - Navigation
C	Frontal Lobe - Higher Brain Functions - Emotions - Learning	- Decision Making
D	Temporal Lobe - Memory (Visual and Verbal)	- Learning
E	Parietal Lobe - Sensory Cortex	- Perceptions
F	Occipital Lobe - Visual Processing	- Perception

FIGURE 1.2   Object-oriented nature of the brain related to game AI systems.

hit in on the low-blocking AI. But another level of AI memory performance would have the AI noticing that pattern, and making adjustments to how it would handle the situation in the future. This would be tantamount to learning about how the player is learning.

Another useful lesson from nature is that the rate of memory reinforcement and degradation in the human brain is not the same for all systems. Usually, memories are created only after repeated exposure to the information. Likewise, already existing memories tend to take a period of time before they either wither through misuse, or will require conscious counter-association in order to quell. Memories associated with pain aversion, however, may never fully extinguish, even if the person only experienced the relation once. This is a good example of nature using dynamic hard coding. The usually plastic changes in the brain can be "locked in" (by stopping the learning process or moving these changes into a more long-term memory) and thus not be allowed to degrade over time. But like the brain, too much hardcoding used in the wrong place can lead to odd behavior, turning people (or your game characters) into apparent phobics or amnesiacs.

Another concept to think about is long-term versus short-term memory. Short-term, or working memory, can be thought of as perception data that can only be held onto for a short time, in a small queue. The items sitting in short-term memory can be filtered for importance, and then stored away into longer-term memories, or simply forgotten about by sitting idle until a time duration is hit or additional data comes in and bumps it off the end of the queue. Varying the size of the queue and the rates of storage creates such concepts as attention span, as well as single-mindedness.

Many games have essentially digital memory. An enemy will see a player and pursue the character for a while. But if the player hides, the enemy eventually forgets about the player and goes back to what he was doing. This is classic state-based AI behavior, but it is also very unrealistic and unintelligent behavior. It's even more unrealistic when the enemy didn't just see the player, but was shot and injured during the exchange. By using a more analog memory model for our opponent, he could still go back to his post, but he'd be much more sensitive to future attacks, would most likely spend the time at his post bandaging his wounds, would probably make it a priority to call for backup, and so forth. For sure, some games do use these types of memory systems. But the vast majority does not.

The brain also makes use of modulators, chemicals that are released into the blood, affect some change in brain state, and take a while to degrade. These are things like adrenaline or oxytocin. These chemicals' main job is to inhibit or enhance the firing of neurons in specific brain areas. This leads to a more focused mind-set, as well as flavoring the memories of the particular situation in a contextual way. In a game AI system, a modulator could override the overall AI state, or just adjust the behavior exhibited within a certain state. In this way, conventional state-based AI could be made more flexible by borrowing the concept of modulation. The earlier-mentioned enemy character that the player alarmed could transition to an entirely different Alerted state, which would slowly degrade and then transition back down to a Normal state. But using a state system with modifiers, the enemy could stay in his normal Guard state, with an aggressive or alerted modulator. Although keeping the state diagram of a character simpler, this would require a much more general approach to coding the Guard state. More on this in Chapter 15, under finite state machine extensions.

The human brain stores things in different memory centers. It does this in a few different ways: direct experience, imitation, or imaginative speculation. With the possible exception of speculation, which would require quite a sophisticated mental model, game characters may gather information in the same ways. Keeping statistics on the strategies that seem to work against the human and then biasing future AI behavior could be thought of as learning by direct experience. Imitation would involve recording the strategies that the human player is successfully using and employing them in return.

The problem that games have had with classical AI learning algorithms is that they usually take many iterations of exposure to induce learning. It is a slippery slope to do learning in the fast-paced, short-lived world of the AI opponent. Most games that use these techniques do all the learning before hand, during production, and then ship the games with the learning disabled, so that the behavior is stable. This will change as additional techniques, infused with both speed and accuracy, are found and made public.

But learning need not be "conscious." Influence maps (see Chapter 19) can be used by a variety of games to create much lower level, or "subconscious" learning, making AI enemies seem smarter without any of the iteration issues of normal learning. A simple measure of how many units from each side have died on each spot of the map could give an RTS game's pathfinding algorithm valuable information necessary to avoid kill zones where an opponent (human or otherwise) has set up a trap along some commonly traveled map location. This learning effect could even erode over time or be influenced by units relaying back that they have destroyed whatever was causing the kill zone in the first place. Influence maps are also being used successfully in some sports games. For example, by slightly perturbing the default positions of the players on a soccer field to be better positioned for the passes the human has made in the past. The same system can also be used by the defensive team to allow them to be better able to possibly block these passes. Influence map systems allow cumulative kinds of information to be readily stored in a quick and accessible way, while keeping the number of iterations that have to occur to see the fruition of this type of learning very low. Because the nature of the information stored is so specific, the problem of storing misleading information is also somewhat minimized.

COGNITION

The flood of data coming from our senses bombards us at all times. How does the brain know which bits of information to deal with first? Which pieces to throw away? When to override the processing it is currently doing for a more life-threatening situation? It does this by using the brain's various systems to quickly categorize and prioritize incoming data. Cognition can be thought of as taking all your incoming sense data, also called perceptions, and filtering them through your innate knowledge (both instinctual and intuitive) as well as your reasoning centers (which includes your stored memories), to come up with some understanding of what those perceptions mean to you. Logic, reason, culture, and all of your personally stored rules can be thought as merely ways of sorting out the important perceptions from the background noise.

Think of the sheer volume of input coursing into the mind of a person living in a big city. He must contend with the sights, sounds, and smells of millions of people and cars, the constant pathfinding through the crowd, the hawkers, and homeless vying for his attention, and countless other distractions. Perceptions are also not all external. The pressures of the modern world cause stress and anxiety that split your attention and fragment your thoughts. Your mind also needs to try to distill the important thoughts inside your own head from the sea of transient, flighty ideas that everyone is constantly engaged in. If your brain tried to keep all this in mind, it would never be able to concentrate sufficiently to perform any task at all. Only by boiling all this information down to the most critical half-dozen perceptions or so at any given time can you hope to accomplish anything.

In game AI, we don't suffer as much from the flood of data because we can pick and choose our perceptions at any level in the process, and this makes the whole procedure a bit less mystical. In Figure 1.3, you can see a mock-up of a sports game using different perceptions for the various decisions being made by the AI player in the foreground. Make sure, when coding any particular AI subsystem that you only use those perceptions you truly need. Be careful not to oversimplify, or you may make the output behaviors from this subsystem too predictable. An auditory subsystem that only causes an enemy character to hear a sound when its location is within some range to the enemy would seem strange when a player sets off a particularly loud noise just outside of that range. A game design should take into account distance and starting volume, so that sounds would naturally trail off as they travel. You might also want to take into account the acoustics of the environment because sounds will travel much longer distances in a canyon than in an office building (or underwater versus open air). These are very simple examples, but you see the notion involved. Perceptions are much more than a single value, because there are usually many ways to interpret the data that each perception represents.

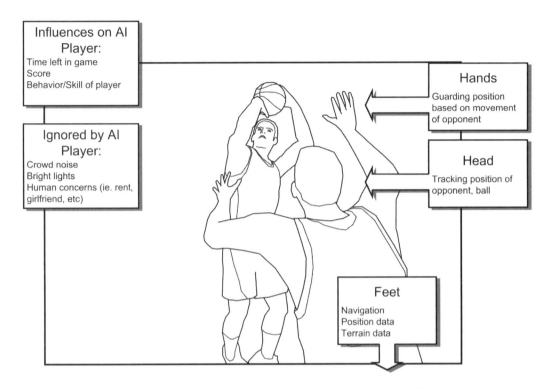

FIGURE 1.3 A visual depiction of various perceptions being taken into account by a game character.

We can think of the systems used in the AI world as filters as well. Whatever technique we are using as our primary decision-making system, to determine the right action to perform, is really just a method of filtering the current game state through all the possible things that the AI can do (or some subset of these possibilities, as defined by some rule or game state). Thus, we see the primary observation many people make about AI in general—that it all boils down to focused searching, in some way or another. This is true to some degree. Most AI systems are just different ways of searching through the variety of possibilities, and as such, the topography of your game's possibilities can be used to conceptually consider the best AI technique to use. This topography is generally called the "state space" of the game. If your game's possible outcomes to different perceptions are mostly isolated islands of response, with no real gray conditions, a state-based system might be the way to go. You're dealing with a set of exclusive possible responses, an almost enumerated state space. However, if the full range of possible responses is more continuous, and would graph out more like a rolling hillside with occasional dips (or another metaphor with more than three dimensions, but you get the idea), a fuzzy system or one using neural nets might be a better fit, as they tend to work better at identifying local minima and maxima in continuous fields of response. We will cover these and the other AI systems in Part III and Part IV of the book; this was merely for illustration.

THEORY OF MIND

One psychological construct that is again being embraced as a major field of investigation by both behavioralists and cognitive scientists is that of the so-called Theory of Mind (ToM). This concept has a good deal of merit in the field of game AI because our primary job is creating systems that seem intelligent. A ToM is actually more of a cognitive capacity of human beings, rather than a theory. It fundamentally means that one person has the ability to understand others as having minds and a worldview that are separate from his own. In a slightly more technical fashion, ToM is defined as knowing that others are intentional agents, and to interpret their minds through theoretical concepts of intentional states such as beliefs and desires [Premack 78]. This isn't as complicated as it sounds. Think of this as having the ability to see intent, rather than just strict recognition of action. We do it all the time as adults, and humanize even the most nonhuman of environmental elements. Listing 1.1 shows a bit of code from a Java version (written by Robert C. Goerlich, 1997) of the early AI program Eliza, which, in its time, did a remarkable job of making people believe it was much more than it really was. The idea of attributing agency to objects in our environment is almost innate in humans, especially objects that move. In simple experiments in which subjects were asked to explain what they saw when shown a scene consisting of a colored spot on a computer screen moving from left to right, closely followed by a different-colored dot, a large portion of people described it as "the first dot was being chased by the second." People give their cars personalities, and even think (at some superstitious level) that if you talk bad about it, or suggest getting rid of it, it will perform poorly.

In human terms, the ability to form a ToM about others usually develops at about the age of three. A commonly used test to determine if the child has developed this cognitive trait is to question the child about the classic "False Belief Task" [Wimmer 83]. In this problem, the child is presented with a scene in which a character named Bobby puts a personal belonging, such as a book, into his closet. He then leaves, and while he's away, his little brother comes and takes out the book and puts it in a cupboard. The child is then asked where Bobby will look for his book when he comes back. If the child indicates the cupboard, he reveals that he has yet to develop the understanding that Bobby wouldn't have the same information in his mind that the child does. He, therefore, does not have an abstract frame of reference, or theory, about Bobby's mind, hence no ToM about Bobby. If the child gives the correct answer, it shows that he can not only determine facts about the world but can also form a theoretical, simplified model of others' minds that includes the facts, desires, and beliefs that they might have; thus providing a theory of this other's mind.

LISTING 1.1   Some sample code from a Java version of Eliza.

```
public class Eliza extends Applet
    {

    ElizaChat        cq[];
    ElizaRespLdr     ChatLdr;
    static ElizaConjugate  ChatConj;
    boolean          _started=false;
    Font             _font;
    String           _s;

    public void init()
        {

        super.init();
        ChatLdr = new ElizaRespLdr();
        ChatConj = new ElizaConjugate();

        //{{INIT_CONTROLS
        setLayout(null);
        addNotify();
        resize(425,313);
        setBackground(new Color(16776960));
        list1 = new java.awt.List(0,false);
        list1.addItem("Hi! I'm Eliza.  Let's talk.");
        add(list1);
        list1.reshape(12,12,395,193);
        list1.setFont(new Font("TimesRoman", Font.BOLD, 14));
        list1.setBackground(new Color(16777215));
        button1 = new java.awt.Button
            ("Depress the Button or depress <Enter> to send to Eliza");
        button1.reshape(48,264,324,26);
        button1.setFont(new Font("Helvetica", Font.PLAIN, 12));
        button1.setForeground(new Color(0));
        add(button1);
        textField1 = new java.awt.TextField();
        textField1.reshape(36,228,348,24);
```

```
        textField1.setFont(new Font("TimesRoman", Font.BOLD, 14));
        textField1.setBackground(new Color(16777215));
        add(textField1);
        //}}
        textField1.requestFocus();
}

public boolean action(Event event, Object arg)
    {
    if (event.id == Event.ACTION_EVENT && event.target ==
                                                        button1)
        {
            clickedButton1();
            textField1.requestFocus();
            return true;
        }
    if (event.id == Event.ACTION_EVENT && event.target ==
                                                        textField1)
        {
            clickedButton1();
            textField1.requestFocus();
            return true;
        }
    return super.handleEvent(event);
}

public void clickedButton1()
    {
    parseWords(textField1.getText());
    textField1.setText("");
    textField1.setEditable(true);
    textField1.requestFocus();

}
public void parseWords(String s_)
    {
    int idx=0, idxSpace=0;
    int _length=0;       // actual no of elements in set
    int _maxLength=200;  // capacity of set
    int _w;

    list1.addItem(s_);
    list1.makeVisible(list1.getVisibleIndex()+1);
    s_=s_.toLowerCase()+" ";
```

```
      while(s_.indexOf("'")>=0)
         s_=s_.substring(0,s_.indexOf("'"))+
                s_.substring(s_.indexOf("'")+1,s_.length());

      bigloop: for(_length=0; _length<_maxLength  &&
                      idx < s_.length(); _length++)
        {
        // find end of the first token
        idxSpace=s_.indexOf(" ",idx);
        if(idxSpace == -1) idxSpace=s_.length();

        String _resp=null;
        for(int i=0;i<ElizaChat.num_chats && _resp == null;i++)
            {
            _resp=ChatLdr.cq[i].converse
                                (s_.substring(idx,s_.length()));
            if(_resp != null)
                {
                list1.addItem(_resp);
                list1.makeVisible(list1.getVisibleIndex()+1);
                break bigloop;
                }
            }
        // eat blanks
        while(s_.length() > ++idxSpace &&
                  Character.isSpace(s_.charAt(idxSpace)));
        idx=idxSpace;

        if(idx >= s_.length())
            {
            _resp=ChatLdr.cq[ElizaChat.num_chats-1]
                                .converse("nokeyfound");
            list1.addItem(_resp);
            list1.makeVisible(list1.getVisibleIndex()+1);
            }
        }
     }
 //{{DECLARE_CONTROLS
 java.awt.List list1;
 java.awt.Button button1;
 java.awt.TextField textField1;
 //}}
 }
 //--------------------
```

```
class ElizaChat
    {

    static int        num_chats=0;
    private String    _keyWordList[];
    private String    _responseList[];
    private int       _idx=0;
    private int       _rIdx=0;
    private boolean   _started=false;
    private boolean   _kw=true;
    public String     _response;
    private String    _dbKeyWord;
    public int        _widx = 0;
    public int        _w = 0;
    public int        _x;
    private char      _space;
    private char      _plus;

    public ElizaChat()
        {
        num_chats++;
        _keyWordList= new String[20];
        _responseList=new String[20];
        _rIdx=0;
        _idx=0;
        _keyWordList[_idx]=" ";

        _space=" ".charAt(0);
        _plus="+".charAt(0);
    }

    public String converse(String kw_)
        {
        _response = null;
        for(int i=0; i <= _idx - 1;i++){
            _dbKeyWord = _keyWordList[i];

            if(kw_.length()>=_dbKeyWord.length()&&
                _keyWordList[i].equals
                    (kw_.substring(0,_dbKeyWord.length())))
                {

                _widx = (int) Math.round(Math.random()*_rIdx-.5);
                _response = _responseList[_widx];
```

```
            _x=_response.indexOf("*");
            if(_x>0)
                {
                _response=_response.substring(0,_x)+
                                kw_.substring(_dbKeyWord.length(),
                                            kw_.length());
                if(_x<_responseList[_widx].length()-1)
                    _response=_response+"?";
                _response=Eliza.ChatConj
                                    .conjugate(_response,_x);
                _response=_response.replace(_plus,_space);
                }
            break;
            }
        }

    return _response;
    }

public void loadresponse(String rw_)
    {
    _responseList[_rIdx]=rw_;
    _rIdx++;
    }

public void loadkeyword(String kw_)
    {
    _keyWordList[_idx]=kw_;
    _idx++;
    }
}
```

It has been routine in philosophy, and the mind sciences in general, to see this ability as somewhat dependent upon our linguistic abilities. After all, language provides us a representational medium for meaning and intentionality; thanks to language, we are able to describe people's actions in an intentional way. This is also probably why Alan Turing gave us his famous test as to a true measure of intelligence exhibited by a computer program. If the program could communicate successfully to another entity (that being a human), and the human could not tell it was a computer, it must be intelligent. Turing's argument is thus that anything we can successfully develop a ToM toward must be intelligent—great news for our games, if we can get them to trigger this response within the people who play them.

Interestingly, further studies in chimpanzees and even some lower primates have shown that they have remarkable abilities toward determining intention and prediction toward each other and us without verbal communication at the human level. So, the ability to form ideas about another's mindset is either biologically innate, can be determined with visual cues, or is possibly something else entirely. Whatever the source of this ability, the notion is that we do not require our AI-controlled agents to require full verbal communication skills to instill the player with a ToM about our AI.

If we can get the people playing our games to not see a creature in front of them with X amount of health and Y amount of strength, but rather a being with beliefs, desires, and intent, then we will have really won a major battle. This superb suspension of disbelief by the human player can be achieved if the AI system in question is making the kinds of decisions that a human would make, in such a way as to portray these higher traits and rise above the simple gameplay mechanic involved. In effect, we must model minds, not behavior. Behavior should come out of the minds that we give our AI creations, not from the programmers' minds. Note that this does not mean we need to give our creations perfect problem-solving abilities to achieve this state. Nor does this mean that every creature in the game must have this level of player interaction and nuance. The main bad guys that will be around for a while or other long-term characters (including the protagonist) would be helped by making them more "rich" in terms of personal connection to the player. One of the primary things a lot of people attribute great movies to is a "great bad guy." Usually it's because the bad guy has been written in such a way that people can really sense his personality and get into his thinking to a certain extent.

What does a realization of this human tendency give us as game producers? It means that as long as we follow some rules, people's brains actually want to believe in our creations. In effect, knowledge of this fundamental, low-level goal (that of brains constantly working to create a ToM about each other) can help give the programmers and designers guidelines about what types of information to show the player directly, what types to specifically not show, and what types to leave ambiguous. As the illusionist says, "The audience sees what I want it to see."

Take for example, an AI-controlled behavior from a squad combat game. In Figure 1.4, we see the layout of a simple battlefield, with the human player at the bottom of the map, and four CPU enemies closing in on him, moving between many cover points. The simple behavioral rules for these enemies are the following:

- If nobody is shooting at the player, and I'm (as the enemy) fully loaded and ready, I will start shooting. Note that only one player can shoot at a time in this system.
- If I'm out in the open, I will head for the nearest unoccupied cover position, and randomly shout something like "Cover me!" or "On your left!" or even just grunt.

- If I'm at a cover position, I'll reload, and then wait for the guy shooting to be finished, maybe by playing some kind of scanning animation to make it look like he's trying to snipe the player.

Now imagine how this battle will look to the human player. Four enemy soldiers come into view. One starts firing immediately, while the other three dive for cover. Then, the one that was firing stops, shouts "Cover me!," and runs forward for cover as a different soldier pops up and starts firing. Here we have a system in which the soldiers are completely unaware of each other (save for the small detail that "someone is shooting"), the player's intentions, or the fact that they're performing a basic leapfrogging advance-and-cover military maneuver. But because the human player is naturally trying to form a ToM about the enemy, the human player is going to see this as very tightly-coordinated, intelligent behavior. Therefore, the ruse has worked. We have created an intelligent system, at least for the entertainment world.

BOUNDED OPTIMALITY

When rationality is a goal of your AI system, the *degree* of rationality you are striving for can be the prime determiner of the overall system design. If your goal is

FIGURE 1.4   Emergent Theory of Mind in a loosely coordinated enemy squad.

near-perfect rationality, you might have to accept that your program is going to need a huge amount of time to run to completion, unless the decision state space you are working with is very small indeed. For most entertainment games, perfect rationality is not only unnecessary, but actually unwanted. As discussed earlier, the goal of game AI is usually to emulate a more human performance level, including all the foibles, falls, and outright screwups.

One of the reasons that humans make all these mistakes is the near certainty of *limited resources*. In the real world, it's practically impossible to get everything you need to come up with the perfect solution. There's always some bottleneck: too few details, not enough time, insufficient money, or just plain limited ability. We try to overcome these hurdles by using what is called *bounded optimality* (or BO), which just means that we make the best decisions we can in the face of resource restrictions. The chances of getting the best possible solution are directly linked to the number and amount of limitations. In other words, you get what you pay for.

BO techniques are prevalent in most academic AI circles (as well as in game theory and even philosophy) because "optimal" solutions to real-life problems are usually computationally intractable. Another reason is that very few real-life problems have no limitations. Given the realities of our world, we need a method of measuring success without requiring absolute rationality.

Like computers, the decision-making ability of people is limited by a number of factors, including the quality and depth of relevant knowledge, cognitive speed, and overall problem-solving skill. But that only covers the hardware and software. We also suffer from environmental limitations that might make it impossible to fully exploit our brains. We live in a "real-time" world, and must make decisions that could save our lives (or merely save our careers) in very short time frames. All these factors come together to flavor our decisions with a healthy dose of incorrectness. So, instead of trying to brute force our programs into finding the ideal solution, we should merely guide our decision making in the right direction and work in that direction for as much time as we have (of course, computing power will eventually get to the level that any time restriction will vanish to the point of nothing, but for now we must still grapple with what we have). The decisions that come out will then, we hope, be somewhat more human and work well with the limiting constraints of the platform and genre of game we are working on. In effect, we create optimal programs rather than achieve optimal actions.

A problem with trying to use BO methods on many types of systems is that they require incremental solutions; that is, solutions that get better by degrees as they are given more resources. Incremental solutions are definitely not universal to all problems, but the types of computationally challenging hurdles that require BO thinking can often be reduced in some way to an incremental level. Pathfinding, for example, can be given several levels of complexity. You might start by pathfinding between very large map sectors, then *within* those sectors, then locally, and then around dynamic objects. Each successive level solves the problem slightly better than the last, but even the earliest level gets the player going in the right direction, at least in a primitive sense.

LESSONS FROM ROBOTICS

Robotics is one of the few academic fields with a good deal of similar tasking to the world of game AI. Unlike other academic endeavors which can deal with large-scale problems and can use exhaustive searches to find optimal results, robots usually have to deal with many real-time constraints like physics, computation speed problems (because of limited on-board computer space), and physical perception of the environment. Robots usually have to deal with the computational issues of solving problems intelligently and must house this technology into a physical construct that must deal with the real world directly. This is truly an ambitious task. As such, academic theories are taken and ground against the stone of reality until finely honed. Many techniques crafted by robotics end up in games because of the inherent optimizing and real-world use that robotics adds to the theoretical AI work done in research labs. The lion's share of the successful pathfinding methods we use in games, including the invaluable A* algorithm, came out of robotics research. Some of the prime lessons that robotics has given us include the following:

SIMPLICITY OF DESIGN AND SOLUTION

Many robotics methodologies, like games, use the "whatever works" model. Robotics in general is a very hard problem, with an ambitious variety of challenges such as navigating undefined terrains, or recognizing general environmental objects. Every true perceptual sense that a researcher bestows on his or her robot translates into a tremendous amount of technology and study necessary to break down the system into workable parts. If the system can be made to work without the sense, then the solution is just as good, if not better, considering that the expense in both time and money was saved by not having to involve a complex perception subsystem. Some of Rodney Brooks's robots illustrate this perfectly: instead of trying to navigate areas by recognizing obstacles and either circumventing or calculating how to surmount them, some of his robot designs are largely mindless; insectile creations that blindly use general-purpose methods (like multiple simple flailing arms) to force their way over obstacles. The lesson here is that while others spend years trying tech-heavy methods for cleverly getting around obstacles and failing, Brooks's designs are being incorporated into robots that are headed to Mars.

THEORY OF MIND

ToM concepts have also been advanced by robotics. Researchers have discovered that people deal better with robots if they can in some way associate human attributes (if not human thought processes) with the robot. Incorporating features into your robot that improve this humanization is a good thing for robotics researchers in that it actually makes the robot seem more intelligent to people, and more agreeable in the eyes of the public. Imagine a robot built to simply move toward any bright light. Humans, when asked to describe this simple behavior, will usually report that the robot "likes lights," or "is afraid of the dark." Neuroscientists usually call this human behavior "attributing agency." This is a fancy way of saying that humans have a tendency to think of moving objects as doing so because of some intentional reason, in most cases by a thinking agent. Think of it this way: you're on a trail in Africa, and you see the bushes rustling. Your brain thinks: "Yikes, there must be a lion over there!" and you head for the nearest tree. You're much more likely to survive (on average) with this response rather than if you were thinking: "Huh, that bush is moving. I wonder why?" It could just be the breeze, but statistically, it is less likely that you'll die if you don't take the chance. The other notion at work here is simple anthropomorphizing. Humans love to think of non-human things as if they were human. How many times have you seen someone at the park pleading with their Golden Retriever to "stop making this so hard, you know I've had a bad week, and I could really use your help with the other dog." It's all complete silliness. Spot isn't making things hard; he's reacting to the smells of the park with mostly pre-described instinctual behaviors. He has no knowledge whatsoever that you've been having a bad week, and for that matter really can't understand English. I've heard practically this same speech given to a computer, a car, and a 12-week-old baby.

By working with people's natural inclination to attribute desires and intentions, instead of raw behaviors, to just about anything, researchers hope to make robots that people will not just tolerate but enjoy working with in the real world. Robotic projects like Cog and Kismet [Brooks 98] continue to push the realm of human-robot interaction, mostly through social cues that deepen and build upon people's ToM about the robot to enliven the interaction itself and the learning that the robot is engaging in. People *want* to believe that your creation has a mind and intentions. We just have to push a little, and give the right signals.

MULTIPLE LAYERED DECISION ARCHITECTURES

Many modern robotics platforms use a system whereupon the decision-making structure of the robot is broken down into layers which represents high-level to low-level decisions about the world [Brooks 91]. This bottom-up behavior design (sometimes called subsumption) allows robots to achieve a level of autonomy in an environment by always having some fail-safe behavior to fall back on. So, a robot might have a very low-level layer whose only goal is to avoid obstacles or other nearby dangers. This "avoidance" layer would get fresh information from the world quite frequently. It would also override or modify behaviors coming from further up the decision structure, as it represents the highest priority of decision making. As you climb the layers, the priority lessens, the amount of interaction with the world lessens, and the overall goal complexity goes up. So, at the highest level, the robot could formulate the high-level plan: "I need to leave the room." In contrast, the bottommost layer might have as its plan "Turn 10 degrees clockwise, I'm going to run into something." The layers within this system know nothing about each other (or as little as possible), they simply build on one another in such a way that the various tasks normally associated with the goal at large are specialized and concentrated into distinct layers. This layer independence also creates a much higher robustness to the system since it means that a layer getting confused (or receiving bad data) will not corrupt the entirety of the structure, and thus, the robot may still be able to perform while the rest of the system returns to normalcy.

A structure of this kind is very applicable to game genres that have to make decisions at many levels of complexity concurrently, like RTS games. By sticking to the formal conventions expressed (as well as experimentally tested) by robotics teams using subsumption techniques, we can also gain from the considerable benefits these systems have been found to exhibit, including automatic fault tolerance (between layers of the system), as well as the robustness to deal with any number of unknown or partially known pieces of information at each level. Subsumption architectures do not require an explicit, start-to-finish action plan, and a well-designed system will automatically perform the various parts of its intelligent plan in an order that represents the best way the environment will allow. This book will cover a general way of breaking down AI engine issues using a method something like this approach in Chapter 23.

SUMMARY

This chapter covered some basic AI terminology that we will use in later chapters, some general psychological theory, and some concepts from other fields that are applicable to AI system design.

- This book will use the term *game AI* to mean character-based behavioral decision making, further refined by concentrating on tasks that require choosing among multiple good decisions, rather than finding the best possible decision.
- Older games used patterns or let the computer opponent cheat by giving it clandestine knowledge that the human player didn't have; both methods are being abandoned because of the increasing power of AI systems being used in games.
- AI is becoming more important in today's games, as players demand better opponents to more complex games. This is true even though many games are going online because most people still play single-player modes exclusively.

- Game AI needs to be smart and fun because this is primarily a form of entertainment. Thus, game AI needs to exhibit human error and personality, be able to employ different difficulty levels, and make the human feel adequately challenged.

- Brain organization shows us the use of object-oriented systems that build upon each other, in complexity order.

- Like the brain, our AI systems can employ long- and short-term memories, which will lead us toward more realistic AI behaviors.

- Learning in a game, like in real brains, can be conscious or unconscious. By using both types, we can model more realistic behavior modification over time, while still focusing our learning on things we deem important.

- Cognition studies lead us to think of AI reasoning systems as filters that take our inputs and lead us toward sensible outputs. Thinking of the nature of the state space that a given game has, and contrasting that with the types of AI techniques available, the right filter can be found for your game.

- By striving to feed into the natural human tendency to build a Theory of Mind about the AI-controlled agents within our game, we can extend the attributes of the agent to basic needs and desires, and therefore extend the realism of his decision making to the player.

- Bounded rationality is a formal concept that we can use to visualize our game AI goals. We are not searching for optimal actions, but optimal incremental programs that give good solutions while working under many constraints.

- Robotics gives us the notion of design and implementation simplicity, extends our desire for cultivating a ToM towards our creations, and provides us with a generic subsumption architecture for designing and implementing autonomous agents from the bottom up.

2   An AI Engine: The Basic Components and Design

In This Chapter

- Decision Making and Inference
- Input Handlers and Perception
- Navigation
- Bringing It All Together
- Summary

I n this chapter, the basic parts of an AI engine will be broken down and discussed. Although this list is neither all-inclusive nor the only way to do things, almost all AI engines will use the following foundation systems in some form or another: *decision making/inference, perception*, and *navigation*. See Figure 2.1 for a basic layout.

DECISION MAKING AND INFERENCE

The workhorse of the engine, the decision-making system is the main emphasis of this book. Inference is defined as the act of deriving logical or reasonable conclusions from factual knowledge or premises assumed to be true. In game terms, this means that the AI-controlled opponent gains information about the world (see "Perception Type," later in this chapter) and makes intelligent, reasonable decisions about what to do in response. Thus, your AI system is defined (as well as restricted) by the kind of information it can gain about the outside world, as well as the richness of the response set (or behavior state space) as defined by the game design. The more things the game allows the AI characters to do, the greater the response set of the game. The technique you choose for your AI engine should be dictated, at least in part, by the size and nature of the state space of the game you are building. More information about this consideration will be given in Parts III and IV, where the different techniques are described.

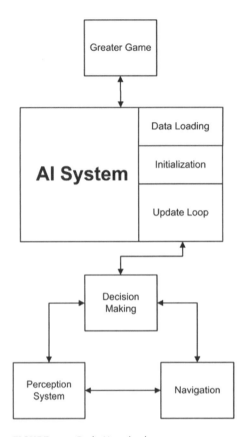

FIGURE 2.1   Basic AI engine layout.

All of the decision-making systems described in this book can be boiled down to different ways of using available inputs to come up with solutions. The main differences we are concerned with are the types of solutions, agent reactivity, system realism, genre, content, platform, development limitations, and entertainment limitations.

TYPES OF SOLUTIONS

The primary game solution types are *strategic* and *tactical*. Strategic solutions are usually long-term, higher-level goals that might involve having many actions to accomplish. Tactical solutions are more often short-term, lower-level goals that usually involve a physical act or skill. An example of the difference between the two solution types is the "Hunt Player" and "Circle Strafe" solutions in a *Quake*-style game. Hunting the player is a high-level goal that involves determining where the player is, physically getting to the player, and then engaging the player in combat.

Circle strafing is merely a way to move while engaged in combat with an enemy. Many games require both strategic and tactical solutions, and this means potentially using different techniques for getting these solutions.

AGENT REACTIVITY

How reactive do your game elements need to be? Scripted systems tend to create characters with much more stylized and contextual response, but they also tend to become locked into these behavior scripts and, thus, lose reactivity. Conversely, fully reactive systems (those that take the inputs, and change responses immediately, with little thought to what was being done before) tend to be considered either spastic or cheating, and are not very human feeling. Highly responsive systems also require a fairly rich response set, or the behavior they exhibit will be very predictable and stale. However, this is great for arcade style, or what are called "twitch" games. This point needs to be addressed based on the type of game being created and the proper balance determined based on the gameplay experience you are looking to create.

SYSTEM REALISM

To be considered "realistic," the decisions and actions that an AI element comes up with need to be regarded as human. Each AI entity requires the intelligence to determine the right thing to do, within the limitations of the game. But being human also means making mistakes. Thus, AI characters need to show human weakness as well. Opponents that block all your punches, or that never miss a basketball shot, or a Scrabble opponent that knows the entire dictionary would only frustrate the player. The goal is to strike a balance between competition and entertainment, so that the player is drawn in by the challenge of the game but also given a constant stream of positive feedback by beating the game. Other realism concerns involve the amount of actual adherence to physical laws the game uses. Can the player jump higher than in real life? Can he fly? Do players heal quickly? All these things are up to the developer.

What this means is that "realism" can be defined as real in *this particular* game world. Care must be taken in fantasy worlds because enemies that arbitrarily break rules are considered to be cheating, not magical. You must take steps to ensure that the player knows the rules of your world and then make sure *you* stick to them. Remember that Earth's physical laws are usually known by most of the people playing your game, whereas special laws might provide your players with an initial stumbling block as they try to get used to the new rules.

Humans also don't perceive randomness very well. In nature few things are truly *random*, as opposed to just infrequent or part of a dynamic system that is too complex for us to see. As such, AI that is random can sometimes feel like it's cheating to the player. If the majority of your players feel this way, you should really look into adjusting your random number generation toward a method that doesn't feel like cheating to people.

The lesson is this: It really doesn't matter if your AI cheats or not, what matters is that your AI doesn't "feel" like it's cheating. An example of this would be the popular puzzle-style game *Puzzle Quest*. This game uses a completely random system for determining what blocks to drop after you clear out a chunk of the board. However, the AI seems to be much luckier than any human opponent. The web is full of discussion about the supposed cheating that the AI does, back and forth over the issue. The truth is that the developers should adjust the algorithm they use for dropping blocks specifically to limit the AI's effectiveness, since it would appear that the majority of people playing the game feel *cheated* and not *unlucky*. People will always determine if you are cheating. This is all but a universal law. However, they will also mark your game as cheating if it "feels to close" to cheating, like *Puzzle Quest*. In this case, the developers should have adjusted things to simply help with that perception.

GENRE

The different broad categories of games require specific types of AI systems. See Part II of the book for an in-depth discussion of each genre. At this level, keep in mind the following factors:

- *Input (or perception) types.* Things to note include the number of inputs, frequency, communication method (polled, events, callback functions, shared memory, etc.), and any hierarchical relationships among inputs. Arcade-style games might have very limited inputs, whereas a character in a real-time strategy game might require quite a few perceptions about the world—to navigate terrain, stay in formation, help friendly units, take orders from the human, and respond to attacking enemies.
- *Output (or decision) types.* Once the perception system collects all the facts about the state of the game world, a decision "output" is generated by the AI system. Outputs can be analog, digital, or complex constructions (like a series of modifying events on top of some ambient behavior). Decisions can involve the entire character (such as diving for cover), merely parts of the character (such as a character turning its head in response to a noise), or multiple characters (such as having your townspeople mine more stone). Outputs can be specific (affecting a single character in a certain way, like jumping into the air), or be high level ("we need to create Dragon units"), which could affect the behavior of many AI characters and change the course of many future decisions.
- *The overall structure of the decisions needed for the genre.* Some games have fairly simple or single-natured decisions. *Robotron* is a good example. The monsters

head towards a player's character, with a set speed and movement type, and try to kill the human player. But a complex game, like *Age of Empires*, requires many different types of decisions to be made during the game. The game involves team-level strategy, group strategy, unit tactics, an array of pathfinding problems (both single unit and group issues), and even more esoteric things, such as diplomacy. Each of these might represent a subsystem in the AI that is using an entirely different technique to get its job done.

CONTENT

Over and above the game's genre are special-case gameplay concerns brought about by special or novel game content. Games like *Black & White* required very specialized AI systems for the basic gameplay mechanism, that of teaching your main animal behaviors by leading it around and showing it how to do things. This requires careful deliberation when designing the framework up front, but can also be aided by early prototype work to flesh out design holes.

PLATFORM

Will the game be made for the personal computer, a home console, an arcade architecture, or for a handheld platform? Although the lines between these differing machines are beginning to blur, each still has its own specific requirements and limitations that must be taken into account. Some AI considerations on each platform include:

- *PC.* Online PC games might require user extensibility (in the form of included level or AI editors), so your AI system would need to handle a more data-driven approach to the world. Single-player PC games usually have fairly deep AI systems, because PC game players are usually a bit older and want a tad more complexity and opponent realism. The standard input mechanism on the PC is the mouse (except for flight simulators or racing games), so remember that if your game requires its human players to perform things that would be either tedious or impossible with the mouse, they'll cry foul. Also, the constantly-changing PC means that the minimum configuration for most games is going to keep climbing, so AI programmers need to predict the minimum configuration that the game will use (usually one to three years after the game is started) when making design decisions. PC game experiences are also usually longer (typically more than thirty hours of gameplay), and thus, the opponent AI needs to vary more often, so that playing against it doesn't get repetitive.
- *Consoles.* The realism constraints in consoles are lifted because console gamers are usually younger and more open to fantasy situations. However, there is a much higher usage of difficulty settings because the overall range of players'

skills is much greater. Memory and CPU budgets are usually much stricter because these machines (at least until recently) have been very limited compared with their PC brothers. Console games have a much higher standard of quality, for the most part—from a quality assurance standpoint, rather than a quality of game-play experience. Games on consoles usually don't crash, although this "PC only" problem has begun to creep into the console world. Because of this higher standard, however, your AI system has to endure much longer and more strenuous testing before it is approved for release. Many companies test their games internally, and then the maker of the console also tests the game before it gets to the shelves. Therefore, any "exotic" AI styles (such as learning systems) that are used in the game might make this testing process longer because of the inherent non-reproducibility of some of these advanced AI techniques.

- *Arcade.* The arcade platform was huge in the 1970s and 1980s when it was cost prohibitive to have advanced graphics hardware in everybody's home and home consoles were much simpler (like the Atari® 2600™ and Coleco-Vision®) in what they could display. Because of today's increasingly powerful home machines, the arcade industry has had to make large changes. Today, most arcade machines are one of three types: large, custom cabinets (such as sit-down racing games or skiing simulators), custom inputs (light gun games, music games), or small games that can be put in the corner of a bar or some other nondedicated arcade environment. Golden Tee golf is a good example of the last type. With the custom arcade machines, the sky is usually the limit in hardware. The entire package is customized, so the developer is free to put as much RAM and processing power as needed (within the limits of reason, of course). Smaller arcade games actually tend to be the opposite, and are sometimes sold as "kits," where the owner of the game can swap out parts from an old game with that of a newer game. Arcade AI is usually still "pattern-based," meaning that the AI follows set patterns instead of reacting to the player, because people assume that's what they're in for when they put in their quarter (or a dollar or more in some of the modern games). Tuning AI for the arcade environment usually involves putting a beta machine in a local venue, and getting statistics back from the machine to determine if areas of the game are too easy, too difficult, or whatever else might be detrimental to the amount of money coming into the machine. So, AI for the arcade world is usually simple, but the tuning is difficult because you are trying to balance fun factor with cash flow.

- *Handheld.* The most restrictive platform, the handheld world has been almost exclusively ruled by the Nintendo® Gameboy®, but has recently become the hot area of game development, with PDAs, cell phones, the Sony® PSP®, and just about every other gadget you can think of now being turned into gaming devices. These machines usually have very little RAM, the number of input buttons is severely limited (this is especially true on cell phones, which are not true game consoles and, thus, not designed to recognize more than one button being pressed at a time), and the graphical power of these mini-machines is very small. In fact, people who used to work heavily in the 8- and 16-bit worlds are finding their talents are marketable again. AI on these platforms needs to be clever, and optimized for both space and speed. As such, these machines usually use throwback techniques for their AI systems: patterned movement, enemies as mindless obstacles, or cheating (by using knowledge about the human that they only have because they're part of the program). However, this will change as more powerful handheld systems are developed, and the handheld/console line will blur.

DEVELOPMENT LIMITATIONS

Development limitations include budgetary concerns, manpower issues, and schedule length. Basically, the AI programmer needs to equate all these things into his or her one primary resource: time. The AI programmer really needs to have a good sense of time. How much time do you have to invest in the design phase, the production phase, and finally the test and tune phase? This last phase of the process is potentially the most important, as has been proven repeatedly by the best games inevitably being the most highly polished. True, designing the system is paramount as well because a well-designed engine will provide the programmer with the ability to add the necessary behavioral content to the game quickly and easily, but even the best-designed games need extensive tuning to get proper feel.

Because the role of AI in a game is inherently higher level (rather than low-level engine code, such as the math library, or the renderer) and because new ideas and behaviors seem to almost inevitably come up late in the production, AI systems are notorious for "feature creep." This is defined as new features being added toward the end of the project, such that the final completion date keeps creeping out into the future. This indicates one of two things: a bad game that requires additional elements to be fun or playable, or a good game that can be made just that much better. If you find yourself in the latter situation, good for you. If management is willing to take the additional investment of time and money to really maximize the product above its initial design, that's great. But tacking on additional elements as quickly as possible to make a questionable or failing game better is a recipe for disaster. A good, up-front game design really is your best line of defense against feature creep, but the production staff also needs to curtail this malady by keeping careful and strict accordance to the schedule.

As you will note in Part II, almost all games use some form of state-based AI, if not as the primary system. This is mostly because of the nature of games in general. People like at least some level of predictability in games—if you're constantly engaged in a never-ending, constantly-changing fight, you'll burn out quickly. The AI (or gameplay experience in general) in most games needs to be somewhat cyclical, with phases of action, followed by a phase of rest, and then repeat. This pacing lends itself well to a state-based approach. However, most games use combination engines, with multiple decision-making sections devoted to the differing AI problems found during the span of the game, so don't feel that a state-based model is the only way to go.

State-based methods are so prevalent because they are a means of organizationally dividing the state space of the entire game into manageable chunks. Instead of trying to tackle the logical connections between decisions across the entire game, you, in effect, split the game into smaller subgames that can be dealt with more easily. Even games that don't lend well to a state-based architecture as a whole can still benefit from the partitioning effect of a high-level state machine that can divvy up the solution state space into convenient pieces. By defining states that are really only *internal* states, a state machine can provide partitioning of the game world. For example, *Joust* is a very dynamic game, every level is pretty much the same (with the exception of the egg stages), and the AI system is more rule-based than state-based (each rider has a set couple of "rules" that govern their behavior). But you *could* divide a normal level of *Joust* into three states: a spawning state (in which the enemies are instantiated), a regular state (during normal gameplay), and an extended state (in which time has run out, and the Pterodactyl is after the human player). Optionally, you could divide the regular state even further. So, you could determine that the AI character is on the bottom layer of the screen, or the middle, or the top, and actually make that a state. The AI system could then respond with specific behavior to each location state. This piece of information could obviously be used as a simple modifier in the regular state (the regular state would have a switch statement dividing up the behavior determination based on the placement of the character, for example). But each resultant state is simpler, as well as easier to edit and extend, as opposed to a more complex, all-encompassing regular state. The correct balance between organizational simplicity and having repetitious code would have to be determined through planning and implementation.

Another reason for the preponderance of state machines in game AI is for testing, tuning, and debugging purposes. If the game's AI system isn't reproducible in some way, the quality assurance staff (QA, or "testers") are going to have a heck of a time determining if the game AI is faulty, or too hard, or outright crashes the computer. Tuning a game made with non-state based techniques is much harder, and adding specific suggestions can be very hard to implement (and we all know that producers are chock full of specific suggestions, sometimes dangerously close to product completion). These types of concerns will be discussed in more detail on a technique-by-technique basis in Parts III and IV of the book.

ENTERTAINMENT LIMITATIONS

Video games have become part of our culture. They've been a part of everyday life for a couple of generations, and show no signs of leaving anytime soon. People have grown up with games, and some of the more archetypical elements of games have become household terms. Games that go against gaming norms, or that don't allow standard gaming conventions can be responded to quite negatively. This includes things like the rock-paper-scissors (RPS) scenario. A commonly used notion in game design is that everything that can be done should have a countermove, thus leading to the RPS comparison. If your game's AI opponents have abilities that cannot be countered by the human player, you'd better have a good reason or your game isn't going to be much fun. But if the human can do something that the AI cannot counter, your game is going to be too easy, and you again lose out. This is the classic game *balancing* that is so crucial to the final success of a game.

How to best use difficulty levels is another entertainment question that must be answered by your AI system. Static skill levels (which are set before the game begins, usually by the player) are typically considered better than dynamic skill levels (levels that change in real time as the player progresses). This is because most players want to know the challenge level they are trying to beat (although you could set up a "static" difficulty level that the player would know is going to adjust as the game progresses). People's skill levels vary a great deal from person to person and at the specific task level. Dynamic skill level adjustments are very hard to tune. It is difficult to implement and still have the game players feel like the game or opponent is balanced and not cheating. Some people enjoy being very anxious about the game, loving the feeling of being just on the edge of their seats, but others just want to sit back and sail through like a tourist, noting the sights and such. Another problem with dynamic skill levels is that you have to somehow filter out exploratory or nonstandard behavior that the human does from behavior associated with being "stuck" or frustrated because of the difficulty.

Because we are making video games, and not movies, there is also a problem with getting across emotion or intent of the AI characters to the player, without being heavy-handed or trite. In movies and TV, this can be done with dramatic camera angles, lots of dialogue, and the inherent expressivity of the human face. In a game, it's much harder to use camera angles because (especially in three-dimensional games) the control scheme might be tied to the camera, or you might need a wide-angle camera in order to play the game (for example, a player might need to see most of the field in a football game, and gameplay would be hurt by even a fairly short close-up of somebody's face). Therefore, we are left with a somewhat limited set of tools to get this type of information across. We can caricature the emotion, which is useful for more cartoonish games, like *Crash Bandicoot* or *Ratchet and Clank.* The use of classic cartoon stretch and squash when animating moves in these games helps to really bring emotion into the characters from afar, without having to use a close-up camera. Dialogue can help but can get repetitive and also requires some level of lip-synching to look good. A character with a sad look on its face, but a generic flapping lower jaw while talking, isn't going to convey a particularly deep level of emotion. We need to realize that most actions have to be fairly obvious to be perceived. Better graphical power in today's platforms is making the problem of conveying emotions a bit easier to resolve. We can actually model more complex characters and use more subtle animations to enliven them, but home consoles still suffer from the limited resolution of regular TV, which means that small details are mostly blended into nothingness on non-HDTVs. Even with high-definition systems, the action should be on the slower side, or subtle details will be lost because you can never be sure where the player is focused.

INPUT HANDLERS AND PERCEPTION

AI perceptions can be defined as the things in the environment that you want the elements in your game to respond to. This might be as simple as the player's position (in *Robotron*, this was the only input to the AI of note, besides the enemy's own position) or something as complex as a record of the units that the computer has seen the human use in a real-time strategy (RTS) game. Usually, these types of data registers are encapsulated into a single-code module, if possible. Doing this makes it easier to add to the system, ensures that you are not repeating calculations in different parts of the AI system, helps in tuning, and distills the computations into an easily optimized central location.

A central perception system can also tag additional data or considerations on each input register, including perception type, update regularity, reaction time, thresholds, load balancing, compilation cost, and preconditions.

PERCEPTION TYPE

The various types of inputs might include standard coding data types like Boolean, integer, floating point, and so on. They might also include static perceptions (a perception needed for logic in a basketball game might be "Ball Handling Skill is greater than 75," which really only needs to be determined once, unless your game allows for that skill to be adjusting during a game).

UPDATE REGULARITY

Different perceptions might only need to be updated periodically because they don't change often or are expensive to recalculate constantly. This could be considered a form of reaction time, but it's more like a polled perception that you don't mind being slightly out of date. Continuing our basketball example, this could be used with line-of-sight check that determines if the ball holder has a clear lane to the basket. That's a pretty expensive check, especially if you use prediction on all the moving characters to determine if they will move out of the corridor in time to allow for passage. So, you might want to check this perception at set time intervals, instead of every update loop.

REACTION TIME

Reaction time is the pause before an enemy acknowledges a change in the environment. With a reaction time of zero, the computer seems just like, well, a computer. By giving a slightly random (or based on some skill attribute) amount of pause time before things are acknowledged by the enemy, the overall behavior of the system seems much more human and fair. This can also be tweaked for difficulty level, to make the overall game more or less difficult as desired. Reaction time can also give a modicum of personality to characters, so faster characters will respond more quickly than slower ones.

THRESHOLDS

Thresholds are the minimum and maximum values to which the AI will respond. This can be for simple data bounds checking but could also simulate a slightly deaf character (his minimum auditory threshold might be higher than that of other characters), or an eagle-eye enemy (who sees any movement at all, instead of large or fast movement). Thresholds can also go down or up in response to game events, again to simulate perception degradation or augmentation. So, a flash grenade would temporarily blind an opponent, but a patrol guard startled by an unidentified sound might actually become a more acute listener because he's paying so much more attention for a short while. This type of behavior is evidenced in the popular *Thief* games, for example.

LOAD BALANCING

In some games, the amount of data that the AI needs to take into account might be too numerous or too calculation-heavy to evaluate on any one game tick. Setting up your perception system so that you can specify the amount of time between updates of specific input variables is an easy way to load-balance the system so that you don't end up using too much CPU time for something that rarely changes.

COMPUTATION COST AND PRECONDITIONS

In addition to load balancing the calculations as just described, you should also consider raw computation cost. You can design your system with any hierarchically linked computations in mind from the start. Simple precondition calculations are done first, and as such, more complex determinations might not have to be done at all. To give an oversimplified example, let us say that in the game of *Pac-Man*, an AI routine for running the main character around needs to make (among others) two calculations: the number of power pills, and the distance to each power pill location. The main character would probably be better off checking the total number of power pills first (by checking some sort of power pill count variable, or polling the various pills to see how many are still active), to make sure there is one, before he recalculates his distance to all the power pills (as this is a more costly calculation).

The perception system you choose for your game will most likely be game-specific because the inputs to which your AI system will respond depend heavily on the type of game, the emphasis of the gameplay, any special powers that the characters or enemies have, and many other things. Some data your AI systems will require are simulated human sensory systems (such as line of sight or hearing radius), whereas others will just use the information straight from the game (like amount of gold left in the world). Make sure you don't go too far with this latter group, or you run the risk of cheating. More likely, you will need to use extended information for these game-specific kinds of input because they would be too costly to compute directly (such as a detailed map of everywhere the AI has been, or modeling a sense that someone is behind a player).

The two main paradigms for updating the perception registers are:

Polling: Checking for specific values to change, or making calculations, on a "game loop by game loop" basis—for example, checking to see if a basketball player is open for a pass every tick. This is necessary for much of the data that your AI will respond to, but it is also the kind of data that is much more likely to need load balancing (see earlier). Use this method for analog (continuous or real valued) inputs, or for values that may vary wildly in some form all the time.

Events: Using events is in some ways the opposite of polling; the input itself tells the perception system that it has changed, and the perception system notes that change. If no events are shunted to the perception system, it does nothing. This is the preferred method for digital inputs (on/off, or enumerative states) that don't change often (rather than thirty times a second or more, like the human player's position, for example). If you're going to have a constant stream of events being registered, queued, and then acted upon, you're really just adding overhead to a polling system (for that particular input) and probably don't want to use an event-based system.

Some games—stealth games in particular—make extensive use of advanced perception systems. This is because the senses of the enemies become a weapon against the player, and a large part of the game experience is about beating the perception system, in addition to the objectives of the game. See Chapter 5, Adventure Games, for more on this.

NAVIGATION

AI navigation is the art of getting from point A to point B. In our search for more realistic/thrilling/dramatic games, the worlds of modern games commonly involve large, complex environments with a variety of terrains, obstacles, movable objects, and the like. The reason we have well-researched AI algorithms for solving problems like this is because of the field of robotics, which has had to deal with trying to get robots to maneuver through tougher and tougher environments. Navigation is typically split into two main tasks: pathfinding and obstacle avoidance.

Pathfinding is an interesting, complex, and sometimes frustrating problem. In early games pathfinding was almost nonexistent, as environments were simple or wide open (like that in *Defender*, where the enemies simply headed in a player's exact direction), or the enemies really didn't head in the player's direction but, rather, random directions that the player had to avoid (like the barrels in *Donkey Kong*). When games started having real worlds in which to move around, all this changed. To have an AI character move intelligently from point A in the world to point B, you're going to need a dedicated system to help the player find the way. Several different schemes have come about to do this, including grid-based methods, simple avoidance and potential fields, map-node networks, navigation meshes, and combination systems. These methods will be discussed a bit more below.

GRID-BASED

In a grid-based system, the world is divided up into an even grid, usually either square or hexagonal, and the search algorithm A* (the heavyweight champ of pathfinding) or some close relative is used to find the shortest path using the grid. Each grid square has a "traversal possibility" value, usually from 0 (cannot pass through at all) to 1 (totally open for travel). Simple systems might use just binary values for the grid, where more complex setups would use the full analog values to show the height of the grid (to make it possible to simulate going uphill being harder than going downhill) or special attributes of the grid squares, such as water or someone standing. (See Figure 2.2.) Concerns with grid-based solutions are sheer memory size of the grid, as well as storage of the temporary data as the system finds the shortest

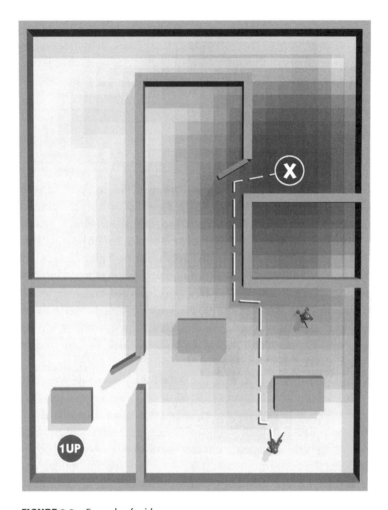

FIGURE 2.2   Example of grid squares.

path. High-resolution grids can become very cost-prohibitive because the amount of work the search algorithm has to do escalates dramatically.

SIMPLE AVOIDANCE AND POTENTIAL FIELDS

With simple avoidance and potential fields, you again separate the map into a grid. You then associate a vector with each grid area that exerts a push or pull on the AI character from areas of high potential to areas of low potential value. In an open world with convex obstacles, this technique can be preprocessed, leading to an almost optimal Voronoi diagram of the space (that is, a mathematically sound optimal "partition" of the space) providing good quality, fast pathfinding. The paths are extracted from the map by simply following the line of decreasing potential as

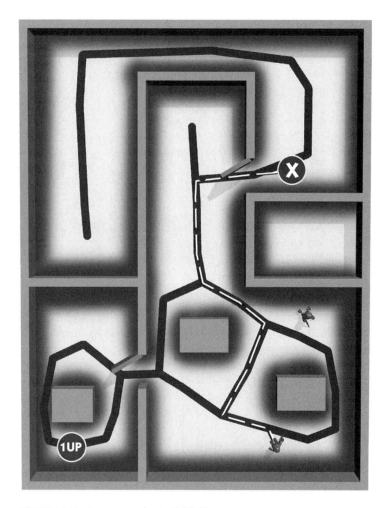

FIGURE 2.3   Preprocessed potential fields.

opposed to heavy searching. (See Figure 2.3.) With convex obstacles, however, you cannot preprocess because the vector would depend on a particular character's approach angle and direction of travel. In this case, the pressure is now on the run-time potential field generator.

MAP NODE NETWORKS

Map node networks are for more expansive worlds, or worlds with heavy use of three-dimensional structures. With this method, the level designers, during world construction, actually lay down a series of connected waypoints that represent interconnectedness among the rooms and halls that make up a particular game

FIGURE 2.4 Map node network systems.

space. (See Figure 2.4.) Then, just like the grid-based method, a search algorithm (most likely A*) will be used to find the shortest connected path between the points. In effect, you are using the same technique as described earlier, but are reducing the state space in which the algorithm will operate tremendously. The memory cost is much less for this system, but there is a cost. The node network becomes another data asset that has to be created correctly to model intelligent paths, and maintained if the level is changed. Also, this method doesn't lend itself well to dynamic obstacles, unless you don't mind inserting/removing the dynamic object locations into and out of the node network. A better way is to use some form of obstacle avoidance system to take care of moving objects, and use the node network to traverse the static environment. The obstacle avoidance system kicks in when a game agent gets too close to a dynamic obstacle, and just perturbs the direction of travel around it. Without a dynamic obstacle, the character would just head to the next path node directly.

NAVIGATION MESH

A navigation mesh system tries to get all the advantages of the map node system, without having to create or maintain the node network. By using the actual polygons used to build the map, this system algorithmically builds a path node network that the AI can use. (See Figure 2.5.) This is a much more powerful system, but can lead to some strange-looking paths if the method of constructing the navigation

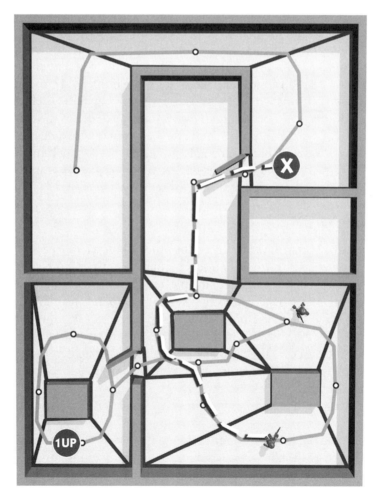

FIGURE 2.5   Navigation mesh systems.

mesh isn't fairly intelligent itself, or the levels were not built with the knowledge that this process was going to be performed.

This type of system is best used for simple navigation, because gameplay-specific path features (such as teleporters or elevators) can be difficult to extract with a general algorithm. You could have the level designers lay down specific connection data associated with these special case gameplay elements, and then your navigation mesh algorithm could use this data in building the network. However, if you're trying to spare the level designers the worry of dealing with navigation issues, this step would somewhat defeat the purpose of autogenerating a navigation mesh in the first place.

COMBINATION SYSTEMS

Some games use a combination of these techniques. Relatively open worlds might use a navigation mesh, but have underground passages that rely on path node networks. Games with lots of organic creature movement (like flocks of birds, or herds of animals) might use a potential fields solution to accentuate the group behavior, but have a fixed pathfinding system for more humanoid creatures, or a special network of nodes that only UFOs can use when flying in the air. By combining, you get the advantage of not having to overtax any one part of the system because you're using that system only for what it does best. You can then rely on another technique when the first one breaks down. It also helps that A* can be used to search through many different types of connected networks, so that you can use the same code to search through the different structures that you're using.

OBSTACLE AVOIDANCE

Dynamic obstacle avoidance, on the other hand, is a much simpler navigation task. It involves getting around objects that are in a player's direct line of travel. Avoidance is akin to dodging, in that a player temporarily changes his or her path to get around objects. The pathfinding system has found the player a legitimate path to get to his or her target location, but the player needs to adjust that path for now because something just got in the way. This temporary nature allows players to handle dynamic obstacles that appear in the world separately from the static pathfinding system. Chapter 20, Steering Behaviors, will cover all this in detail, but for now we shall introduce these concepts.

Avoidance is commonly done in a couple of different ways:

Potential fields: If your design already uses the potential fields for your primary pathfinding, you could use a similar method for avoidance. The various dynamic obstacles simply apply a repellant force away from their center, pushing invaders away. Make the force get stronger as the invader gets closer, until it finally stops the invader at some minimum distance.

Steering behaviors: Back in 1987, Craig Reynolds released a paper [Reynolds 87] detailing a system of behaviors for what he called "boids," creatures that moved in groups and had somewhat organic behavior without complex planning. In 1999, he updated his research by releasing another paper entitled, "Steering Behaviors for Autonomous Characters," [Reynolds 99] and games have been borrowing from it ever since. In it, he illustrated that with only a few mathematical forces you could very easily simulate realistic motion patterns for AI-controlled characters. The most popular application of Reynolds's techniques have been in the implementation of "flocking" systems (dealing with large groups of creatures, such as birds and fish). The same system can also be used for general movement, including avoidance. By using very simple sensors to determine future collisions, and then reacting accordingly with simple steering behaviors, avoidance can just be another element in your steering solution.

There are many, many articles and papers on pathfinding. So many early games did this task poorly, and were taken to task by critics, that this AI task is actually one of the more heavily explored problems in the AI world. This book will not be delving into implementation of specific pathfinding systems, but see the companion CD-ROM for links to materials concerning this important AI engine subsystem.

BRINGING IT ALL TOGETHER

By taking all of these considerations into account, and noting the strengths and weaknesses of the different AI techniques (as described in later parts of this book), you will assuredly find a solution to your game's AI needs. The basic steps involved in AI engine design are thus:

1. **Determine the different sections of your AI system:** Consider that you might have to treat these different parts as separate pieces to your engine. Each piece of your AI system may pose a problem that needs a specific AI technique to solve. Some of this is genre-specific. If you will be coding on a straightforward fighting game, you might need one real type of AI system (on most fighting games, the AI is usually heavily data-driven). But if you're going to be coding a large RTS, you might need several subsystems to accomplish the many levels of AI that encompass this genre.
2. **Determine the types of inputs to the system:** Will they be digital (on/off), some series of enumerative states, full floating-point analog values, or any combination of these?
3. **Determine the outputs that the system will use:** Along the same lines as the inputs, you may have very distinct outputs, like playing a specific

animation or performing in a very constrained behavior. You could have a number of analog outputs, such as speed, where you can be at 1.5 mph or 157.3 mph. But you might also have layered outputs; an example would be characters that can play different animations for the upper and lower parts of their body. This character's lower half might be connected strongly with movement, whereas the upper body could then be concerned mostly with holding a weapon, and aiming, or playing some taunt animation. In effect, you are now governing two outputs concurrently, and they are being layered onto the character in some way.

4. **Determine the primary logic you are going to need to link the inputs to the outputs:** Do you have real, hard, and steadfast rules? Do you have very general rules and a ton of exceptions? Do you have no rules at all, and merely modes that can layer onto each other to convey an overall logic? All of these setups are prevalent in today's games.

5. **Determine the type of communication links in your system:** Between objects in your game, between the AI systems you might need to code, and between the other game systems. Are you going to need continuous communication, or a more event-driven situation? Are you going to be getting back multiple messages from things within any particular game tick every so often, or almost always?

6. **Consider the attributes of each AI technique:** These types of considerations will give you a list of additional requirements that you will need from your individual AI entities, as well as the overall system. Take note of all the other limitations that your game will endure. Platform-specific concerns are a big category here. Schedule length is another issue, which is a hard one to deal with when you're first tackling an AI project. There are so many places to get tangled, and the high-level nature of AI work means that you're also relying on other people in the team to provide you with technology or art resources along the way. You have to be reasonable about the amount of work that you can accomplish, given these types of concerns, but also remember that if you work yourself into the ground, you'll go crazy or burn out.

At this point, you can consider the pros and cons of each AI technique, as detailed in Parts III and IV of the book, and you will find something that you can use to implement your system. If you can't seem to find the right technique, it might be because you haven't broken the problem down enough and are trying to tackle too large of a chunk at once. Try looking at the system (or subsystem) you are designing, and ensure that you aren't trying to pack too much functionality into a single AI technique, and choking it with complexity or exceptions.

Theory will only get you so far. Take the skeletal code included with this book and do some prototyping in your game. You might find specific failings with a particular method, discover that it is difficult to scale a technique to the level you require, or need additional elements for side AI issues. Consider this prototyping to be a part of the design phase of your AI engine. It will help you find holes in your plan, as well as break up the somewhat tedious task of class and structural design. Your final product will be better for it.

SUMMARY

This chapter covered the foundation systems inherent in a game AI engine and described the primary points to consider when designing and building an engine. The three main portions of an AI engine are decision making, perception, and navigation.

- The type of decision-making technique you use should rely on game-specific factors like types of solutions, agent reactivity, system realism, genre, special content, platform, and development and entertainment limitations.
- Perception systems are usually central locations for input data calculations for the AI characters. By keeping it central, the AI system prevents excessive recalculation and aids debugging and development.
- Perception systems can also take into account low-level details, including update regularity, reaction time, thresholds, load balancing, and computation cost and preconditions.
- Navigation systems for game AI usually fall into one of four main paradigms: grid-based, simple avoidance and potential fields, map node networks, and navigation meshes. Some games use combinations of these hierarchically.
- Obstacle avoidance is a more local system dealing with short-term goals.
- When designing your AI system, use the following process:
  1. break down the overall system into sections
  2. determine inputs and input types, determine outputs and output types
  3. determine logic needed to unite the two
  4. determine communication types needed
  5. determine other system limitations
  6. consider the attributes of each AI technique
- If you're having trouble fitting a system into a technique, you might need to simplify (by subdividing) the current system you're working on, or maybe a different technique will be better.
- Prototyping your AI system as part of the design phase will help to ensure that your system is flexible enough to handle everything you will need from it, and will quickly point out holes in design or implementation, which will be much more easily fixed before the full production cycle is underway.

3   AIsteroids: Our AI Test Bed

In This Chapter

This chapter will introduce the small application that will become the test bed for the various AI techniques, AIsteroids. As the name implies, it is a very simplified version of an *Asteroids*-style game, with only rocks (represented by circles), an AI or human-controlled ship (represented by a triangle), and powerups that increase your shot power (represented by squares) to begin with. The ship can turn, thrust (forward and reverse), use "hyperspace," and shoot. Later we will incorporate additional elements (an alien craft, different weapons, and powerups) as the need arises to show off particular AI techniques. This application was picked because of its simplicity and because the various AI methods could be implemented within the program easily.

Before we begin dissecting the code of the basic classes within the AI system, a quick note on some of the coding practices used in this book:

- All variables are in CamelCase (meaning that multiword names are all stuck together, with each new word capitalized; examples are `thisVariableIsLocal` and `nextItemInList`).
- All class member variables start with the "m_" prefix. Examples are `m_lifeTimer` and `m_velocity`.

- All local variables begin with a lower case letter. Examples are `index` and `someVariable`.
- Class member Functions begin with an uppercase letter. Examples are `Update()` and `Draw()`.
- Global utility functions are in all uppercase. Examples are `DOT` and `MIN`.
- Global macro functions are in all lowercase. Examples are `randflt` and `randint`.

Figure 3.1 shows the layout of the various classes used. This fairly flat hierarchy has only one major base class, the `GameObj`. The dynamic objects in the game—asteroids, bullets, explosions, powerups, and ships—are all `GameObj` children. This allows the `GameSession` class, which is the main game logic depository, to have a complete list of `GameObjs` on which it can act. There are three other main files:—`Aisteroids.cpp` and the `utility.cpp` and `utility.h` files. `Aisteroids.cpp` is the main loop, as well as the initialization code for the OpenGL Utility Toolkit (GLUT). The `utility.cpp` and `utility.h` files include some useful math functions, several game-related definitions, and functions for drawing text to the screen under GLUT.

THE `GameObj` CLASS

As shown in Listing 3.1, the `GameObj` class is very straightforward. The class encapsulates object creation, collision (both checking for physical collisions and any special code that needs to run in the event of a collision), basic physical movement, and `Draw()` and `Update()` methods. `Explode()` handles the spawning of explosions for object types that explode when they collide.

Note the enumeration for object types. They have been made bitwise values instead of a straight integer enumeration so that the code can also use these types for collision flags. Each object must register for the specific object types with which it will collide, and this bitwise representation allows an object to register collisions with multiple object types. Collisions for all game objects are handled with simple collision spheres that test for intersection.

Also, notice that by default a plain `GameObj` does not draw, explode, or perform any special code at collision time. Children of this class must override these member functions to facilitate each action.

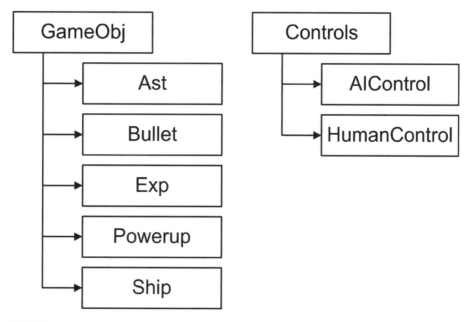

FIGURE 3.1   Alsteroids class structure.

LISTING 3.1 Header for the GameObj class.

```
class GameObj
{
public:
    //constructors/functions
    GameObj(float _size = 1);
    GameObj(const Point3f &_p,
            const float _angle,
            const Point3f &_v);
    virtual void Draw(){}
    virtual void Init();
    virtual void Update(float t);
    virtual bool IsColliding(GameObj *obj);
    virtual void DoCollision(GameObj *obj) {}
    virtual void Explode() {}

    //unit vector in facing direction
    Point3f UnitVectorFacing();
    Point3f UnitVectorVelocity();

    enum//collision flags/object types
    {
        OBJ_NONE     = 0x00000001,
        OBJ_ASTEROID = 0x00000010,
        OBJ_SHIP     = 0x00000100,
        OBJ_BULLET   = 0x00001000,
        OBJ_EXP      = 0x00010000,
        OBJ_POWERUP  = 0x00100000,
        OBJ_TARGET   = 0x01000000
    };

    //data
    Point3f      m_position;
    Point3f      m_axis;
    float        m_angle;
    Point3f      m_velocity;
    float        m_angVelocity;
    bool         m_active;
    float        m_size;
    Sphere3f     m_boundSphere;
    int          m_type;
    unsigned int m_collisionFlags;
    int          m_lifeTimer;
};
```

THE GameObj UPDATE FUNCTION

Listing 3.2 is the base class update function, which updates the base physics parameters (m_position and m_angle) and decrements the optional m_lifeTimer, which is a generic way of having game objects last for a set period of time and then automatically removing themselves from the world. This feature is used for bullets, explosions, and powerups. In this game, positions are essentially two-dimensional. We are keeping true three-dimensional positions for each object, but the Z component is always set to 0, and thus the world represents a flat two-dimensional plane.

LISTING 3.2   The base game object update () function.

```
//——————————————
void GameObj::Update(float dt)
{
    m_velocity  += dt*m_accelleration;
    m_position  += dt*m_velocity;
    m_angle     += dt*m_angVelocity;
    m_angle      = CLAMPDIR180(m_angle);

    if(m_position.z() !=0.0f)
    {
        m_position.z() = 0.0f;
    }
    if(m_lifeTimer != NO_LIFE_TIMER)
    {
        m_lifeTimer -= dt;
        if(m_lifeTimer<0.0f)
            m_active=false;
    }
};
```

THE Ship OBJECT

The ship object is a GameObj, with the addition of controls and the ability to fire bullets. Listing 3.3 shows the class header. The majority of the class methods represent the behaviors available to the ship: the controls of the craft, powerup management, bullet firing, and bookkeeping. The m_invincibilityTime integer sets the initial period of invincibility when a level starts, or when the main ship respawns. The variable m_shotPowerLevel is an accumulator for powerups that affect a player's shooting power level. If you were to create additional powerup types, you would probably want to give the structure accumulator variables for those as well. The Update() function is only mildly different from the base class; the Update() function checks to see if m_thrust is true, and if so, calculates an acceleration, and then updates velocity, position, and angle. The function also updates the m_invincibilityTime, if required.

LISTING 3.3   The ship class header.

```
class Ship : public GameObj
{
public:
     //constructor/functions
     Ship();
     virtual void Draw();
     virtual void Init();
     virtual void Update(float t);
     virtual bool IsColliding(GameObj *obj);
     virtual void DoCollision(GameObj *obj);

     //ship controls
     void ThrustOn()    {m_thrust=true; m_revThrust=false;}
     void ThrustReverse(){m_revThrust=true; m_thrust=false;}
     void ThrustOff()    {m_thrust=false; m_revThrust=false;}
     void TurnLeft();
     void TurnRight();
     void StopTurn()    {m_angVelocity=0.0;}
     void Stop();
     void Hyperspace();

     //Powerup Management
     virtual void GetPowerup(int powerupType);
     int GetShotLevel()  {return m_shotPowerLevel;}
     int GetNumBullets(){return m_activeBulletCount;}
     void IncNumBullets(int num = 1){m_activeBulletCount+=num;}
     void MakeInvincible(float time){m_invincibilityTimer = time;}

     //bullet management
     virtual int MaxBullet();
     void TerminateBullet(){if(m_activeBulletCount > 0)
                            m_activeBulletCount-;};
     virtual void Shoot();
     virtual float GetClosestGunAngle(float angle);
```

```
        //data
        Control* m_control;
private:
        int      m_activeBulletCount;
        Point3f  m_accelleration;
        bool     m_thrust;
        bool     m_revThrust;
        int      m_shotPowerLevel;
        float    m_invincibilityTimer;
};
```

THE OTHER GAME OBJECTS

Exp (explosions) and Powerup are very simple objects that simply instantiate, last
for their preset lifetime, and then disappear. If a ship collides with a powerup,
however, that ship will call its GetPowerup() function in response to the collision.
Asteroids are simple objects that just float around, don't have a maximum lifetime, and will split apart when struck by a bullet, if big enough. The target object
is for debugging (unless you wanted to implement it for something else, such as
homing missiles), and is simply a game object with no logic that displays itself
as an X.

Bullets require one further collision step, as shown in Listing 3.4.

LISTING 3.4 The bullet special collision code.

```
void Bullet::DoCollision(GameObj *obj)
{
    //take both me and the other object out
    if(obj->m_active)
    {
        obj->Explode();
        obj->DoCollision(this);
    }
    m_active=false;
    if(m_parent)
    {
        Game.IncrementScore(ASTEROID_SCORE_VAL);
        m_parent->TerminateBullet();
    }
}
```

In this simple function, the bullet also increments the score, and calls its parent's `TerminateBullet()` function (this depends on whether you set this bullet to have a ship parent because bullets can be freely instantiated as well), which just decrements the number of shots the ship has active. The bullet will also kill off the other object with which it collides. The general collision system only calls the—`Explode()` and `DoCollision()` functions for the first object in the collision, for optimization reasons. Therefore bullets, which require both objects to run collide code, need this special case consideration.

THE GameSession CLASS

The overall game structure is shown in Listing 3.5. Most of the class is public because it will be accessed by the main game functions. The game is divided into a few high-level states: `STATE_PLAY`, `STATE_PAUSE`, `STATE_NEXTWAVE`, and `STATE_GAMEOVER`. These are very basic game flow states and serve only as modifiers to the draw and control codes. For this demonstration program, there are two `Control` classes that are instantiated, a `HumanControl` class that handles the keyboard events, and an `AIControl` class, which for right now does nothing but will eventually be where we put our AI code for the game.

LISTING 3.5   The `GameSession` class header.

```
typedef std::list<GameObj*> GameObjectList;
Class GameSession
{
public:
    //constructor/functions
    GameSession();
    void Update(float dt);
    void Draw();
    void DrawLives();
    void Clip(Point3f &p);
        void PostGameObj(GameObj*obj)
          {m_activeObj.push_back(obj);}

    //game controls
    enum
    {
        CONTROL_THRUST_ON,
        CONTROL_THRUST_REVERSE,
        CONTROL_THRUST_OFF,
```

```
        CONTROL_RIGHT_ON,
        CONTROL_LEFT_ON,
        CONTROL_STOP_TURN,
        CONTROL_STOP,
        CONTROL_SHOOT,
        CONTROL_HYPERSPACE,
        CONTROL_PAUSE,
        CONTROL_AION,
        CONTROL_AIOFF
};
void UseControl(int control);

//score functions
void IncrementScore(int inc)    {m_score += inc;}
void ResetScore()               {m_score = 0;}

//game related functions
void StartGame();
void StartNextWave();
void LaunchAsteroidWave();
void WaveOver();
void GameOver();
void KillShip(GameObj *ship);

//data
  Ship*         m_mainShip;
  HumanControl* m_humanControl;
  AIControl*    m_AIControl;

bool  m_bonusUsed;
int   m_screenW;
int   m_screenH;
int   m_spaceSize;
float m_respawnTimer;
float m_powerupTimer;
int   m_state;
int   m_score;
int   m_numLives;
int   m_waveNumber;
int   m_numAsteroids;
bool  m_AIOn;

enum
{
```

```
            STATE_PLAY,
            STATE_PAUSE,
            STATE_NEXTWAVE,
            STATE_GAMEOVER
        };
    private:
        GameObjList m_activeObj;
        };
```

The list of dynamic objects for the game is stored in a Standard Template Library (STL) `list` structure called `m_activeObj`. This program was written for simplicity, so it does things like `new` and `delete` memory while in game, whereas most real games try to achieve a solid memory allocation beforehand to prevent memory fragmentation (one method could be to allocate a large pool of the different `GameObj` structures, and then manage their use as needed). By placing all the game objects in this structure, the `Update()` function for `GameSession` is very simple and generic. The discussion of this function will be shown split into eight parts, so that each part of the update can be discussed separately. See Listings 3.6.1 through 3.6.7.

PRIMARY LOGIC AND COLLISION CHECKING

Listing 3.6.1 is the primary part of the update loop. It sets up a `for` loop to iterate through all the game objects, and then for each object, runs its `Update()` method and clips its position to the viewport (which also wraps the position around, asteroids style). The function then checks for any collisions with other objects, by looping through the objects and calling the `IsColliding()` method on each. The collision calculations are optimized by the following rules:

1. An object must be registered to collide by having its `m_collisionFlags` variable not contain the `GameObj::OBJ_NONE` bit.
2. The object will only do collision checks against objects of the types for which it is registered.
3. An object cannot collide with another object that isn't active (it `m_active` member is false).
4. Objects cannot collide with themselves.

LISTING 3.6.1   `GameSession`'s update loop, section 1: update and collision checking.

```
void GameSession::Update(float dt)
{
```

```
GameObjectList::iterator list1;
for(list1=m_activeObj.begin();
    list1!=m_activeObj.end();++list1)
{
    //update logic and positions
    if((*list1)->m_active)
    {
        (*list1)->Update(dt);
        Clip((*list1)->m_position);
    }
    else continue;

    //check for collisions
    if((*list1)->m_collisionFlags !=
        GameObj::OBJ_NONE)
    {
        GameObjectList::iterator list2;
        for(list2=m_activeObj.begin();
            list2!=m_activeObj.end();++list2)
        {
            //don't collide with yourself
            if(list1 == list2)
              continue;

            if((*list2)->m_active        &&
              ((*list1)->m_collisionFlags &
                (*list2)->m_type)        &&
              (*list1)->IsColliding(*list2))
            {
                (*list1)->Explode();
                (*list1)->DoCollision((*list2));
            }
        }
    }
    if(list1==m_activeObj.end()) break;
}//main for loop
}
```

OBJECT CLEANUP

Objects that were destroyed by a collision or an object that has outlived its life counter variable will be removed from the object list by the code shown in Listing 3.6.2, and then erased. The functor that checks for the inactive condition (RemoveNotActive) is also in charge of deleting the actual memory taken up by the object; the erase function just takes it out of the GameSession object list.

LISTING 3.6.2 GameSession's update loop, section 2: killed object cleanup.

```
//get rid of inactive objects
    GameObjectList::iterator end    = m_activeObj.end();
    GameObjectList::iterator newEnd =
            remove_if(m_activeObj.begin(),
                m_activeObj.end(),RemoveNotActive);
    if(newEnd != end)
        m_activeObj.erase(newEnd,end);
```

SPAWNING MAIN SHIP AND POWERUPS

Listings 3.6.3 and 3.6.4 are simple parts of the update function that check a couple of timers, m_respawnTimer and m_powerupTimer. The respawn timer is used when the main ship has been destroyed; it takes a small pause before respawning. This is so the player has time to realize his ship has exploded. The powerup timer provides for the pause between each powerup spawning. If this time is up, the game spawns a new powerup with random position and velocity and adds it to the main object list.

LISTING 3.6.3 GameSession's update loop, section 3: respawn main ship.

```
//check for no main ship, respawn
    if(m_mainShip == NULL || m_respawnTimer>=0)
    {
        m_respawnTimer-=dt;
        if(m_respawnTimer <0.0f)
        {
            m_mainShip = new Ship;
            if(m_mainShip)
            {
                PostGameObj(m_mainShip);
                m_humanControl->SetShip(m_mainShip);
                m_AIControl->SetShip(m_mainShip);
            }
        }
    }
```

LISTING 3.6.4 GameSession's update loop, section 4: spawn powerups.

```
//occasionally spawn a powerup
    m_powerupTimer -=dt;
    if(m_powerupTimer <0.0f)
    {
```

```
        m_powerupTimer = randflt()*6.0f + 4.0f;
        Powerup* pow = new Powerup;
        if(pow)
        {
            pow->m_position.x()= randFlt()*m_screenW;
            pow->m_position.y()= randFlt()*m_screenH;
            pow->m_position.z()= 0;
            pow->m_velocity.x()= randFlt()*40 - 20;
            pow->m_velocity.y()= randFlt()*40 - 20;
            pow->m_velocity.z()= 0;
            PostGameObj(pow);
        }
    }
```

BONUS LIVES

Listing 3.6.5 does a simple score check, and every 10,000 points, it awards the player another life. This is fairly straightforward and is a common practice in these kinds of games.

LISTING 3.6.5   `GameSession's` update loop, section 5: bonus lives.

```
//check for additional life bonus each 10K points
    if(m_score >= m_bonusScore)
    {
        m_numLives++;
        m_bonusScore += BONUS_LIFE_SCORE;
    }
```

END OF LEVEL AND GAME

The next two listings (3.6.6 and 3.6.7) check for two important game conditions, the end of the current level (determined when no asteroids are left for the player to shoot), and end of the game (determined when the player has no more lives left). Each of these conditions calls a function, `WaveOver()` or `GameOver()`, which sets some critical flags, and also advances the overall game state to either STATE_NEXTWAVE or STATE_GAMEOVER.

LISTING 3.6.6   `GameSession's` update loop, section 6: end of level.

```
//check for finished wave
    if(!m_numAsteroids)
    {
```

```
        m_waveNumber++;
        WaveOver();
    }
```

LISTING 3.6.7   GameSession's update loop, section 7: game over.

```
//check for finished game, and reset
    if(!m_numLives)
        GameOver();
```

THE Control CLASS

To give commands to a ship, the system makes use of the Control class. Control's base class contains the barebones structure, including Update(), Init(), and an m_ship pointer to the ship to be controlled. This class is the parent to both the human control system (HumanControl) and to the AI (AIControl). The HumanControl class is a bit different in that it doesn't use its update function. Rather, it's just the depository for the global callbacks that the program passes to GLUT to perform keyboard checks and notifications. If the game were more complex, we would implement a state-based control scheme (or some other way of separating the system functionality) and use the full functionality of the Control class. Later in the book, when we implement the various AI methodologies, we'll start by creating a specific AIControl class to house the particulars of each AI method.

THE AI SYSTEM HOOKS

The GameSession class checks to see if the AI system is turned on, and if so, the Update() function for the AIControl class is called. This update function is stubbed out in AIControl.cpp, meaning that the AI system does nothing here. Again, this is just the framework for the future implementations of each AI technique. We will later make child classes of this barebones AIControl class that will run specific code for each technique.

The only other things of note in the base class are some debug data fields, which were used in developing the demo programs in this book and were left in to serve as a good start for any additional debugging information you might add. It's good practice to include debugging hooks in your system right from the start, so that you don't have to spend precious time during development trying to patch debugging output into your AI engine.

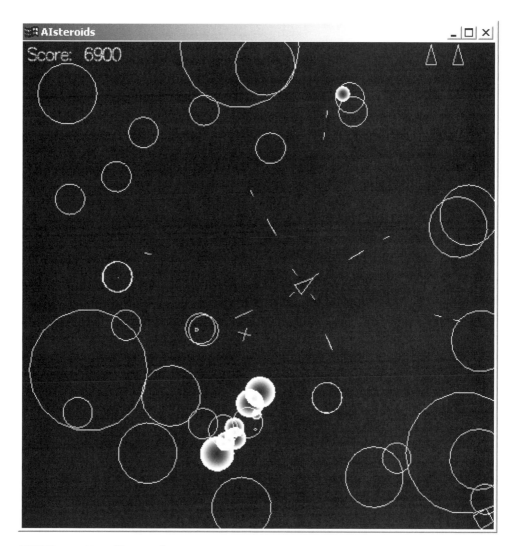

FIGURE 3.2   AIsteroids screenshot.

The two update functions, `Update()` and `UpdatePerceptions()`, deal with system-level data objects. These functions are separated to emphasize the separation of game *objects* from game *perceptions*. `UpdatePerceptions` handles the refreshing of all the game variables that the objects in your game will use to make decisions (all of these inputs to the system could be called *perceptions*), whereas the regular update function handles all the functions for the game objects themselves. Figure 3.2 shows a screenshot of the test bed running the finite state machines (FSM) AI system from Chapter 15.

GAME MAIN LOOP

AIsteroids.cpp is the main game file for the project. It initializes GLUT and sets up the callback pointers for updating the game, drawing the game, and handling all the input from Windows or the user (the global functions that handle the keyboard are in the HumanControl.cpp file).

SUMMARY

This chapter described the primary test-bed application the book will use for implementing each AI technique in Parts III and IV. The overall class structure was discussed, as were the notable sections of the base class code.

- GameObj is the basic game object class. It takes care of physics and handles object drawing and updating.
- The current objects in the game include asteroids, bullets, explosions, powerups, ships, and a debugging target object.
- GameSession is the singular game class. It takes care of all the variables and structures needed to run a game. It has the primary update and draw functions for the game. It spawns all additional game elements and manages object-to-object collision checking.
- Aisteroids.cpp is the main loop file, and it includes all the initialization of GLUT and all the GLUT callbacks for running the game.
- The Control class handles the logic for a ship object. This logic can be in the form of an AI technique or keyboard functionality for a human player.
- The AIControl class will be the branching point for our AI to hook into the system. By overriding the class with a specific AI method class (for example, FSMAIControl, discussed in Chapter 15), we can use this game application with CPU-controlled opponents. The keyboard control will still be enabled, but this is to facilitate the application as a test bed (we still want to be able to send keyboard events to the game when the AI system is running).

4 Role-Playing Games (RPGs)

In This Chapter

- Common AI Elements
- Useful AI Techniques
- Examples
- Exceptions
- Specific Game Elements That Need Improvement
- Grammar Machines
- Quest Generators
- Better Party Member AI
- Better Enemies
- Fully-Realized Towns
- Summary

As personal computers became more mainstream, one of the first new game genres to appear was the *role-playing game,* or RPG. RPGs became popular because they were a radical departure from the fast, twitch-based action games that had dominated the arcades. They allowed for more thoughtful strategy, and were able to give the player much more interesting input opportunities by using the keyboard found on personal computers rather then an arcade-style controller and a button or two. They also enveloped the player in a rich storyline, and gave the player a high degree of identification with the hero since the game took so long to complete. Arcade-style games, which in those days were mostly shooters or platformers, were typically designed to be over quickly (for profit reasons, but also because of limited complexity) so a game that takes a long investment in time and effort was a complete departure from the arcade norm. The RPG allowed for characters that grew and morphed over time, thus permitting players to really get to know, and affect the development of the main characters.

The earliest RPGs were either text based (like *Adventure* or *Wumpus*) or had art crafted out of ASCII characters like *Rogue* and *NetHack* (see Listing 4.1 for a code snippet from *NetHack*—the listed function is a generic method for determining and defining missile attacks from an AI-controlled enemy). The gameplay tended to be mostly exploratory (leading many of these games to be called "dungeon crawlers"), with random monster encounters and turn-based combat systems. Typically, the dungeon itself is randomly generated, and as such you could continue to advance and discover deeper dungeons pretty much forever.

The next wave of RPGs finally came out with graphical art, but the images were static, like *The Bard's Tale* and *Wizardry*. Typically, these games were just graphically upgraded versions of early RPGs, but some started to craft specific locations and included backstory and secondary characters. They also typically had an "ending," in which players actually defeated the final bad guy and saved the world (or something along those lines).

Modern RPGs are generally fully open, sprawling worlds filled with other characters, monsters, places to explore, and tons of interaction with both people and objects in the game. Today, both console and computer RPGs have blurred the platform line, with games like *Diablo* being a computer game with simple, console-like action-oriented gameplay; and the new online persistent RPGs on the consoles are all but identical to their personal computer brothers.

LISTING 4.1   Code snippet from the Open Source ASCII RPG, NetHack.

```
     Distributed under the NetHack GPL.
/* monster attempts ranged weapon attack against player */
void
thrwmu(mtmp)
struct monst *mtmp;
{
    struct obj *otmp, *mwep;
    xchar x, y;
    schar skill;
    int multishot;
    const char *onm;

    /* Rearranged beginning so monsters can use polearms not in a
            line */
    if (mtmp->weapon_check == NEED_WEAPON || !MON_WEP(mtmp)) {
        mtmp->weapon_check = NEED_RANGED_WEAPON;
        /* mon_wield_item resets weapon_check as appropriate */
        if(mon_wield_item(mtmp) != 0) return;
    }

    /* Pick a weapon */
    otmp = select_rwep(mtmp);
```

```
if (!otmp) return;

if (is_pole(otmp)) {
    int dam, hitv;

    if (dist2(mtmp->mx, mtmp->my, mtmp->mux, mtmp->muy) >
            POLE_LIM ||
        !couldsee(mtmp->mx, mtmp->my))
    return;     /* Out of range, or intervening wall */

    if (canseemon(mtmp)) {
    onm = xname(otmp);
    pline("%s thrusts %s.", Monnam(mtmp),
            obj_is_pname(otmp) ? the(onm) : an(onm));
    }

    dam = dmgval(otmp, &youmonst);
    hitv = 3 - distmin(u.ux,u.uy, mtmp->mx,mtmp->my);
    if (hitv < -4) hitv = -4;
    if (bigmonst(youmonst.data)) hitv++;
    hitv += 8 + otmp->spe;
    if (dam < 1) dam = 1;

    (void) thitu(hitv, dam, otmp, (char *)0);
    stop_occupation();
    return;
}
x = mtmp->mx;
y = mtmp->my;
/* If you are coming toward the monster, the monster
 * should try to soften you up with missiles.  If you are
 * going away, you are probably hurt or running.  Give
 * chase, but if you are getting too far away, throw.
 */
if (!lined_up(mtmp) ||
    (URETREATING(x,y) &&
        rn2(BOLT_LIM - distmin(x,y,mtmp->mux,mtmp->muy))))
    return;

skill = objects[otmp->otyp].oc_skill;
mwep = MON_WEP(mtmp);          /* wielded weapon */

/* Multishot calculations */
multishot = 1;
if ((ammo_and_launcher(otmp, mwep) || skill == P_DAGGER ||
```

```
    skill == -P_DART || skill == -P_SHURIKEN) && !mtmp->mconf) {
    /* Assumes lords are skilled, princes are expert */
    if (is_prince(mtmp->data)) multishot += 2;
    else if (is_lord(mtmp->data)) multishot++;

    switch (monsndx(mtmp->data)) {
    case PM_RANGER:
        multishot++;
        break;
    case PM_ROGUE:
        if (skill == P_DAGGER) multishot++;
        break;
    case PM_NINJA:
    case PM_SAMURAI:
        if (otmp->otyp == YA && mwep &&
        mwep->otyp == YUMI) multishot++;
        break;
    default:
    break;
    }
    /* racial bonus */
    if ((is_elf(mtmp->data) &&
        otmp->otyp == ELVEN_ARROW &&
        mwep && mwep->otyp == ELVEN_BOW) ||
    (is_orc(mtmp->data) &&
        otmp->otyp == ORCISH_ARROW &&
        mwep && mwep->otyp == ORCISH_BOW))
    multishot++;

    if ((long)multishot > otmp->quan)
            multishot = (int)otmp->quan;
    if (multishot < 1) multishot = 1;
    else multishot = rnd(multishot);
}

if (canseemon(mtmp)) {
    char onmbuf[BUFSZ];

    if (multishot > 1) {
    /* "N arrows"; multishot > 1 implies otmp->quan > 1, so
        xname()'s result will already be pluralized */
    Sprintf(onmbuf, "%d %s", multishot, xname(otmp));
    onm = onmbuf;
    } else {
```

```
        /* "an arrow" */
        onm = singular(otmp, xname);
        onm = obj_is_pname(otmp) ? the(onm) : an(onm);
        }
        m_shot.s = ammo_and_launcher(otmp,mwep) ? TRUE : FALSE;
        pline("%s %s %s!", Monnam(mtmp),
          m_shot.s ? "shoots" : "throws", onm);
        m_shot.o = otmp->otyp;
    } else {
        m_shot.o = STRANGE_OBJECT;
            /* don't give multishot feedback */
    }

    m_shot.n = multishot;
    for (m_shot.i = 1; m_shot.i <= m_shot.n; m_shot.i++)
        m_throw(mtmp, mtmp->mx, mtmp->my, sgn(tbx), sgn(tby),
            distmin(mtmp->mx, mtmp->my,
                        mtmp->mux, mtmp->muy), otmp);
    m_shot.n = m_shot.i = 0;
    m_shot.o = STRANGE_OBJECT;
    m_shot.s = FALSE;


        nomul(0);
}
```

RPGs, in general, follow a simple formula: the player starts with nothing, performs tasks for treasure and money (mostly killing monsters and going on quests), trains his or her skills, and eventually builds his or her character into a powerhouse figure that can then right the ultimate wrongs of the land. Some games include a whole party of adventurers, so the player is in effect building up a whole team of characters. Whatever the technical details, the name of the game is immersion: getting the player to identify with the main character, and caring enough to invest the vast amount of time necessary to build the character up and eventually finish the game.

The enemy-filled, constantly hostile world of most RPGs might seem odd, but not to teenagers. In a way, young people somewhat *relate* to a character who is solitary in the world, against everyone, universally misunderstood and attacked. It's what gives RPGs their appeal to many of the youth who play them. The inclusion of a small band of party members ties nicely into the clique-ish world of most teens, in which they form a small group of intense friends, and extend the "me against the world" fight to include these people as well. This argument is not to say that older or younger people cannot enjoy RPGs but, rather, speaks to a theoretical reason why some people find these types of games popular.

RPGs are fairly AI-intensive, because they are usually expansive games, with varying types of gameplay and many hours of gaming experiences per title. As such, the apparent intelligence of the varying game elements has to be higher than most, or at least more heavily scripted. The sheer number of hours people invest in an RPG will make any behavioral repetition much more obvious, as well as making small annoyances (like pathfinding hangups) in AI behavior appear larger.

On home computers, users demand a minimum of 40 or so hours of gameplay from an RPG. Consoles are a bit lower, usually 20 to 40. This formula seems to be somewhat fixed in the minds of game players (a strange mix of the approximate amount of time a game can keep a player's interest, and marketing education about how much gameplay a buyer can expect for their money), but there are exceptions, like *Baldur's Gate* for the PC having 100+ hours of play.

Because of these hefty gameplay *quantity* demands, your game needs a variety of gameplay types (such as puzzles, combat, crafting, different types of travel, etc.) or your primary combat system had better be *very* fun and addicting. The *Diablo* games fall into the latter category. The gameplay is very repetitive, but also very addictive. Some have theorized that the game somehow awakens our inherent "hunter-gatherer" lineage, and we just can't stop clicking the mouse.

COMMON AI ELEMENTS

RPGs contain a number of commonly AI-controlled elements. These include both antagonistic characters (enemies, bosses, and non-player characters), as well as good or neutral characters (shopkeepers, and other party members). Since RPGs' main gameplay revolve in many ways around character interaction, either combat or otherwise, each of these elements can be quite complex.

ENEMIES

The majority of the population of most RPG worlds is *enemies*. An almost endless supply of enemies is needed to provide the player with something to dispatch and get experience points, money, and powerful new items. RPGs in the past used almost exclusively what can be described as *statistical* AI, in that the attributes (strength, size, hit points, etc.) of the monsters determined everything about them: the attacks they use, the way they fight, how tough they are in general, what treasure they drop when they die, and so on. Today's games go a bit further and have enemies that are more hand-tailored. These modern enemies also use more complex behavior patterns, including running away, healing themselves, fighting in groups by surrounding a player and using complementary attack methods, and so forth.

Since enemies in RPGs usually come in such numbers during a game, the AI is specifically set up to be more *A* and not so much *I*. Turn-based RPGs of the past (*Bard's Tale, Phantasy Star, Chrono Trigger*), the so-called real-time combat RPG (*The Legend of Zelda,* the later *Ultima*™ games, *Diablo, Terranigma*), and the fusion variants brought about recently (*Baldur's Gate* or *Icewind Dale,* which are real-time games that can be paused and, thus, made to act turn-based) all pretty much boil down the enemies to be combination *containers* (of wealth and experience points) and *obstacles* (by being "walls" of a certain number of hit points that the hero must destroy to get by). Very few games go beyond this kind of simple-style enemy to create anything with personality, ingenuity, or shifting strategy.

This is done by design, of course. When a player who has spent 60 or more hours playing your game goes into a room and sees a monster approach that looks like an enemy character he has seen before, he should feel one of three ways:

1. **I can beat this guy.** I know what attacks he uses, approximately how many hit points he has, and that I have a weapon that affects this enemy.
2. **I think I can defeat this guy.** He looks a lot like an enemy I've already fought, but is a different color, or a special name, that makes him unusual and possibly more advanced. In effect, I believe he belongs to an enemy "type," but I'm not sure about his toughness.
3. **I cannot beat this guy.** He's too tough, or I don't have the weapon necessary to get through his armor. I know because I've tried before, and failed, or somebody in the game has warned me.

This is another way of immersing the player in the game and making him feel a part of the world, in that he "knows" the enemies by experience. If a lowly Orc suddenly pulls out a grenade (after futilely running up and using a rusty dagger in the last fifty encounters) and nukes the player, the player is going to feel somewhat cheated. However, this basic guideline can be occasionally sidestepped, if the player is allowed to save the game whenever he wants, or the game actually autosaves quite frequently. In this way, a highly unusual encounter with a special enemy might kill the player, but he won't have lost much playing time if he has a save. Yes, this leads to more "save, then round the corner, kill one monster, then save" behavior from the player, but it also gives you more freedom to put elements of surprise into your random encounters.

BOSSES

Bosses are larger, more complex game characters, either humanoid or creature, found at the end of each level (or game world, or subsection) after defeating a horde of lesser enemies. They are usually equivalent to monster *leaders,* the Kings of the Monsters. These are specific, usually unique enemies that can break all the previous rules. Players expect to be surprised by the power, skills, weapons, and so forth used by these characters. Bosses are even thought of as *treats* in the RPG world, and a good boss creature can make up for a lot of game shortcomings, either in the areas of average gameplay, or merely a period of tedious leveling-up necessary to continue on in the game world.

As such, Boss monsters are usually heavily scripted, with specialty attacks and behaviors that only they perform. Boss monsters also usually communicate with the player, in the form of plot advancing information, or pure invectives. So the AI for these creatures needs to include use of the dialogue system for the game. The *Final Fantasy* series' Boss monsters are a wonder of specialized coding, with encounters that might take hours of real time, complete with various stages of battle and conversation. These encounters are strictly paced by the developers, with planned volleys of the player's advantage, followed by the enemy's advantage, scripted interruptions with other enemies or special game events, and whatever else the designers can think up.

Another tried-and-true Boss tactic involves the "can't be killed . . . yet Boss." This involves a Boss that the players can bring to near death, only to miraculously escape, shouting "I'll be back!" and promising to be bigger and badder next time. Although somewhat trite, this is the gaming equivalent of simple character development, with the Bad Guy developing over the course of the game as much as you are.

Some games use the designation of "sub-boss" to further stratify the monsters in the game, although they are usually just very tough versions of regular creatures, like the "unique" creatures that heavily populate the *Diablo* series. But even *Diablo,* which many considered an "RPG-lite" click fest, also uses much more specialized Boss creatures that employ additional dialogue, animations, spell and weapon effects, and special powers.

The Boss designation also includes the final creature (wizard/god/evil doer) that the player will need to defeat to win the game, also called the *End* Boss. This character is very important indeed, and many a good game has received bad marks for having a disappointing or anticlimatic End Boss. The player should have to perform every trick he or she has learned during the game, and stretch the acquired skills to the limit to destroy this character, and the End Boss itself should be able to do things that the player has never seen before in the game. The End Boss should be tough from a statistics point of view, of course (with lots of hit points and immunities to weapons or spells), but the End Boss should also be capable of behaviors beyond the typical. That's why the character is the End Boss in the first place.

Nonplayer Characters (NPCs)

NPCs are defined as *anybody in the game that is not a human player.* Usually, however, the term *NPC* refers to characters in the game that the player can interact with in ways other than combat. NPCs are the characters who inhabit the towns, the half-dead soldiers on the trail who give the player valuable clues to the danger ahead, and the occasional old man who offers the player's character money to rescue the old man's daughter. Typically, NPCs can be grouped into one of two types:

1. One-shot characters (meaning they have something for the player once during the course of the game, but afterwards will only greet the player with gratitude), like the people that are involved in a side quest.
2. Information-dumping characters, that a player can keep conversing with at different points during the game. These characters might know something additional about whatever is currently "new" in the game flow.

NPCs are generally not very intelligent; they usually don't have to be. Anything they add beyond information or story advancement is just flavor for the game. However, they also represent one of the largest sources of information the player has about the flow of the storyline. NPCs can also serve as in-game help that can bring a stuck or lost player back into alignment with the objectives of the game. As such, many games have experimented with differing ways of doing NPC conversation. Some games give the player keywords that represent questions the player is posing to the NPC (as in the *Ultima* games), others give the player a choice between a number of complete sentences that represent the different attitudes the player can take with the NPC.

The evolution of these systems will continue as grammar systems become better, faster, and more generally accepted. Some day, players may converse directly with a general AI NPC who can give wide-ranging responses by indexing the character's knowledge base and forming sentences on the fly. Until then, we do what we can.

SHOPKEEPERS

Shopkeepers are special NPCs that do business with the player; buying and selling gear, teaching the player new skills, and so on. Shopkeepers usually aren't much smarter than regular NPCs, but they get special mention because they usually have extended interfaces, which, in turn, require special code so they seem intelligent and usable. Sometimes shopkeepers might be part of a scripted quest or game sequence, in that they only become shopkeepers later in the game, or after a task has been completed. A shopkeeper thus might have a notion about whether or not he likes the player, which would then affect his attitude, and prices, when dealing with that player. Some games have a general charisma attribute for characters within the game (or some derivative; the meaning is "How well other people perceive you naturally," considering first impressions, the player's looks, and the player's speaking ability), as well as some form of a reputation system that represents a sort of "rating" depicting the amount of good versus evil deeds a player has, as well as flags representing specific things the player has done that NPCs can notice and respond to.

There is a natural human tendency to give inanimate things human qualities, and this tendency is tied directly to the amount of time we have to spend dealing with something. There is also a correlation with how much that object has cost us. Very few people would attribute human qualities to their shoes, but many people name their cars, know its gender, know how to identify if it's having a bad day, and will even plead with it if it isn't running well. Both objects (shoes and cars) do roughly the same thing: help protect our bodies from the rigors of traveling, so why the disparity? The answer is obvious. With no moving parts, and a simple procedure that we learned when we were three years old, we put on our shoes in the morning, and forget about them. Buying a new pair doesn't require a credit check. Our cars are exactly the opposite.

The same is true with Shopkeeper AI. If you have a one-shot NPC within your game, you can pretty much do whatever you want with his behavior, dialogue, and interactions with the player. The player isn't expecting much and will take most things at face value. But with a shopkeeper, especially one that the player will have to keep coming back to for a large part of the game, every nuance, reply, and animation frame will be carefully watched, memorized, and humanized.

Do you have a bartering system (which in reality takes the player's charisma score, adds in a random factor, and determines a small discount that a player can bargain for) within your game? Over time, a human player will start to imagine intricate rules involving the order of the items he does business with, the time of day, the shopkeeper's moods, and a host of other factors that may not actually exist. It is precisely this humanizing tendency that allows game makers to get away with so little detail in their games because the human player will fill in all the complexity where there is none. The lesson is that shopkeepers do more than provide your players with an economy interface; they also give richness to the world and provide the player with other facets of the game to consider.

PARTY MEMBERS

Members of a player's adventuring party are also special NPCs, except that they travel with the player, and are either completely player-controlled (in turn-based RPGs, or in later games that allow players to pause the action so they have time to give detailed commands) or have AI code associated with them. These AI-based party members need careful coding because stupid party members will drive potential players away quickly. Many of the real-time combat games use simple party AI, so that the player can predict (and rely on) what each party member is going to do during a fight.

A large factor to remember with real-time combat RPGs is pathfinding. In turn-based combat systems, a player's party members are just attached to the player, or follow the player around directly (like the *Final Fantasy* games, or even the early *Bard's Tale*), but in real-time games, they actually have to pathfind to follow the player. In a semi-enclosed space (such as an underground dungeon, for instance) with no room to manuever, one or more party members might go running off to take some extra-long scenic route that the pathfinder managed to find. Blind pathing can be supremely frustrating to the player, as it can cause these confused party members to run through packs of monsters in other parts of the map, even bringing unfriendlies running into the room behind the "helpful" friends to join in the fight.

Here's a place where an intelligent party member might say, "Hmm, I can't get around that guy directly to use my sword. But I do have a bow and arrow in my pack, and I'm decent at archery, maybe I'll try a ranged attack." A simpler solution might be "Can't get around directly, so I can't attack. Maybe I should tap my weaker buddy on the shoulder, who's being mauled by a creature, and *replace* him on the front line." These kinds of "smarts" (rather than ignorant pathfinding and script following) are the difference between useful party members, and ineffective accomplices that the player needs to babysit. If the characters a player adventures with frequently screw up, do the right thing in the wrong way, or are constantly getting themselves (or worse, the player) killed, the player is not going to want to continue playing with them.

Baldur's Gate (and its descendents) even allows users to edit the scripts that govern the party members' AI, so that users have even more control over this crucial game element. Some users in the community have created very advanced AI scripts and put them up on fan websites for all to use. See the section on "Scripting" that follows.

Adding a scripting system to edit a party AI is a careful balance. If you make it too easy to use and don't provide enough complexity and functionality, it's worthless. But if the system is too powerful, then it can overwhelm the casual gamer, and again becomes worthless to a large part of your audience.

A technique that many sports games use to allow players to adjust the AI in their games is to expose specific *tendencies* of behavior as "sliders" (scroll bars that tie to a variable) that the player can set. For sports games, this means that the players could set up a basketball game where the AI never tries to steal the ball, doesn't guard as well, and is better at three point shots all by setting sliders to certain points. A similar system could be used to give more casual gamers access to AI editing without having to write script code. Even some of the more complex uses of a scripting system, like setting up when specific spells would be cast by an AI mage character, could be represented as sliders that are specific to that spell. This does translate to many potential sliders, but again, it's definitely more accessible to a larger audience than script files are.

USEFUL AI TECHNIQUES

Along with the many types of AI-controlled entities within RPGs come the many AI techniques that are useful when constructing RPG-style games. These include scripting (because of the heavy story-based element in the genre), finite-state machines (for their general usefulness), and messaging (since so many RPG tasks are flag-based events).

SCRIPTING

Most RPGs are heavily scripted because these games tend to follow a very specific storyline. Scripts are used for a variety of game constructs, including dialogue, game event flags, specific enemy or NPC behavior, environmental interaction, and many others.

Scripting is used because most RPGs are linear, or at most branching linear, and so work well with the scripted interface. You can design parts of the game to play out almost exactly as specified, with choke points and flags embedded into the scripts so that the players are forced to follow the game flow from point A to point B, even if they first wandered over to points C, D, E, and F in the meantime. Plus, the conversational nature of many RPGs also lends itself to this technique. You can think of scripts as a data-based way of hardcoding the assorted events that come up during the overall story. See Listing 4.2 for an example of a short script from the Black Isle game, *Baldur's Gate*. Here you can see a very basic attack script, which determines whether to attack an enemy based on the enemy's distance to the character, and then also determines whether to use a ranged or melee weapon. It does perception checking (the range calculations) as well as perception scheduling (by saying how often the script should be run). It also has some randomness, in that the determination for ranged or close combat is determined by a random number (33 percent of the time, it chooses melee, the rest of the time, it chooses ranged).

LISTING 4.2   Sample Warrior AI user-defined script from *Baldur's Gate*.

```
IF
    // If my nearest enemy is not within 3

    !Range(NearestEnemyOf(Myself),3)

    // and is within 8

    Range(NearestEnemyOf(Myself),8)
```

```
THEN
    // 1/3 of the time

    RESPONSE #40
      // Equip my best melee weapon
      EquipMostDamagingMelee()
        // and attack my nearest enemy, checking every 60 ticks
         // to make sure he is still the nearest

      AttackReevalutate(NearestEnemyOf(Myself),60)

      // 2/3 of the time

    RESPONSE #80

      // Equip a ranged weapon

      EquipRanged()

      // and attack my nearest enemy, checking every 30 ticks
          // to make sure he is still the nearest

      AttackReevalutate(NearestEnemyOf(Myself),30)
END
```

FINITE-STATE MACHINES (FSMS)

The staple of game development, FSMs are useful in RPGs, just as they are useful in any game—they allow the developer to split the game into explicit states. In each state, specific characters can perform different behaviors, and manage these with discrete code blocks. Thus, you could have an NPC who first meets a player and gives the player a quest (for example, state before meeting the player is state_intro, changing to state_quest after giving the player information about a quest). Then, after the player finishes the quest, the NPC becomes a shopkeeper and sells the player things at a discount as a reward (state_shopkeep). Note how earlier the script from *Baldur's Gate* is only applicable if an enemy is close by. Any other game state would require additional scripting, or it could fall back on some default script, which would most likely do some idle behavior.

By having a state-based system, but scripting the entry and exit to those states, many RPGs hide the "hard" state transitions (meaning, it's difficult to notice the difference in game state, because the transition was a seamless scene that moves us from one state to another). Other games do not, like Nintendo's classic *The Legend of Zelda*, in which the game was split into two globally distinct states: the overworld and the dungeons of the underworld. The game's music would change, the character itself would look a little different (because of the "lighting"), and if the player died, the game acted a little differently (by allowing the player to continue in the same dungeon, if the player wanted), all because of this basic state change.

MESSAGING

With so many elements in an RPG world, the need to communicate between entities is high, so a messaging system is useful in this genre. Information can be passed between party members quickly and easily, facilitating group combat or dialogue. Door keys (or whatever your game is using) can message locks to open, and out-of-place wall stones could cause entire sequences of events to occur when pushed. Because of the sheer number of uses within an RPG, messaging systems can really give you a lot of flexibility and ease of implementation.

One thing that should be watched for, because it breaks the illusion of reality, is for instant messaging being used by the game. If a party kills some creature on the far side of the world, they then teleport back to town (because of a special magic item), and *everyone* back in town already knows about the battle, that the party won, and that the player is the hero. The townspeople obviously got the message and have switched on the game state-specific behavior for it. Wouldn't a better reaction be that the first character the player talks with *doesn't* know (unless the player took the long way home, and gave everybody time to find out on their own), and the player has to tell him? Then, *that character* runs into the streets and spreads the good news? Build messaging into the game, and use it to set game flags that change game behavior, but don't overuse it, or abuse the system by allowing game states to change instantaneously in ways that couldn't possibly have occurred. If the mayor of the town has his own wizard who saw everything happen through his crystal ball, that's a different story, but it should be portrayed as such.

EXAMPLES

Classic games like *Wizardy,* the early *Ultimas, Phantasy Star, Might and Magic,* and the *Bard's Tale* had mostly statistic-based enemies, with little special case code. They all used a simple "key and lock" puzzle system (using some sort of key or jewel or Skull of Muldark or what have you) that had to be found and used in the right place at the right time. This was most likely coded as a system of flags that the elements of the game would access to determine the particulars of the game progression.

Usually, the gameplay diagram for these games would include a town state, a "travel" state, and a combat state. The differences between these games were pretty much the overall game's graphic quality, how the player conversed with NPCs, and the combat interface.

Strangely enough, some massive multiplayer online RPGs (MMORPGs) are using this exact game style to create huge worlds in which people can play. The only real gameplay addition has, of course, been the vast number of people who are also playing the game at the same time, leading to more human-to-human interactions.

Modern RPGs such as the later *Final Fantasy* games, *Neverwinter Nights,* *Baldur's Gate,* and *System Shock* are much more scripted affairs, with some of the attribute-based enemies of these games, but with a large portion of hand-tailored encounters and environments along the way to provide the player with a more crafted gameplay experience. Only recently have the online RPGs tried this tactic (such as the *Final Fantasy* online game) because of the enormous amount of work associated with creating custom quests and encounters for a world that may be inhabited by thousands of people at all hours of the day. But, the demand is there for higher quality content, so game companies will provide it.

EXCEPTIONS

Bethesda Softworks makes the excellent *Elder Scrolls* series of RPGs (see Figure 4.1 for a screenshot from *Elder Scrolls: Arena,* the first in the series), which it touts as being open ended, meaning that you can solve the game and perform the various quests in a nonlinear fashion. The games do deliver this promise to a much larger degree than any other RPG. A large amount of freedom is granted through the lack of time limits on the quests you receive, so you can collect quests, and do them in any order. The quests are still mostly scripted (a number of quest types are used as templates, with different characters and locations) and usually simple in nature to facilitate this (although the newer games in the series have vastly improved the variety and complexity of quests). The main quest is still linear, facilitated by scripted encounters with unique NPCs, but it allows the player to take time completing many other side quests as well.

Neverwinter Nights is another recent game that was supposed to change everything. By allowing players to control a character in the game and actually be in the Dungeon Master role (as borrowed from the pen and paper world), the game was supposed to be *Dungeons and Dragons (D&D)* fully brought to the computer. To some degree it succeeded, but in many ways, all it really showed was that the average person is pretty bad at coming up with good game content. Patches have fixed some of the problems, and the title is nothing if not created

FIGURE 4.1   Elder Scrolls: Arena screenshot. © 1993. Bethesda Softworks LLC, a ZeniMax Media company.

for longevity, so this will surely change, and good modules will make their appearance on the Net.

SPECIFIC GAME ELEMENTS THAT NEED IMPROVEMENT

Any established genre can use some improvements pushing forward through the sea of established storylines and gameplay mechanics. RPGs have their share of issues when it comes to perennial issues. Some specific issues that could use some fresh insight include making role playing more then just endless combat, grammar machines, quest generators, better enemy and party member AI, and fully realized towns. A game with all these elements would truly be an epic adventure, with something new behind every door.

ROLE PLAYING DOES NOT EQUAL COMBAT

The definition of "role playing" is typically "acting like someone else in an escapist fantasy." There is a vast array of possible behaviors that you could engage in. Acting means a lot of things; everything from behaving like another person to using their manner of speaking. It can also mean subtle (yet very important) distinctions like taking on the other identity's core beliefs (maybe the character being role played is whole-heartedly evil, whereas the person doing the role playing might be a Girl Scout), or holding grudges against others that have done the character wrong within the role playing universe. All of these things give role playing a rich, usually dramatic, and freeing sense of open-endedness that make it an activity with nearly limitless potential.

However, in most RPGs, right from the start, most of the time spent role-playing is actually time spent *killing,* mainly because of some seminal influences: two really old pen-and-paper RPGs (*Dungeons and Dragons* and, earlier than that, *Chainmail*) centered their gameplay systems on fighting against fantastical creatures. The rulebooks were filled with combat statistics, magical spell lists, and weapon descriptions. There really wasn't a single chapter anywhere in the rulebooks about creating realistic stories, locales, and people to inhabit them. Novel combat scenarios are much easier to model and invent than an actual story with plot, characters, drama, and so on.

Consider this: nonkiller classes in most RPGs are only useful for the small set of contrived circumstances that the designers have included to justify these classes. Thieves are one of the more classic types with problems, even in paper *D&D.* If you allow thieves to *really* do what they do, they're too powerful because they don't have to follow the rules like everybody else does (just like in real life; the Mafia is more powerful than a police officer).

So games hobble them. Thieves can disarm traps, and pickpocket. But, if they disarm incorrectly, they generally die, and if they pickpocket unsuccessfully, they are generally always caught. Fun is nowhere to be seen. Think of the myriad wonderful professions that players can choose from in the average Massive Multiplayer Online Role Playing Game (MMORPG). In *Ultima Online,* a player could be a baker. Unfortunately, the player could spend months playing the game, become a Master Baker, a true *King* of baking, and then be almost instantly killed the second the player stepped outside of town by an extremely low-level fighter with a rusty spoon.

In today's MMORPGs, people tend to be tanks (meaning fighter types with huge amounts of health and armor; human walls that absorb damage), or casters (someone who stands behind a tank and can either damage creatures with spells, or heal the tank so he can continue to bash and be bashed). Specialty classes have somewhat dissolved into these two basic groups.

Huge areas of compelling potential gameplay are hidden within RPG worlds, but that involves thinking about ways of creating content that doesn't involve killing and that takes advantage of nonlethal skills in a meaningful way, not just to affect your prices for new swords. The task involved here is not an easy one, and writing AIs to support these new quest types will also be hard. But our RPGs will definitely be better for it.

GRAMMAR MACHINES

Grammar machines (GMs) make for better conversations. A lot of the interaction with other characters in RPGs is through conversation, usually in the form of choosing from a list of responses, and then reading the character's scripted response. *Ultima* used a keyword system, so a player would say "thieves," and the other character would tell the player about the local thieves, mentioning toward the end that someone named Blue is their boss. A new keyword, "Blue," would show up in the player's list, and the player could ask for additional information in this way. Old text-adventure games actually had rudimentary grammar engines that could handle semicomplex sentences. A fully functional grammar system used to converse with NPCs in a modern RPG has yet been implemented. This might change because of the advent of better and better speech recognition software. Eventually, RPGs might use this system instead of a slow, clumsy text interface to allow the user to really ask questions. Our job as AI programmers will then be to fully flesh out a grammar engine, and fill a text database with enough knowledge to dutifully answer those questions.

QUEST GENERATORS

The *real* quest (for game developers) is quest generators that don't churn out derivative or repetitive content. Sort of the Holy Grail of large-scale RPGs, an advanced quest generator could make up new quests that the player could tackle without having to be explicitly set up and scripted by a game designer. Games like *World of Warcraft*, which are played around the clock online, could benefit greatly from a system that could come up with novel challenges for any number of party members, and of any skill level. As of now, only a few games have "random" quests, and they usually fall into the "Fed Ex" quest realm. That is, go somewhere, get something, and bring it back to me.

An improvement might be a system set up ad-lib style; using templates to create custom quests (or strings of connected quests) that included multiple characters, locations, rewards, and different actions to be done. These templates, connected to a database of potential ad-lib names and locations, as well as some way of scoring quests for skill level and such, could make RPG games truly unique experiences (at least for side quest interactions). The game could even keep track of which quests the player liked (by keeping records of quests turned down or never finished versus successful and repeated types) and adjust the kinds of quests given to a specific player. Also, by making the ad-lib machine extensible, you could add content continually (through mods, patches, or expansion packs to individual products), and the ad-lib system would just incorporate it into the mix.

BETTER PARTY MEMBER AI

Party AI that can be extended and modified, both implicitly and explicitly, is another big area in need of concern. Early real-time RPGs (like *Ultima 7*, pictured in Figure 4.2) had simple party AI that mainly just followed a player around the map and tried to help during combat. *Baldur's Gate* has contributed heavily to real-time RPG party AI becoming a greater priority. The level of adjustment that can be accomplished within their simple script form is pretty

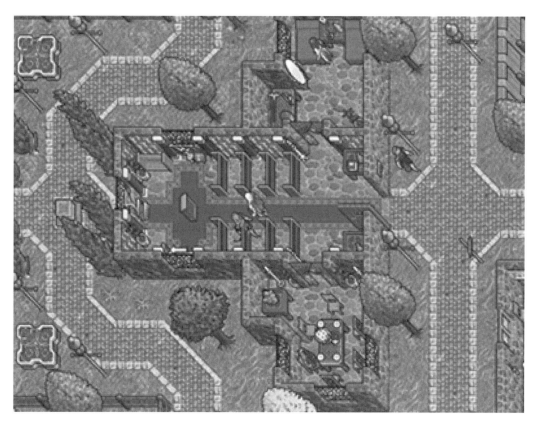

FIGURE 4.2   *Ultima*™ *7* screenshot.

astounding, but it could be better. The character could keep track of the sorts of actions the player has the character do, and could incorporate them into automatic behavior.

Think of this as simple learning by imitation. Does the player always retreat from a certain character (like a weak mage, perhaps)? After two or three times of doing this manually, the mage could retreat automatically. Does the player drink a health potion whenever the player gets to one-third health, but only after the battle is over or after running away from immediate danger? The characters should perceive this and parrot these simple behaviors.

Imagine how the player's game experience is going to evolve and change as the game progresses, instead of micromanaging very tedious actions again and again during hours of gameplay. It might even be possible to show the player this learned behavior list and allow the player to edit it by deleting things, or changing the priorities of these behaviors.

BETTER ENEMIES

Instead of just mobs (groups of monsters that turn toward the player, advance until in range, and attack), enemies should work together from multiple fronts, using plans and the environment to their advantage. They should set ambushes, make traps, find your weakness and try to exploit it, and do everything else that a human player would do. This is, of course, a universal problem. As stated earlier, most RPG enemies are supposed to be relatively mindless, so the player can quickly kill enough of them to rise in rank at a rate that feels good. The problem is that this need creates very monotonous battles, one after another, with exceedingly stupid monsters. One popular answer to this is sub-bosses or mildly scripted and slightly more strenuous enemies that will make the player feel like the whole of creation is not filled with senseless drones, all attacking in the same manner as the last. *Dungeon Siege* (Figure 4.3) and the *Diablo* games used this technique relatively successfully, as areas of the map would always have a native type of creature, and some larger, stronger version of that creature type would be leading them. This unique creature would not be tied to any quest (although some were) but, rather provided a bit of variety to the constant stream of cannon fodder.

These sub-bosses could be developed as more than just tougher versions of regular monsters, to a level where they are truly small boss monsters that rule that part of the game world. Sub-bosses could be little generals, giving sophisticated orders to their armies, and doing things that a leader would do. By killing this creature, the player would weaken the attack of all the creatures the sub-boss led, until another leader is promoted.

FIGURE 4.3   *Dungeon Siege* screenshot. © 2002 Gas Powered Games Corp. All rights reserved. Gas Powered Games and Dungeon Siege are the exclusive trademarks of Gas Powered Games Corp. Reprinted with permission.

An aside about *Dungeon Siege*, however, is that the game did *too many* things automatically for the player. At times, the game seemed to be playing itself, with hardly any input from the user. If this automatic behavior could have been modified or tweaked (maybe even just a slider so that the player could set the level of automation he liked), the game might have felt better to a larger audience.

FULLY-REALIZED TOWNS

The towns that constitute the trade and information centers of these games are usually pretty dull, filled with people either standing around, or moving between two locations. These townsfolk usually say the same thing over and over and don't appear to have a "life" at all. Obviously, this is not reality. By using simple rules, and a data-driven approach to town creation, even large villages could be populated with characters who have jobs, go to school, shop for groceries, or whatever it is that people do in your RPG world. If you employ a system like this, you would also have to make it easier for the human player to find people in the town (this is *why* most games have people standing in one place, so that the user knows where to find them). But this is a problem that can be solved (perhaps you have certain important NPCs that can be found in one of three different places, based on time of day). The overall effect of a living, breathing town would make the game world much more interesting and immersive.

Implementing this kind of town could be done a few different ways. You could use a *need-based* system (like *The Sims*), in which each NPC would have a number of needs and would autonomously determine how to fulfill those needs. As an arbitrary example, let's say that a certain part of town contains 100 NPCs. Each NPC has three needs: hunger, business, and family. Each need is satisfied when the NPC performs tasks that are suited to the particular need (eating to hunger; trading, training, talking, and so forth to business; and parenting, providing, and so on to family). The game could then use a "need pathfinding" system to give information on how to fulfill its needs to each NPC. The streets would be busy with people, going to and fro, buying bread, painting fences, or looking for their kids. The given action of each townsperson is defined by what need is the highest.

Another way to write this system would be to write a number of different scripts, each of which would define a chain of actions, and just assign these little scripts to each NPC in the map. The second method saves a lot of computation (because you don't have to do any sort of planning, or need tracking), but isn't as general (you could implement a hundred different places for a need-based NPC to satisfy his hunger and the AI would use them all, whereas you'd need to write a hundred different scripts in addition to creating the hundred different places in the scripted system).

SUMMARY

As a game genre, RPGs have been around a long time and people still love them; they show no sign of falling out of favor. They provide people with an escape from their ordinary lives by allowing users to take on another persona. The AI systems in this genre are quite complex, with many different AI needs across the entire game.

- Enemies and Boss Enemies are necessary to give the player something to fight, and to provide story motivation.
- NPCs and Shopkeepers provide the player with more personal interactions (other than combat), and give the world a living feel, complete with an economy.

- Party-member AI needs special attention, especially in real-time combat-based RPGs.
- AI Scripting is a prime weapon to use in developing RPGs, but FSMs, and messaging systems are also staples for this genre.
- Some areas in which RPGs need improvement include grammar machines for better conversations, quest generators for more varied and long-lasting gameplay situations, better enemy and party member AI, and fully-realized towns to give the player a greater sense of immersion in the world.

5 Adventure Games

In This Chapter

- Common AI Elements
- Useful AI Techniques
- Areas That Need Improvement
- Summary

A dventure games and early personal computers were made for each other. The spectacularly limited abilities of early PCs required a truly creative game to give the player a rich experience. This was challenging given the fact that the game could only give the player feedback by spelling things out in black and white text on the screen, or showing a few blocky shapes in limited colors. What was needed was a great story and some way of interacting with that story, letting the player's own imagination create the striking visuals. Plus, PCs gave the game industry something they'd never really had before: a full keyboard interface. In the late 1970s and early 1980s, adventure games were some of the first games to make entertainment use of the clunky PCs that were just starting to become popular.

The so-called *text-based* adventure games (the original being *Collosal Cave Adventure,* another being the famous *Zork* series) were our first taste of the genre. These games got their names because they had no graphics whatsoever—a text description of the room you were in and your imagination were all that you had to utilize. The player would type commands into a parser, and the game would either respond in kind with the result of the action the user had entered or inform the user that it didn't know what he or she was talking about (if the user typed something in that wasn't in the game's command language). The player traveled from room to room collecting elements used to unlock puzzles, which would in turn allow the user access to other areas and further the story.

Eventually, people started attaching pictures to these puzzle-filled stories, including games like the *King's Quest* series, LucasArts'® seminal *Day of the Tentacle* and *Monkey Island* games, and the *Leisure Suit Larry* games. LucasArts also did away with full-text parsers, instead relying on a highly simplified keyword and iconic interface.

In 1993, a small company called Cyan released a game called *Myst. Myst* took the adventure game and removed most of the story, leaving a very pretty world (it was one of the first CD-ROM games and used prerendered backdrops, which looked amazing compared with the simplistic real-time 3D worlds that people were used to seeing in other games at the time) and a large number of puzzles to solve. A player couldn't die, but there was also no help to guide the player through the game; it was pure exploration mixed with trial and error. Although this sounds like a simple premise, *Myst* was *the* runaway hit of its time and is still widely credited as one of the best-selling computer games of all time. It spawned five sequels (the entire series has sold more than 12 million copies worldwide) and countless similar games tried to follow its formula.

Today, the *classic* adventure game has all but disappeared. Nobody seems to know why. The *Myst* games may have given the genre sales numbers (adventure games had never been very big sellers), but they also may have been the reason for the dearth of new titles. People started to associate the adventure game title with slow, casual gaming that was merely a collection of puzzles and forgot (or had never heard) about the well-written, rich storylines of the earlier titles. Players have instead headed for the instant gratification of the more action-oriented adventure-game variants that have begun to take over the genre today.

This book will not concentrate on the classic style of adventure game, which has also been called *interactive fiction*. We mention them for historic note only, since the level of AI elements inherent in these games is usually so low that they don't require even moderate levels of decision-making potential. They are usually coded with state-based characters; most have only static elements, and only certain games even have actors that can move from room to room. Also, because the human could solve the puzzles in many of these games in any order, the AI for the characters is something more akin to a database of flags then to an actual decision structure. That being said, creating a classic-style game would require a parsing system, which is very akin to the scripting engine described in Chapter 18.

Instead, this book will focus on the modern alternatives that have all but taken over the genre. These new takes on the adventure game (sometimes called action adventure) are usually variations of the first-person shooters/third-person shooters (FTPS) genre that focuses on noncombat-based gameplay situations: a mostly exploratory game (like *Tomb Raider*), or the more recent *stealth* games.

The stealth game involves a main hero who cannot shoot his way out of the primary situations in the game but instead must use elements of stealth and guile to slip past the guards (such as the recent *Metal Gear* games, or the *Thief* series). Stealth games have proven hugely popular because of the varying gameplay elements, and the heightened sense of tension that comes from having to come up with alternative means of traversing the level and solving problems other than "pull the trigger."

This transcends the FTPS roots of the games, bringing players back to the feeling of constant puzzle solving and a great storyline, but in a real-time game environment, so these are now considered adventure titles.

Another variation, which does contain some combat elements, is called the survival horror game. Titles such as *Resident Evil* still have a lot of combat, mostly projectile attacks, but these are mostly three-dimensional exploration titles with lots of puzzle-elements to drive the player around the map.

COMMON AI ELEMENTS

Adventure games are in somewhat the same realm as role-playing games. They also have enemies, non-player characters, and cooperative elements. But the modern adventure game also tends to sport advanced perception systems and specialized cameras that require AI programming effort.

ENEMY AI

Enemies in stealth games tend to be implemented with scripted movement sequences or very simple rules. The player needs to sneak by guards and other enemies and has to be able to identify patterns of movement to determine ways of exploiting these patterns. Once alerted to the player's presence, however, the enemy's behavior can get a whole lot smarter, and enemies can become quite involved. Guard characters usually employ multiple stages of attention, from "Did I hear something?" to a guard *pretending* he didn't hear the player's character as the guard slowly patrols in the player's direction while taking the safety off his gun. Guards also perform basic behaviors like calling for backup, hunting the player down, and so forth. Remember that as an AI designer, you don't want the enemies to be too diligent, or a player's character would wake up the whole complex by setting off one guard, which would be frustrating to the human player.

For other types of adventure games, pretty much anything goes. Some games use somewhat mindless hunter-style enemies, as in the simpler FTPS games. Other games have smart enemies that are constrained to zones (as in the *Thief* games), so a player might find himself being tracked down by an alerted guard, but the player won't set off the whole world if he can escape his territory within a reasonable time.

The survivor horror titles use *very* simple enemy AI, usually because the monsters involved are zombies, or something similar. The combat interface is mostly secondary to the exploration and puzzle interaction, so the enemies are slow, and the action isn't as *twitch*-oriented (reliant on fast reflexes).

NONPLAYER CHARACTERS (NPCs)

Just as in RPGs, NPC characters are noncombatant inhabitants of the game world. They are placed there to give the player information, or to bring the world to life for visual support. The AI used for these characters is quite varied, from both an ability level and an implementation level, and can be anything from a static dialogue and actions to a much more complex system involving paths, goals, and a conversation engine with which to engage the player. This is all determined by the design goals of your game.

COOPERATIVE ELEMENTS

Cooperative characters go beyond the realm of NPCs. These characters assist the player directly, by showing the player new items, locations, or quests. In the case of action-oriented adventure games, cooperative characters will sometimes assist by helping players fight against the enemy creatures in the game. They can even be secondary main characters. Other games involve the player constantly switching primary control back and forth, in episodic or mission-based chunks of time, between different game characters. Switching control like this is a great way to decrease the perceived linearity of your game and to break the action into manageable chunks for the player.

The state of the guards in a stealth-based game *is* the game, so to speak. The player is essentially balancing his exploration and discovery goals with trying to sneak around unseen and unheard, so as to slip past all the guards without "setting off the system" (meaning, causing the guards to become alerted to his presence), and bringing ruin upon himself. In order to be challenging at all, many of these games use smart *chains* of guards. This refers to guards that talk to one another, overlap each other's territory, and generally share in patrolling an area. Connected guards lead to what can be thought of as a *tightly coupled system*. Each guard is in many ways coupled to other guards. The player cannot just get past one guard at a time, but must contend with systems of guards that are working together. Because of this touchy nature of stealth games, the programmer must make sure that an AI helper in that specific genre isn't going to do anything that would set off the guards, or else we're back to player frustration.

PERCEPTION SYSTEMS

For stealth games, most of the complexity of the AI model is contained within the perception system. Different techniques have been developed for each of the senses—to model each sense such that it translates well to the videogame world.

Thief, from LookingGlass™ Studios, took the stealth game to an entirely new level, with the main thrust of the gameplay being constant sneaking, hiding in shadows, pickpocketing specific characters when they're not looking, and so on. A good breakdown of the perception system of *Thief* was given by one of the programmers who worked on the game at the 2002 Game Developer's Conference; the paper can be found online at the following site: *http://www. gamasutra.com/gdc2003/features/20030307/ leonard_01.htm* under the heading *Building an AI Sensory System.* This is highly suggested reading if you plan to do a system of this complexity. Also, see the CD-ROM for additional links and materials.

CAMERA

Most adventure games are three-dimensional (a notable exception is the two-dimensional *Commandos* series) and third person, so again the problems associated with bad camera placement are inherent. However, because of the much slower pace of these types of games, this is usually an easier problem to fix, and cinematic-style camera cuts with precise camera placement are usually the norm. Certain sections of the game may require a free-form camera system, and thus need programmer attention. Stealth games also frequently require an *around the corner* camera angle for hiding behind cover and watching a guard walk by. This can be an algorithmic camera that comes up when the player crouches next to a corner, or specific camera parameters can be set up in the level editor for particular cover positions.

USEFUL AI TECHNIQUES

The various AI elements used in adventure games once again give rise to the need for a varied AI toolset in order to solve all the required logic problems. The techniques that work well in adventure games include: finite-state machines, scripting and messaging systems, and fuzzy logic systems.

FINITE-STATE MACHINES (FSMs)

Many elements of stealth and exploration adventure games lend themselves well to FSM-based AI systems. If the game is digitally triggered, such as guards having an alerted state of *yes* or *no*, or if the game has an enumeration of states (like neutral, annoyed, alert, mad, berserk), then state machines provide the best bang for the buck. Because of the nature of state machines, you can make parts of your AI fairly simple, with other parts having many more states and thus much more complexity. For games with limited AI complexity and a large number of very straightforward AI tasks, you might want to stay with a state-based system.

SCRIPTING SYSTEMS

Some adventure games use very cinematic camera placement, lots of in-game dialogue, and sequences that show the results of solving a particular puzzle somewhere else in the level. Scripting systems allow the programmers (and designers) to easily put extra tailoring into specific parts of the game, and this technique is readily used for the linear story that these games employ.

The combination of triggered events setting off scripted sequences, and having the trustworthy game mechanic of having to "unlock" later parts of the game by accomplishing tasks (which is essentially changing certain game-state flags) gives the best of both worlds; it allows game designers to have many places within a game in which to get specific things to happen, while still giving the player some feeling of being able to roam around uncontrolled.

MESSAGING SYSTEMS

The event-driven nature of typical adventure-game puzzles (push lever A, door goes up; move three stones into certain pattern, hidden chamber opens; and so forth) lends well to the use of messaging systems. Passing messages means that the disparate elements in the game don't require direct code access to each other to communicate. The advanced perception systems of stealth games can use messages for determining perceived sounds and the like, as well as providing enemy guards an easy method for alerting others or calling for help.

FUZZY LOGIC

The perception systems used by stealth games can be quite complex. In the face of numerous, sometimes conflicting, sensory inputs, AI opponents need to incorporate fuzzy decision making to make full use of the rich information. Many of the challenges in stealth titles involve getting past guardians, and using a fuzzy-state-based system can help make guard states feel forgiving to the player (the player can sneak by if the player doesn't push the boundaries *too* much—like being able to push on a pinball table: some movement is legal, but if you overdo it, you tilt).

Frequently, part of the gameplay is having the guards deal with situations such as player-initiated distractions, diversions, ambushes, and other kinds of slighting. These sorts of interactions are often scripted. Another implementation could use fuzzy logic to allow the guards a fuller and more flexible model of the world, in order to deal with the kind of imperfect information that a diversion might provide. The guard's notion of his territory might be fairly clear—he hasn't seen or heard anything suspicious in a while. Then, the player throws a rock into a dark corner. The guard hears it, his suspicion level goes up a bit, he adds a suspicion target to his internal list, and he focuses most of his attention on it because it's his only area of concern right now. The player tosses another rock; the guard reacts by getting more suspicious, adds another target to his list of things to investigate. He yells, "Who's there?" and cocks his weapon, moving slowly toward the corner. You get the picture. The ebb and flow of suspicion, directed toward however many targets, is determined by the guard's *very* unclear, sparse picture of the world, which is determined by his perceptions.

Note however, that this kind of system is typically much harder for the player to figure out. Scripted systems are usually quite telegraphed: the smart player can watch the guard for a bit, and notice that every two minutes he gets up and goes to the balcony to look outside, giving the player a window of time to make his or her move. A fuzzy system would instead be blending many different inputs into a final behavior; the player might not pick up on all the elements that are giving the guard his final behavior, and as such have difficulty determining what he or she needs to do in order to affect changes in the guard's actions.

In practice, most of this fuzziness would be better used within the perception system itself, rather than in the decision structure. An FSM with fuzzy transition logic is much easier to program then a full fuzzy logic system is.

Examples

After the classic adventure games began to wane in popularity, crossover genres started to appear. *Tomb Raider* was the early hit that started us off on the crossover from shooter to adventure game. Other earlier games included *Alone in the Dark,* and *Shadow Man,* which added horror elements, and eventually gave us *Resident Evil. Resident Evil* in turn spawned a slew of more fully horror-based exploration titles like *Silent Hill,* American McGee's *Alice in Wonderland,* and *Nightmare Creatures.* These action-adventure games still had lots of combat involved, because the AI systems were still borrowing heavily from their FTPS brothers. The designers just increased the exploration and item-gathering challenges to round out the overall experience.

As the AI engines got better, and perception systems became complex and had gameplay depth, the stealth games came out, with *Thief, Deus Ex,* and *Metal Gear Solid* initially leading the pack. These games made it fun to *not* kill your enemies but, rather, to never even let them see you. *Commandos* was an overhead two-dimensional stealth game: the gamer's job was to accomplish missions by infiltrating increasingly complex enemy bases and sneaking from spot to spot unseen. The game was spectacularly hard, but very well done. The line of sight of all the guards was actually shown as moving cones on the ground, so players could much more intimately time their movements to ensure their secrecy. This is a great example of giving the human player more information in order to deepen the game mechanic.

Another notable hybrid adventure game was *Blade Runner,* which touted real multiple endings and storylines, and a somewhat alive world. The NPCs in the game were engaged in semi-autonomous behavior, moving through the city to get to stores, jobs, and so forth. The overall effect was mostly cosmetic, though, as interactions with the NPCs were still very state- and/or event-based.

Although a new classic-style adventure game is rare, it is not fully extinct. Some great examples of these games in recent years include *Full Throttle, Grim Fandango,* and *Circle of Blood.* These games have expanded the old formula, with better (and more involved) puzzles, great graphics, and much more varied gameplay elements (*Full Throttle* even included a motorcycle combat stage).

The interaction system that these games use has gone up and down in complexity over the years. With the initial text adventures, the player could type pretty much anything, and the game's parser would either recognize the command or say otherwise. Players would eventually learn the commands that the parser knew. Later, with LucasArts' SCUMM system (which stands for *Script Creation Utility for Maniac Mansion,* a great example of a tool being built for a specific game becoming the cornerstone of an entire suite of games, as the SCUMM engine was eventually used in no less than eighteen games. SCUMM still has a rabid fan base online, with new games created by fans still coming out. Visit *http://www. scummvm.org/* for more details), the possible commands were given to the player as buttons on the graphical interface, and the player could apply these commands to various elements on screen. *Full Throttle* went even more abstract, with icons depicting the player's eye, mouth, or hand being used as context-sensitive commands to apply to game objects. So, if a player used his mouth with an NPC, the player would talk, whereas if the player used his mouth with a beer, the player would drink it.

The simplification of possible inputs from the human to facilitate ease of interfacing with the game led the NPCs to become much more simplistic as well. The level of communication with the player is inherently limited, simply because the player no longer has any means by which to respond intelligently. If an NPC asks a player for the time, does the player click on the character with the mouth icon to talk, or with the hand icon to check the character's watch? If the player chooses the wrong response, and the NPC asks what's wrong, then what? This limited interface may streamline the game somewhat, but it definitely takes away from the feeling of living in an organic, much more interactive environment like Zork. Sure, most of the nonsense things you typed in Zork were ignored by the response "I don't know what that means" but you were still allowed to type them. In the games with the simpler interface, you were left to just shout at the screen.

AREAS THAT NEED IMPROVEMENT

As with any game genre, there are always areas within the family of released games for improvements in the AI realm. In adventure games, these include: additional types of steal goals, returning to traditional adventure game roots, better NPC communication, and user interface designs.

ADDITIONAL TYPES OF STEALTH GOALS

In addition to the classic stealth mechanic of patterned movement that has to be circumvented, *Deus Ex* gave players many different ways to accomplish key story goals. For example, to get through a particular door, the player could shoot the guard and take his key, and then fight the other four guards that would come when they heard the shot. The player could also cause some kind of diversion, and then use a hacking skill to open the unguarded lock. Or, the player could climb through a ventilation shaft and find a different way in. The player could even find a guard uniform and use it to walk right by the guard. By doing this, the game designers made each encounter and area of the world into a puzzle. The player had to really experiment with the situation to uncover the hidden gameplay gems. The player didn't have to sneak down one particular hallway and open one particular door. This forced *Deus Ex*'s guard AI to be more open ended, instead of being heavily scripted, because there were potentially so many ways to get around them.

A RETURN TO TRADITIONAL ADVENTURE ROOTS

Traditional interactive fiction provided computer gamers with some of the most popular games released in the 80s and 90s. Many of the classic LucasArts and Sierra games have loyal followings. Today's exploratory and more action-oriented games must meld with classic roots of the genre to bring adventure games alive again. In many ways, the genre has become too action oriented. There is still a place for complex logic and exploration puzzles, as well as deep storylines with interesting NPC characters that have full personalities. Today's "run and gun" adventure games sometimes suffer from not having the time necessary to build up the intricate stories of yesterday's game titles.

BETTER NPC COMMUNICATION

The inherent noncombat nature of modern stealth adventure games lends itself well to having additional story-driven elements included as part of the experience. By giving NPCs in adventure games real grammar systems, or even allowing branching storylines within the full umbrella of the greater game story, the world in which the adventure is occurring could become more real, and much more personal to the player. This, of course, would require an immense amount of additional work in story design to make up for branching and consistency problems.

USER INTERFACE

When we lost the full-text parsers of the original text adventures, we also lost the ability to have rich interactions with in-game characters. After going to a graphical interface, the complexity was gradually degraded until eventually some adventure games had as few as three or four basic commands that could be used with elements in the world. Today, with the more action-oriented variants, little interaction occurs other than a player positioning his or her character well and using quiet weapons or tools when necessary.

Imagine *Sam and Max* with a full-voice interface, or some other kind of general interface where the player could get a much richer kind of connection to the game if he or she spent the time to explore the capabilities of the parser. Eventually, a new interface could help adventure games regain some of their traditional depth, without having to resort to typing long sentences into a computer.

SUMMARY

Adventure games are continuing to evolve from their initial roots, which was a string of puzzles wrapped into a story, and were definitely not played in real time. The modern stealth games and the more action-oriented exploration games are modern variants of the classic adventure formula that will continue to give game players challenges and new worlds to explore.

- The first adventure games were text-based and required the user to type commands to a parser. These eventually gave way to the graphical adventure game, which added a graphical user interface to save the user from typing.
- Modern adventure games are variants on the FTPS genre, and emphasize non-combat situations such as exploration and stealth.
- Enemy AI in stealth games can be somewhat pattern-based because the object of the game is to note patterns and circumvent confrontations. In the more exploratory combat-style games, enemy AI can be much more varied.
- Most adventure games have a number of NPCs, as well as cooperative characters, that give the player information or new gear. The AI level of these agents varies greatly.
- Perception systems are paramount for stealth games because overcoming the guards' perceptions is the goal of the game.
- Camera AI is usually necessary for these adventure games because they usually are done in 3D.

- FSMs, scripting, fuzzy logic, and messaging AI systems are commonly used within the adventure genre.
- New stealth challenges (possibly by infusing the current game schemes with more intelligent enemies) is an area of improvement for the adventure genre.
- A return to the classic adventure game roots is needed to help revive the lineage of the genre.
- Increased NPC communication and story branching might give adventure games additional personal connections to the player.
- An advanced user interface could help give back the richer interaction level of more traditional adventures to modern games.

6 Real-Time Strategy (RTS) Games

In This Chapter

- Common AI Elements
- Useful AI Techniques
- Examples
- Areas That Need Improvement
- Summary

The AI systems used in RTS games are some of the most computationally intensive of all videogames. They usually involve large armies that must coordinate their behavior and technology trees that must be navigated to perform goals. They must also share CPU time with the rest of the game technology, like collision detection and drawing routines, which also contend with numerous units.

Although RTS games have been around for years (the 1990 game *Herzog Zwei* for the Sega® Genesis™ console is usually considered the first), AI performance has been nowhere near the level of good human players. The AI in RTS games has to fight against many factors: huge numbers of characters to give orders to, very incomplete information about the game world (the fog of war is the most obvious example), heavy emphasis on micro actions (meaning that actions have limited effect on the overall game), and having to run in real time. By contrast, consider the types of games in which AI has achieved expert (or at least very good) level: turn-based games, with perfect information, in which most moves have global consequences and in which limited human-planning abilities can be outsmarted by mere brute force enumeration. This type of game includes chess and the like. Thus, almost every aspect of RTS games is considered non-optimal for AI performance. The burden lies on game designers to overcome these problems in a believable fashion.

COMMON AI ELEMENTS

RTS games are some of the largest consumers of AI programmer time. There are many differing elements within RTSs that require AI logic, which include: individual units, economic units, high-level strategic AI, commanders and other medium-level strategic units, town building, indigenous life, pathfinding, and tactical/strategic support systems.

INDIVIDUAL UNITS

The real *player* in RTS games is the "overseeing general" of the "army" (or whatever name you wish to give to the forces; military names are being used because the vast majority of these games involve military based setups), either the CPU or the human user. The goals each player is fighting for can involve the entirety of their society. However, this doesn't mean that individual units are worry-free. Individual behaviors in RTS games are usually considered secondary, by temporarily overriding the primary order given by a user. Most of this local intelligence falls into the categories of pathfinding, obstacle avoidance, concentrating attacks, and falling back when the player cannot win.

The question of how much intelligence to put at this secondary *tactical* level is tricky. The amount of micromanagement your RTS is trying to achieve should determine this. The more individual intelligence a unit has, the less often a player has to check every unit in his or her army. However, for games with low-level tactical AI, if the CPU opponent micromanages its individual-unit AI too much (giving it the appearance of better individual AI), it will be seen as cheap AI trick because it isn't possible for the human to replicate the computer's efforts as fast or easily. One simple example of this is the archer behavior in the *Age of Empires* games. The computer will send in many weak projectile units, which then shoot, retreat, shoot, retreat. This very simple behavioral micromanagement makes these weak units become much more powerful because they will string out and separate guards in all directions, a behavior that would be very difficult (or at least tedious) for a human to do. Reliance on the power of this simple individual behavior has also made the *Age of Empires* games not attempt more common strategic techniques, such as setting up a wall of melee fighters and putting the archers (or other long-range attackers) behind them for support, which is something that almost all human players do.

ECONOMIC INDIVIDUAL UNITS

Sometimes called *peons* (the "builders" and "gatherers"), economic individual units are those that usually do not fight but are, instead, employed as the economy on which the player gains resources for creating his or her armies. Much like other individual units, the level of AI has to be carefully tuned to the level of micromanagement the game requires. *Age of Empires* recently addressed common dislikes about this area of the game's AI by making peons automatically start gathering resources after building a resource-associated building, and also making food gathering easier by the ability to "queue up" farms instead of having to check back and replant them manually. Other common peon management techniques include:

- *Order queues.* In most RTS games, the interface allows a player to tell a unit to perform multiple actions, one after another. This is a very powerful addition to the genre because it allows smart players to plan the behavior of their economic units ahead, so the player can then continue play, assured that their economic units will be busy during more battle-oriented points of the game. However, the interface still requires the player to set it up, so the AI of each individual unit doesn't have to be bloated with special-case code designed to make the peons appear smart.
- *Auto-retreating.* Peon units can rarely fight (or aren't skilled at fighting), so most RTS games have some sort of autoretreat AI for these units. Usually it's just leaving the attack range of the enemy, however. This aspect could definitely be improved by getting to a building for protection, or running to the nearest military unit (while shouting "Help!"). Also, noticing when the danger is over and going back to work would be another welcome addition.

HIGH-LEVEL STRATEGIC AI

High-level strategic AI might be thought of like the general of a real army. This is the layer that most closely maps to trying to mimic the human player. Performing commands and plans from this level of direction might involve numerous units, or require whole sections of the economy to shift. High-level plans usually include actions at many different levels of AI to complete. The perceptions at this level are typically built on information from the lower levels to determine what the enemies are doing. Given all this feedback, the high-level AI makes plans to deal with threats exposed in the perception data. In this way, the strategic level affects everything from the individual soldier (as part of a larger group of soldiers who are told by a commander level to respond by moving) to the entire economic system for the AI player (when shifting the allocation of units that are retrieving resources to bias a particular type that will support the high-level plans).

Frequently, the high-level AI is multifaceted, in that it is running resource allocation between several different aspects of the game (defense versus offense versus research versus economy), and thus represents most of a given RTS civilization's *personality.* Race #1 might value offense and have a strong economy. Race #2 might be cautious and studious. Coupled with specialty units for a given AI type, and some tunable parameters, the system designer can differentiate different types of AI opponent races easily, just from this level of the AI.

COMMANDERS AND MEDIUM-LEVEL STRATEGIC ELEMENTS

Some games directly use "commanders" to bolster groups of units (such as *Total Annihilation,* which used its commander unit as a primary builder in addition to a super unit). In other games, commanders are used internally by the AI system to group units into fighting elements and control them in a larger war sense. This can be considered a medium-level AI, because it requires much more than simple individual actions (such as shoot or go somewhere) and is not a fully high-level strategy (line taking command of a particular resource, or defending a base).

A simple example is a commander choosing a new destination for a group of units (medium level), but the individual units decide how to stay in formation and use the terrain features to get there (low level). By dividing the labor in this way, it makes the system easier to write. You can write higher-level systems to cover large troop movements, and lower-level code to get over and around the map. The part of the system that's trying to get troops into position doesn't have to worry about keeping the long-range units behind the short, or figuring out the quickest way through a maze-like canyon.

A more complex example: the general decides that attacking player #3 is the best course of action (high level). The commander (medium level) would then direct twenty infantry to attack from the west, followed by a group of ranged weapon units, and some tanks in from the south to take out towers that could harm the infantry along the way. As always, the low-level pathfinding and avoidance AI would get all those units around the map in the best way possible given the lay of the land.

This middle level of strategic RTS game AI is usually sorely lacking, by and large because it is the most complex to create and tune. High-level goals can be somewhat direct, almost simple. Think of the high-level goal "Take command of Hill #3." Stripped of all the details necessary to actually accomplish the goal, the entire plan is only five words. Low-level goals are also straightforward, involving very atomic behaviors and local, small-scale perceptions. In contrast, the commander level requires large collections of feedback information from many sources. It has to combine all these perceptions into short- and medium-range plans that coordinate group movements, resource allocation, and in some games, form secondary goals involving diplomacy and trade.

TOWN BUILDING

Most RTS games involve collecting resources in order to build a town (base, settlement, colony, etc.) that will then provide the player with the tools and technology to create larger and better-equipped armies. Laying out the initial headquarters, as well as planning the advanced AI bases, is a difficult problem in its own right. A player will want to place structures somewhat close together, for ease of protection (by surrounding walls, or force fields, etc.). But the player will also want to spread them out a bit, to get better visibility and guard against area-effect weapons. Finding this balance, while keeping a fluid economy running, can be quite challenging. Many games use hard rules for town building (which are broken up into difficulty levels) that start out fine, but may or may not be able to cope with changing world conditions, and as such can look silly by the end of the game.

The decisions about where to place key structures need to account for many different elements. Economic structures need to be placed next to the resource they are going to store; military structures need clear exit lanes and proximity to the front line (if possible). Guard structures need to maximize visibility effects and be able to back each other up and watch over the largest possible number of other units.

INDIGENOUS LIFE

Most RTS games have some kind of native inhabitants within their game worlds. Games like *Warcraft* have sheep walking around in them, and *Age of Empires* actually uses the indigenous fauna as a resource that can be gathered. Other games treat the locals as a hazard, or even a source of powerups. AI for these entities is usually minimal, but some games give them a certain degree of intelligence.

Depending on the nature of these elements within your game (be it resource or hazard), you might need to balance the distribution of these elements, otherwise your players may not have fun. *Age of Empires* games using random maps can sometimes be thrown off by having a wolf too close to a player's initial town, and this random element can diminish the starting capabilities of that player tremendously if the wolf inadvertently kills one or more of that player's initial peons.

PATHFINDING

Pathfinding is one of the biggest CPU concerns for RTS games. In the worst-case scenario, a huge number of units could be simultaneously ordered to go to wildly different faraway locations across the map. The pathfinding system must correctly find quality paths for everyone, load balance the CPU cycles necessary to find these paths, and use other optimizations to make pathfinding feasible for so many separate entities. Other types of movement elements such as formations, flocking techniques, and follow-the-leader-type systems will vastly improve the speed of per-unit pathfinding.

Other pathfinding concerns include handling friendly units blocking paths, dealing with special case choke points like bridges, and dynamic path elements such as user-constructed walls or level debris.

TACTICAL AND STRATEGIC SUPPORT SYSTEMS

Many RTS games are increasingly using extended AI techniques to make the actions taken by their games smarter. These advanced support systems include the following:

■ *Terrain analysis.* By dividing the terrain into manageable chunks and then breaking down various characteristics of each piece, the AI can glean huge amounts of data that can be useful for strategic decision making. Terrain bottlenecks and odd landscape features can be identified and recorded for the pathfinding system, so that the pathfinder can more easily and quickly develop intelligent paths. The system can keep track of enemy base locations and resources, and also find holes in the player's (or other player's) defenses. Most of this can be done by using an influence map, which is really just a fancy name for grid-based map attributes. The AI divides the game world up into an even grid, and then associates each location with data specifically describing certain features of each grid square. Terrain analysis data can be created offline during level creation, but the system becomes much more powerful when the game's AI dynamically updates it during the course of the game, as scouting information comes in or allies offer up counsel.

  Some RTS games have a special multiplayer mode in which a certain resource is located all in one spot on the map, leading to a vicious fight over this precious supply point by all the players. Human players can see quite easily that control of the scarce resource is the only way to win in this style of map. AI opponents, unless specifically analyzing the terrain for features like this, are usually ineffective at seeing the long-term problem with this type of map. Typical RTS AI will only head for far-off resources when local ones are depleted and will usually be overrun by human players who have already taken control. The same sort of situation can arise in game maps that have strong movement choke points, like a river crossing or a bridge across a deep canyon. A human player can seek out terrain elements like these and set up strong defenses on one side, and then wait for the computer opponents to waste a lot of resources trying to get through.

■ *Opponent modeling.* In games with imperfect information, like RTS games (or poker, for another example), a player cannot use standard AI opponent assumptions. AI systems for games like chess routinely are built around the premise "My opponent will make roughly the same decisions as I do, because we both use the same optimal search algorithms for the state space of this game." In RTS games, the AI might not know the abilities of the other players (since it can only guess by observation as to what units and technology players have researched, as well as where players have located all their forces), and thus has no basis on which to make predictions about the other players.

By observing and noting both physical abilities of the opponents (like seeing a Dread Mage, or hearing a dragon scream), as well as opponent behaviors (the opponent has always attacked the base from the right, or has always built a tower near the opponent's own gold mines), the AI can build a model of its opponents. Keeping this model as up-to-date as possible is very important, so the AI can use the model to make much more appropriate decisions in dealing with its opponents.

By noting which players have specialty units in their army, the AI can build a fairly accurate tech tree for its opponents and know what other technologies or units each opponent has access to, and can plan for future attacks that might use these. By recording player behavioral tendencies (which types of units the player favors, the time between player attacks, the usual kinds of defenses the player uses, etc.), the AI can better assign defenses and build the correct units to answer upcoming challenges from its opponents. In essence, this is what human military generals do, as well as the meaning of the age-old saying, "know your enemy."

- *Resource management.* Most RTS games (*Myth* was a notable exception) have an economy that must be tended to as much, if not more, than the battles. Raw resource requirements such as gold or wood and the need for secondary resources like combat units and research structures must be balanced during the course of the game. Most games' AI handle this complex task by starting the AI off with a build order (a string of things to build, one after another, that will jump-start a thriving economy), which is a technique that even human players use. This leads to very predictable AI behavior, however, because experienced human players are quick to discover this build order and, from it, learn the approximate times for attacks and when AI defenses will come online so they can exploit defensive holes.

  A better arrangement might involve resource allocation systems that recognize supply deficiencies and rectify them by using a planner to organize goals necessary to fill these needs. By using a need-based system, AI opponents could be implemented that bias heavily toward certain units or resources and would rely much more on map type and personality, rather than blindly following a build order and then reacting to the outcome of the initial first large battle. Even humans who use a build order are quick to adapt the build order to specific things that they see (either in the form of map resources or enemy activity, through their scouts) so that they are not blind-sided. An early RTS game, *Enemy Nations*, used this exact approach with excellent results.

- *Reconnaissance.* Most of these games have some form of "fog of war," which is a mechanism for visually representing two things: unexplored terrain and line of sight. To combat these perception deficiencies, players must use units to explore the map, to uncover map features, such as borders or resources, and to find the enemy and its forces. This is a difficult assignment.

Most AI opponents in RTS games do a good job of exploring the map, simply because they can micromanage a scout unit much more effectively than most humans, but the concept of keeping tabs on enemy movements and encampments through additional recon is uncommon. Humans have to use continual scans to see what kinds of threats the AI (or other human players) are building up against them, as well as noticing any changes to the area that have occurred since the last time a scout went through (like the creation of guarding structures, or the depletion of resources by other players).

One way that some games have tackled this problem is to have the AI-controlled player use a scattered methodology when building its structures. The AI player doesn't have to remember where anything is, so it can create very random and scattered towns that give the AI system the greatest amount of line of sight possible. Then, advancing armies from other players are sure to enter the line of sight of one of these forward buildings, thus alerting the system to invasion early on. This does lead to somewhat greater building loss by the AI, though, because the human will make sure that these forward buildings are taken down as they are passed. A better system would be the more complex wall building and guard-post placement that most humans use.

- *Diplomacy systems.* One of the underused places for AI in today's RTS games is in the area of diplomacy, which is defined as different players working together toward a victory. *Age of Empires* takes AI diplomacy to mean "we won't kill each other," and that players also share map visibility information. It doesn't go into such areas as supporting an ally's troop movements, specialization ("my opponent will develop many units; I'll mine gold and build towers"), or even simply timing attacks to coincide more readily with allies. Human players manage all these diplomatic tasks very well, and AI systems should develop these tasks further. Of course, this involves additional AI work and additional user interface work because the human would need ways to communicate to the AI ally that he's planning an attack from the south in sixteen minutes, or that he needs help in sector six.

USEFUL AI TECHNIQUES

All those specialized game elements requiring AI call for one of the largest required tool sets of any AI game engine. Some of the techniques that work well with RTS games include messaging, finite-state machines, fuzzy-state machines, hierarchical AI, planning, scripting, and data-driven systems.

MESSAGING

With such a huge number of potential units in the game, polling for game state changes or enemy events would be computationally wasteful. Instead, messaging systems can be used for broadcasting events and game flags to a large number of registered units quickly and easily.

FINITE-STATE MACHINES (FSMs)

Never to be left out, FSMs can always be useful somewhere within the numerous AI tasks that are part of the RTS world. Individual-unit AI (most likely implemented as stack-based FSMs, so that they can be temporarily interrupted, then restored easily), systems within the strategy level (a city builder AI could be constructed as an FSM making use of an offline-created build-order script that has been proven to work), and many other game elements can take advantage of the loyal FSM. Small-scale modules are a great fit for FSMs, because they are easy to create and their primary disadvantage, that of not scaling well to large problems, isn't an issue if used in this way.

FUZZY-STATE MACHINES (FuSM)

RTS games' higher-level strategic requirements are some of the few game genre problems that don't lend themselves well to regular state-machine-based solutions. The preponderance of imperfect information about the opponents and the world, combined with the number of micro decisions that need to be made, make for a game in which the AI opponent usually has multiple directions to play toward, all of which are winning decisions.

A better system is fuzzy-state machines (FuSM), which provide the structure and reproducibility of state machines, while accounting for the somewhat "flying blind" nature of RTS decision making. The AI might not know how many tanks the enemy has, or how much gold the opponent has in reserve to purchase additional reserve troops, but must still try to thrust forward toward victory. FuSMs allow this type of gameplay decision, without using the more straightforward method of just cheating and giving the AI knowledge of its opponent's positions and army makeup (which it then uses to make "intelligent" decisions based on some randomness and the difficulty level of the game).

The parallel nature of FuSMs allows an AI system to determine, separately, how much effort to spend on each facet of command that might require attention at any given time. Thus, the complete *blend* of behavior that the AI is exhibiting is going to be much more varied and contextual, and will not rely on omniscient cheating to help the AI.

HIERARCHICAL AI

RTS games have multiple, sometimes conflicting AI requirements. A computer opponent needs to move an army from point A to point B, but along the way, a small ambush happens and its units are being attacked. Do the endangered units break off and return fire, does the entire army stop and make sure the problem is quelled, or do all the troops ignore the threat and march on? The answer is determined by the amount of individual versus commander (or strategic versus tactical) AI, but also the interface between these differing layers and how one can influence the other. Hierarchical systems provide a means for RTS games to form high-level goals but also appear smart at a unit level, without choking the primary AI system for resources.

PLANNING

Goal planning is a large part of the RTS AI world. To accomplish higher-level tasks (for example, to guard the left side of a player's camp against air attack) any prerequisite tasks must also be added to the AI's current plan. Thus, for the just-mentioned task, the AI would have to also (1) gain any foundation technologies in the tech tree (for example, a player might need to make guard towers before he can build antiaircraft towers, or the game could require a communications building so that a player's weapons could use radar to detect incoming planes), and (2) determine the necessary resource units to spend (which, if deficient, might spawn a secondary goal to gain more of the needed resources).

Tech-tree navigation is only one area of planning, however. Specific offensive or defensive goals require planning to appear intelligent as well. It has even been researched that to look truly intelligent, even simple tasks like running away from a threat need some level of forward thinking (beyond just pathfinding). So large troop attacks could use planning to coordinate smaller groups to work in concert. A diplomatic planner could determine how to "save up" the resources that an ally has requested in order to trade for a much-needed technology.

SCRIPTING

Although RTS games usually don't use scripting to the same extent as other genres, it is still used to extend the story elements of certain games, or to more rigidly describe the behavior of certain units under certain conditions. Some titles seem to be concentrating on fewer units and more scripted and rich interactions between these units (such as *Warcraft III*). This emphasis on so-called superunits has led to scripting being used more heavily in this style of game, in much the same way that *Half-Life* led to more scripting in FPS games.

Another place that scripting is useful within RTSs is the aforementioned build-order scripts that most RTS games employ. Some of these scripts can become quite complex, and even include options for building based on early enemy attacks or proximity to certain resources.

DATA-DRIVEN AI

Many of the larger RTS games are putting large portions of the AI decision making into non-code form, be it simplistic parameter setting (like the early *Command and Conquer* games) to actual rule definitions (such as the *Age of Empires* scripts). This allows two things: Designers working on the games gain easier access to the game so they can tune the AI, and people who buy the game can tweak the AI settings themselves. *Age of Empires* especially needed a system like this, with upwards of a dozen civilizations. See Listing 6.1 for an example of a user-defined *Age of Empires* script.

LISTING 6.1   A sample *Age of Empires* AI user-defined script showing simple rule definitions.

```
; attack
(defrule
    (or (goal GOAL-PROTECT-KNIGHT 1)
        (goal GOAL-START-THE-IMPERIAL-ARMY 1))
    (or (unit-type-count-total knight-line >= 25)
        (soldier-count >= 30))
=>
    (set-goal GOAL-FAST-ATTACK 1)
    (set-strategic-number sn-minimum-attack-group-size 8)
    (set-strategic-number sn-maximum-attack-group-size 30)
    (set-strategic-number sn-percent-attack-soldiers 100)
    (attack-now)
    (disable-timer TIMER-ATTACK)
    (enable-timer TIMER-ATTACK 30)
    (set-strategic-number sn-number-defend-groups 0)
    (disable-self)
)


(defrule
    (current-age == feudal-age)
    (soldier-count > 30 )
    (goal GOAL-FAST-ATTACK 1)
=>
    (set-strategic-number sn-number-explore-groups 1)
    (set-strategic-number sn-percent-attack-soldiers 100)
    (attack-now)
    (set-goal GOAL-FIRST-RUCH 0)
    (disable-timer TIMER-ATTACK)
```

```
        (enable-timer TIMER-ATTACK 30)
        (disable-self)
    )

    (defrule
        (current-age == feudal-age)
        (soldier-count > 20 )
        (or    (players-current-age any-enemy >= castle-age)
            (players-population  any-enemy >= 20))
    =>
        (set-goal GOAL-FAST-ATTACK 0)
    )

    (defrule
        (current-age >= feudal-age)
        (soldier-count > 20 )
    =>
        (set-goal GOAL-FAST-ATTACK 1)
    )

    (defrule
        (current-age == feudal-age)
        (goal GOAL-FAST-ATTACK 1)
        (timer-triggered TIMER-ATTACK)
        (soldier-count > 20 )
    =>
        (set-strategic-number sn-percent-attack-soldiers 100)
        (attack-now)
        (set-strategic-number sn-number-defend-groups 0)
        (disable-timer TIMER-ATTACK)
        (enable-timer TIMER-ATTACK 30)
    )
```

EXAMPLES

Herzog Zwei, the granddaddy of RTS games, was really more an action game with the added twist that players had to acquire money to get more equipment. With no real pathfinding, enemies constantly got stuck. A player could trick the AI builder unit so that it was impossible for it to fight back. For the most part, *Herzog* was probably coded using a very simple state machine, with the states defined as get money, attack, and defend.

Westwood Studio's® *Dune: The Building of a Dynasty* came out two years later and started the standard RTS formula that mostly continues today, in which players build a town, mine resources, span a tech tree, and fight enemies. The game didn't have the best AI, but understandably so, given the minimal system requirements of the game. *Dune* used an initial defense build order, followed by a phase of finding the opponent's base, and then attacking. It wouldn't really rebuild its defenses (because they were only built during the opening phase), it wouldn't attack anywhere but the side of its opponent's base facing its base (no real flanking or trying to find weaknesses), and it cheated extensively (the AI never seemed to run out of money, and it could build its structures unconnected from each other, whereas the human could not).

The golden age of RTS games included the *Command and Conquer* series, *Warcraft, Starcraft,* and many spin-offs and imitations. During this time, the AI continued to push forward, the biggest improvement being pathfinding. But the games were still plagued by AI exploits that human players would find very quickly. This was mainly because the AI didn't have the processing power or memory space necessary to use things like influence maps for full terrain analysis or better planning algorithms.

More modern games—such as the *Age of Empires* series, *Empire Earth, Cossacks,* and the like—have built on these modest foundations and created full-featured games with plenty of challenge and fairly good AI opponents. Although some problems are perennial (such as formations interfering with pathfinding, and diplomacy AI being all but absent), these games can, and will, give human players a challenge without cheating (for the most part) and without exploits. Most of these titles use some form of advanced terrain costing to further their pathfinding. Most do some planning to determine goals and subgoals. Starting build orders are still quite popular, simply because of their ease of implementation and the tunable way that they affect difficulty level.

Some modern RTS games have changed direction a bit, with *Warcraft III, Command and Conquer: Generals,* and *Age of Mythology* being notable examples. These games have started emphasizing the use of superunits, or *champions*, instead of throngs of mindless units. These champion units are tougher, more capable, and more expensive to build and to lose. They also employ a much higher amount of mission scripting, so that the game has a much more crafted feel, instead of many of the missions of earlier RTS games where players were just pitted against larger and larger opposition forces.

AREAS THAT NEED IMPROVEMENT

RTS games, like all genres, could use some fresh perspective and new direction in gameplay. Many things were done unintelligently in the past due to CPU constraints, and have remained unintelligent due more to convention than anything else. Some of the areas in the RTS world that could use improvement include: learning, determining when an element is stuck, helper AI, opponent personality, and using more strategy with less tactics.

LEARNING

RTS AI too often gets caught in the same trap repeatedly. A simple example is readily seen in most RTS titles, in which the computer will march one or two units past a tower (which will kill them) over and over. The AI should definitely take into account successful travel information about map locations (using the influence mapping techniques described earlier) so that it can stop being kill-zoned by smart players who notice lines of migration.

Other learning opportunities for RTS games could include opponent modeling opportunities like keeping track of the direction of player attack, noting which types of units the player favors, or even keeping track of game strategies across multiple games against a particular player. Does the player use early rushes? Does the player rely on units that require a lot of a certain resource? Does the player frequently build a number of critical structures in a poorly defended place? Are the player's attacks balanced, or does the player build many rocks, many paper, but never any scissors? When you start attacking a remote base, how long does it take the player to respond? The answers to these kinds of questions could be stored along with statistics that would allow a smart AI system to adapt to these kinds of issues and more.

Using this kind of information doesn't mean that the AI slowly becomes unbeatable; it just means that the human has to switch tactics to win, somewhat forcing the player to investigate other areas of the game's complexity. An AI opponent that is shutting down specific player offensive maneuvers doesn't necessarily mean that the AI *itself* has to be aggressive, unless the player has set the difficulty very high.

DETERMINING WHEN AN AI ELEMENT IS STUCK

At some point, in almost every game, an AI element (from the lowliest economic peon, to an entire group of tanks) might get into a situation where it doesn't know what to do at all. Maybe all the resource-gathering centers are gone, there's not enough money to build another one, and a peon has an armload of coal but doesn't know what to do with it. Or a group of tanks is being hounded by an aerial unit (and cannot fight back), but is also trapped in a close-quarters area, and stuck in a pathfinding/fleeing cycle that keeps the tanks going in circles as they try to get away, but trip each other up, over and over again. This type of nasty feedback loop can make an AI element look extremely stupid, but it is precisely the kind of behavior that almost every RTS game has in some form. Detecting this kind of "stalling" and either having a contingency plan, or some kind of bailout behavior, is essential to help the intelligence of these games.

Another case of this is the classic problem in which a player has to kill all the units in the enemy's army to win, and the AI has one peon unit, hidden behind a tree, somewhere on the huge world map. This leads to the player scouring the map, for an hour and a half, until the player happens upon the peon, who was just sitting there frozen with nothing to do. The AI in RTS games should be able to recognize when it's been beaten (most do, but even the best get confused sometimes) and offer surrender. If the player *wants* to hunt down the last peon, the player can; but the designer should also give the player the chance to see his hard-won "Victory!" screen without spending all day hunting for some foolish unit.

HELPER AI

To alleviate micromanagement tasks that a human player performs repeatedly during the game, helper AI is an area that screams for exploration by developers. Also mentioned in Chapter 4 during the discussion of RPG party members, "automatic" behavior that units perform on their own could be improved. A flexible system could add new behaviors (if the game recognizes that the player is always doing a specific small behavior), exhaust unwanted behaviors, and perform with mild intelligence. It would make playing RTS games much more flavorful than the current "build up, attack, build up, attack" click-fest, in which the person who knows the best build order and can get things done the fastest wins. Sometimes, yes, that is exactly the game some people want to play. But right now we don't have much of a choice, as it seems to be the way most RTS games are set up.

In effect, this system would recognize small behavior macros (groups of behaviors that the human is repeatedly doing) and then either ask the player if he needs help in doing that or just take over the task (possibly with some sort of "It's taken care of" message communicated to the player). The player could select the level of macro help he'd like, with level 0 being no help, level 5 would find things repeated more than five times and would extinguish these behaviors if the player cancelled out of them more than once, and at level 10 it would discern anything the player repeated more than twice; the macro would never extinguish these rules. At any rate, you would probably also want little macro "flags" to appear somewhere onscreen (or in some quick menu), so that the player could cancel any that the player wanted to at any time.

OPPONENT PERSONALITY

One of the earliest RTS games, *Herzog Zwei,* had two opposing AI personalities (heavily offense-based and heavily defense-based). Each offered a very different playing experience. A player had lots of time to build forces against the defensive opponent, whereas the player had almost no time at all before the more offense-based AI would be at the player's main base with invaders.

Imagine getting variation not just in difficulty level of the AI, but in other attributes as well. We do this in sports games or fighting games, why not in RTS games? By using resource allocation systems to describe bias toward specific units, or specialization in different branches of the tech tree, we could generate opponents with much more flavor. In the development phase, different stable personalities could be tuned and played against each other, to find the combinations that lead to victory. These personalities could even be replaced by a singular AI opponent over time, so the AI opponent would start play with a very balanced game, but after a brutal combat loss might get "mad" and use a much more aggressive resource allocation table to force out more units, for retribution.

This would not only flavor the AI battle, but could carry over into the diplomacy game. A player might reconsider allying with an AI character that the player knows has a tendency to turn on its allies, or is a hothead and will become angered by the smallest incursion, turning the supposed ally into a liability if the AI character is off hunting a perceived enemy instead of sticking to a larger agreed-upon battle plan.

More Strategy, Less Tactics

AI micromanagement leads to better per-unit behavior. To be considered human-like, however, RTS games need better strategic team leadership, not individual-unit intelligence that outdoes the human in speed or tedium. Instead of better planning algorithms and squad (or commander)-level AI, which is more analogous to the way a human plays, most games rely on the computer's ability to quickly micromanage attacking units on an individual basis.

Another commonly used technique is to have unit AI that is not present when a human player is under control, which makes it *feel* like micromanagement. This leaves the AI able to do things that are near impossible for a human, which leads to frustration, and a feeling that the AI is cheating.

Perhaps the AI could be given limits on the amount of micromanaging it can do in a given timeframe, to simulate the time it takes a human to scroll around, clicking the mouse and hitting hotkeys. In any case, better strategic systems in RTS games will go a long way toward making the AI in these games more human and, ultimately, more fun to play against. Some things that a superior strategic system should accomplish are these:

■ *Grouping units by type, and then using groups to back up other groups, or respond to specific threats with the correct counter type of units.* Right now, most battles initiated by the AI opponent are started by the AI generating a mix of units based on a scripted combination that works well together, affected by the resources the AI has, and to some lesser degree by the types of units they expect to see from the human player. This is a good start, but that's where the strategic AI in most games ends. Once a war party actually reaches the human's forces, the AI could respond to the dangers it finds there more efficiently by using a commander level of AI decisions that targets enemies with good counter units and makes adjustments as the battle ensues, just like a person would, by setting up attack lines to take advantage of multiple fronts, and also leave support lines open for additional forces to come in.

Again, most RTS games suffer from using the individual-unit AI far too much once the battle has begun. They also don't use much in the way of attack scheduling. Splitting up an army, and coming from two sides, is a technique used when an advancing enemy places units where they are not protected very well. But it requires that these two fronts be timed so that they happen concurrently, otherwise all you've done is split your army in two.

■ *Using terrain features to set up optimal wall structures.* Wall construction separates good RTS AI from the truly great. Some games use a random map generator to keep multiplayer games fresh, so the need for a dedicated wall constructor is paramount to make quality, useful walls that still use terrain features to their advantage.

Schedule retreats if they are foreseeable, or just initiate them if everything falls apart. Battles with large numbers of units "going kamikaze" should only happen if there are bigger motives at play. You could use their sacrifice as a diversion (to attack another front, or make a run for a particular resource, etc.). The attack could be specifically designed to fight against some entrenched enemy defense. Retreats from a losing battle should be a bit more elegant than just selecting every unit and giving them a destination of home base.

Set up ambush situations, or cover lines of retreat for advancing armies. A common strategy that human players employ is to keep a large force back from the front lines, and then have a few fast units go forward and draw some enemy forces from their entrenchments and back to this waiting ambush. Or, the human will use these fast units to draw a considerable number of the defensive forces away from one side of the enemy's main base, and then send in the larger force to this less-protected area. Either way, the essential strategy the AI needs to employ is to protect the line of retreat of any of the AI's forces. If they have to fall back, the AI won't have to worry about fast enemy units following the retreat line and picking off slower units trying to flee.

SUMMARY

RTS games have given game players the amazing opportunity to be generals in charge of an entire army, complete with an economy to replenish that army. Because of the tremendous number of units and possible actions going on in real-time throughout the map, the AI challenges in RTS games are particularly large.

■ Individual-unit AI gives personality to units, without clogging the higher-level AI systems.

■ Economic AI needs to be carefully tuned so that human players don't have to micromanage too much, or too little.

■ Commander-level and team-level AI provide increasingly more strategic layers to the system, and can help keep each layer simple and easy to maintain.

■ Town building AI is a unique challenge that must account for factors such as protection, visibility, and forward planning to look intelligent.

■ Pathfinding takes up a large percentage of CPU cycles because of the numbers of units and the complex terrains. A good pathfinder implementation is paramount to the success of the game.

■ Support AI systems that are important to RTS games include terrain analysis, opponent modeling, resource management, reconnaissance, and diplomacy systems. Each delivers an important part of the RTS experience.

■ Messaging is a very important AI technique for RTS games because of the high-level communication that needs to occur.

■ FuSMs are a good way to model the huge amount of imperfect information that RTS AI systems have to process, along with the many directions that a team has to split its resources and attention.

■ Hierarchical AI systems, as well as planning algorithms and scripting systems, are also key elements to many RTS AI engines.

■ Learning, either directly, or through secondary means (like influence maps) can make the AI in RTS games far more adaptive.

■ Determining when a unit (or entire game element) is stuck is a problem that many RTS games have not solved very well.

■ Helper AI could be used when a human is playing the game to help alleviate micro tasks by giving the player the option of AI taking them over automatically.

■ Opponents in RTS games rarely exhibit any personality, and as such, your human players might find it hard to really connect with their opponents.

■ RTS games need to concentrate on more strategic battle elements, and less on individual-unit tactical AI.

7 First-Person Shooters/ Third-Person Shooters (FTPS)

In This Chapter

- Common AI Elements
- Useful AI Techniques
- Examples
- Areas That Need Improvement
- Summary

Like RTSs, First-Person Shooter/Third-Person Shooter (FTPS) games are the other major genre that has been blessed by both deep development from inside the industry, and research within the classical academic community.

One reason for this is because of early efforts by Id Software. Most of Id's games have pushed the envelope for graphics and network programming, and have been groundbreaking in the area of user extensibility. Other leading games have followed suit. Many FTPSs include tools that people can use to add levels, change weapons, script new AI elements, and even perform what is called a "total conversion," meaning that the entire game has been changed radically. An entire "mod" (short for modification) scene has sprung up with many Web sites where people can get information about customizing their favorite game, as well as download mods created by other users.

One type of mod that specifically uses AI techniques is called a "bot." Short for *robot*, this is what the FTPS world refers to as an autonomous agent. Bots can navigate a map, find enemies, and attack them intelligently. Bots respond to injury, powerups, and so on. See Listing 7.1 for a sample of code from a *Quake* bot.

Some bot writers have gone on to get legitimate jobs in game development because of their independent work in the mod world. A good example is Steve Polge, writer of the Reaper Bot (one of the earlier and more famous bots), going on to be the AI programmer for *Unreal*. Many level editors have gotten their start in the mod community as well. Interviews with companies doing FTPS games are often preceded by showing the interviewer levels or modifications that a candidate has done independently, often with good reviews from community sites.

LISTING 7.1 *QuakeC* sample of user-defined script for an AI-controlled bot.

```
void (float dist) ai_run = {

   local vector delta;
   local float axis;
   local float direct;
   local float ang_rint;
   local float ang_floor;
   local float ang_ceil;

   movedist = dist;
   if ( (self.enemy.health <= FALSE) ) {

      self.enemy = world;
      if ( (self.oldenemy.health > FALSE) ) {

         self.enemy = self.oldenemy;
         HuntTarget ();

      } else {

         if ( self.movetarget ) {

            self.th_walk ();

         } else {

            self.th_stand ();

         }
         return ;

      }

   }
   self.show_hostile = (time + TRUE);
   enemy_vis = visible (self.enemy);
```

```
     if ( enemy_vis ) {

        self.search_time = (time + MOVETYPE_FLY);

     }
     if ( ((coop || deathmatch) && (self.search_time < time)) ) {

        if ( FindTarget () ) {

           return ;

        }

     }
     enemy_infront = infront (self.enemy);
     enemy_range = range (self.enemy);
     enemy_yaw = vectoyaw ((self.enemy.origin - self.origin));
     if ( (self.attack_state == AS_MISSILE) ) {

        ai_run_missile ();
        return ;

     }
     if ( (self.attack_state == AS_MELEE) ) {

        ai_run_melee ();
        return ;

     }
     if ( CheckAnyAttack () ) {

        return ;

     }
     if ( (self.attack_state == AS_SLIDING) ) {

        ai_run_slide ();
        return ;

     }
     movetogoal (dist);

};
```

Because of this extensibility (and the product's stability), some of Id's games have become test beds for AI research in academia. Many diverse research labs are using their games, with heavily modified code, to test AI techniques under conditions that are much closer to modeling real-world situations than used in the lab before, and with much more realistic time constraints. Various techniques have been tested from new ways to store environment information, to faster planning algorithms, to complete rule inference systems. There have been many presentations of these extensions given back to game developers at industry gatherings, so that their ideas and techniques are exchanged in something of a "feedback loop" that has been beneficial to both groups.

Another type of FTPS game that has become popular lately is the squad combat game (SCG). This is an FTPS game in which the main character isn't a single person but, rather an entire squad (usually about three to ten people) working toward a common goal. SCG games started out as a multiplayer game mode in some regular FTPS games, called Capture the Flag. (In Capture the Flag, both teams have a flag. If you can get the other team's flag and return it to your base while you're still in possession of your own flag, your team gets a point.) This concept was then expanded into full-blown military squad simulations. The AI for these types of games can be very complex, since squad group maneuvers and multi-agent coordination is a much harder problem to solve than the problems inherent in the more straightforward FTPS games.

COMMON AI ELEMENTS

FTPS games have a number of typically common AI controlled parts. These include: enemies, boss enemies, deathmatch opponents, weapons, cooperative agents, squad members, pathfinding, and spatial reasoning.

ENEMIES

FTPS games are, by definition, shooters, and shooters require targets. Thus, the main thrust of FTPSs is to have enemies—and lots of them. So the AI used in these enemies is vital to the longevity of the product. Many games have touted "better enemy AI" for their game, only to have it shot down by exploits almost immediately upon release.

Certain FTPSs have used what some call *arcade* AI, which is the simple pattern AI of old-style arcade games. *Doom* and the modern *Serious Sam* games use this technique very well. They give the player a chance to simply run around with the biggest gun and destroy everything in his or her path, which is just what some people want. Still other games, such as *Half-Life,* provide a much more scripted, intelligent, and rich gameplay experience, and were also successful.

How much work you put into your enemies is directly related to the type of gameplay experience you are striving for. Strange, though, is the notion that both the arcade and scripted types of FTPS games are hard to do well. *Doom* hit a perfect balance with its mindless enemies, great level design, and weapon balance. It spawned countless copy-cats, almost all of which were not as good. *Half-Life* did the same with scripted content in an FTPS game. It sported a great story, many hand-tuned situations complete with complex nonplayer character behavior, and good atmosphere. These efforts were followed by a vast number of games seeking to do the same, with few succeeding.

Boss Enemies

Some of the action-based FTPS games, such as *Serious Sam,* also contain Boss enemies as might a basic shooter or a role-playing game. At the end of any given level, you would come face to face with a (usually) larger and more powerful enemy, complete with special attacks and unique abilities. Even the more complex games like *Half-Life* had some really big creatures to tackle. These creatures are generally very tough but have some weakness that can be exploited if discovered. Some even required you to use elements of the environment to kill them.

Deathmatch Opponents

The AI opponents necessary for FTPS games fall into two basic categories: regular *monster* enemies and deathmatch *bots.* Monsters are creatures that are expected to act like beasts, or at best, evil humanoid killers. They provide the fodder for parts of your game that require masses of enemies for the user to gun down. As stated, they could be human, but are more likely animals, zombies, or some other unthinking mob-style agents.

Bots, on the other hand, are trying to closely model human behavior and performance during deathmatch games. Some bots have been created to caricature certain behaviors (such as bots that only use a particular weapon and are always jumping, for instance), but they are mostly trying to model good, solid, human deathmatch execution.

If you plan to add a multiplayer portion to your product, you are going to need bot AI so that players can have a multiplayer experience if they don't have a means of connecting to someone else, or just want to practice. Unlike the regular enemies in a FTPS game, these characters are supposed to be as smart and as human as possible (with difficulty levels, of course) to provide the player with a fun, yet challenging, run through the deathmatch environments.

Bot difficulty levels usually involve tweaking different aspects of the bot's behavior, such as aggressiveness, how often the bot will retreat and load up on health powerups, the appropriateness of weapon usage (or does the bot have a favorite weapon that it uses much better), as well as how good the bot's aim is.

Another activity gradually finding its way into bot behavior in new FTPS games is using chat messages. Examples include sending a quick message to taunt players recently killed, or commending another player on a good shot. Although still very simplistic, the effect is becoming better as games continue to use it. In the future, we may see the equivalent of full chat bots within our FTPS games, to make them seem even more human.

WEAPONS

FTPS weapons have run the gamut from the seminal rocket launcher to the very odd "voodoo doll" in *Blood* that had players stick pins in their enemies from afar. With weapons that bounce around corners, leave trails of deadly goo, or have to be steered like heat-seeking missiles, sometimes it takes intelligence just to *use* some of the weapons that these games employ.

Other weapon intelligence issues involve specific concerns like not shooting splash damage weapons when the bot itself might be hurt by the effect, or strange usages of weapons, such as the electricity gun discharge in the first *Quake* game (if a player shot the electricity gun into a pool of water, it would instantly kill anybody immersed in the pool, including the original gun owner). It could even be said that knowing which weapon to pick is a definite intelligence test: taking into account weapons that match well against other weapons, player types, enemy range, and amount of ammunition.

COOPERATIVE AGENTS

An element that started showing up within more complex, story-driven FTPS games, cooperative agents are "helper" bots, or special NPC types that inhabit a level. When the player interacts (other than in a killing sense) with these special characters, they might offer help, or a new weapon, etc. Some of these characters are quite complex, following a player around a level, helping with enemies, and pointing out features of the map.

Games that have used this element successfully are *Half-Life, Medal of Honor: Underground*, and many others. Just as with RPGs, cooperative agents need to have enough "smarts" so that the player doesn't feel like the agent requires babysitting; otherwise, the player will quickly abandon the agent, or become frustrated with the game.

SQUAD MEMBERS

If you're constructing a game based on squad combat, then you're going to be spending a large amount of time making the individual squad member AI as smart as possible. Squad-based maneuvers range from the simple (leapfrogging forward movement while providing cover) to the very complex (part of a squad breaking off, to take out a guard post, while the main group continues forward, to remove a different guard, and then both groups meet at some point).

The AI that controls squad members needs to be *reactive* (the "thinking" process here is, if you're being fired at don't keep running to a spot because the player told you to earlier; rather, get behind some cover, look for the source of attack, and then use some smart means of either communicating back to the commander, or using the terrain features to get to the target safely), *proactive* (if a grenade gets lobbed into our trench, someone should pick it up and lob it back, or jump on it . . . don't wait for my orders), and *communicative* (give me feedback about success and failure, any slowdowns the forces are incurring, additional information they have uncovered, etc.).

If you're making an SCG game that is a not military-based (for example, a game where a player and his virtual family have to defend their home against alien attack), you would need to account for some additional personality issues, including being calm under fire, dealing with injuries, panic, and the shock of seeing violence. These are all things that a professional soldier is trained to do well, but if a player sees the eight-year-old sister doing fine and giving the player a thumb's up while under heavy laser fire with a serious leg wound, the player might think it was pretty unrealistic. Of course, this might be what you're going for (maybe you're designing the game to be specifically campy).

On top of all this, squad-level AI systems need to make the team competent, but not unstoppable. Such is the fine line of game *balance.* If the squad is *too* capable, the player feels like a bystander and not needed, but if the squad is not capable enough, the player might start to feel surrounded by idiots. This is where extensive gameplay testing is imperative.

PATHFINDING

Pathfinding is one of the primary AI systems in an FTPS. In real-time strategy (RTS) games, pathfinding usually encompasses only terrain management. FTPS pathfinding further involves using in-game elements (such as elevators, teleporters, levers, etc.) and specialized movement techniques (the "rocket jump," crossing underwater sequences that might hurt if not done correctly, etc.). As such, pathfinding in FTPS games usually employs a combination of specialized level data, alongside custom pathfinding "costing," which can help account for special movement oddities.

Local pathfinding for dynamic objects, or *obstacle avoidance,* is used to help with more immediate problems. Avoidance can complement or completely override the normal pathfinding system, based on context. If a character has his back to a corner, and he's being pinned there by some other player or environmental element, the pathfinding system needs to recognize this state as being "stuck" and have some sort of exit contingency for the character. Your autonomous AI-controlled characters can and will find every sticky spot on the map to get wedged into, and the look of your pathfinding system will suffer dramatically in that they stay that way for any length of time. By leaving nothing (or near nothing) to chance, you can allow the level designers free rein to create any environments they want to, and still give your creations a fighting chance to navigate them successfully.

SPATIAL REASONING

In the same way that RTS AI systems use terrain analysis to find expoitable elements in the game world (such as bottlenecks and crucial resource sites), FTPS games need to model the kinds of spatial determinations that humans make about areas of the game world. Humans are very good at looking at an environment and finding sniper locations, choke points, good environmental cover, and such.

However, this is a pretty difficult problem to tackle in a real-time, three-dimensional environment (RTS games can use a cut-down, overhead two-dimensional version of the map to simplify things). So again, this problem is usually solved with another step in the level-design process, by tagging areas of the map with helper data that the AI opponents can discern and use to their advantage. Systems that can perform this process automatically on a level have been developed, usually as a preprocessing stage that produces this spatial reasoning data in some usable form. Typically this autogenerated data is used in conjunction with designer-placed data.

USEFUL AI TECHNIQUES

In order to achieve all the required AI for these games, a number of different AI methods have proven themselves useful. These include: finite-state machines, fuzzy-state machines, messaging systems, and scripting.

FINITE-STATE MACHINES (FSMs)

The staple of the AI programming world makes its appearance again. FSMs can be used exclusively (*Serious Sam*), or as part of a larger AI system (as in *Half-Life*). The life span of most enemies in these games can be very short; no real forward planning is usually needed. Deathmatch AI for these games involves a minimum of states, usually along the lines of attack, retreat, explore, and get powerup. The rest of the intelligence comes from special navigation systems, the movement model for the bot, and other support routines. See Listing 7.2 for a snippet of the AI FSM code from *Quake 2*.

This function is used to determine if certain AI states (namely `ai_run` and `ai_stand`) should transition to `ai_attack`. Note the comment line labeled JDC, the initials of John Carmack. Also notice the `//FIXME:` comment that is in the final released code. It's good to know that John is still human.

LISTING 7.2   *Quake 2* AI code snippet. © Id Software, licensed under the GPL.

```
/*
=============
ai_checkattack

Decides if we're going to attack or do something else
used by ai_run and ai_stand
=============
*/
qboolean ai_checkattack (edict_t *self, float dist)
{
    vec3_t      temp;
    qboolean    hesDeadJim;

    // this causes monsters to run blindly to
        // the combat point w/o firing
    if (self->goalentity)
    {
        if (self->monsterinfo.aiflags & AI_COMBAT_POINT)
            return false;

        if (self->monsterinfo.aiflags & AI_SOUND_TARGET)
        {
            if ((level.time - self->enemy->teleport_time) > 5.0)
            {
                if (self->goalentity == self->enemy)
                    if (self->movetarget)
                        self->goalentity = self->movetarget;
                    else
                        self->goalentity = NULL;
                self->monsterinfo.aiflags &= ~AI_SOUND_TARGET;
                if (self->monsterinfo.aiflags &
                        AI_TEMP_STAND_GROUND)
                    self->monsterinfo.aiflags &=
                        ~(AI_STAND_GROUND | AI_TEMP_STAND_GROUND);
            }
            else
            {
                self->show_hostile = level.time + 1;
                return false;
            }
        }
    }
```

```
enemy_vis = false;

// see if the enemy is dead
hesDeadJim = false;
if ((!self->enemy) || (!self->enemy->inuse))
{
    hesDeadJim = true;
}
else if (self->monsterinfo.aiflags & AI_MEDIC)
{
    if (self->enemy->health > Ø)
    {
        hesDeadJim = true;
        self->monsterinfo.aiflags &= ~AI_MEDIC;
    }
}
else
{
    if (self->monsterinfo.aiflags & AI_BRUTAL)
    {
        if (self->enemy->health <= -8Ø)
            hesDeadJim = true;
    }
    else
    {
        if (self->enemy->health <= Ø)
            hesDeadJim = true;
    }
}

if (hesDeadJim)
{
    self->enemy = NULL;
    // FIXME: look all around for other targets
    if (self->oldenemy && self->oldenemy->health > Ø)
    {
        self->enemy = self->oldenemy;
        self->oldenemy = NULL;
        HuntTarget (self);
    }
    else
    {
        if (self->movetarget)
        {
            self->goalentity = self->movetarget;
```

```
                    self->monsterinfo.walk (self);
        }
        else
        {
            // we need the pausetime otherwise the stand code
            // will just revert to walking with no target and
            // the monsters will wonder around aimlessly trying
            // to hunt the world entity
            self->monsterinfo.pausetime = level.time +
                                        100000000;
            self->monsterinfo.stand (self);
        }
        return true;
    }
}

self->show_hostile = level.time + 1;// wake up other monsters

// check knowledge of enemy
enemy_vis = visible(self, self->enemy);
if (enemy_vis)
{
    self->monsterinfo.search_time = level.time + 5;
    VectorCopy (self->enemy->s.origin, self->
                                monsterinfo.last_sighting);
}

// look for other coop players here
//    if (coop && self->monsterinfo.search_time < level.time)
//    {
//        if (FindTarget (self))
//            return true;
//    }

enemy_infront = infront(self, self->enemy);
enemy_range = range(self, self->enemy);
VectorSubtract (self->enemy->s.origin, self->s.origin, temp);
enemy_yaw = vectoyaw(temp);


// JDC self->ideal_yaw = enemy_yaw;

if (self->monsterinfo.attack_state == AS_MISSILE)
{
    ai_run_missile (self);
```

```
            return true;
        }
        if (self->monsterinfo.attack_state == AS_MELEE)
        {
            ai_run_melee (self);
            return true;
        }

        // if enemy is not currently visible, we will never attack
        if (!enemy_vis)
            return false;

        return self->monsterinfo.checkattack (self);
    }
```

FUZZY-STATE MACHINES (FuSMs)

Fuzzy-state machines have also been implemented within these games, especially because the number of fuzzy variables is usually low, so you don't run into the problems of combinatorial calculation growth that hurts fuzzy systems. Also, the states of inputs from which FTPS opponents must make their determinations are rarely as crisp as finite states are considered to be. An AI-controlled opponent might be at 23 percent health, but have a really good weapon, and is also coming up behind the human player, unseen by the player. So, even though the AI opponent is very damaged, should the AI opponent take the shot? The answer is probably yes, but only when you think of the system using a combination of the various fuzzy inputs to this agent. Again, this is only relevant when you consider the types of enemies you are programming. Shooting the player in the back isn't very entertaining behavior (for the human), unless you are creating a deathmatch opponent.

This technique also works well because of the way many of these games portray their animation. The upper and lower bodies of the characters are usually almost completely decoupled from each other. The lower half tries to play some running animation that corresponds to the direction of travel, while the upper half aims, fires, and switches weapons. This leads nicely to a fuzzy solution where two states might be activated at lower levels, a character might be shooting at a player, but also running for a health powerup, the result of a fuzzy-state system that treats "50 percent shoot, 50 percent get powerup" as a solution.

MESSAGING SYSTEMS

In most deathmatch-style FTPSs, the thrust of the gameplay could be described as "a physics model with input handlers" (meaning that the gameplay is basically just taking input from the humans, using the physics code to move everything around, and keeping track of when the missile weapons collide with the players). Because of this, using a messaging system within this genre is a natural fit, in that a stable underlying system (the physics system, the renderer) runs constantly, with events marking any interesting happenings (such as firing a rocket, or player X entering the #23 teleporter).

Most of these games include an online multi-player element, and quite a few use the server-client network model. The client of a message-based game could employ a simple state-based AI system, with changes in state initiated by events from the server. One major reason this type of setup is common with online multiplayer FTPSs is that it helps guard against cheating, in that all game information comes directly from the server.

Messaging also works well in SCGs because of the need to pass information back and forth among squad members, including sharing a lot of information about visible threats, positions, status, and much more.

SCRIPTING SYSTEMS

Some modern developers use a high level of scripting in their FTPS games. Everything, including elements in the environment, enemies, conversations, player interaction with specific game objects or agents, and in-game cut scenes are all (or in part) scripted. Scripting, in general, makes direct storytelling easier, so if your FTPS has a strong story element, then this is the way to go. In the more action-heavy titles, however, the only scripted elements are probably cut scenes, camera moves, or the more stylized attack patterns of a boss-type creature.

EXAMPLES

Old-school FTPS games, such as *Doom* and *Duke Nukem 3D,* used simple AI. Most of the enemies are directly placed in the level by a level designer. The enemies are generally restricted to a specific part of the level, to keep pathfinding (if it even exists) to a minimum, and the nature of the levels themselves (what was sometimes called 2.5D because the rendering engine could only handle elevations but not stacked rooms) allowed for fairly direct movement and combat maneuvers.

Later games converted to full three dimensionality (one of the first was *Descent*) and started using complex pathfinding systems to get around. However, the brains of the AI enemies were still pretty simplistic. Typically the only difficult opponents were the boss creatures, but their toughness was generally because of sheer hit points, damage potential, and the fact that many times players were locked in a small room with them as opposed to clever tactics. Games such as *Hexen, Blood,*

Heretic, and the like are all good examples of games that fell into this category. *Heretic* was one of the early third-person shooter games to really give the new formula a great interface.

With the next level of FTPS games, we suddenly got a full taste of our true new addiction, online multi-player deathmatch. Before this time, only those lucky enough to work at a computer company with a LAN, or with more than one in-home computer that they could string a null modem between had experienced this exciting mode. But finally, programmers discovered ways of getting decent gameplay over the Internet, even with a dialup connection, and gamers wanted in on it. The games got better, *Quake* and *Unreal* being the top two.

Also during this period, Id made *Quake* highly extensible for the end user (with *Unreal* following suit) and, thus, led to the development of the deathmatch bot, which forever changed the FTPS AI world. People started to see what an FTPS enemy could do, given a degree of intelligence, and started demanding more challenging enemies in the single-player portion as well. This led to a much higher level of AI complexity across the board.

Today, a new variant on these games is taking over people's free time. It's called squad combat, and some of the best are *Socom* and *Tom Clancy's Rainbow Six.* These games include all the regular FTPS AI, and also involve the coordination of multiple team members in real-time combat missions against teams of enemies. There is a fine balance in these games between the high-level commands that a player sends to his or her team members and the realistic tactical AI that they need to perform to operate well in concert.

The last batch of FTPS games to come out have been almost completely (besides sequels to our perennial favorites, including *Unreal*) based in the realm of war-themed games. *Battlefield: 1942, Call of Duty,* and *Battlefield: Vietnam* are very popular games that capture much of the grit of real war, while still looking very good and playing well. Purists of war gaming are not amused by some of the license that has been taken with historical details, or weapon details, but the medium-level shooter crowd really enjoys the inclusion of a more realistic world (without having to worry who's going to come around the corner with the BFG and blow a hole in the entire world), as well as the inclusion of all the vehicle types that many of the war FTPS games include, like tanks, boats, and even planes.

AREAS THAT NEED IMPROVEMENT

Inevitably, as with all game genres, there are things to try and strive for, new techniques or gameplay roads we could travel to make the genre grow and mature. These improvement areas include: learning and opponent modeling, personality, creativity, anticipation, better conversation engines, motivation, and better squad AI.

LEARNING AND OPPONENT MODELING

Holes in the AI's behavior are found and exploited in FTPS games, just like any other game genre. Because FTPSs are often played online in multi-player situations, however, these holes are found even faster, and people will pass on this knowledge very quickly. FTPSs run the risk of becoming very repetitive, simply because even if you design a new game which changes the location, the enemy, and the weapon, the players are still just hunting enemies down and shooting them.

Therefore, FTPS games run the risk of becoming boring very quickly. AI enemies need to react much more to the personal playing style of their opponents to ensure game longevity. Enemies could keep track of various statistics to affect their gameplay style, such as the following:

- *The weapons the human uses most.* Most people specialize, either because the damage of a certain weapon is high (such as the rocket launcher that players seem to love in the various *Quake* games), or because they have an affinity for a certain weapon and have practiced special techniques with it (such as the nail gun in the original *Quake,* which bounced around corners and could be really nasty if the player took the time to find spots to fire at that would bounce to commonly-tread areas of the map; or the devilish places people found to put *Duke Nukem 3D* trip mines).
- *The routes through the map the human uses.* One popular method of playing these games is to learn a good route through the map that puts the player in contact with all the major powerups while keeping the player moving so they don't get caught napping. The AI could discern these routes and either watch for the player along the route, or fire rockets and such down corridors that the human routinely uses, forcing the player to change his or her game.
- *The close-quarters combat style of the human.* If the human always circle strafes to the left, for instance, the AI could use this to better dodge the oncoming fire.
- *The type of player the human is.* This mostly refers to the level of movement that the human employs while playing. It usually goes from a high level of movement (or a hunter type), to medium movement (or a patroller type), to almost no movement (a sniper, or what is known as a camper type).

Tracking other player statistics could lead you to differentiate AI play in other ways, but all of the above mentioned systems would lead to better, more human-like AI opponents. By knowing this type of information about the player, the AI opponent can fine tune how it looks for the player, how it attacks, and how it can out-perform players that don't mix up their playing style. By getting players to change their playing style frequently, we can force players to explore different ways to play, new weapons to master, and thus continue to further enjoy our games.

PERSONALITY

Even though the bots of today play well, and usually employ a minimum of out-right cheating, they fall far short of having the kind of personality that players can sense when playing against another human. Especially when someone plays against a particular human opponent regularly, the player can get a sense of the other person's personality (aggression level, how rattled the other person gets under fire, does the opponent camp, etc.) and the range of the human opponent's personality (for example, the opponent is usually even-headed, but in the final three minutes of a game, he or she goes berserk).

Bot "personality" has typically involved their weapons of choice, and their overall difficulty level. More personality would actually lead to a more immersive exchange, as players learn the ins and outs of the bot's styles and tendencies. It can be very difficult to convey a bot's personality, however, since player interaction is often limited to a short-duration exchange of gunfire. Obviously there's a lot of tuning that needs to be done to make bot personalities work. One thing to consider would be to only fully work out personalities for sub-boss or boss level creatures that are either recurrent (meaning they come back several times after retreating from the fight before dying) or take such a spectacularly long time to kill that you can actually get their personality across during the fight.

CREATIVITY

Playing against humans, gamers can see the vast array of new and unique ways to use the weapons and environment that people have found. Many humans bounce around the map by jumping or using the backlash from weapons, and it makes them much harder to hit. An FTPS with a solid physics model (with few special cases, to allow for stable math) could either note human player trajectories and figure out how the human got there (by jumping and then firing a rocket sideways, to send the player flying high speed to another ledge), or could randomly try different ways of traversing a given game area and then tag their internal model of the level with these new ways of progression.

Although true creativity might be beyond the scope of an AI system, AI programmers could come up with a much richer degree of environment usage by the AI, and the overall effect would be that of a bot that "really knows the level well," an affectation usually given to players that can move around the level in novel ways and attack their opponents by strange means.

ANTICIPATION

One thing that good players employ all the time in FTPS games is anticipation. A player might watch an opponent go into a room, and because there is only one door, time the firing of an area effect weapon so that it will hit the player as he comes back out the door.

This would require the AI to keep a mental model of the other player, and estimate how long it would take the player to enter the room, go to whatever powerup made the player enter the room in the first place, and then come back out. The AI would then set up the shot, or a more personal ambush, to match the AI's model of when the player will emerge. Shot anticipation would be a fairly advanced move, but if a human player truly wants to practice what online play is like, this is the type of AI opponent the player will need to acclimate to, since humans *will* use behavior like this.

A more mild anticipatory behavior would be to set up ambushes, either by reasoning that another player will use a certain doorway and lying in wait for the other player to come along, or by getting the attention of an enemy, running away, and waiting in some safe spot that the AI has scouted out earlier for the enemy to follow.

BETTER CONVERSATION ENGINES

Right now, the state of the art for FTPS AI talk-back is along the lines of canned one-liners that the AI shouts when it's just killed a human player, or the player has, instead, killed the AI. Action movie cliches like "Enjoying lunch? I see you're having the rocket surprise" or "Not your day, is it" kind of banter gets repetitive quickly and is almost never contextual or interesting. With a small grammar system and some semblance of a sentence engine, the AI could use more contextual shouts that actually work, thus drawing the player in by bringing a sense of realism. The bots used in classic MUD (Multi-User Dungeon) games such as *Eliza* or *Julia* may have much to offer here. Instead of generic canned sentences, an intelligent system would construct a snappy comeback using an ad-lib style template (that takes into account the weapon used, the length of the fight, the relative scoring, etc.), or possibly even a full blown AI system (like a decision tree) that takes into account large numbers of game perceptions, including player-to-player history, and carefully crafts something to shout at the player that will be contextually seamless as well as poignant and personalized.

MOTIVATIONS

Currently, AI FTPS bots have two primary motivations: to stay alive and to kill the player. Some don't even care if they stay alive. But human players don't fight like that. They get angry, sometimes with specific people. Or, they get rattled and retreat for a while until they settle down. AI systems need to model this behavioral flexibility, to mimic their human counterparts more truthfully.

Imagine AI bots that call for a temporary truce with the player, to team up on other human players, or that can't stand campers (people who sit in hidden spots and snipe players from afar) and hunt them down exclusively. These types of more emotional behavior, combined with a bit higher verbal output, might just make them seem much more human.

BETTER SQUAD AI

Most of the squad-based games have relied on very simple team member commands (cover me, follow, stay here, etc.). These types of commands are obviously easier to code, but were also used because the interface necessary to run a squad needs to be simple, so that it can be used quickly and efficiently during battle.

A context-based menu of possible answers to the current situation would be better, like playbooks for football. The commander could choose which one he wanted to use, and the squad would start it up. From there, the commander could direct single soldiers to do something different, or change the entire "play."

With this system, the designers could implement a number of base strategies for any given incursion, custom tailoring squad formations, and the types of actions that each play entails. The human player could vary from this formula by directing certain soldiers to do other things, but these plays could be used to quickly set up each soldier with a workable plan. The different types of solutions presented to the player for each game situation might be attitude-based (aggressive versus defensive), goal-based (save ammo, spread out, etc.), or even time-based (use extreme caution versus run now). Thus, the type of commands employed by the human player would create the overall battle flavor. The player could experiment with the different solutions to find the one that he or she felt most comfortable with, as well as the types of formations that left the player open for more victories, or even more interesting game situations.

SUMMARY

FTPS games involve some fairly disparate types of AI programming, from simple creatures to deathmatch bots with personality and style. The mindless enemies of the genre's roots have been replaced by intelligent systems that are capable of almost human-level play.

- Early FTPS games set the stage for AI research to be done on their games by making most game code accessible and extensible; this led to user-made modifications, or mods.

■ Deathmatch bots were one of the mod types that brought another level of AI depth to the genre, by creating fully autonomous agents that explored the level, hunted players, used weapons and powerups intelligently, and generally acted like regular human players.

■ Regular enemies in a FTPS game refer to those implemented in the single-player campaigns, either the mindless arcade-style enemies, or the more scripted story-following style of enemy.

■ Deathmatch AI is also required if you want to provide for people who don't have access to an Internet connection, or just want to practice. Deathmatch AI allows anyone to play in a deathmatch setting against an opponent.

■ Cooperative AI bots have given some games an infusion of story and broken up the action by providing the player with human-style help during parts of the game, or by interacting with them in some way other than combat.

■ Squad AI refers to the systems that need to be in place for games in which the player is controlling more than one character, and the others need to be CPU-controlled. The intelligence of these bots needs to be high, but the competence needs to be closely tuned, so that the player feels important, but not alone.

■ Pathfinding in FTPS games can be especially tricky because the environments are usually fully three-dimensional and can have very complex constructions. They also include a number of additional gameplay elements, such as ladders, elevators, teleporters, and the like that require pathfinding attention.

■ Spatial reasoning provides the AI-controlled characters with ways in which to find level-specific areas of concern, such as sniper points or good places for cover and visibility.

■ FSMs are put to work in FTPS games, but so are FuSMs because of the nature of inputs in FTPS games.

■ Messaging makes a lot of sense in this genre. Regular FTPS games can benefit from it because of the inherent event-driven gameplay (move, shoot, get hit, etc.), and the nature of a server-based online model. SCGs can also use the messaging system to coordinate information back and forth between characters easily.

■ Scripting is used in those FTPS games that are going for a more handcrafted feel, rather than the classic "we made the rules, and a bunch of levels" mentality.

■ By endowing our creations with even modest learning and opponent modeling, we stop the stale breaking down of gameplay into finding the best weapon, and using it repeatedly by getting the player to mix up the action a bit.

■ Creative solutions to movement and attack positions would give AI opponents a considerable advance toward true deathmatch intelligence.

■ Anticipation of impending events would allow AI characters to set up direct, as well as impromptu, ambushes by keeping a mental model of the possible future.

■ Better conversation engines might change the canned shouts and taunts in today's games to more context-based, and thus more realistic, banter.

■ Giving AI opponents the ability to change motivation might lead to advanced concepts, such as temporary truces, or to showing some sort of emotional flare-up.

■ The AI employed by most squad games is very simple, and could lend itself well to a contextual, quick command system that would lead to better-looking squad maneuvers and quicker control of the situation by the human.

8   Platform Games

Platform games are the primary staple of the console world. From the classic *Donkey Kong* to the modern epic *Ratchet and Clank,* platform games are one of the consummate gaming exercises and will most likely always be with us in some form or another.

Early platform games were mostly two-dimensional, single-screen, *Mario Bros.*-style setups due to the limitations of system capabilities and memory. The main character starts on the bottom of the screen. He then has to navigate enemies and the environment using mostly jumping (hence the name, "platformer," stemming from the need to leap from platform to platform). Platformers were very popular in the arcade world because they presented a new type of gaming challenge: timing. Before platformers, most arcade games were almost completely about recognizing (and memorizing) patterns, either shooters with patterns of enemies coming at the player like *Galaga,* or simple enemy patterns to be avoided like *Pac-Man* and *Frogger.* Platform games kept the patterned enemies (because the technical reasons for using patterns hadn't gone away), but now the player was also expected to precision-time jumps over enemies and from ledge to ledge to traverse the level and gain the summit.

Later, this concept was expanded into the scrolling platform game, which pushed the genre forward. The side-scroller is almost identical to the early platform game, but adds the notion of a continuing world, which scrolls by as the player runs forward. Now, instead of an ascending single screen, the game offers an entire world of challenges that slowly reveal themselves as the player progresses into the level. *Super Mario Bros., Sonic the Hedgehog,* and *Mega Man* (see screenshot in Figure 8.1)

FIGURE 8.1 *Mega Man* screenshot. © Capcom Co., Ltd. Reprinted with permission.

were influential games in this category, each spawning many sequels and hundreds of imitators.

In 1995, a PC game called *Abuse* was released by a company called crack.com, which later released the entire source code for the product. *Abuse* was an advanced two-dimensional scroller, with fully networked multi-player support, and an almost first-person/third-person shooter (FTPS) game feel. Listing 8.1 is a sample from the source code of the enemy AI in *Abuse*, written in the programming language LISP. You will note that the basic setup for the AI of this creature (in this case, an ant) is a finite-state machine (FSM) implemented as a `select` statement with various states.

LISTING 8.1   Sample LISP source code from an enemy in the side scroller *Abuse*.

```lisp
(defun ant_ai ()
    (push_char 30 20)
    (if (or (eq (state) flinch_up) (eq (state) flinch_down))
    (progn (next_picture) T)
    (progn

    (select (aistate)
        (0   (set_state hanging)
             (if (eq hide_flag 0)
             (set_aistate 15)
             (set_aistate 16)))

        (15 ;; hanging on the roof waiting for the main character
         (if (next_picture) T (set_state hanging))
         (if (if (eq (total_objects) 0);; no sensor, wait for guy
             (and (< (distx) 130) (< (y) (with_object (bg) (y))))
           (not (eq (with_object (get_object 0) (aistate)) 0)))
             (progn
                 (set_state fall_start)
                     (set_direction (toward))
                 (set_aistate 1))))

        (16 ;; hiding
         (set_state hiding)
         (if (if (eq (total_objects) 0);; no sensor, wait for guy
             (and (< (distx) 130) (< (y) (with_object (bg) (y))))
           (not (eq (with_object (get_object 0) (aistate)) 0)))
             (progn
                 (set_state fall_start)
                     (set_direction (toward))
                 (set_aistate 1))))

        (1 ;; falling down
         (set_state falling)
         (scream_check)
         (if (blocked_down (move 0 0 0))
             (progn
                 (set_state landing)
                 (play_sound ALAND_SND 127 (x) (y))
                 (set_aistate 9))))

        (9 ;; landing /turn around(gerneal finish animation state)
         (if (next_picture) T
```

```
        (if (try_move Ø 2)
        (progn
          (set_gravity 1)
          (set_aistate 1))
          (progn (set_state stopped)
            (go_state 2)))))   ;; running


    (2 ;; running
     (scream_check)
     (if (eq (random 2Ø) Ø) (setq need_to_dodge 1))
     (if (not (ant_dodge))
       (if (eq (facing) (toward))
       (progn
         (next_picture)
         (if (and (eq (random 5) Ø) (< (distx) 18Ø)
                                    (< (disty) 1ØØ)
              (can_hit_player))
            (progn
               (set_state weapon_fire)
               (set_aistate 8))  ;; fire at player
               (if (and (< (distx)1ØØ)(> (distx) 1Ø)
                    (eq (random 5) Ø))
          (set_aistate 4)  ;; wait for pounce

            (if (and (> (distx) 14Ø)
             (not_ant_congestion)
             (not (will_fall_if_jump)))
             (set_aistate 6)

          (if (> (direction) Ø)
             (if (and (not_ant_congestion) (blocked_right
                                       (no_fall_move 1 Ø Ø)))
             (set_direction -1))
             (if (and (not_ant_congestion) (blocked_left
                                       (no_fall_move -1 Ø Ø)))
                (set_direction 1)))))))))
         (progn
           (set_direction (toward))
           (set_state turn_around)
           (set_aistate 9)))))

    (4 ;; wait for pounce
     (if (ant_dodge) T
```

```
      (progn
        (set_state pounce_wait)
        (move 0 0 0)
        (if (> (state_time) (alien_wait_time))
        (progn
           (play_sound ASLASH_SND 127 (x) (y))
           (set_state stopped)
           (go_state 6))))))

(6 ;; jump
 (setq need_to_dodge 0)
 (if (blocked_down (move (direction) -1 0))
     (progn
        (set_aistate 2))))

(8 ;; fire at player
 (if (ant_dodge) T
   (if (eq (state) fire_wait)
   (if (next_picture)
       T
     (progn
        (fire_at_player)
        (set_state stopped)
        (set_aistate 2)))
        (set_state fire_wait))))

(12 ;; jump to roof
 (setq need_to_dodge 0)
 (set_state jump_up)
 (set_yvel (+ (yvel) 1))
 (set_xacel 0)
 (let ((top (- (y) 31))
   (old_yvel (yvel))
   (new_top (+ (- (y) 31) (yvel))))
   (let ((y2 (car (cdr (see_dist (x) top (x) new_top)))))
     (try_move 0 (- y2 top) nil)
     (if (not (eq y2 new_top))
     (if (> old_yvel 0)
       (progn
          (set_state stopped)
          (set_aistate 2))
       (progn
         (set_state top_walk)
         (set_aistate 13)))))))
```

```
(13 ;; roof walking
 (scream_check)
 (if (or (and (< (y) (with_object (bg) (y)))
          (< (distx) 10) (eq (random 8) 0))
        (eq need_to_dodge 1))  ;; shooting at us, fall down
        (progn
           (set_gravity 1)
           (set_state run_jump)
           (go_state 6))
      (progn
        (if (not (eq (facing) (toward)))
             ;; run toward player
        (set_direction (- 0 (direction))))
        (if (and (< (distx) 120) (eq (random 5) 0))
        (progn
          (set_state ceil_fire)
          (go_state 14))
      (let ((xspeed (if (> (direction) 0) (get_ability
                                             run_top_speed)
            (- 0 (get_ability run_top_speed)))))
        (if(and(can_see (x)(- (y) 31)(+(x) xspeed)(- (y) 31) nil)
             (not (can_see (+ (x) xspeed) (- (y) 31)
                        (+ (x) xspeed) (- (y) 32) nil)))
           (progn
             (set_x (+ (x) xspeed))
             (if (not (next_picture))
                (set_state top_walk)))
             (set_aistate 1)))))))


(14 ;; cieling shoot
 (if (next_picture)
     T
   (progn
     (fire_at_player)
     (set_state top_walk)
     (set_aistate 13))))

)))


 T)
```

In 1996, *Mario64* came out, presenting us with the next chapter in platform game development: the fully three-dimensional platform game. *Mario64* took scrolling levels into the realm of a fully-realized, three-dimensional land, but somehow kept all the positive elements of its earlier brothers. This game is still the blueprint by which modern platformers measure themselves and serves as a model of great gameplay, beautiful camerawork, and a highly polished overall experience.

Today, platform games predominantly feature three elements: exploration (the need to figure out where things are hidden, and how to get there), puzzle solving (either through specific gameplay or through combining elements found in the world), and physical challenges (timed jumps, performing chains of specific moves, overcoming a time limit, etc.). Game designers in this genre are continually pushing the envelope of new gameplay mechanics, new types of challenges, and new ways to make this genre fun and engaging.

COMMON AI ELEMENTS

Platform games tend to contain many of the same AI controlled entities. These include: enemies, boss enemies, cooperative elements, and the camera.

ENEMIES

Enemies within platformers are typically simple, with basic behaviors, because enemies are usually considered little more than obstacles in the platform world. They complement the difficulty of the exploration challenges (for example, by being placed in the exact location that an inexperienced player might jump to, or by forcing an incoming player to then perform another immediate jump). In this way, placement of enemies becomes another level of tuning for designers because they can find the setups that lead to the precise difficulty level for which they are striving.

However, some enemies are more general, being either crafty or highly skilled (such as the little blue thieves in the *Golden Axe* games who are almost impossible to stop). In the *Oddworld* games, many of the enemies were actually invincible, at least to direct attack. Players had to find the way to disable these enemies, by affecting the environment or another character, and thus *indirectly* removing the threat. *Oddworld* was almost an extended puzzle game, with each enemy being another puzzle that the player had to determine how to disarm.

But generally, platformers are more about physical challenges (jumping, climbing, etc.), so the enemies sometimes ride in the back seat. Many games have also used the concept of enemies that *are* platforms, in which the player is walking on the backs of large enemies like stepping stones, but that doesn't mean the enemy has to like it. Thus, the enemy can fight back, tip the player off, and so forth.

Boss Enemies

Modern platform games usually have large, scripted, end-of-level boss creatures. Most games use scripted patterns for the boss monsters (which the player will learn over time), and in addition, will usually force the player into performing some sort of advanced jumping challenge or other game mechanic exhibition (for example, blasting away pieces of the floor, so that the player's available landing positions become less, or temporarily covering large portions of the floor with damaging fire, spikes, or explosions).

Boss enemies are extremely important to the platform game experience, as in all games that use them. They provide a break from the regular gameplay mechanics and help with pacing; commonly, their large size and surprising abilities make for interesting game experiences.

Cooperative Elements

A lot of platformers were used as marketing vehicles to push mascot characters onto the public in the form of action figures, TV shows, even cereal in some cases. Mario, Sonic, and Crash Bandicoot were all very popular players in the platforming world. Eventually some games also included a supportive character, such as Rush, the helper dog that was added to the later *Mega Man* games.

The support character is either under direct control of the user, or functions automatically, helping as needed. In the latter case, AI code must control this character, usually as secondary attacks, some form of powerup retrieval, or some combination move that augments the gameplay. Consequently, the AI is usually not overly complex for these game agents and is mostly reacting to what the player is doing.

In some ways, you do not want an overly powerful helper because a helper that could do too much would eventually make the player feel less important. Most helpers are about 80 percent autonomous (meaning they run a small script or element that reacts to the player), and the rest of their use is in their response to some kind of "action" key initiated by the player. *Come here, pick me up,* or *go get that* are all examples of a controlled callable action for which the player is allowed to use the helper.

Camera

Once platform games made the switch to three dimensions, they faced the problem that has felled many games involving precise positioning and environmental challenges in three-dimensional space: *where to place the camera for the best viewing advantage.* Today, with more dynamic environments and faster gameplay, this problem is even more pronounced.

Some games have used the higher graphical power of the more modern game consoles to try to remedy this by having environmental elements that occlude visibility by becoming transparent, so the player can see through them to the action. Although this does help to some degree, it distances the player from the game experience by making the player feel like an observer to the action, rather than the main character. Clever camera code, and a tight integration with the level itself, can be used to create a camera system that can give players good visibility, while maintaining connection with the character. Camera AI is usually created with a few different methods:

- *Algorithmically placing the camera behind the main character toward his or her direction of travel (or some other vector).* This leads to, at the very least, dependable camera movement, and with camera-relative controls, allows the least amount of surprise movement by the human player (meaning, that the camera will not suddenly cut to a dramatically different angle to the player, and hence affect the direction of the controls). The problem with an algorithmic system is that it is very hard to use it to account for things like special terrain features, dynamic enemy placement, special moves that might propel the character very rapidly or in some strange direction, and so forth. In effect, an algorithmic solution helps with only one-half the problem. You need a good general solution, but also a means of approaching all the special cases that a game might confront because of gameplay mechanics or level design.

- *Laying down tracks of level data for placement and orientation.* This method, usually used in combination with the first technique, involves the level designers placing a number of camera paths in the map. At a specific location within the map, the camera knows where to position itself and orient toward by taking cues from the map data. This leads to a much greater use of environmentally-affected camera angles, and can create dramatic camera shots that give the player a sense of "being there." It can also help the user determine the direction of play within a particularly large or open world. For instance, in your game, you might have a very deep pit with many platforms that a player would have to drop down onto. Using a camera system like this one, the camera could help the player to know the general direction of the next platform, by biasing the position of the camera as the player approached the edge of each stage.

- A *free camera mode.* Usually meaning a "first-person" mode, in which the player has direct control of the orientation of the camera, looking out from the eyes of the main character. Most games include this mode because of the frustration of getting the other two modes to be all-inclusive.

    Even in games in which the automatic camera almost never fails, some developers give the player this option anyway, so that the player can pause occasionally and appreciate the game environment (or just feel more in control).

USEFUL AI TECHNIQUES

Platformers handle their AI tasks just like any other game type: by matching the challenges to the methods best suited to help organize and formulate solutions. The techniques most useful to platform games include: finite-state machines, messaging, scripting, and data-driven architectures.

FINITE-STATE MACHINES (FSMs)

State machines are useful in platform games as well. These games have very straightforward enemies, with usually only a few behaviors exhibited by any one enemy (except bosses, perhaps, although boss enemies in platformers are usually *very* state- or script-based). Also, these behaviors are usually very crisp, meaning there is little gray area between them. The ghouls in *Maximo*, for example, are either walking very slowly in some random direction, or they see the player and charge directly toward that player very quickly.

MESSAGING SYSTEMS

The puzzle-style nature of most platform games lends itself well to using event messages to notify enemies and environment elements about game-state change because the game would have to poll for an undisclosed period as the human figures things out, which is a wasteful way to do things. Thus, puzzle elements could themselves send out an event that would advance the state of the game. For instance, after the game hero has found the magic green button on top of the roof of the correct house and pressed it, an event is triggered so that the gate blocking the green cave will retract.

SCRIPTED SYSTEMS

Because of the pattern-based nature of boss enemies, not to mention some normal game enemies, scripting is a natural way to craft the AI for these elements. Scripting allows for a very fine control to be exerted over the flow of a particular part of the game, say that of a boss encounter, or an in-game cinematic sequence that gives the player information.

Some of the more complex platformers have an in-game help character that follows the player around for the first level and shows the player how to perform all the moves and special powers that the main character has at his or her disposal. Scripting would allow you to add all of this helper character's actions, as well as dialogue, and tie it into the control scheme of the game so that the helper will wait for the player to practice the moves, explore on his or her own, or even ask questions and have the helper repeat part of the script.

DATA-DRIVEN SYSTEMS

The camera for three-dimensional platformers can become very complex. If a suitable algorithmic camera solution cannot be found, camera paths must be constructed within the level editor for these games. Designers can also do a lot of level tuning when they populate the levels with enemies, by knowing the patterns of movement for different types of creatures, as well as the effect these placements will have on the human traversing that section of the level. These games can become very data driven if enough forethought is put into the types of challenges the designer wants to incorporate, as well as the limits of the level editor and the control needed by the designers for level tuning.

EXAMPLES

Classic platform games like *Donkey Kong, Castlevania, Sonic the Hedgehog, Mario Bros.,* and *Metroid* are some of the big names in the platform game hall of fame. *Castlevania* was almost too hard. *Sonic* was almost too fast. Samus, the main character from *Metroid,* was definitely "too cool." Consumers loved them all. Each of these games used state-based enemies, often singular-state enemies. Usually, these enemies employed simple movement patterns (such as moving back and forth between two objects), or they would "hide" until a player got close, and then they'd jump out at the player. Many of these games used the concept that enemy contact hurts the player, so enemies rarely had more to their attack strategy than ramming into players, although some did have simple projectiles.

The next generation of platform games offered titles like *Mario64 (the* three-dimensional platformer, in which many of the techniques later used by other companies were all but invented by Nintendo's prime game designer Shigeru Miyamoto), *Spyro the Dragon,* and *Crash Bandicoot.* The jump to three-dimensional play provided new challenges because of the added complexity of moving within three-dimensional worlds, but also brought a new evil: the bad camera system.

The games continued to use most of the earlier styles of AI implementation, with patterned or scripted enemies, and slightly more complex level bosses. Sadly, during both the two- and three-diemnsional eras of platform games, many platformers became showcases for cutesy new characters instead of gameplay. Gamers were inundated with edgy, *slightly* bad attitude and somewhat cute animals of all kinds, trying to hawk games that were derivative at best. Lucky for us, the industry got over that hurdle.

Today, platform games are doing better than ever. Platform game players are being given stunningly cinematic games with increasingly devious puzzles, smarter enemy AI, and more interactive and intricate level design. Games like

Ratchet and Clank, Jak and Daxter, and *Super Mario Sunshine* continue to push the envelope. Some of these games still use simple FSM and scripted AI, but augment it when necessary with smarter opponents and clever sidekicks. The camera systems of these modern games, although still somewhat problematic, continue to get better, with heavily-layered camera systems getting closer to always pointing in the right direction, while maintaining and enhancing the overall feel of the game.

AREAS THAT NEED IMPROVEMENT

Platform games have been around the block a good many times. But even a mature genre needs a push now and again. Two areas where platforms can always be improved are camera work and help systems.

CAMERAWORK

As good as some games' cameras are, very few games have had total success with camerawork, partly because players have different expectations for the camera and partly because it is a difficult problem. In some ways, the camera needs to somehow *anticipate* the movements of the player (or even the intent to move, which is even more impossible) and move the camera to show the player what is in that direction.

The problem is also very game-specific. Characters that can jump a long way need to see farther out; characters engaged in heavy combat need to have bearings so that they can land hits on a nearby enemy, who may be returning attacks with much better accuracy.

In the future, we may even get a specialized peripheral, such as the microphone headset being used in some games today with voice recognition, except that it would track certain movements to help with the camera. In some ways, this was the promise of head-mounted virtual reality displays, but they proved far too costly and unwieldy when they first came out in the early 1990s.

HELP SYSTEMS

Some platformers are simply too difficult for some people, or a given location puzzle can stump a player for an overly long time. This kind of slowdown in the flow of the game can ruin the experience very quickly. If the game could discern that the human is stuck, and needs help, it could possibly offer hints to get the player moving again. This could be an option that the player could turn on or off, so that diehard players who want to find everything themselves wouldn't have the surprise ruined for them. But casual gamers might appreciate the helping hand after spending four hours trying futilely to make an impossible jump because they don't realize that they need to walk around the corner and use the invisible catapult to get across the chasm.

The goal-oriented nature of these games would make it possible to have a help manager that could be goal-based. Thus, each small section of gameplay could keep track of the attempts being made by the human to solve that atomic portion of the game, and note failures. In addition, puzzles of the same type later in the game could respond more quickly because the game passes on the information that the player had difficulty with similar earlier challenges.

But a "watchful eye" isn't the only way that you can handle help. Your platformer companion could specifically watch out for you, offering hints and tips to make things flow more smoothly. Just make sure you don't turn your sidekick into the helper paperclip from Microsoft Word.

Again, this kind of system would have to be a difficulty setting (which could be turned on or off, or be some level of help), but could be turned on by default in the first "training" level, or whatever system your game will use.

SUMMARY

Platform games have gone from simple affairs, to grandiose living worlds, all within ten years. Even with this vast change in the landscape, many companies have managed to keep the fun formula intact, with careful adherence to the genre's strengths and by minimizing the effect on all the additional technology to the gameplay mechanics with clever controls and good AI systems.

- Most enemies in platform games are very simple, with patterned or simple movements, to facilitate the fact that killing enemies is secondary to the physical challenges of the game.
- Boss enemies are generally much larger, and more powerful, but are generally still scripted. The trick is to discover the pattern, then use it against the creature to beat it.
- Cooperative elements in platform games are more like semi-intelligent powerups, in that they usually just augment the main character.
- The camera system, if the game is three-dimensional, is vital to the overall quality level of the game because seeing the right thing at the right time is complicated heavily by the bigger and more open worlds. Techniques involving algorithmic solutions, camera tracks laid down in an editor, and a free-look camera are typical methods of approaching the problem.
- FSMs are used heavily in these games because of the simple nature of the AI enemies and such.

- Messaging systems make sense in this genre because of the event-driven nature of the puzzles and interactions.
- Scripting will aid in the creation of the patterned movements of enemies, and give in-game, cinematic events a means by which to tailor custom animation and audio sequences.
- Camerawork needs to strive toward giving the player a system with the best angle, without sacrificing control.
- Help systems could be implemented, to give hints (or outright aid) to players who are stuck on a puzzle or physical challenge, if they so desire it. This will help frustrated players, but does require a significant amount of AI to achieve.

9 Shooter Games

In This Chapter

- Common AI Elements
- Useful AI Techniques
- Exceptions
- Examples
- Areas That Need Improvement
- Summary

The term *shooter games* refers to the fairly open genre encompassing classic shooters (static as well as horizontal or vertical scrolling) and the modern variation, which is played using a light gun. Most of these types of games use simple AI or patterns for their enemies. The trick to any given game level is finding the enemy patterns (or AI weak point) and exploiting that knowledge to reach the next level or enemy. Some shooters throw enough enemies at players that even if players know the pattern, survival is still questionable.

Shooters usually involve a spaceship, or some other kind of character, who faces monstrous waves of enemies that come at the player in patterns. The player kills as many enemies as possible while avoiding (or in some light games, ducking behind cover) the enemy's incoming shots. Along the way, players pick up powerups and fight bosses (which tend to be massive affairs in these games).

Simple control schemes are generally the law of the land; players usually can't look down to find a button in the middle of a sea of enemy bullets. A notable exception was *Defender II: Stargate*, a truly classic horizontal shooter, that had no less than seven controls: the one axis up/down joystick, thrust, reverse (to turn around), a hyperspace button (which randomly teleported a player), a shoot button, an "inviso" button (which was an invincible shield of sorts), and a smartbomb button (which killed all the on-screen enemies). The game was devilishly hard and was made even more so by the nature of the control scheme. But it was a gigantic hit and continues to be a classic favorite. Again, the rule seems to be that if the game is good enough, people will take the time to learn how to play it well.

Shooters originated in the arcades, and although they have made a decent showing on the various home consoles, they never really found a huge following within the personal computer world.

An interesting exception to the PC rule is that numerous independently-made shooters can be downloaded from the Web. Many game designers get their start by home programming a two-dimensional shooter of some sort. This is the kind of game that one person can still program on his or her own (possibly with some help on the art). Listing 9.1 shows some of the enemy AI code from the open-source game *Wing*, which the author (Adam Hiatt) jokingly mentions is a recursive acronym that stands for "Wing Is Not Galaga." Notice that Adam's game uses a simple implementation of a finite-state-based AI system, in which he has various behaviors written (Attack_1 through Attack_5), and the enemies cycle between them in patterns.

LISTING 9.1 Sample AI code from *Wing*, by Adam Hiatt. Licensed under the GNU.

```
//=================================================================
void EnemyTYPE :: UpdateAI ( int plane_x, int plane_y )
{
    EnemyNodeTYPE * scan = enemy_list;
  for (; scan != NULL; scan = scan -> next)
  {
     if ( scan -> health <= 0 && scan->explode_stage ==
                                  ENEMY_EXPLODE_STAGES - 1 )
       DeleteNode ( scan );
     else
     {
       if ( scan -> attacking )
       {
          if ( (scan -> xpos >= plane_x && scan -> xpos < plane_x
               + PLANE_WIDTH) ||
              (scan -> xpos + EnemyWidths [scan->TypeOfEnemy] >=
              plane_x && scan -> xpos + EnemyWidths [scan->
              TypeOfEnemy] < plane_x + PLANE_WIDTH))
          {
             if(timer - scan -> TimeOfLastFired > BULLET_PAUSE &&
                 (plane_y > scan -> ypos + EnemyHeights [scan->
                 TypeOfEnemy] && timer- scan->TimeOfLastFired >=
                 BULLET_PAUSE))
             {
                scan -> TimeOfLastFired = timer;
                enemy_bullets.Fire (scan -> xpos, scan->ypos,
                       XBulletVelocities [scan->weapon],
```

```
                                          -(YBulletVelocities [scan->
                                          weapon]), scan->weapon );
                    }
                }

            switch ( scan->state )
            {
                  case ATTACKING_1 : Attack_1 ( scan );
                                              break;
                  case ATTACKING_2 : Attack_2 ( scan );
                                              break;
                  case ATTACKING_3 : Attack_3 ( scan,plane_x );
                                              break;
                  case ATTACKING_4 : Attack_4 ( scan );
                                              break;
                  case ATTACKING_5 : Attack_5 ( scan );
                                              break;
                  case ATTACKING_6 : Attack_5 ( scan );
                                              break;
                  default          :          break;
            }
            scan -> state_stage ++;
            if ( (scan -> ypos < -80 || scan -> ypos>SCREEN_HEIGHT) ||
                  (scan -> xpos + EnemyWidths[scan->TypeOfEnemy] < 0 ||
                   scan -> xpos > SCREEN_WIDTH ) )
            {
                scan -> attacking = false;
                num_enemies_attacking —;
            }
        }
      }
    }
  }
}
//================================================================
void EnemyTYPE :: Attack_1 ( EnemyNodeTYPE * enemy )
{
    if ((enemy->xpos >= SCREEN_WIDTH - 75 && enemy->dx > 0 )||
       (enemy->xpos <= 5 && enemy->dx < 0))
        enemy->dx = -(enemy->dx) ;
    else if ( enemy -> state_stage % 20 == 0 )
    {
       if( enemy->xpos < SCREEN_WIDTH / 2 )
       {
          if ( enemy -> xpos <= 160 && enemy -> dx < 0 )
```

```
                    enemy->dx /= 2;
              else if ( enemy ->dx < 8 && enemy ->dx > -8 )
                    enemy->dx *= 2;
            if ( enemy->dx == Ø )
                    enemy-> dx = 1;
        }
        else
        {
            if ( enemy-> xpos >= SCREEN_WIDTH-16Ø && enemy-> dx > Ø )
                    enemy->dx /= 2;
            else if ( enemy ->dx < 8 && enemy ->dx > -8 )
                    enemy->dx *= 2;
            if ( enemy->dx == Ø )
                    enemy-> dx = 1;
        }
    }
    enemy->ypos += enemy->dy;
    enemy->xpos += enemy->dx;
}
//================================================================
void EnemyTYPE :: Attack_2 ( EnemyNodeTYPE * enemy )
{
    if ( enemy -> ypos == INIT_ENEMY_Y )
    {
    enemy -> dy = 4;
        if ( enemy -> xpos < SCREEN_WIDTH / 2 )
        enemy -> dx = 3;
        else
            enemy -> dx = -3;
    }

    if ( (enemy -> ypos) % 16Ø == Ø)
        enemy->dx = -(enemy->dx);

    enemy->ypos += enemy->dy;
    enemy->xpos += enemy->dx;
}
//================================================================
void EnemyTYPE :: Attack_3 ( EnemyNodeTYPE * enemy, int plane_x )
{
    if ( enemy -> ypos == INIT_ENEMY_Y )
    {
        enemy -> dy = 6;
        if ( enemy -> xpos < SCREEN_WIDTH / 2 )
```

```
                    enemy -> dx = 3;
            else
                    enemy -> dx = -3;
        }
    else if ( enemy -> ypos > 175 )
    {
        if ( enemy -> dy == 6)
        {
            enemy -> dy = 4;
            if ( enemy -> xpos > plane_x  )
                enemy -> dx = -10;
            else
                enemy -> dx = 10;
        }
        if ( enemy -> state_stage % 20 == 0 )
            enemy -> dx /= 2;
    }
    enemy->ypos += enemy->dy;
    enemy->xpos += enemy->dx;
}
//=============================================================
void EnemyTYPE :: Attack_4  ( EnemyNodeTYPE * enemy )
{
    if ( enemy -> ypos == INIT_ENEMY_Y )
    {
        enemy -> dy = 4;
        if ( enemy -> xpos < SCREEN_WIDTH / 2 )
            enemy -> dx = 3;
        else
            enemy -> dx = -3;
    }

    if ( (enemy -> ypos) % 160 == 0)
        enemy->dx = -(enemy->dx);

    if ( enemy-> ypos > 0 )
    {
        if ( enemy -> state_stage % 40 == 0 )
        {
            enemy-> dx = rand() % 13;
            enemy-> dy = rand () %13;
        }

        if ( enemy->dx > 7 )
```

```
                    enemy->dx = -rand ()%7;
            if ( enemy->dy > 7 )
                enemy->dy = -rand ()%7;
    }
    else
        enemy-> dy = 4 ;


    enemy->ypos += enemy->dy;
    enemy->xpos += enemy->dx;


}
//================================================================
void EnemyTYPE :: Attack_5  ( EnemyNodeTYPE * enemy )
{
    if ( enemy -> ypos == INIT_ENEMY_Y )
    {
        enemy -> dy = 4;
        if ( enemy -> xpos < SCREEN_WIDTH / 2 )
            enemy -> dx = 3;
        else
            enemy -> dx = -3;
    }

    if ( (enemy -> ypos) % 16Ø == Ø)
        enemy->dx = -(enemy->dx);

    if ( enemy-> ypos > Ø )
    {
        if ( enemy -> state_stage % 3Ø == Ø )
        {
            enemy-> dx = rand() % 13;
            enemy-> dy = rand () %13;
        }

        if ( enemy->dx > 6 )
            enemy->dx = -rand ()%6;
        if ( enemy->dy > 6 )
            enemy->dy = -rand ()%6;
    }
    else
        enemy-> dy = 3 ;

    if ( enemy->xpos + enemy->dx < Ø || enemy->xpos + enemy->dx +
        EnemyWidths [enemy->TypeOfEnemy] > SCREEN_WIDTH )
```

```
        enemy->dx = -(enemy->dx);

    enemy->xpos += enemy->dx;
    enemy->ypos += enemy->dy;
}
```

COMMON AI ELEMENTS

Shooters typically employ a few classic categories of AI-controlled agents: enemies, boss enemies, and cooperative elements.

ENEMIES

Shooter enemies are usually distinctly patterned, so that players successively learn more of the pattern and get farther into the game. As such, the AI for these games is not usually intelligent at all. The light gun games are the same basic mechanic: a pattern of enemies will pop out from behind things, and players have to shoot them before the enemies shoot the players.

Some games do stray from this basic formula and make AI enemies that readily seek the player or use almost first-person shooter/third-person shooter (FTPS) "bot-like" behavior, using decent intelligence to counter the human player. However, even games with advanced enemies generally keep the player on some kind of *rail* (a set path through the map, so-named because to the player it feels like he or she is in a slow traincar riding along on rails), which keeps the player constrained within the game world and allows quick opponents to duck off screen to escape the player's attacks. Movement rails are used in both conventional shooters and light gun games, mainly to control pacing of the game (rails were originally created in arcade games to limit players' progress to a certain rate during gameplay).

Other games use large, moving creatures (such as the dinosaurs in *Jurassic Park: The Lost World*) that occasionally display vulnerable spots that players shoot at. This behavior is basically the same as targets jumping out at players, but the increased on-screen movement of this system adds a lot to the look and feel of the game.

BOSS ENEMIES

Just like in role-playing games (RPGs), bosses in shooter games are frequently considered a treat that players find at the end of each level. Shooters usually go overboard on the boss enemies because of the fairly repetitive gameplay inherent in the genre. Good boss creations can sometimes make the experience of the average shooter much better and more memorable. As such, the AI system for the bosses is very important and should be flexible enough to encompass any sort of specialized needs that each boss in the game requires. The bosses of scrolling shooters are usually huge, horribly beweaponed monoliths, spewing bullets of every shape and size in all directions. They generally attack in waves (which translate to *states* as far as implementation is concerned), with phases of heavy attack, followed by a brief respite, followed by another blindingly large gun blast, and then it all repeats again. Bosses are most times impervious to all damage, except for key locations (typically colored red, or glowing in some way), that may or may not *also* be state-based (in that they are sometimes covered by a protective shell of some sort).

During hectic boss battles, many scrolling shooters have what hardcore players refer to as *safe zones,* which are specific locations on the screen where a player could sit and never be hit by an enemy bullet, but still get an occasional shot at the boss. Some games embraced this, making the boss very difficult, almost impossible, and counting on the human to find the safe spot. Other games went the other way, discouraging safe zones by adding an occasional "homing" shot to ferret out nonmoving players.

COOPERATIVE ELEMENTS

Some shooter games include an AI-controlled drone or some sort of helper object that is either an integral part of the gameplay mechanics (like the TOZ in *Gaires*), or something that becomes a weapon and, once found, helps the player (the "Option" powerup in the *Gradius* games). These elements are usually pretty simple, but this determination is completely up to the game designer. You don't want a drone doing too much of the work, however. You also don't want to have to *babysit* the drone, since the player's attention is really at a premium in this genre.

USEFUL AI TECHNIQUES

Shooters have pretty straightforward AI requirements, and the techniques used to conquer those requirements are equally straightforward. Finite-state machines, scripted systems, and data-driven architectures tend to be in heavy use when creating shooter games.

FINITE-STATE MACHINES (FSMs)

State machines continue their usefulness in this genre, mostly because of the simple, straightforward nature of the AI in most of these games. The organization of the games themselves (level-based), with an easy start period, followed by a buildup, and then a boss, also lends well to a state-based architecture. Many of the enemies in this genre have only one state, such as the main creature in the classic game *Centipede,* which used a simple rule for its AI. It moved forward until it hit a mushroom. It then moved down one row and reversed its left/right direction. The only other behavior it had was the speed increase if only one segment of the creature was left. A very simple rule, and the layout of the level provided the variance in the gameplay. In modern AI programming, this is called *emergent* behavior. The elements of *Centipede* combine, and the final behavior emerges from, the interactions. Back then it was just called good game design. Emergent behavior is a critical aspect of a game's design as it often gets the player believing that the AI is actually "smarter" or "better" than it truly is—an important and very desirable conclusion!

SCRIPTED SYSTEMS

The boss enemies in shooters are usually immobile behemoths with one or two well-guarded vulnerable spots. Even if they are more mobile, they are most likely just scripted affairs. Boss monsters rarely react to the human's actions (although they might slowly head in in a player's direction, or jump on top of a player, or something along those lines). Rather, they tend to move in patterns while spitting out waves of bullets and other things to harm the player. These simple chains of behavior are textbook uses for a simple scripting system.

By adding in the ability to randomly branch within a script, you give a degree of variety to your pattern scripts (because each chunk will be executed in some random order). Scripts also make it very easy to tag specific enemy spawns with difficulty-level information (so that more enemies will attack the player in harder games, or from different angles and locations), so that the same script can be used for easy, normal, and hard levels of difficulty.

DATA-DRIVEN SYSTEMS

The general enemy AI for shooters (if following the patterned waves paradigm) is very open for a full data-driven structure. The basic types of enemy movement and firing patterns could be defined using code, and then a designer (or whomever) could quite easily set up a database table of when and where these patterns would appear in the levels, or they could actually be placed into some form of level editor that would then generate these appearance tables. In this way, the designer could tweak and tune the enemy content of the levels quickly and easily, without programmer help. Of course, new patterns might require programmer intervention. But even this could be set up in an editor if need be, by providing the designer even more basic building blocks to construct behavior patterns by him- or herself.

EXCEPTIONS

Zanac, an 8-bit Nintendo Entertainment System (NES) game from 1986, claimed to have "automatic level of difficulty AI code," which would take into account the player's attack patterns and skill level. The implementation they used involved checking a few stats (like the player's rate of fire, the player's hit percentage, and how long the player had been alive) and then adjusting the number, speed, and aggression of enemies. If a player survived too long, killed every ship, and used a turbo button-enhanced controller, it would take this system about ten minutes of game playing to be at the point of filling almost the entire screen with bullets. This was a great concept: Make the game's difficulty scale adjust with the ability of the player. Right? Not really. The player could dupe the system by not killing all the enemies, missing shots, and occasionally dying on purpose. All of which brings up a big failing of games that try this method of difficulty scaling: You must consider the performance of the human player, and you have to filter malicious or odd behavior, so that the system can't be fooled into helping the AI defeat itself.

EXAMPLES

Shooters were some of the very first true videogames. Sure, the *Pong* types ran the roost for a few years, but then came 1978 and *Space Invaders*, what some consider to the be first true videogame—complete with a score field, lives, and enemies that crept ever closer, firing away at the player. Over the years, shooter controls have grown more involved, the enemy patterns have grown more complex, and the powerups have grown more elaborate and powerful. But in all actuality, the very first video game of them all, *Spacewar!*, first built on a DEC PDP-1 in 1962, was a shooter game. This genre really has been here since the beginning.

Other games like *Gradius, 1943, Raiden*, and *R-Type* further defined the genre. They involved a player versus an appalling number of enemies, and the enemies only stopped coming so that the huge end boss could slip in and throw some death in the player's way.

Along the way, players can pick up numerous powerups, which turned their simple ship into a bullet-producing factory. These games continued to use patterned movement for their enemies. The advancing waves of enemy craft would move in back-and-forth patterns, various serpentine or circular shapes, or combination lines like a football play: Move straight across to the left until the enemies are lined up with the player, then double the enemies' speed and charge at the player.

During the late 1980s and early 1990s, the popularity of shooters started to wane, but then along came the light gun game. Games like *Duck Hunt, Wild Gunman* (which even made its way into the second *Back to the Future* movie), *House of the Dead, Time Crisis,* and *Point Blank* (see the screenshot in Figure 9.1) are all great examples of this variant. These games were functionally just like their predecessors, but with a different input medium. Most still require players to dodge enemy fire

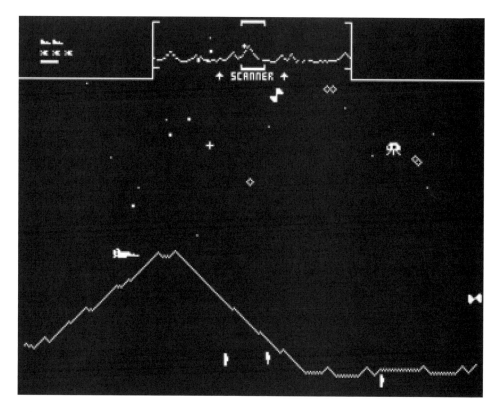

FIGURE 9.1 *Point Blank* screenshot. POINT BLANK® © 1994 Namco Ltd., All rights reserved. Courtesy of Namco Holding Corp.

in some fashion, by requiring the player's on-screen persona to duck behind cover, or to have the player shoot *and* move a character around (like *Cabal*). Most just required the player to shoot first. Almost all of them include powerups that give players more powerful weapons or more health and the like.

Some shooter games in the arcade arena have tried to get some additional gameplay out of the genre by using strange control methods. *Robotron* and *Smash TV* used two joysticks, so players could move in one direction and shoot in another. *Cabal* and *Blood Bros* used a trackball that controlled the player's weapon's aim and that of a third-person character at the bottom of the screen. Players had to aim while dodging the enemy fire directed at this character. Light gun games follow this same trend, with games that use different guns (such as automatic weapons, large rifles, pistols, etc.), or specialty guns (such as *Silent Scope,* which included a small LCD screen to simulate a sniper scope; or even *Brave Firefighters,* which puts players in control of a fire hose that they use to put out fires as they appear in the game).

AREAS THAT NEED IMPROVEMENT

Shooter games have fallen from grace since the early part of the new millenium. This is probably because the old methods of pattern recognition and finding boss vulnerabilities have been done so many times that the concept is wearing thin. The light gun variant brought about a temporary return to these kinds of games, but eventually this small gameplay addition will be tired as well.

Some of the additions that could potentially revive this tired genre include: actual AI, story-driven content, and additional innovation in gameplay mechanics.

INFUSION OF ACTUAL AI

Possibly, the gameplay could remain, but enemies with actual AI decision making could be written. Scrolling shooters with this type of AI would almost be more like FTPS deathmatches, with the essential shooter gameplay mechanic and the bot opponents of the FTPS games. Making a shooter deathmatch game with online play and (because of the simplified two-dimensional playing field) possibly many more simultaneous players might be the way to continue the dynasty of shooter-style games on the PC.

STORY-DRIVEN CONTENT

A technique that has invigorated other aging genres is to inject the gameplay with elements of drama and tension by winding the game through an elaborate single player, story-driven experience. Games like *Half-Life* almost single handedly saved the FTPS game, and the *Grand Theft Auto* series really gave racing games a boost. There are definitely some that would say the *Star Control* games were some of the most compelling games ever to grace our joysticks. This technique has proven itself again and again to take gameplay mechanics that have been around forever and really make them feel new again.

INNOVATIVE GAMEPLAY MECHANICS

Just like any genre, there is always a balance to be kept between keeping the control scheme "standard" for the genre, so that old fans will be able to pick up your new game and learn quickly, with infusing fresh gameplay mechanics into the game in an attempt to evolve the genre as well as bring in new players. Shooters have to become a bit riskier with this balance, and try out a few new things, since more of the same appears to not sell well. People are ready to try something new, while still playing a shooter, and we should provide it for them.

SUMMARY

Shooter games are an old genre and are starting to seem stale because of the lack of innovation in gameplay and content. The light gun variation gave the genre additional fuel for a while, but the shooter game needs something new to continue to be a viable genre.

- Enemies in shooter games are patterned; the object is to figure out the pattern to get further into the game.
- Boss enemies are considered a treat and are very important elements of the shooter genre.
- Cooperative elements are usually advanced powerups that involve additional gameplay techniques.
- FSMs and/or data-driven AI are usually the methods used in shooters. The simple nature of the AI-controlled enemies, coupled with the fact that each level of a shooter is usually one long, scripted pattern of appearing enemies, lends well to these two approaches.
- Either more complex FSMs, or a full-scripting system might be useful for the larger boss enemies.
- An infusion of actual AI techniques, story-driven content, and innovative new gameplay mechanics could possibly liven up this genre; a possible direction might be creating AI-controlled bots capable of fighting the player in a deathmatch-style mode of play, except within a shooter gameplay world.

10 Sports Games

In This Chapter

- Common AI Elements
- Useful AI Techniques
- Examples
- Areas That Need Improvement
- Summary

Sports games have been a part of the video gaming world since its advent. Technically, *Pong* was a tennis game. The combination of instantly recognizable gameplay (everybody knows the rules to your game) combined with head-to-head action gives sports games a mass appeal that many other genres can only dream of. Coupled with a sea of rabid fans that buy perennial titles in multiple sports, the genre has become *the* money-making enterprise for companies that can capture the minds of sports gamers.

AI has become increasingly important in sports games. Early sports games were like action games, in that players learned the patterns exhibited by the other team and exploited them to win the game. Remember back to the handheld LED football games, where players could score a touchdown easily by steering their red dot around the "defenders" very quickly and without stopping. If players were fast enough, they could keep going for a very long time before the defense would react. This kind of system is no longer acceptable.

Today's sports gamers want the computer opponents to play like they do in real life, with intelligence, quickness, and a modicum of style. Games where the AI opponents are merely *more powerful,* or employ other forms of "cheating" using the stats of the opponents, are quickly called out for their unfair number-juggling ways and are just as quickly taken back to the store.

Most competitive sports games fall into two basic categories:

1. **Fluid gameplay sports.** Sports like soccer, hockey, or basketball, in which the game is quick, dynamic, and continues for long periods with few or no

stops. The nature of these games' constantly-changing playfield conditions mean that even the simplest strategies need to be watched closely, to determine when a given *play* (a series of coordinated movements designed to score on the other team) isn't working, and recover gracefully by responding to the next set of game conditions. State-based AI tends to break down in these types of games because so many states are connected to other states that a spider web results instead of a nice flow diagram. State hierarchies help with this problem, but the structure of working hierarchies tends to be anything but intuitive, as game designers tend to have more difficulty breaking things into tree structures instead of state-based structures.

2. **Resetting gameplay sports.** These are games that stop and reset after a set event or time, such as football and baseball. The AI team in this style of game gains the benefit of being able to frequently reset and start from scratch, so the organization of the AI system can be designed with this in mind. This type of game lends itself much better to a state-based system because the sport itself is divided nicely into distinct game-flow states.

One benefit of working on the AI engine for a sports title is that the game is usually fully designed before production starts. At least, the basic game you are trying to model is. If you're making a basketball derivative that uses robots and weapons, you're somewhat on your own. But a straight sports simulation has the advantage of a vast amount of information about how to play a successful game, with years of research and player statistics to back it up.

However, this strength is also a profound weakness. Everywhere you look, there are sports people. People who eat, drink, and breathe these games. People who know all the stats, follow their teams, and are very passionate about the game and the players. These are the kinds of people who buy sports games in the first place. The primary audience of your game is armed with this vast array of intimate knowledge of the sport, so it places great pressure on the developer. If you are making a pure simulation, you had better do it well. Someone who plays your game will know if the behavior he sees a player exhibit would never happen in real life. Some of the players that your game might be trying to model are celebrities, and their actions and performance level is a signature that people either recognize being correctly represented by your system, or not. Getting this wrong will greatly impact the feel and believability of your game.

COMMON AI ELEMENTS

Sports AI is actually quite complex, and as such there are quite a few tasks that need intelligence to solve when trying to simulate the workings of a professional sport.

These include: coach- or team-level strategic AI, player-level AI, pathfinding, camera, miscellaneous elements, and mini-games.

COACH- OR TEAM-LEVEL AI

Consider coach- or team-level AI the *strategic* AI found in real-time strategy (RTS) or chess games. High-level AI makes decisions, such as which play to call, or to substitute a player because he's in foul trouble and the smart coaching move would be to save the player for the last quarter. Without this level of a sports game AI system, the gameplay of the team can seem random, or simply without an overall purpose. Which is, of course, exactly the case.

The team layer encompasses whole team-level decisions, but might also handle slightly smaller tasks that still involve more than one player (in a coordinating fashion), such as a handoff in football or a player setting an offensive pick for the ball handler in basketball. Usually, this level in the system uses some kind of shared data area (such as a blackboard system, or a team singleton class) that encapsulates the workings of the team level, and also provides a central place for the various other game elements to reference when they need access to the team decisions.

A common mistake when coding this section of a sports game AI system is to not break down the tasks or use any kind of attribute data at this level. Most sports games make almost *constant* use of attributes when working at the player level (so that some hit the ball better than others, or are much faster), but this same type of thinking should be used when coding the team level. Using *team*-level attributes and overall goals, the same system can also simulate the various ways that particular teams play the game. Team personality is particularly important in games in which the coach (the physical person himself) is one of the more important elements in determining how a team plays. College basketball is a prime example. The players are good but inexperienced, so the coaches call almost all the plays and strategies. Two college teams might have wildly different play styles, even though the players on each team have similar skill levels.

PLAYER-LEVEL AI

At the player level, AI decisions are concerned with the more personal, tactical behaviors that involve *just* the player: making a quick juke move ("juke" is a basketball term referring to a fast movement meant to throw your defender off balance so that you can quickly change direction and leave the defender behind) to try and evade the defender, leading off from first base, or just the way that the player catches a ball. The decisions and behaviors coming out of this layer are heavily based on the personal attributes of the particular player involved, so as to be a reflection of his real-life counterpart (if any).

By perturbing the behavior of the AI with real statistics, human players will feel like they are playing with a character commensurate with the skill level of the real sports player. In this way, the AI of sports games must include a large element of simulation. You don't want to design a game in which everybody is a superhero. Instead, players who are bad passers should actually miss more often, and poor defenders should break down and allow the offensive players to perform well more frequently.

The player level of an AI engine is actually more like two separate systems: the tactical decision-making part that decides upon a behavior, and selection of a specific animation once the specific behavior has been assigned (see Chapter 25, "Distributed AI Design," for more on this). As an example, let's look at the thought process behind trying to get open for a pass in football.

The strategic decision-making system decides that it wants a particular player to get open for a pass. The player in question has a defender watching his every move, keeping him from easily doing so. The player must juke in order to shake off his defender. So, the type of juke move to play (based on attributes, personal preference, and defensive match-up) and the direction of movement (calculated because of proximity to other players and court boundaries, as well as court position in general) are determined.

The animation selection process would then take this behavior data and use it to determine the exact animation that the player will use to juke. Other factors that the animation layer will account for: the *type* of player (big, small, fast, showy, or some signature move), the speed of the player, the direction change (small changes might just rotate the player, bigger changes necessitate turnaround-type transition moves), some randomness so that the same animation doesn't play all the time, and many other factors, depending on the behavior.

Complex animation selection can sometimes become a secondary step of almost every action the player does in sports games. Many sports titles use motion-captured animation for most moves in the game. "Motion capture" refers to the technique of using a setup involving a special camera arrangement and a live actor wearing a custom suit to scan specific bobdy moves directly into animations for use in a game. Motion capture provides the signature moves of the stars, and shows the richness of secondary body movement (which is notoriously difficult to hand animate, and as such is usually only caught with motion-capture techniques). For some moves (such as football end zone dances or basketball dunks), players demand a huge variety of animations because they become the in-game taunts that allow players to rub their victory in the face of their opponents.

With this flood of available animations for a given behavior, systems must be put in place that can accurately pick the most contextually correct animation from the large number of available animations using current game conditions. Generalized data-driven animation selection techniques (such as table-based or scripted systems) can be used to describe the links between the attribute data (as well as spatial, preferential, and any other determinants) and the various animations for each action. This can vastly improve the overall organization of your AI and limits duplicate code by using data-driving methods. This approach also makes it easier to expand or add to animations with future update packs or add-ons, an important consideration when dealing with season-to-season sports.

Animation selection is not generally considered purely part of the AI system because the human player requires this same functionality when performing the player behaviors. However, the process is generally delegated to the AI programmer because of the high level of context-sensitive determination involved (meaning that process can be unique on a behavior-by-behavior basis). General approaches can quickly make your game look bland or inappropriate. The kinds of variables and factors that you must take into account to make correct animation selection can overlap considerably with the overall AI decision-making requirements.

PATHFINDING

Finding good movement paths during the frenzy of a sports game can be truly frightening. Sure, the number of characters visibly on screen is limited, and the environment is usually free of static obstacles (although not always, you do have a large net in hockey and soccer), but the dynamic obstacles (the other players and possibly a referee) are in almost constant motion, making traditional path planning too slow and cumbersome. Lightweight, CPU-optimized methods must be used to make players move around each other as they do in the real game.

Navigation in most sports titles also requires game-specific information to be considered when choosing paths. For example, in basketball, if the player's team is on offense, the player will not want to run right in front of the ball holder if it can be helped. Even though the player has technically avoided the ballholder, the player has also cut off the ballholder's movement and probably even caused a traffic jam right in front of the ballholder, which is not desirable. In football, which has even more rules of this type, finding good paths (or closing them) is actually a major part of the game.

CAMERA

The camera system for a modern sports game usually has two very conflicting goals: 1) to show the action in the best possible way to facilitate good gameplay, and 2) to look like TV broadcast sports games. These two goals focus the kinds of camera angles, cuts, and movement styles that can be used with the game, while still being playable. The balance of these two goals can only be determined by the design of the specific game. Are you shooting for the experience of "being the player"? Then you could probably experiment with different camera angles that are almost first-person or heavily skewed toward a certain player's perspective.

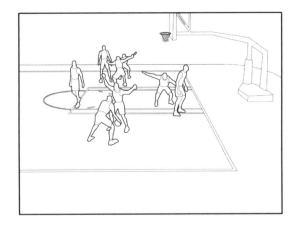

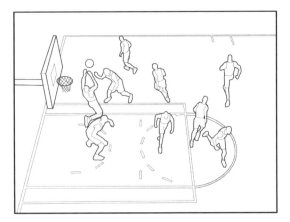

FIGURE 10.1   Different camera styles used in sports games can affect gameplay.

Are you trying to get the human to feel like he's "at the game"? Then you'll want to expand your camera focus, giving the human a wider, whole-court viewpoint on the action. Other camera styles that might be analogous to game-design types include "be the coach," "watch the game on TV" (a very popular choice), "old school" (the overhead, almost two-dimensional view used by many older games), and so on. See Figure 10.1 for two examples of these styles in use.

MISCELLANEOUS ELEMENTS

Miscellaneous elements include things like cheerleaders, mascots, sideline coaches, the crowd, and everything else that makes up the side characters during sports games. Although they usually use very simple AI, these elements can really add up to making your game look much more real by supplying the player with elements that are alive in the world, regardless of his direct interaction.

Mini-Games

Something that most sports games make use of to extend feature sets for their games is the concept of mini-games. These are very small game mechanic concepts that form limited scope experiences, that while remaining true (at least in some form) to the sport involved, represent separate small games unto themselves. Basketball games have things like dunk contests, or skills challenges. *Madden* NFL Football even implemented a full foosball game that you could play from the skybox of certain arenas. This is a very open area in sports games.

Useful AI Techniques

The heavy simulation aspect of these games means that data-driven systems are typically used. Multi-agent communication lends itself well to message based technology. State machines (both fuzzy and finite) of course are always useful.

Finite-State Machines (FSMs) and Fuzzy-State Machines (FuSMs)

Games that fall into the "resetting gameplay" category are much easier to fit into a purely state-based AI model than are their more dynamic brethren. However, all games follow a set game flow (even basketball has tip-off, inbound, gameplay, and freethrow states that flow from one into another). But inside certain states within this overall game flow, the decisions the coaches and players must make is anything but clear-cut. Indeed, fuzzy decisions must be made at almost every level of sports games, and FuSMs can be used to provide this type of cloudy decision making.

Another way to incorporate a level of fuzziness is at the perception level in your sports game. The states themselves can remain somewhat crisp, but the activations for each state get a little blurry. So, a perception variable that refers to whether or not a player has an open look to take a slap shot would have a bit of fuzziness in its calculation (using a reaction time, a value hysteresis, and taking into account some player-level attributes; instead of just shooting a ray from the puck to the net and declaring it clear of obstacles), so that the crisp "shoot the puck" state would therefore only be activated under this more fuzzy determination.

Listing 10.1 includes some example code from Sony's basketball game *NBA Shootout 2004 (PS2)*. This code shows some (roughly 10 percent) of the high-level behavior states that the AI player holding the ball could perform. The system was implemented using a hierarchical FSM.

LISTING 10.1 Example FSM Behaviors from *NBA Shootout 2004*. Code © Sony Computer Entertainment America. Reprinted with permission.

```
//-------------------
//-------------------
//AlleyOop
//-------------------
//-------------------
void gAlleyOop::Update(AIJob* playerjob)
{
    playerjob->ShowGoalLabel("Alley Oop");
}
bool gAlleyOop::GetPriority(AIJob* playerjob)
{
    bool doTheOop = false;
    int shotDistanceType = playerjob->m_pPhysic->
                                       GetShotDistanceType();
    t_Player* oopPlayer = NULL;

    if( (fmodf(GameTime::GetElapsedTime(),BP_ALLEY_OOP_INTERVAL) <
      GameTime::GetDeltaTime())&& Random.Get(BP_ALLEY_OOP_CHANCE) &&
      ( ( shotDistanceType == t_BallAI::distance_outside ) ||
        (shotDistanceType == t_BallAI::distance_three_point ) ) )
    {
        AlleyOopCoach.SetPasser( playerjob->m_Player );

        if((oopPlayer = AlleyOopCoach.FindAlleyOopReceiver())!= NULL)
        {
            if( oopPlayer->GetBallHandlerJob()->
                GetNumberOpponentsLineOfSightColumn( Basket.
                GetPosition(), BP_LINE_OF_SIGHT_WIDTH ) <= 1 )
              doTheOop = playerjob->m_Player->
                    GetBallPlayerSkill()->AlleyOop(oopPlayer);
        }
    }
    return doTheOop;
}
//-------------------
//-------------------
//LastDitchShot
//-------------------
```

```
//-------------------

void gLastDitchShot::Update(AIJob* playerjob)
{
    playerjob->ShowGoalLabel("Last Ditch Shot");
    Team[playerjob->m_Player->team].ClearMiniPlay();
    ((BallHandlerJob*)(playerjob))->DoShootBall();
    return;
}

//-------------------

bool gLastDitchShot::GetPriority(AIJob* playerjob)
{
    if( Court.IsBehindBackboard(playerjob->m_Player) )
        return false;
    if(Team[playerjob->m_Player->team].m_humanOnMyTeam &&
    playerjob->m_Player->GetBallHandlerJob()->m_justReceivedBall)
        return false;

    // last ditch effect
    return( GameState.GameClock.GetTime() <= 2.0f ||
                GameState.ShotClock.GetTime() < 2.0f );
}
//-------------------
//-------------------
//FastBreak
//-------------------
//-------------------

void gFastBreak::Update(AIJob* playerjob)
{
    playerjob->ShowGoalLabel("Fast Break");

    //try passing, it won't do it if it cannot
    ((BallHandlerJob*)(playerjob))->DoFastBreakPass();

    Vec3 basket = Basket.GetPosition();
    Vec3 target;
    target.x    = (playerjob->m_pPhysic->position.x+basket.x)/2.0f;
    target.y    = 0.0f;
    target.z    = (playerjob->m_pPhysic->position.z+basket.z)/2.0f;

    playerjob->m_pPhysic->SetDestDirection
                ( Basket.GetPlayerDirection(playerjob->m_Player) );
```

```
        playerjob->m_pPhysic->SetTargetPositionBallHandler( target );
        playerjob->m_pPhysic->SetCPUGotoAction( PHYS_TURBO );
}


//-------------------

bool gFastBreak::GetPriority(AIJob* playerjob)
{
    if( !GameState.isFastBreak )
        return false;

    if(playerjob->m_Player->GetPlayerSkill()->m_inCollision )
        return false;

    return true;
}
//-------------------
//-------------------
//LongHold
//-------------------
//-------------------

void gLongHold::Update(AIJob* playerjob)
{
    playerjob->ShowGoalLabel("Long Hold");

    t_Player* passTo = playerjob->m_Player->m_pBestPassTo;
    int chance = (Basket.GetPlayerDistance(playerjob->m_Player) >
                FEET(15.0f) && playerjob->m_Player->
                m_pHasDefenderInPlace)? 90 :playerjob->m_Player->
                Personality->passes ;
    bool wouldPass = Random.Percent( chance );

    if( passTo != NULL && wouldPass)
    {
        GoalOffPass.Update(playerjob);
    }
    else
    {
        ((BallHandlerJob*)(playerjob))->DoJumpShot();
    }
}

//-------------------
```

```
bool gLongHold::GetPriority(AIJob* playerjob)
{
    //the point guard on the initial bring up
        //shouldn't be limited as much
    if(Rules.shotClock == LowmemGameRules::ON && playerjob->
            m_Player->position == POINT_GUARD &&
            GameState.ShotClock.GetTime() > 9.0f)
          return false;

    Time stillTime = 0.0f;
    stillTime = playerjob->m_Player->GetBallPlayerSkill()->
                m_ballHoldTimer.Get();

    Time decisionTime = lerp(playerjob->m_Player->Personality->
                             dribbles/100,3.0f,5.0f);
    if(playerjob->m_Player->m_isOut)
    {
        if ( GameState.period >= 3 &&
            GameState.GameClock.GetTime() < 60.0f)
            decisionTime = 60.0f;
        else
            decisionTime = lerp(playerjob->m_Player->Personality->
                                playsPerimeter/100,3.0f,6.0f);
    }

    if( Court.IsInKey( playerjob->m_Player ) )
        decisionTime = 1.5f;

    bool result = false;

    if ( stillTime > decisionTime )
    {
        dbgprintf( "Long hold timeout: decision - %f still - %f\n",
                decisionTime, stillTime );

        result = true;
    }

    return result;
}

//--------------------
//--------------------
//OffPass
```

```
//-------------------
//-------------------

void gOffPass::Update(AIJob* playerjob)
{
    char msg[80];
    sprintf(msg,"Offense pass, chance:%d",chance);
    playerjob->ShowGoalLabel(msg);

    t_Player* m_passTo  =  playerjob->m_Player->m_pBestPassTo;
    //if invalid, try the team stuff
    if((!m_passTo || m_passTo == playerjob->m_Player))
        m_passTo = Team[playerjob->m_Player->
                            team].m_bestPlayerToShoot;
    if(!m_passTo || m_passTo == playerjob->m_Player)//failsafe
        m_passTo = playerjob->m_Player->
                GetClosestPlayerToPlayer(playerjob->m_Player->team);

    if(m_passTo && (((m_passTo==GameRules.LastPossession.player) &&
    (playerjob->m_Player->GetBallPlayerSkill()->
     m_ballHoldTimer.Get()>1.0f)) ||
    ( m_passTo != GameRules.LastPossession.player ) ) )
    {
      playerjob->m_Player->GetBallPlayerSkill()->PassBall(m_passTo);
        playerjob->m_Player->GetOffenseSkill()->
                    m_targetTimer.Clear();//go back to where ya from
    }
}


//-------------------

bool gOffPass::GetPriority(AIJob* playerjob)
{
    //if nobody to pass to...
    if(!playerjob->m_Player->m_pBestPassTo)
        return false;

    if(playerjob->m_Player == playerjob->m_Player->m_pBestPassTo)
        return false;

    chance =0;
    if(playerjob->m_Player->IsInsidePlayer())
    {   //inside players
        if(Basket.GetPlayerDistance(playerjob->m_Player) <=
```

```
                    FEET(2.Øf))
        chance       = 1Ø;//basket is close
    else if(playerjob->m_Player == t_Team::m_pDoubledOffPlayer)
        chance       = (playerjob->m_Player->position==CENTER)?
                            7Ø:8Ø;
    //double team
    else if(playerjob->m_Player->m_pHasDefenderInPlace)
    {
        if(playerjob->m_Player->GetPlayerSkill()->m_canDribble)
        {
            if(playerjob->m_Player->Ratings->insideShooting<75)
                chance  = (playerjob->m_Player->
                            position==CENTER)? 6Ø:5Ø;
                //covered, can dribble, low inside shot
            else
                chance  = (playerjob->m_Player->
                            position==CENTER)? 2Ø:4Ø;
                //covered, can dribble, high inside shot
        }
        else
            chance  = (playerjob->m_Player->
                        position==CENTER)? 5Ø:7Ø;
            //covered, can't dribble
    }
    else
        chance = 1Ø;//not covered (or dteamed, or really close)
}
else // outside players
{
    if(!playerjob->m_Player->GetPlayerSkill()->m_canDribble)
        chance       = 1ØØ;//can't dribble
    else if(playerjob->m_Player->m_pHasDefenderInPlace)
        chance       = 3Ø;//covered
    else
    {
        if(!playerjob->m_Player->m_pHasDefenderInPlace)
            chance       = 1Ø;//wide open
        else
            chance       = 3Ø;//not covered, no lane
    }
}


//offset for longer holds, greater increase if
//you're inside or can't dribble
```

```
        float modVal;
        if(playerjob->m_Player->IsInsidePlayer() ||
           !playerjob->m_Player->GetPlayerSkill()->m_canDribble)
        {
            modVal = GameTime::GetGoalDeltaTime();
        }
        else
        {
            modVal = Ø.1f;
        }

        float rem = fmodf(playerjob->m_Player->GetBallPlayerSkill()->
                    m_ballHoldTimer.Get(), modVal);
        int holdAdj = int(rem/GameTime::GetGoalDeltaTime());
        chance += holdAdj;

        //now check for tendencies
        bool wouldI = Random.Percent( playerjob->m_Player->
                                        Personality->passes);

        return (wouldI && Random.Percent(chance));
}

//-------------------
//-------------------
//Dunk
//-------------------
//-------------------

void gDunk::Update(AIJob* playerjob)
{
    playerjob->ShowGoalLabel("Dunk");
    if(playerjob->m_Player->GetBallPlayerSkill()->DunkBall())
        playerjob->m_Player->Task.SetCPUSequence(TaskDoChargeMove);

}

//-------------------

bool gDunk::GetPriority(AIJob* playerjob)
{
    //don't try if you can't
    if(!playerjob->m_Player->m_canDunk)
        return false;
```

```
    //always dunk if you're wide open
    else if(playerjob->m_Player->m_laneCoverage <= 0.1f)
        return true;

    //otherwise, use personality
    return(Random.Percent(playerjob->m_Player->Personality->dunks));
}
```

DATA-DRIVEN SYSTEMS

With huge numbers of players and callable plays, vast statistical data, and a huge amount of animation, almost all sports games rely on at least some data-driven AI. Plus, with a push toward ever more realistic sports AI as well as online play, data-driven systems will make it much easier to tune the AI, and to update it online with changes that reflect either real-life player statistical changes or further game-balancing polish. Some things that are commonly performed with data driven techniques are:

- *Playbooks.* Instead of creating plays for the AI system, a better system is to create atomic behaviors that the AI-controlled players can perform, and then have an editor that designers can use to chain these behaviors into full plays to create the playbook for the teams in your game. In this way, the designers can experiment with new plays and handpick the best ones (or the ones that each team likes to use most in real life), and the AI programmer can now concentrate on additional behaviors, instead of trying to tune hardcoded plays.
- *Animation picking.* By being able to specify (through a visual editor or some kind of scripting tool) the types of conditions that specify the best animation for a given behavior, designers can quickly spell out the kinds of animations that make sense for each in-game action and can change or expand these animation lists as needed, without any code changing.
- *Player statistics.* At this level, the players need statistical data that approaches the levels represented by their real life counterparts, and additional in-game statistics must be created so that the myriad attributes can be related in some way to the game simulation.

MESSAGING SYSTEMS

With many players having to communicate to each other, and such a dynamic environment, it makes good sense to include a messaging system into the AI framework for your sports game. Everything from coordinating plays between two players (or even collision events), to noting actions by the human, could be sent through the messaging system, with the AI responding to only those messages that it is interested in, instead of having to monitor the entire playing field continuously. Different levels of the AI system can use the same system as well so the physics layer will respond to the collision event, in which the team level will respond to a coordination event between two players.

EXAMPLES

Early sports games, such as *Football* and *Basketball* on the Intellivision and Atari, couldn't even support the full number of players on each team, since the hardware just couldn't push that many sprites. They also used simplified AI, with opponents that more closely resembled pillars players had to negotiate around, instead of the reactive players that we are used to in modern games.

Sports games really began to come into the spotlight with the NES game system, as programmers finally had the processing and graphical power necessary to do a much better job of approximating the games, although still at a somewhat primitive level. Games like *RBI Baseball, Tecmo Super Bowl, Ice Hockey,* and *Double Dribble* are still loved by sports games fans. The gameplay employed by these titles was simplified, but did approach a simulation of actual play, and we finally started to see a greater use of statistics (instead of two equal teams playing against each other).

Many of today's games, even with their greater graphical look, still employ most of the gameplay institutions that were created during this early period, which has in some ways stalled sports games gameplay evolution. But it has the advantage of making most games instantly playable by longtime fans because the control scheme, overall game mechanics, and general game strategies are still somewhat familiar. A similar situation occurred in the fighting game genre when most of the "copycat" games borrowed *Street Fighter*'s six-button control layout and special joystick moves.

The 1990s continued seasonal versions of all the popular games, now in 16-bit versions and beyond. As the games incrementally increased in quality and scope, and as the consoles began to use more sophisticated controllers, the games gave players more controls and options. This means the AI has to follow suit, so its complexity increases.

Today's sports games are marvels of AI, with perennial games like *Madden NFL*, Sega's *NBA* and *NFL 2K* series, and *World Soccer* playing sophisticated simulations of their sports, while showing the personalities of the players and giving the game player a great sports experience. These games use a variety of AI systems, including complex FSMs to make play calling and tactical decisions against the human player, data-driven systems to choose the correct animations based on several factors, sophisticated simulation calculations to make game characters perform like they do in real life, and even more in an increasing attempt to make the games more realistic and fun.

AREAS THAT NEED IMPROVEMENT

Sports games, being annual titles that are sold largely to the same people year after year, live and die by their incremental improvements. But, considering the amount of time and money being spent on these games, they have tended to play it safe in many areas that could benefit greatly from extended AI programming. These include: learning, game balance, and gameplay innovation.

LEARNING

Sports game AI continues to fall the victim of exploits, with even the best AI-controlled team losing because the human did something repeatedly that the AI is poor at stopping. If the AI could compensate for this by specifically targeting this repetitive behavior, it would force the human player to either change his game tactic, or stop scoring so easily.

Team AI could also learn from this, by discerning favorite plays that the human employs and better defend against that play if it were to happen again. This type of sports learning has been implemented using influence maps (by incrementally changing positioning data to reflect more winning positions) and by statistical learning (by keeping track of behaviors that work, or don't work, and adjusting future decisions appropriately). This system doesn't have to increase difficulty of the game; it will just stop exploits from ruining the overall performance of the AI system. In the end, this system will merely cause the player to change his game plan a bit more often, and the overall experience will just be that much closer to a real game.

Of course, this same system *can* be used to increase difficulty, because the system can learn the kinds of things that the human is poor at stopping quite quickly, and have bias toward those kinds of behaviors (in effect, the system is finding exploits against the human's intelligence).

GAME BALANCE

The primary issue with sports games is the problem of game balance. Certain sports tasks, like defense in basketball, are much harder to do than others (the reason for this is that basketball is a very fast sport, and the actions of the defense are by definition reactive, thus always slightly behind the offense). How do we support basketball defense for the human (to make this task fun), without killing the balance of the game by making it too easy to defend, and therefore shutting down the offense? As this issue continues to evolve, on a case-by-case basis, it will continue to consume AI programmers' time as they come across problems that require decisions based on the game at hand and the fun factor of the game.

Online play further complicates the task of game balancing. So far, there has been an inherent lag associated with all but the fastest connections in online games because of bandwidth limitations, as well all the related problems dealing with packet confirmation and loss. The kinds of highly reactive behaviors in sports games end up suffering visually because of it, more so than in more physics-based games like FTPS, which have very simple animations and can use physics to predict character and projectile movement to fill in the gaps caused by lag.

Another issue in online sports games is that of *discontinuity*. Basically, this means that one of the players sees behavior that actually hasn't happened, or that is dramatically different from what really happened. Think of it as a much worse version of normal online game lag, where you think you shot a guy in an online *Quake* game but you have a slow network connection and he actually moved out of the way.

Most online games are written such that both machines are running the game in a synched fashion, such that the same exact game is running on both player's machines. The network code then sends each player's joystick inputs back and forth to the other, so that the two games can continue to play, still synched, with both players seeing the same results. Discontinuity will occur if a bug in the code, or a bad network connection, causes the two games to somehow get out of synch with each other.

If an event-based networking scheme is employed (where game events are passed instead of player input, and each player's game essentially "catches up" to the other by performing these events as they come in) then the game will have a much greater chance of showing discontinuous moments. If one player sees that he caught the pass, but the server machine says that he did not, then the first player is going to be pretty confused when he suddenly doesn't have the ball anymore. If this happens once, it might be overlooked as an online jitter. But if it is a systemic problem, where the clients of your game are continually catching up to the server's reality, by popping animations, behaviors, and positions, the game becomes unplayable in a hurry.

GAMEPLAY INNOVATION

Sports games have become increasingly similar in how they play, and hence the genre is somewhat stagnant. Marketing has driven innovation almost out of this highly profitable sector of the game industry. Even *Madden*, arguably one of the best and most successful franchises in all of sports gaming, hasn't done anything really innovative in many years. The *Madden* team has incrementally improved graphical quality, presentation, and animations and have also made some small changes to the interface. But, the game is almost identical, gameplay wise, to the some of the earliest *Madden* football games. It's just a lot prettier. Is this really what the consumer wants? Or is this what the consumer has been given? The motivation, of course, is to not lose any market share by scaring people off with strange gameplay mechanics or AI behaviors that people either don't enjoy immediately or can't learn quickly enough. No matter what marketing thinks, people will buy a game and actually spend the time to learn a new interface or game mechanic if the experience is good enough. Nobody knew how to control a basketball game when the first one came out, yet customers still bought it.

There is plenty of room for innovation in the sports game world, both in gameplay and in competitive and cooperative AI. We must strive to offer something new to the consumers, lest this genre grows stale and dies. Imagine an AI system in football that discusses things with you during a huddle and helps to develop a plan against the other team. Imagine a commentator AI system that does television-style slow motion while remarking about the play and drawing things on the screen for emphasis. Imagine more intuitive voice controls for these games, where you could shout "toward" a certain player (with head movement tracking or some other means) and get an appropriate response. These are the kinds of things that will keep the genre fresh and growing.

SUMMARY

Sports games have come a long way from the incredibly simplistic versions that were first created for home consoles in the 1970s. With ever more realistic visuals and gameplay, the need for high-quality AI-controlled athletes is greater. Sports games are some of the highest money making games in the business right now, and the players who shell out that money demand quality in every element.

- The two main categories of sports gameplay are fluid and resetting games. Fluid refers to games that have mostly nonstop gameplay, with very dynamic situations. Resetting games are those that have periodic resets or stops in the action, and so are more linear.
- The common sports game purchaser has a high level of sports knowledge, and that means that a higher level of detail needs to be to be implemented for simulation-style sports titles.
- A coach- or team-level AI layer provides the system with more far-reaching decision making and provides a means for coordinating actions among multiple players.

- Player-level AI systems are usually more tactical than the coach-level and usually include both decision-making and animation selection elements.
- Pathfinding in sports games usually involves much higher numbers of dynamic obstacles and needs to take into account special means of travel with the rules of a specific game.
- Animation selection systems are very important to sports games because the system needs a fast way to query a large database of animations and make intelligent decisions.
- Miscellaneous elements make the world bigger than the game court and give the player a greater sense of immersion.
- FSMs and FuSMs are used widely in sports games. The type of game (fluid or resetting) can sometimes be a factor when using these techniques, but because of the inherent nature of any sports game, some degree of state machine will be used in the construction of the game.
- Data-driven systems help offload some of the tremendous amount of detail that needs to be addressed on a player, team, and animation level.
- Messaging will help the various layers of the AI system communicate and provides a quick means of cutting through the very dynamic environment.
- Learning will help to solve the problem of AI exploits and could aid the player in learning the system.
- AI systems need to extend their abilities in those areas in which game balance and fair gaming need to be addressed because additional intelligence in the system will give more aid to the player, but may wreck game balance.
- The genre must continue to innovate in gameplay and opponent and cooperative AI systems, so it doesn't go stale.

11 Racing Games

In This Chapter

- Common AI Elements
- Useful AI Techniques
- Areas That Need Improvement
- Summary

The racing genre is an interesting one, both from a gameplay standpoint and from an AI standpoint. The genre is divided into two main groups for the most part—vehicular and specialty. The two groups have a common thread, which is that gameplay has at least some resemblance to a physics-based simulation of racing. For our purposes, racing is loosely defined as moving about a set course in a timed competition against others.

Early games like *Pole Position* (or even its granddad, the 1974 Atari game, *Gran Trak*) are much more along the lines of action games, in that the processing power of the hardware at that time didn't allow for much simulation. They were really just fun gameplay systems. Most racing games (even modern ones) take liberties with their physics, but that's what videogames are about. We keep some areas of reality that we don't mind being limited by, and strip out the parts of reality that we do. This means we mostly want controls that provide realistic cornering and handling (which gives us more control over the game by providing recognizable feedback like a real vehicle), but we also want to be able to jump a car over ten semi-trucks and still be able to drive away after landing (because we've always dreamed of doing it in real life). This is much like the gamers who don't mind having to reload a rocket launcher between shots, but they would mind if they could only carry three rockets at a time; they want a hundred shots in the backpack, never mind that a load like that would probably weigh far more than the character could carry for any distance, much less jump with.

Two variants of vehicular racing games appeared early, and the split stuck. They are differentiated by their camera perspective: the first-/third-person racing game (such as *OutRun*, or *Stun Runner*) and the overhead view (*RC Pro-AM*, or *Ivan Stewart's Off Road Challenge*). The overhead games tended to be skewed toward the action-oriented, simpler arcade-style game, with very unrealistic physics. The other group stayed more true to its roots, with a more reasonable simulation of vehicular physics.

The specialty racing games are mostly fad-driven—they involve the trendy racing-style sport at the time. Past examples that received some degree of success include snowboarding, skiing, boating, wave runners, hovercraft, dirt bikes, and the like. These games had to augment traditional racing AI with sport-specific behaviors, such as performing tricks or dealing with futuristic or non-traditional physics systems.

One last subtype is the cart racing game (made popular by *Mario Kart*, but since has seen decent success with quite a few different characters), which simplifies the driving portion of the game and adds obstacles, strange tracks, and other action elements. By calling this style of racing "cart racing," players know that the vehicles are more like go-carts, which are very simplified cars. Most go-carts only have a gas pedal and a brake, and this is also usually the control setup of most cart-style racing games.

Pure vehicular simulation can be a fairly technology-intensive undertaking. You need complex mathematical solutions to deal with the different suspension systems used in modern vehicles, good multibody collision handlers, AI opponents that can adjust to differing road conditions (especially for off-road racing or in games that include rain, oil, or ice hazards), as well as any special concerns your game might bring. Some of the best racing games have been showcases for the computational and graphical power of new game systems as they first are released. The physics models and control schemes that these games use have been so highly polished that they need almost no tweaking at all. Designers work on a nice graphics engine, produce some higher-quality car models, and deliver a finished, high-quality launch title.

Overall, the AI of pure racing games has gotten very advanced over the years, with many great examples of track AI that does a competitive job without cheating. In fact, the racing genre was starting to lose popularity because of a lack of freshness. Too many games came out in which the primary driving simulation was so good, and so close to reality, that almost nothing could be done better. The genre needed a shot in the arm to revive it.

In 1995, *Twisted Metal* was released, and the first true vehicular combat game was born (although other games released earlier had cars and weapons, they were usually more cartoony, like *Mario Kart*, or just plain action games, like *SpyHunter*. So they weren't really driving simulations, but they were definitely an influence on the genre). *Twisted Metal* was a moderately realistic driving simulation (for its time), coupled with arena-style levels and weapons. People forgave the subpar graphical quality and the very strange control setup because the additional gameplay elements were truly original, and it was very fun to play. It wasn't enough, however, mostly because the single-player experience suffered from bad AI (both the performance as well as the difficulty level), and the gameplay was repetitive when the player was not playing against another human (trash talking side by side with friends, and hearing them scream as they are killed, seems to add replay value for most gamers). Other games came out, including the stylish *Interstate '76*, which added the concept of a linear story and an overall "bad ass" attitude that worked well. But it also suffered from the replayability and single-player problems of *Twisted Metal*. Again, the genre needed more.

Recently, something more has arrived. By going one step further, and adding complex adventure and story elements to the racing genre in addition to weapons, racing games have opened enormous possibilities. *Grand Theft Auto* started out in 1997 as a somewhat primitive, overhead two-dimensional game with a very simple concept: provide a living city in which the player can perform many different activities, including driving, to eke out a life as a thuggish-criminal.

Over the years, the concept remains, but it has since moved to the full splendor of a completely realized three-dimensional world, with a realistic, if somewhat over-the-top driving simulation, and a high degree of sex, violence, and rock music. It has also become one of the best selling games of all time, with the four games in the series selling a combined total of more than 70 million copies as of 2008. The combination of providing open-ended gameplay and adult content has proved hugely popular.

Many other games have since capitalized on this formula, so the full-blown vehicular action genre has picked up where the pure racing simulation and the combat games have left off. The action elements of these games venture quite far into the adventure or first-person shooters/third-person shooters (FTPS) game's territory, but the primary gameplay system is vehicular, or at least it has been until now.

COMMON AI ELEMENTS

Classic racing games didn't require much AI, but modern games, with their emphasis being on cross-pollination into other genres, can require quite a few AI elements. Some of these include: track AI, traffic, pedestrians, enemies and combat, non-player characters, and other competitive behaviors.

TRACK AI

The most obvious of racing AI requirements is the system needed to keep a CPU-controlled car on a racetrack (or city street) at high speed and within the rules of the game. Usually, this is a state-based system, with the different vehicle states detailing the main ways that a racer can exist on the track (most likely OnTrack, OffTrack,

**Path of Minimum
Curvature**

FIGURE 11.1   Track with path of minimum curvature shown.

WrongWay, and Recovering, or something similar). Each vehicle state would have ways of steering and applying the throttle and brake to best serve the particular state the vehicle is in, combined with the vehicle's position, and its place relative to the position of the other racers. As guidelines, most games use a combination of physics and "optimal lines of travel" (which are either data paths laid down in the track editor, or calculated automatically by a technique known as "finding the path of minimum curvature," as shown in Figure 11.1) that mimic the invisible lines of travel that humans use when they race on tracks and roads. In addition, there are also optimal offset positions, if the true optimal position is already occupied. These optimal lines of travel are then modified by the particulars of the vehicle involved (one vehicle might be lighter and more agile, and can thus take a turn more aggressively then another).

Another form of "track AI" is to actually embed the "AI" into the track itself . . . that is, the *track* guides the cars and makes decisions for each non-player vehicle based on conditions in the game at the moment. This approach is generally simpler than customizing an AI for each car's peculiar capabilities, but requires a more thorough cycle of planning to avoid every car behaving the same way.

Some racing games don't occur on roads. There are racing games on water (with boats or jet-skis), snowy mountains (with snowboarding), or even more exotic terrains (like the tubes and chutes of *Stun Runner*). Thus, they might not use a pure version of the minimum curvature technique because the dynamics of the surface might entail other types of optimal maneuvers.

TRAFFIC

A number of these games are built around racing in functional cities, so they have working traffic simulations, complete with stoplights, highway systems, and numerous cars. The traffic in these games is usually just good enough to be realistic *looking*, but rarely does traffic react much to the player's movements (in fact, the games are usually intentionally designed this way; gamers wouldn't want everyone getting out of their way and ruining the excitement).

Some games, however, use complex traffic systems that are very realistic, with lane changes, cars pulling over for police vehicles, proper use of traffic lights and intersections, and so on. These are mostly FSM-based behaviors, with a lot of synchronization to ensure that accidents don't happen (unless some rowdy human happens along at 130 mph), and some randomness to ensure that these actions and events don't look repetitive.

PEDESTRIANS

Ever since race games started appearing with cities for backdrops, pedestrians have been part of the equation. Different games take different approaches. The *Midtown Madness* games, being a bit more family friendly, have the pedestrians walking around on paths randomly, and if a car gets too close they dive out of the way. Other games, like *Grand Theft Auto* or *Carmageddon,* let the user pretty much run over anybody he wants. The pedestrians *try* to get out of the way, but clever violence hounds will always find some means, and the people will fall. In fact, *Grand Theft Auto* has quite a range of pedestrian types, all of which are running different AI, based on function. In most games, this type of behavior is state-based, probably with some global messaging.

Other systems use very simple flocking-type behaviors, with areas in the level being assigned particular values of attract and repel (thus, certain storefronts might attract people, who would look in the window for a while and then walk toward the next attractor, whereas a dead body might be a powerful repelling force, so that people look like they're avoiding the accident). *State of Emergency* made good use of a system similar to this. The crowds were very fluid and reacted well to most of the action.

Enemy and Combat

This is the car equivalent of deathmatch bot code. Some games allow full combat either car-on-car, or pedestrian-on-car, or some other combination. This code needs to combine the race AI mentioned earlier with the bot AI from FTPS games, including the human-level performance-checking that would do things like making the AI misfire and drive into walls occasionally, to ensure that the player doesn't feel cheated (or merely that the player is being pursued by a relentless evil robot, unless that's your design intention). It might also include multiple cars working together, as in police cars taking different streets to cut off multiple escape routes, or two cars boxing the player in so it is impossible for him to turn.

Nonplayer Characters (NPC)

NPCs are the *other* people players deal with in the game world, usually not in combat, such as characters who are going to give the player information, or sell the player a better car. As in role-playing games, NPCs usually have scripted behaviors and dialogue to facilitate these encounters. They generally aren't very reactive because most of these games don't have sophisticated conversation engines (it's really not the point; if people want that, they'll play an RPG), so most NPCs are usually handled in a non-interactive cut scene.

Other Competitive Behavior

Some racing games also require specialized behavior from their AI opponents, such as performing tricks in snowboarding or motocross games. These systems need to have either scripted chains of moves that look well together or a decent understanding of physics and timing so that they pick moves that they can pull off successfully and stylishly.

   This kind of decision structure is more like a fighting game, taking into account the appropriateness and timing of moves. Each move would have some length of time associated with it (that is, how long it takes to perform the move as well as recover). The AI makes its move determinations based on how much time it has (from simple physics calculations that take into account speed and height achieved), as well as skill level and personality.

USEFUL AI TECHNIQUES

As in any genre, FSMs make themselves useful in racing game engines. Scripted systems make the story-driven elements of these games easier to develop. The heavy synchronization required by pedestrian and traffic systems means ample places for messaging systems to be taken advantage of. Finally, racing games are one of the primary users of an advanced AI technique, that of genetic algorithms, although it is typically an offline usage.

FINITE-STATE MACHINES (FSMs)

Race games have a fairly straightforward AI layout, mostly defined by the laws of physics, and the (usually) simple objectives of the current "race" (be it to get to the finish line first, or to pick up a package and bring it back while surviving the attacks of the other players). Also, the state layout for the game flow of most classical racing games is very straightforward (start, racing, off the track, overtake, pacing, pit). FSMs make themselves useful again.

SCRIPTED SYSTEMS

The vehicular action genre usually follows a story of some sort (although some are extremely open-ended) and work well with the scripting paradigm. Also, some of the ambient pedestrian and traffic systems can lend themselves well to a scripted system, in which various patterns of movement are scripted and interact with the street layout of the city. Sometimes this is just a first layer, with overriding reactive systems in place to affect this scripted behavior when the need arises. So, if you have a crowd milling about in a mall, checking out the merchandise, using the escalators, and such, this could be a series of small scripts that each AI-controlled person would use to look like the character has intimate knowledge of the environment. But if a car suddenly comes crashing through the window, the pedestrians' flee behaviors would kick in, overriding the normal script, in a mad dash to escape being crushed.

MESSAGING SYSTEMS

The ambient traffic and pedestrian systems most commonly use messaging systems to talk to one another and coordinate movement in the complex ways that these things happen in real life. Of course, it is also possible to code these types of behavior using FSMs (even if you use a messaging system, you'll still probably want to control overall behavior of traffic and pedestrians with scripting or state machines), but if you're going to have a large number of ambient vehicles and walkers, and want them to respond to periodic or situational events either singly or in coordination, this is probably the way to go.

GENETIC ALGORITHMS

Some of these games have an enormous number of cars (*Gran Turismo 2* has more than 500), each of which require tuning of their handling and performance abilities to be as close to reality as possible. In response, some companies have used techniques to automate this tuning task with a simple offline genetic algorithm application used to modify the car's performance parameters until optimal results are achieved. These results are then stored and used directly during actual gameplay. This is a very straightforward use of genetic techniques (as a preprocessor that optimally tunes a system of parameters), and the amount of time the genetic algorithm will take to perform these calculations is dramatically less than the time it would take a programmer or designer working within the game using trial and error. Note that none of these games use genetic algorithms to tune behavior *after* the game has shipped. As neat as this might sound, it has the potential to lead to too much chaos with individual players. This approach is used solely to tune cars during development and testing.

Examples

Driving games have been with us almost from since the beginning of video games themselves, with the earliest ones coming out in the beginning of the 1970s. These early driving titles were little more than a scrolling field of two small lines that players had to stay between. But this simple representation is all the mind needs to engage the competitive spirit, if also given a steering wheel and a gas pedal.

The driving game has come a long way, with the older *Pole Position* and *SpyHunter* looking dated next to the almost movie-quality visuals of today's *Gran Turismo*. Also, the arcade-style, fast-and-loose gameplay of the past has been all but lost to the almost perfect rendition of the handling and performance modeling in today's better racing games. Not that gamers missed realism in games like *Crazy Taxi*, however. *Midtown Madness* gave players great city traffic, *The Simpsons: Hit and Run* successfully extended the game model to a comic license and managed to keep the comedy, *Interstate '76* infused a degree of style and a good story into the mix, and *Carmageddon* actually had players using the windshield wiper to clean off the blood.

AREAS THAT NEED IMPROVEMENT

Classical racing simulation games have been all but mastered. If your racing simulation doesn't include a well-built, solid physics model combined with a polished, intuitive control scheme, ultrarealistic visuals, and some way to differentiate yourself from the games that already have accomplished all these things, don't even bother putting it on the market. However, the new variations of incorporating vehicular racing with other elements of gameplay still have many areas in which to improve.

AREAS OF INTEREST OTHER THAN CRIME

To possibly push these games more mainstream (which is hard to imagine considering the many millions of units these types of games have already sold), more parent-palatable game types could be found—most mothers do not want to see their child running over a prostitute for her wallet. Violence in videogames does sell, but it doesn't have to be as extreme as in *Grand Theft Auto.*

MORE INTELLIGENT AI ENEMIES

Imagine you are being chased by teams of cars, but instead of working together to set up roadblocks and head you off, the whole event becomes a Blues Brothers–style chase with one lead vehicle being trailed by forty cop cars. This scenario is pretty much the norm for the genre, but more complex maneuvers could (and should) be used for the opponents. Just give the human "criminal" player a police scanner, so the player can hear about the roadblocks slightly ahead of time and circumvent capture. Some games are making headway in this area, but they are rare.

Other problems can be seen in simple overtake maneuvers in some games. AI-controlled cars sometimes pay very little attention to other AI-controlled cars; they do adjust their speed and turning to some degree, but the collision between AI vehicles is tuned to minimize the effect they have on each other to simplify the overall race simulation. Thus, AI cars in some games don't use real overtake moves to get by each other—one car will bump the other out of the way, in a subtle way that looks okay from afar, but doesn't hold up to close scrutiny. Instead, why not give each vehicle a more realistic AI race model, so that the human doesn't notice this AI cheat? In real life, race drivers are members of larger teams, and multiple cars will work together on the track to win races.

PERSISTENT WORLDS

A vehicular action game has not yet been adapted to the multi-player online model, but this could be a big boon to the genre. Imagine a game based on the *Autoduel* world (the 1985 game from Origin™ based on the Steve Jackson *Car Wars* pen-and-paper RPG—it's sort of a Mad Max after the collapse of civilization scenario), or *Grand Theft Auto*, for that matter. The dynamics of these kinds of story worlds lend themselves well to the gameplay mechanics of racing with the large, open worlds that online games require.

The problems lie in simple computing power; driving the complex mathematics of the vehicle simulations and running traffic AI for an entire city (rather than a small sphere of traffic centered on the player, as is used in *Midtown Madness*) does not work well with the limited bandwidth capabilities of the Internet. Online game choppiness caused by CPU usage spikes (which is somewhat tolerated and can be compensated for in some game types) might make the game unplayable. We shall see whether or not these limitations can be breached and bring racing-style gameplay to the online community.

SUMMARY

Racing games went from very simplistic toys in the 1970s arcades, to some of the most graphically and technologically sound games of all time. This quick rise in quality came at the price of gameplay innovation, however, and the genre almost stalled out. The modern infusion of additional gameplay elements into racing games has truly invigorated the genre and given it a new life.

- The racing genre is globally defined as a game using a somewhat physics-based model of racing.
- Vehicular racing games involve the more common types of vehicles: cars, motorcycles, F1 racers, and so on. The vehicles can be on- or off-road, and involve an actual racetrack, or take place in a city or other locale.
- Specialty racing games involve competitive racing of some other type, like jet skis, snowboarding, or the like.
- The creation of vehicular combat games increased the gameplay potential of the genre. Adventure and action elements were also eventually added into the mix, extending to the vehicular action game.
- Track AI is the system by which CPU-controlled racers maintain control while racing over the terrain within the confines of the physics system and rules of the game.
- For games that take place within urban areas, traffic and pedestrian systems greatly add to the visual and situational realism of the city.
- Combat AI is required in games that use additional gameplay elements beyond the racing competitions.
- NPC AI would be required if your game uses additional character interaction other than combat or specialized areas of economy or information.
- Other competitive elements would also require AI work, if your game was such that it involved doing tricks or other actions while racing.
- FSMs make themselves useful in this genre because of the linear nature of most race scenarios.
- Scripting lends itself well to the story of a vehicular action game, as well as to the nature of traffic and pedestrian systems.

- Messaging will ease the need for communication between game elements in complex race and traffic AI systems.
- Genetic algorithms can help automate the process of tuning the handling and performance parameters of the hundreds of cars that are sometimes represented in a large racing game.
- Areas of interest other than crime need to be explored for vehicular action games. This will continue the push toward mass appeal and provide appropriate games for children.
- The opponent AI needs additional intelligence because the level of pathing through cities and overtaking on racetracks is still inferior to human level.
- A persistent world game for Internet use in this genre could do much to extend the genre.

12 Classic Strategy Games

In This Chapter

- Common AI Elements
- Useful AI Techniques
- Areas That Need Improvement
- Summary

Game theory can be roughly thought of as *the study of human behavior when dealing with interactions in which the outcomes depend on the strategies of two or more persons who have opposing or, at best, mixed motives.* John von Neumann virtually founded the field in 1928 by studying the concept of bluffing in poker and discovering that the analysis had significant ramifications for economics. He *officially* fathered the field in 1944 with the publishing of his classic *Theory of Games and Economic Behavior* (written with Oskar Morgenstern). The book took his earlier researched work on minimax theory (discussed later in the chapter) and extended it to include more complex games, like economics.

In game theory, the concept of a *game* takes on special meaning. Instead of the more common entertainment-oriented definition of the word, game theory uses a more broad meaning; a *game is an undertaking in which several agents strive to maximize their payoff by taking actions, but the result relies on the actions of all the players.* By discovering that this generalization exists across different types of "games," game theory hopes to explain some kinds of human interactions across many varying playfields, from business to war, and from the checkerboard to overpopulation.

Some of the classic "games" that have been studied under game theory include barbarians at the gate, mutually assured destruction, the prisoner's dilemma, and *caveat emptor*. These are all mathematical constructs that attempt to define what are called dominant strategies of the various human behaviors that each detail.

In some of his earliest work, von Neumann made a very important discovery, with one very large requirement. The discovery was that for some games, *rationality* (meaning the best action to take) could be mathematically calculated, given the strategies and payoffs inherent in the game. The requirement was that the game be what is called a *zero-sum* game, which is *a game in which one player's winning actions directly result in another's equivalent loss.* In other words, these are games in which a number of players engage in a system of pure competition, in which there is only one winner.

This is not a trivial requirement. Many of the more socially important problems that game theory had hoped to tackle (such as economics, dealing with use of natural resources, and political systems) are not zero-sum games. Although game theory can still give insights into these other kinds of games, it cannot help define game-specific rationality like it can in the limited world of zero-sum games.

Von Neumann's work became a foundation for early AI researchers' work, as they set out to create programs that could accomplish complex tasks requiring rationality. How best to test their creations than by finding some abstract version of worldly problems, that also manages to fit neatly into a clean mathematical model, so that rationality can be assured? Zero-sum games answered the call and are still some of the most studied of all AI problems.

Classical strategy games such as chess, checkers, tic-tac-toe, and even poker are all examples of zero-sum games. It also turns out that non-zero-sum games like *Monopoly* (in which it might be possible that two people could form an alliance, and both "win" money from the bank) can be converted to a zero-sum game by considering one of the players to be the board itself (or the bank, in *Monopoly*). This ghost player is in essence losing the sum of the amount won by the players, and thus all the formal assumptions and proofs concerning zero-sum gaming can be employed.

Researchers began using computers to build an "intelligent program" capable of playing these games almost as soon as computers made their appearance. Alan Turing (of the Turing test fame) and Claude Shannon wrote some of the first chess programs in 1950, barely five years after ENIAC came online. Both men put forth that a program that could competently play these games epitomized the definition of something requiring (and exhibiting) intelligence.

This brings up an interesting parable about AI problems in general. In the past, if a task was too difficult for a computer to accomplish, it was said that if someone could devise a program to do that task, then that program would be intelligent. But, after years of work, when someone finally does release a program that performs the task, the detractors declare it to be simple brute force search (or whatever computer technique the program uses), and not real intelligence. Thus, AI never gets to actually solve any problems. In effect, the bar keeps moving.

Researchers turned to games for a number of reasons. They are more complex and lend themselves more to real-world situations than so-called *toy* problems do and represent a more uncertain and (somewhat) exciting world than massive search ventures like the traveling salesman problem (finding the optimal non-repeating route a salesman should take to connect a number of cities), or integrated circuit design.

Classic strategy games also personify the optimal conditions for classic AI search techniques. They are games of perfect information (both players know everything about the game world), the moves are mostly global in effect (rather than within some small sphere of influence). The games are turn-based, which gives the computer time to think. Strategy games are also very complex (in terms of state space), thus requiring intelligent methods for finding rational solutions.

This is precisely the list of attributes that typically make a good computer AI simulation. However, because these games also add the element of an opponent, they provide the problem with elements of uncertainty and, more specifically, directed uncertainty. Undirected uncertainty would be randomness introduced by dice or some similar means, and is thus unbiased and is merely part of the cost of playing. But directed uncertainty deals with things like bluffing, mixing strategies to appear random, or using irrational moves to confuse your opponent.

If you consider the previously mentioned optimal conditions for AI problem solving, it is easy to determine the parts of strategy games that will be weak for an AI system. Closed chess endgames (the term "closed" refers to a state with a number of interlocked pawns across the middle of the board; see Figure 12.1) are notoriously difficult for traditional AI systems. The reason? The moves are no longer global, in effect. Suddenly, we can cut up the chessboard into separate chunks and throw off the computer by making diversionary moves on the other side, to make the AI system think something is going on. Tactics like this are one way that Gary Kasparov beats many of the computer chess programs (and because he's one of the best chess players in the history of the game, of course).

What separates most academic studies from more traditional entertainment versions of classical game playing programs is the notion of a time limit. Given the unreasonable request of an infinite amount of time, the best solution can almost always be found. But given the limits of the real world, gameplaying programs always have some form of time limitation, and we must make do with the amount of time that we have allotted to us. Of course, as computation speeds increase, we are getting closer and closer to the point when brute force methods will be possible, given even modest time constraints. But there will always be another, more complex game that will force AI researchers to use alternate methods to find better solutions fast, without relying on total brute search.

AI researchers have "solved" several of these games, meaning that the entire state space has been mapped out and can be easily searched by today's computers to result in optimal performance (that being a win for the first player to move, or a draw). Games that have been solved include tic-tac-toe, checkers, *Connect Four*, *Go-Moku*, and *Othello*. Several others are in various states of being solved. Chess is getting close. The highest-classed chess programs use a stored "opening book"

FIGURE 12.1   A closed chess game position.

(chains of moves that have been researched over the centuries by chess masters to give good play) for the opening moves. They use a smart search technique of some kind for the transitory middle game phase, and then have another stored database of good moves for the endgame phase. See Figure 12.2 for a listing of solved and partially solved games. Bear in mind that while much was made of IBM's *Deep Blue* beating Gary Kasparov in 1997, most chess programs were able to beat most human players long before that (the first real computer chess programs that came out in the late 1950s could surely have beaten most human players).

Solved

- ☑ **Awari**
- ☑ **Connect Four**
- ☑ **GoMoku**
- ☑ **Hex (up to 9 x 9)**
- ☑ **Nim**
- ☑ **Nine Men's Morris**
- ☑ **Three Men's Morris**
- ☑ **Qubic**
- ☑ **Tic-Tac-Toe**

Partially Solved

- ☐ **Checkers**
- ☐ **Chess**
- ☐ **Go (up to 4 x 4—game is usually 19 x 19)**
- ☐ **Reversi**

FIGURE 12.2   Classic games that have been solved, in whole or partially.

Some games can have such huge state spaces (the game of *Go* has a game tree size of around 10^{400}, which is a number larger than the amount of atoms in the universe, give or take) that they are all but immune to brute force search methods and, thus, require either very clever directed search routines within recognized portions of the state space, or intelligent algorithms to develop novel solutions given the game rules. Either way, these are some of the most classically-defined AI problems there are.

Listing 12.1 shows the search() and think() functions from the open source chess program, *Faile*, written by Adrien M. Regimbald. The entire source is on the CD-ROM, along with its corresponding Web links for more information. *Faile* is a very compact (the entire source zip file is 42 K), yet full-featured, alpha-beta search system, which gives this tiny little program expert-level AI play capability.

Notice that the search function uses bounded optimality, in that it has a time limit, and will make decisions based on the best move it has seen given the time it has left, and will even make decisions on whether to continue searching or not based on time. More detail will be given on this later in the chapter when alpha-beta search is discussed.

LISTING 12.1 `search()` and `think()` from *Faile*. Distributed under the MIT license.

```
long int search (int alpha, int beta, int depth, bool do_null) {

  /* search the current node using alpha-beta with negamax search */

  move_s moves[MOVE_BUFF], h_move;
  int num_moves, i, j, ep_temp, extensions = 0, h_type;
  long int score = -INF, move_ordering[MOVE_BUFF],
           null_score = -INF, i_alpha,h_score;
  bool no_moves, legal_move;
  d_long temp_hash;

  /* before we do anything, see if we're out of time
         or we have input: */
  if (i_depth > mindepth && !(nodes & 4095)) {
    if (rdifftime (rtime (), start_time) >= time_for_move) {
      /* see if our score has suddenly dropped, and if so,
              try to allocate some extra time: */
      if (allow_more_time && bad_root_score) {
    allow_more_time = FALSE;
    if (time_left > (5*time_for_move)) {
      time_for_move *= 2;
    }
    else {
      time_exit = TRUE;
      return 0;
    }
      }
      else {
    time_exit = TRUE;
    return 0;
      }
    }
    #ifndef ANSI
    if (xb_mode && bioskey ()) {
      time_exit = TRUE;
      return 0;
    }
    #endif
  }
```

```
/* check for a draw by repetition before continuing: */
if (is_draw ()) {
  return 0;
}


pv_length[ply] = ply;


/* see what info we can get from our hash table: */
h_score = chk_hash (alpha, beta, depth, &h_type, &h_move);
if (h_type != no_info) {
  switch (h_type) {
    case exact:
  return (h_score);
    case u_bound:
  return (h_score);
    case l_bound:
  return (h_score);
    case avoid_null:
  do_null = FALSE;
  break;
    default:
  break;
  }
}


temp_hash = cur_pos;
ep_temp = ep_square;
i_alpha = alpha;

/* perform check extensions if we haven't gone past maxdepth: */
if (in_check ()) {
  if (ply < maxdepth+1) extensions++;
}
/* if not in check, look into null moves: */
else {
  /* conditions for null move:
     - not in check
     - we didn't just make a null move
     - we don't have a risk of zugzwang by being in the endgame
     - depth is >= R + 1
     what we do after null move:
     - if score is close to
         -mated, we're in danger, increase depth
     - if score is >= beta, we can get an early cutoff and exit */
```

```
if (do_null && null_red && piece_count >= 5 &&
        depth >= null_red+1) {
  /* update the rep_history just so things don't get funky: */
  rep_history[game_ply++] = cur_pos;
  fifty++;

  xor (&cur_pos, color_h_values[0]);
  xor (&cur_pos, color_h_values[1]);
  xor (&cur_pos, ep_h_values[ep_square]);
  xor (&cur_pos, ep_h_values[0]);

  white_to_move ^= 1;
  ply++;
  ep_square = 0;
  null_score = -search (-beta, -beta+1,
                          depth-null_red-1, FALSE);
  ep_square = ep_temp;
  ply-;
  white_to_move ^= 1;

  game_ply-;
  fifty-;

  xor (&cur_pos, color_h_values[0]);
  xor (&cur_pos, color_h_values[1]);
  xor (&cur_pos, ep_h_values[ep_square]);
  xor (&cur_pos, ep_h_values[0]);
  assert (cur_pos.x1 == compute_hash ().x1 &&
      cur_pos.x2 == compute_hash ().x2);

  /* check to see if we ran out of time: */
  if (time_exit)
return 0;

  /* check to see if we can get a quick
         cutoff from our null move: */
  if (null_score >= beta)
return beta;

  if (null_score < -INF+10*maxdepth)
extensions++;
  }
}
```

```
/* try to find a stable position before passing
        the position to eval (): */
if (!(depth+extensions)) {
  captures = TRUE;
  score = qsearch (alpha, beta, maxdepth);
  captures = FALSE;
  return score;
}

num_moves = 0;
no_moves = TRUE;

/* generate and order moves: */
gen (&moves[0], &num_moves);
order_moves (&moves[0], &move_ordering[0], num_moves, &h_move);

/* loop through the moves at the current node: */
while (remove_one (&i, &move_ordering[0], num_moves)) {

  make (&moves[0], i);
  assert (cur_pos.x1 == compute_hash ().x1 &&
      cur_pos.x2 == compute_hash ().x2);
  ply++;
  legal_move = FALSE;

  /* go deeper if it's a legal move: */
  if (check_legal (&moves[0], i)) {
    nodes++;
    score = -search (-beta, -alpha, depth-1+extensions, TRUE);
    no_moves = FALSE;
    legal_move = TRUE;
  }

  ply--;
  unmake (&moves[0], i);
  ep_square = ep_temp;
  cur_pos = temp_hash;

  /* return if we've run out of time: */
  if (time_exit) return 0;

  /* check our current score vs. alpha: */
  if (score > alpha && legal_move) {
```

```
      /* update the history heuristic since we have a cutoff: */
      history_h[moves[i].from][moves[i].target] += depth;

      /* try for an early cutoff: */
      if (score >= beta) {
   u_killers (moves[i], score);
   store_hash (i_alpha, depth, score, l_bound, moves[i]);
   return beta;
      }
      alpha = score;

      /* update the pv: */
      pv[ply][ply] = moves[i];
      for (j = ply+1; j < pv_length[ply+1]; j++)
   pv[ply][j] = pv[ply+1][j];
      pv_length[ply] = pv_length[ply+1];
   }

}

/* check for mate / stalemate: */
if (no_moves) {
  if (in_check ()) {
    alpha = -INF+ply;
  }
  else {
    alpha = 0;
  }
}
else {
  /* check the 50 move rule if no mate situation
          is on the board: */
  if (fifty > 100) {
    return 0;
  }
}

/* store our hash info: */
if (alpha > i_alpha)
  store_hash (i_alpha, depth, alpha, exact, pv[ply][ply]);
else
  store_hash (i_alpha, depth, alpha, u_bound, dummy);
```

```
    return alpha;


}
//--------------------
move_s think (void) {

  /* Perform iterative deepening to go further in the search */

  move_s comp_move, temp_move;
  int ep_temp, i, j;
  long int elapsed;

  /* see if we can get a book move: */
  comp_move = book_move ();
  if (is_valid_comp (comp_move)) {
    /* print out a pv line indicating a book move: */
    printf ("0 0 0 0 (Book move)\n");
    return (comp_move);
  }

  nodes = 0;
  qnodes = 0;
  allow_more_time = TRUE;

  /* allocate our time for this move: */
  time_for_move = allocate_time ();

  /* clear the pv before a new search: */
  for (i = 0; i < PV_BUFF; i++)
    for (j = 0; j < PV_BUFF; j++)
      pv[i][j] = dummy;

  /* clear the history heuristic: */
  memset (history_h, 0, sizeof (history_h));

  /* clear the killer moves: */
  for (i = 0; i < PV_BUFF; i++) {
    killer_scores[i] = -INF;
    killer_scores2[i] = -INF;
    killer1[i] = dummy;
    killer2[i] = dummy;
    killer3[i] = dummy;
  }
```

```
for (i_depth = 1; i_depth <= maxdepth; i_depth++) {
  /* don't bother going deeper if we've
          already used 2/3 of our time, and we
     have finished our mindepth search, since
          we likely won't finish */
  elapsed = rdifftime (rtime (), start_time);
  if (elapsed > time_for_move*2.0/3.0 && i_depth > mindepth)
    break;

  ep_temp = ep_square;
  temp_move = search_root (-INF, INF, i_depth);
  ep_square = ep_temp;

  /* if we haven't aborted our search on time,
          set the computer's move
     and post our thinking: */
  if (!time_failure) {
    /* if our search score suddenly drops, and
            we ran out of time on the
       search, just use previous results */
    comp_move = temp_move;
    last_root_score = cur_score;
    /* if our PV is really short, try to get some
            of it from hash info
       (don't modify this if it is a mate / draw though): */
    if (pv_length[1] <= 2 && i_depth > 1 &&
            abs (cur_score) < (INF-100) &&
        result != stalemate && result != draw_by_fifty &&
        result != draw_by_rep)
        hash_to_pv (i_depth);
    if (post && i_depth >= mindepth)
      post_thinking (cur_score);
  }

  /* reset the killer scores (we can keep the
          moves for move ordering for now, but the
          scores may not be accurate at higher depths, so we need
     to reset them): */
  for (j = 0; j < PV_BUFF; j++) {
    killer_scores[j] = -INF;
    killer_scores2[j] = -INF;
  }

}
```

```
/* update our elapsed time_cushion: */
if (moves_to_tc) {
  elapsed = rdifftime (rtime (), start_time);
  time_cushion += time_for_move-elapsed+inc;
}

return comp_move;

}
```

COMMON AI ELEMENTS

Classic strategy games don't typically require too much in the way of overall AI-controlled content. An opponent to play against, and in some cases a helper or tutorial system, is really all that these types of games implement.

OPPONENT AI

By definition, a zero-sum game must have an opponent to challenge. In an entertainment sense, this opponent must become another "person," in effect, and play the rules with some semblance of personality. For most games, this personality is simply represented by a difficulty rating. By playing against the program enough times at each rating, a human being will eventually determine the kinds of moves that the particular AI-controlled player will make and not make.

HELPER AI

Consumer games like chess usually include a tutor mode, in which the computer offers players a number of drills and lessons to improve their game. Although some games only provide minimal tutoring content in the form of scripted lessons, others actually include intelligent help systems that see flaws in the player's game and can steer to the person-scripted lessons, or give advice about a board setup in real time. Many people buy chess products for this feature alone, because they want to learn or improve their games by getting instruction and practice from the AI system. Other games like *Bridge* that have somewhat large or confusing rule sets also use helper-AI systems to teach the basic strategies of the game. It is very important, however, that such systems not be intrusive and can be ignored or switched off by the player so they don't feel "nagged" by the computer.

Useful AI Techniques

Classic strategy games tend to use different techniques than most other game genres. That doesn't stop them from using FSMs, though. In addition, the classic strategy genre also makes use of alpha-beta search, neural nets, and genetic algorithms.

Finite-State Machines (FSMs)

Most of these games are fairly linear (although some only have one basic state change: that of ending the game). The gameplay can be broken down into smaller parts (as in the opening, midgame, and endgame phases of chess), which are easily identifiable and can therefore allow the system to switch between different AI methods based on these sub-states.

Alpha-Beta Search

This is pretty much the *de facto* standard for search in classical games that need minimax trees searched. Minimax trees are specially set-up game-state trees, with the layers of the tree comprising nodes representing the choices each player can make, and in which the values associated with each node of the tree depict its closeness to a winning value (see Figure 12.3 for a simplified example of a minimax tree). The algorithm then follows at each choice, the first opponent moves with the max score at his level of the tree, and the other player plays the minimum scored at his. This is because the first player is trying to maximize his score, and the second player is trying to minimize the first player's score. This technique leads to an optimized move

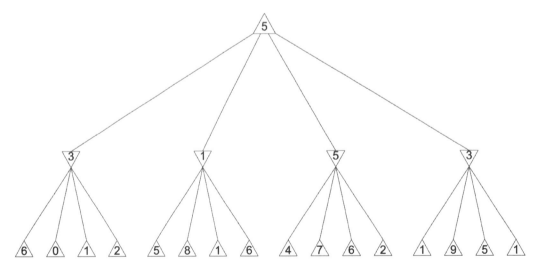

FIGURE 12.3 Simplified example of a minimax search tree showing one turn or "ply" for each player.

direction for these types of games, but has the problem of assuming a completely rational and defensive second player.

Minimax methods can be extended to games that also contain an element of pure chance, such as backgammon. This extension is called an *expectimax* tree and merely adds the element that a pure minimum and maximum value cannot be calculated at each tree node, thus introducing *chance* nodes that use an estimate of the random values that are being introduced into the game.

The problem with a full minimax search is that it takes into account the whole tree. Consider chess, for which, at any given board position, there are usually about 35 legal moves. This means that a 1-level search is 35 entries, 2 levels is 352, 6 levels is almost 2 billion entries, and a 10-level search (which is in reality only 5 moves per player) is more than 2 quadrillion tree nodes.

It is important to search as deeply as possible (average human players can usually make decisions based on looking 6 to 8 moves ahead, and grandmaster players sometimes make decisions 10 to 20 moves ahead). An alpha-beta search allows us to prune whole tree branches with total safety, so this vastly reduces the number of comparisons to perform, unless you get unlucky enough to have your game-state tree set up in the worst-case scenario, which would mean that the optimization would be completely nulled out, and you would end up performing a regular minimax search.

NEURAL NETS (NNs)

Strategy games with larger state spaces or somewhat strange evaluations of board positions (such as *Go*, in which most of the position scoring involves very esoteric things like "influence" and "territory") have lent themselves well to the kinds of esoteric knowledge that can be stored in NNs. However, this kind of data structure is fiendishly hard to train, and even harder to debug. It is used in these sorts of situations because nothing else will really do the job.

GENETIC ALGORITHMS (GAs)

GAs can be considered another type of search, the so-called *random walk* search. This means searching the state space for solutions using some form of guided randomness. In this case, we use natural selection as our guide, and random mutation as our random element. We will discuss more of the specifics of this family of algorithms in later in this book.

Examples

Chess computer programs have been with us since the creation of the computer, starting in the early 1950s; they are still among the more popular classic games played as an entertainment. Early commercial games, like *Sargon*, weren't terribly intelligent and ran quite slowly. Today, chess games have improved so much that you can go to the store and buy a grandmaster-level, very fast chess program to play against for less than thirty dollars. Over the years, some companies have tried to mix up the formula, while still keeping the same game, such as *Battle Chess* (1988), which showed animated death sequences whenever players took an opponent's piece.

Most strategy games play straightforwardly, without malice or bias. However, some people have crafted their games to have some semblance of personality, such as *Checkers with an Attitude*, from Digenetics™, a game using various neural nets to play a very good, and distinctly personable, game of checkers.

AREAS THAT NEED IMPROVEMENT

As with any game genre, there are always things that could be better. Classic strategy games can be a bit stuffy. Some advanced technqiues that give AI opponents creativity could give the genre some life. Plus, more CPU horsepower will always improve the overall speed of these games, such that they'll make better decisions in less time.

CREATIVITY

Extended use of GAs might lead these types of AI opponents to find increasingly nonintuitive solutions, which GAs are known for. GAs have the ability to find correlating features across a much larger number of variables simultaneously than many other techniques, sometimes leading them to surprising results. Also, different heuristic-based searches could be implemented with NNs or GAs determining the heuristic, again so that creative, local solutions could be found. In an indirect way, these solutions could be thought of as "creative" ways of playing the games, and could even change the way that people play. Real creativity might be a tall order, but by building strategy games to incorporate some of these more exotic techniques, games could eventually appear to players to utilize novel tactics and strategies.

SPEED

Speed is always an overriding factor in game AI programming, *especially* in strategy games, which may entail tremendous amounts of searching. By improving our brute-force methods, we may eventually find clever ways of arriving at decisions, without taking the time necessary to search massive trees to find the best solution. Or, the computers will just get so fast that the optimal search can be done trivially, and we'll take our AI somewhere else to play.

SUMMARY

Classic strategy games were some of the first to use academic AI techniques to build opponents because they represent the ideal candidate for AI-directed search methods. Strategy games have shown the entertainment industry the benefit of using real AI solutions for these types of problems (and for far less ideal situations like videogames) and have even provided us with most of our data structures and methodologies.

- Classic strategy games are defined as being zero-sum games of perfect information, with mostly global moves that are turn-based.
- The type of opponent AI you are coding is based on the type of game: a competition opponent requires optimal performance, but an entertainment opponent must use difficulty settings and such.
- Helper AI in entertainment strategy games is sometimes included for teaching and giving advice during practice games.
- FSMs can still be used in these games to break the state space into smaller chunks.
- Alpha-beta search is the primary opponent modeling means by which most classical strategy games consider opponent moves during planning.
- Genetic algorithms and neural nets can help facilitate directed search in new ways, or find unintuitive solutions.
- Creativity is a common lacking element in these games; they usually use more brute force in their search for the correct answer.
- Speed of the AI system is always a concern for these kinds of games because AI represents the largest percentage of the CPU time that the game is using.

13　Fighting Games

Fighting games are a strange mix of the action and opponent puzzle genres. In the arcades of the 1980s and 1990s, fighting games used to be *the* genre, easily outnumbering all other types of coin-operated games.

Early fighters, simple side-scrolling games with tough-sounding names *and* main characters (sometimes referred to as "brawlers" or "beat-em-ups," like *Double Dragon, Bad Dudes,* and *Final Fight*) were more like horizontal scrolling shooter games, in which you used martial arts instead of projectiles. Other types of early brawlers included boxing games (like Nintendo's *Punch Out*) and wrestling competitions (*Pro Wrestling,* for the NES). All these games were popular, but fighting games were still just another genre.

However, the fighting genre reached the height of popularity in the early 1990s with *Street Fighter 2: The World Warrior (SF2)* from Capcom (screenshot in Figure 13.1). *SF2* leapt onto the scene by taking the simple brawler formula and making the combat the entire experience, going over the top with concepts like combos, blocks, super moves, and in-your-face man-against-man action (although an earlier game, *Karate Champ,* did some of these things first, *SF2* did them all so much better that it stole the title of first real head-to-head fighter).

Arcades moved all their other machines out, and lined up *SF2* machines. People everywhere got in line, "put their quarter up" on the ledge of the machine, and waited their turns. One important thing that *SF2* did was to reintroduce the concept of complex game controls to the game world. The special moves that *SF2* required of its advanced players were unlike anything the game world had seen before, and people loved being able to pull off monster combinations using complex hand movements that took days or even weeks of practice.

FIGURE 13.1   *Street Fighter 2: The World Warrior* screenshot. © Capcom Co., Ltd. Reprinted with permission.

The game proved to be so popular that it is usually credited with being a major reason that the Super Nintendo console finally caught up in sales to the Sega Genesis; because the Super Nintendo version of *SF2* was a better version, fans couldn't get enough, and the sales of *SF2* and the SNES were 1 for 1 (meaning for every SNES console that was sold, a copy of *SF2* was also sold) for many months.

Fighters, like the other genres, gradually made the switch to three-dimensions, but not all the way. While games like *Virtua Fighter* and *Tekken Tag Tournament* (screenshot in Figure 13.2) carved niches for themselves using three-dimensional combat methods, the *Street Fighter* series stayed in the two-dimensional realm and instead created deeper systems of gameplay that couldn't be replicated in three-dimensions because of the problems with cameras, targeting, and the super-quick timing necessary to pull off the advanced moves.

Wrestling games didn't really suffer from the transition to three dimensions, however. Wrestling involves grappling (by definition), so the kinds of character interactions become much more numerous, and you can set up very deep chains of moves as the characters move into and out of various locks and takedowns by initiating attacks and counterattacks. The characters are grappled together, so they don't have the problems of lining up with their opponent, and the camera can be more tightly positioned because of the proximity of the wrestlers.

FIGURE 13.2   *Tekken Tag Tournament* screenshot. TEKKEN TAG TOURNAMENT® ©1994, 1995, 1996, 1999 Namco, Ltd., All rights reserved. Courtesy of Namco Holding Corp.

In recent years, even though fighting games have fallen from their number-one spot, they are still around and are invading other genres with games like *Buffy the Vampire Slayer,* which could be described as half-fighter and half-adventure game.

Such is the trend of all genres: start with a bang, and then develop until a level of maturity (and complexity) is reached. From there, any additional improvement is incremental at best. Languish in unpopularity for a while, and then in semidesperation, merge with other genres to add content and flavor to the experience.

COMMON AI ELEMENTS

Fighting games, like any genre that has started to merge with other genres, can sometimes contain a large number of AI-controlled components. Some of the commonly used elements in fighting games include: enemies, collision systems, boss enemies, cameras, and action adventure elements.

ENEMIES

The enemies in fighting games use some of the most heavily tuned and balanced opponent AI code ever written. One of the biggest selling points of most successful fighters was that the game was balanced; no one character was intrinsically easier to win with than any other. Some might be harder or easier to control, but with practice, you could be equally deadly with any of them.

Because of this, precise control over individual characters' moves, down to the single frame of animation level, was exercised by the game developers. As such, most of these games use a form of scripting language that can describe events on a frame-by-frame basis, including sounds, particle effects, turning on/off defensive and offensive collision spheres, marking points in the animation where branches are possible (for combos), and anything else the move might need to trigger. Character scripters would spend months working balance issues out of the game.

In some fighting games, the background is more than just a backdrop and might contain elements that can be used in battle, or hidden behind, or simply smashed to receive some kind of powerup. Enemies in these games need to be able to react intelligently with these elements as well. For instance, an enemy approaching the main character for a fight has a big wooden crate sitting in between himself and his opponent. Does he use an avoidance system to move around it? Does he pick it up and throw it either out of the way or at his opponent? Does he jump over it? Does he jump on top of it to gain a height advantage at the expense of agility of movement? Or does he just smash through it with a huge punch? These are the kinds of advanced decisions that your enemies might have to make if you're working on a fighting game with background interactions.

COLLISION SYSTEMS

Collision systems at the character level are also supremely important to the fighting genre. Each character typically had a number of collision areas, each of which might change size for any given animation frame, or even be disabled for certain periods of time. To facilitate gameplay, the collisions were never really physics-based but, rather, relied on tuned data that detailed such things as the amount of knock-back felt by each player, the animation to play upon collision, a sound or effect to spawn, any "recover" time associated with the move (meaning, the amount of time after a move that a player can't throw another move at all), and a host of other data values that the games needed.

BOSS ENEMIES

Like RPGs and some other genres, certain fighting games use boss enemies to treat the player to a bigger, nastier enemy at the end of the game, or each level. In the two-dimensional brawlers, these were sometimes the only memorable enemies in the whole game, another similarity to horizontal scrolling shooter games. Head-to-head fighting games traditionally only had one boss, the character a player had to fight after the player defeated everybody else. This character was traditionally very tough to beat, the difficulty being much harder than whatever the rest of the game was set at.

CAMERA

In the three-dimensional fighting games, you run into the problem of camera positioning, just as in three-dimensional platformers. However, because of the fast-paced nature and camera-relative controls that the fighting character is using, the camera for three-dimensional fighters needs special attention; otherwise, it will ruin the fighting game by messing up combos, causing moves to miss the target because of orientation problems, and generally make the game a mess to play.

Another difference from platform games is that the player really doesn't have the time to use a free-look camera because the player is engaged in close-quarters combat. Also, because there are potentially two (or more) human players, a free-look camera wouldn't be viable from a control or visibility standpoint. Therefore, a good algorithmic or tracked camera system is essential.

ACTION AND ADVENTURE ELEMENTS

Some of the genre-crossing variants to the fighting genre are using more action or adventure game ingredients. Some involve heavy amounts of exploration and puzzle solving similar to adventure games. But some also involve the jumping and climbing challenges of the platform game world. By blending in these additional game elements, developers are keeping the fighting game alive, while inventing new combinations of gameplay experiences that keep games fresh.

USEFUL AI TECHNIQUES

Fighters typically are not that complex in regard to code. Their development instead tends to be design intensive, so the techniques associated with them are typically more geared to designer implementation. FSMs still make a showing, but data-driven and scripted systems are the commonly used techniques here.

FINITE-STATE MACHINES (FSMs)

Fighting games are usually state-based, with the AI-controlled opponent performing a move, sitting there, or responding to a collision. A simple FSM can keep most fighter games in line and provide the developer with more than enough structure to add complexity without maintenance headaches. Usually the structure of any particular character's FSM is data driven in some way, to facilitate the fact that during tuning and play testing, the state diagram of any given character might change dramatically and often.

DATA-DRIVEN SYSTEMS

Fighting games employ a huge number of characters, moves, blocks, throws, and combos. Given the level of tuning and balance that these games require, driving the primary fighting engine with designer-accessible scripting is really the only way to go.

Usually, each move is scripted to allow very precise determination of attack, defense, combo branching, sound effects, collision times, and size of collision area, as well as damage inflicted. The collision system is usually quite complex (even the first *SF2* game had many collision areas per enemy sprite, with separate head, arms, body, legs, etc.), with data tables detailing the animations to play if areas on the enemy are hit, blocked, or whatever. Additional tables would describe the "personality" of each fighter, by listing out bias values on moves and combos, how aggressive the player was defensively, and just about everything else about the character.

SCRIPTING SYSTEMS

In addition to the notion that the designers need strict control over fighting animations (thus, they usually require a script to detail everything that needs to happen during each move), story elements and the like are still very prevalent. This occurs in some of the adventure-style fighting game variants especially, so scripting systems are used in fighters frequently.

Scripting systems are also useful for in-game cinematic moments, for example, when the fight starts and the characters enter the arena, or after someone wins and the winner exhibits some kind of victory dance. Hugely complex moves (sometimes called "super combos" or the like) might also require a level of scripting because super combos are usually constructed from other moves, all strung together in a specific fashion. Of course, you could implement this kind of behavior with state machines, but if your game is going to require scripting for other things, you might as well incorporate its use in other areas as well.

Examples

Early fighters were simple affairs. You usually had a punch button, or maybe a punch and kick button. Games in this realm were the side scrollers (or brawlers), such as *Bad Dudes, Kung-Fu Master, Golden Axe,* and *Ninja-Gaiden.* The enemies had very simple AI—usually they would just try to surround the player and throw whatever simple move or combination of moves they had in their arsenal. The side-scrolling fighters had boss characters, but the bosses were usually just very fast, or had a lot of hit points, or some huge weapon; they were almost never smarter.

Then the head-to-head fighters started appearing, and were so popular that many different game franchises were started: *Samurai Showdown, King of Fighters, Mortal Kombat,* and of course, the *Street Fighter* series. As the years progressed, sequels continued to be better, with more complex, more technically enhanced games.

The AI-controlled enemies in head-to-head fighting games were completely fleshed-out fighting opponents, with the full abilities of almost any human, and usually beyond. The difficulty of the AI could be set by the operator (in the arcades) or by the player (on the home consoles) to fit any user skill level—everything from totally inept to almost invincible. This was only possible because in the course of constructing these games, with their finely-tuned input windows, animation frame counting, and rigorously adjusted collision systems, the game developers allowed the entire system to be scaled up or down by raw difficulty, as well as time scaling (for various turbo speed modes of play). The scripts and data associated with each move could handle sliding skill levels internally.

The three-dimensional brawlers have also come a long way, with initial games like *Battle Area Toshinden* (the game that came with a lot of people's first Playstation console), all the way to the current brands: *Soul Calibur, Dead or Alive,* and the *Virtua Fighter* games. These games use all the data-driven AI systems of their two-dimensional brothers. They also use extensive camera work, and some even use a degree of pathfinding because of the advanced terrain usage.

Games like *Buffy the Vampire Slayer* (which used a popular license and lots of exploration challenges), *The Mark of Kri* (with its great integration of cinematics), and *Viewtiful Joe* (a throwback game that took today's advanced technology and married to it to a hardcore old-style brawler) are all examples of the use of heavy fighting systems in various other game types. All of these titles have used techniques from pure fighting games to solve specific combat problems, as well as have had to deal with the AI challenges preset in mainstream action and adventure games.

AREAS THAT NEED IMPROVEMENT

The primary interaction between players and AI-controlled fighting game characters is single combat. There will most likely always be room for games of this type, simply because this is a simple human please, that of man-on-man competition. It is a simplified "king of the hill" sort of game experience that resonates deeply with many game players. Some ways in which we could improve the fighting game experience include learning and additional crossover/story elements.

LEARNING

Fighting games are like most video games; eventually, the human will find a weak point and exploit it repeatedly to make the game easier for himself. This was evident even in *SF2*, where continually jumping and doing a fierce punch over and over again could almost always defeat the usually difficult character, Zangief. If poor Zangief had even a smidgen of learning AI, he could have eventually seen the pattern of the human's attacks, and taken precautions. A learning system could also help with general case exploits and actually help keep the gameplay even (against the computer at least) by having the AI notice if the human is repeating a single, very powerful attack and circumventing it.

An AI set to lower difficulty could even help out the player by adjusting its attack patterns if some of its attacks were always hitting. In this way, the fight would be a bit more interesting, even if the human kept making the same mistakes.

ADDITIONAL CROSSOVER/STORY ELEMENTS

Fighting games have barely begun to scratch the surface of genre crossover. Role playing elements have yet to be deeply explored. Imagine an open world game, where you find new fighting techniques, master them, and then fight in competitions against AI-controlled enemies or other human players. Boxing games are still very arena based, as opposed to having to build up your fighter outside the ring with an overall story thread that could take you from amateur to world champ.

Several fighting games (including *Fighter Maker* and *Mortal Kombat Armageddon*) included "create a fighter" modes within their games. However, these almost all used pre-made moves (that you could rename at best) and were more for making characters that you then used to play. Imagine a more open ended fighting game creation mode, where players would not only craft visual character distinctions, but could tweak the AI of a character so that they could custom create whole new characters complete with new ways of attacking the player. A game with a mode like this could become a sort of "gladiator" system, where players could pit fight their creations against one another to determine king of the hill status indirectly through the performance of the player's creations.

SUMMARY

Fighting games, both two-dimensional and three-dimensional, give the player a level of character control that most other games do not. They appeal to both twitch gamers (who love fast action, button-mashing style gameplay), as well as to tacticians who study the various blocking-and-attack systems looking for advantages as well as crowd-pleasing mega combos.

■ Fighting games started out as two-dimensional side-scrolling brawlers, with simple controls and little strategy.

■ Head-to-head fighters infused the genre with the depth of gameplay it needed to survive, and also made it the most popular genre for almost a decade.

■ Fighting game characters and boss enemies require heavy tuning to preserve game balance. This needs to be taken into account when coding them.

■ The collision systems used in fighters are also very complex, requiring much higher resolution of targets then most games.

■ The camera system (for three-dimensional fighters), and any additional action or adventure elements may also require AI code.

■ FSMs and scripting (or some other form of data-driven AI) constitute the most common means by which fighting game AI is created. Data driving a fighter is important because of the high amount of tuning and designer input that needs to occur at many levels of gameplay.

■ Learning in fighting games could help against AI exploits and keep gameplay from becoming repetitive. Continuing to explore crossover/story elements will extend the fighting game universe.

14 Miscellaneous Genres of Note

Although most games fall into the general categories explored in the previous chapters, many games are either hard to categorize, or in a class all by themselves. This chapter will highlight some of the most notable of these games and will briskly discuss the artificial intelligence methodologies used in their creation.

CIVILIZATION GAMES

Civilization (or civ) games are turn-based strategy games. These are *big* turn-based strategy games; sometimes with monstrous amounts of units to control, and hundreds of things for the player to manage and tweak on any given turn. Almost exclusively a PC genre (mostly because of interface concerns), there are a few console games of this type—*Final Fantasy Tactics* and even the handheld game *Advance Wars* are good examples.

The genre is almost owned by one man, Sid Meier. He was designing a spin-off of the 1989 hit game *SimCity*™ (which will be discussed later, with God games) when he came up with the idea, and two years later managed to create an entirely new genre. The game was called *Civilization,* and has since spawned an entire series, as well as dozens of other civ games. The *Civilization* series (Figures 14.1 and 14.2 show the evolution from *Civilization* to *Civilization 3*), as well as the recent *Alpha*

FIGURE 14.1 *Civilization* screenshot. Sid Meier's Civilization® and Sid Meier's Civilization® III courtesy of Atari Interactive, Inc. © 2004 Atari Interactive, Inc. All rights reserved. Used with permission.

Centauri and many others, are all civ games, with incredibly deep strategy, challenging AI systems, good interfaces, and almost infinite replay value. Some other great examples of civ games are *X-Com*, the *Heroes of Might and Magic* games, and the *Master of Orion* series.

In a turn-based interface, players (a mix of humans and AI opponents) take turns issuing orders to their armies, cities, etc., and then watch the turn's total activities unfold. This process continues, back and forth, until the game is over. The player can control everything: which battles are instigated, what cities and towns are producing, what types of research are being studied, what new inventions are having resources allocated to them, and so forth. These games can last a long time—many hours or even days. But, because of this turn-based mechanic, both sides have longer time in which to make decisions, and so deep gameplay strategies can emerge. The concept of bounded optimality discussed in Chapter 1, "Basic Definitions and Concepts," really takes effect here; the time restriction felt by more real-time AI systems is all but lifted for the AI-controlled opponents of these games. Humans don't really enjoy waiting for the computer to make moves and decisions, so the AI engines for most civ style games do many calculations while the human is performing his turn and, thus, can limit the amount of time taken for the computer opponent's turn.

FIGURE 14.2 *Civilization 3* screenshot. Sid Meier's Civilization® and Sid Meier's Civilization® III courtesy of Atari Interactive, Inc. © 2004 Atari Interactive, Inc. All rights reserved. Used with permission.

Unlike real-time strategy (RTS) games, these games have very little unit-based intelligence. Almost all decisions are strategic, with the conflicts between individual combat units (or even between units and defended cities) reduced to random rolls based on the unit's strength and defense numbers. This leads to more of a simulation feel, rather than the action element that individual combat adds to the RTS genre.

Typical AI systems used in civ games have the following attributes:

- They use most of the same types of AI methods required by RTS games, including finite-state machines (FSMs), fuzzy-state machines (FuSMs), hierarchical AI systems, good pathfinding, and messaging systems.
- Civ games borrow most of the support systems also used by RTS games, including terrain analysis, resource management, city planning techniques, and opponent modeling.

- A heavy data-driven element is usually employed because of the number of civilization types (as well as the many types of units, technologies, resources, etc.) usually represented in these games, as well as the heavy tuning required for balancing.

- Robust planning algorithms are used because these games usually have expansive technology trees and huge game worlds. See Listing 14.1 for a very small sample of AI code from *FreeCiv*, an open-source recreation of *Civilization*. *FreeCiv* has a huge following and has been ported to many platforms.

- Civ games have advanced AI systems for counselors and diplomacy. Many of these games have such a large amount of "work" to be done that some people would find it boring or tiresome to do everything, so the concept of counselors was introduced. These AI characters can offer to help the player with parts of the game that the player finds tedious or confusing by offering advice when asked. This system uses the AI decision-making engine to pass over the game world while the human is in control, and then inform the human what the computer would do right now, as a suggestion that can be taken or discarded. Typically, these counselors were specialized into the various parts of the game, such as trade, or research, or government. In that way, the player only needs to consult those counselors that the player wants to and can ignore the counselors at other times. Diplomacy systems are also much more complex. Different groups will make alliances, and leaders might manipulate, outright lie, or hold grudges. The states of mind of these diplomatic types varies greatly during a game, and satisfying everybody is not possible, just like in real life. In fact, in the original *Civilization,* it is all but impossible to run an entirely bloodless game, in which the civs all live in peace and prosperity until someone wins through technical superiority.

LISTING 14.1 Sample AI code from *FreeCiv.*

```
/**************************************************************
   Buy and upgrade stuff!
**************************************************************/
static void ai_spend_gold(struct player *pplayer)
{
  struct ai_choice bestchoice;
  int cached_limit = ai_gold_reserve(pplayer);

  /* Disband troops that are at home but don't serve a purpose. */
  city_list_iterate(pplayer->cities, pcity) {
    struct tile *ptile = map_get_tile(pcity->x, pcity->y);
    unit_list_iterate(ptile->units, punit) {
      if (((unit_types[punit->type].shield_cost > 0
            && pcity->shield_prod == 0)
```

```
          || unit_has_role(punit->type, L_EXPLORER))
        && pcity->id == punit->homecity
        && pcity->ai.urgency == 0
        && is_ground_unit(punit)) {
      struct packet_unit_request packet;
      packet.unit_id = punit->id;
      CITY_LOG(LOG_BUY, pcity,
                    "disbanding %s to increase production",
              unit_name(punit->type));
      handle_unit_disband(pplayer, &packet);
    }
  } unit_list_iterate_end;
} city_list_iterate_end;

do {
  int limit = cached_limit; /* cached_limit is our gold reserve */
  struct city *pcity = NULL;
  bool expensive; /* don't buy when it costs x2 unless we must */
  int buycost;

  /* Find highest wanted item on the buy list */
  init_choice(&bestchoice);
  city_list_iterate(pplayer->cities, acity) {
    if (acity->anarchy != 0) continue;
    if (acity->ai.choice.want > bestchoice.want &&
                                  ai_fuzzy(pplayer, TRUE))
        {
      bestchoice.choice = acity->ai.choice.choice;
      bestchoice.want = acity->ai.choice.want;
      bestchoice.type = acity->ai.choice.type;
      pcity = acity;
    }
  } city_list_iterate_end;

  /* We found nothing, so we're done */
  if (bestchoice.want == 0) break;

  /* Not dealing with this city a second time */
  pcity->ai.choice.want = 0;

  ASSERT_REAL_CHOICE_TYPE(bestchoice.type);

  /* Try upgrade units at danger location
        * (high want is usually danger) */
```

```
if (pcity->ai.danger > 1) {
  if (bestchoice.type == CT_BUILDING &&
          is_wonder(bestchoice.choice)) {
    CITY_LOG(LOG_BUY, pcity,
                "Wonder being built in dangerous position!");
  } else {
    /* If we have urgent want, spend more */
    int upgrade_limit = limit;
    if (pcity->ai.urgency > 1) {
      upgrade_limit = pplayer->ai.est_upkeep;
    }
    /* Upgrade only military units now */
    ai_upgrade_units(pcity, upgrade_limit, TRUE);
  }
}

/* Cost to complete production */
buycost = city_buy_cost(pcity);

if (buycost <= 0) {
  continue; /* Already completed */
}

if (bestchoice.type != CT_BUILDING
    && unit_type_flag(bestchoice.choice, F_CITIES)) {
  if (!city_got_effect(pcity, B_GRANARY)
      && pcity->size == 1
      && city_granary_size(pcity->size)
         > pcity->food_stock + pcity->food_surplus) {
    /* Don't build settlers in size 1
         * cities unless we grow next turn */
    continue;
  } else {
    if (city_list_size(&pplayer->cities) <= 8) {
      /* Make AI get gold for settlers early game */
      pplayer->ai.maxbuycost =
                        MAX(pplayer->ai.maxbuycost, buycost);
    } else if (city_list_size(&pplayer->cities) > 25) {
      /* Don't waste precious money buying settlers late game */
      continue;
    }
  }
} else {
  /* We are not a settler. Therefore we
```

```
              * increase the cash need we
     * balance our buy desire with to
            * keep cash at hand for emergencies
     * and for upgrades */
    limit *= 2;
}

/* It costs x2 to buy something with no shields contributed */
expensive = (pcity->shield_stock == 0)
              || (pplayer->economic.gold - buycost < limit);

if (bestchoice.type == CT_ATTACKER
    && buycost > unit_types[bestchoice.choice].build_cost * 2) {
    /* Too expensive for an offensive unit */
    continue;
}

if (!expensive && bestchoice.type != CT_BUILDING
    && (unit_type_flag(bestchoice.choice, F_TRADE_ROUTE)
        || unit_type_flag(bestchoice.choice, F_HELP_WONDER))
    && buycost < unit_types[bestchoice.choice].build_cost * 2) {
  /* We need more money for buying caravans. Increasing
     maxbuycost will increase taxes */
  pplayer->ai.maxbuycost = MAX(pplayer->ai.maxbuycost, buycost);
}

/* FIXME: Here Syela wanted some code to check if
 * pcity was doomed, and we should therefore attempt
 * to sell everything in it of non-military value */

if (pplayer->economic.gold - pplayer->ai.est_upkeep >= buycost
    && (!expensive
        || (pcity->ai.grave_danger != 0 &&
                assess_defense(pcity) == 0)
        || (bestchoice.want > 200 && pcity->ai.urgency > 1))) {
  /* Buy stuff */
  CITY_LOG(LOG_BUY, pcity, "Crash buy of %s for %d (want %d)",
           bestchoice.type != CT_BUILDING ?
                 unit_name(bestchoice.choice)
           : get_improvement_name(bestchoice.choice), buycost,
           bestchoice.want);
  really_handle_city_buy(pplayer, pcity);
} else if (pcity->ai.grave_danger != 0
           && bestchoice.type == CT_DEFENDER
           && assess_defense(pcity) == 0) {
```

```
      /* We have no gold but MUST have a defender */
      CITY_LOG(LOG_BUY, pcity,
                "must have %s but can't afford it (%d < %d)!",
          unit_name(bestchoice.choice),
                pplayer->economic.gold, buycost);
      try_to_sell_stuff(pplayer, pcity);
      if (pplayer->economic.gold - pplayer->ai.est_upkeep >=
              buycost) {
        CITY_LOG(LOG_BUY, pcity,
                      "now we can afford it (sold something)");
        really_handle_city_buy(pplayer, pcity);
      }
      if (buycost > pplayer->ai.maxbuycost) {
        /* Consequently we need to raise more money through taxes */
        pplayer->ai.maxbuycost =
                              MAX(pplayer->ai.maxbuycost, buycost);
      }
    }
  } while (TRUE);

  /* Civilian upgrades now */
  city_list_iterate(pplayer->cities, pcity) {
    ai_upgrade_units(pcity, cached_limit, FALSE);
  } city_list_iterate_end;

  if (pplayer->economic.gold + cached_limit <
          pplayer->ai.maxbuycost) {
    /* We have too much gold! Don't raise taxes */
    pplayer->ai.maxbuycost = 0;
  }

  freelog(LOG_BUY, "%s wants to keep %d in reserve (tax factor %d)",
          pplayer->name, cached_limit, pplayer->ai.maxbuycost);
}
#undef LOG_BUY

/*********************************************************************
 cities, build order and worker allocation stuff here..
 *********************************************************************/
void ai_manage_cities(struct player *pplayer)
{
  int i;
  pplayer->ai.maxbuycost = 0;
```

```
city_list_iterate(pplayer->cities, pcity)
  ai_manage_city(pplayer, pcity);
city_list_iterate_end;


ai_manage_buildings(pplayer);


city_list_iterate(pplayer->cities, pcity)
  military_advisor_choose_build(pplayer, pcity,
                                   &pcity->ai.choice);
  /* note that m_a_c_b mungs the seamap, but we don't care */
  establish_city_distances(pplayer, pcity);
      /* in advmilitary for warmap */
  /* e_c_d doesn't even look at the seamap */
  /* determines downtown and distance_
      * to_wondercity, which a_c_c_b will need */
  contemplate_terrain_improvements(pcity);
  contemplate_new_city(pcity);
      /* while we have the warmap handy */
  /* seacost may have been munged if we found
      * a boat, but if we found a boat we don't rely on the seamap
      * being current since we will recalculate. — Syela */


city_list_iterate_end;


city_list_iterate(pplayer->cities, pcity)
  ai_city_choose_build(pplayer, pcity);
city_list_iterate_end;


ai_spend_gold(pplayer);


/* use ai_gov_tech_hints: */
for(i=0; i<MAX_NUM_TECH_LIST; i++) {
  struct ai_gov_tech_hint *hint = &ai_gov_tech_hints[i];

  if (hint->tech == A_LAST)
    break;
  if (get_invention(pplayer, hint->tech) != TECH_KNOWN) {
    pplayer->ai.tech_want[hint->tech] +=
    city_list_size(&pplayer->cities) * (hint->turns_factor *
                        num_unknown_techs_for_goal
                        (pplayer,
                         hint->tech) +
                        hint->const_factor);
```

```
        if (hint->get_first)
     break;
     } else {
       if (hint->done)
     break;
     }
   }
 }
```

On October 28, 2003, Activision® released the source code for *Call to Power II,* an offshoot from the main *Civilization* line. The game has been heralded by its many fans for the level of extensibility it allows. It contains a very powerful scripting system (in fact, before the source was released, a number of actual bugs in the game code had clever game players creating script-based workarounds and distributing them on the Internet).

GOD GAMES

Another genre that is unique and virtually owned by a few franchises is the "God game." They are called God games because the player takes the role of creator, over-seer, and the force of change for the entirety of the game, yet does not have *direct* control over the other inhabitants of the game.

In some ways, this makes the experience much like an artificial life (alife) game, but on a much larger scale. Alife games are usually about molding just one creature (or maybe a few) by training and caring for them somewhat directly. God games give players more global control, affecting the lives of many. The two fathers of the genre, Will Wright and Peter Molyneux, designed and created the earliest God games. Wright's game, released in 1987, is called *SimCity*™ (see Figures 14.3 and 14.4 for screens from *SimCity* and *SimCity 2000*™). *SimCity* was a real-time game, in which the player builds an ever-growing city and tries to keep the AI-controlled city inhabitants happy and healthy. In 1989, Molyneux released *Populous*™ (screenshot in Figure 14.5), which took the concept one step further by casting the player in the position of the Supreme Being over the land.

The player could create and destroy land elements, used far reaching powers to create plagues or volcanoes, and tried to get the game's inhabitants to worship the player which added to the player's power. Over the years, both Wright and Molyneux have both released additional games in this genre, including *SimCity* variants (*SimAnt*™, *SimEarth*™, *SimFarm*™, etc.) from Wright's camp, and games like *Dungeon Keeper*™ and *Populous 2* from Molyneux. Both men are

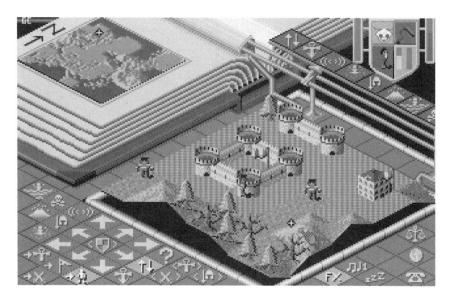

FIGURE 14.3   *SimCity* screenshot. Populous, SimCity, SimCity 2000 and Ultima 7 screenshots
© 2004 Electronic Arts Inc. Populous, SimCity, SimCity 2000, SimAnt, SimEarth, SimFarm,
Dungeon Keeper, The Sims and Ultima are trademarks or registered trademarks of Electronics
Arts Inc. in the U.S. and/or other countries. All rights reserved.

currently working on projects that evolve more into the alife genre and will be
discussed later.

This style of game requires a large quantitiy of strategic AI for the opponent,
if there is one. But in many of these games, especially the *SimCity* variants, there
are no strategic AI systems at all. The human supplies all the strategic decisions for
his or her side, and the "opponent" is merely the force of entropy. The game will
incrementally add elements to the simulation that require player supervision, or
constantly try to tear down whatever structure, city, and so forth that the player
is trying to build with random accidents, durability issues, increasing occupants,
resource demands on the system, and the like.

All these games have one type of AI element in common—the somewhat autonomous characters that the player rules over as a supreme being, be they humans or
ants, etc. They are the beings that will inhabit and live under the light of the player's
rule. Generally, these individual characters are brought into the game world as a collection of needs: each being needs X amount of food, Y amount of space, and Z
amount of happiness (or the equivalent for any particular game). They will wander
through the game world, looking for ways in which to satisfy these needs, and if a
player has set up the city, world, or ant farm correctly, the characters will find satisfaction. If not, the characters get angry or leave, costing the player simulation setbacks.

FIGURE 14.4   *SimCity 2000* screenshot. Populous, SimCity, SimCity 2000 and Ultima 7 screenshots © 2004 Electronic Arts Inc. Populous, SimCity, SimCity 2000, SimAnt, SimEarth, SimFarm, Dungeon Keeper, The Sims and Ultima are trademarks or registered trademarks of Electronics Arts Inc. in the U.S. and/or other countries. All rights reserved.

Typical AI systems used in God games are the following:

■ Like civ games, this genre uses the same strategic AI systems as RTS games, but only if there is an opponent god that competes with the player for followers or control of the world and that would require this kind of decision-making ability.

■ Autonomous characters most likely use a state-based system of needs. At the top level, each basic need would be tied to a state, such as GetFood or GetAHouse, the activation of which would be the perception that the characters were hungry or homeless. The actions the characters take during each state would then get them the required resource, ending the perception that they need it, and thus, changing their state. A well-balanced game of this type will almost never have an autonomous character needing nothing; characters will always be in a state of getting something, and always be busy.

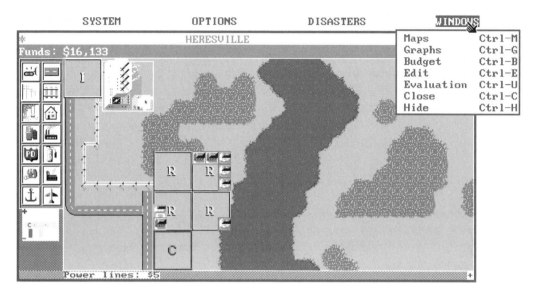

FIGURE 14.5 *Populous* screenshot. Populous, SimCity, SimCity 2000 and Ultima 7 screenshots © 2004 Electronic Arts Inc. Populous, SimCity, SimCity 2000, SimAnt, SimEarth, SimFarm, Dungeon Keeper, The Sims and Ultima are trademarks or registered trademarks of Electronics Arts Inc. in the U.S. and/or other countries. All rights reserved.

■ The "world" AI level determines that the player's town is attractive enough so that more people would flock to it, or sets off random events to further challenge the player. This includes the so-called *rules* of the game, which in most games includes things like the physical laws, as well as provisions for magic or respawning when a character dies. In God games, however, the rules might be the actual opponent with whom the player is competing. So, the player must keep in mind rules such as "There must be 50 square feet of living space for each person in the city," and "For every 300 worshippers, you must build another temple," lest the player's control over the game starts to slip away.

WAR GAMES

Not referring to the recent glut of war-themed FTPS games (like *Battlefield:1942* or *WW2Online*), this group instead pertains to the classic turn-based strategy war games with no or very indirect control of an economy to restock armies. These games try to restage historic battles so that armchair generals can see if they have the same instincts as the professionals, or could have even done it better. These games have always been a niche market, even in their original form as very complex board games. Avalon Hill is the company that created most of the better-known board games, and most of the successful computer war games have some basis, or are actually renditions of, the classic Avalon Hill games.

These games require much more realistic simulation than do regular strategy games because historic recreation is the entire point. If elements don't act the way they did in real life, the game will be unacceptable to the tiny niche market the game designer is shooting for in the first place. Things like terrain traversal, line-of-sight calculations, realistic weather simulations, and statistical modeling of almost every angle of combat are paramount to the success of the war simulation.

Some examples of good war games include the *Combat Mission* games and the *Airborne Assault* series. Listing 14.2 shows a function, buildObjective(), from the open-source project *Wargamer: Napoleon 1813*. The game, originally published in 1999 by Empire® Interactive, is a deep simulation of some of Napoleon's most famous battles and has been taken over by the open-source community. The sample function is part of a higher-level system that the AI is using to determine strategic plans for the future.

LISTING 14.2 buildObjective() from *Wargamer: Napoleon 1813*. Distributed under the GNU license.

```cpp
bool AIC_ObjectiveCreator::buildObjective(const AIC_TownInfo& tInfo)
{
#ifdef DEBUG
    d_sData->logWin("Assigning units to %s", d_sData->campData()->
                                        getTownName(tInfo.town()));
#endif

    /*
     * Pass 1:
     *     build list of units and keep track of SPs removed from
     *     other objectives
     *
     *     Ony units that would not destroy an objective with
     *     a higher townImportance can be used
     */

    std::map<ITown, int, std::less<int> > otherObjectives;
    std::vector<TownInfluence::Unit> allocatedUnits;

    SPCount spNeeded = d_townInfluence.spNeeded();
    SPCount spAlloced = 0;
    SPCount spToAllocate = d_sData->rand(spNeeded,
                            d_townInfluence.spAvailable());
```

```
    TownInfluence::Unit infUnit;
    while((spAlloced < spToAllocate) &&
      d_townInfluence.pickAndRemove(&infUnit))
    {
        ASSERT(infUnit.cp() != NoCommandPosition);

        if(infUnit.cp()->isDead())
          continue;

        AIC_UnitRef aiUnit = d_units->getOrCreate(infUnit.cp());
        TownInfluence::Influence unitInfluence = infUnit.influence();
        // friendlyInfluence.influence(aiUnit.cp());

        float oldPriority = d_townInfluence.effectivePriority(aiUnit);
        if(unitInfluence >= oldPriority)
        {
            SPCount spCount = aiUnit.spCount();

#ifdef DEBUG
            d_sData->logWin("Picked %s [SP=%d, pri=%f / %f]",
              (const char*) infUnit.cp()->getName(),
              (int) spCount,
              (float) unitInfluence,
              (float) oldPriority);
#endif

            /*
             * If it already has an objective
             * Then update the otherObjective list
             */

            AIC_Objective* oldObjective = aiUnit.objective();
            if(oldObjective)
            {
              ITown objTown = oldObjective->town();

              if (spAlloced > spNeeded)
              {

#ifdef DEBUG
                d_sData->logWin("Not using %s from %s because we already have
                enough SPs",
                  (const char*) infUnit.cp()->getName(),
                  (const char*) d_sData->campData()->
                              getTownName(objTown));
#endif
```

```
                continue;
            }


        if (objTown != tInfo.town())
        {
            const AIC_TownInfo& objTownInf =
                        d_towns->find(objTown);
            if(objTownInf.importance() >= tInfo.importance())
            {
                int* otherCount = 0;
                if(otherObjectives.find(objTown) ==
                    otherObjectives.end())
                {
                    otherCount = &otherObjectives[objTown];
                    *otherCount = oldObjective->spAllocated() -
                                oldObjective->spNeeded();
                }
                else
                    otherCount = &otherObjectives[objTown];

                if(*otherCount >= spCount)
                    *otherCount -= spCount;
                else
                {
#ifdef DEBUG
                    d_sData->logWin("Can not use %s because it would break
objective at %s",
                        (const char*) infUnit.cp()->getName(),
                        (const char*) d_sData->campData()->
                                    getTownName(objTown));
#endif
                    continue;
                }
            }
        }
    }

    allocatedUnits.push_back(infUnit);
    spAlloced += spCount;
    }
}
```

```
    if (spAlloced < spNeeded)
    {
#ifdef DEBUG
        d_sData->logWin("Can not be achieved without breaking more important
        objective");
#endif
        return false;
    }

    /*
     * Assign the allocated Units to objective
     */

    Writer lock(d_objectives);

    AIC_Objective* objective = d_objectives->
                            addOrUpdate(tInfo.town(), tInfo.importance());
    ASSERT(objective != 0);
    if(objective == 0)    //lint !e774 ... always true
        return false;

#ifdef DEBUG
    d_sData->logWin("Creating Objective %s", d_sData->campData()->
                                        getTownName(tInfo.town()));
    d_sData->logWin("There are %d objectives", (int)d_objectives->size());
#endif

    objective->spNeeded(spNeeded);

    for (std::vector<TownInfluence::Unit>::iterator it =
            allocatedUnits.begin();
        it != allocatedUnits.end();
        ++it)
    {
        const TownInfluence::Unit& infUnit = *it;

        AIC_UnitRef aiUnit = d_units->getOrCreate(infUnit.cp());
        TownInfluence::Influence unitInfluence = infUnit.influence();
        // friendlyInfluence.influence(aiUnit.cp());

#ifdef DEBUG
        d_sData->logWin("Adding %s",
            (const char*) infUnit.cp()->getName());
#endif
```

```
      // Remove unit from its existing Objective
      // Unless it is already attached to this one

      AIC_Objective* oldObjective = aiUnit.objective();

      if(oldObjective != objective)
      {
         if(oldObjective != 0)
         {
            // Remove Unit from Objective
            // If objective does not have enough SPs then
            // remove the objective

            removeUnit(infUnit.cp());
         }

         ASSERT(aiUnit.objective() == 0);

         // Add it to the objective table

         aiUnit.objective(objective);
         objective->addUnit(infUnit.cp());
      }

      // Set priority to a higher value to
      // reduce the problem of objectives being
      // created and destroyed too quickly.

      const float PriorityObjectiveIncrease = 1.5;
      aiUnit.priority(unitInfluence * PriorityObjectiveIncrease);
   }

#ifdef DEBUG
   if(d_objectiveDisplay)
      d_objectiveDisplay->update();
   if(campaign)
      campaign->repaintMap();
#endif

   return true;
}
```

Typical AI systems used in war games are the following:

1. The same level of strategic AI found in civ games is used, but in war games, the AI is focused more on direct combat experiences.
2. Data-driven systems are often employed because most of these games have huge numbers of battles in which the can engage, as well as numerous statistical details for each piece of equipment, tactical unit, and location.
3. Scripting comes into play quite regularly, to accurately model unusual or signature battle movements and strategies that were used by specific commanders in particular battles.

FLIGHT SIMULATORS (SIMS)

Another niche market, flight simulators (sims), try to accurately model the piloting of specific planes and give the player a realistic cockpit view and all the controls the player would use in an actual aircraft. The most popular example is the *Microsoft Flight Simulator,* which originally came out in 1982 and is still going strong today. Even though pure flight sims have no real AI (players are basically fighting gravity, trying not to crash), some variants to the flight sim model were released, in an attempt to make a more mass-appeal game.

Some of the most famous of these "popularized flight sims" were based on the Star Wars universe, such as *X-Wing* and *Tie Fighter.* Both of these games were much lighter on their flight sim elements (there were only a handful of cockpit controls, and players flew in outer space, so they didn't have stalls or strange atmospheric disturbances). They simulation was just enough to immerse the player in the Star Wars world without overwhelming the player, and gave many more people a taste for the flight sim experience than had ever tried it before. The *Wing Commander* series was also in this category, though perhaps focusing even less on realism and even more on an immersive experience.

Other games, like *Descent,* took the flight sim to the world of the FTPS game. *Descent* was deathmatch play with flying vehicles. The *Privateer* and *Freelancer* games added a full story to a light flight sim, and did very well. Also in this grouping are the numerous war-based flight sims, in which players perform historic missions, just like in war games, but from the cockpit of one of the planes involved, for a more personal feel.

Typical AI systems used in flight sims are the following:

1. The pure flight sims have no competitive AI elements—players are simply fighting the forces of physics, mostly gravity and aerodynamics, to keep control over an aircraft. Some of these games do have a form of AI system

for teaching the player how to pilot the plane, but it is usually just scripted sequences to show the various aircraft systems and abilities. Listing 14.3 shows the main AI loop for the open-source flight sim project *FlightGear*, which has simple AI elements that will engage in dogfights with the player.

2. Action-oriented flight sims are like action racing games in that they need AI systems that can competently handle the vehicles of the game, as well as deal with the additional elements (combat, using powerups, etc.) that the game brings. These games might also include land-based AI-controlled enemies and require additional functionality beyond simple vehicular control. These games are much like other complex, genre-combining games and use a mixture of FSMs, messaging, and scripting.

LISTING 14.3 Main AI Loop from *FlightGear*. Distributed by the GNU license.

```
void FGAIAircraft::Run(double dt) {

  FGAIAircraft::dt = dt;

  double turn_radius_ft;
  double turn_circum_ft;
  double speed_north_deg_sec;
  double speed_east_deg_sec;
  double ft_per_deg_lon;
  double ft_per_deg_lat;
  double dist_covered_ft;
  double alpha;

  // get size of a degree at this latitude
  ft_per_deg_lat = 366468.96 - 3717.12 *
                   cos(pos.lat()/SG_RADIANS_TO_DEGREES);
  ft_per_deg_lon = 365228.16 * cos(pos.lat() /
                   SG_RADIANS_TO_DEGREES);

  // adjust speed
  double speed_diff = tgt_speed - speed;
  if (fabs(speed_diff) > 0.2) {
    if (speed_diff > 0.0) speed += performance->accel * dt;
    if (speed_diff < 0.0) speed -= performance->decel * dt;
  }

  // convert speed to degrees per second
  speed_north_deg_sec = cos( hdg / SG_RADIANS_TO_DEGREES )
                        * speed * 1.686 / ft_per_deg_lat;
```

```
speed_east_deg_sec  = sin( hdg / SG_RADIANS_TO_DEGREES )
                       * speed * 1.686 / ft_per_deg_lon;

// set new position
pos.setlat( pos.lat() + speed_north_deg_sec * dt);
pos.setlon( pos.lon() + speed_east_deg_sec * dt);

// adjust heading based on current bank angle
if (roll != 0.0) {
  turn_radius_ft = 0.088362 * speed * speed
                      / tan( fabs(roll) / SG_RADIANS_TO_DEGREES );
  turn_circum_ft = SGD_2PI * turn_radius_ft;
  dist_covered_ft = speed * 1.686 * dt;
  alpha = dist_covered_ft / turn_circum_ft * 360.0;
  hdg += alpha * sign( roll );
  if ( hdg > 360.0 ) hdg -= 360.0;
  if ( hdg < 0.0) hdg += 360.0;
}

// adjust target bank angle if heading lock engaged
if (hdg_lock) {
  double bank_sense = 0.0;
  double diff = fabs(hdg - tgt_heading);
  if (diff > 180) diff = fabs(diff - 360);
  double sum = hdg + diff;
  if (sum > 360.0) sum -= 360.0;
  if (fabs(sum - tgt_heading) < 1.0) {
    bank_sense = 1.0;
  } else {
    bank_sense = -1.0;
  }
  if (diff < 30) tgt_roll = diff * bank_sense;
}

// adjust bank angle
double bank_diff = tgt_roll - roll;
if (fabs(bank_diff) > 0.2) {
  if (bank_diff > 0.0) roll += 5.0 * dt;
  if (bank_diff < 0.0) roll -= 5.0 * dt;
}

// adjust altitude (meters) based on current vertical speed (fpm)
altitude += vs * 0.0166667 * dt * SG_FEET_TO_METER;
double altitude_ft = altitude * SG_METER_TO_FEET;
```

```
// find target vertical speed if altitude lock engaged
if (alt_lock) {
  if (altitude_ft < tgt_altitude) {
    tgt_vs = tgt_altitude - altitude_ft;
    if (tgt_vs > performance->climb_rate)
      tgt_vs = performance->climb_rate;
  } else {
    tgt_vs = tgt_altitude - altitude_ft;
    if (tgt_vs  < (-performance->descent_rate))
      tgt_vs = -performance->descent_rate;
  }
}

// adjust vertical speed
double vs_diff = tgt_vs - vs;
if (fabs(vs_diff) > 1.0) {
  if (vs_diff > 0.0) {
    vs += 400.0 * dt;
    if (vs > tgt_vs) vs = tgt_vs;
  } else {
    vs -= 300.0 * dt;
    if (vs < tgt_vs) vs = tgt_vs;
  }
}

// match pitch angle to vertical speed
pitch = vs * 0.005;

//#########################//
// do calculations for radar //
//#########################//

// copy values from the AIManager
double user_latitude  = manager->get_user_latitude();
double user_longitude = manager->get_user_longitude();
double user_altitude  = manager->get_user_altitude();
double user_heading   = manager->get_user_heading();
double user_pitch     = manager->get_user_pitch();
double user_yaw       = manager->get_user_yaw();
double user_speed     = manager->get_user_speed();

// calculate range to target in feet and nautical miles
double lat_range = fabs(pos.lat() - user_latitude) *
                          ft_per_deg_lat;
```

```
   double lon_range = fabs(pos.lon() - user_longitude) *
                                   ft_per_deg_lon;
   double range_ft  = sqrt(lat_range*lat_range +
                                   lon_range*lon_range );
   range = range_ft / 6076.11549;

   // calculate bearing to target
   if (pos.lat() >= user_latitude) {
      bearing = atan2(lat_range, lon_range) * SG_RADIANS_TO_DEGREES;
        if (pos.lon() >= user_longitude) {
           bearing = 90.0 - bearing;
        } else {
           bearing = 270.0 + bearing;
        }
   } else {
      bearing = atan2(lon_range, lat_range) * SG_RADIANS_TO_DEGREES;
        if (pos.lon() >= user_longitude) {
           bearing = 180.0 - bearing;
        } else {
           bearing = 180.0 + bearing;
        }
   }

   // calculate look left/right to target, without yaw correction
   horiz_offset = bearing - user_heading;
   if (horiz_offset > 180.0) horiz_offset -= 360.0;
   if (horiz_offset < -180.0) horiz_offset += 360.0;

   // calculate elevation to target
   elevation = atan2( altitude_ft - user_altitude, range_ft )
                     * SG_RADIANS_TO_DEGREES;

   // calculate look up/down to target
   vert_offset = elevation + user_pitch;

/* this calculation needs to be fixed
   // calculate range rate
   double recip_bearing = bearing + 180.0;
   if (recip_bearing > 360.0) recip_bearing -= 360.0;
   double my_horiz_offset = recip_bearing - hdg;
   if (my_horiz_offset > 180.0) my_horiz_offset -= 360.0;
   if (my_horiz_offset < -180.0) my_horiz_offset += 360.0;
   rdot =(-user_speed * cos(horiz_offset * SG_DEGREES_TO_RADIANS ))
             + (-speed * 1.686 * cos( my_horiz_offset *
                                      SG_DEGREES_TO_RADIANS ));
*/
```

```
    // now correct look left/right for yaw
    horiz_offset += user_yaw;

    // calculate values for radar display
    y_shift = range * cos( horiz_offset * SG_DEGREES_TO_RADIANS);
    x_shift = range * sin( horiz_offset * SG_DEGREES_TO_RADIANS);
    rotation = hdg - user_heading;
    if (rotation < 0.0) rotation += 360.0;


}
```

RHYTHM GAMES

A popular genre of game that has recently been developed is the rhythm game. In some ways, they are the videogame equivalent to the 1978 classic handheld electronic game *Simon,* in which the player is supposed to repeat increasingly long sequences of a musical and visual pattern. The first rhythm game was the 1997 game *PaRappa The Rapper.* Since then, games have included everything from singing, to playing various instruments, to dancing. They all follow the same *Simon* formula, for the most part. These games are really puzzle games, but are much more patterned, so that players who continue to replay the games can get further and further along.

In 2005, a new rhythm game property was created by Harmonix Music Systems, called *Guitar Hero.* This game came out for the Playstation 2 platform, and included a large plastic guitar-like peripheral which served as the player's controller instead of the standard pad. This did two things: it gave the player a much more immersive guitar experience, and also propelled *Guitar Hero* from mere game into the realm of cultural phenomenon, selling over 1.5 million copies. Subsequent sequels have pushed the franchise to earnings of over $1 billion, at more than 21 million units as of 2008. In 2007, a "competitor" finally appeared, in the guise of *Rock Band.* Calling this game a competitor is strange because the creator of *Rock Band* is also Harmonix, having been removed from creating further *Guitar Hero* games in 2006 following several corporate acquisitions. But things worked out for the best. Now we have two franchises that are very well done, and differentiated enough that they're not stealing each other's thunder. The *Rock Band* franchise has also sold millions of copies, and with its ability to download additional music packs, it has created an entirely new income stream for EA, who distributes the game.

Both of these games build on *PaRappa's* use of the *Simon* formula by timing the hitting of streaming "notes" using the controller. But with the immersive quality of the controllers (*Rock Band* actually includes a multitude of instruments, including bass/lead guitar, drums, and a microphone), and the very addictive social aspects of the game (some bars have *Guitar Hero* night somewhat like karaoke, and people will gather for large *Rock Band* parties at a friend's house) these franchises have proven to be a world-spanning hit for the developers, and one that it sure to stick around for a while.

Although many of these games just have the player battling against the actual notes of the music, some do include opponents that are trying to outperform the player. Even *PaRappa* had a final freestyle stage to finish the game. But, the AI involved even in these opponents is at best very scripted. The script that is played *could* take into account the level of playing by the player, forcing the opponent to step up to the challenge, as they say. But actual improvisational music using AI that would sample the types of things the human was doing and build on them with more complexity (similar to real jam sessions) has definitely not been used in these games yet.

Typical AI systems used in rhythm games are the following:

1. Scripting matches the AI-controlled character's movements and dialogue to the songs, as well as sets up story elements.
2. Data-driven gameplay, in which a general lightshow system (or other visuals) might be tied to music analysis software, and a large number of songs are included with the game. Examples of this are *Vib Ribbon*, *Frequency*, and *Amplitude*.
3. Some rhythm games have additional elements, like *Rez* (which was a scrolling shooter) and *Chu Chu Rocket* (a sort of puzzle or party game along the lines of *Bomberman*). These games use fairly simple state-based or scripted intelligence systems, which also works with the music.

PUZZLE GAMES

Puzzle games are small, simple games of skill, which usually continue forever, but increase in difficulty over time. They usually have very simple interfaces, and even simpler descriptions of how to play. But, because of this simplicity, they are also some of the most addictive and widely played games in the world. It has been said that the main reason the Nintendo Gameboy became a worldwide phenomenon was because of a little game called *Tetris* (shown in Figure 14.6), and the most played computer game of all time is still *Freecell*, the card game that comes with Microsoft Windows. These games require very little of a player's attention, or time. Players can play ten minutes of a game, and then just shut it off. The very nature of these games allows players to have a little taste of challenge, without having to commit to anything in terms of emotion or time.

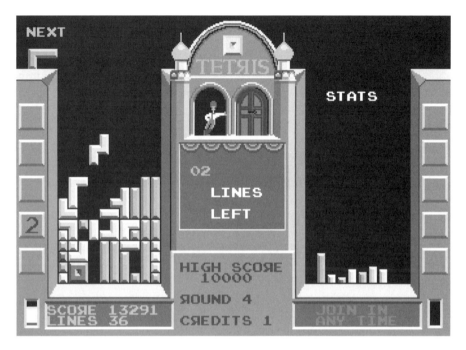

FIGURE 14.6   *Tetris* screenshot. Tetris®: Elorg 1987. Reprinted with permission.

Two areas have become major selling points for these games: the online world and cell phones and PDAs. Online, puzzle games make a lot of sense. Designers can code a puzzle game with minimal resources (perfect for keeping download speeds low) and allow people everywhere to come to the game site to play the games for free, or for next to nothing. This minimal game size also lends itself well to the space-restrictive world of cell phones and PDAs. People want some kind of distraction that they can use if they're stuck in an airport, or waiting for the bus, and most people have one of these devices already. It was a natural mix, once the hardware could support it. The bad news is that most puzzle games don't really use AI, the gameplay comprises simple patterns or specific setups that the player must overcome or unravel. However, some games do use AI, such as PopCap's *Mummy Maze*, although it is usually very simple state-based behavior.

Typical AI systems used in puzzle games are simple state-based behaviors, if a game has any elements of AI usage at all.

ARTIFICIAL LIFE (ALIFE) GAMES

These titles are not considered games by some people, but are more like videogame-based pets of a sort. There are not many of these games, but some of them use some of the most cutting-edge game AI programming we have so far.

These represent the pinnacle of exotic AI techniques in a real-time game experience. Other games in the alife genre are not so complex, AI-wise, but represent an additional way of constructing AI systems to maximize traditionally difficult elements to model.

The first of these games were actually small electrical gadgets, called *Tamagotchi*, that were a huge craze in Japan. They were essentially small (key chain–sized) LCD-based units that had a lumpish looking creature pictured on it.

The creature would demand to be fed, or to be petted, or whatever, based on a set of needs. The human then pushed the corresponding button that gave the creature what it wanted. If the human failed to perform the correct tasks for too long, the creature might become angry with its "owner," or even die. But if human players did things right, the creature would flourish, and live a long, full life, all the while growing and getting small visual differences that people could use to differentiate their pets. Although this is a very strange concept by gaming standards, it was also a very popular one.

These toys eventually lead game developers to create videogames using this premise. Some examples are *Seaman* (a game in which players caretake a very rude fish with a man's head), the *Monster Rancher* games (which use random data from any CD to create unique creatures that players then train for battle), and the *Petz* games (pure *Tamagotchi*-style pets).

Another series of products in this same line is the *Creatures* series developed by Cyberlife. These games are notable because of the actual systems they use to evolve their game characters. Whereas the other games use mostly some kind of advanced fuzzy-state machines (FuSMs), or just keep a lot of statistics about human interaction and hash that into large behavior lookup tables, the *Creatures* games have gone the high-tech route. Their games use advanced neural nets (NNs) to model learning and emotion *and* use a kind of genetic system to allow users to cross breed and evolve the creatures through genetic selection. The products are barely games, more like high-tech fish bowls, and even the developers consider it a technology demo. They are CPU intensive and have to run constantly for quite a bit to learn things, but they are quite impressive from a game AI standpoint.

Other types of alife games strive to make a bit more of a true game experience, and this includes Wright's newest batch of games, *The Sims*™, as well as *Black & White*, from Molyneux.

In *The Sims,* the simulated element players now control is a *person's life.* At the start of the game, players are given a Sim, a semiautonomous character that has a number of needs. Sims are semiautonomous in that they will perform need procurement to survive (if there's food around and the character is hungry, the Sim will eat), but to really excel or progress, the human player has to basically baby-sit the Sim, getting it to perform its duties faster and more efficiently, and encouraging additional interactions, especially those with other Sims. The game has broken new ground by creating a simple AI paradigm known as *smart terrain*. In this concept, the agent has only basic needs that require fulfillment, is smart enough to get around the world to reach things that can satisfy those needs, and has a fuzzy system that allows it to have some biases and rudimentary learning. But the true brains of the system are spread over the land by embedding AI in the objects that populate the game world. Every object in the game that the Sims can interact with contains all the information about how this interaction will take place and what it will give the Sim, including the animation to play. In this way, new items can be added to the world at any time and can be instantly used by the Sims (which is easy to see, considering the number of expansion packs that have come out for the game). Because of its massive open endedness, its mass appeal because of its mostly nonviolent nature, and the sheer customization and expansion capabilities of the game, *The Sims* has become one of the best-selling games of all time.

Black &White takes the God game concept and adds a twist. Each player must take care of a small village of people that worship the player. The twist is the addition of a totem animal which serves as the physical manifestation of the player's power within the game world. This totem character is controlled by a sophisticated AI system (at least by game AI standards), including dynamic rule building and decision-tree creation, as well as the use of simple neural networks (called perceptrons) to allow the player's totem animal to learn new behaviors directly from the player's instruction.

To facilitate this learning, the game allows a number of different ways for these totem animals to gain knowledge: by direct command, by observation, by reflection, and by behavioral feedback from the player (players could slap or stroke the creature, communicating to the creature that he recently did something bad or good). By allowing the creature so many ways to learn, all of which would affect the creature's beliefs and desires, the overall behavior set of the creature was very malleable, and thus, unique from creature to creature. It also led to more rapid learning than might be gained from any one method.

Typical AI systems used in alife games include the following:

1. FuSMs are heavily used because they are easier to train and provide more directed behavior patterns.
2. Neural nets are becoming increasingly researched and used, as developers find better ways to train and tune neural nets, and to watch out for the wildly wrong behaviors they might cause.
3. Genetic algorithms are being used in some of these games, facilitating breeding programs, and helping generations of game characters to evolve in various ways.
4. A solid helping of standard game AI techniques are in use, including regular FSMs, messaging, and scripting.

SUMMARY

In this chapter, we've covered a broad range of game types. Every game, from the most sweepingly epic war game to the lightest puzzler, requires highly proprietary AI code in order to challenge players. The list of covered genres in this chapter (plus the other game genre chapters) is by no means a complete list of all game types. The hope is that you can begin to see the patterns for which AI techniques work best with the various AI challenges inherent in the various styles of games.

- Civilization games require much of the same technology as RTS style games. FSMs, FuSMs, hierarchical systems, pathfinding, messaging, and data-driven techniques are all useful. Support systems like terrain analysis, resource management, city planning, opponent modeling, tech-tree planning, and counselor/diplomat AI are also usually necessary for a full-fledged civ game.
- God games, if they have an "opponent God" element, will use the same kinds of AI technology as civ games. They additionally have (typically) simple autonomous agents beneath/beholden to the player's "God."
- The war game genre again uses the same technologies as the civ genre, with a lot more combat focus. They rely heavily on data-driven techniques and scripting in order to model real battles and equipment.
- Flight sims are broken into two major genres: "pure" flight sims (which usually have no AI elements at all; they sometimes use scripted tutorials, or dogfighting opponents), and "action-oriented" flight sims. This latter category is like the racing game category, and tends to employ a mix of FSMs, messaging, and scripting.
- Rhythm games use the data-driven systems, including scripting. They also use FSMs like so many other of the game genres.
- Puzzle games are typically devoid of anything but the simplest of AI, and usually require nothing but FSM support.
- Artificial life games use some of the most advanced AI techniques being used in games today. Some of the recent examples of this genre have employed FuSMs, neural nets, and genetic algorithms. They also make use of more common AI systems, like FSMs, messaging, and scripts.

15 Finite-State Machines

In This Chapter

- FSM Overview
- FSM Skeletal Code
- Implementing an FSM-Controlled Ship into Our Test Bed
- Example Implementation
- Performance of the AI with This System
- Extensions to the Paradigm
- Optimizations
- Design Considerations
- Summary

In the world of game AI programming, no single data structure has been used more than the finite-state machine (FSM). This simple yet powerful organizational tool helps the programmer to break an initial problem into more manageable subproblems and allows programmers to implement intelligence systems with flexibility and ease. Even if you have not used a formal FSM class, you have probably used the principles that this structure follows, as it is a basic way of thinking about software problems in general. If your game uses a more exotic AI technique for some element of decision making, you will probably also use some form of state-based paradigm in your game.

FSM OVERVIEW

At its heart, a state machine is a data structure that models the behavior of a system. FSMs help organize a system by dividing it into separate, discernable circumstances. An FSM contains three things: the states inherent in the object being modeled, the transitions that serve as the lines of connectivity between the states, and the conditions that must be met to engage each transition. It's really just that simple. A given state will continue to run until a transition condition becomes true, at which point the machine takes the transition to the correponding new state.

Classically, an FSM is a pure data structure. The FSM is initialized by first declaring all the states, then declaring each state's transitions with its required conditions (which are typically just events). To update the machine, the game calls the FSM's Update() function (passing it a list of the game events that occurred during this game loop). The Update() function then returns the current state of the machine, after it has determined if any state transitions have occurred.

This book packages the individual states into full-fledged C++ classes. The state class will include all the in-state logic and behavior in its update code, as well as all the transition logic. The separate state machine class keeps track of the current state, and serves as the master controller for the state collection. Figure 15.1 shows the differences between the classic FSM and the "modular" system used in this book.

Classic FSM

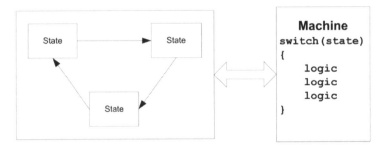

Modular Approach

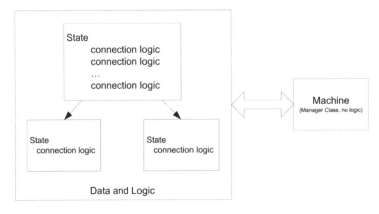

FIGURE 15.1 Comparison of execution flow between classic and modular FSMs.

The reason behind this architectural difference is that it keeps the machine class from becoming the repository of all the game logic. Instead, each state is a stand-alone module that has its update logic, transition logic, and special code such as enter and exit functions. This modularity makes the overall system more manageable and scaleable.

Another difference between the standard implementation and the one this book uses is the transition system. In classic FSM methods, the transitions are expressed as events, usually an enumerated list of some kind, that the perception system can use to trigger transitions. Each state then registers its transitions into a list constituting an input-output matching (e.g., PLAYER_IN_RANGE and AttackState, or SHOT_IN_HEAD and DeathState). The transition checking is then accomplished by sending all the states in the machine the current input events, and determining if any state has a transition that responds to any of the input events.

The modular states in this book will instead use an internal member function for checking transitions. In this way, the skeletal framework given in this book is more than capable of emulating the classical FSM setup by creating an enumeration of input types and then testing to see if any of them have been triggered in the transition function of the current state. This also allows for much more complex computations to determine state transition, on a state-by-state basis.

In electrical engineering terms (from which computer science borrows the concept of the FSM in the first place), most FSMs in games are coded using the Moore model, which just means that you put your actions inside the state. If you initiate actions on the transitions between states, you are instead following the Mealy machine model. Thus, during the Sit state, you want the character to play a sit animation. In the Moore model, the update function itself starts the animation. In a Mealy machine, the character would start the sit animation during the transition between the StandState and the SitState and would do nothing during the SitState except wait for a transition out.

However, with just a bit of clever code placement, you can achieve either effect with the generic structures in this chapter. Specifically, you could use the Enter() function to launch animations, which simulates the Mealy model, or use the Moore method by placing action code within the Update() function directly.

Let's look at a simple FSM example in Figure 15.2. Here we see an FSM diagram for Blinky, the red ghost from Pac-Man. Blinky was the aggressive ghost, the one that most directly chased the player. All the ghosts start life in the Rise state because they're currently located in the center part of the maze. During this state, the ghost gets another body (if it doesn't have one), and then exits the center box. Doing this triggers the FSM to transition to Blinky's primary state, ChasePlayer. Blinky will stay in this state until one of two things happens: the player dies, or eats a power pellet.

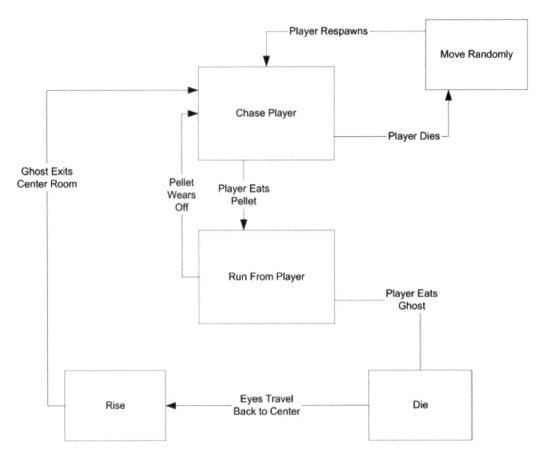

FIGURE 15.2 Simple FSM diagram of the red ghost from *Pac-Man*.

If the player dies, Blinky will then transition to MoveRandomly. The other exit is to the state RunFromPlayer, which will cause Blinky to flee now that Blinky has been turned blue by the power pellet. When running away, Blinky will transition back to chasing the player if the power pellet wears off. If Blinky is eaten by Pac-Man, he then transitions to the Die state, which converts Blinky to a set of eyeballs and walks Blinky back to the center of the maze. As soon as Blinky enters the center, he transitions to Rise, and the whole thing starts over again.

You can see the clear delineation between states of being and transition lines in the diagram. By diagramming out the overall behavior in this way you can also see the atomic actions that need coding to achieve the entire FSM. Dividing the behavior of your AI system into atomic units is very useful, especially if you are going to have different AI-controlled characters that differ in only a few ways, or have specific behaviors missing.

The state diagram for Inky, another ghost in *Pac-Man* that was not as aggressive as Blinky, might be very similar. An entirely different personality is created by simply having different reasons for switching between the three movement states: RunFromPlayer, ChasePlayer, and MoveRandomly. Inky could transition between these states randomly (totally erratic behavior), based on the physical distance to Pac-Man (avoidance or a limited line-of-sight simulation), or maybe just change his mind every so often (so that Inky appears to be single-minded, but flighty). Inky would, of course, still need to have the same power pellet and death logic as Blinky because that is basic ghost behavior, rather than each ghost's personality (which could be defined by the ghost's movement style within the maze).

This very simple FSM controlling Blinky's state *could* be coded as in Listing 15.1, using a simple switch statement. In fact, many games still use this type of free-form FSM for simple game elements. However, if this were not *Pac-Man* but, rather, *Madden Football,* and thus many hundreds of times more complex, you can imagine how this level of organization would be incredibly inadequate, and excessively complex. The priority of transitions becomes harder and harder to determine because it depends on the order of execution. The function housing this switch statement will get progressively larger as more states are added to the game. The modular system this book uses will give you a formal organizational model for combating these problems.

LISTING 15.1   Free-form FSM implementation for *Pac-Man.*

```
switch(m_currentState)
{
case STATE_RISE:
    if(AtCenter())
        GetNewBodyAndExitCenter();
    else
        ChangeState(STATE_CHASEPLAYER);
    break;

    case STATE_DIE:
    if(!AtCenter())
        ChangeToEyesAndMoveBacktoCenter();
    else
        ChangeState(STATE_RISE);
    break;

    case STATE_RUNFROMPLAYER:
    if(!PoweredPacMan())
        ChangeState(STATE_CHASEPLAYER);
```

```
        else if(Eaten())
            ChangeState(STATE_DIE);
        else
            MoveAwayFromPacMan();
        break;

        case STATE_CHASEPLAYER:
        if(PoweredPacMan())
            ChageState(STATE_RUNFROMPLAYER);
        else if(!PacMan)
            ChangeState(STATE_MOVERANDOMLY);
        else
            MoveTowardsPacMan();
        break;

        case STATE_MOVERANDOMLY:
        if(PacMan)
            ChangeState(STATE_CHASEPLAYER);
        else
            MoveRandomly();
        break;

        default:
        PrintError("Bad Current State");
        break;

    };
```

FSM SKELETAL CODE

The code for a skeletal FSM will be implemented within the following classes:

■ The FSMState class, the basic *state* in the system.
■ The FSMMachine class, which houses all the states and acts as the *state machine*.
■ The FSMAIControl class, which houses the state machine, as well as game-specific code such as perception data.

The next sections will discuss these classes in more detail, and will then discuss the specific implementation of the FSMAIControl class and each FSMState needed for our AI test-bed application.

THE FSMState CLASS

When implementing a state system, it is best to code each state as if it is the only state in the world, with no knowledge of other states, or of the state machine itself. This leads to very modular states, which can be arranged in any order without prerequisite or future requirement. At its most basic, each state should have the following functions:

Enter(). This function is always run immediately upon first entering the state. It allows the state to perform initialization of data or variables.

Exit(). This function is run when you are leaving the state and is primarily used as a cleanup task, as well as where you would run any additional code that you wanted to happen on specific transitions (for Mealy-style state machines).

Update(). This is the main function that is called every processing loop of the AI when this state is the current state in the FSM (for Moore-style state machines).

Init(). Resets the state.

CheckTransitions(). This function runs through the logic by which the state will decide to end. The function should return the enumeration value of the state to run, coming back with the same state if no change is needed. Note that the order in which the logical state transitions are determined becomes the priority of the different transitions. So, if your function first checks for a switch to the AttackingState, and then checks for the DodgingState, the AI will be much more offensive than if those checks were reversed.

The skeletal code header for this class can be seen in Listing 15.2. The class complexity has been kept to a minimum, so that this code can be the foundation for any system that you might need to build using an FSM. The class also contains two data members, m_type, and m_parent. The type field is used by both the overall state machine and by the interstate code to make determinations based on which particular state is being considered. The enumeration for these values is stored in a file called FSM.h, and is currently empty, containing only the default FSM_STATE_NONE value. When you actually use the code for something, you would add all the state types to this enumeration, and go from there. The parent field is used by individual states, so they can access a shared data area through their Control structure.

LISTING 15.2   Base class header for state.

```
class FSMState:
{
public:
        //constructor/functions
```

```
        FSMState(int type=FSM_STATE_NONE,Control* parent=NULL)
          {m_type = type;m_parent = parent;}
        virtual void Enter()                    {}
        virtual void Exit()                     {}
        virtual void Update(int t)              {}
        virtual void Init()                     {}
        virtual void CheckTransitions(int t) {}


        //data
      Control* m_parent;
        int     m_type;
    };
```

THE FSMMachine CLASS

The state machine class (see Listing 15.3 for the header) contains all the states associated with machine in an STL vector. It also has a general case `UpdateMachine()` function, the implementation of which is shown in Listing 15.4. It also contains functions for adding states to the machine and setting a default state. Notice that the state machine is actually derived from the state class. This is to facilitate a state that is actually a completely different state machine. Again, like the state class, the machine class has a type field, the types of which are declared in an enumeration in `FSM.h`, which is essentially empty for now.

LISTING 15.3 FSMMachine header.

```
class FSMMachine: public FSMState
{
    public:
    //constructor/functions
    FSMMachine(int type = FSM_MACH_NONE)
        {m_type = type;}
    virtual void UpdateMachine(int t);
    virtual void AddState(FSMState* state);
    virtual void SetDefaultState(FSMState* state)
        {m_defaultState = state;}
    virtual void SetGoalID(int goal) {m_goalID= goal;}
    virtual TransitionState(int goal);
    virtual Reset();


    //data
    int m_type;
```

```
private:
    vector<FSMState*> m_states;
    FSMState* m_currentState;
    FSMState* m_defaultState;
    FSMState* m_goalState;
    FSMState* m_goalID;
};
```

LISTING 15.4   The machine class `UpdateMachine( )` function.

```
void FSMMachine::UpdateMachine(int t)
{
    //don't do anything if you have no states
    if(m_states.size() == 0 )
        return;

    //don't do anything if there's no current
    //state, and no default state
    if(!m_currentState)
        m_currentState = m_defaultState;
    if(!m_currentState)
        return;

    //update current state, and check for a transition
    int oldStateID = m_currentState->m_type;
    m_goalID = m_currentState->CheckTransitions();

    //switch if there was a transition
    if(m_goalID != oldStateID)
    {
        if(TransitionState(m_goalID))
        {
            m_currentState->Exit();
            m_currentState = m_goalState;
            m_currentState->Enter();
        }
    }
    m_currentState->Update(t);
}
```

The `UpdateMachine()` function is very simple. It has two quick optimizations: It will bail out if the machine wasn't given any states, and will also return if there is no current state set and no default state to fall back on. The next block calls the current state's `CheckTransition()` function, followed by a block that determines if the state triggered a transition. If so, the function `TransitionState()` queries the machine's list of states to see if the machine actually has the new state that was requested, and if it exists, calls `Exit()` on the state the system is leaving, and `Enter()` on the new state. Finally, the current state's `Update()` function is called.

THE FSMAICONTROL CLASS

The final part of the basic FSM system (and also the beginning of the game-specific code) is the Control class (which was covered briefly in Chapter 3, "AIsteroids: Our AI Test Bed"). As you recall, this class is the behavior controller for the main in-game ship. It also serves as the branching point between the human controls and the primary location for the AI framework. For an AI-controlled ship, we inherit from `AIControl` and create the child class `FSMAIControl` (see Listing 15.5 for the header).

LISTING 15.5   `FSMAIControl` header.

```
class FSMAIControl: public AIControl
{
    public:
    //constructor/functions
    FSMAIControl(Ship* ship = NULL);
    void Update(int t);
    void UpdatePerceptions(int t);
    void Init();

    //perception data
    //(public so that states can share it)
    GameObj*      m_nearestAsteroid;
    GameObj*      m_nearestPowerup;
    float         m_nearestAsteroidDist;
    float         m_nearestPowerupDist;
    Point3f       m_collidePt;
    bool          m_willCollide;
    bool          m_powerupNear;
    float         m_safetyRadius;

private:
    //data
    FSMMachine* m_machine;
};
```

The `FSMAIControl` class contains the standard `Update()` function, which updates the state machine and runs the `UpdatePerceptions()` method. This class also includes the game-specific blackboard data members that will be shared by all the states in the machine. If this was a much more complex game, with large numbers of these kinds of global data members (or a variety of data members that require extensive management), it would be much better to construct a full-perception manager class and then have the FSMAIController contain a pointer to the perception manager for this game. But for the simple needs of our test-bed demo, storing the perceptions directly into the controller will do fine. Having a minimal list of data members to maintain, we don't have to worry about the calculations taking too long, or having to wade through an unwieldy long perception update function.

IMPLEMENTING AN FSM-CONTROLLED SHIP INTO OUR TEST BED

To get our AIsteroids program to use an FSM, we first need to determine the entire state diagram for the behavior exhibited by a ship during a game of asteroids that we want our system to model. For our purposes, Figure 15.3 should perform fine.

As Figure 15.3 shows, there are five basic states to an AI-controlled AIsteroids ship:

1. Approach, which will get the ship within range of the closest asteroid.
2. Attack, which will point the ship toward the closest asteroid within range, and then fire.
3. Evade, which will initiate avoidance of an asteroid on a collision course.
4. GetPowerup, which will try to scoop up powerups within some range.
5. Idle, which will just sit there if nothing else is valid.

The game also needs the following conditions to make the necessary logical connections between these states:

- *Asteroid in firing range.* A simple distance check, but it also requires that we keep track of the closest asteroid.
- *Asteroid on collision course.* Another distance check, but also a trajectory intersection. The intersection is more costly, so we'll only do it if the asteroid is within the distance check.
- *Powerup in pickup range.* One more distance check, this also requires that we keep track of the closest powerup.

Notice one other thing about the state diagram: Every state needs to check for the condition "Asteroid on collision course," to then switch to the Evade state. This shows one of the inherent weaknesses of building the logic into each state. This type of determination would have to be repeated in each state.

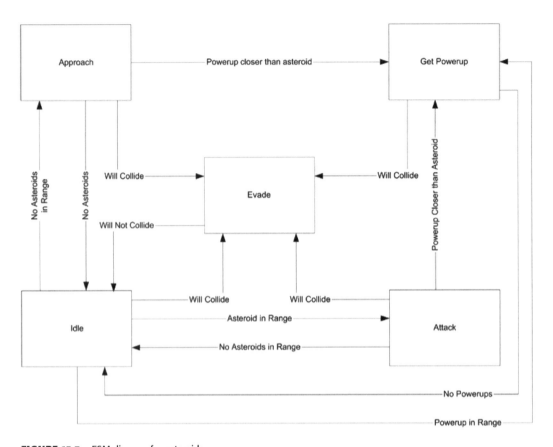

FIGURE 15.3   FSM diagram for asteroids.

However, this implementation uses the `Control` class's `UpdatePerceptions()` function as a global data location, essentially using the `Control` class as a central location that will hold calculations common to the entire state machine. This gives us the best of both worlds, by keeping the number of recalculations to a minimum (through a central storage location) and giving us the ability to separate out the nonrepetitious portions of the calculations to be done only when needed (by putting logic and calculations within specific states).

EXAMPLE IMPLEMENTATION

Now we will take the FSM classes we have discussed and use them to construct a working AI ship for our test application. We will first set up the `Control` class, and then implement each of the requisite states for the system.

CODING THE CONTROL CLASS

The controller class for the FSM model (see earlier Listing 15.5 for the header, and Listing 15.6 for the implementation of the important functions) contains the state machine structure, as well as the global data members for this AI model.

The constructor for the class builds the FSM structure, by instantiating the machine class, and then adding an instantiation of each requisite state. The constructor also sets the default state, which is also used as the startup state for the machine.

The Update() method is straightforward and ensures that the ship this class is controlling exists, and if so, updates the perceptions and the state machine.

The UpdatePerceptions() function is where all the action is. The closest asteroid and powerup are noted, the ship's distance to these objects is determined, and the status variables are set (m_willCollide and m_powerupNear). These perceptions allow all the transition checking in the individual states to be simple comparisons, instead of having to calculate these things individually. This approach also consolidates this code—better or faster methods can be implemented here and the effects will be seen throughout the states.

LISTING 15.6   FSMAIControl function implementations.

```
//--------------------
FSMAIControl::FSMAIControl(Ship* ship):
AIControl(ship)
{
    //construct the state machine and add the necessary states
    m_machine = new FSMMachine(FSM_MACH_MAINSHIP,this);
    StateApproach* approach = new StateApproach(this);
    m_machine->AddState(approach);
    m_machine->AddState(new StateAttack(this));
    m_machine->AddState(new StateEvade(this));
    m_machine->AddState(new StateGetPowerup(this));
    m_machine->AddState(new StateIdle(this));
    m_machine->SetDefaultState(approach);
}


//--------------------
void FSMAIControl::Update(int t)
{
    if(!m_ship)
    {
        m_machine->Reset();
        return;
    }
```

```
            UpdatePerceptions(t);
        m_machine->UpdateMachine(t);
    }


    //--------------------
    void FSMAIControl::UpdatePerceptions(int t)
    {
        //store closest asteroid and powerup
        m_nearestAsteroid = Game.GetClosestGameObj
                            (m_ship,GameObj::OBJ_ASTEROID);
        m_nearestPowerup  = Game.GetClosestGameObj
                            (m_ship,GameObj::OBJ_POWERUP);


        //asteroid collision determination
        m_willCollide = false;

//small hysteresis on this value, to avoid
//boundary oscillation
        if(m_willCollide)
            m_safetyRadius = 30.0f;
        else
            m_safetyRadius = 15.0f;
        if(m_nearestAsteroid)
        {
            float speed = m_ship->m_velocity.Norm();
            m_nearestAsteroidDist = m_nearestAsteroid->
                        m_position.Distance(m_ship->m_position);
            float dotVel;
            Point3f normDelta = m_nearestAsteroid->m_position -
                                m_ship->m_position;
            normDelta.Normalize();
            float astSpeed = m_nearestAsteroid->
                                m_velocity.Norm();
            if(speed > astSpeed)
                dotVel   = DOT(m_ship->UnitVectorVelocity()
                               ,normDelta);
            else
            {
                speed = astSpeed;
                dotVel= DOT(m_nearestAsteroid->
                        UnitVectorVelocity(),-normDelta);
            }
            float spdAdj = LERP(speed/AI_MAX_SPEED_TRY
                                ,0.0f,50.0f)*dotVel;
```

```
                    float adjSafetyRadius = m_safetyRadius + spdAdj +
                                            m_nearestAsteroid->m_size;

                    //if you're too close, and I'm heading somewhat
                    //towards you, flag a collision
                    if(m_nearestAsteroidDist <= adjSafetyRadius
                       && dotVel > 0)
                        m_willCollide = true;
                }

            //powerup near determination
            m_powerupNear = false;
            if(m_nearestPowerup)
            {
                m_nearestPowerupDist = m_nearestPowerup->m_position.
                                       Distance(m_ship->m_position);
                if(m_nearestPowerupDist <= POWERUP_SCAN_DIST)
                {
                    m_powerupNear     = true;
                }
            }
        }
    }
```

CODING THE STATES

The five listings discussed below (15.7 to 15.11) are the implementations for the necessary states. These states include: StateApproach, StateAttack, StateEvade, StateGetPowerup, and StateIdle. They will be discussed separately, followed by the relevant listing.

StateApproach

This state's purpose is to turn to face the nearest asteroid and then thrust toward it. For simplicity's sake, the AI system for this demo doesn't try to deal with the wraparound effect of the game world—that would require more math, and is not the focus of this text.

The Update() function does some calculations to find the approach angle to the nearest asteroid and will add a *braking* vector if the speed of the ship is overly high. This is to keep the AI-controlled ship from occasionally getting into trouble because of too much speed.

After the angle is computed, the code then turns the ship in the proper direction, or turns on the appropriate thruster if the ship is already pointing correctly. This type of movement is a bit more digital than most human players, so it looks a little more robotic than human. It could be made more natural-looking by using the thrusters during turning (which is what most humans do), but again, this would complicate the calculations and this example is being coded specifically for readability, not to show the optimal implementation.

The `CheckTransitions()` function is straightforward enough, checking in turn for the three possible transitions from this state, FSM_STATE_EVADE (if you're going to collide), FSM_STATE_GETPOWERUP (if there's one nearby), and FSM_STATE_IDLE (if there's no asteroid to approach).

The `Exit()` function assures the system that anything the state sets in the larger game world will be reset. In this case, the ship's turn and thrust controls may be turned on, so this function turns them both off.

LISTING 15.7 The `StateApproach` class functions.

```
//-------------------
void StateApproach::Update(int t)
{
    //turn and then thrust towards closest asteroid
    FSMAIControl* parent = (FSMAIControl*)m_parent;
    GameObj* asteroid = parent->m_nearestAsteroid;
    Ship*    ship      = parent->m_ship;
    Point3f deltaPos  = asteroid->m_position -
                             ship->m_position;
    deltaPos.Normalize();

    //add braking vec if you're going too fast
    float speed = ship->m_velocity.Norm();
    if(speed > AI_MAX_SPEED_TRY)
        deltaPos += -ship->UnitVectorVelocity();

    //DOT out my velocity
    Point3f shpUnitVel = ship->UnitVectorVelocity();
    float dotVel = DOT(shpUnitVel,deltaPos);
    float proj = 1-dotVel;
    deltaPos -= proj*shpUnitVel;
    deltaPos.Normalize();

    //find new direction, and head to it
    float newDir = CALCDIR(deltaPos);
    float angDelta = CLAMPDIR180(ship->m_angle - newDir);
    if(fabsf(angDelta) <2 || fabsf(angDelta)> 172)
    {
        //thrust
```

```
            ship->StopTurn();
            if(speed < AI_MAX_SPEED_TRY ||
                parent->m_nearestAsteroidDist > 40)
                  fabsf(angDelta)<2? ship->ThrustOn() :
                                     ship->ThrustReverse();
            else
                ship->ThrustOff();
        }
        else if(fabsf(angDelta)<=90)
        {
            //turn when facing forwards
            if(angDelta >0)
                ship->TurnRight();
            else
                ship->TurnLeft();
        }
        else
        {
            //turn when facing rear
            if(angDelta<0)
                ship->TurnRight();
            else
                ship->TurnLeft();
        }

        parent->m_target->m_position = asteroid->m_position;
        parent->m_targetDir = newDir;
        parent->m_debugTxt = "Approach";
}


//--------------------
int StateApproach::CheckTransitions()
{
    FSMAIControl* parent = (FSMAIControl*)m_parent;
    if(parent->m_willCollide)
        return FSM_STATE_EVADE;

    if(parent->m_powerupNear&&(parent->m_nearestAsteroidDist
    >parent->m_nearestPowerupDist)&& parent->m_ship->
    GetShotLevel() < MAX_POWER_LEVEL)
        return FSM_STATE_GETPOWERUP;

    if(!parent->m_nearestAsteroid ||
        parent->m_nearestAsteroidDist < APPROACH_DIST)
```

```
            return FSM_STATE_IDLE;

        return FSM_STATE_APPROACH;
    }

    //-------------------
    void StateApproach::Exit()
    {
        if(((FSMAIControl*)m_parent)->m_ship)
        {
            ((FSMAIControl*)m_parent)->m_ship->ThrustOff();
            ((FSMAIControl*)m_parent)->m_ship->StopTurn();
        }
    }
```

StateAttack

The StateAttack class will turn the ship toward the nearest asteroid, and then fire the cannon. The class accounts for multiple guns (awarded to the player when the player obtains powerups) by calling the ship function GetClosestGunAngle(), which will pass in the closest gun to an angle parameter.

Update() calculates the position of the nearest asteroid, and must also perform some additional calculations to find the projected position of the asteroid, to find the leading angle to fire a bullet toward in order to hit the asteroid while it's moving. After finding this position, it gets an angle to it, turns the ship, and fires the guns.

CheckTransitions() for this state is just like StateApproach, with branches to FSM_STATE_EVADE, FSM_STATE_GETPOWERUP, and FSM_STATE_IDLE.

This state potentially turns the ship, so the Exit() function must concern itself with resetting that particular flag.

LISTING 15.8 The StateAttack class functions.

```
    //-------------------
    void StateAttack::Update(int t)
    {
        //turn towards closest asteroid's future position,
        //and then fire
        FSMAIControl* parent = (FSMAIControl*)m_parent;
        GameObj* asteroid    = parent->m_nearestAsteroid;
        Ship*    ship        = parent->m_ship;

        Point3f futureAstPosition = asteroid->m_position;
```

```
    Point3f deltaPos = futureAstPosition - ship->m_position;
    float dist  = deltaPos.Norm();
    float time = dist/BULLET_SPEED;
    futureAstPosition += time*asteroid->m_velocity;
    Point3f deltaFPos = futureAstPosition - ship->m_position;
    deltaFPos.Normalize();

    float newDir   = CALCDIR(deltaFPos);
    float angDelta = CLAMPDIR180(ship->GetClosestGunAngle
                                (newDir) - newDir);
    if(angDelta >1)
        ship->TurnRight();
    else if(angDelta < -1)
        ship->TurnLeft();
    else
    {
        ship->StopTurn();
        ship->Shoot();
    }

    parent->m_target->m_position = futureAstPosition;
    parent->m_targetDir = newDir;
    parent->m_debugTxt = "Attack";
}


//--------------------
int StateAttack::CheckTransitions()
{
    FSMAIControl* parent = (FSMAIControl*)m_parent;
    if(parent->m_willCollide)
        return FSM_STATE_EVADE;

    if(parent->m_powerupNear && parent->m_nearestAsteroidDist
       >parent->m_nearestPowerupDist && parent->m_ship->
       GetShotLevel() < MAX_POWER_LEVEL)
        return FSM_STATE_GETPOWERUP;

    if(!parent->m_nearestAsteroid ||
       parent->m_nearestAsteroidDist > APPROACH_DIST)
        return FSM_STATE_IDLE;

    return FSM_STATE_ATTACK;
}
```

```
//-------------------
void StateAttack::Exit()
{
    if(((FSMAIControl*)m_parent)->m_ship)
        ((FSMAIControl*)m_parent)->m_ship->StopTurn();
}
```

StateEvade

This important state simply tries to stop collisions with asteroids, by both performing thrusting maneuvers, as well as firing the guns to possibly clear the way.

The Update() function computes a steering vector that comprises a sideways
normal vector to the line between the player and the asteroid and adds in a braking
vector if the player is headed at the asteroid. The Update() function then calculates
the angle to this thrust vector, and like StateApproach, turns the ship and thrusts
when appropriate, but will also fire the ship's guns when using its thrusters, which
has the added benefit of sometimes clearing out the area.

CheckTransition() has only one state to check for, that of FSM_STATE_IDLE.
We could check for transitions to the other states directly, but this is undesirable. By keeping the state connections to a minimum, we lessen the CPU requirements of running the state machine (especially if the transition determinations
are more complex than simple comparisons) and make the overall state diagram
simpler and easier to add to in the future when we want to insert more states into
the system.

The Exit() method for StateEvade is like any other state that controls movement,
in that it must reset the turning and engine status of the ship being controlled.

LISTING 15.9 The StateEvade class functions.

```
//-------------------
void StateEvade::Update(int t)
{
    //evade by going to the quad opposite as the asteroid
    //is moving, add in a deflection,
    //and cancel out your movement
    FSMAIControl* parent = (FSMAIControl*)m_parent;
    GameObj* asteroid   = parent->m_nearestAsteroid;
    Ship*    ship       = parent->m_ship;
    Point3f vecSteer = CROSS(ship->m_position,asteroid->
                       m_position);
    Point3f vecBrake = ship->postion - asteroid->m_position;
    vecSteer += vecBrake;
```

```
    float newDir = CALCDIR(vecSteer);
    float angDelta = CLAMPDIR180(ship->m_angle - newDir);
    if(fabsf(angDelta) <5 || fabsf(angDelta)> 175)//thrust
    {
        ship->StopTurn();
        if(ship->m_velocity.Norm() < AI_MAX_SPEED_TRY ||
           parent->m_nearestAsteroidDist< 20 +asteroid->
           m_size)
            fabsf(angDelta)<5?
                ship->ThrustOn() : ship->ThrustReverse();
        else
            ship->ThrustOff();

        //if I'm pointed right at the asteroid, shoot
        ship->Shoot();
    }
    else if(fabsf(angDelta)<=90)//turn front
    {
        if(angDelta >0)
            ship->TurnRight();
        else
            ship->TurnLeft();
    }
    else//turn rear
    {
        if(angDelta<0)
            ship->TurnRight();
        else
            ship->TurnLeft();
    }


    parent->m_target->m_position=asteroid->m_position;
    parent->m_targetDir = newDir;
    parent->m_debugTxt = "Evade";
}

//--------------------
int StateEvade::CheckTransitions()
{
    FSMAIControl* parent = (FSMAIControl*)m_parent;

    if(!parent->m_willCollide)
        return FSM_STATE_IDLE;
```

```
        return FSM_STATE_EVADE;
}

//-------------------
void StateEvade::Exit()
{
    if(((FSMAIControl*)m_parent)->m_ship)
    {
        ((FSMAIControl*)m_parent)->m_ship->ThrustOff();
        ((FSMAIControl*)m_parent)->m_ship->StopTurn();
    }
}
```

StateGetPowerup

This state recognizes the locality of a powerup and will attempt to force a collision with the powerup, to gain its effects.

Update() is much like in StateApproach, only we need a more precise collision, instead of just moving in the general direction. So, this state must compute projected movement of the powerups. Also like StateApproach, it tries to keep the maximum velocity of the ship under check, by imposing a braking factor if the ship is moving too fast. As in some of the other states, Update() then computes a new direction, turns to it, and fires up the engines.

CheckTransitions() has determinations for both exit clauses from this state, FSM_STATE_EVADE and FSM_STATE_IDLE.

Exit() must reset the ship's turn and thrust controls to ensure leaving them in a neutral manner.

LISTING 15.10 The StateGetPowerup class functions.

```
//-------------------
void StateGetPowerup::Update(int t)
{
    FSMAIControl* parent = (FSMAIControl*)m_parent;
    GameObj* powerup     = parent->m_nearestPowerup;
    Ship*    ship        = parent->m_ship;

    //find future position of powerup
    Point3f futurePowPosition = powerup->m_position;
    Point3f deltaPos = futurePowPosition - ship->m_position;
    float dist  = deltaPos.Norm();
    float speed = AI_MAX_SPEED_TRY;
```

```
float time = dist/speed;
futurePowPosition += time*powerup->m_velocity;
Point3f deltaFPos = futurePowPosition - ship->m_position;
deltaFPos.Normalize();

//add braking vec if you're going too fast
speed = ship->m_velocity.Norm();
if(speed > AI_MAX_SPEED_TRY)
    deltaFPos += -ship->UnitVectorVelocity();

//DOT out my velocity
Point3f shpUnitVel = ship->UnitVectorVelocity();
float dotVel      = DOT(shpUnitVel,deltaFPos);
float proj        = 1-dotVel;
deltaFPos        -= proj*shpUnitVel;
deltaFPos.Normalize();

float newDir   = CALCDIR(deltaFPos);
float angDelta = CLAMPDIR180(ship->m_angle - newDir);
if(fabsf(angDelta) <2 || fabsf(angDelta)> 177)//thrust
{
    ship->StopTurn();
    if(speed < AI_MAX_SPEED_TRY ||
       parent->m_nearestPowerupDist > 20)
        fabsf(angDelta)<2?
        ship->ThrustOn() : ship->ThrustReverse();
    else
        ship->ThrustOff();
}
else if(fabsf(angDelta)<=90)//turn front
{
    if(angDelta >0)
        ship->TurnRight();
    else
        ship->TurnLeft();
}
else//turn rear
{
    if(angDelta<0)
        ship->TurnRight();
    else
        ship->TurnLeft();
}
```

```
        parent->m_target->m_position = futurePowPosition;
        parent->m_targetDir          = newDir;
        parent->m_debugTxt           = "GetPowerup";
    }

    //--------------------
    int StateGetPowerup::CheckTransitions()
    {
        FSMAIControl* parent = (FSMAIControl*)m_parent;

        if(parent->m_willCollide)
            return FSM_STATE_EVADE;

        if(!parent->m_nearestPowerup || parent->
           m_nearestAsteroidDist < parent->m_nearestPowerupDist)
            return FSM_STATE_IDLE;

        return FSM_STATE_GETPOWERUP;
    }

    //--------------------
    void StateGetPowerup::Exit()
    {
        if(((FSMAIControl*)m_parent)->m_ship)
        {
            ((FSMAIControl*)m_parent)->m_ship->ThrustOff();
            ((FSMAIControl*)m_parent)->m_ship->StopTurn();
        }
    }
```

StateIdle

The last necessary state is merely a catchall—a purely transitory state. The state machine for this simple demo has so few states that StateIdle connects to every other state in the machine, but high connectivity is rare, in general. If we added additional behaviors to this game (such as specialized attack states, or game-specific environment elements) then these would be more isolated in the state graph. But the simple nature of this game leads this state to be a common return point from all the other states. After finishing any of the other states, the ship will always fall back into idle.

The Update() function of this state does nothing, except provide the debugging system with a label to use when drawing debug information to the screen.

CheckTransitions() has determinations for all the other states in the game because of the foundation nature of the idle state in this game.

There is no Exit() function for this state, as it changes nothing in the greater game sense.

LISTING 15.11   The StateIdle class functions.

```
//--------------------
void StateIdle::Update(int t)
{
    //Do nothing
    FSMAIControl* parent = (FSMAIControl*)m_parent;
    parent->m_debugTxt = "Idle";
}

//--------------------
int StateIdle::CheckTransitions()
{
    FSMAIControl* parent = (FSMAIControl*)m_parent;

    if(parent->m_willCollide)
        return FSM_STATE_EVADE;

    if(parent->m_nearestAsteroid)
    {
        if(parent->m_nearestAsteroidDist > APPROACH_DIST)
            return FSM_STATE_APPROACH;

        if(parent->m_nearestAsteroidDist <= APPROACH_DIST)
            return FSM_STATE_ATTACK;
    }

    if(parent->m_nearestPowerup)
        return FSM_STATE_GETPOWERUP;

    return FSM_STATE_IDLE;
}
```

PERFORMANCE OF THE AI WITH THIS SYSTEM

The AI is quite able to play a good game of asteroids with this simple framework, being able to occasionally achieve scores well over 2 million. The added behavior of shooting while in the StateEvade state seems to be key to the ability of the system to survive later levels because the craft is almost continuously evading the extreme numbers of asteroids. However, by just watching it for a while, you will notice a number of things that could be improved:

- *The addition of some specialty states.* Getting the first powerup significantly improves the AI's chance of survival, so this could be a priority state. Specifically filling up on powerups when the number of asteroids is low would be a big help, so that it will start the next level with maximum guns. Also, humans can play this game forever if they just get full powerups and then sit in the middle of the screen and continuously rotate and fire. This "spiral death blossom" attack is something that the AI could do at appropriate times, such as when it's surrounded. Taking advantage of invincibility would be another state—the AI ship could make a beeline for powerups or ignore evasion tactics when invincible.

- *Increased complexity of the math model.* This gives the AI system the ability to deal with the world coordinates wrapping. Right now, the AI's primary weakness is that it loses focus when things wrap in the world, and considering this during targeting and collision avoidance would greatly increase the survivability of the AI ship.

- *Bullet management for the ship.* Right now, the ship just points, and then starts firing. There is no firing rate on the guns, so it tends to fire clumps of shots toward targets. This is somewhat advantageous; when it fires a clump of shots into a large asteroid, the remaining shots will sometimes kill the pieces as the asteroid splits. But this can get the ship in trouble when it has fired its entire allocation of bullets and must wait for them to collide or expire before it can shoot again, leaving it temporarily defenseless.

- *Better positioning the ship for attacks.* This means the ship doesn't miss fast-moving targets quite so often. Humans tend to move to some position that the asteroid will eventually travel by, and then stop at that position and wait for the asteroid to come. Because the math was specifically kept simple for the demo, the system moves directly toward the asteroid. Even this simple method is really only a problem because of the world-wrapping effect. This method of play doesn't really look as intelligent as the human scheme.

- *Better evade behaviors.* Right now, the ship is using simple steering behavior (modified slightly, because we can only thrust forward and reverse) for obstacle avoidance. Humans use a much more complex determination for avoidance, including shooting though a potential collision (not making any thrust adjustments), noting clumps of asteroids coming and evading them as a group, preemptive positioning before an asteroid gets too close, or even braking to a stop to just slow down the action a bit. A bit of simple playfield analysis would help the AI with some of these actions. By knowing which parts of the map had the lesser concentrations of asteroids, it could perform evasion tactics in the general direction of "more space," or even set itself up in low-concentration areas preemptively to give itself a better chance for survival.

PROS OF FSM-BASED SYSTEMS

FSMs are easy and intuitive to picture, especially when dealing with Moore-style machines. Our implementation into the test bed, which used a Moore-style state machine, in which the actions are in the states (rather than the transitions), is how most people tend to think about AI behaviors. Even within this paradigm, however, you could have coded the FSM in many ways for the demo game to achieve similar performance.

FSMs are also easy to implement, as you've seen in this chapter. Given a well-thought-out state diagram, the structure of the state machine practically writes itself. Its simplicity is its greatest strength because the nature of the methodology lends itself well to splitting AI problems into specific chunks and defining the linkages between them. After a while, writing FSM structures becomes a fairly rote task for most programmers.

State-based systems are easy to add to because the game flow is very deterministic and connections between states are so explicit. In fact, it is a good idea to make a paper copy of your FSM diagram (or specific portions of it, if it is very large) and continue to keep it current as you extend the system. This will augment your ability to maintain a mental picture of the overall FSM structure and will help you find logical holes or areas where you need a connection but don't have one. This kind of bookkeeping could even be achieved by inserting special debugging code into your states, so that the state diagram could effectively be written to a file by your game and examined offline, to look for any transitions that you missed or are misplaced.

FSM methods are also very straightforward to debug. The deterministic nature of state machines makes it easy (usually, that is) to replicate bugs, and the centralized nature of the FSMMachine class makes an easy code location to trap specific AI characters or behaviors when they occur. Visual debugging is also simplified in this paradigm because it is trivial to output state information to the screen on an individual character basis and watch the AI make determinations on the fly. This kind of information can also be useful written to a file as a log of the state transitions leading up to a certain condition.

Finally, because of their nonspecific nature, FSM systems can be used for any number of problems, from simple game flow between screens, to the most intricate of NPC dialogues. This inherent general-purpose quality means that at some level, almost every game will have some sort of state-based element to them. Not that very simple state systems need a full, formal framework to run, but almost every game will use FSMs in some form simply because they can be applied to such a vast array of different game issues.

Cons of FSM-Based Systems

The primary strength of FSM systems, their ease of implementation, tends to be their greatest weakness as well. Projects can run into problems when state-based systems weren't initially designed with a static framework from the start and, instead, used more "switch and case"-based FSMs, mixed in with more formal-state machines. Programmers sometimes code a behavior quickly (during a crunch period, or during a moment of experimentation) and then don't bother to go back and reimplement it correctly into the overall game structure.

This kind of willy-nilly implementation leads to fragmented systems that have logic spread out in directions and places that are not organizationally sound, leading to maintenance problems.

FSM systems also tend to grow in complexity during the project, as more specialized behaviors are found (such as those mentioned earlier that could improve the asteroids-playing FSM from the start of this chapter). Although it is good to try to improve the abilities of your AI systems over time, FSMs tend to not scale well to this kind of iterative work. The state diagram will become incredibly complex as the number of transitions grows exponentially to the number of new states and, as such, resolving transition determination and priority of actions becomes unwieldy.

Another downfall of the state-based model is the issue of state oscillation. This occurs when the perception data boundary that separates two or more states is too crisp—that is, there is no room for overlap. For example, let's say that a game creature (see Figure 15.4) has only two states, Flee and Stand. Flee runs directly away from any enemy less than four feet from the creature, and Stand causes the creature to simply sit there. Now, an enemy character enters the scene, and stands 3.99 feet from the creature. The creature enters its Flee state, but as it starts its animation, the creature's position changes slightly, and suddenly, it's instead 4.001 feet from the enemy. So the creature transitions to Stand. The Stand state plays a different animation, and in transitioning back to the standing animation, it might move the creature back a touch, and start the whole situation over again. Although this is a very specific and simplistic example, the lesson is that the inherent crispness of the state system can lead to vacillating states like

FIGURE 15.4 Common state-based problem of oscillation.

this unless care is taken. Some ways to fight this problem will be given in the following section.

Extensions to the Paradigm

Because of the extremely open-ended implementation of FSMs, a number of useful variants have been used over the years to combat the weaknesses of FSM systems. Some of the more useful of these extensions are covered here.

Hierarchical FSMs

Sometimes, a given state in an FSM will be quite complex. In our AIsteroids example, the Evade state could be made much more complicated in an attempt to make it more foolproof. Special case code could be written to separate situations such as when the ship is surrounded, or a tight grouping of asteroids is coming toward the player. Other code could try to preempt collisions by moving to more open areas, or shooting straight through oncoming traffic. Some of these things could be taken care of within the current Evade::Update() method, but a better way to approach this would be to make the Evade state an entirely different state machine. Within this state machine, you could deal with threats iteratively and separate code into more manageable sections. So, the Evade state machine would contain states for first dealing with being surrounded, then dealing with any immediate threats by either shooting or dodging, and then trying to get to a safer location so that the code can exit the Evade state completely.

This technique is a great way to add complexity to an FSM system without creating undue connectivity within the greater state machine. In effect, you are grouping states into more locally scoped areas, and taking advantage of similarities among these local states. By grouping similar states within their own state machine, the "super state" that contains this new machine can also house common functionality and shared data members, much like the FSMAIControl structure does for the AIsteroids example.

Substates do not have to be true states, either. Another commonly used technique is to have a state in the larger FSM contain many substates, all of which are treated as equal choices. The specific resultant substate can either be chosen randomly, or because of some combination of perception triggers. This is the same as having two or more states as equal branches in a classic state diagram, but having the logic for which branch to take embedded in a state Update () method, instead of indirectly through perception order priority or some other roundabout manner.

MESSAGE- AND EVENT-BASED FSMS

In some games (or merely some states), transitions may happen infrequently. If this is the case, and if your game also contains numerous states or the computations to determine transitions are complex, then it becomes computationally expensive to check for transitions in a polling model. Instead, an FSM system can be implemented easily that uses messages as triggers instead of having to poll.

The *overall* structure of our state-machine framework could be converted to use this type of system. The game (most likely through the Control class in some way) would have to pass messages down to the state machine, which would then distribute them to the various states. The FSMMachine::UpdateMachine() method would become the message pump for the state machine, and each state's CheckTransitions() function would become a switch statement (or the like) for handling the various messages that it wants to consider. The rest of the code would remain mostly unchanged. Even the Enter(), Exit(), and Update() functions could be triggered by automatically sending messages through the system. Note that combination systems could be implemented, in which each state could store a flag indicating whether it is a polling or event-driven state, and the UpdateMachine() function could handle it appropriately.

FSMS WITH FUZZY TRANSITIONS

FSMs can be written so that instead of events or some kind of perception trigger causing transitions in the machine, fuzzy determinations (such as simple comparisons or calculations) can be used to trigger state transitions. Because of the way the framework in this chapter has been coded, this technique requires no code changes to implement. In fact, the implementation of AIsteroids laid out earlier in the chapter uses this technique. If it had been coded using the more traditional style of FSM, then all state transition logic would have been performed in the Control class, and each state's CheckTransition() method would have just been triggered by input events.

For example, in the StateIdle state, the CheckTransition() function checks whether there is a nearby asteroid, and if so, then checks the distance to it, and then assigns a transition. A classically designed FSM would have done the existence and distance checking from the Control class, and passed (or set a Boolean value that the function could check for) the input type ASTERIOD_CLOSE_TO_PLAYER, which the idle class would have then used to assign the transition to the Attack state. In this example, the transitions are still crisply defined, but they could have a fuzzier determination that takes into account a ramping-up phase (so that it wouldn't notice the asteroid for some set *reaction time*), or some set minimum time (so that the ship couldn't break out of a state until after some minimum has passed), or any other types of calculations you might want.

By allowing a more flexible means by which to assign transitions, the code framework opens the door to other, richer methods of assigning transitions. It also keeps some of the proprietary logic calculations within the confines of the state itself, instead of within a large controller class that would perform all the logic within its perception functionality.

STACK-BASED FSMs

Another variation on regular FSM layout is to extend the `m_currentState` member in the state machine class to instead be a stack data structure. As the machine makes transitions from state to state, it keeps a history of the preceding states by pushing them onto the stack. Once a state is completely finished, it is popped off the stack, and the next topmost state is made current again. This allows characters to have a limited form of memory, and their tasks can be interrupted (by a command from another character, or to deal with more pressing concerns, like being shot suddenly), but after the interruption is taken care of, they then return to whatever it was they were doing before.

Care must be taken when using this variant that interruptions clean up any errant stack problems when entering and leaving current status. So, let's say that an AI-controlled character that was in a `Patrol` state is interrupted by being sniped by the player and immediately switches to a `Take Cover` state. If the character were hit, it really wouldn't make sense for the character to go back to `Patrol` after the sniping danger is clear. The `Patrol` state being interrupted by the `Take Cover` state should actually be flagged as a *replacement* behavior, in that it replaces `Patrol` as the topmost behavior on the stack. This new state might also want to set an exit behavior, based on whether or not the character was wounded, so that the AI will have some state to go to that makes more sense. In that way, when the character comes out of hiding, the character won't just blindly start patrolling again but would, instead, call for help (if wounded), or investigate the area from which the shot came. Unless, of course, that's what you want your game to do.

MULTIPLE-CONCURRENT FSMs

The question of synchronizing or coordinating multiple FSMs is split into two categories: FSMs between multiple characters, and multiple FSMs controlling a single character. Multiple-character coordination is usually handled by a manager of some type, an observer class that gives both characters orders from above and can set up complex scenarios as a puppeteer of sorts. Some games handle this kind of activity with clever use of regular FSM systems that simply play off each other, state-wise, but really don't know anything about each other.

A situation that is a bit uncommon is multiple intracharacter FSM interaction. This requires that characters can be truly doing two things at once. This could be as simple and straightforward as a *Robotron* AI character using one FSM for movement and another for shooting (although these two systems are so completely separate in *Robotron* that it might be better to use a fuzzy state machine here; see Chapter 16, "Fuzzy-State Machines"). It could also be as complex as a series of FSMs running alongside each other for a real-time strategy (RTS) game AI opponent. An RTS opponent would need separate decision state machines for resource management, research, combat, and so on.

These FSMs might communicate with one another through an observer of some kind (possibly even another FSM, a "general" FSM that uses output from the other FSMs as transition conditions), through a shared data area (like in our AIsteroids FSM implementation), or by passing messages and event data between states and state machines.

Things to watch for in this kind of system would be problems that network code or parallel processing systems encounter. One state machine might overwrite a shared data member that a different state machine needs, two state machines might be in a feedback loop with each other, causing oscillation, there might be an inherent order to some calculations that cannot be guaranteed because of process timing issues, or the like.

DATA-DRIVEN FSMS

The push toward more richly defined AI behavior sets has led many developers to think about creating their FSM systems such that their construction is mostly done by nonprogrammers (likely designers and producers). This means that new (or im-proved) behaviors can be added to the system without much programmer involve-ment, giving more people on the project the ability to shape gameplay. There have been many different methods for implementing a data-driven FSM system. Some of the more popular ways to accomplish this are the following:

■ Scripted FSMs, using actual text files, or a simple macro language from within a regular code environment. This is probably the simplest to create, but also calls for a greater technical effort from the designers, especially because most scripting languages end up being subsets of a regular language anyway (most are generally a light version of C, although Python, LISP, or even assembly code-style scripting languages are not unheard of). A simplified version of a scripting system might comprise solely generic comparison evaluators (>, <, ==, !, =, etc.), and the script writer would set up the state machine by defining the transition connections between states by using predefined variables and values. Macro languages are a bit simpler to implement than a full language parser is (except for extremely simple languages) and have the advantage of being actual code, making them easier to debug. They have the disadvantages of code as well: Your designers now have to compile the game to run their new scripts (as well as obviously requiring the company to buy additional copies of the programming environment), although this is offset by being able to use modern source control tools on these macro files and, hence, provide for things like multiple people working on the same file with automatic merging, as well as setting up protected files that cannot be changed without permission.

- Visual editors have been written that allow designers to set up FSMs in much the same way as they would prototype them using standard FSM diagrams to show state connectivity and flow of the system. This kind of system is very easy for designers to use, but calls for a much greater commitment to coding than other systems do. The regular game has to be written to expose states, transition conditions, and other information to the editor, so the designers can build the FSM diagrams from these elements as this list grows or changes in the game. In addition to this, the editor itself must be written and maintained over the life of the product (and beyond, in some cases).

INERTIAL FSMS

One of the problems with FSMs is the concept of state oscillation (as detailed earlier in the chapter). This is caused when the events that cause transitions between states are too close in onset. An example might be a perception in a basketball game that keeps track if a player has an open lane to the basket. This perception *could* be created by doing a line-of-sight check between the player and the basket, and then checking that line of sight for collisions against all the other team's players. If this check is being performed very often (let's assume you have no optimizations in yet, and it is actually being checked every frame), then you can see how it would be very easy for this player to fluctuate wildly between the Stand state, and the DriveToTheBasket state because the line-of-sight collisions might vary slightly on each frame as other players moved about the court. This is exactly the kind of behavior you have to avoid, otherwise your characters will look very twitchy as they switch back and forth quickly between two or more behaviors.

The way to combat this is to introduce the notion of *inertia* into the system. This simply means that if a state has been actuated, it stays actuated for some time, or that new states have to overcome some inertia before they can fire in the first place. This can be done at either (or both) of two levels: the states themselves, or the perceptions that fire the states.

At the state level, the state machine itself can keep track of the current state and enforce minimum running times; this would model *inertia to change*, or what could be thought of as the single-mindedness of the AI system, "how often does it change its mind?" Oncoming states need to request promotion several times before actually becoming the current state; which models *static inertia*, analogous to some kind of environmental awareness, or what might be called reaction time. In this way, the perceptions would be kept as raw as possible, and the state machine would sample the perception stream to take notice of trends (instead of individual data change spikes) in the perception variables, and use this to make state changes. Also at the state level, you could also employ time functions when checking for transitions; the longer a state has been the current state in the machine, the more possible transitions out of it become. The transitions out always exist, they just become more freely accessible as time goes on. Say a game character is waiting for you to perform some feat in order to give you a prize. He could patiently wait until you performed the specific task to unlock his next state transition, or his AI system could recognize that a huge amount of time has passed within the game, and determine that the character should relax his requirements in order to advance the story. This could be done by giving the player a hint, or just giving him a secondary prize and some remark.

Inertia at the perception level is precisely the opposite. The state transitions are crisp, but the actuations of perception events are modeled in such a way that they represent the inertia in the system. Perceptions can take multiple firings to actuate (reaction time), require a certain level of perception to fire (sensitivity), continue to keep actuation after the perception has finished (ramp down, or extinction sensitivity), or even require another perception to fire before they themselves will fire, even in the event of the first perception's values becoming true (prerequisite conditions, or cascading actuation). An example from a basketball sports game: a condition called, "Has open line to the offensive basket" is used as a prerequisite for another condition, "Should I take the ball to the Hoop?" The second condition requires that the first condition be true for a number of game loops, so that the higher-level decision of taking the ball somewhere doesn't happen after a tiny, momentary opening in the defense.

Inertia from the perception side is sometimes more desirable because perceptions might be shared as triggers across many different states, and so building inertia into a single, commonly used perception might stop oscillation in a large part of the system. But, state-side inertia is more general and has the potential to be quicker to implement. A combination of the two methods can be used quite easily to get the exact level of smoothness (versus reactivity) that you want from your system.

Finally, remember that if your AI system requires extreme reactivity (in an action game, for instance, with very fast gaming requirements and instant AI player reactions), you might need to forgo these kinds of decision-smoothing techniques to rely instead on things such as the animation engine to help smooth out twitchy character artifacts. If the animation engine has a degree of inertia built into the blending system, or simply doesn't change the animation for a tick or three when actions change, the AI system could effectively jump around quite a bit and the overall look of the game wouldn't be harmed too much. In the end, however, this level of reactivity is rarely necessary because enemies that react at 1/60th of a second (or less) are not usually considered more intelligent and rarely end up being much fun. However, if the game includes a Boss monster with superhuman reactions, and the player has to use a magic item that will slow down the Boss, then it's a whole different story.

OPTIMIZATIONS

FSMs are easy to code and are probably the most efficient of all AI methodologies because they logically break the code into manageable chunks, both organizationally and computationally. There is room for optimization for both the algorithm (in speed of processing) and the overall data structure (for memory usage and such), so long as the code doesn't become too "overdesigned" as a result—you are trying to develop an FSM for your game, after all, not develop a generic class usable for any purpose. The common techniques are explored here.

LOAD BALANCING BOTH FSMS AND PERCEPTIONS

Load balancing refers to spreading the amount of computation to be done over time to lessen the immediate load on the processor. Think of it as buying something on credit: You get the object, but there's an increased cost. In purchasing, that cost is interest payments. In our system, the cost is overhead of having to create either time scheduling systems for our AI and perception systems or having to create incremental algorithms.

Load balancing is generally tackled one of two ways (both methods working just as well at both the AI and perception level): by having the system run at a set or scheduled rate (e.g., twice a second, or every other second), or by having a system that gives incrementally better results the more time it is given. Many pathfinding systems work under the latter system, in which they initially just give a rough direction to move toward, then give better and better paths as the time spent in the algorithm increases. Another kind of system along this path is an interruptible FSM system, in which the entire machine can be stopped after a set time limit, and then will start right where it left off when it gets another time slice from the system.

This kind of computational complexity isn't necessary for everything because simple time scheduling will work fine for most perceptions (we're modeling human behavior, and humans' own perception systems rarely work at 60+ frames per second), as well as for general AI decision-making systems (again, humans also rarely change their minds at 60+ fps). If the number of things needing scheduling becomes large, a good way to handle spreading out all the computations is to use an automated load-balancing algorithm to try to minimize the spikes in processing that invariably occur, while the system programmer keeps rough control over update scheduling. These kinds of algorithms keep statistical data on computation times and use extrapolation to predict future needs by the various game elements, and then use this data to determine the order in which to update objects to try to smooth out the processing.

LEVEL-OF-DETAIL (LOD) AI SYSTEMS

Level-of-detail (LOD) systems were originally (and still are) used by 3D graphics programmers to ease the amount of work that the rendering pipeline needs to perform, by having objects that are far away be displayed using models comprising fewer polygons and textures because the player won't notice the difference anyway. In some games, in which the player can see a very long way off, some LOD systems will actually reduce a game character to a single triangle with a certain color. But because it's so far off, the player can't tell, and the rendering engine isn't spending all the time it would take to compute everything for the 2,000 polygon model that it would usually use for that character.

This same sort of thinking is starting to migrate into AI work because we are now struggling with CPU-intensive AI routines, and we still have a limited player view of the world. So, why not simplify things for the AI when the player might not notice? Instead of generating a real path from A to B using the pathfinding system, a character in another part of the world from the human might just estimate how long it would take to get to some destination, and just teleport there after that time was up (a better way would be to teleport there in chunks, to minimize the chances of this behavior screwing things up or being noticed). A retreating character that manages to escape the human player might just get its health back after a set time, instead of actually having to hunt down health powerups and use them. This sounds a bit like cheating, and it can be if overused. However, by simulating the effect of things over time, as well as assuring that the human won't run into somebody in the wrong LOD or that the AI uses it too soon after the human is out of view, the feeling of cheating can be mitigated.

The problem with LOD systems in the AI world, as opposed to the graphics world, is that AI systems are unlike LOD systems for graphics rendering, which are mostly automatic. Some graphical LOD systems require special art be worked out for each step of LOD, but others autogenerate these additional detail levels. Then, the graphics engine just has to determine line of sight and distance from the player to determine the correct LOD to display the character at. With AI programming, behavior usually needs to be specially written for each LOD, so it should only be used in situations where there will be a significant savings in CPU expense that will not hinder gameplay. Consider a game that has dynamic crowds that mill about and interact with the environment. At the closest LOD, the crowd members could use full avoidance, collision response, interact with each other using facial expressions and animations, and spawn other objects like trash that they throw away. At the farthest LOD, they would still probably look pretty good as single polygons that have no collision at all, don't animate, and are simply moving along set path lines laid down in the city.

SHARED DATA STRUCTURES

This is one of the most basic and powerful techniques to optimize FSM computation speed. FSMs (at some level) need a system in which environmental conditions are triggering state transitions, and these conditions may be in some way shared by differing states, so an immediate speedup can ensure that different conditions are not recomputed by each state but, rather, are computed in some common area that is shared by the states. This is done in the AIsteroids demo by having some determinations directly in the states' `CheckTransitions()` methods, while having other calculations performed in the `FSMAIControl` structure's `UpdatePerceptions()` function.

Sometimes this functionality is so basic to the engine of the game that an entire shared-data framework paradigm is used when building the game engine. The *blackboard* architecture model is one such paradigm; it provides a formal way for any game object to publish information to a central data area, and interested objects can request this information or be given an event message with a location to look if they are concerned.

DESIGN CONSIDERATIONS

Before deciding to plunge fully into a state-based system, you should consider all the factors discussed in Chapter 2, "An AI Engine: The Basic Components and Design," concerning your game, and note the types of systems that FSMs model well: types of solutions, agent reactivity, system realism, genre, content, platform, development limitations, and entertainment limitations.

TYPES OF SOLUTIONS

Because of their general-purpose nature, FSMs can be adapted to any kind of solution type, both strategic and tactical. They are most at home with (obviously) *state* types of solutions, however, so note that the more specific the solution you require from your system, the more specific the state will have to be that provides that solution. Or, this means that you will require hierarchical FSMs to achieve more specificity. In general, FSMs really show their power if the number of states in a game is relatively small and the states themselves are much more separate and discrete. A system comprising 400 states that are all the same with small differences is going to incur quite a bit of overhead by an FSM structure, with little benefit.

AGENT REACTIVITY

FSM systems can be tuned to provide the system with any level of agent reactivity because of the simple nature of their processing models. In fact, most FSM systems run fast enough that decision stability needs to be a factor when you build FSMs (discussed with state oscillation in the Cons of FSMs section). The time it takes to make a transition decision by an FSM is practically instantaneous; the real cost is in the perception calculations.

This isn't how humans make decisions, however (except for very simple, hard-wired behaviors like reflex actions or instinctive acts). Humans are deliberative, have reaction times, and are affected by their environments when making decisions. When an AI makes decisions too fast, it seems robotic and jittery. This type of decisional jitter can be dealt with at either (or both) of two levels: the state machine itself, or at the perception level. Given that FSMs make all their transition determinations as a result of changes in perception, we can stop jitter in the state machine by stopping jitter in the perceptions.

You can handle this by implementing some of the techniques discussed in Chapter 2's section "Input Handlers and Perception," or this chapter's section on "Inertial FSMs." Thus, the reactivity of the AI-controlled characters can be explicitly controlled at many levels in an FSM system.

SYSTEM REALISM

FSM-based decision making tends to be unrealistic, unless the FSM system involved is very complex and the modeled behaviors wanted from the system are somewhat narrow. FSMs are static, and unless you have a complex hierarchical system that covers every possible event, they will respond in the manner in which the subset of possibility is shown to them through their perceptions. By their very nature, they can only respond to changes in the game with the states they've been provided with.

Humans tend to be very good at finding AI patterns of FSM behavior and can locate "missing" perceptions or states that can be exploited by the player very quickly. This might be what your game requires (for instance, in coding the Boss monster in a shooter game, the Boss might follow a set pattern of states for the duration of the battle, and finding this pattern is the player's key to getting past the Boss). Thus, FSM behavior models are usually used for more static behavior sets, or where unchanging lines of reaction are the goal of the system.

GENRE

FSMs have been used in every genre of game, again because of their lack of problem-specific context and simplicity of design. They thrive in genres with perceptions that can be calculated in simple terms, as well as unique sets of terms, so that the input space can be divided into usable states by the system. Our demonstration program, AIsteroids, is actually not an ideal candidate for FSMs because the gameplay is mostly similar across the whole of each wave (attack everything and get powerups), and the types of behaviors are so similar (usually turning and thrusting toward some target).

However, FSMs can be built in such a modular way that they can be used for a given subset of a game's decision structure, and not bleed into the rest of the AI engine. This means that if your game has a specialized element that is very state oriented, you can use this type of paradigm for just that part. This is usually the case in most games and is one of the reasons that FSMs are used in almost every game in some form or another.

CONTENT

This varies depending on the game being created. Does your game require decision-making elements that follow a state driven flow? Can this additional behavior be split into specific states, that are connected in some way by a system of transitions? If so, then an FSM can be used to control it. But if not, then you might need other types of control structures to capture the behavior of specialized systems that result from specific game content designs. One of the other techniques in this book might be a fit.

PLATFORM

FSMs are also platform independent because they don't have large demands of computing power or memory footprint. Old-style arcade games used to be somewhat more FSM dependant, because of these low demands. In fact, some very old arcade games used actual solid-state logic for their AI opponents (or patterns of enemy movement), and used FSMs in the electrical engineering sense.

DEVELOPMENT LIMITATIONS

FSMs lend themselves well to games with heavy development limitations because of their speed of development and debugging. Especially in very short projects, FSMs don't usually have the time to get convoluted by excessive additions and tweaking, which can plague FSM systems in the long run. Also, smaller-scale games that only have one AI programmer (or possibly a few) are also good candidates for FSMs, if everything else is a match, of course. It is easier for a limited number of people to remember the changing structure and connectivity of a developing state machine than it is for large teams or extremely separated teams.

Additional gameplay elements can be folded into FSMs much more easily than some systems, simply because if you can fit a new state into the state diagram completely, then the system can be coded to incorporate this change. FSM systems are easy to understand by incoming programmers; unlike more exotic AI systems that may require extended learning curve periods by new staff. Quality assurance is also generally quite painless with state-based models—behavior is usually quite simple to reproduce, and behavior logs and the like are trivial to implement and use.

ENTERTAINMENT LIMITATIONS

Entertainment concerns, especially difficulty levels and game balancing, are easily handled by state-based systems. If the difficulty level of gameplay is going to change during the game, then this setting itself might be controlled by an FSM that is responding to particular happenings in the game to respond with difficulty level switching. Game balance is made more straightforward because the system requires a state to respond to a change in any given perception state, in effect enforcing a rock-paper-scissors scenario. Thus, if your opponent is coming at you in the Rock state, you should be transitioning to the Paper state. Obviously, this assumes that your FSM model is working under reactive conditions, instead of predictive conditions, but there's no rule that says that the perceptions being fed into the state machine cannot be computed using predictive methods.

SUMMARY

FSMs are the duct tape of the game industry. They are simple, powerful, easy to use, and can be applied to almost any AI problem. However, just like duct tape, the resulting solution may work, but won't be pretty, is marginally hard to extend and modify, and might break if flexed too often.

- A state machine is defined as a list of states, and a structure that defines connectivity between the states given certain conditions.
- The FSM framework given in this book is more modular than most, in that it encapsulates the types of transitions and the transition logic within a single state. Each state is modular because it contains everything it needs to interact with the other states. This also allows more complex transition determinations than the classical input event method.
- The FSM system in this book comprises three main classes: FSMState, FSMMachine, and FSMAIControl.
- Our implemented FSM, in the AIsteroids test bed, uses only five states (Approach, Attack, Evade, GetPowerup, and Idle) to achieve fairly high performance, if a little superhuman.

- Extensions to the test bed for better performance include the addition of states, better math to handle wrapping, bullet management, and better attack and evade maneuvers.

- The pros of FSM systems are their ease of design, implementation, extension, maintenance, and debugging. They are also such a general problem-solving methodology that they can be applied to a broad range of AI issues.

- The cons of FSM systems are organizational informality, inability to scale, and state oscillation problems.

- Hierarchical FSMs allow increased complexity while allowing the overall state machine to maintain a level of organization through grouping. Code and data can also be shared locally to these states, instead of cluttering the global FSM structure.

- Message-based FSMs are great for systems that have a large number of states, or sporadic transition events. This system will broadcast transitional information instead of individual states having to poll perception systems for transition triggers.

- Stack-based FSM variants allow states to be interrupted by more pressing activities, and then returned to by means of the simple "memory" of a state stack.

- Multiple FSMs can control different aspects of a single AI-controlled character and tackle separate portions of the character's decision-making problems but still keep the system simple from an organization point of view.

- Data-driven FSMs using scripts or visual editors are a great way to empower designers to take control of the AI decision flow of a character, as well as add to the speed of creation and the extensibility of the product.

- Load-balancing algorithms can be applied to FSM systems, as well as to their perception systems, to achieve more stable CPU usage.

- Level-of-detail (LOD) AI systems can dramatically reduce CPU usage in games with many AI-controlled characters or large worlds that may be partially hidden to the human player.

- Shared data structures help curtail repetitive condition calculation in transitional logic for the various states in an FSM.

16 Fuzzy-State Machines (FuSMs)

In This Chapter

- FuSM Overview
- FuSM Skeletal Code
- Implementing an FuSM-Controlled Ship into Our Test Bed
- Example Implementation
- Coding the Control Class
- Performance of the AI with This System
- Extensions to the Paradigm
- Optimizations
- Design Considerations
- Summary

In the last chapter, we covered finite-state machines, which involved transitions between distinct states, only one of which could be occupying the system at a time. This chapter will cover a variant, but fairly far removed version of state machines called fuzzy-state machines (FuSMs).

FuSM Overview

FuSMs are built on the notion of fuzzy logic, commonly defined as a *superset of conventional (Boolean) logic that has been extended to handle the concept of partial truths.* It should be noted that FuSMs build on this notion, but do not represent actual fuzzy logic systems.

While the concept of partial truths is a very powerful notion, FuSMs are much less general in scope than regular FSMs. Like FSMs, FuSMs keep track of a list of possible game states. But, unlike FSMs, which have a singular current state and then respond to input events by transitioning into a different state, FuSMs instead have the possibility of being in any number of their states at the same time, so there are no "transitions." Each state in a fuzzy system calculates an *activation level,* which determines the extent to which the system is engaged in any given state. The overall behavior of the system is thus determined by the combination of the currently activated state's contributions.

FuSMs are really only useful for systems that *can* be in more than one state at a time and have more than simple digital values, such as on or off, closed or open, and alive or dead. Fuzzy values are more like halfway on, almost closed, and not quite dead.

A way of quantifying these kinds of value types is to use a unitary coefficient (a number between 0.0 and 1.0) that represents the condition's membership to each end state (0.0 == fully off, 1.0 == fully on), although being unitary is not necessary to the workings of the FuSM. It is simply an easy way to not have to remember specific limits on each state's membership, as well as ensuring ease of comparison between state membership values (both in direct comparison, as well as the multiplicitive value of a unitary value; you can multiply unitary numbers together and get an average value overall).

There is some confusion about what exactly FuSMs are (in the game AI community), because there are several FSM variants that are in the same family as FuSMs. These variants (which will be covered in further detail later in the chapter) include the following:

- *FSMs with prioritized transitions.* This model is still an FSM, so each state still has a list of possible transitions. In this model, the activation level of each applicable state is computed, and whoever has the highest activation level wins and becomes the new current state. This is how many programmers use the concept of fuzziness to enhance their decision-state machines, but the reality is that the system is still an FSM, and the predictability of the behaviors output by a system like this is only mildly less than that of a regular FSM.
- *Probabilistic FSMs.* In this form of FSM, there are probabilities placed on transitions out of states, so that the traversal of the FSM is more nondeterministic and thus less predictable. These probabilities could change over time, or could be set within an FSM, with the game using multiple FSMs to group together different probability sets.

    This is sometimes used when certain transitions have a number of *equivalent* output states. For example, approaching an enemy might cause an AI character to want to switch to one of three states (of equivalent value): `Punch`, `Kick`, or `HeadButt`. If there is only one output state in a given transition, the FSM functions as normal. But if there are multiple states, then probabilities are assigned to the multiples (either evenly, for total equivalence of choice, or biased toward certain states, or more complex determinations that consider whether one branch was recently taken or if the human keeps blocking a certain move, etc.).

- *Markov models.* These are like probabilistic FSMs, but the transition logic is completely probability-based, so they are useful for inducing some change in coupled states. As an overly simplistic example, say you have two states, `Aim` and `FireWeapon`. In this game, these two states are normally totally linked, in that whenever you're done aiming, you will fire your weapon. But, suppose instead you wanted to model a more realistic gun model, and so 2 percent of the time, `Aim` will instead transition to `WeaponJam`. This type of state transitioning is sometimes referred to (in other fields that use Markov models) as *reliability modeling.*

  In this example, the weapon is 98 percent reliable. Markov models are mainly used for these kinds of statistical modeling because one of the assumptions of the system is that the next state is related through probability to the current state. Thus, Markov models are very useful in fields such as risk assessment (in determining rates of failure), gambling (in finding ways to increase house profits), and engineering (to determine the tolerances necessary in fabrication to ensure reliability of the finished product to acceptable levels).

  A reactive videogame may have some elements that fall under this category, but because the main reasons that AI opponents may be changing states is in answer to the folly of a human player's actions, this kind of state prediction is rarely the norm. An interesting usage of this kind of system might be to actually model the *accidents* expressed by humans occasionally. An AI opponent could occasionally trip, drop the ball, or shoot himself in the foot.

  All these accidents could be handled at the basic run, hold ball, or shooting action level and could just happen from time to time by taking very unlikely branches in the tightly coupled animations of these activities. Whether or not this kind of realistic behavior fits in your game simulation, or is entertaining to the player at all, is left up to you.

- *Actual fuzzy-logic systems.* Contrary to popular belief, FuSMs are not really fuzzy-logic systems. Fuzzy logic is a process by which rules expressed in partial truths can be combined and inferred from to make decisions. It was created because many real-world problems couldn't always be expressed (with any degree of accuracy) as finite events, and real-world solutions couldn't always be expressed as finite actions. Fuzzy logic is merely an extension of regular logic that allows us to deal with these kinds of rule sets.

  The simplest form of actual fuzzy rule in game usage (which is very common), is straightforward if . . . else statements (or their equivalents, through a data table or some kind of combination matrix) that describe changes in behavior. For example, the statement "If my health is low, and my enemy's health is high, I should run away" is a straightforward fuzzy rule. It compares two perceptions (my health and my enemy's health) in a fuzzy manner (low versus high) and assigns it an action (run away). This statement has probably been written as an if statement in hundreds of games over the years. This represents the barest minimum of an actual fuzzy system. A real fuzzy-logic system would comprise many general fuzzy guidelines for any given combination of the player's health, the enemy's health, and all the other variables of concern into matrices of rules that will give a response action through algorithmic combination.

This tends to be a powerful way of getting results from a fuzzy system, but suffers when there are many fuzzy variables (each of which may have numerous possible value states or ranges) by creating a necessary rule set of quickly unmanageable size, a problem called *combinatorial explosion*. This can be worked around using a statistics technique called Combs method, which can reduce the required rule set, but also reduces accuracy.

FuSMs (as well as the previously mentioned similar variants) are rapidly becoming much more common in game AI usage. The predictability of FSMs is becoming undesirable, and the overall content of many games is becoming rich enough to warrant the additional design and implementation complexity of FuSMs.

FuSMs definitely require more forethought than their finite brothers do. The game problem must really be broken into the most independent elements that the problem allows. An FSM could be implemented within the confines of an FuSM system, by calculating digital activation levels and designing the system so that there is no overlap in state execution. Some people do this by accident (or through ignorance) when setting up a fuzzy system. It is much more natural for many problem situations to think in a finite way, so if you are finding it hard to come up with a methodology for FuSMs in your game, then it's probably because you shouldn't be using the fuzzy method in the first place. FuSMs are not as suited to the general range of problems as FSMs are. FuSMs are a kind of FSM that simply allow for the activation of multiple states as the current state, as well as being able to have a level of activation equivalent to the degree that the game situation merits each state.

In fact, many people will contend that FuSMs are not even really state machines at all (because the system isn't in a solitary state) but, rather, are more like fuzzy knowledge bases where multiple assertions can be partially true at the same time. But, by coding independent states to take advantage of these multiple assertions, we can use FuSMs to accomplish our AI goals that require this kind of blended behavior.

A very simple example of how a system like this might be used would be in coding a decision-making system for an AI-controlled enemy in *Robotron*. An FSM state diagram for a straightforward *Robotron* player is shown in Figure 16.1. There are three main states (this game is very similar to *Asteroids*, so the FSMs should look familiar): `Approach`, `Evade`, and `Attack`. In a strict FSM-based system, to move and shoot at the same time, the code would need to be written so that the `Approach` and `Evade` states start movement in a particular direction, but don't stop movement

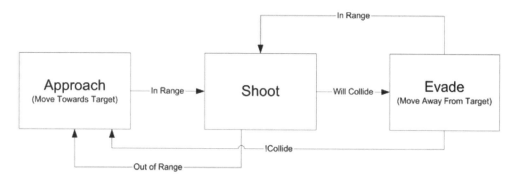

FIGURE 16.1   FSM diagram for a *Robotron* player.

when the state is changed. Thus, when the Attack state is in control, the player would still be moving from the last movement state that it was in. This works, but isn't very clean. The Attack state would have to keep checking for transitions to the other states, so that the player wouldn't run into enemies while shooting in another direction, or end up in a corner far away from all the enemies. A better way would be to create a FuSM for this game. Then, the player could Approach, Evade, and Attack all at the same time.

Like FSMs, FuSMs can be written in a free-form way. You could write an FuSM to better accomplish the FSM Robotron behavior as shown in Listing 16.1. Here you see the Update() function for a Robotron player using three different functions that will update if a condition has been met. The player class encapsulates both the methods to handle the different aspects of the overall behavior and the determination functions that establish which methods to use.

This is fine for relatively simple examples like this one, but generally is insufficient in a complex system. Consider an real-time strategy game in which you have an FuSM running the decision-making engine; it would divide the time it has for computation based on the activation levels of each independent decision-making system that needs updating, be it combat, resource, building, strategic, or whatever. You want to separate this logic into the various modules, making the system more organized, readable, and approachable by more than one programmer at a time.

LISTING 16.1   Update code for a free-form FuSM *Robotron* player.

```
void RobotronPlayer::Update(float dt)
{
    float urgency;
    if(CalculateApproachUrgency(urgency))
        Approach(dt,urgency);
```

```
        if(CalculateEvadeUrgency(urgency))
            Evade(dt, urgency);
        if(CalculateAttackUrgency(urgency))
            Attack(dt, urgency);
}
```

Also notice in this *Robotron* example that one of the states, Attack, really can't be completely fuzzy. The player is either shooting, or not shooting, because you cannot partially fire a laser (although you could think of a partial attack as one meant to cripple instead of to kill). This is not the case with the other states, in which movement can be expressed as a smooth gradient between not moving and moving at full speed. This "defuzzification" of the Attack state doesn't hurt the rest of the system, however, and doesn't invalidate the method. FuSMs can easily blend in more digital states by having the activation level be calculated in a digital way; the system will still respond to this digital state just like the others.

FuSM Skeletal Code

Like FSMs, the code for FuSMs will be implemented in three main classes:

1. The FuSMState class, the basic fuzzy *state*.
2. The FuSMMachine class, the fuzzy-state machine.
3. The FuSMAIControl class, the AIControl class that handles the working of the machine, and stores game-specific information and code.

The FuSMState Class

At their most pure level of implementation, states in an FuSM system are wholly disconnected systems. Each state will use perception variables (from the Control class, or a more complex and dedicated perception system) to determine *activation level* (which will be represented in this book by a number between 0 and 1), which is the measure of how fully active the state needs to be to respond to the perceptions. The activation level could correspond to the amount of some value in the game, such as aggression; an activation level of 0.0 means the character is not aggressive at all, 1.0 means it is completely consumed with rage.

The minimum requirements for an FuSM state are much like an FSM state:

■ Enter(). This function is always run as soon as you enter the state. It allows the state to perform initialization of data or variables.

- Exit(). This function is run when you are leaving the state and is primarily used as a cleanup task, or where you would run (or start running) any additional code that you wanted to occur on specific transitions (for Mealy-style state machines).
- Update(). This is the main function that is called every processing loop of the AI, if this state is the current state in the FSM (for Moore-style state machines).
- Init(). This function initializes the state.
- CalculateActivation(). This function determines the fuzzy activation level of the state. It returns the value, and stores it in the state as the m_activationLevel data member. As you will see later in the chapter, more digital states (such as the Attack state in our test bed) can be modeled here by returning Boolean values instead of the normal unitary value.

The header for this class is given in Listing 16.2. Again, this class has been created to be as general as possible to allow for the maximum flexibility in implementing it into your game. As you can see, it is very similar to the FSM class, with the exception of the m_activationLevel data member. In fact, this data member could be combined into the FSM class, and a hybrid system could be developed that uses both kinds of states interchangeably.

LISTING 16.2   FuSMState header.

```
class FuSMState
{
public:
    //constructor/functions
    FuSMState(int type = FUSM_STATE_NONE,
              Control* parent = NULL)
        {m_type = type;m_parent = parent;
         m_activationLevel = 0.0f;}
    virtual void Update(float dt){}
    virtual void Enter()           {}
    virtual void Exit()            {}
    virtual void Init()            {m_activationLevel = 0.0f;}
    virtual float CalculateActivation()
                        {return m_activationLevel;}

    virtual CheckLowerBound(float lbound = 0.0f)
            {if(m_activationLevel < lbound)
              m_activationLevel = lbound;}
    virtual CheckUpperBound(float ubound = 1.0f)
            {if(m_activationLevel > ubound)
              m_activationLevel = ubound;}
```

```
    virtual CheckBounds(float lb = 0.0f,float ub = 1.0f)
            {CheckLowerBound(lb);CheckUpperBound(ub);}


    //data
    Control*    m_parent;
    int         m_type;
    float       m_activationLevel;
};
```

The class has three bounds-checking functions, which are really just floor and ceiling checkers for your activation levels. You can call any of these from your states, or none at all if you want totally raw activation levels.

Like normal FSMs, the class also contains two data members, m_type, and m_parent. The type field can be used by both the overall state machine and the interstate code, to make determinations based on which particular state is being considered. The enumeration for these values is stored in a file called FuSM.h and is currently empty, containing only the default FuSM_STATE_NONE value. When you actually use the code for something, you would add all the state types to this enumeration, and go from there. If you wanted to be more data-driven and not pollute the base class at all, you could set up a system in which you register all the state types with the base class. The parent field is used by individual states, so they can access a shared data area through their Control structure.

THE FuSMMachine CLASS

This class (the header is Listing 16.3) contains all the states that the machine needs to keep track of, just like the equivalent FSMMachine class. It also contains a list of all the currently activated states. Also like the FSMMachine, the fuzzy machine is a child of the FuSMState class, so that hierarchical FuSMs can be constructed by making a particular fuzzy state be an entire FuSM.

LISTING 16.3   FuSMMachine header.

```
class FuSMMachine: public FuSMState
{
public:
    //constructor/functions
    FuSMMachine(int type = FUSM_MACH_NONE,Control* parent = NULL);
    virtual void UpdateMachine(float dt);
    virtual void AddState(FuSMState* state);
    virtual bool IsActive(FuSMState* state);
    virtual void Reset();
```

```
    //data
    int m_type;
protected:
    std::vector<FuSMState*> m_states;
    std::vector<FuSMState*> m_activatedStates;
};
```

UpdateMachine(), which runs the general fuzzy machine, is shown in Listing
16.4. As you can see, the system is simple: run each state's CalculateActivation()
function, separate out the activated states, Exit() all the nonactivated states as a
group, and then call Update() for all the activated states. Although it might seem
attractive to simply call the exit or update method for each state in turn, rather than
store the states in separate vectors, it would be very restrictive to do so. It needs to
be done in this manner because the Exit() function from some nonactivated states
might reset some things that activated states have turned on or need to change
while updating.

LISTING 16.4   FuSMMachine::UpdateMachine() function.

```
void FuSMMachine::UpdateMachine(float dt)
{
    //don't do anything if you have no states
    if(m_states.size() == 0)
        return;

    //check for activations, and then update
    m_activatedStates.clear();
    std::vector<FuSMState*> nonActiveStates;
    for(int i =0;i<m_states.size();i++)
    {
        if(m_states[i]->CalculateActivation() > 0)
            m_activatedStates.push_back(m_states[i]);
        else
            nonActiveStates.push_back(m_states[i]);
    }

    //Exit all non active states for cleanup
    if(nonActiveStates.size() != 0)
    {
        for(int i =0;i<nonActiveStates.size();i++)
            nonActiveStates[i]->Exit();
    }
```

```
        //Update all activated states
        if(m_activatedStates.size() != 0)
        {
            for(int i =0;i<m_activatedStates.size();i++)
                m_activatedStates[i]->Update(dt);
        }
    }
```

THE FuSMAIControl CLASS

Finally, Listing 16.5 shows the control class for the FuSM system. It is virtually identical to the FSM control class and contains the global data members necessary to run the system, as well as a pointer to the fuzzy machine structure. In more formalized games, with many global data members, or complex perception update calculations, it would probably be better to create a dedicated perception system instead (controlled through the control class), but this small list being updated directly with the UpdatePerceptions() method is fine for our test application.

LISTING 16.5 FuSMAIControl header.

```
class FuSMAIControl: public AIControl
{
public:
    //constructor/functions
    FuSMAIControl(Ship* ship = NULL);
    void Update(float dt);
    void UpdatePerceptions(float dt);
    void Init();

    //perception data
    //(public so that states can share it)
    GameObj*    m_nearestAsteroid;
    GameObj*    m_nearestPowerup;
    float       m_nearestAsteroidDist;
    float       m_nearestPowerupDist;
    bool        m_willCollide;
    bool        m_powerupNear;
    float       m_safetyRadius;

private:
    //data
    FuSMMachine* m_machine;
};
```

IMPLEMENTING AN FuSM-CONTROLLED SHIP INTO OUR TEST BED

The AI system necessary to run our AIsteroids main ship doesn't lend itself to the fuzzy system, because most states are just transitions to other states (you have to turn to shoot, but also turn to thrust). So, in our FuSM test bed example, we have a second kind of ship, the Saucer, which is dramatically different from our main ship. The Saucer doesn't require turning to thrust. It flies with anti-gravity, and thus doesn't suffer from inertia or slow acceleration. It can thrust in any direction it wants and has dampeners internally to keep the pilot safe. Because of this amazing ability, it has also been equipped with a gun turret that can fire in any direction. It also has a tractor beam that it can use to drag objects toward itself.

This kind of craft has independent systems and is relatively free from having to connect the different parts of its decisions (movement is almost completely separate from attacking, and grabbing objects has also been decoupled), so it is now a good candidate for an FuSM system to run it. Given some basic perceptions, each system (guns, engines, tractor beam) can operate independently, and concurrently. Thus, our ship will no longer use a state system, in that it progresses from one state to another but, rather, will operate under the fact that each independent activity will control whether or not it is contributing to the overall behavior of the ship.

EXAMPLE IMPLEMENTATION

In the following sections, the necessary classes to implement the `Saucer` and an FuSM controlling its behavior will be introduced and fully described.

A NEW ADDITION, THE Saucer

The `Saucer` is the game implementation of the new ship type (see the header in Listing 16.6). As you can see, it is very similar, although the `GetClosestGunAngle()` method just returns the passed-in angle because the turret can fire in any direction.

LISTING 16.6 `Saucer` header.

```
class Saucer : public Ship
{
public:
    //constructor/functions
    Saucer(int size = 7);
```

```
        void Draw();
        void Init();

        //bullet management
        virtual void Shoot();
        virtual float GetClosestGunAngle(float angle)
                                     {return angle;}
    };
```

OTHER GAME MODIFICATIONS

To allow the saucer to work, several other systems were included. The base ship class was given controls to deal with the tractor beam and the AG thruster (antigravity, or noninertial drive). It was also given a vector for the direction of the AG drive m_agNorm. This vector can be assigned in two different ways: you can use AGThrustOn(vector) to turn on the drive and set the direction to the normalized value of the passed in vector, or you can use AGThrustAccumulate(vector), which will turn on the drive but then add the vector into the m_agNorm variable. It will then be normalized as it is used by the ship's update method for movement. This is an important part for the fuzziness of the system. Each state that requires movement will use the AGThrustAccumulate() method to request ship movement and will scale the vector it will pass in by multiplying it by its current activation level. By doing this, a state with a high activation level will contribute more to the ship's direction of movement than will a state with a low activation level. The base class ship Update function then checks whether the AG drive is turned on, and if so, applies the m_agNorm vector to the position of the ship, thereby giving it instant acceleration and the ability to ignore inertia.

Another addition to the code is the new GameSession::ApplyForce() function. This function is overloaded twice, the first takes an object type, a force vector, and a delta time as parameters to apply the force. It will run through the game's object list and add the force to any objects of the types passed in. The second ApplyForce() method takes an object type, a force line, the force vector, and a delta time to apply the force. We will be using this method to simulate the tractor beam, as it first checks if the object has collided with this force line before it will apply the force.

THE FuSM SYSTEM

In Figure 16.2, you can see the diagram of the FuSM. Unlike the FSM implementation for the asteroids game, there are only four states instead of five. An FSM system is essentially a closed loop and must have a current state at all times. In the FSM implementation, the Idle state worked as the primary branching point for all

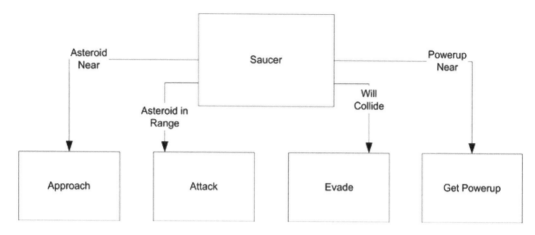

FIGURE 16.2   FuSM diagram for the asteroids game.

the other states in the system, serving as the state of last resort. But, an FuSM can run any number of states (including none), so this state isn't necessary in the fuzzy system. As seen in Figure 16.2, these basic states are the following:

- Approach, which will get the ship within range of the closest asteroid.
- Attack, for the saucer, is merely firing the guns in the direction of the nearest asteroid. The ship has forward-firing weapons and needs to turn and face its target, but the saucer has a gun turret.
- Evade, which will initiate avoidance of an asteroid on a collision course by monitoring the ship's speed.
- GetPowerup, which will try to scoop up powerups within some range. Unlike the ship, however, the saucer has a tractor beam that it will use to grab the powerups.

The FuSM requires a few bits of data so it can calculate each state's activation level. These are the following:

1. The distance to the nearest asteroid is used to determine the activation of three of the states, Approach, Evade, and Attack. The closer an asteroid is, the more the craft will evade and attack; the further away, the greater the activation of the approach behavior.
2. The distance to the nearest powerup. This affects the activation of the GetPowerup state. The closer the saucer is to the powerup, the more it will try to get it.

There are a few things to notice about the system. Each fuzzy state has no information about other states in it. Each state is only concerned with the perception checks that directly deal with itself only. In the FSM implementation, almost every state needed to watch for the m_willCollide field to be true, to transition to the Evade state.

Also note the reduction of redundant state transition checks that are found in the finite system. Many of the states in our asteroids FSM example were interconnected because of the somewhat even priority rating of all the states in the FSM. If you find that your FSM is employing an almost completely connected state diagram, your system may be a good candidate for an FuSM. This is not always the case, but if your game can traverse from any state to any other, the likelihood is that there isn't too much in the way of prerequisite, linear behavior being exhibited by your system.

CODING THE CONTROL CLASS

The controller class for the FuSM model (see Listing 16.7 for the header, Listing 16.8 for the implementation of the important functions) contains the state machine structure, as well as the global data members for this AI model.

LISTING 16.7   FuSMAIControl class header.

```
class FuSMAIControl: public AIControl
{
public:
    //constructor/functions
    FuSMAIControl(Ship* ship = NULL);
    void Update(float dt);
    void UpdatePerceptions(float dt);
    void Init();

    //perception data
    //(public so that states can share it)
    GameObj*    m_nearestAsteroid;
    GameObj*    m_nearestPowerup;
    float       m_nearestAsteroidDist;
    float       m_nearestPowerupDist;
    bool        m_willCollide;
    float       m_safetyRadius;

private:
    //data
    FuSMMachine* m_machine;
};
```

The fuzzy control class is much simpler from a perception point of view. However, we can attribute this to breaking the rules of asteroids (such as the saucer having no inertia, a gun turret, and a tractor beam), not because we're using an FuSM. It is simply easier, mathwise, to get the saucer to move to and avoid specific locations because it doesn't have to worry about its own velocity as much.

The FSM AI data member `m_powerupNear` is no longer necessary; it was more of an event trigger that the FSM could respond to, but the fuzzy system uses the distance from the powerup to directly relate to the activation level of the `GetPowerup` state.

The `Update()` method is exactly the same as in the FSM implementation. It won't run the controller if there is no ship to control, and it simply updates the perceptions and the fuzzy machine itself.

LISTING 16.8   `FuSMAIControl` important function implementations.

```
FuSMAIControl::FuSMAIControl(Ship* ship):
AIControl(ship)
{
    //construct the state machine and add the necessary states
    m_machine = new FuSMMachine(FUSM_MACH_SAUCER,this);
    m_machine->AddState(new FStateApproach(this));
    m_machine->AddState(new FStateAttack(this));
    m_machine->AddState(new FStateEvade(this));
    m_machine->AddState(new FStateGetPowerup(this));
}


//--------------------
void FuSMAIControl::Update(float dt)
{
    if(!m_ship)
    {
        m_machine->Reset();
        return;
    }

    UpdatePerceptions(dt);
    m_machine->UpdateMachine(dt);
}


//--------------------
void FuSMAIControl::UpdatePerceptions(float dt)
{
    if(m_willCollide)
        m_safetyRadius = 30.0f;
```

```
        else
            m_safetyRadius = 15.0f;

    //store closest asteroid and powerup
    m_nearestAsteroid = NULL;
    m_nearestPowerup  = NULL;
    m_nearestAsteroid = Game.GetClosestGameObj(m_ship,
                            GameObj::OBJ_ASTEROID);
    if(m_ship->GetShotLevel() < MAX_SHOT_LEVEL)
        m_nearestPowerup  = Game.GetClosestGameObj(m_ship,
                            GameObj::OBJ_POWERUP);


    //asteroid collision determination
    m_willCollide = false;
    if(m_nearestAsteroid)
    {
        m_nearestAsteroidDist = m_nearestAsteroid->
                    m_position.Distance(m_ship->m_position);
        float adjSafetyRadius = m_safetyRadius +
                            m_nearestAsteroid->m_size;

        //if you're too close,
        //flag a collision
        if(m_nearestAsteroidDist <= adjSafetyRadius )
            m_willCollide = true;
    }

    //powerup near determination
    if(m_nearestPowerup)
        m_nearestPowerupDist = m_nearestPowerup->
                    m_position.Distance(m_ship->m_position);
}
```

CODING THE FUZZY STATES

The four state implementations: FStateApproach, FStateAttack, FStateEvade, and FStateGetPowerup (Listings 16.9 to 16.12) will be discussed separately in the following sections.

FStateApproach

FStateApproach merely computes the vector to the closest asteroid and uses it as a thrust vector for the antigravity drive of the saucer. There's no magic here; the antigravity drive simply works as discussed earlier by directly affecting position instead of acceleration.

The CalculateActivation() method returns a zero if there aren't any nearby asteroids; otherwise it returns a normalized value that is between 0.0f (when the distance to the asteroid is almost zero) and 1.0f (when the distance is at or above FU_APPROACH_DIST). The CheckBounds() call ensures that the activation value falls in this range.

Finally, the Exit()function stops the AG drive because this is the only mode that the state dealt with.

LISTING 16.9 FStateApproach implementation.

```
//--------------------
void FStateApproach::Update(float dt)
{
    //turn and then thrust towards closest asteroid
    FuSMAIControl* parent = (FuSMAIControl*)m_parent;
    GameObj* asteroid = parent->m_nearestAsteroid;
    Ship*    ship     = parent->m_ship;
    Point3f deltaPos  = asteroid->m_position −
                        ship->m_position;


    //move there
    ship->AGThrustAccumulate(deltaPos*m_activationLevel);

    parent->m_target->m_position = asteroid->m_position;
    parent->m_debugTxt = "Approach";
}


//--------------------
float FStateApproach::CalculateActivation()
{
    FuSMAIControl* parent = (FuSMAIControl*)m_parent;
    if(!parent->m_nearestAsteroid)
        m_activationLevel = 0.0f;
    else
        m_activationLevel = (parent->m_nearestAsteroidDist −
         parent->m_nearestAsteroid->m_size)/FU_APPROACH_DIST;
    CheckBounds();
    return m_activationLevel;
}
```

```
//-------------------
void FStateApproach::Exit()
{
    if(((FuSMAIControl*)m_parent)->m_ship)
        ((FuSMAIControl*)m_parent)->m_ship->StopAGThrust();
}
```

FStateAttack

FStateAttack is also a bit simpler than the FSM version. Again, the saucer doesn't have to turn like the regular ship, so all it needs to do is calculate a leading angle and fire.

The activation function for this state is digital, either 0 or 1, because you cannot partially fire a gun at something. In a more complex game, we could create a more analog system by strategically targeting specific areas of a target (like the shield generators on a large spacecraft) or to discriminate between targets. The state is simply on if there is an asteroid and it is within firing range, or it is off.

There is no Exit() method for this state because the shoot command is not an on/off toggling command. It only fires one shot at a time.

LISTING 16.10 FStateAttack implementation.

```
//-------------------
void FStateAttack::Update(float dt)
{
    //turn towards closest asteroid's future position, and then fire
    FuSMAIControl* parent = (FuSMAIControl*)m_parent;
    GameObj* asteroid = parent->m_nearestAsteroid;
    Ship*    ship     = parent->m_ship;

    Point3f futureAstPosition = asteroid->m_position;
    Point3f deltaPos = futureAstPosition - ship->m_position;
    float dist  = deltaPos.Norm();
    float time = dist/BULLET_SPEED;
    futureAstPosition += time*asteroid->m_velocity;
    Point3f deltaFPos = futureAstPosition - ship->m_position;

    float newDir = CALCDIR(deltaFPos);
    ship->Shoot(newDir);

    parent->m_target->m_position = futureAstPosition;
    parent->m_debugTxt = "Attack";
}
```

```
//--------------------
float FStateAttack::CalculateActivation()
{
    FuSMAIControl* parent = (FuSMAIControl*)m_parent;
    if(!parent->m_nearestAsteroid)
        m_activationLevel = 0.0f;
    else
        m_activationLevel = parent->m_nearestAsteroid &&
            parent->m_nearestAsteroidDist < FU_APPROACH_DIST;
    return m_activationLevel;
}
```

FStateEvade

This state follows suit with the other movement states. It calculates a vector away from the nearest asteroid and sets up the AG drive to thrust in that direction.

Its activation level goes up as it gets to the nearest asteroid, to simulate getting more single-minded about evasion as it closes in on a collision.

It turns off the AG engine when exiting, like other states that use the antigravity system.

LISTING 16.11   FStateEvade implementation.

```
//--------------------
void FStateEvade::Update(float dt)
{
    //evade by going away from the closest asteroid
    FuSMAIControl* parent = (FuSMAIControl*)m_parent;
    GameObj* asteroid = parent->m_nearestAsteroid;
    Ship*    ship     = parent->m_ship;
    Point3f vecBrake = ship->m_position - asteroid->
                                              m_position;
    ship->AGThrustAccumulate(vecBrake*m_activationLevel);

    parent->m_target->m_position = parent->
                          m_nearestAsteroid->m_position;
    parent->m_debugTxt = "Evade";
}


//--------------------
float FStateEvade::CalculateActivation()
{
    FuSMAIControl* parent = (FuSMAIControl*)m_parent;
    if(!parent->m_nearestAsteroid)
```

```
            m_activationLevel = 0.0f;
        else
            m_activationLevel = 1.0f - (parent->
                            m_nearestAsteroidDist - parent->
                            m_nearestAsteroid->m_size)/
                            parent->m_safetyRadius;
        CheckBounds();
        return m_activationLevel;
    }


    //--------------------
    void FStateEvade::Exit()
    {
        if(((FuSMAIControl*)m_parent)->m_ship)
            ((FuSMAIControl*)m_parent)->m_ship->StopAGThrust();
    }
```

FStateGetPowerup

Unlike the normal ship, the saucer is equipped with a powerful tractor beam that drags powerups toward itself when activated. It still will approach the powerup, and the urgency of the approach will be controlled by the state's activation level. The state will also turn on the tractor beam to drag the powerup in.

The activation calculation method is much like the FStateEvade state, in that the closer to the powerup, the stronger the activation. This is so that the saucer will make more of an effort (with its maneuvers) to pick up the powerup if it is very close by. Otherwise, the tractor beam will do most of the work.

The Exit() method needs to turn off both the tractor beam and the AG engine because it uses both.

LISTING 16.12 FStateGetPowerup implementation.

```
    //--------------------
    void FStateGetPowerup::Update(float dt)
    {
        FuSMAIControl* parent = (FuSMAIControl*)m_parent;
        GameObj* powerup = parent->m_nearestPowerup;
        Ship*    ship    = parent->m_ship;

        Point3f deltaPos = powerup->m_position -
                        ship->m_position;
```

```
    ship->AGThrustAccumulate(deltaPos*m_activationLevel);
    ship->TractorBeamOn(-deltaPos);

    parent->m_target->m_position = powerup->m_position;
    parent->m_debugTxt = "GetPowerup";
}


//--------------------
float FStateGetPowerup::CalculateActivation()
{
    FuSMAIControl* parent = (FuSMAIControl*)m_parent;
    if(!parent->m_nearestPowerup)
        m_activationLevel = 0.0f;
    else
        m_activationLevel = 1.0f - (parent->
                    m_nearestPowerupDist - parent->
                    m_nearestPowerup->m_size)/
                    FU_POWERUP_SCAN_DIST;
    CheckBounds();
    return m_activationLevel;
}


//--------------------
void FStateGetPowerup::Exit()
{
    if(((FuSMAIControl*)m_parent)->m_ship)
    {
        ((FuSMAIControl*)m_parent)->m_ship->StopAGThrust();
        ((FuSMAIControl*)m_parent)->
                            m_ship->StopTractorBeam();
    }
}
```

PERFORMANCE OF THE AI WITH THIS SYSTEM

With the FuSM system in place, as well as the much more lenient gameplay rules that the saucer has to follow, it is all but unstoppable at destroying the asteroids in the test-bed game. It will play as long as you let it, and it has survived several hours of continuous play in testing. Figure 16.3 shows the saucer going to work. It does still die occasionally, but could be made completely unstoppable with the same kinds of improvements that would help the FSM system.

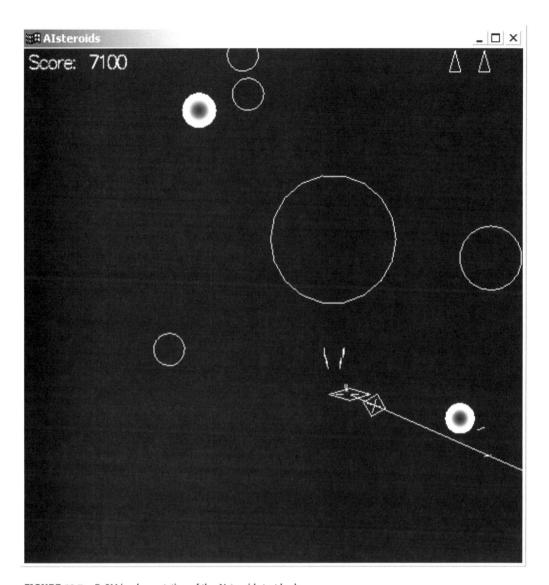

FIGURE 16.3   FuSM implementation of the AIsteroids test bed.

Increase the complexity of the math model to give the AI system the ability to deal with the world coordinates wrapping. Right now, the AI's primary weakness is that it loses focus when things wrap in the world, so accounting for this during targeting and collision avoidance would greatly increase the survivability of the AI ship. Even this weakness is considerably lessened by the saucer's capabilities over the regular ship because the saucer never floats across a border like the ship does.

Bullet management for the ship. Right now, it just points, and then starts firing. With such a fast firing rate on the guns, the saucer tends to fire clumps of shots toward targets. This is somewhat advantageous; when firing a clump of shots into a large asteroid, the remaining shots will sometimes kill the pieces as the asteroid splits. But this can get the ship in trouble when it has fired its entire allocation of bullets, and must wait for them to collide or expire before it can shoot again, leaving it temporarily defenseless.

PROS OF FuSM-BASED SYSTEMS

FuSMs are very straightforward to design, for the right problems. If your AI situation involves independent, concurrent systems, then this model allows you to design the separate systems as just that: separate systems without any concern for each other. Therefore, you don't incur the effort of designing the transition events and links between states that FSM systems require. The model provides a simple way in which to activate each state according to a scale that you can define for the particular problem. FuSMs also allow digitally activated states to be mixed in freely with the more fuzzy ones by simply setting up the activation calculator to return digital values.

Implementating an FuSM system is typically easier than FSMs because of the lack of transitions. Each state can be implemented in a pure vacuum, with only the global perception data (stored in the control class) as the glue holding the system together.

Extending a fuzzy system is as uncomplicated as finding other states that will freely mix with the system. In our asteroids example, another state could be added to aid evasion in the form of a repulsion beam, the opposite of the tractor beam. This would shoot out from the ship and deflect incoming asteroids. Adding a state that controlled the use of the repulsion beam to the FuSM would be almost effortless; by copying the `GetPowerup` state and changing a few lines to affect the nearest asteroid instead of powerups and changing the direction of the force that will be applied to the rocks.

Debugging a fuzzy system is also quite straightforward. Because of the uncoupled nature of the states, you can disable any that you are not concerned with at the time, and then concentrate on the remaining active states. You can see how minimal the evasion code for the saucer is by disabling the attack state. The saucer will try to evade the rocks, but because it is taking only one asteroid into account at a time, it will invariably be surrounded and crushed. To extend the abilities of the craft, advanced evasion techniques (possibly involving moderate pathfinding or some form of influence map analysis) could be implemented and tested, without having to worry about the very efficient attack behavior mowing everything down and clearing the way for the saucer.

FuSMs scale very well, again because of the disconnected nature of the states. The only problem that you have to deal with is the notion of too much blending, which might lead to very average or muddy behaviors on the whole. Say that our test bed not only had Approach, Evade, and Get Powerup behaviors vying for the movement of the ship. Instead, it also has states trying to dock with floating bases, maneuvering for the use of transportation gates of some kind, responding to formation requests from other friendly saucers, and maybe even responding to emergencies like wormholes. Eventually, so many states would be affecting the direction of thrust for the AG drive that the ship might not be able to move at all. The more states that are blending into a particular trait of the system, the more diluted each individual state's contribution becomes. This dilution can be overcome by trying to combine states into like-minded groups (the previous example of a transportation gate-handling state could possibly be considered a different kind of powerup, and the wormhole handler could be grouped into Evade, for instance).

Fuzzy systems allow a much greater range of behavioral personality to be exhibited by your AI-controlled agents. The current FuSM saucer implementation can be made more "aggressive" by lowering the FU_APPROACH_DIST define. By upping the priority of the evasion behavior and raising the overall activation level of the powerup state, you would end up with a more defensive character, which would even appear greedy when powerups were present. Different saucers could be coded using separate classes that redefined the CalculateActivation() methods of the various states, or they could use a data-driven interface that would access a list of attributes to tweak the overall mix of behaviors toward specific personality traits.

The FSM problem of state oscillation is nonexistent in the FuSM world. FuSMs can actually be in every state at once, or none at all, so there is no real concept of switching back and forth between states. The problem is somewhat replaced by the notion of *behavior* oscillation, however, and is discussed in the next section.

CONS OF FuSM-BASED SYSTEMS

FuSMs are not as general a problem solver as FSMs. FSMs are a way of modeling behaviors that happen, one after another, in sequence; they represent a circular, progressive system that allows reactivity, proactive tasking, and prerequisite actions. FuSMs are better suited to a complex behavior system that can be constructed by blending smaller, unconnected behaviors together. This concept of blending is key. FuSMs are uniquely qualified for dealing with gradients of behavior. Games don't always require or even want this kind of behavior, because subtle behavioral differences are often lost in the fast movement, low graphical resolution, fixed animation, and simplified art assets of the game world. In the future, when advances in facial animation and physics-based movement systems (which would model movement based on the forces acting on a person, rather than a hand made or motion captured animation that is being played by a character) are the norm, FuSMs will be an integral part of bringing the full range of emotion and ambiance to AI-controlled characters. For right now, pure FuSM systems are a niche technique useful for specific groups of behaviors.

Badly designed FuSMs can exhibit *behavior oscillation*. This is when an AI-controlled character cycles one or more behaviors on and off in a rapid fashion. With our asteroids saucer, we don't have to worry about this because the only states that might fight each other are *exact* opposites, the Approach and Evade states. However, they cancel each other out if both states are at maximum values, and the ship will sit still. But if Approach and Evade used nonopposite vectors, and Approach wanted to get closer than Evade wanted to allow, the ship might behave oddly: it might move in circles or with some kind of cyclical diagonal zigzagging. The way to solve this is precisely the way that our asteroids saucer does: model behaviors like the human body uses its muscles, with complementary yet opposite states that get the job done and work together to mute activation inconsistencies.

EXTENSIONS TO THE PARADIGM

As discussed at the start of this chapter, FuSMs are somewhat misunderstood. The various reasons that people employ FuSM-like behavior structures are many. Some of the more useful of these extensions and variants will be covered here.

FuSMS WITH A LIMITED NUMBER OF CONCURRENT STATES

You might have a system where you want a series of behaviors that have a smooth gradient of activation, but only one or possibly a few behaviors are going to be able to update. FuSMs can be easily extended to treat the activation level of each state as a priority function, and the winner (or some number of the highest priority states) will end up being the only one to update. With a single state, this system becomes more like the FSM with fuzzy transitions variant discussed in Chapter 15.

If you still allow multiple current states, you could think of this method as a means of fighting the dilution problem discussed earlier in the previous section. Particular fuzzy states could be tagged with subtypes, and the highest priority subtype would win for that particular subtype category. In our AIsteroids example, attack would be a subtype, along with movement and tractor beam. So, Approach and Evade would fight to be the winner of the sole movement state that gets to function. This works to help with dilution, but also defuzzies the system because you are taking additional blended elements out of the overall behavior. Limiting the max number of executing states can also be employed as a computation cost-saving optimization for games in which CPU time is a concern.

An FuSM Used as a Support System for a Character

Although fully fuzzily-controlled characters are somewhat rare (look at how many rules we had to break in the original AIsteroids example to get a good candidate for FuSMs), specific parts of a character might be extremely good places for this method. A facial expression system might be a very good fit for this kind of scheme. Each state would be a particular emotion: happy (would curl the mouth and squint the eyes), sad (would arch the eyebrows and droop the mouth), mad (bares the teeth, brings together eyebrows, opens eyes), and so on. Each emotion would activate to a level based on separate perceptions, and the whole system would run concurrently with whatever the rest of the AI system was doing.

An FuSM Used as a Single State in a Larger FSM

Even though not all the states or behaviors a given character employs might be independent or fuzzy, specific sections might. A simple example is a character that runs a normal state machine while running around the map, getting items and interacting with others. But when the character stands still, a fuzzy state might start up that would blend together three separate behaviors: looking around (the shorter time he's been in this environment, the more inquisitive he is about it), fidgeting (the more tasks he has, or the longer he's waited, or the less time since his last enemy encounter, the more nervous he is), and whistling (the more safe he feels, the noisier he'll be when standing around). This idle behavior is the overall FSM's current state, but it will also be running any or all of these fuzzy substates to model the standing behavior of the character.

Hierarchical FuSMs

Just like FSMs, FuSMs can easily be made hierarchical. The skeletal code has the FuSMMachine class inheriting from the FuSMState class to facilitate this. However, this isn't the most useful notion, design-wise. Multiple states could be running simultaneously, so there is little reason to group states together, except for organization. If you are combining some of these variant methods, this would be more useful. You could use an FuSM to contain additional FuSMs that use the "limited number of current states" method mentioned earlier. Each sub-FuSM would return the highest priority state within its subtype, and then all the winners would run under the parent FuSM.

Another type of combination system might be an FSM in which each state is an FuSM. This becomes, in effect, a fuzzy system that can switch out its entire fuzzy-state system based on game events or perception changes. This is a very powerful and general-purpose system.

Imagine a hierarchical FSM containing states that are either FuSMs (for more dynamic and emergent behavior), or regular FSMs (for more static or semiscripted reactions to game events), giving the programmer the ability to use the exact system that best suits the specific state of the game.

DATA-DRIVEN FuSMs

Data driving an FSM usually means allowing designers some method (either in script or through a visual interface of some kind) to set up states and be able to show transition connectivity between the states, as well as assign conditions to the transitions.

In FuSMs, the control is changed, in that the designers would instead decide which states they want to add to the total machine (which will become the different elements that are blended to become the end behavior), and then control the activation calculations of each state, either by laying down conditions and simple equations directly, or by affecting a standard calculation with modifiers (such as adjusting the state's activation level boundaries, or by applying some scale factor). This kind of data could be tweaked on a per-character level, to get different personality types out of the system, or on a difficulty basis, to affect how behaviors are selected to affect the overall difficulty of the game.

OPTIMIZATIONS

FuSMs have the potential of running many different states concurrently, and so can become more computationally expensive than their FSM brothers. FuSMs do not incur the transition calculations of a finite system, but have their own activation computation costs. The same kinds of optimizations that FSMs use apply to fuzzy systems: load balancing, level-detail systems, and shared data.

DESIGN CONSIDERATIONS

FuSMs are good for AI problems that are quite different from those that their FSM brothers handle. The checklist of considerations when deciding on an FuSM-based system include types of solutions, agent reactivity, system realism, genre, platform, development limitations, and entertainment limitations.

TYPES OF SOLUTIONS

FuSMs are another very general problem-solving tool and can be used to implement many kinds of solution types. FuSMs are a bit paradoxical, in that they work very well for very high-end solution types, and for very low-end solution types. The reason being is that both tend to be organic solutions that combine several elements to achieve a final solution. More stylized or scripted behaviors (the kinds that end up being in the middle of the road, behavior-wise) tend to be more suited to state-based systems because they usually have a lot of prerequisite activity and are typically activated by crisp perceptions.

A high-level decision maker for an RTS game might combine the output of several fuzzy states such as reconnaissance, resource gathering, diplomacy, combat, and defense to determine its overall activity. An even higher-level decision process could have a *counselor* state for each of these areas, and then blend the advice from these counselors to form an overall decision about how to run a civilization as a whole. Lower-level, or tactical decision-making examples might include blending immediate orders or goals (go here, attack this unit, gather this resource) with secondary states of behavior (motioning to other units for support, combat evasion when that unit is not a combat unit, fleeing when badly hurt, etc.).

AGENT REACTIVITY

Given a sparsely connected state structure, FuSMs are generally more reactive than FSMs because there isn't a transition structure that the character has to traverse to reach a goal. But, with simple FSMs or interconnected FSMs, there is very little cost difference between the two methods, and almost any level of reactivity can be built into each state of the system. The techniques described in the section on Inertial FuSMs can be used to help tune the level of agent reactivity that your game requires.

SYSTEM REALISM

Games based on FuSMs can have a much greater sense of realism because the final behavior of the system is a continuous curve of perception reaction. This feels much more realistic than does a character hitting some threshold and then changing to some other state. A well-designed FuSM will react to perception changes in a realistic manner, by *adjusting* its current behavior, not completely changing to something new. Most people respond to a new situation by slightly modifying their ongoing behavior (unless the new situation is life-threatening or very shocking, although even then the new behavior is initiated as a delta from what the person was already doing, but this kind of quick change in behavior can be modeled by an FuSM as well).

GENRE

FuSMs, because they are a fairly general technique, will work with any genre of game in some limited fashion. When considered as a *primary* game-wide AI framework, they are definitely limited by genre. You wouldn't want to try to implement a linear, scripted game using a fuzzy-state system. But even in a game that doesn't require this kind of problem solving generally, there might be a use for the kind of fuzzy behaviors that FuSMs can accord.

The perception system of a game could be written using an FuSM as the framework. Perceptions are usually independent and can usually be coded with very little thought to any other perception. The fact that perceptions have arbitrary output values (Booleans, continuous floating-point values, enumerated types, etc.) is fine with the FuSM system. An FuSM doing this kind of work would use the different states to represent each perception, with the state's `Update()` method computing the perception value, and the activation level operating as the indicator that the game needs to update the perception. All the secondary perception calculations, such as reaction time, load balancing, and so on could be handled through the `CalculateActivation()` function. Time-scheduled updates could be handled within special data members of the `FuSMState` class, which could keep records for any scheduling system, so that the fuzzy machine could decrement timers or determine triggers for updating states.

PLATFORM

The memory and CPU requirements for FuSMs are as minimal as any other basic game AI technique, and so FuSMs are generally platform independent. However, they do lend themselves to more subtle behavior, which is usually the realm of PC games. Whether to use them or not is usually more a game design issue.

DEVELOPMENT LIMITATIONS

If your AI problem falls into the kinds of situations that FuSMs handle well, then there is no better means by which to implement them. FSMs are easy to understand and implement, but FuSMs are not much more difficult and provide a much richer and more dynamic product. FuSMs are just as straightforward to debug as FSMs; even though they have a greater range of behavioral outputs, they are still deterministic (unless you have specifically set them up not to be).

ENTERTAINMENT LIMITATIONS

Tuning difficulty settings, balancing specific behaviors, and other entertainment concerns are generally quite easily performed with FuSM based behavior. They can be tuned from a state-by-state basis, at the perception level, or any combination. Some behaviors might have a synergistic effect with another behavior (such as the attack state's ability to bail out the simplistic `Evade` state in the AIsteroids implementation), and make some tuning a careful affair, but usually individual states can be tuned separately.

SUMMARY

FuSMs build on the straightforward FSM system, by allowing complex behaviors that can be broken into separate, independent actions to be constructed by blending these actions together at different levels of activation. This powerful extension to the FSM concept gives the FuSM method the ability to create a much broader range of output behavior, but adds the requirement of this style of aggregate behavior-building.

- The definition of FuSMs is somewhat hazy, with confusion existing between real FuSMs and similar systems, such as FSMs with fuzzy transitions, probabilistic FSMs, Markov models, and actual fuzzy-logic systems.
- FuSMs do not use a single current state but, rather, can have any number of active states, each with a variable level of activation.
- Some states in an FuSM can have digital activation levels, and this defuzzification of some part of the system is fine and will not affect the overall method.
- The skeletal FuSM framework discussed in this book is built on three base classes: `FuSMState`, `FuSMMachine`, and `FuSMAIControl`.
- The original game doesn't fit well into the FuSM model, so we added a new ship class, the saucer, that flies with antigravity (no inertia or acceleration), has a gun turret that can fire in any direction, and a tractor beam to drag powerups toward itself. This provides us with a much more ideal candidate for an FuSM control structure because the saucer uses mostly independent systems, most of which have variable levels of activation.
- The implementation of an FuSM into the AIsteroids test bed needs only four states: `Approach`, `Attack`, `Evade`, and `GetPowerup`. Its state implementations are much simpler than those of the FSM system, and the perception calculations are also simpler, but this is more because of the saucer breaking some of the game rules that the regular ship was following, rather than because of the switch in AI techniques. However, the saucer is superior to the FSM implementation in performance and can play almost indefinitely.
- Extensions to the AIsteroids game for better performance would be to figure world wrapping into attacking and evasion, and bullet management routines.
- The pros of FuSM systems are their ease of design (for the right style of problems), implementation, extension, maintenance, and debugging. They allow a much greater range of behavioral personality and do not suffer from the FSM problem of state oscillation.
- The cons of FuSM systems are that they are not as general of a solution system as FSMs are, and they can have behavioral oscillation problems if designed poorly, but this can easily be countered with forethought.

- FuSMs with a limited number of current states can be written to tune the level of fuzziness you want to use in your game. You can have one current state, a few, or limit current states within subtypes of states.
- An FuSM used as a support system for a character is a great way of adding fuzziness only where it is needed in the implementation of complex characters, such as in a facial expression system.
- An FuSM used as a single state in a larger FSM can be used to represent a character that has very fuzzy behavior determination, but only within the confines of a larger finite game state.
- Hierarchical FuSMs are usually quite rare in their most pure form because they don't make much sense, but when combined with other state machine variants, their true power is seen.
- Data driving FuSMs involves designer control over the particular states a character might use, as well as affecting activation level calculation.
- FuSMs can benefit from the same kinds of optimizations used in regular FSMs.

17 Message-Based Systems

In This Chapter

- Messaging Overview
- Messaging Skeletal Code
- Client Handlers
- Example Implementation in Our AIsteroids Test Bed
- Coding the States
- Performance of the AI with This System
- Extensions to the Paradigm
- Optimizations
- Design Considerations
- Summary

I n the world of modern game programming, only one technique is used more than state machines. That technique is the use of messaging (or events, as they are also called). The concept of messaging is simple. Instead of game entity A checking game entity B for particular changes every tick, or even on some time schedule, A is informed of changes from a *message* that is delivered to A from B only when the change has occurred. This means that nobody has to waste computation cycles or code space by making checks throughout the game engine to determine if things are happening. The game informs the entity with messages about the kinds of occurrences it is interested in, and then goes about its merry way, not worrying about it until another message comes in for delivery.

MESSAGING OVERVIEW

Unlike many of the other techniques discussed in this book, messaging is not a decision-making structure, per se. It is more of a communication technique that can be used in the game to help with organization, optimization, and ease of communication between disparate objects and classes in the game. Messaging serves as a secondary system that resides below the underlying decision structure of your game. It is used in games in which this type of communication is cost-effective, and as games become more complex, that category is growing. Most modern games can benefit from using messaging systems in their engines.

AI systems have two main traits that make them good candidates for using message-based communication:

1. AI-controlled characters are most often created to be reactive, in that they regularly depend on an outside perception change to affect the behavior of the character. This makes sense; we are reacting to the human player interacting with the game. But this also means that AI systems can do a lot of waiting for perception changes or perform many computations determining those perception changes. AI characters might be completely inactive, especially if they are not visible to the human player, for large chunks of gameplay time. Spending time performing calculations during these periods would be wasteful.

2. AI is a very high-level part of game development. The AI programmer might have to communicate with many other game systems (including animation, character and world physics, gameplay, controls, sound, etc.) when creating the condition checks and behaviors for the AI system. Without some form of abstraction when performing this communication between parts of the engine, your game will be strapped with an AI system that has access into every other area in the game engine. Although this gives the AI programmer a lot of power (to do harm as well as good), this is generally considered bad programming methodology and can lead to un-maintainable systems that are all but impossible to extend, debug, and understand.

   Messaging is uniquely qualified to conquer these issues. It creates a system that is completely reactive because the system is only responding to event messages. It also decouples data from the code, so that AI systems can request data from other areas in the game, and not have to have full access to the underlying class structure of those systems. It provides a central way of moving data and events between AI code sections and the greater game, so that the underlying AI system can change, without having to recode the entire process of getting information from the rest of the game.

   This chapter will lay the framework for a general case event messaging system that you can use for your entire game, or for parts of a game. This general framework will comprise three main parts: a message object, the

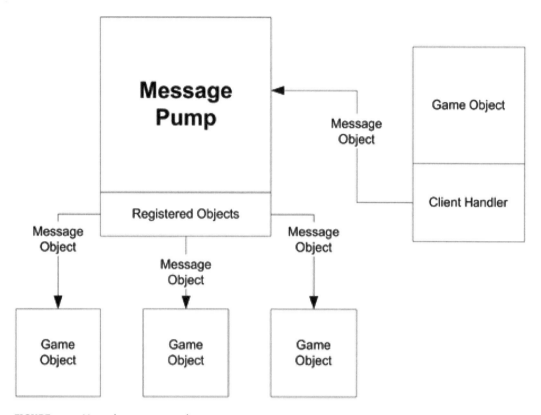

FIGURE 17.1   Messaging system overview.

message pump, and client handlers. See Figure 17.1 for a visual representation of this architecture.

MESSAGING SKELETAL CODE

The general messaging system this chapter will introduce is implemented using these base classes:

- The Message class that stores the individual information requirements of a message.
- The MessagePump class, which is the central message router.
- Client handlers, which run code to accommodate any given incoming message.

In the following sections, each of these classes will be fully discussed.

THE MESSAGE OBJECT

The message object is a general structure that is used to store a message. You can see that the header in Listing 17.1 contains only a few data fields:

m_typeID is the type of message.

m_fromID is the unique ID of the object that sent the message. This is an optional data field for a message because messages can be sent anonymously.

m_toID, is the ID of the object that the message is to be delivered to. Again, this is an optional field because the message pump can also have messages that have been registered for delivery by a given object, so the message itself doesn't need to specify.

m_timer is used for setting delays in delivering messages.

m_delivered is used by the message pump to mark messages that have been processed so that they can be removed from the queue.

DataMessage is also included in the file and is a simple template class that has a single data field of whatever type you pass in. You can use this class to pass messages with simple data fields, but you'll have to implement additional types of messages if you require more complex data sending. In any case, a message handling callback function would just cast the incoming message to the type it knows it is (from the message ID type) and access the data through the cast pointer.

LISTING 17.1   Message class header.

```
class Message
{
public:
    //constructor/functions
    Message(int type = MESSAGE_DEFAULT){m_typeID =
                type;m_delivered = false;m_timer = 0.0f;}
    ~Message(){}

    //data
    int    m_typeID;
    int    m_fromID;
    int    m_toID;
    float m_timer;
    bool  m_delivered;
};

//simple template message class for simple data passing
template <typename T>
```

```
class DataMessage: public Message
{
public:
    DataMessage(int type, T data):Message(type){m_dataStorage = data;}
    ~DataMessage(){}

    //data member
    T m_dataStorage;
};
```

THE MessagePump

The MessagePump is the class that will store all the possible message types, as well as be the central location that messages are delivered to and from. The MessagePump will keep track of delayed messages, broadcast messages to interested objects, and generally act as the post office for the system. Listing 17.2 shows the header for the class, and Listing 17.3 shows the important method implementations.

As the header shows, we will be implementing the MessagePump as a singleton, which is a software design pattern that just means that there will be only one global instance of this class for the entire game. The #define at the bottom of the header provides clean access to the singleton class structure.

LISTING 17.2   MessagePump header.

```
typedef std::list<Message*> MessageList;
typedef std::map<int,MessageType*> MessageTypeMap;

class MessagePump
{
public:
    static inline MessagePump& Instance()
    {
        static MessagePump inst;
        return inst;
    }

    static void Update(float dt);
    static void AddMessageToSystem(int type);
    static  int RegisterForMessage(int type, int objected,
                                 Callback& cBack);
    static void UnRegisterForMessage(int type, int objectID);
    static void SendMessage(Message* newMessage);
```

```
protected:
    MessagePump();
    MessagePump& operator= (const MessagePump&){}

private:
    static MessageTypeMap m_messageTypes;
    static MessageList    m_messageQueue;
};

#define g_MessagePump MessagePump::Instance()
```

The implementation listing shows the important functions for the `MessagePump` class.

The `Update()` method checks each message in the queue, and either decrements its timer if it is a delayed message, or delivers the message to anyone that has registered for that message by supplying a callback function. The function then removes all the delivered messages from the queue.

`AddMessageToSystem()` is used to insert message types into the pump's list of possible messages. This can be performed at any time, whether it is class creation or as you get new objects that require the system to store information on new message types.

`RegisterForMessage()` requires two things: that the message type be in the system, and that you aren't already registered for the message. If both of these things are true, it will add you to the notification list for the specific message type that you passed in.

`UnRegisterForMessage()` does just what its name implies. It cycles through all the registrations for a specific message and removes the player from the list.

LISTING 17.3   `MessagePump` **implementation.**

```
//-------------------
void MessagePump::Update(float dt)
{
    if(m_messageQueue.size() == 0)
        return;

    //process messages
    MessageList::iterator msg;
    for(msg=m_messageQueue.begin();
        msg!=m_messageQueue.end();++msg)
    {
        if((*msg)->m_timer > 0)
        {
            //delayed message, decrement timer
```

```
                            (*msg)->m_timer -= dt;
                    }
                    else
                    {
                        //check for registrations
                        MessageTypeMap::iterator mType;
                        mType = m_messageTypes.find((*msg)->m_typeID);
                        if(mType == m_messageTypes.end())
                            continue;

                        MessageRegList::iterator msgReg;
                        for(msgReg=(*mType).second->
                            m_messageRegistrations.begin();
                            msgReg!=(*mType).second->
                            m_messageRegistrations.end();++msgReg)
                        {
                            //deliver message by launching callback
                            if((*msgReg)->m_callBack)
                                (*msgReg)->m_callBack.function
                                        ((*msgReg)->m_objectID,(*msg));
                        }
                        (*msg)->m_delivered = true;
                    }
                }

            //remove all delivered messages from queue
            MessageList::iterator end    = m_messageQueue.end();
            MessageList::iterator newEnd = std::remove_if
                        (m_messageQueue.begin(),m_messageQueue.end(),
                         RemoveIfDelivered);

        if(newEnd != end)
            m_messageQueue.erase(newEnd,end);
    }

//--------------------
void MessagePump::AddMessageToSystem(int type)
{
    //ensure that this type isn't already in the system
    MessageTypeMap::iterator mType;
    mType = m_messageTypes.find(type);

    if(mType == m_messageTypes.end())
    {
        MessageType *newType = new MessageType;
```

```
            newType->m_typeID = type;
            m_messageTypes[type] = newType;
    }
}


//--------------------
void MessagePump::SendMessage(Message* newMessage)
{
    m_messageQueue.push_back(newMessage);
}


//--------------------
int MessagePump::RegisterForMessage(int type, int objectID,
                                        Callback& cBack)
{
    //only register once
    MessageTypeMap::iterator mType;
    mType = m_messageTypes.find(type);

    if(mType == m_messageTypes.end())
        return REGISTER_ERROR_MESSAGE_NOT_IN_SYSTEM;

    MessageRegList::iterator msgReg;
    for(msgReg=(*mType).second->
        m_messageRegistrations.begin();
        msgReg!=(*mType).second->
        m_messageRegistrations.end();++msgReg)
    {
        if((*msgReg)->m_objectID == objectID)
            return REGISTER_ERROR_ALREADY_REGISTERED;
    }
    //add new registration
    MessageReg* newRegistration  = new MessageReg;
    newRegistration->m_callBack  = cBack;
    newRegistration->m_objectID  = objectID;

    (*mType).second->m_messageRegistrations.
                    push_back(newRegistration);
    return REGISTER_MESSAGE_OK;



}
```

```
//-------------------
void MessagePump::UnRegisterForMessage(int type, int objectID)
{
    //find entry
    MessageTypeMap::iterator mType;
    mType = m_messageTypes.find(type);

    if(mType == m_messageTypes.end())
        return;

    MessageRegList::iterator msgReg;
    for(msgReg=(*mType).second->
        m_messageRegistrations.begin();
        msgReg!=(*mType).second->
        m_messageRegistrations.end();++msgReg)
    {
        if((*msgReg)->m_objectID == objectID)
        {
            (*mType).second->
                m_messageRegistrations.erase(msgReg);
            delete (*msgReg);
            //you can exit out here, there is only one
            //registration allowed per message type
            return;
        }
    }
}
```

CLIENT HANDLERS

In this implementation, the message handler functions will be written as callbacks. Callbacks are functions that, when the message is delivered to a particular game object, represent the code that the game object wants to run to respond to the message.

Another type of general message handling system that is often used is simply having a `ProcessMessage()` function, which would, in essence, be a big switch statement with either code or function calls to answer any passed-in message type. Using callbacks offers a more flexible system than this, and avoids the cumbersome, all-encompassing processing function.

C++ doesn't allow direct member functions to be used as callbacks, so we will be using the common method of having a dummy callback class (with a virtual function representing the form of the callback method), for callback objects to inherit from. These callback objects are then used in the place of traditional C-style callbacks. Listing 17.4 shows the dummy callback header, as well as an example function using the interface.

LISTING 17.4 `Callback` system, with example.

```
class Callback
{
public:
    virtual void function(int pid, Message* msg);
};

class EvadeCallback : public Callback
{
    void function(int pid, Message* msg);
};
```

EXAMPLE IMPLEMENTATION IN OUR AISTEROIDS TEST BED

In this section, we will rework the FSM version of our test bed to use messaging to perform all state transitions, as well as use the system to effect other game changes, such as giving orders to the ship from a state. To do this, we will need to make some changes to the original finite-state system and incorporate the new code for the transition callbacks and messaging functions.

The AIsteroids test bed really isn't a game that demands this technique. The state transitions happen frequently. There is very little time when the main ship is waiting for something to do. Very few objects in the game world require a clear channel of communication or interaction. Messaging in this game will actually add overhead, and probably slow down the system a bit, because it will be continually registering and unregistering for messages as it changes states. This implementation is really just to show practical application of the method, but should not be taken as a good example of when to use messaging in a game environment.

THE MessState CLASS

Listing 17.5 shows the header for the `MessState` class. Very little has to change from the original state class that we used in the FSM chapter. We no longer need the `CheckTransition()` function because this logic will no longer be in each individual state. Instead, the `Control` class will do the calculations and send off the correct messages to set off the transition callbacks.

The `Enter()` and `Exit()` methods will now be responsible for setting up the message registrations for the state, as well as any other cleanup functionality. In this way, messages are scoped to the particular state because any given state will then respond only to those messages that have meaning within the state.

The `Init()` method can be used to add any additional message types to the system that the state requires. This is useful for self-directed messages that a state might use. For example, a state called `Flee` might first notice the enemy, wait for a half second (simulating a reaction time), and then start to flee. You could set this up as two states (`Notice` and then `Flee`), or the `Flee` state itself could, upon entry, put itself in a wait mode (during which the previous behavior of the character wouldn't change) and send itself a wakeup message delayed for half a second. When this message comes back, it would change the wait status of the character, and the character would then flee.

LISTING 17.5   `MessState` header.

```
class MessState
{
public:
    //constructor/functions
    MessState(int type = FSM_STATE_NONE,Control* parent = NULL)
                                    {m_type = type;m_parent=parent;}
    virtual void Enter()        {}
    virtual void Exit()         {}
    virtual void Update(float dt)  {}
    virtual void Init()         {}

    //data
    Control*    m_parent;
    int m_type;
};
```

THE MessMachine CLASS

The state machine itself has only one change from the finite version, in the `UpdateMachine()` function. As Listing 17.6 shows, a single line is missing from this method, where the current state's `CheckTransitions()` function is called. This model will not poll for transition changes. Instead, messages for state transitions will be sent from the individual states to the control class, which will respond to those messages by directly setting the m_goalID member of the MessMachine.

LISTING 17.6 MessMachine update implementation.

```
void MessMachine::UpdateMachine(float dt)
{
    //don't do anything if you have no states
    if(m_states.size() == 0 )
        return;

    //don't do anything if there's no current
    //state, and no default state
    if(!m_currentState)
        m_currentState = m_defaultState;
    if(!m_currentState)
        return;

    //check for transitions, and then update
    int oldStateID = m_currentState->m_type;

    //switch if there was a transition
    if(m_goalID != oldStateID)
    {
        if(TransitionState(m_goalID))
        {
            m_currentState->Exit();
            m_currentState = m_goalState;
            m_currentState->Enter();
        }
    }
    m_currentState->Update(dt);

}
```

THE MessAIControl CLASS

Listing 17.7 contains the header for the MessAIControl class, as well as the call-back class that the controller will use to respond to requests to change the state of the machine. You will notice that it is very similar to the regular FSM controller. The real difference between the controllers is in their implementation; Listing 17.8 shows the relevant functions in the message controller file.

LISTING 17.7   MessAIControl header.

```
class ChangeStateCallback : public Callback
{
    void function(int pid, Message* msg);
};

class MessAIControl: public AIControl
{
public:
    //constructor/functions
    MessAIControl(Ship* ship = NULL);
    void Update(float dt);
    void UpdatePerceptions(float dt);
    void Init();
    void SetMachineGoalID(int state);

    //perception data
    //(public so that states can share it)
    GameObj*    m_nearestAsteroid;
    GameObj*    m_nearestPowerup;
    float       m_nearestAsteroidDist;
    float       m_nearestPowerupDist;
    bool        m_willCollide;
    bool        m_powerupNear;
    float       m_safetyRadius;

private:
    //data
    MessMachine* m_machine;
    ChangeStateCallback m_changeStateCallback;
};
```

The implementation differences are much more noticeable. The constructor must also set up the messaging system for the game, so it has to add all the applicable message types to the pump. The constructor also registers for the change state message because the controller will now be causing the state-machine transitions by responding to message requests from the states.

The biggest change is in the UpdatePerceptions() method. Here you can see that some of the logic that was contained in the CheckTransitions() state functions has been transferred here instead. This does go against the modular organization model that the initial FSM system was written to incorporate, and this code showing up here is a sure sign that you shouldn't be using this method for your game. Although this function is straightforward enough in this simple test application, even a moderately complex game would require a great deal more logic to generate the messages necessary to perform all the transitions. Again, this implementation is merely showing the code in use, but is not warranting this as a good game usage.

LISTING 17.8   `MessAIControl` **implementation.**

```
//-------------------
MessAIControl::MessAIControl(Ship* ship):
AIControl(ship)
{
    //construct the state machine and add the necessary states
    m_machine = new MessMachine(FSM_MACH_MAINSHIP,this);
    MStateApproach* approach = new MStateApproach(this);
    m_machine->AddState(approach);
    m_machine->AddState(new MStateAttack(this));
    m_machine->AddState(new MStateEvade(this));
    m_machine->AddState(new MStateGetPowerup(this));
    m_machine->AddState(new MStateIdle(this));
    m_machine->SetDefaultState(approach);

    g_MessagePump.AddMessageToSystem(MESSAGE_WILL_COLLIDE);
    g_MessagePump.AddMessageToSystem(MESSAGE_NO_ASTEROIDS);
    g_MessagePump.AddMessageToSystem(MESSAGE_NO_POWERUPS);
    g_MessagePump.AddMessageToSystem(MESSAGE_ASTEROID_NEAR);
    g_MessagePump.AddMessageToSystem(MESSAGE_ASTEROID_FAR);
    g_MessagePump.AddMessageToSystem(MESSAGE_POWERUP_NEAR);
    g_MessagePump.AddMessageToSystem(MESSAGE_POWERUP_FAR);
    g_MessagePump.AddMessageToSystem(MESSAGE_CHANGE_STATE);

    g_MessagePump.RegisterForMessage(MESSAGE_CHANGE_STATE,
                       m_ship->m_ID,m_changeStateCallback);
}

//-------------------
void ChangeStateCallback::function(int pid, Message* msg)
{
    ChangeStateMessage* csMsg = (ChangeStateMessage*)msg;
    int newState = *((int*)(csMsg->m_data));
    ((MessAIControl*)Game.m_AIControl)->
                          SetMachineGoalID(newState);
}
```

```
//--------------------
void MessAIControl::SetMachineGoalID(int state)
{
    m_machine->SetGoalID(state);
}


//--------------------
void MessAIControl::Init()
{
    m_willCollide   = false;
    m_powerupNear   = false;
    m_nearestAsteroid = NULL;
    m_nearestPowerup  = NULL;
    m_safetyRadius    = 15.0f;

    m_target = new Target;
    m_target->m_size = 1;
    Game.PostGameObj(m_target);
}


//--------------------
void MessAIControl::Update(float dt)
{
    if(!m_ship)
    {
        m_machine->Reset();
        return;
    }

    UpdatePerceptions(dt);
    m_machine->UpdateMachine(dt);
}


//--------------------
void MessAIControl::UpdatePerceptions(float dt)
{
    if(m_willCollide)
        m_safetyRadius = 30.0f;
    else
        m_safetyRadius = 15.0f;

    //store closest asteroid and powerup
    m_nearestAsteroid = Game.
          GetClosestGameObj(m_ship,GameObj::OBJ_ASTEROID);
```

```
if(m_ship->GetShotLevel() < MAX_SHOT_LEVEL)
    m_nearestPowerup  = Game.
        GetClosestGameObj(m_ship,GameObj::OBJ_POWERUP);
else
    m_nearestPowerup = NULL;

//reset distance to a large bogus number
m_nearestAsteroidDist = 100000.0f;
m_nearestPowerupDist  = 100000.0f;

//asteroid collision determination
m_willCollide = false;
if(m_nearestAsteroid)
{
    float speed = m_ship->m_velocity.Norm();
    m_nearestAsteroidDist = m_nearestAsteroid->
                m_position.Distance(m_ship->m_position);
    float dotVel;
    Point3f normDelta = m_nearestAsteroid->m_position -
                m_ship->m_position;
    normDelta.Normalize();
    float astSpeed = m_nearestAsteroid->
                                    m_velocity.Norm();
    if(speed > astSpeed)
        dotVel  = DOT(m_ship->UnitVectorVelocity(),
                      normDelta);
    else
    {
        speed = astSpeed;
        dotVel = DOT(m_nearestAsteroid->
                    UnitVectorVelocity(),-normDelta);
    }
    float spdAdj = LERP(speed / AI_MAX_SPEED_TRY, 0.0f,
                        50.0f)*dotVel;
    float adjSafetyRadius = m_safetyRadius + spdAdj +
                            m_nearestAsteroid->m_size;

    //if you're too close, and I'm heading
    //somewhat towards you, flag a collision
    if(m_nearestAsteroidDist <= adjSafetyRadius &&
       dotVel > 0)
    {
        m_willCollide = true;
        Message* msg = new Message(MESSAGE_WILL_COLLIDE);
```

```
            g_MessagePump.SendMessage(msg);
        }
        else
        {
            Message* msg = new Message(MESSAGE_WONT_COLLIDE);
            g_MessagePump.SendMessage(msg);
        }

    }
    else
    {
        Message* msg = new Message(MESSAGE_NO_ASTEROIDS);
        g_MessagePump.SendMessage(msg);
    }

    //powerup near determination
    m_powerupNear = false;
    if(m_nearestPowerup)
    {
        m_nearestPowerupDist = m_nearestPowerup->m_position.
                            Distance(m_ship->m_position);
        if(m_nearestPowerupDist <= POWERUP_SCAN_DIST)
            m_powerupNear = true;
    }
    else
    {
        Message* msg = new Message(MESSAGE_NO_POWERUPS);
        g_MessagePump.SendMessage(msg);
    }

    //arbitrate asteroid/powerup near messages
    if(m_powerupNear && m_nearestAsteroidDist >
                    m_nearestPowerupDist)
    {
        Message* msg = new Message(MESSAGE_POWERUP_NEAR);
        g_MessagePump.SendMessage(msg);
    }
    else if(m_nearestAsteroid)
    {
        if(m_nearestAsteroidDist > APPROACH_DIST)
        {
            Message* msg = new Message(MESSAGE_ASTEROID_FAR);
            g_MessagePump.SendMessage(msg);
        }
```

```
        else
        {
            Message* msg =new Message(MESSAGE_ASTEROID_NEAR);
            g_MessagePump.SendMessage(msg);
        }
    }
}
```

CODING THE STATES

The individual states themselves are barely changed. This book will show one of them, the Idle state, to illustrate the differences. Listing 17.9 is the MStateIdle header (including all the required callback object declarations), and Listing 17.10 shows the implementation differences from the regular FSM method.

LISTING 17.9 MStateIdle header.

```
//callbacks for handling messages
class EvadeCallback : public Callback
{
    void function(int pid, Message* msg);
};
class ApproachCallback : public Callback
{
    void function(int pid, Message* msg);
};
class AttackCallback : public Callback
{
    void function(int pid, Message* msg);
};
class GetPowerupCallback : public Callback
{
    void function(int pid, Message* msg);
};

class MStateIdle : public MessState
{
public:
    //constructor/functions
    MStateIdle(Control* control):
            MessState(FSM_STATE_IDLE,control){}
    void Enter();
```

```
        void Exit();
        void Update(float dt);

        EvadeCallback       m_evadeCallback;
        ApproachCallback    m_approachCallback;
        AttackCallback      m_attackCallback;
        GetPowerupCallback  m_getPowerupCallback;

};
```

LISTING 17.10 MStateIdle implementation differences beyond the normal FSM version.

```
//--------------------
void MStateIdle::Enter()
{
    g_MessagePump.RegisterForMessage(MESSAGE_WILL_COLLIDE,
                              m_parentID,m_evadeCallback);
    g_MessagePump.RegisterForMessage(MESSAGE_ASTEROID_FAR,
                           m_parentID,m_approachCallback);
    g_MessagePump.RegisterForMessage(MESSAGE_ASTEROID_NEAR,
                             m_parentID,m_attackCallback);
    g_MessagePump.RegisterForMessage(MESSAGE_POWERUP_NEAR,
                         m_parentID,m_getPowerupCallback);
}

//--------------------
void MStateIdle::Exit()
{
    g_MessagePump.UnRegisterForMessage(MESSAGE_WILL_COLLIDE,
                                       m_parentID);
    g_MessagePump.UnRegisterForMessage(MESSAGE_ASTEROID_FAR,
                                       m_parentID);
    g_MessagePump.UnRegisterForMessage(MESSAGE_ASTEROID_NEAR,
                                       m_parentID);
    g_MessagePump.UnRegisterForMessage(MESSAGE_POWERUP_NEAR,
                                       m_parentID);
}

//--------------------
void EvadeCallback::function(int pid, Message* msg)
{
    DataMessage<int>* newMsg = new DataMessage<int>
              (MESSAGE_CHANGE_STATE,MFSM_STATE_EVADE);
```

```
        newMsg->m_fromID  = pid;
        g_MessagePump.SendMessage(newMsg);
    }


    //--------------------
    void ApproachCallback::function(int pid,Message* msg)
    {
        DataMessage<int>* newMsg = new DataMessage<int>
                        (MESSAGE_CHANGE_STATE, FSM_STATE_APPROACH);
        newMsg->m_fromID  = pid;
        g_MessagePump.SendMessage(newMsg);
    }


    //--------------------
    void AttackCallback::function(int pid,Message* msg)
    {
        DataMessage<int>* newMsg = new DataMessage<int>
                        (MESSAGE_CHANGE_STATE, FSM_STATE_ATTACK);
        newMsg->m_fromID  = pid;
        g_MessagePump.SendMessage(newMsg);
    }


    //--------------------
    void GetPowerupCallback::function(int pid,Message* msg)
    {
        DataMessage<int>* newMsg = new DataMessage<int>
                        (MESSAGE_CHANGE_STATE, FSM_STATE_GETPOWERUP);
        newMsg->m_fromID  = pid;
        g_MessagePump.SendMessage(newMsg);
    }
```

In Listing 17.10, you can also see the use of the DataMessage template, for sending messages with additional data. The DataMessage contains the member m_dataStorage, the type of which is passed into the template on instantiation. When this message is delivered, the receiving callback function can cast the incoming message pointer to the correct type of DataMessage structure, and gain access to the data. More complex data would use the same system. If a message passed multiple data fields, the message would only need to be created with a struct containing the necessary data fields. At send time, the struct's fields would be initialized to the relevant values, and the receiver would again just cast the incoming message pointer to the type of the DataMessage struct used.

PERFORMANCE OF THE AI WITH THIS SYSTEM

The game performance of this system is virtually identical to that of the regular FSM implementation. Nothing has changed other than the method by which transitions occur. As previously discussed, however, the actual CPU performance has most likely gone down a bit because we are using the messaging system somewhat wastefully; the states are registering and unregistering themselves from specific messages whenever they enter or exit.

One thing that is different from the regular FSM implementation is that this version has much more difficulty evading asteroids. This shows one of the drawbacks of making a state machine use messages to drive the state changes, that of transition priority. The state changes are currently being triggered by callbacks that have been registered for message events, so we no longer have control of the priority of multiple callbacks that could occur within a single game loop. The system simply changes state on the first incoming message. In fact, the system will change state for each incoming message (because the message pump updates before the state machine does), and so the only state change that matters ends up being the last state change message in the queue.

This could be fixed by simply arbitrating the priorities at the perception level, but then you lose the decoupling of logic that the messaging system is giving you in the first place. You end up only sending out the highest priority messages, and essentially the system becomes a very convoluted way of calling a member function. A better way could be an incoming queue of state change requests to the machine, which could then determine priorities. This method isn't very clean either; you will again be centralizing logic that should be at the state level. The real solution for this problem would be to implement a change state queue, as mentioned before, but also assign priority numbers on the messages themselves, and use these numbers for arbitration. Messaging priority will be discussed later in this chapter in the "Extensions" section.

PROS OF MESSAGING SYSTEMS

Messaging systems, in effect, optimize the client-side code. In our game, this means that the states, which represent the client side, are optimized in that they do not have to worry about transition determinations. The server side (the controller class in our game) has to perform the necessary calculations, and the states merely wait until they get the correct signal from the server. We're really not saving anything (the code is moving from the states to the controller), so it might not seem like anything special.

The limited test bed implementation is only the beginning of what could be done with the messaging system. We could also have run the collision system with messages, informing game objects that they've collided. Powerups could send a message to the ship when collected, to inform the ship of the results, instead of the switch statement that the ship class has for getting powerups. Individual asteroids could check for proximity to the main ship and could send out messages when within a set boundary or when a collision is imminent, which would speed up the colliding determination in the controller class' `UpdatePerception` method. When all these examples are incorporated, as well as the many other ways the game could take advantage of a general messaging system, then the real power of the technique comes into play. The decoupling of class-level communication frees the programmer to use the messaging system to do things that previously would have required full-class access between game areas.

Most of the system is event-driven, so debugging the system can be aided by logging the message stream. If the system is written for it, the message stream could even be recorded and played back through the system to reproduce bugs or specific game behavior directly.

By using the messaging system as the primary means of communication with disparate game sections, a class can be written in a completely modular way. This will speed up compile time for the class (because it doesn't need to include files from all over the place to gain access to other classes) and make it easier for internal methods to change over time because the only interface to the outside is through the messages passed in and out. How the messages are determined and sent from each class doesn't matter anymore, it is only important that they are sent.

Cons of Messaging Systems

Messaging systems have very few detracting points because their simplicity and common sense understandability make them easy to work with, and their very nature (distributed computation with notification instead of centralized, polled computation) makes them less CPU-intensive. Event-driven architectures usually have an additional memory footprint, caused by having to keep track of messages (and any attached data). But with simple messaging systems (such as the one implemented in this chapter), there are no insurmountable problems.

Even with systems that require huge numbers of incoming and delayed messages and large amounts of passed data, load-balancing techniques can be applied to the message pump, which could smooth out processing of the system, as well as address memory concerns. But even without that level of complexity, a simple system can provide a game engine with most of the advantages of messaging.

There is the notion of too much of a good thing, however. Systems that try to incorporate messaging completely might suffer from specialization. If your game framework is completely event-driven, certain parts of your game might find it hard to perform the polling functionality that it requires, or the overhead involved in polling within the messaging system might become cumbersome if the number of polled objects is large. Monitoring CPU usage to notice this would be important, and you (and your game engine) should be flexible enough to allow a module that uses a more optimized approach to getting the data it requires.

Another downside is the problem discussed earlier in the chapter dealing with messaging in the AIsteroids game, that of message priority. Without extending the system by giving messages a level of priority, you lose much of the control of incoming messages implicit in a normal state-based system.

EXTENSIONS TO THE PARADIGM

The messaging system presented in this chapter is very straightforward and simple. It is easy to understand, use, and add to the system. Some things that would advance the system include message priority, message arbitration, and automatic and extended message types.

MESSAGE PRIORITY

By attaching a priority to messages, the message pump could sort the messages so that the more important messages get processed first. This is especially useful in games in which the message system is given a finite amount of time and has to allocate its time in the most urgent direction.

However, this can cause the new problem of message *starvation*. Care must be taken that low-priority messages eventually grow in priority (the longer they are in the queue) so that they don't sit at the bottom of the queue forever, continually pushed back by a steady stream of higher-priority messages. Starvation is okay if you have ambient messages that do not *require* attention, but are merely fallback status events. But in an online game that is using the messaging system to keep up-to-date across a network, message starvation might lead to a complete loss of game synchronization.

MESSAGE ARBITRATION

Another common messaging technique is that of arbitration. This is a sort of bookkeeping procedure that is performed by reading through the list of incoming messages, before processing, and looking for things such as message redundancy, message collision (two messages effectively canceling each other out), starving messages, or any other problems that the system sees a need to fix on the fly. The arbiter would then deal with each problem according to built-in rules. Message collisions might result in both messages being removed from the queue. If the two messages don't completely cancel each other out, they might be removed and require a small cleanup code segment to be run.

Message redundancy might simply involve removing the excess messages, unless there is some meaning to the redundancy, such as additional messages having slightly different and more recent data elements, even though they're the same *type* of message. In this case, they should all be thrown out except for the last one. This kind of message preprocessing can be taken quite far, with many levels of optimization and clean up. An arbitration system can become quite complex (if allowed to be), so care must be taken that a nice clean message-based system doesn't become convoluted because of a messy arbitration phase.

AUTOMATIC AND EXTENDED MESSAGE TYPES

Message types can streamline the messaging process and make frequent or automated tasks more convenient. Other message types might include special case messages that are handled differently by the system. Several common types of messages that are used include the following:

- *Periodic messages.* These are messages that happen on a constant time schedule, such as every second, or twice a minute. Some games that are heavily event-driven use an update message that happens automatically every game tick and is what signals all the objects in the game to call their Update() method.
- *Debugging messages.* Messages can be embedded into the system that will be perceived by a central debugging system (a very easy system would emulate asserts; instead of stopping program execution, it would merely trap the program in a central place for observation or to ignore the asserted code). The debugging system could discern these hidden messages (in that the rest of the game doesn't know or care that they exist), as well as normal game variables to provide the programmer with whatever he or she needs to fix/tune code segments. These messages can be written so that they are compiled by setting a define, so that the final code isn't slowed down by debugging information and processes.
- *Confirmation messages.* Some systems might require stalling messages; when game object A sends B a message, A then waits (or *stalls*) for a response from B before continuing. Confirmation could be sent automatically to the sender upon receipt of a message, and this behavior could thus be accommodated.
- *Immediate messages.* In the current implementation, messages are stored in a queue and are processed all at once every game loop. *Immediate* messages would skip this convention, and be sent immediately to the other game object for processing. This is necessary when you have overriding messages

that require immediate attention, or have some game states that are more important than others but don't have a priority system built into your messaging structure.

OPTIMIZATIONS

Event-driven AI is fairly optimized (compared with the more traditional polling models), but only for systems that contain an event-friendly environment. Otherwise, messaging can add overhead and complexity.

As we saw in our AIsteroids test bed, some games don't lend themselves well to a messaging paradigm. Although implementing messaging into the test bed (that of having the transitions be event-based) may be a questionable example, other parts of the game would benefit from messaging, and later game extensions could then take advantage of an already instantiated event system.

DESIGN CONSIDERATIONS

Messaging systems can find their way into almost any game, given that they are a very straightforward and efficient means of communicating between game objects and code sections. They allow fast, unconnected systems that have a centralized means for passing data and events back and forth without complicated, heavily coupled class structures. They can also make it easier to add network capabilities to an otherwise solo game if desired.

TYPES OF SOLUTIONS

Messaging usually helps more with higher-order types of solutions, strategic versus tactical. This is because strategic thinking is more about coordinating multiple elements (either separate game entities, or even different aspects of a singular game entity) toward a greater goal, which implies a large degree of communication between disparate game elements.

Tactical solution types, on the other hand, have more to do with physical actions in response to a given order, or to determine the best way to go about a simple task. Even at the tactical level, however, messaging provides a good means for tactical feedback to the strategic systems for increased strategic response. So, messaging works from the top down (by providing an efficient means for distributing strategic plan information to many elements), but also from the bottom up (by providing the means for many separate game elements to provide feedback into the system).

AGENT REACTIVITY

Event-driven agents are all about reactivity because they are simply waiting for something to happen so they can respond. With the proper perception system, any level of reactivity can be implemented with messaging-based agent communication.

SYSTEM REALISM

Event-driven games need to be watchful that their possible event list isn't too narrow, otherwise the AI-controlled characters will be too predictable and static, behaviorally. This is not to say that event-driven systems themselves are predictable. But some games drive the actual behavior of the characters almost completely from perception events, and this can dull the richness of the character dramatically. In effect, you've limited the total number of states that the system can be in.

Usually, event-driven characters also need to use other techniques, such as scripting, to respond to key game events with proprietary, rich behavior. This is only one example of how messaging could be combined with another AI technique to provide additional realism or depth of play.

GENRE AND PLATFORM

Genre and platform are of almost no concern to messaging methods. Messaging excels with games that have either numerous game objects that require communication (such as RTS games with huge armies that are being ordered around and are sending back constant feedback), or very rich interaction between game objects (such as a football game, in which two or more players are responding to each other's positions relative to each other, are engaged in complex collision with each other, and are dealing with other factors during a play). Messaging systems do require additional memory, but usually make up for it by simplifying the code base and can be implemented on even the smaller, more restrictive platforms.

DEVELOPMENT LIMITATIONS

Development limitations might actually push a team toward a message-based system, which provides amazing bang for the buck, and can speed up implementation of game features that require cooperation between classes and game objects. Message-based systems (if done properly) are generally quicker to compile and build, because of the class decoupling that the method enforces. Debugging systems can be integrated directly into the messaging stream (or at the object level) and provide many access points for fixing potential problems and logging behaviors for review.

ENTERTAINMENT LIMITATIONS

Tuning difficulty settings, balancing specific behaviors, and other entertainment concerns are generally independent of messaging system use, so are not usually a problem.

SUMMARY

Messaging systems can provide a variety of decision-making paradigms with additional flexibility in communication between game objects, as well as between separate code segments that must act in concert.

- AI characters are usually reactive, which lends itself well to an event-driven methodology.
- AI systems are usually high level, meaning that they have access to many separate parts of the game engine, so they can perform the kinds of determinations and behaviors necessary. Messaging provides a clean interface for this access to occur without giving global class access.
- The simple messaging system in this chapter was implemented in three parts: the message pump, the message object, and client handlers.
- The client handlers in this method will be coded as callback objects to facilitate greater flexibility and organization over more centralized methods, such as a general `ProcessMessage()` function.
- The test bed will be implemented so that all transitions occur because of events. Although this is not the ideal messaging example, it does show off the power of the technique and provides a clear example of how messaging can be used.
- Message-based systems work best when most of the game takes advantage of the system. Debugging and other secondary systems can also use the messaging engine to ease those tasks as well.
- Messaging does require additional memory to store messages and attached data, but load-balancing and arbitration systems can optimize the level of CPU and memory necessary.
- Adding the ability to set message priority, allow message arbitration, and add automatic or extended message types to the system can extend the use of messaging beyond its most simple implementation.

18 Scripting Systems

So far, we have explored ways of constructing game logic and behavior in code. This results in custom AI systems that are tied closely to the product and can be optimized to perform well. But, as we have seen, this requires dedicated programmers to implement, debug, and extend. However, programmers may not be the people that are creatively overseeing the product. Considerable roadblocks can exist in communicating the creative vision to the programmers. More commonly, the level of creative content that must be included in the game is simply too great to allow a limited number of programmers to custom code everything to the quality level required.

SCRIPTING OVERVIEW

A common technique for getting more hands into the guts of the AI system without having to hire more programmers is called scripting. Scripting means using a simplified programming-style language (although scripting tools can be made visual, as well as written) to build AI elements, logic, or behaviors. The conversation tree in a role-playing game, the cinematic movement and visuals of various characters

363

during story sequences, the specifics of each move in a complex fighting game, or the way that groups of enemies coordinate attacks can and have all been performed using scripting systems in various games.

Scripting languages range from the very simple (sometimes called *predicate languages*), to full-fledged programming languages (*Neverwinter Nights* uses Java as its scripting language).

Making a scripting language for your product is not a trivial task. You are essentially creating another product, with a specific user (in this case, game designers or end users who are creating mods for your game), input and output requirements, and a design, implementation, and debug schedule separate from the actual game you intend on creating. The design phase of your scripting system requires careful thought to many different technical and creative elements:

■ *The kinds of functionality that the language will require.* Does your game need linear triggering of events, or does the script need to include conditional branches? Will the scripters need variables? Essentially you are defining the complexity of the scripting system. Let us consider an example, that of a vertical shooter. In this game, you will fly a ship along a set length of game world, with attacking enemies flying in patterns along the way. A simple scripting system for this game could be one that merely allows the scripter to define the points at which specific enemy types spawned and could even modify starting parameters for each enemy as the scripter saw fit.

The specifics of the enemy behavior would be left in code. A more complex system might allow the scripter to define enemy movement patterns within script and allow assignment of these patterns to enemies. An even more involved system might completely drive the creation of enemies: A scripter would define each as a set of attributes (body type, speed, duration, armor level, etc.) and behavior types (attack method, movement style and pattern, etc.) from a laundry list of possibilities that the game engine can complete. Finally, a system could be implemented that would also allow enemies to assess game-side values and respond to them within scripted sequences. This would allow the scripters to write reactive systems that could account for the state of the player or other enemies in the game.

■ *Will the runtime engine interpret the scripts, or will they be precompiled into some kind of bytecode?* Interpreted scripts tend to be slower and larger. But they also allow more flexibility (you could enter a new script from an in-game console, and it could then be reinterpreted by the engine on the fly). Interpreted scripts are a little simpler to implement because of the lack of the intermediary compilation step. Precompiled scripts generally run faster, because the compiler parses the script into codes that the system can execute directly.

- *How big will the scripts be in size?* Code tends to compile down into small chunks, whereas script code (especially interpreted script) does not. Care must be taken that the platform for which you are developing has enough memory (or memory bandwidth, if you will be streaming scripts into the game from disk) to accommodate the sum of the script requirements for the game. Remember also that you might require additional memory buffers for decompressing and/or parsing.
- *Who will be using the scripting language?* If junior programmers will be using the language, it can be fairly complex and full featured. Are the primary users high-level designers who don't have much technical knowledge? For the severely nontechnical, the scripting system needs to be simple enough to use, robust enough to handle errors without crashing, and include a decent amount of debugging hooks to be useful.

A very common mistake in creating a scripting system is to make something that is far too complex and powerful for nontechnical designers. They usually end up overwhelmed by the system and not using it to its full potential. Better to make the initial system easy to use, then gradually add more advanced features as the designers become comfortable with the system. If you are going to expose your scripting language (and your scripting development tools, potentially) to the public to make modding your game easier, realize that the average person who might try and use it may have very little programming experience.

The learning curve can be simplified if your scripting language follows similar rules to an already established language (this is the primary reason for the large number of "C-like" scripting languages), or is so simple that a few example scripts can be included with the game to show how to use all the functionality.

EXAMPLE IMPLEMENTATION IN OUR AISTEROIDS TEST BED

This chapter covers two different approaches to developing a scripting system within a game. First, we will implement a simple configuration scripting system that will allow you to bind in-game variables or actions to scripting tokens. Second, we will cover a more general and full-featured method, by discussing the Lua language and how it can be embedded within a game application as well as exposing game functions and variables to Lua.

A CONFIGURATION SCRIPT SYSTEM

The first scripting system we cover is basic and allows the programmer to set up a simple grammar using keywords and parameters. There are no variables, scoping, parameter passing, or any other of the more advanced language constructs, but it still allows for barebones "languages" that can be used to set up transition rules, triggers, or simple behaviors. Think of this system as a formalized way of configuring or initializing variables from within a script. You expose whatever flags, values, and triggers you want to the scripting language, and then a script can be written that uses the correct tokens to perform the setup tasks that you require.

The implementation we will use for the AIsteroids game is split into four parts: a parser, a list of tokens, in-game token callbacks, and the actual script files.

1. The *parser* is the code that loads in the script file, scans it for applicable tokens, and then executes any tokens it finds.
2. *Tokens* comprise a token name, and a corresponding `Execute()` function, which is called by the parser when it finds each token. Executing a token involves scanning the file for any additional parameters that the token expects, and then sending the game a message that includes this data.
3. The *in-game callbacks* are the functions that respond to the messages sent by the token `Execute()` calls. This is where you will actually bind real-game variables to incoming script data.
4. The *scripts* themselves can be written in any text editor. The only real grammar that the system uses is that each line must end in a semicolon. The example scripts included in this implementation (see Listing 18.1 for the file test.txt) use the general grammar "Token= parameter;" but the = sign is actually part of the token name, so it could be anything you want. The "comment" lines at the top of the file do not require the comment signifier //, they are just there for readability. In fact, if a real token had been included in the comment line, it would have been found and parsed.

LISTING 18.1   `test.txt` script file.

```
//don't need to put anything in a certain order,
//the parser ignores whitespace after the = sign,
//all lines begin with a token and end in a semicolon,
//and tokens are case insensitive
//all values in the script Override the default values
//that are set up in the Init() functions.

PowerupScanDist= 150.0;
SeekPowerups= true;
MaxSpeed= 80.0;
ApproachDist= 180.0;
AttackDist= 260.0;
SafeRadius= 15.0;
```

To initialize the system, register the parser with all the Tokens (Listing 18.2 is the header) you intend on using in your script. As the code shows, each token stores an ID, an internal value m_matchPos (used by the parser when scanning for tokens), and the name string that is used to identify the token in a script file. The Get functions are all standard retrieval methods to extract the various kinds of parameter types from a text file. If you had any other widely used parameter types (be they different data types, or more complex data structures) you could add methods for loading them here. The enum stores all the ID types for the tokens used in the game.

LISTING 18.2   Token header information.

```
class Token
{
public:

    enum
    {
        TT_NONE,
        TT_POWERUPDIST,
        TT_POWERUPSEEK,
        TT_APPROACHDIST,
        TT_ATTACKDIST,
        TT_MAXSPEED,
        TT_SAFERADIUS,
    };

    //constructor/functions
    Token(int type = TT_NONE, char* name = "")
        {m_tokenAsStr=new char(MIN(strlen(name),MAX_TOKEN_LENGTH));
         m_tokenAsStr = name;m_tokenID = type;m_matchPos = 0;}
    ~Token(){}
    virtual void Execute(_iobuf* fileName) {}

    //Additional data acquisition
    float GetFloat(_iobuf* fileName);
    char  GetChar(_iobuf* fileName);
    int   GetInt(_iobuf* fileName);
    bool  GetBool(_iobuf* fileName);
    void  GetString(_iobuf* fileName, string& storageStr);

    //data
    int             m_tokenID;
```

```
    int             m_matchPos;
    char*           m_tokenAsStr;
};
```

The parser (Listing 18.3 is the header, 18.4 is the important function implementations) is about as simple as a file parser can get. As the header shows, it only stores one data structure: a pointer to the list of tokens, passed in when you instantiate the parser. This facilitates using the parser in a general sense for the whole game; you can change the token list and reparse a file, or parse a different file. You could have different token lists for many disparate occurrences within your game engine: different states of the game, different game levels, or for various specialized systems within the AI engine that you might use scripting.

LISTING 18.3 Parser header information.

```
class Parser
{
public:
    Parser(TokenList *tList = NULL):m_tokenList(tList){}
    int         CheckForToken(char currentChar);
    bool        ParseFile(char* fileNameStr);
    void        Reset();
    void        SetTokenList(TokenList *tList){m_tokenList = tList;}

protected:
    TokenList*  m_tokenList;
};
```

The parser works on a "single character at a time" basis. It gets a character out of the file, and then checks that against the list of tokens. If it finds a token with a matching character, it adds to its m_matchPos variable. Any time it finds a token that has matched all its characters to the incoming stream, it flags the incoming phrase as a token, resets all other parsing-related variables, and returns. If it is in the middle of a token string, and an incoming character doesn't match, it resets the count because the matches need to be in order. Two things to notice:

1. Tokens are scanned for using *case insensitivity.* Users can enter tokens in either upper- or lowercase. If nontechnical people are going to be the primary users of this system, using case-insensitive tokens will save you some of the headache of looking for bugs caused by mistyping. Notice too that the GetBool() method in Token.cpp will accept a variety of

symbols as true or false so that it makes it easier for nonprogrammers to use.

2. Tokens whose names are subsets of other tokens' names might be a problem. If you had two tokens, "Shout=" and "Out=", you will have collision problems because "out=" is in both strings. So, based on the order in which they were registered, only one token will ever be called. You could either extend the system to allow for this (by flagging tokens for execution and then batch executing them after scanning, or whatever means you see fit), or by simply keeping the token names from colliding with each other (you can enforce the convention verbally to the programmers, or make a `RegisterToken()` function and have it flag incoming name collisions as an error).

LISTING 18.4   `Parser` implementation.

```
//-------------------
int Parser::CheckForToken(char currentChar)
{
    TokenList::iterator tListiterator;
    for (tListiterator = m_tokenList.begin();
         tListiterator != m_tokenList.end(); ++tListiterator)
    {
        Token* pToken = *tListiterator;
        if (tolower(currentChar) ==
            tolower(pToken->m_tokenAsStr[pToken->m_matchPos]))
        {
            // if the currentChar matches the requested
            // character of the current token,...
                // increase the "match-position" counter
            pToken->m_matchPos++;

            if (pToken->m_matchPos == strlen(pToken->m_tokenAsStr))
            {
                // if the counter equals the length of the current
                // token, we found a token. Thus,...
                // ...reset the counters of all the
                    // other tokens and...
                Reset();
                // ...return the token found
                return pToken->m_tokenID;
            }
        }
    }
```

```
            else
            {
                // if the currentChar does *not* match the requested
                // character of the current token,...
                // reset the corresponding counter
                pToken->m_matchPos = 0;
            }
        }
        return NO_TOKEN;
}

//--------------------
void ZeroPosition(Token* pToken)
{
    pToken->m_matchPos = 0;
}

//--------------------
void Parser::Reset()
{
    for_each(m_tokenList.begin(),m_tokenList.end(),ZeroPosition);
}

//--------------------
bool Parser::ParseFile(char* fileNameStr)
{
    FILE* pFile;
    if ((pFile = fopen(fileNameStr,"r")) == NULL)
    {
        return false;
    }

    char buffer;
    Reset();
    while (fread(&buffer, 1, 1, pFile) == 1)
    {
        int currentToken = CheckForToken(buffer);
        if(currentToken == Token::TT_NONE)
            continue;
        else
        {
            TokenList::iterator tListiterator;
            for (tListiterator = m_tokenList.begin();
                tListiterator!=m_tokenList.end();++tListiterator)
```

```
        {
            Token* pToken = *tListiterator;
            if(pToken->m_tokenID == currentToken)
                pToken->Execute(pFile);
        }
    }
}

    fclose(pFile);
    return true;
}
```

Once a token is found, its `Execute()` call is performed (Listing 18.5 shows
the execute method for a couple of the example tokens). The `Execute()` method is
responsible for retrieving any additional parameters from the file, then setting up
and sending the correct message to the engine. The method allows for any implementation you want, so this could be used for any kind of structure.

The single parameter shown in the examples could be extended to multiple parameters separated by commas, or a token could be a kind of state indicator. An "if"
token's execute method can be an entirely new parse phase that looks for any number of additional conditions. It can have its own list of conditional tokens and call
the parser on the current file with this new token list. A "then" token would mark
the latter phase of the "if" clause; it would stop looking for conditions and instead
start scanning for actions to perform. This style of complex, nested structure might
actually read in many lines of the script, all triggered by a single token (if). Again,
because of the generic structure of this parsing system, you can implement almost
anything you require for simple parsing situations.

LISTING 18.5   Some `execute` method implementations.

```
//--------------------
void TokenSafeRadius::Execute(_iobuf* fileName)
{
    float safeRad = GetFloat(fileName);

    //send out message with data of incoming token
    DataMessage<float>* newMsg = new DataMessage<float>
                (MESSAGE_TOKEN_SAFERAD,safeRad);
    g_MessagePump.SendMessage(newMsg);

}
```

```
//--------------------
void TokenPowerupSeek::Execute(_iobuf* fileName)
{
    bool seekPowerups = GetBool(fileName);

    //send out message with data of incoming token
    DataMessage<bool>* newMsg = new DataMessage<bool>
                      (MESSAGE_TOKEN_POWSEEK,seekPowerups);
    g_MessagePump.SendMessage(newMsg);

}
```

PERFORMANCE OF THE AI WITH THIS SYSTEM

Our simple example scripting setup is built directly on top of the messaging-based system from the last chapter. It is used solely to set up initial variables, so it performs exactly like the purely message-based method. The small file that is parsed at load time adds negligible time to level start up, and even a large configuration file with a huge number of possible tokens would still not be much of a concern to the game's performance.

EXTENSIONS TO THE CONFIGURATION SCRIPT PARADIGM

This solution is so open and generic that you could technically code whatever kind of advanced token type you needed for your game. You could construct tokens that require any number of parameters. You could use the "//" token to signify a comment, and discount parsing the rest of the entire line. A more complex addition would be tokens that effectively put the parser into a special mode, so that it's then looking for different tokens. This would be roughly equivalent to a *block* signifier within a regular programming language. For example, when the C compiler sees an if token in the code, it then looks for a left parenthesis (signifying the start of an expression block), or else there's a syntax error. After the expression, the C compiler then looks for a single statement, which may be a curly brace, signifying another block. Your language could technically build any type of block structure that it wanted to give the script advanced organization and structure. Of course, with the simplistic and rough parsing being done in this system, you would probably have a bit of a hurdle dealing with the possible errors that scripters might introduce trying to follow anything but a very basic grammar within this code.

EMBEDDING LUA

In this section, we will take an entirely different scripting route, and embed Lua in a game environment as a substitute for creating our own scripting language.

We will cover a light review of the Lua language, and then move on to the details of integrating the language into your game and passing information back and forth between Lua and a C/C++ program environment.

LUA OVERVIEW

Lua is a lightweight programming language developed by a team at the Computer Graphics Technology Group at the Pontifical Catholic University in Brazil. In addition to being used as a stand-alone language, many developers are using Lua as a general-purpose scripting and extension system for their games.

You might decide to go in this direction for a number of reasons. You might not have the time to write, debug, and maintain your own custom system. You might have many areas in your game that you would like to use scripting with to allow maximum extensibility, and thus, want a very general scripting system to encompass the many areas of your game code you want to affect. You might even have a number of people on your staff that already know the Lua language because it has been around for a while, and has been used in a number of well-known commercial games (*Baldur's Gate* and *Grim Fandango* are two examples).

Lua is slowly but surely beating out older embedded languages like Python for many reasons:

- It is generally faster, has a smaller memory footprint, and is easier to learn.
- Its syntax is largely procedural and has dynamic typing.
- It can be interpreted from script or compiled bytecode.
- It has automatic memory management with garbage collection facilities.
- It is easy for both programmers and nontechnical people to learn, with a sort of free-form Pascal syntax (at the 2003 Game Developer's Conference, it was discussed that seasoned programmers should pick it up in an hour or so, and nontechnical people would need just a bit longer for simple Lua tasks).
- The biggest reason that Lua is gaining steam is its abilities in the area of integration with other languages. Instead of implementing numerous internal language features, Lua includes an easy-to-use API for exchanging data back and forth between your game and Lua. In this way, Lua can be thought of as a tool for building game-specific languages. You are effectively building a set of functions (in Lua and your code) that allow designers, or whoever is using the scripting system, to write game-specific scripts to perform actions within your game. Coupled with the very forgiving syntax of Lua, very usable and human-readable code can be generated quickly and easily. This also keeps the core language small and fast.

LUA LANGUAGE FUNDAMENTALS

In this section, we will give a brief overview of the Lua language. It is not meant to be exhaustive but, rather, to simply show some of the primary language features.

For a much broader look at how Lua is programmed, go directly to the source: *http://lua-users.org/wiki/TutorialDirectory*, which has a nice selection of topics that are covered well. These tutorials can be followed easily because the stand-alone interpreter can be run, and Lua commands can be entered directly into an internal prompt for immediate execution. Lua's syntax is easy to pick up if you have any experience programming more high-level languages. Listing 18.6 shows some example Lua code, which will be used for illustration. Some of the basic language features include the following:

1. *Very simple scoping.* All Lua statements are in the global environment. The only way to restrict scoping is to assign a variable local status within a smaller block of code (this block being delimited by a control structure, within a function, etc.).
2. *Dynamic typing.* Lua does not require variable types to be declared. These types can be intermingled to an amazing degree. Lua only recognizes seven different types:
   a. nil
   b. boolean (*nil* counts as false, but the number zero and the empty string " " counts as true)
   c. number (all numbers in Lua are considered floats)
   d. string
   e. table
   f. function
   g. thread
   h. userdata (a type specifically designed to allow for arbitrary C pointers to be stored; they are essentially void* variables).
3. *Tables.* Tables are *the* free-form data construct in Lua. Much like a *list* structure in LISP, you can put any combination of types into a table, and tables can contain other tables. Each member of a table is essentially stored like an STL map, in that it has a key and a value. Simple tables (like one declared `table = {1,2,3}`) are also called *numerically indexed* because all the keys are implied as array indices. A corresponding nonnumerically indexed table would could be declared as `table = {name = "Bob", number = "5551212", hometown = "Somewhere"}`. In this second table, you would access members by key name, for example, `table.name == "Bob"`. Tables can also contain functions, which could be thought of as object-oriented "methods."
4. *Control structures.* Lua provides a number of standard control blocks, including `do` loops, `while..do` loops, `repeat..until`, `if..then..else.. elseif` blocks, and `for` loops. Each control structure (except for `repeat.. until`) must be delimited with an "end" identifier.
5. *The stack.* Lua uses a "stack" to pass values to and from C programs. Even though it is referred to as a *stack,* it really isn't a classical stack data structure.

Usually, stacks are only accessed with push and pop commands. Lua stacks are more like an indexed set of registers that are used during the communication between programs and scripts. Anytime you call a C function from Lua, a new, independent stack is created for passing data back and forth. The default size for these stacks (as defined in lua.h as LUA_MINSTACK is 20, usually more than enough unless you're pushing a bunch of things to the stack from within the function or passing huge structures), but it can be grown using the function lua_checkstack(). In addition to the expected push and pop functions, Lua stacks have commands for inserting, removing, and replacing specific elements, as well as recognizing pseudo-indices (by using negative values, you can index relative to the top, and positive values index relative to the bottom) to make random stack access easier. The last chunk of code in Listing 18.6 shows a small block of C code that manipulates stack values for illustration.

LISTING 18.6   Simplistic Lua syntax demo.

```
—examples declaring different types

varNumber    = 5
varFloat     = 5.5
varFunction = function(i) return i-1 end
varNumber    = varFunction(56)
varTable     = {1,false,6,8,{12,"string",7.99}}
v1,v2,v3     = 12,"apple",-5.6

—examples of control structures
index = 1
do
  index = 5
  print("Index = "..index)—should print 5
end
print("Index = "..index)—should print 1
—===========
index = 1
while index < 5 do
    print("Been here "..index.." times")
end
—===========
num = 1
repeat
    print(num)
    num = num * 3
```

```
until num > 100
—===========
function min(a,b)
    local minimum
    minimum = a
    if b < a then
        minimum = b
    end
    return minimum
end
—===========
if x == 3
    print("X equals 3")
elseif x < 1
    print("X is not 1")
else
    if x > 0
            print("X is positive, and less than 1")
    else
            print("X is negative")
    end
end
—===========
for index 1,50,3 do
    print("Loop value ="..index)
end

varTable = {name="marvin",look="monkey",job="ceo"}
for key,value in varTable do
    print(key,value)
end

—examples of table usage
table = { 23,44.5,18, color="blue", name="luxor" }
print(table[1])—will print 23
print(table[color])—will print blue



- - - - - - - - - - - - - - - - - - - -


//examples of stack usage, C code
//As an example, if the stack starts as 10 20 30 40 50*
//(from bottom to top; the '*' marks the top
```

```
lua_pushnumber(L, 10);// -> 10*
lua_pushnumber(L, 20);// -> 10 20*
lua_pushnumber(L, 30);// -> 10 20 30*
lua_pushnumber(L, 40);// -> 10 20 30 40*
lua_pushnumber(L, 50);// -> 10 20 30 40 50*


lua_pushvalue(L, 3);//  -> 10 20 30 40 50 30*
lua_pushvalue(L, -1);// -> 10 20 30 40 50 30 30*
lua_remove(L, -3);//    -> 10 20 30 40 30 30*
lua_remove(L, 6);//     -> 10 20 30 40 30*
lua_insert(L, 1);//     -> 30 10 20 30 40*
lua_insert(L, -1);//    -> 30 10 20 30 40* (no effect)
lua_replace(L, 2);//    -> 30 40 20 30*
lua_settop(L, -3);//    -> 30 40*
lua_settop(L, 6);//     -> 30 40 nil nil nil nil*
```

INTEGRATION

Integrating Lua scripts into your game is simple. You link your game with the Lua libraries, instantiate an instance of the Lua interpreter, and then either perform Lua commands directly, or load and parse an entire file. Listing 18.7 shows the code necessary to start up the interpreter.

The secondary libopen functions initialize parts of the interpreter that you might need (input/output, advanced string functions, and math functions, respectively). The `lua_settop()` call clears the stack of any random values that were left there by the library initializations.

The last part of the whole process is to expose game-side functions and values to Lua, and vice versa. The code in this book will use a very simple extension to Lua, the LuaPlus Call Dispatcher, written by Joshua Jensen, to help with the exposing process. This single-header file is a nice compilation of templates that allows very simple registration of C++ code and data elements, whether global, members of a class, or even virtual members in the case of functions. The reason for using this is that normally any function exposed to Lua from C needs to be a static function of the type `static int Function(lua_state* ls)`, and all arguments and return values being passed on the stack. These are called *glue functions,* in that they provide a middle layer between your real C++ methods and Lua scripts. The LuaPlus Call Dispatcher merely uses some very clever template coding to provide these glue functions for us, as well as handling the stack manipulation necessary to pass the arguments and return values. Listing 18.8 shows examples of exposing variables and code from C++ to Lua, and back.

LISTING 18.7 Simple Lua interpreter startup code.

```
#include "luaPlusCD.h"
extern "C"
{
    #include "lua.h"
    #include "lualib.h"
}


//and this code must be in an actual function

m_luaState          = lua_open();
lua_baselibopen(m_luaState);
lua_iolibopen(m_luaState);
lua_strlibopen(m_luaState);
lua_mathlibopen(m_luaState);
lua_settop(m_luaState,0);
```

LISTING 18.8 Examples of exposing variables and data to and from Lua.

```
//from C++ to Lua
//-------------------

//variable data
int integerVariable  = 42;
char stringVariable[] = "doughnut";

lua_pushnumber(m_luaState,integerVariable);
lua_setglobal(m_luaState,"intVar");
lua_pushstring(m_luaState,stringVariable);
lua_setglobal(m_luaState,"strVar");
/////////////////////////////////////
//static functions using barebones Lua
//function takes a number argument,
//and returns 3*the number and 4*number
static int MyCFunction(lua_state* L)
{
    int numArgs = lua_gettop(L);//should be one
    float arg[numArgs];
    int i;
    for(i=0;i< numArgs;i++)
        arg[i] = lua_isnumber(L,1);
```

```
    for(i=0;i<numArgs;i++)
    {
        lua_pushnumber(L,arg1*3.0f);
        lua_pushnumber(L,arg1*4.0f);
    }
    return 2*numArgs;//number of results
}
lua_register(m_luaState,"MyCFunction",MyCFunction);
//Lua script can then say:
// a,b = MyCFunction(25)
//with results: a==75, b==100
//...or...
// a,b,c,d = MyCFunction(4,5)
//with results: a==12,b==16,c==15,d==20
////////////////////////////////////

//regular functor examples using LuaPlusCD
//(example taken from author's website)
static int LS_LOG(lua_State* L)
{
    printf("In static function\n");
    return 0;
}


class Logger
{
public:
    int LS_LOGMEMBER(lua_State* L)
    {
        printf("In member function. Message:%s\n",
                                    lua_tostring(L,1));
        return 0;
    }

    virtual int LS_LOGVIRTUAL(lua_State* L)
    {
        printf("In virtual member function\n");
        return 0;
    }
};

lua_pushstring(L, "LOG");
lua_pushfunctorclosure(L, LS_LOG, 0);
lua_settable(L, LUA_GLOBALSINDEX);
```

```
Logger logger;
lua_pushstring(L, "LOGMEMBER");
lua_pushfunctorclosure(L, logger, Logger::LS_LOGMEMBER, O);
lua_settable(L, LUA_GLOBALSINDEX);

lua_pushstring(L, "LOGVIRTUAL");
lua_pushfunctorclosure(L, logger, Logger::LS_LOGVIRTUAL, O);
lua_settable(L, LUA_GLOBALSINDEX);

//and the package can also set up direct calls, which are much
//more natural to C programmers...
void LOG(const char* message)
{
    printf("In global function: %s\n", message);
}


class Logger
{
public:
    void LOGMEMBER(const char* message)
    {
        printf("In member function: %s\n", message);
    }

    virtual void LOGVIRTUAL(const char* message)
    {
        printf("In virtual member function: %s\n", message);
    }
};


lua_pushstring(L, "LOG");
lua_pushdirectclosure(L, LOG, O);
lua_settable(L, LUA_GLOBALSINDEX);

Logger logger;
lua_pushstring(L, "LOGMEMBER");
lua_pushdirectclosure(L, logger, Logger::LOGMEMBER, O);
lua_settable(L, LUA_GLOBALSINDEX);

lua_pushstring(L, "LOGVIRTUAL");
lua_pushdirectclosure(L, logger, Logger::LOGVIRTUAL, O);
```

```
lua_settable(L, LUA_GLOBALSINDEX);
//////////////////////////////////////

//from Lua to C++
//-------------------

//variables
int intVar;
char strVar[20];
lua_getglobal(m_luaState,"intVarName");
intVar = lua_tonumber(lua_gettop(m_luaState));
lua_getglobal(m_luaState,"strVarName");
strVar = lua_tostring(lua_gettop(m_luaState));
//////////////////////////////////////

//functions
//Lua function looks like:
//     function multiply(x,y)
//          return x*y
//     end

//C code would require:
float x = 123.0f;
float y =  55.0f;
lua_getglobal(m_luaState,"multiply");
lua_pushnumber(m_luaState,x);
lua_pushnumber(m_luaState,y);
float result = lua_tonumber(lua_call(m_luaState,2,1),-1);
```

EXAMPLE IMPLEMENTATION IN THE AISTEROIDS TEST BED

To run Lua scripts from the test bed, we need just a few additions. We will be building on the messaging-based system from Chapter 17, just like our simple scripting example. Essentially, we are going to expose the necessary perception data members to our Lua script, which will store the logic to determine the current status of the ship's state machine. Listing 18.9 shows the changes to the code, and Listing 18.10 shows some small sample Lua scripts that can be used to control the AI ship for this demo. Notice that the second script only uses the Evade and Approach states. It relies on the fact that the Evade state shoots the guns if you line up with an asteroid. Not really a great way to play the game, this is just to show contrast between the real script and this one.

LISTING 18.9 `MessAIControl` changes needed to use Lua scripting.

```
#include "luaPlusCD.h"
extern "C"
{
#include "lualib.h"
}

//--------------------
MessAIControl::MessAIControl(Ship* ship):
AIControl(ship)
{
    g_MessagePump.AddMessageToSystem(MESSAGE_SHIP_TOTAL_STOP);
    g_MessagePump.AddMessageToSystem(MESSAGE_CHANGE_STATE);

    //construct the state machine and add the necessary states
    m_machine = new MessMachine(MFSM_MACH_MAINSHIP,this);
    m_machine->AddState(new MStateApproach(this));
    m_machine->AddState(new MStateAttack(this));
    m_machine->AddState(new MStateEvade(this));
    m_machine->AddState(new MStateGetPowerup(this));
    MStateIdle* idle = new MStateIdle(this);
    m_machine->AddState(idle);
    m_machine->SetDefaultState(idle);
    m_machine->Reset();

    m_messReceiver = new MessageReceiver;

    //default values
    m_safetyRadius      = SAFETYRADUIS;
    m_powerupScanDist   = POWERUP_SCAN_DIST;
    m_maxSpeed          = MAI_MAX_SPEED_TRY/Game.m_timeScale;
    m_appDist           = MAPPROACH_DIST;
    m_attDist           = MATTACK_DIST;
    m_powerupSeek       = true;

    m_luaState          = lua_open();
    lua_baselibopen(m_luaState);
    lua_settop(m_luaState,0);//clear the stack

    //bind const values to lua variables
    lua_pushnumber(m_luaState,MAX_SHOT_LEVEL);
    lua_setglobal(m_luaState,"gvMaxShotPower");
    lua_pushnumber(m_luaState,MFSM_STATE_APPROACH);
```

```
    lua_setglobal(m_luaState,"gsSTATEAPPROACH");
    lua_pushnumber(m_luaState,MFSM_STATE_ATTACK);
    lua_setglobal(m_luaState,"gsSTATEATTACK");
    lua_pushnumber(m_luaState,MFSM_STATE_EVADE);
    lua_setglobal(m_luaState,"gsSTATEEVADE");
    lua_pushnumber(m_luaState,MFSM_STATE_GETPOWERUP);
    lua_setglobal(m_luaState,"gsSTATEGETPOWERUP");
    lua_pushnumber(m_luaState,MFSM_STATE_IDLE);
    lua_setglobal(m_luaState,"gsSTATEIDLE");

    //bind state change function for lua to use
    lua_pushstring(m_luaState,"ChangeState");
    lua_pushdirectclosure(m_luaState,*this,
        &MessAIControl::SetMachineGoalState,0);
    lua_settable(m_luaState,LUA_GLOBALSINDEX);
}
//--------------------
void MessAIControl::Update(float dt)
{
    if(!m_ship)
    {
        m_machine->Reset();
        return;
    }

    UpdatePerceptions(dt);

    //update exposed lua variables
    lua_pushnumber(m_luaState,m_nearestPowerupDist);
    lua_setglobal(m_luaState,"gvDistPowerup");

    lua_pushnumber(m_luaState,m_nearestAsteroidDist);
    lua_setglobal(m_luaState,"gvDistAsteroid");

    lua_pushboolean(m_luaState,m_willCollide);
    lua_setglobal(m_luaState,"gvWillCollide");

    lua_pushboolean(m_luaState,m_isPowerup);
    lua_setglobal(m_luaState,"gvIsPowerup");

    lua_pushboolean(m_luaState,m_isAsteroid);
    lua_setglobal(m_luaState,"gvIsAsteroid");

    lua_pushnumber(m_luaState,m_ship->GetShotLevel());
    lua_setglobal(m_luaState,"gvShotPower");
```

```
        //run lua script, which handles state transitions
        lua_dofile(m_luaState,"script1.lua");

        m_machine->UpdateMachine(dt);
    }
```

LISTING 18.10 Sample Lua scripts to control the ship.

```
    —Lua script for simple asteroids state Logic


        if gvWillCollide then
            ChangeState(gsSTATEEVADE)
        elseif gvIsPowerup  and gvShotPower < gvMaxShotPower then
            ChangeState(gsSTATEGETPOWERUP)
        elseif gvIsAsteroid then
            if gvDistAsteroid < 200 then
                ChangeState(gsSTATEATTACK)
            else
                ChangeState(gsSTATEAPPROACH)
            end
        else
            ChangeState(gsSTATEIDLE)
        end

    —Another asteroids Lua script
        if gvWillCollide then
            ChangeState(gsSTATEEVADE)
        else
            ChangeState(gsSTATEAPPROACH)
        end
```

Lua script is being used to handle the state transition logic for the state machine. Because of the way the test bed is written (with the script being executed by calling the lua_dofile() function), you don't even have to shut off the game to change the AI behavior. If you edit the script1.lua file, and then save it, in the next game tick the file will be loaded and executed. You can change the script in a text editor and see the results every time you hit save. In a real game situation, however, you would probably not want frequent disk access during gameplay. Lua provides for this; you can load a script file into a buffer, and then execute it from memory instead of using the direct file access method. You could still keep fast iterative script changing by providing functionality from within your game to reload this buffer on command.

You could also just leave the random file access in for development and switch to the buffered system when shipping your final product.

The Lua script encapsulates all the state transition logic into a single if… then…else block, so it might seem like this is a step back, design wise and organizationally. We could do the exact same construct from within our C++ program, and the program would also run faster. The simple state-machine logic necessary to run our test bed is small enough that this method is fine, but in a game of any size or complexity, this would definitely not be true. But recognize that these simple transition definitions can now be traded back and forth, be made specific to each character in your game, and potentially be authored by non-programmers.

A DESCRIPTION OF A BETTER SYSTEM

In a large-scale game, you might create a simple, barebones FSM system on the game side, with the logic behind it being completely data-driven. The game-side state machine would consist of a list of states and a block of perception data (that is exposed to your Lua scripts). The game-side code would also include a list of "behaviors," which encapsulated the code necessary to actually perform actions within the game world. The scripts themselves would be organized as separate Lua functions for each game state; each function would consist of behavior calls and the transition logic for just that state.

Each time the AI engine would call the Lua script, it would first update a global variable in Lua that stored the name of the current game state, which could then directly translate into the corresponding Lua function to handle that state. To add another state to the game, the scripters would just make a new function in Lua and put the new function or game-state name into a global table of function or game states that is exposed to the game side. When the game loads (or reloads), it would grab this global table of game states and construct a barebones state-machine structure at run time. Listing 18.11 shows a simple C++ example, along with the Lua script that would be used.

LISTING 18.11   A better way of handling Lua-controlled FSM transitions.

```
//FSM Game code
LuaPerceptionExport();
UpdatePerceptions();

lua_pushnum(m_luaState,m_currentState);
lua_setglobal(m_luaState,"gCurrentState");
lua_doFile(m_luaState,"transitions.lua");
```

```
    UpdateMachine();


    _____

    —example.lua

    —game state functions
    function gsStateStand()
        —start/stop behaviors based on Perception data

        —check for transitions
        —would call a "ChangeState() function, which would
        — change the C++ m_currentState variable
    end

    function gsStateRun()
        —do run state
    end

    function gsStateSit()
        —do sit state
    end

    —global table of functions, C code can
    —access this in order to find out the number of
    —game states in the system, and their order
    funcs = {gsStateStand,gsStateRun,gsStateSit}

    —executes the current state function
    funcs[gCurrentState]()
```

A system like the one just described would have the scripters themselves declaring all the possible game states and, hence, would not need a programmer to be involved in adding or removing them. The result is that you separate your game content into two "camps": perceptions and behaviors are in the code, and logic and configuration parameters (things like attributes or numbers that require tuning and balancing) are covered by scripting. The scripters can arbitrarily set up game states, to facilitate any logic tree they desire, and their only requirement of the programmers would be the list of available game perceptions and behaviors that are implemented in the game code.

PERFORMANCE OF THE AI WITH THIS SYSTEM

Our script is very small, so the performance hit of running through the script file, and interpreting the entire script every frame is negligible. The game runs quite well with this system and is easy to tune and tweak given that you can edit the game logic as the game runs.

However, this system will not scale well for larger games. What if you had hundreds of character states, as well as hundreds of different characters? You would need to execute huge files, repeatedly traversing large scripted if blocks. This is not a system you would want to work on. Performance would be atrocious, debugging would be a nightmare, and extending the system would be hard work indeed. Instead, you would want to split up your system into some kind of modular organization, possibly using the setup detailed earlier under "Description of a Better System."

For larger implementations of an embedded Lua system, or for games built in a multithreaded environment, you can also use the more advanced Lua constructs: threads and coroutines. Threads are separate, full Lua environments, whereas co-routines are just re-entrant functions that can be paused and resumed at will. By using a system of co-routines, you could set up many different scripts to run the various AI entities in your game world and, with clever programming, not worry about any one script eating up all your CPU resources.

PROS OF SCRIPTING SYSTEMS

Scripting within an AI engine provides a means by which less technical staff can create and extend logic, tune systems and behaviors, and even completely change whole AI constructs (if the engine is set up to be fully data driven). Some of the things that scripting does well include rapid prototyping, increased accessibility, speed of tuning, user extensibility, and easy scaling. They also tend to make your level designers much happier since they don't have to try to describe how something should function for the programmer to code it—they simply build and test the scripts themselves.

Rapid Prototyping

Any time you are forced to abstract game perceptions and behaviors to a higher level (as you will have to do when deciding what to expose to your Lua scripts), you tend to distill your game down to the most foundational concepts; to basic principles. These principles represent the core perceptions that must be taken into account by an intelligent agent in order to make quality decisions within your game world. These basic concepts are created in the perception system, and the basic behaviors are built. Then the scripters can immediately begin scripting logic and strings of behavior, as well as start tuning in-game settings and events. Having fast turnaround when developing scripts (by providing script reloading in-game) accelerates the rate at which decent content can be added to the system.

Increased Accessibility

By using a more focused, higher-level language, you remove the barriers from entry that a real programming language incurs. You allow more people to feel confident to try to "get under the hood," if you will. Imagine how many more people might try and fix their own cars if they knew that the parts involved were simple, straightforward, and intuitive. By designing an easy-to-use scripting system for your game, you actually entice designers (and end users, if you allow it) to dig in and make script changes and additions.

Speed of Tuning

Scripting allows for much faster tuning of AI behavior (than is afforded by code changes, followed by a compile and link, followed by a game restart), as well as making available an open means by which more people can perform the tuning. In game script, interpreters also allow for parameter setting directly if you implement a console feature. A console is an in-game command prompt from which you can launch commands. The user could check or set variables, check memory, read in new AI files, save log information, and all manner of other activities that will dramatically speed up development.

Provides a Means for User Extensibility

The same system used to encode the AI and gameplay content for the production game can be included in the release of the product. Some companies include a full suite of development tools along with their games. This has especially become the norm in the PC FTPS genre, in which user-created mods have increased the shelf life of games from months or weeks to many years.

Some of the scripting languages included in these highly open games rival real programming languages in complexity (like *QuakeC*, or *UnRealScript*). They also allow the end user to control, change, and create almost any effect within the game. Through extensive use of built-in scripting languages, people have created flight sims, racing games, and platformers within FTPS game engines.

Easy Scaling

As the number of sections of your game under the control of the scripting engine increases, the real power of scripting becomes apparent. The overhead that scripting brings becomes less of a factor the more that you can leverage the data-driven paradigm. Each individual system within your game might have separate script functionality and resources. You can have one chunk of functions exposed for use in scripting behaviors, other game functions can be designated to script-state logic, or cinematic sequences. All these systems can be built on one unified scripting platform, if that platform is open and flexible enough to allow it.

CONS OF SCRIPTED SYSTEMS

Scripting does have some negative points, but these can generally be overcome with careful design, forethought, and the heavy processing power of today's game machines and PCs. Some of the things to consider when designing your scripting system include speed of execution, debugging difficulty, scripting, power, and the number of systems needing maintenance.

Speed of Execution

Any interpreted system is going to be slower than programs that have been compiled into native machine code. Lua scripts can be precompiled into bytecode, which give it a small speed boost (and has the added effect of being unreadable, in case you don't want users looking into the particulars of your scripts), but not much.

This is one reason why most scripting systems are made to be easily integrated with the regular compiled language used by your game, like C/C++. Then you can create the functions that require speed in the compiled language, while using script to develop the parts of the game that aren't as performance sensitive.

Debugging Can Be Difficult

The primary beef against scripting systems has always been in the realm of debugging. Two separate issues are usually the main problems.

First, scripting environments (especially custom-developed scripting languages) don't have the level of mature debugging tools (dedicated debuggers, profilers, asserts and internal error checking, syntax checking during compilation, etc.) that the big languages have, unless you specifically code them yourself.

Second, the people who usually write the scripts are not as technically trained as dedicated programmers (that was the point, right?). Even simple logic gymnastics (this AND that OR not this OtherThing AND these; now invert the whole thing) are sometimes beyond the grasp of purely creative types. So, non-technical staff tend to lack some "common sense" debugging techniques.

These debugging techniques include *binary* bug hunting, useful for scripts in which a bug makes the system stop dead, with no indication of what is wrong. In simple terms, run *half* the script. If there is no error, run the other half, if possible (if not, you would instead just run the first half, as well as a little more). Error? Then split that chunk in half and keep going.

Other common debugging methods include using print statements to watch script variables change while the game runs, or putting error checking directly into the scripts themselves, so that they can somewhat recover from mistakes or bad data on their own.

Usually, non-technical people learn to debug over time (just like most programmers do), and languages with long, flat learning curves are best for this. Languages that designers can get into fast, but take time to master. Lua, Python, and some of the other full-featured scripting languages offer this. You can write very simple scripts quickly, and as you progress through the learning curve, learn advanced features of the language in order to accomplish more powerful actions.

Looking Scripted

For a while, games used scripting languages just like Hollywood used scripts, to define large chunks of game behavior that was essentially being *performed* in front of the player, in a non-interactive way.

For example, as the player enters a room, control would be taken away, the camera would swing dramatically in to reveal three monsters emerging from some portal. They would then take their places, a leader type would approach, yell some invective to the player, and tell all about how he was going to end the player's life. Meanwhile, the room begins filling with fog, and the weird hat the player found in the last room starts glowing with some special purpose.

This is all very nice, at least the first couple of times you see it. But if players have to replay this battle many times because it is a difficult encounter, or this type of scenario occurs many times during a game, it starts to grate on players; they feel like they're not really playing the game but, rather, are being led around by their nose to witness the "next great vision" that will be presented to them.

Some games do this very well, and people love it. But many more games do this badly, and it becomes a kind of torture to have to sit through countless lengthy sequences of noninteractive silliness. But looking scripted doesn't have to include long cinematic sequences. It could just be that every time you talk to the drunk at the bar, he burps, then falls down, then says, "Leave me alone!" and then gets back up and reseats himself. If the player talks to the drunk three times in a row, he's going to know there's a very simple script that controls the drunk's behavior. Even though it may actually be a small piece of game code, today this kind of action is usually branded as scripting.

The richer you make your scripted responses, the better they will look the first time. The next time, all the illusion will be destroyed, and your static script will be discovered. The way to fight this is, of course, to not do it. Granted, some games definitely want that exact behavior, and this is fine as long as they don't overdo it. Also beware of using long static scripts in difficult parts of the game; a scripted reaction sequence is going to become a tedious ordeal for a player who is already having trouble with a particular section of your game (and thus is having to replay the area embedded with the script).

The Question of How Much Power

One problem with data-driven AI systems in general is the question of *when to stop* data driving. You've made the state transitions script-based. But in doing so, you've noticed that with a little more extension to the system, you can offload the state-machine definitions to the scripters. A little more engine code, and they could define the vast majority of actual AI behaviors. A touch more functionality to the scripting language, and they could also define perceptions, including the actual equations for calculation, the update frequency, and so on.

The problem is this: If you make too little script functionality, you've added overhead to the game for very little payoff, but if you add too much functionality, you run the risk of overwhelming the scripters with the entire job of coding a game, except in a scripting environment that is only half as user-friendly as a real programming language and that runs at three-quarters the speed.

Where to stop scripting is a serious question that needs careful attention when designing an engine. The answer lies in the type of game on which you are working, the level of functionality you need in your scripts to perform the things you need, and the level of organization and control you want of the content in your game.

You're Now Maintaining Two Systems

When you elect to write a script-based AI system, you're really choosing to provide another completely separate product in addition to your game. You now have two jobs. First, you are producing a game with a target audience that has specific needs and assumptions about how the game should look, feel, and play. Second, you are producing a light programming language, with a completely different target audience (although in some cases the scripting system will be given to the end-product users), who also has very specific needs and desires about how the scripting system should work.

When deciding to incorporate a scripting engine into your AI system, you are going to have to become somewhat of a people person. The difference between a good scripting language and a bad one lies in how easy it is for your scripters to use it; this initially means "How good are you at teaching your scripting language to others."

Be prepared to minimally write many example scripts (and they'd better be decent quality because they will most likely be cut and pasted directly into the game with minor changes for quite a while, as the scripters learn how to use the system). You'll also find yourself fielding questions regarding everything from debugging to simple programming methods: things like basic logic, organization methods, and different styles of using loops and data.

In addition, the feeling of power that scripting gives to people who were previously nonprogrammers is both contagious and can have a snowball effect. The more things you allow scripters to change in the game, the more things they're going to *want* to be able to change, and therefore the more features they're going to want you to add to the scripting language. You must allow for flexibility in the system for future extensions. But remember the last point in the list of cons: too much functionality in the scripting system can be a problem as well.

EXTENSIONS TO THE SCRIPTING PARADIGM

Scripting systems, by their very nature, open up to a whirlwind of possibilities. Extensions to a scripted environment are many, and are only restricted by the game and your scripter's needs. Some advanced features for scripting systems include custom languages, built-in debugging tools, a smart IDE for writing scripts, automatic integration into the game, and self-modifying scripts.

COMPLETELY CUSTOM LANGUAGES

A common means of creating a scripting system for your game is to go the way of the classic "Lex & Yacc" route. These are tools specifically for creating compilers, but they can also be used to streamline the creation of custom scripting languages.

The process is fairly straightforward: First, you generate a *grammar* file, which details the lexicon for the language you're developing, with the help of Lex. It allows you to set up all the rules for your language. These are actually special rules called *context-free grammars,* which is another way of saying that these grammatical rules can have wildcards, or nested definitions. You then run Yacc (which stands for Yet Another Compiler Compiler, aptly enough) on the grammar file, and it generates the C code necessary to parse a file using your specified grammar.

Games that use these tools tend to keep Yacc around as the in-game interpreter, a process that is sometimes called just-in-time (JIT) compiling, which refers to the fact that the script is compiled "just in time" for the game to use it. By using these tools, you can generate completely custom languages that still allow the flexibility and powerful parsing ability shown by more commonly used compilers, without having to code your system completely from scratch. Your scripting language can still use complex block structures, a variety of different operators and keywords, with whatever syntax works best for your game.

BUILT-IN DEBUGGING TOOLS

Of paramount importance if your system is going to be large and/or complex is a means for determining why things aren't working. By putting debugging functionality directly into the scripting system, or with an embedded system, giving the scripters immediate game-side functions to call that allow them to track down bugs and their causes is a great way to build a scripting system in the first place. Simple tools like "watch" functionality (allowing a variable's value to be constantly visible), break statements (which would stop the game if a specific line of script code is reached), and the ability to single step through a script (running the script one line at a time while being able to see variables and such) will accelerate debugging scripts just as they do regular code.

Also, visual debugging functionality that is visible *in game* is very useful. The scripters should be able to set up things within a script to write out text to the game screen, or icons, lines, and anything else they might need to depict what's going on inside the script, as well as allow scripters to test their code. These elements could be ignored once a game goes to production, by simply setting flags within the script parser to ignore them or only compiling the functionality into debug projects and not released code.

A Smart IDE for Writing Scripts

Obvious bugs in code are sometimes the hardest to find. This is even more true for nonprogrammers, who might stare at the line heroHitPoints = 0 for days and never realize that they needed to use a double equal sign (==) instead of a single. A function call in all lowercase letters instead of having the correct capitalization can be invisible to a scripter. By providing a full integrated development environment (IDE, typically defined as a combination editor/compiler/debugger all within one user interface), or at least some kind of dedicated editor for your scripting system, you can provide users with on-the-fly syntax checking (by interpreting the script within the editor for syntactical issues). Other common editor features include keyword finishing (you type the first few letters of a keyword, and then pressing tab will finish it, as well as correct the case), showing local variables and/or functions, and the like. These features will help to erase simple bugs before they ever enter the game and will make the system easier to learn and use overall.

Automatic Integration with the Game

Integration of new content with the game code can be handled a number of different ways. You can have your tool define meta-data to be used by the script, and the game engine itself when defining key in-game data structures. The game reads this data, as well as the scripts, and rebuilds the entire system's sets of objects or properties.

Another method, if there must be some programmer work for any new addition, is to simply use the scripting system as a kind of feedback tool for the programmers, as sort of a *request based* system. Any time a new "widget" is requested (through whatever means you use; be it a special editor data file, or just the inclusion of a RequestedWidget command from within a script itself), the system would just add it to a special list that programmers would have access to, to find out what the scripters require for new functionality. A useful addition is to allow the scripters to give a short description when requesting a new feature, so that the request is not just an empty shout in the dark. The programmers would then implement the requested widget, add it to the game-side code base, and the next time the scripts get loaded, the system could recognize that the requested widget has been completed, and move on.

SELF-MODIFYING SCRIPTS

Scripting systems, being data-based, open the door for a rarely-used technique in the realm of code-based AI: self-modifying behavior. Any given script can potentially change itself, so that the next time it is interpreted it will lead to different behavior. You could have script that changes small parameters within itself, or that changes large portions of the script itself.

A script-based system could keep track of specific behaviors that work (and don't work), and bias them up or down accordingly by actually writing data back into the script files. The system could append additional rules onto its script (or remove some) as the consequence of some event during a game.

Behavior like this could be thought of as a kind of learning, or it could go even further than learning. There is a field of AI called genetic programming that deals with this phenomenon. Unlike genetic algorithms, which strive to use genetically derived methods to tune algorithms for finding solutions to problems, genetic programming deals with using genetic methods to actually write whole programs to solve problems. In effect, the system is searching for the ideal script in which to perform its job, instead of the ideal parameters to use within a script.

The problem with using real code in genetic programming is that most genetically-created code segments are garbage, and wouldn't even compile, much less run. This is akin to the fact that most real genetic mutations don't lead to successful new variations on an established species. Your program might have to run for a very long time indeed to genetically "grow" a program that would run at all, much less be an ideal solution.

However, with a more abstract, high-level scripting system, you can begin to see the possibilities. A suitably robust system could generate scripts, test them, and genetically find superior programs that the AI could run to perform tasks. This is obviously a very different and ambitious path to take, but to the victor go the spoils.

OPTIMIZATIONS

The performance of any given scripting system relies both on the level of its use within the game and on the functionality of your language and how structured your overall system is. The simple configuration language implemented early in the chapter is barely more than a file parser and could be run with little to no impact on a game (especially because it is primarily designed for setting variables and flags during level load time, rather than during gameplay). If you were to use it as a base to write a serious scripting system (which isn't advised because it has none of even the simplest scripting niceties), you might have to perform considerable file-based gymnastics to get everything working.

Lua is a fairly lightweight language, and as such runs pretty fast for an interpreted system. But you still wouldn't want to write your AI navigation system's pathfinder in a Lua function. A well-written pathfinding system requires many tight search loops and a great deal of data being passed around. This is exactly the opposite of what you want to do within a scripter. Make sure that you're not using your scripting system just to use it. Low-level functionality should almost always be written in code.

For simple scripts that are just declaring behaviors in reaction to some event, a scripted AI system might actually make your game AI *faster* than if it were trying to calculate all the things necessary to get the AI to procedurally perform all the actions that a script might encapsulate. The scripted AI is simply being given a list of things to do, without recalculating anything midscript.

When dealing with large scripts, however, filled with heavy amounts of logic and game-side function calls, you might run into performance issues. Thread or co-routine-based scripting languages can help if you find that your AI scripts are taking too much time. These systems allow you to run your scripts over more than one frame, so you have to make sure that your AI solutions are reentrant, meaning they can be incrementally solved through a few game loops.

DESIGN CONSIDERATIONS

Scripting systems have a home in many different styles of games: in old-school games that relied on set patterns to portray behavior, and modern games that increasingly depend on large quantities of richly designed and detailed content.

Scripting systems allow nonprogrammers to define game content in a fast, generally game-safe way, without the bottleneck of having to rely on dedicated coders to help. These systems also allow fast tuning and the like because they allow changing game behavior without actually changing the game code itself and requiring a recompile.

TYPES OF SOLUTIONS

Scripting systems work equally well in the venues of low-level solutions (where scripts might be used to describe behaviors, animation selections, or simply set up game variables with tuned settings that radically change game actions), as well as high-level AI solutions (including strategic decisions involving many game elements, or scripted events that require many behaviors to be linked sequentially). They are a bit better suited toward the high-level work because they usually have an even higher abstracted view of the game world than the game code side of the AI system.

AGENT REACTIVITY

Scripted systems can give any level of reactivity you require, although it does depend on the kinds of scripts your game allows. If you can only use scripted behavioral responses that are somewhat limited or lengthy, your system might be seen as being too scripted, and as such, not very reactive. But if you use your scripting system to merely encode logic for a state-based AI system, then you can expect the reactivity of your agents to be commensurate with the update frequency of your system.

SYSTEM REALISM

Scripted systems have some of the largest ability to perform realistic, unique behavior in response to a given game event among many of the various game AI methodologies. The problem is that the richer and more scripted the behavior is, the more proprietary it is. It can only be used in one limited part of the game; in some cases it can only be used once.

Thus, if you have a completely state-driven, reactive game, and suddenly one part of your game launches a massive single-shot script giving everyone realistic behaviors, it's either going to seem out of place, or it's going to make the rest of your game seem boring.

Thus, rich content can force even *more* rich content to be built into your game. In addition, overly scripted behavior very quickly loses its realism if the player can cause it to repeat, as it will make the game characters seem very robotic and unresponsive, which is the opposite of what you were striving. Outside of the issue of *overly* scripting a game, however, scripting systems can allow increased realism without overly robotic behaviors simply because they allow a greater amount of overall behavioral content to be included in the game given the same development-time restrictions.

Genre and platform are of almost no concern to scripting systems. Games with a large number of AI entities or differing game situations are ideal for scripting systems because the main reason for using them in the first place is that you require more content or tuning than can be easily handled directly (or indirectly) by the programmers on your project.

If you are making a game with one main character, one enemy, and three behaviors apiece, you could most likely write everything in code and easily tune the entire system from the game side. You still might want to use a configuration script system to set game-specific variables and properties from data, so that you can set tuning values and not have to recompile the game, but this would depend on your preference. Scripting systems do require additional memory (in overhead for the parser, interpreter, and data size), but usually make up for it by simplifying the code base so they can be implemented on even the smaller and more restrictive platforms.

Care must be taken because, unless specifically designed otherwise, scripted code will always run somewhat slower then compiled code, and this kind of performance hit must be considered.

DEVELOPMENT LIMITATIONS

Development limitations are one of the most important things to consider when deciding on using a scripting system in your AI engine. You have to determine if you have the time to implement the language, the time to teach it to your scripters, and the extra time and effort needed to debug the scripts and the game code. You will save time when it comes to tuning the final product, but this may not offset the costs incurred by all these hurdles.

ENTERTAINMENT LIMITATIONS

Tuning difficulty settings, balancing specific behaviors, and other entertainment concerns are generally the reasons why a team chooses to implement a scripting system because these issues are either very important to the product, or the level of this kind of work is incredibly large. Scripting, using either a basic or a full system, will aid in all these endeavors.

SUMMARY

Scripting systems provide game makers with a means to get more content into their game without needing more programmers. Scripting systems typically use a simplified programming system to build AI elements, logic, and/or behaviors. Scripting languages can be anything from simple, representational token-based systems, to full-fledged programming languages themselves.

- When designing your scripting system, consider the kinds of functionality that the language will require, how the runtime engine will interpret the scripts, the overall size of the scripts, and the potential users of the language.
- A configuration script system is a simple, text-parsing system employing user-defined tokens.
- The simple configuration scripting code included in this chapter is broken down into three parts: Token, Parser, and a number of callbacks, each one associated with a particular `Token`.

- Because of the generic nature of the simple scripting system given here, extensions to the method are unlimited. However, the lack of any real features found in more robust scripting systems might keep you from investing any time and effort with such a rudimentary foundation.

- Embedding Lua as a scripting language is becoming a popular shortcut to rolling your own language. Lua is small, fast, easy to learn, and integrates well with C/C++.

- Lua features include dynamic typing, garbage collection, LISP-like associative arrays called tables, and a random access stack structure for passing values back and forth between scripts and the host language.

- To integrate Lua into a game environment, you compile the libraries into your game, include the header files, instantiate a `lua_state` interpreter, register any host language functions with the interpreter, and finally pass the interpreter data, direct commands, or whole files to execute. When the game is done, you close the interpreter.

- Scripts can be compiled into bytecode, which makes them execute a bit faster, but also encrypts them so they cannot be read.

- The test-bed implementation places all the state transition logic into a Lua script. Given a large-scale game, a more robust implementation would be to put the entire state machine into Lua, and just pass perception data and register behaviors with the scripting system. Each state could have its own script function for modularity and maintainability.

- Lua supports threads and coroutines for use in large scripts that must be completed across game loops, in sequentially written scripts that have pauses, or in multithreaded game environments.

- The pros of scripting involve rapid prototyping, increased accessibility, speed of tuning, and easy scaling.

- The cons of game scripting, which can in most cases be overcome, involve speed of execution, debugging difficulty, becoming "scripted looking," balancing the power versus ease of use of the script system, and that you now must produce two products (the game and the scripting language).

- Extensions to base scripting systems commonly are built-in debugging tools, smart environments for script writing, automatic integration with game-side code, and self-modifying script code.

- Optimizing a scripting system involves the specific game in question and the specific scripting system in question. Some scripting might actually improve game performance because the AI character would be just "following a script," instead of calculating a response. For re-entrant problems, threading or co-routine-based scripts might help with performance problems.

19 Location-Based Information Systems

In This Chapter

- Location-Based Information Systems Overview
- How These Techniques Are Used
- Influence Mapping Skeletal Code and Test-Bed Implementation
- Pros of Location-Based Information Systems
- Cons of Location-Based Information Systems
- Extensions to the Paradigm
- Optimizations
- Design Considerations
- Summary

This chapter, like Chapter 17, "Message-Based Systems," will cover a family of AI techniques that are secondary to an overall game AI decision-making system. However, unlike messaging, which is more of a communication technique, location-based information systems (LBI) are helper routines that augment decision making by providing additional information to the intelligence engine. This extra information is brought forward in the form of a centralized bank of data that is tied to the game world itself in some fashion. LBI could be thought of as specialized perception data, which might also include embedded logic or lower-level intelligence.

LOCATION-BASED INFORMATION SYSTEMS OVERVIEW

The discussion of LBI will be broken into three common (but not exclusive) categories in this book: influence maps, smart terrain, and terrain analysis. The first part of this chapter will briefly discuss each of these categories. Later, we will implement some simple influence mapping techniques. The other two techniques are considerably more complex and much more game-specific (and hence, a full implementation would go beyond the scope of the method explanation), so this chapter will not fully implement these techniques, but will broadly discuss implementations of smart terrain and terrain analysis, both for our test application and for real-world games.

INFLUENCE MAPS (IMs)

Influence mapping is slowly becoming one of the most commonly used secondary AI techniques in games. Its generic structure and open-ended usage make it second only to finite-state machines (FSMs) in ease of implementation and adaptability to different game AI problems.

The term *influence map* refers to using a simple array of data in which each element represents information about a specific world position. IMs are usually conceptually thought of as a 2D grid overlaid on the world. The resolution of this grid (and thus the number of elements in your influence array) depends on the minimum size of game space that you need to tag with information. Where your game can compromise between data size and influence accuracy will also determine this resolution. So, if you absolutely need specific information for every square inch of a large game world, your IM will have a very high resolution (and take up a lot of memory in doing so).

Many games employ multiple IMs, to either help with memory and searching costs, or to provide different levels of game space resolution to the various AI systems. An example within a real-time strategy (RTS) game might have an IM with very low resolution (say, each element is an entire game screen) that reflects the amount of each resource within. The game could use this low-res IM for high-level planning when base building as well as determining the best direction in which to expand the base as the game progresses. You would want to expand your base (and thus your main defenses) toward more resourceful areas to facilitate future expansion. Our example RTS game could also employ another IM, with a much higher resolution (each element is now approximately equal to four of the smallest units standing together). This one keeps track of the number of units that have been killed in each grid square. It is used to affect the pathfinding engine so that units will not continue to take paths into areas with high mortality scores.

In games with worlds that are heavily 3D, a more complex data structure is necessary; these can be represented with layered IMs, or by building the influence data into the navigation mesh used for pathfinding. Another technique might be to only use IMs where you need them, or *local* IMs.

For example, a battle between forces in an RTS game might start anywhere on the map. You might want to have a heavily detailed IM during battles to coordinate forces, but not want to use the memory to have a global IM for the game world with the resolution necessary to provide the level of information it would require.

Instead, you could implement a heavily detailed, but local IM. The system would detect a battle and set the coordinates of the local battle planning IM to be some distance out from the "center" of the battle. The center of the battle could be determined using a different, lower-resolution IM that keeps track of population data or fighting locations. Thus, the size of the global IM is still constrained, but local information can become quite detailed.

The nature of IM's generic structure can be used to construe location-specific data in an infinite number of different and useful ways, limited only by your imagination and the relevance to your game in particular. In fact, this basic system can be (and usually is) the central repository for the other two LBI techniques to communicate with the rest of the game.

SMART TERRAIN

Made popular by the Sims games (in fact, the term was coined by Will Wright, the Sims creator), this technique places logic and behavior data for how to use various world features and game objects into the objects themselves.

In the Sims, characters in the game were motivated by *needs* that could be satisfied by interfacing with the various objects in the game. The Sims's programmers could apply different attributes to each object, which corresponded to particular needs that the game characters required. Thus, a microwave oven satisfied the Food need, and a bed fulfilled the Sleep need. The character then navigates around the world, trying to gratify his or her unmet needs at any given time, doing so by listening for broadcast messages from any nearby smart object. These messages would communicate to the character the need categories each object satisfied, and the character would then be free to use any world object to satiate him- or herself. Of course, this is a simplified view of the workings of the Sims game, but it illustrates the general idea.

The technique also bundles all the interaction animations, sounds, and any other special data that a character would need to use the object into the object itself, thus making the object completely self-contained. In this way, new objects could be added whenever the developers wanted and would require only two things: that the new object contained all the data that the game requires to be a fully functional game object, and that the new object assuaged one or more of their basic needs so that the characters would actually seek out and use the new object.

TERRAIN ANALYSIS (TA)

Tracking various attributes and statistical data within an IM is only part of the problem. The AI system must also *make use* of this data. TA is a family of methods that have used IM techniques to provide AI systems with increased strategic information about maps, especially randomly generated maps that haven't had the benefit of ever being touched by a level designer. Even with custom-created maps that have had preprocessed analysis, most games have some element of dynamic change within the game world, which again calls for additional, on-the-fly analysis of the map.

TA methods are best described as specialized pattern recognition within an IM data array. The system searches through the IM array, looking for motifs that can be exploited or that deal with strategic and tactical decision making. Even simple analysis done on a medium-resolution IM array can be computationally expensive because of the large amount of searching required for many pattern-matching algorithms. To counter this, some games use TA systems employing non-brute force methods to determine patterns, such as neural nets or fuzzy-logic systems, that can algorithmically find patterns within the IM array.

HOW THESE TECHNIQUES ARE USED

IMs are increasingly common in game AI, especially RTS games (although other genres, like role-playing games, and action and adventure games are following suit). Some examples of how games use IMs include occupance data, ground control, pathfinding, danger signification, rough battlefield planning, simple terrain analysis, and advanced terrain analysis.

OCCUPANCE DATA

Occupance data means tracking various populations within the game. An easy use of an IM is to keep track of the number of specific game objects within a certain area. You might want to keep track of all combat units, specialized resource locations, important quest items, or any other in-game object. Simple occupance data can be used to help with obstacle avoidance (overriding the pathfinding system with local detours around occupied terrain), give rough estimates of various game perceptions (army size, town density, the direction to the most powerups, etc.), or any other task that requires quick access to localized population data.

A common usage of the occupance IM is the familiar fog of war line-of-sight system that almost all RTS games employ. Initially, this fog covers the map completely, so that players are forced to explore the map to find resources and enemy towns. Exploring the terrain removes the fog and allows a player to see the physical details of the land, but the player must have a unit within line of sight of any given location to see the current activity within it. The game uses occupance within the map to uncover areas of the map that are visually within line of sight of any of a player's units.

GROUND CONTROL

Ground control is finding actual influence of game ground. Although the term *influence map* is used in game AI as a loosely defined data structure, the phrase historically refers to techniques derived from the field of thermodynamics (in determining heat transfer) and field analysis in general (such as electromagnetic fields). These same equations can be used in a game setting and can quickly determine which player has control over which part of the game map.

The algorithm for this is simple: First, zero out the entire map. Then, assign each grid square a value based on its team-specific control (the magnitude represents the degree of control, the sign differentiates teams; a positive value for player A's units, a negative value for player B's units, with more complex schemes for more than two players). Then go over the map again, and for each map square, add up the values of the squares surrounding it, scale by some amount (to prevent value overflow), and add that to the square's value. Repeat a few times to disperse the influence out until you achieve a stable state. Player A controls the squares that have positive values, and player B controls negatively valued squares. This technique will provide the AI engine with a way of measuring global, as well as local, control. In areas where no one has direct positional control, the influence numbers will have propagated from the nearest units that do have direct control. The IM analyzer can then determine large regions of contiguous control, which carve the game world into areas of player affect. The game could then sum all the areas to determine who has the most control over the map, for king of the hill scenarios.

PATHFINDING SYSTEM HELPER DATA

When provided with additional information about a specific area, the pathfinder can help smooth the solution through a tricky part of the map by giving a shortcut, or allowing the AI-controlled character to use a specific map feature such as a teleporter or ladder. The pathfinder data may include things like passability relative to terrain features (such as hills or cliffs) and to terrain type (land versus sea) or even which player currently controls the areas of the map you want to traverse.

Some games use a simplistic potential field-like technique for augmenting a path node-based system, implemented by placing designer-authored influence data throughout the map, or to be procedurally determined. Usually, this would be used to help (or force) steering of AI characters away from hazards or places the game developer just doesn't want a bunch of roving monsters to congregate. A potential field IM might also change and adapt to game conditions over time, giving characters the appearance of learning as the game progresses. An in-game example of this might be in a sports setting (for example, a hockey game), in which a small offset IM field is used in conjunction with a formation system. When the game starts, the offsets are all zeroed out, so the CPU team uses the standard formation for positioning. But as the human player starts to play against the CPU team, the offset IM is used to perturb the formation of the computer players toward places that the human often uses for travel or for passing the puck. In this way, the human is forced to change his game to continue to score effectively because the computer team is continually fine-tuning its formations to the human's style of play.

DANGER SIGNIFICATION

Another useful implementation of IMs is to keep track of areas where bad things have happened over a period of time. This data can then adjust the regular AI behavior, so that the AI doesn't continue to perform the same actions that result in the continuation of this harm.

An example mentioned in the RTS chapter would be the human placing an attacking tower in the midst of a pathfinding route that the AI uses regularly. The tower then proceeds to kill the single line of units that continually trickle by the tower. If the AI had a danger signification system in place, the units would eventually stop walking by the tower (because the AI would use the danger data to influence the pathfinding cost of traveling through that area), and better yet, would send out an attack group to investigate what is causing the danger in the area. Another example would be an AI deathmatch bot in a FTPS game remembering areas where the bot was ambushed or sniped, so that the bot could avoid those areas, or just approach them differently.

ROUGH BATTLEFIELD PLANNING

The ground control method detailed earlier can be used to quickly point out areas of interest in the midst of battles. By looking for regions of low-control value, you can easily find where armies are directly fighting for control of an area. This will tell you where the conflicts are, and where the front line of any given battle is. Large areas of near-zero values are, by definition, places where no one is in control. When a human player knows where the brunt of his force is, in relation to the main body of the other army (as well as the relative size of each army), the player can focus attack direction, determine chances of winning to initiate additional charges or retreats, send reinforcements more intelligently, and coordinate attacks on multiple fronts more cleanly.

SIMPLE TERRAIN ANALYSIS

Simple TA includes mathematical determinations such as *cover* (how much a given position is open to attack from any given angle), *visibility* (in some ways, the opposite of cover, but also considers lighting concerns and line-of-sight issues), and *height factors* (many games allow greater missile weapon range from higher ground and better visibility). The best areas of cover that have height advantage become sniping spots. Areas with low visibility might become sneaky back doors to other map areas. An area with high visibility might work as the target of an ambush if it is surrounded on some sides by high-cover terrain.

ADVANCED TERRAIN ANALYSIS

RTS games routinely require much more advanced TA methods to appear even remotely intelligent when playing against a human opponent.

Finding good choke points in a map, meaning places where movement or visibility are severely restricted, is a common way to use IMs. By scanning maps for this feature the AI can set up ambushes if a choke point exists between two or more major map zones, especially if it's a *perfect* choke point (meaning there is no other way to travel between the two zones, and the other player has to travel through to win the game). Walls can be built inside natural choke points to minimize the amount of walls that need to be built to close off a map area. Walls can also be used to create artificial choke points to force opponents into dicey manuevers.

Another key usage of IM information is in determining the best way to build a town, defenses, or other structures. Towns should be built with some preplanning, to keep *crowding* under control (for pathfinding as well as for protection because buildings that are too close together can be splash damaged by large artillery type weapons en masse), to maximize future *growth* (by growing toward additional resources and minding routes of travel from older buildings), and yet allow *maintenance* (watch so that the town doesn't have too many flanks, and spread out the town's defenses to prevent weak flanks).

The AI might want to use impassable terrain to its advantage by building the base of a town against it, therefore removing a line of attack. Humans build walls to slow down or redirect AI enemies that are pathfinding through an area (Figure 19.1 shows a human-made kill zone constructed of a maze of walls). These same sorts of tricks could be employed by an AI system to trip up players who don't micromanage their forces. But setting up these measures would require the AI system to scout for good places in which to do so, or else the behavior of the AI would look silly.

Determining important map areas (such as maps with severely limited resources or key strategic positions) is something at which humans are extremely skilled. Given a snapshot of the map layout (see Figure 19.2), a good human player will quickly ascertain that the player has to control area "A" because it contains most of the powerups and is fairly defensible. AI systems are usually quite bad at this type of determination, but an IM tracking this type of information (powerup location density, cover information, and choke points) would be quick to help with this shortcoming.

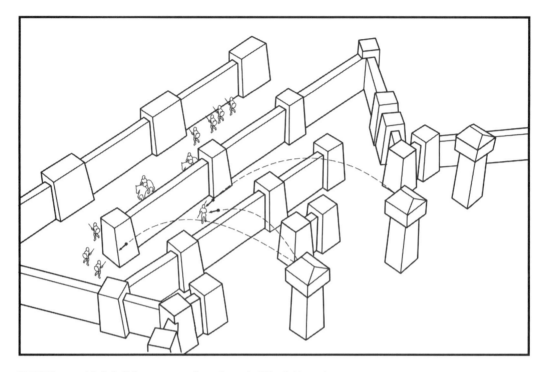

FIGURE 19.1   Walls built in a maze configuration to hold back AI attackers.

INFLUENCE MAPPING SKELETAL CODE AND TEST-BED IMPLEMENTATION

In this section, we will implement a few different kinds of basic IMs into the test-bed application. The implementation will be for illustrative purposes and will not affect the decision-making process of the AI subsystem within the test bed. Rather, it will show how easy it is to gather information and centralize it within an IM, and will display this information visually by means of a debugging system that allows both the grid and the cell contents to be drawn during the game. After each implementation, a discussion will follow about how the particular method could have been used by the test bed to improve performance.

Three simple types of IMs will be implemented, to show different ways to use them. These are the following:

1. **Occupance-based IM:** tracks where a given game object is in the world.
2. **Control-based IM:** uses a gradient to show an area of control around each game object and uses the notion of player sides.
3. **Bitwise IM:** splits the IM element's value into bitwise data components.

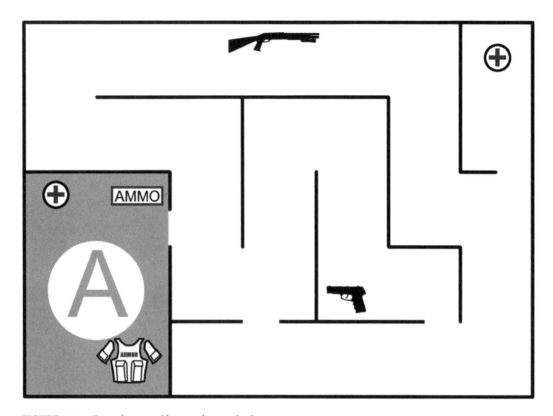

FIGURE 19.2   Example map with several strategic elements.

Each IM type inherits from the basic IM class, `InfluenceMap` (see Listing 19.1 for the header, 19.2 for the function implementations). As you can see, the first item of interest in the base class is the IM array, `m_map`, which is an array of `int` (an unsigned 16-bit field). If you needed more or less storage within your IM array, you could change this to whatever you needed. You could even make a custom `struct` that the array would be composed of, but then you would have to change the class to accommodate this.

LISTING 19.1   `InfluenceMap` header information.

```
struct RegObj
{
    GameObj*    m_pObject;
    int         m_objSizeX;
    int         m_objSizeY;
    int         m_objType;
    Point3f     m_lastPosition;
    bool        m_stamped;
};
```

```
typedef std::list<RegObj*> RegObjectList;

class InfluenceMap
{
public:
    //constructor/functions
    InfluenceMap(int type):m_influenceType(type)
                        {m_drawGrid = false;m_drawInfluence = false;}
    ~InfluenceMap();
    virtual void Update(float dt) {}
    virtual void Draw();
    virtual void DrawTheGrid();
    virtual void DrawTheInfluence();
    virtual void Init(int sizeX, int sizeY, int wSizeX, int wSizeY);
    virtual void Reset();
    virtual void RegisterGameObj(GameObj* object);
    virtual void RemoveGameObj(GameObj* object);
    virtual void StampInfluenceShape(int* pMap,Point3f& location,
                                    int sizeX,int sizeY, int value);
    virtual void StampInfluenceGradient(int* pMap,Point3f& location,
                                        int initValue);
    int  SumInfluenceShape(int* pMap,Point3f& location,
                            int sizeX,int sizeY);
    int  GetInfluenceValue(int* pMap,Point3f& location);
    void SetType(int type) {m_influenceType = type;}
    void DrawGrid(bool on = true){m_drawGrid = on;}
    void DrawInfluence(bool on = true){m_drawInfluence = on;}
    int  GetSizeX(){return m_dataSizeX;}
    int  GetSizeY(){return m_dataSizeY;}

    //influence map types
    enum
    {
        IM_NONE,
        IM_OCCUPANCE,
        IM_CONTROL,
        IM_BITWISE
    };

protected:
    //data members
    int*    m_map;
    RegObjectList m_registeredObjects;
```

```
    int     m_dataSizeX;
    int     m_dataSizeY;
    int     m_numCels;
    int     m_worldSizeX;
    int     m_worldSizeY;
    float   m_celResX;
    float   m_celResY;
    int     m_influenceType;

    bool    m_drawGrid;
    bool    m_drawInfluence;
};
```

The influence system works by maintaining a list of registered game objects within its `m_registeredObjects` list. Game objects are thus freed of having to worry about updating themselves within the IM, because the system keeps its own list, but must remember to remove themselves from the IM system when they die in general.

Two functions, `StampInfluence()` and `StampInfluenceGradient()`, are used to actually write values to the IM. The plain version merely writes a value to a chunk of the array that is passed in size and position. The gradient version writes a decreasing value square gradient into the array starting at a certain position. These are generic enough that they are in the basic class, but they can be overridden by any subclass you create to perform custom writes to the IM array.

`GetInfluenceValue()` is an accessor for the map, and `SumInfluence()` is a generic function that merely sums the influence values at a position in a specific shape. Notice that all the functions dealing with the IM element map take an array pointer as a parameter. This is to facilitate custom IM types that may require additional scratch maps to perform multiple pass actions on the overall IM array.

LISTING 19.2   `InfluenceMap` implementation of important functions.

```
//-------------------
InfluenceMap::~InfluenceMap()
{
    if(m_registeredObjects.size() == 0)
        return;
    RegObjectList::iterator listObj;
    for(listObj=m_registeredObjects.begin();
```

```
            listObj!=m_registeredObjects.end();++listObj)
    {
        delete (*listObj);
    }
    m_registeredObjects.clear();

}
//-------------------
void InfluenceMap::Init(int sizeX, int sizeY, int wSizeX, int wSizeY)
{
    m_dataSizeX     = sizeX;
    m_dataSizeY     = sizeY;
    m_numCels       = m_dataSizeX*m_dataSizeY;
    m_map           = new int[m_numCels];

    //clear out the map
    memset(m_map,0,m_numCels*sizeof(int));

    m_worldSizeX    = wSizeX;
    m_worldSizeY    = wSizeY;
    m_celResX       = m_worldSizeX / m_dataSizeX;
    m_celResY       = m_worldSizeY / m_dataSizeY;
}

//-------------------
void RemoveAll(RegObj* object)
{
    delete object;
}

//-------------------
void InfluenceMap::Reset()
{
    //clear out the map
    memset(m_map,0,m_numCels*sizeof(int));

    //get rid off all the objects
    if(m_registeredObjects.size() == 0)
        return;
    for_each(m_registeredObjects.begin(),
            m_registeredObjects.end(),RemoveAll);
    m_registeredObjects.clear();
}
```

```cpp
//--------------------
void InfluenceMap::RegisterGameObj(GameObj* object)
{
    int sizeY,sizeX;
    sizeX = sizeY = 1;

    RegObj* temp;
    temp = new RegObj;
    temp->m_pObject      = object;
    temp->m_objSizeX     = sizeX;
    temp->m_objSizeY     = sizeY;
    temp->m_lastPosition = object->m_position;
    temp->m_stamped      = false;
    m_registeredObjects.push_back(temp);
}


//--------------------
void InfluenceMap::RemoveGameObj(GameObj* object)
{
    if(m_registeredObjects.size() == 0)
        return;

    RegObjectList::iterator listObj;
    for(listObj=m_registeredObjects.begin();
        listObj!=m_registeredObjects.end();++listObj)
    {
        RegObj* temp = *listObj;
        if((*listObj)->m_pObject == object)
        {
            m_registeredObjects.erase(listObj);
            delete temp;
            return;
        }
    }

}


//--------------------
void InfluenceMap::StampInfluenceShape(int* pMap,Point3f& location,int
sizeX, int sizeY, int value)
{
    int gridX = location.x()/ m_celResX;
    int gridY = location.y()/ m_celResY;
```

```
    int startX = gridX - sizeX/2;
    if(startX < 0) startX += m_dataSizeX;
    int startY = gridY - sizeY/2;
    if(startY < 0) startY += m_dataSizeY;

    for(int y = startY;y<startY + sizeY;y++)
    {
        for(int x = startX;x<startX + sizeX;x++)
        {
            pMap[(y%m_dataSizeY)*m_dataSizeY+(x%m_dataSizeX)]+=value;
        }
    }
}


//--------------------
int InfluenceMap::GetInfluenceValue(int* pMap,Point3f& location)
{
    int gridX = location.x()/ m_celResX;
    int gridY = location.y()/ m_celResY;
    return pMap[gridX,gridY];
}


//--------------------
int InfluenceMap::SumInfluenceShape(int* pMap,Point3f& location,
                                    int sizeX,int sizeY)
{
    int sum = 0;
    int gridX = location.x()/ m_celResX;
    int gridY = location.y()/ m_celResY;

    int startX = gridX - sizeX/2;
    if(startX < 0) startX += m_dataSizeX;
    int startY = gridY - sizeY/2;
    if(startY < 0) startY += m_dataSizeY;

    for(int y = startY;y<startY + sizeY;y++)
    {
        for(int x = startX;x<startX + sizeX;x++)
        {
            sum+=pMap[(y%m_dataSizeY)*m_dataSizeY+(x%m_dataSizeX)];
        }
    }
    return sum;
}
```

```
//--------------------
void InfluenceMap::StampInfluenceGradient(int* pMap,Point3f&
                                          location, int initValue)
{
    int gridX = location.x()/ m_celResX;
    int gridY = location.y()/ m_celResY;

    int stopDist = fabsf(initValue)*0.75f;//*(m_dataSizeX/32);
    int halfStopDist = stopDist / 2;
    int startX = gridX - halfStopDist;
    if(startX < 0) startX += m_dataSizeX;
    int startY = gridY - halfStopDist;
    if(startY < 0) startY += m_dataSizeY;

    for(int y = startY;y<startY + stopDist;y++)
    {
        for(int x = startX;x<startX + stopDist;x++)
        {
            int value;

            int distX = fabs(x - (startX + halfStopDist));
            int distY = fabs(y - (startY + halfStopDist));

            value = initValue*( halfStopDist –
                        MAX(distX,distY))/halfStopDist;
            pMap[(y%m_dataSizeY)*m_dataSizeY +
                    (x%m_dataSizeX)] += value;
        }
    }
}
```

THE OccupanceInfluenceMap

Now that you have been given the basic system, we can go forward to the specific implementations. Listing 19.3 and 19.4 give the header and implementation of the class OccupanceInfluenceMap, which is a simple IM that tracks population data within the IM of the different game objects.

LISTING 19.3   OccupanceInfluenceMap header.

```
class OccupanceInfluenceMap:public InfluenceMap
{
public:
    //constructor/functions
    OccupanceInfluenceMap():InfluenceMap(IM_OCCUPANCE){}
```

```
    ~OccupanceInfluenceMap();
    virtual void Update(float dt);
    virtual void RegisterGameObj(GameObj* object);
    virtual void RemoveGameObj(GameObj* object);
    virtual void DrawTheInfluence();
};
```

As Listing 19.4 shows, the `Update()` function is where most of the work is being done. Here, too, you can see two different ways that IM data is handled. In the update method, you can see a call to `memset` that is commented out, above a small chunk of code that unstamps the old locations before the new locations are stamped. These two code blocks represent both ways of dealing with the "old" values in the IM map, roughly analogous to the old graphics frame buffer during rendering. Having the function unstamp the old locations before continuing is akin to a "dirty rectangles" scheme of graphics drawing, in which you only redraw the elements that need it, rather than the entire scene. If your game world is small and you have many objects to write, like our test bed, it's much more reasonable to just wipe the IM array and start over (by using the direct `memset` call). But in the midst of a very large game world, with few game objects, or a game with static IM data (such as terrain features or specialized IM flags), you could instead use the dirty rectangles method, so that you don't radically upset the buffer or are forced to reconstruct a lot of feature data. Notice also that because this class was written using the unstamp process, the `RemoveGameObj()` method for this class must unstamp the removed object, so no artifacts are left behind.

`RegisterGameObj()` also sets the size of the influence for the object. This probably could have been a more algorithmic process, but for converting the mostly round game objects into square IM shadows for the test bed, this proved to be a fine solution. In the `DrawInfluence()` function, notice that we're drawing a grayscale polygon for each IM array element and that it reaches maximum value at 10 objects within the cell.

LISTING 19.4 `OccupanceInfluenceMap` implementation of important functions.

```
//- - - - - - - - - - - - - - - - - - -
void OccupanceInfluenceMap::Update(float dt)
{
    //bail out if nobody to update
    if(m_registeredObjects.size() == 0)
        return;

    //clear out map
//    memset(m_map,0,m_numCels*sizeof(int));
```

```
RegObjectList::iterator listObj;
//unstamp old locations
for(listObj=m_registeredObjects.begin();
    listObj!=m_registeredObjects.end();++listObj)
{
    if((*listObj)->m_pObject->m_position ==
        (*listObj)->m_lastPosition)
        continue;
    if((*listObj)->m_stamped)
        StampInfluenceShape(m_map,(*listObj)->
                            m_lastPosition,(*listObj)->
                            m_objSizeX,(*listObj)->m_objSizeY, -1);
}


//stamp new locations
for(listObj=m_registeredObjects.begin();
    listObj!=m_registeredObjects.end();++listObj)
{
    if((*listObj)->m_pObject->m_position ==
        (*listObj)->m_lastPosition)
        continue;
    StampInfluenceShape(m_map,(*listObj)->m_pObject->
                        m_position,(*listObj)->m_objSizeX,(*listObj)->
                        m_objSizeY, 1);
    (*listObj)->m_stamped = true;
    (*listObj)->m_lastPosition = (*listObj)->m_pObject->m_position;
}
}


//--------------------
void OccupanceInfluenceMap::RemoveGameObj(GameObj* object)
{
    if(m_registeredObjects.size() == 0)
        return;

    RegObjectList::iterator listObj;
    for(listObj=m_registeredObjects.begin();
        listObj!=m_registeredObjects.end();++listObj)
    {
        RegObj* temp = *listObj;
        if((*listObj)->m_pObject == object)
        {
            if((*listObj)->m_stamped)
```

```
                   StampInfluenceShape(m_map,(*listObj)->
                                 m_lastPosition,(*listObj)->
                                 m_objSizeX,(*listObj)->m_objSizeY, -1);
           m_registeredObjects.erase(listObj);
           delete temp;
           return;
       }
   }

}

//--------------------
void OccupanceInfluenceMap::RegisterGameObj(GameObj* object)
{
    int sizeX,sizeY;
    if(object->m_size <4)
    {
        sizeX = m_dataSizeX/16;
        sizeY = m_dataSizeY/16;
    }
    else if(object->m_size<11)
    {
        sizeX = m_dataSizeX/10;
        sizeY = m_dataSizeY/10;
    }
    else if(object->m_size<33)
    {
        sizeX = m_dataSizeX/8;
        sizeY = m_dataSizeY/8;
    }
    else if(object->m_size <49)
    {
        sizeX = m_dataSizeX/5;
        sizeY = m_dataSizeX/5;
    }
    else if(object->m_size <65)
    {
        sizeX = m_dataSizeX/4;
        sizeY = m_dataSizeX/4;
    }
    else
    {
        sizeX = m_dataSizeX/3;
        sizeY = m_dataSizeX/3;
    }
```

```
        //set minimum size of 1 in each direction
        sizeX = MAX(1,sizeX);
        sizeY = MAX(1,sizeY);

        RegObj* temp;
        temp = new RegObj;
        temp->m_pObject      = object;
        temp->m_objSizeX     = sizeX;
        temp->m_objSizeY     = sizeY;
        temp->m_lastPosition = object->m_position;
        temp->m_stamped      = false;
        m_registeredObjects.push_back(temp);
    }

//--------------------
void OccupanceInfluenceMap::DrawTheInfluence()
{
    glPushMatrix();
    glDisable(GL_LIGHTING);
    glTranslatef(0,0,0);
    glEnable(GL_BLEND);
    glBlendFunc(GL_ONE, GL_ONE);
    for(int i=0;i<m_numCels;i++)
    {
        if(m_map[i])
        {
            int y = i / m_dataSizeY;
            int x = i - y*m_dataSizeY;
            float grayscale = m_map[i]/10.0f;
            glColor3f(grayscale,grayscale,grayscale);
            glBegin(GL_POLYGON);
            glVertex3f(x*m_celResX,            y*m_celResY,           0);
            glVertex3f(x*m_celResX,            y*m_celResY+m_celResY,0);
            glVertex3f(x*m_celResX+m_celResX,y*m_celResY+m_celResY,0);
            glVertex3f(x*m_celResX+m_celResX,y*m_celResY,           0);
            glEnd();
        }
    }
    glDisable(GL_BLEND);
    glEnable(GL_LIGHTING);
    glPopMatrix();
}
```

To use the system, you instantiate the map, and then initialize it with the grid resolution and the size of the game world you want. You then register any objects you want tracked with the IM. In our test bed, all game objects are being registered with the IM, and another data member of the class GameObj has been added, the Boolean m_influence, so you can prevent particular game objects from affecting the influence system.

USES WITHIN THE TEST BED FOR AN OCCUPANCE IM

Figure 19.3 shows a screenshot of the test bed with this system engaged. The IM is being drawn for debugging purposes. Use of an occupance IM system within the AIsteroids test bed could help to improve the Evade state to steer the player away from heavily congested areas. You could even put a static occupance ring around the extents of the world, and the Evade state would then try and keep the ship from

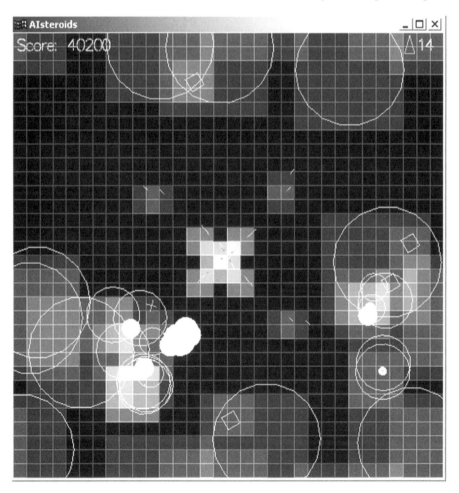

FIGURE 19.3   AIsteroids test bed with an occupance IM engaged.

staying too near the edges of the world, which tends to get the ship killed by fast-moving asteroids that world wrap and catch the ship off guard.

The `Attack` state could also check the occupance of the map and send that many bullets toward it, so that multiple asteroids at the same location would all be targeted.

THE `ControlInfluenceMap`

The next system we will cover tracks control of game areas. Game objects will have a gradient of control written to the map, the magnitude of which is determined by the overall size of the object (except for some special objects, which are given control magnitudes directly). It also assigns the ship and bullets to have positive influence values, and the asteroids to use negative values. All object influence values are added to the map, so the more positive an influence value an IM element contains, the more ships or bullets are inhabiting that element, and the converse holds for negative values and asteroids. Listings 19.5 and 19.6 give the header and implementation of the `ControlInfluenceMap` class.

LISTING 19.5 `ControlInfluenceMap` header.

```
class ControlInfluenceMap:public InfluenceMap
{
public:
    //constructor/functions
    ControlInfluenceMap():InfluenceMap(IM_CONTROL){}
    ~ControlInfluenceMap();
    virtual void Update(float dt);
    virtual void RegisterGameObj(GameObj* object);
    virtual void DrawTheInfluence();

};
```

Notice that within this class, there is no unstamping of influence values, we simply wipe the IM array clean every update. The amount of change within the IM array is quite large considering the gradient information being constantly updated. Because of this, the entire field is usually "dirty" and as such it is much faster to just clean out the array completely instead of trying to localize the changes.

The `ControlInfluenceMap` class uses a type for its registered objects, of which only `OT_FRIENDLY` or `OT_ENEMY` are counted for updates (`OT_BULLET` is just a special type of `OT_FRIENDLY`). It then uses this type to determine whether to write positive or negative control values to the map.

In the `DrawInfluence()` function, we're now drawing a colored polygon for each IM array element, based on the magnitude of control at each location and the sign of that control.

LISTING 19.6 `ControlInfluenceMap` implementation of important functions.

```
//-------------------
void ControlInfluenceMap::Update(float dt)
{
    //bail out if nobody to update
    if(m_registeredObjects.size() == 0)
        return;

    //clear out map
    memset(m_map,0,m_numCels*sizeof(int));

    //stamp obj locations
    RegObjectList::iterator listObj;
    for(listObj=m_registeredObjects.begin();
        listObj!=m_registeredObjects.end();++listObj)
    {
        //only care about "control" objects, not miscellaneous
        if((*listObj)->m_objType == OT_MISC)
            continue;

        if((*listObj)->m_objType == OT_FRIENDLY)
            StampInfluenceGradient(m_map,(*listObj)->
                                    m_pObject->m_position, 16);
        else if((*listObj)->m_objType == OT_BULLET)
            StampInfluenceGradient(m_map,(*listObj)->
                                    m_pObject->m_position, 8);
        else
            StampInfluenceGradient(m_map,(*listObj)->m_pObject->
                        m_position, -(((*listObj)->m_pObject->
                                        m_size)/2));
        (*listObj)->m_lastPosition = (*listObj)->m_pObject->
                                                    m_position;
    }
}

//-------------------
void ControlInfluenceMap::RegisterGameObj(GameObj* object)
{
    int sizeX,sizeY;
    sizeX = sizeY = 1;
```

```
    RegObj* temp;
    temp = new RegObj;
    temp->m_pObject     = object;
    temp->m_objSizeX    = sizeX;
    temp->m_objSizeY    = sizeY;
    temp->m_lastPosition = object->m_position;
    temp->m_stamped     = false;
    if(object->m_type == GameObj::OBJ_SHIP ||
       object->m_type == GameObj::OBJ_SAUCER)
        temp->m_objType = OT_FRIENDLY;
    else if(object->m_type == GameObj::OBJ_BULLET)
        temp->m_objType = OT_BULLET;
    else if(object->m_type == GameObj::OBJ_ASTEROID)
        temp->m_objType = OT_ENEMY;
    else
        temp->m_objType = OT_MISC;
    m_registeredObjects.push_back(temp);
}


//--------------------
void ControlInfluenceMap::DrawTheInfluence()
{
    glPushMatrix();
    glDisable(GL_LIGHTING);
    glTranslatef(0,0,0);
    glEnable(GL_BLEND);
    glBlendFunc(GL_ONE, GL_ONE);
    for(int i=0;i<m_numCels;i++)
    {
        if(m_map[i])
        {
            int y = i / m_dataSizeY;
            int x = i - y*m_dataSizeY;
            float color = m_map[i]/16.0f;
            if(color > 0)
                glColor3f(0,0,color);
            else
                glColor3f(-color,0,0);
            glBegin(GL_POLYGON);
            glVertex3f(x*m_celResX,y*m_celResY,0);
            glVertex3f(x*m_celResX, y*m_celResY+m_celResY,0);
            glVertex3f(x*m_celResX+m_celResX,
                           y*m_celResY+m_celResY,0);
            glVertex3f(x*m_celResX+m_celResX,
                           y*m_celResY, 0);
```

```
                    glEnd();
                }
        }
        glDisable(GL_BLEND);
        glEnable(GL_LIGHTING);
        glPopMatrix();
    }
```

USES WITHIN THE TEST BED FOR A CONTROL-BASED IM

Figure 19.4 shows a screenshot of the test bed with the control-based system engaged and being drawn for debugging purposes. Tracking control within the AIsteroids test bed allows many improvements.

The Evade state could be made much more intelligent by staying within areas of control, if possible (providing much more active evasion, rather than the reactive evading that the game currently uses), as well as providing a platform for simple pathfinding to be performed on the IM array to find clear lanes of travel. Evasion could be improved even more if the control positioning considered velocity, either by perturbing the shape of the control gradient in the direction of travel, or by computing a future position for the object and using that as the position sent to the stamping function. Like the occupance IM, you could put a static ring of "asteroid control" around the extents of the game world, so that the Evade state would try to avoid getting near the edges. This type of IM data would give more of a fuzzy effect—the ring of static control could be a smooth gradient, making the avoidance stronger the closer the ship was to the edge.

The GetPowerup state could increase its priority if the closest powerup is within the area of the ship's control. It could also sum the total control of the asteroids and, when low enough, make filling up on powerups a total priority (so that when there are very few asteroids remaining, the ship will max out its shot power and vastly increase its chances of surviving the next wave).

THE BitwiseInfluenceMap

The last simple IM design we will cover shows how you can use each bit in an array element as a separate Boolean value. This very generic usage of an IM array allows you to custom tailor the information that you are tracking within your IM system. In our test bed application, we will be tracking two main things: object type, and direction of travel. The bottom 8 bits of each array element correspond to the type of object, and bits 9 to 12 are set if the object is moving in any of the cardinal directions. This is a somewhat arbitrary usage of the system and is just for illustration of

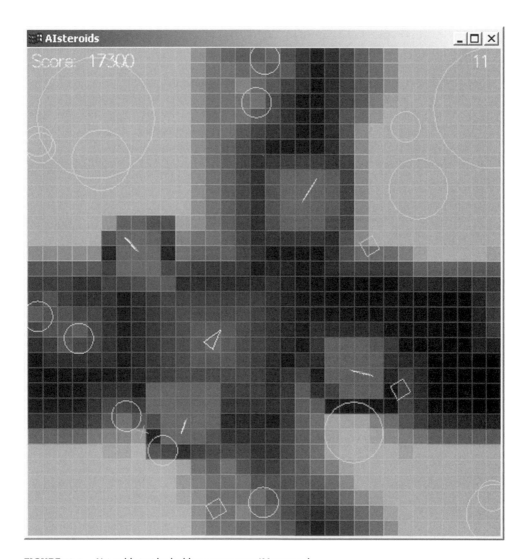

FIGURE 19.4   Alsteroids test bed with an occupance IM engaged.

the method, not an example of something that needs to be done. Listings 19.7 and 19.8 give the header and implementation of the BitwiseInfluenceMap class.

LISTING 19.7   BitwiseInfluenceMap header.

```
class BitwiseInfluenceMap:public InfluenceMap
{
public:
    //constructor/functions
    BitwiseInfluenceMap():InfluenceMap(IM_BITWISE){}
```

```
    ~BitwiseInfluenceMap();
    virtual void Update(float dt);
    virtual void RegisterGameObj(GameObj* object);
    virtual void DrawTheInfluence();
    virtual void StampInfluenceShape(int* pMap,Point3f& location,
                    int sizeX,int sizeY, int value, bool undo = false);
    int GetVelocityDirectionMask(GameObj* object);
    int  GetInfluenceType(int* pMap,Point3f& location);
    int  GetInfluenceDirection(int* pMap,Point3f& location);
};
```

This class is much like the others, with the small changes necessary to handle bitwise array access. The stamp function use logical operators, and even though the current implementation doesn't require the use of the unstamping (because the map is zeroed out each update), the stamp function does have the ability to undo stampings.

The debug draw function is a little different for this setup because it draws three polygons for each IM element. The bottom half of the square is the type of object inhabiting the square. The top left quarter is colored if the object is moving up or down, and the top right quarter is colored if the object is moving right or left. A good debugging system for a real game would use more explanatory and intuitive visual debugging aids than simple colors (such as small status icons or text display, for example), but this will be fine for a test application.

LISTING 19.8 `BitwiseInfluenceMap` implementation of important functions.

```
//--------------------
void BitwiseInfluenceMap::Update(float dt)
{
    //bail out if nobody to update
    if(m_registeredObjects.size() == 0)
        return;

    //clear out map
    memset(m_map,0,m_numCels*sizeof(int));

    //stamp new data
    RegObjectList::iterator listObj;
    for(listObj=m_registeredObjects.begin();
        listObj!=m_registeredObjects.end();++listObj)
    {
        RegObj* temp = *listObj;
        //have to update the bits, since you can
        //change direction continuously
```

```
            temp->m_objType = (char)temp->m_objType |
                          GetVelocityDirectionMask(temp->m_pObject);
            StampInfluenceShape(m_map,(*listObj)->m_pObject->
                        m_position,(*listObj)->m_objSizeX,(*listObj)->
                        m_objSizeY,(*listObj)->m_objType);
            (*listObj)->m_stamped = true;
            (*listObj)->m_lastPosition = (*listObj)->m_pObject->
                                                    m_position;
        }
    }
}


//--------------------
void BitwiseInfluenceMap::RegisterGameObj(GameObj* object)
{
    int sizeX,sizeY;
    if(object->m_size <4)
    {
        sizeX = m_dataSizeX/16;
        sizeY = m_dataSizeY/16;
    }
    else if(object->m_size<11)
    {
        sizeX = m_dataSizeX/10;
        sizeY = m_dataSizeY/10;
    }
    else if(object->m_size<33)
    {
        sizeX = m_dataSizeX/8;
        sizeY = m_dataSizeY/8;
    }
    else if(object->m_size <49)
    {
        sizeX = m_dataSizeX/5;
        sizeY = m_dataSizeX/5;
    }
    else if(object->m_size <65)
    {
        sizeX = m_dataSizeX/4;
        sizeY = m_dataSizeX/4;
    }
    else
    {
        sizeX = m_dataSizeX/3;
        sizeY = m_dataSizeX/3;
    }
```

```
        //set minimum size of 1 in each direction
        sizeX = MAX(1,sizeX);
        sizeY = MAX(1,sizeY);


        RegObj* temp;
        temp = new RegObj;
        temp->m_objType = object->m_type;
        temp->m_objType |= GetVelocityDirectionMask(object);

        temp->m_pObject       = object;
        temp->m_objSizeX      = sizeX;
        temp->m_objSizeY      = sizeY;
        temp->m_lastPosition  = object->m_position;
        temp->m_stamped       = false;
        m_registeredObjects.push_back(temp);
    }

    //--------------------
    int BitwiseInfluenceMap::GetVelocityDirectionMask(GameObj* object)
    {
        int velDir = 0;
        if(object->m_velocity.x() > 0)
        velDir |= DIR_RIGHT;
        else if (object->m_velocity.x() < 0)
        velDir |= DIR_LEFT;
        if(object->m_velocity.y() > 0)
        velDir |= DIR_UP;
        else if (object->m_velocity.y() < 0)
        velDir |= DIR_DOWN;
        return velDir<<8;
    }

    //--------------------
    void BitwiseInfluenceMap::DrawTheInfluence()
    {
        glPushMatrix();
        glDisable(GL_LIGHTING);
        glTranslatef(0,0,0);
        glEnable(GL_BLEND);
        glBlendFunc(GL_ONE, GL_ONE);
        for(int i=0;i<m_numCels;i++)
        {
            if(m_map[i])
```

```
{
    int y = i / m_dataSizeY;
    int x = i - y*m_dataSizeY;
    //determine color for type
    Point3f color(0,0,0);
    for(int index = 0;index<8;index++)
    {
        int bitset = (m_map[i] & (1<<index));
        if(bitset)
            color += colorArray[index];
    }
    glColor3f(color.x(),color.y(),color.z());
    glBegin(GL_POLYGON);
    glVertex3f(x*m_celResX,y*m_celResY,0);
    glVertex3f(x*m_celResX,y*m_celResY+m_celResY*0.5f,0);
    glVertex3f(x*m_celResX+m_celResX,y*m_celResY+
                                     m_celResY*0.5f,0);
    glVertex3f(x*m_celResX+m_celResX,y*m_celResY,0);
    glEnd();

    color = Point3f(0,0,0);
    //get colors for direction
    int direction = m_map[i]>>8;
    if(direction & DIR_LEFT)
        color = colorArray[COLOR_SILVER];//left
    if(direction & DIR_RIGHT)
        color = colorArray[COLOR_PURPLE];//right
    glColor3f(color.x(),color.y(),color.z());
    glBegin(GL_POLYGON);
    glVertex3f(x*m_celResX,y*m_celResY+m_celResY*0.5f,0);
    glVertex3f(x*m_celResX,y*m_celResY+m_celResY,0);
    glVertex3f(x*m_celResX+m_celResX*0.5f,y*m_celResY+
                                     m_celResY,0);
    glVertex3f(x*m_celResX+m_celResX*0.5f,y*m_celResY+
                                     m_celResY*0.5f,0);
    glEnd();

    color = Point3f(0,0,0);
    if(direction & DIR_UP)
        color = colorArray[COLOR_OLIVE];//up
    if(direction & DIR_DOWN)
        color = colorArray[COLOR_TEAL];//down

    glColor3f(color.x(),color.y(),color.z());
    glBegin(GL_POLYGON);
```

```
                    glVertex3f(x*m_celResX+m_celResX*0.5f,y*m_celResY+
                                            m_celResY*0.5f,0);
                    glVertex3f(x*m_celResX+m_celResX*0.5f,y*m_celResY+
                                            m_celResY,0);
                    glVertex3f(x*m_celResX+m_celResX,y*m_celResY+
                                            m_celResY,0);
                    glVertex3f(x*m_celResX+m_celResX,y*m_celResY+
                                            m_celResY*0.5f,0);
                glEnd();
            }
        }
        glDisable(GL_BLEND);
        glEnable(GL_LIGHTING);
        glPopMatrix();
}


//--------------------
void BitwiseInfluenceMap::StampInfluenceShape(int* pMap,Point3f&
                    location,int sizeX, int sizeY, int value, bool undo)
{
    int gridX = location.x()/ m_celResX;
    int gridY = location.y()/ m_celResY;

    int startX = gridX - sizeX/2;
    if(startX < 0) startX += m_dataSizeX;
    int startY = gridY - sizeY/2;
    if(startY < 0) startY += m_dataSizeY;

    for(int y = startY;y<startY + sizeY;y++)
    {
        for(int x = startX;x<startX + sizeX;x++)
        {
            if(undo)
                pMap[(y%m_dataSizeY)*m_dataSizeY + (x%m_dataSizeX)]
                    &= ~value;
            else
                pMap[(y%m_dataSizeY)*m_dataSizeY + (x%m_dataSizeX)]
                    |= value;
        }
    }
}
//--------------------
int BitwiseInfluenceMap::GetInfluenceType(int* pMap,
                                        Point3f& location)
```

```
    {
        int gridX = location.x()/ m_celResX;
        int gridY = location.y()/ m_celResY;
        return pMap[gridX,gridY] & 0x0f;
    }

    //-------------------
    int BitwiseInfluenceMap::GetInfluenceDirection(int* pMap,
                                                   Point3f& location)
    {
        int gridX = location.x()/ m_celResX;
        int gridY = location.y()/ m_celResY;
        return pMap[gridX,gridY] >> 8;
    }
```

USES WITHIN THE TEST BED FOR A BITWISE IM

Figure 19.5 shows the bitwise system up and running in the test bed game. Even using the somewhat arbitrary variables that we tracked in the example, the AI ship would benefit. By checking the IM under approaching asteroids, the ship could use the general direction flags to steer his evasion in better directions. The direction of travel could also help him with asteroids that are soon to wrap, because his evade state could watch for asteroids moving away from him against the opposite edge of the game.

Both evading and approaching asteroids could use the general direction of travel logged into the IM as a way to either steer clear efficiently, or to proactively approach along a parallel direction, which is more like how humans play asteroids. Humans rarely fly directly at asteroids, knowing that they will shoot them. Rather, they usually approach from a safe side path of travel, and then turn and shoot. If other variables had been tracked within the bitwise system, any number of different behaviors could be gleaned from the system.

OTHER IMPLEMENTATIONS

All these example IM implementations are just a sampling of what can be accomplished with the basic influence paradigm. Some other examples within our test bed might be the following:

■ A danger measurement (small, slow-moving asteroids headed away from us get low numbers; fast, large asteroids on collision courses with the ship get the highest) tracked within the IM would enable the ship to evade much more effectively. This would be similar to the control type of map, but more specialized for evasion.

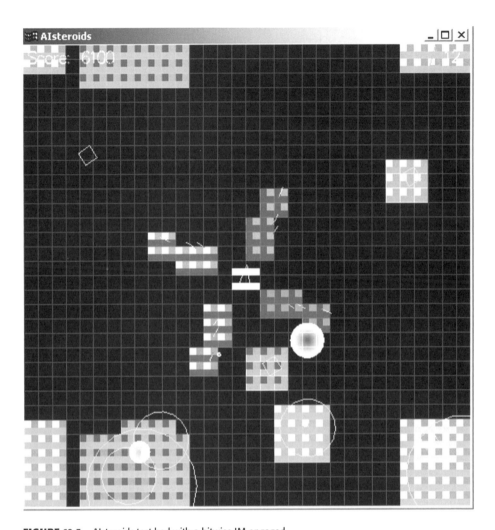

FIGURE 19.5   AIsteroids test bed with a bitwise IM engaged.

■ If the game had additional powerups, enemy ships, or environmental objects (such as static planetoids or black holes, for example) several more complex states would be needed to handle them within the AI system. An IM would help by further specializing the different pathfinding tasks, providing "control" information for objects that require more complex interactions, and being a platform for terrain analysis.

■ If the game world were much larger, or oddly shaped, the IM array would be a good place to do game object searches because a pathfinder could find better targets than the simple "Closest asteroid or powerup" system currently being used. The IM could be tagged with connectivity data so that object searches take the wrapping borders into account, and irregularly shaped worlds would wrap as usual.

■ The IM array could keep a short duration record (10 seconds should be long enough) of the occupance data, and maybe the movement direction of the occupance. The ship could use this information to try to keep out of highly traveled areas of the map, or line up next to one of these "routes," and the next time the asteroid comes along, the ship could attack then. This system might only be turned on when there are only a few asteroids left, and only if there are fast-moving asteroids, so that the ship doesn't do a lot of unnecessary movement to chase down a straggler asteroid.

Adding smart terrain techniques on top of our IM system would be useful for a number of reasons. Using smart terrain within the test bed would require four things:

1. An extension to the `GameObj` class (`SmartObj`, namely) that includes a new `Update()` function, where it would broadcast a message about the type of object it is, and possibly some other information (position or distance from the main ship, and some kind of priority value). Each `SmartObj` would also need an `Interact()` function that the ship would call to properly use each object. Using an object would be context-sensitive, so using an asteroid might mean shooting or dodging it, but using a powerup would mean collecting it. Notice that objects do not have to move and could be static structures within the game world, but they still must be represented by an object at some level.

2. A new decision system for the ship (a simple FSM would suffice) that listens to the incoming messages, and decides on a primary object for the ship to interact with. Based on a number of factors, the ship might also interact with several secondary targets (calling the `Interact()` function on six asteroids might only uncover one asteroid that causes the ship to fire; the other five additively thrust the ship to perform avoidance or lead the ship toward an alternate path), so the ship would keep a list of the objects that it cares about and calls each object's `Interact()` method. If the interaction is fairly complex, then the smart object's `Interact()` call would likely be better off written as an FSM or a script of some sort.

3. To be fully smart, each object would also need to include all the additional code and data necessary for the ship to interact with it. So, if you make a new powerup for the game that requires the ship to dock with it by playing a special animation, the object would have to include that animation data. Other special case data would include sound effects, powerup effects, any necessary code to incorporate it into the IM system the game is using (if any), and so on.

4. Game code that deals with some object interactions would need to be removed. The `GetPowerup()` code needs to be removed from the ship class,

and most of the behavior code will be moved from the ship's states and into the smart object's interaction functions. This might seem a bit backward, but notice that when this refactoring process is finished, adding new pow-erups, weird space anomalies, or enemies would become a process of just setting up the smart object, and letting it loose into the game.

PROS OF LOCATION-BASED INFORMATION SYSTEMS

LBI systems are a generic interface for games, and as such, almost any specialized location data requirement can be built within the system. LBIs are intuitive and easy to program and scale well to large and small problems. Debugging LBI systems is generally very simple; employing visual feedback is straightforward (as the dem-onstration implementations show).

Generally, IM systems tend to simplify the perception search space by lowering the resolution of the data that the AI needs to consider when making decisions. IM systems also represent a kind of shared knowledge base about the world that AI char-acters can use to act more intelligently. Thus, even though the ship hasn't personally made every little calculation about the asteroids in the map, it can consult the IM for a wealth of info about each asteroid and make far smarter decisions in less time.

CONS OF LOCATION-BASED INFORMATION SYSTEMS

LBI systems do have trade-offs, however. IM arrays tend to be expensive to memory budgets, especially in games with large data requirements, large world sizes, and high array resolutions. You need to be smart in implementing your IM system, using multiple levels of resolution to limit data size and using local, relocatable higher resolution IMs for more detailed work instead of an all-encompassing IM.

Terrain analysis can be computationally expensive because of the many searches through the array that need to be performed to glean all the necessary information. Almost any pattern-matching algorithm is going to be costly and prone to error. However, this is also the only way to better emulate human analysis and perfor-mance within complex games.

EXTENSIONS TO THE PARADIGM

The LBI systems implemented in this chapter are very rudimentary, meant to dem-onstrate the breadth of things possible within the model. The only limits to the different ways that you can use these basic principles in your game are the type of game you are working on, the data size you are allotted for your IM, and the CPU time you can spend searching the map for useful patterns that you can exploit.

Almost any genre can find a suitable use for these techniques. FTPS games could use them for king-of-the-hill-style matches, to track control. RTS games are the biggest potential users of these methods, with the possibility for many different areas of the game using a shared IM for a variety of tasks. Even genres like classic adventure games could use LBI methods; you could keep track of where the user is clicking with the mouse, and if he seems to be clicking everywhere, or the same places over and over again, he's probably stuck or doesn't understand some puzzle element and could use some contextual help.

OPTIMIZATIONS

IMs deal with a large contiguous block of memory, so writing and reading from IMs becomes a problem similar to using early software graphics engines. You are almost "blitting" influence data to the array, and reading values back out again. Thus, many of the optimizations that people used for early graphics also apply to IM optimizing, which is where the dirty rectangles analogy came from earlier when we were discussing the occupance IM implementation. Instead of drawing every element into the array every update, you draw the small areas where objects moved. Other similar optimizations might include finding out the size of the data bus on the machine you're developing for and ensuring that the size of the usual data element you write or read out of it fits within the bus, to ensure fast data transfer, as well as better cache usage.

The other optimizations talked about during the rest of the chapter, such as levels of IMs with increasing resolutions (level of detail IM arrays), as well as local IMs that use much more detail, will save you both memory and computation time because you only apply as many CPU resources to IM tasks as you need.

TA functionality needs to be optimized on a per-case basis because TA tasks differ so greatly in terms of many factors: what they are trying to accomplish, the scope of their search within the IM array, the kinds of patterns they are seeking to find, and the frequency that the given TA task must be updated.

DESIGN CONSIDERATIONS

LBI systems are usually found in the more AI-heavy games, such as RTS, death-match FTPS, and RPGs, because they require a level of intelligence that the more action-oriented genres do not need from their AI opponents. LBI have an open architecture for location-specific information and allow proven search methods to be applied to this data in a central location.

TYPES OF SOLUTIONS

LBI can be used to solve both tactical and strategic types of AI problems. Tactically, an IM can help guide pathfinding and dynamic obstacle avoidance. It can provide a character with secondary behavior cues so that he looks more engaged in the world. At the strategic level, TA can provide an AI system with pattern matching necessary to really use the terrain, and plan large-scale battles or building whole towns.

Objects within a smart terrain system are typically more tactical because they don't tend to add much to the strategic intelligence of an AI character. You don't see Sims characters planning very far ahead to satisfy a need. They mostly roam, seeking the next object that will help them. Yes, the characters go to work to get money, but that's more of a game-state mechanism rather than a plan in which a Sims character "thinks" about wanting something and then goes off to earn the money to buy it. This is because each object is an island unto itself and doesn't know about any of the other objects in the world except for the thing that object has been programmed to interact with.

AGENT REACTIVITY

LBI is a secondary system, so reactivity is more a question of what primary AI technique is being used. LBI systems can help make a character much more proactive in its reactions, however, so that should be considered.

SYSTEM REALISM

IM-enabled games are not necessarily more realistic. In the real world, the microwave certainly doesn't broadcast that it will feed you. But with the right level of IMs and analysis, a game could make much more realistic, humanlike decisions. Using a central map of information is much more like the human approach to these kinds of problems, rather than knowing everything like a computer opponent and/or cheating. Smart terrain objects aren't really a realistic way of modeling things, but they do allow a much richer environment because new objects can be added so readily, and they do abstract objects and environmental elements into categories, which is a realistic human behavior.

GENRE AND PLATFORM

The genres listed earlier—RTS, deathmatch FTPS, and RPGs—are the usual suspects for IM systems and TA. Smart terrain has only found its way into a small number of titles so far, but it is much more general, relative to genre. Any game that needs a no-nonsense level of interaction between arbitrary objects and the environment could benefit from a smart objects system—both for ease of writing the primary AI decision system and from an expandability point of view. The only real platform concern with LBI is the memory requirements of an IM array, but with proper forethought and optimizations, this can be overcome.

DEVELOPMENT LIMITATIONS

Development limitations are not really a concern for LBI systems. LBI information actually might help debugging of a game, so that isn't an issue. IMs are another way to decouple AI characters from the rest of the code (by providing a central data location for them to search in, instead of making gamewide code calls) and help the AI system become more modular. Smart terrain objects, by their nature, allow modular implementation, so they tend to be debuggable and scaleable.

ENTERTAINMENT LIMITATIONS

Tuning difficulty settings, balancing specific behaviors, and other entertainment concerns are generally independent of LBI system use, so they are not usually a problem.

SUMMARY

Location-based information systems can provide a variety of decision-making paradigms with additional flexibility in dealing with location-specific data, as well as decoupling the AI characters from the rest of the game by providing them with a central data location or encapsulating logic and data for interactions.

- The three main categories of LBI systems covered were influence maps, smart terrain, and terrain analysis.
- IMs are a generic data structure usually represented as a 2-D grid of data elements laid over the game world. The data contained within, or even the structure of the data within, is completely arbitrary to the method.
- Smart terrain is a technique whereby logic and behavior data showing how to use various world features and game objects are stored in the objects themselves. This provides a modular and expandable world for the game characters to live in, but limits the amount of interaction that can be done with any one element.
- Terrain analysis is a family of methods that can be performed on terrain data to search for usable patterns that can lead to better strategic decisions.
- The demonstration implementation was done in four parts: the basic IM, and the three various versions: occupance, control, and bitwise IMs.
- LBI methods within a game can be implemented in many other ways than were demonstrated in this chapter.

- The pros of LBI systems include ease of implementation and debugging, generic interface, and centralizing AI data.
- The cons of LBI systems include large memory requirements for IM arrays, and possible high computation costs for heavy TA.
- IM functions can sometimes be optimized along the lines of early graphics routines because you are writing and reading data from large contiguous arrays.

20 Steering Behaviors

In This Chapter

- Steering Behavior Overview
- Steering Skeletal Code
- Implementing a Steering-Controlled Ship into Our Test Bed
- Performance of the AI with This System
- Extensions to the Paradigm
- Optimizations
- Design Considerations
- Summary

Sometimes, the creatures you're building in your game don't require advanced intelligence. High-level decision making simply is not necessary. Instead, you need organic, natural-looking behaviors. You may desire behaviors that move characters around in realistic ways, either separately or within large groups. In 1986, Craig Reynolds began experimenting with creating computer simulations of large numbers of birds or fish flocking. These flocking (or schooling, in fish terms) behaviors gradually grew into what he called *steering behaviors*. The concept, as well as implementation, of steering is so simple and at the same time so useful in many areas of game character creation that this chapter is presented to fully explore steering behaviors so that you can immediately start using them in your games.

STEERING BEHAVIOR OVERVIEW

So far in this book, we have covered systems that are mostly high-level, strategic decision-making architectures. Steering behaviors are different. They represent much lower-level decision making. Instead of representing an overall plan for an AI-controlled character's actions, steering behaviors are only concerned with which direction a character should steer. Where does the character want to go, at what speed, and along which path? In fact, characters that use steering behaviors exclusively are sometimes called *autonomous agents*, meaning that they are typically just set in motion, and don't require additional help from the programmer or scripted elements in order to perform within the game world.

Think of games in which the main character has to run through large moving crowds of people that are milling about. These types of NPCs are generally coded as autonomous agents using steering behaviors to give them lifelike reactions to each other (and the player) with minimal effort on the programmer's part. Notice that these characters don't have *total* autonomy. If you walk up to a crowd and take out a crowbar from your backpack, the closest crowd member probably won't come over and ask if you need help, or even look at you directly. But what he'll probably do is turn and walk around you, essentially continuing on his way without being blocked by your intrusion. Movement is generally the only behavior that is modeled using steering, so that is the part of the AI behavior that is generally thought of as autonomous within this type of system. However, it can be used for other things, some of which will be discussed later in the chapter under "Extensions to the Paradigm."

Reynolds called his original creatures "boids," a play on *birds*. He found that with very simple rules, he was able to model startlingly realistic-looking, complex flocking behaviors. In fact, his initial implementation involved only three behaviors: alignment, cohesion, and separation. See Figure 20.1 for a depiction of these behaviors.

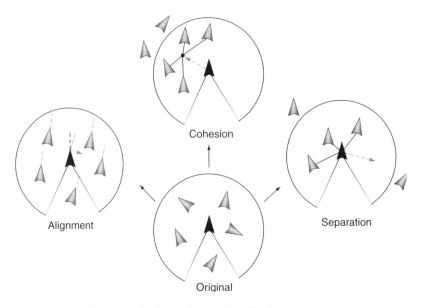

FIGURE 20.1   Alignment, cohesion, and separation behaviors.

- **Alignment** represents the individual's attempt to position itself such that it's heading in essentially the same direction as the rest of the group.
- **Cohesion** is the force keeping the group together; keeping the collection tight and focused.
- **Separation**, which can be seen as somewhat the opposite of cohesion, gives the group members a "personal space bubble" so that they don't crowd each other too much, and every individual has room to operate.

The boids took into account these simple behaviors, but they didn't concern themselves with all members of the flock, only those in their immediate neighborhood (in Figure 20.1, the area that looks something like a Pac-man character is the neighborhood description Reynolds used; notice that in each behavior the boid not inside the neighborhood is not taken into account). These few perceptions paid real dividends. Reynolds's simulations produced some of the most realistic-looking group dynamics seen on a computer screen, and the level of *emergent* behavior from these few rules was very exciting to watch and tinker with. These group dynamics were created from a distributed behavior model: Each member of the group is "doing its own thing," without modeling the group directly.

In later work, Reynolds added some additional behaviors, namely obstacle avoidance and goal seeking, and created several demonstrations (small graphical movies, since computers back then weren't fast enough to show complex 3D environments in real time), which were presented at the annual conference on computer graphics, SIGGRAPH (which is short for Special Interest Group on **GRAPH**ics and Interactive Techniques) and to the world at large. The reason for these additional behaviors was to directly facilitate the demos, which used static obstacles (pillars or rock outcroppings) and had the boids following a scripted path in order to show the rich movement that the simulations allowed.

As mentioned earlier, the key element of Reynolds's model was the level of emergent behavior that sprang forth. Emergent behavior is something like the holy grail of game programming, where the combination of simple local rules lead to very complex global behaviors. In many cases, the emergent elements can even be suprising or unexpected. Each individual rule is inherently nonlinear in that it is an analog response to only local stimulus. This would move the group to a more chaotic state over time. But, negative feedback from the main controller brings the overall group behavior back into a more ordered state. It is this push and pull between chaos and order that makes the overall effect lifelike. Life itself has been called "order on the edge of chaos" by Christopher Langton, a biologist and computer scientist who founded the field of artificial life.

Reynolds has stated that one of the significant properties of realistic lifelike behavior is that of *unpredictability* over moderate time scales. Watching a flock of boids move, trying to predict anything but short-term changes in the flock's behavior is impossible. Half a second from now, most of the flock members will be heading in the same general direction, at approximately the same speed as before. But where will any given member of the flock be in a minute? Prediction is all but impossible.

STEERING SKELETAL CODE

The code will be implemented in the following classes:

- The SteeringBehavior class, which is the basic behavior definition in the system.
- The SteeringBehaviorManager class, which houses and controls all the behaviors, and combines all the steering vectors.
- The SteeringControl class, the primary controller class, contains the SteeringBehaviorManager as well as sets up the priority for the different behaviors, and handles other game-specific code not covered by the steering behaviors (like perceptions, and in the case of our AI testbed, shooting at asteroids).

The next sections will discuss these classes in more detail, and we will then cover the specific implementation of the SteeringAIControl class and each SteeringBehavior needed for our AI test bed application.

THE SteeringBehavior CLASS

SteeringBehavior has been implemented as an almost purely virtual class, with only two real functions: SteerTowards and SteerAway. These are simple helper functions that most steering behaviors will require, that of heading towards a particular calculated target using the standard formula:

calculated vector to target − current velocity vector

SteerAway is just included for completeness; you could pass in a negative steering vector to SteerTowards and get the same result.

Steering behaviors all have an Update() function, a Draw() call, and a Reset(), which are just stubs in the base class.

The skeletal code header for this class can be seen in Listing 20.1. The class also contains some data members:

- *m_name*. Just a text string used for debugging display purposes
- *m_weight*. Used by the manager class when using the simple weighted combination method (which will be discussed in detail later)

- *m_parent*. Used by the individual state classes, to access shared data and/or functions
- *m_probablility*. Used by the manager class when using the prioritized dither combination method (which will also be discussed in detail later)
- *m_disable*. Used by the manager class when a particular steering behavior needs to be turned off for any reason
- *m_lastForceMagApplied*. Another field used for debugging purposes. This stores the magnitude of the force that the behavior calculated the last time it was updated

There are many classicly implemented steering behaviors, some of which we'll be discussing after we finish our look at the framework code. Some of the behaviors we'll be discussing include: pursuit, evade, arrive, wall avoidance, and the flocking behaviors. More on this in the implementation section.

LISTING 20.1 SteeringBehavior header file.

```
class SteeringBehavior
{
 public:
     //constructor/functions
     //constructor/functions
     SteeringBehavior(AIControl* parent,char* name = NULL)
     {
            memcpy(m_name,name,strlen(name)+1);
            m_parent = parent;
            m_disable = false;
            m_lastForceMagApplied = 0.0f;
     }
     virtual bool Update(float dt,Point3f& totalForce) {return false;}
     virtual void Reset()   {}
     virtual void Draw()    {}
     virtual void SteerTowards(Point3f& target,Point3f& result)
     {
            Point3f desired = target - m_parent->m_ship->m_position;
            float targetDistance = desired.Length();
            if(targetDistance > 0)
            {
                    desired = desired.Normalize() *
                        m_parent->m_ship->m_maxSpeed;
                    result = desired - m_parent->m_ship->m_velocity;
            }
```

```
                else
                        result.SetZero();
        }
        virtual void SteerAway(Point3f& target,Point3f& result)
        {
                Point3f desired = m_parent->m_ship->m_position - target;
                float targetDistance = desired.Length();
                if(targetDistance > 0)
                {
                        desired = desired.Normalize() *
                                m_parent->m_ship->m_maxSpeed;
                        result = desired - m_parent->m_ship->m_velocity;
                }
                else
                        result.SetZero();
        }

        //data
        AIControl*      m_parent;
        float           m_weight;
        float           m_probability;
        char            m_name[30];
        bool            m_disable;
        float           m_lastForceMagApplied;
};
```

THE SteeringBehaviorManager CLASS

This class serves as the overall behavior handler. It has a container holding all the behaviors, and will in turn update them and then combine each individual steering vector into a total steering force that the ship will consume.

Any time you set up creatures that are using steering behaviors, you will quickly find that the best way to design and use them is to keep individual behaviors very simple, and combine multiple behaviors together in order to get the full creature behavior that you desire. The dynamic interaction between steering behaviors is the key to achieving true emergent behavior. Actually *combining* steering forces is a touchy issue however—if combined poorly or randomly, the behavioral interaction can be meaningless or seem patternless (which in turn doesn't look lifelike).

In the simplest combining system, you would just add all the forces together, and then clamp the sum to some upper bound so that your creatures wouldn't suddenly accelerate to lightspeed and be gone. This almost never works out. If the behaviors being combined are completely complementary, meaning that they support one another and tend to layer nicely, this simple method can work.

But most steering behavior combinations tend to be antagonistic, leading to more interesting dynamics as the behaviors push and pull against each other. However, using a simple summing combination method with this can lead behaviors to cancel each other out. *Totally* antagonistic behaviors (like running away and running towards) can be somewhat easily tweaked so that they work better together (by adjusting range of effect, or other considerations), but it becomes much more difficult to build a large number of behaviors in which the sum of steering effects does not cause cancelling out issues. So we must turn to a more structured way of combining steering forces. There are several ways to do this, the most popular are:

- **Simple Weighted.** This is a slight variation on the method discussed earlier, in that we sum up all the individual steering forces. However, we apply a weight multiple to each force vector before we add it into the running sum. This allows you to determine just how much of an effect each steering behavior is allowed to have on the overall system. Tweaking these weights is a much easier way of tuning steering behaviors to work well together, but can lead the programmer down a long road of adjusting small numbers up and down in an effort to find a good balance.
- **Prioritized Sum.** Another problem with the simple summation methods we've discussed include the fact that they update every steering behavior a creature has every time the system loops. This can be expensive on CPU time. In the Prioritized Sum method, we store our behaviors in a prioritized list. As we update each one, we sum the result into an accumulated steering force, just like before. The magnitude of the incoming force is also subtracted from a *maximal force* that the programmer has set. So, when we finally get to the point where the incoming steering force is larger then what's left of the maximally allowed total, we truncate the incoming force to fit, and then stop updating our behaviors.

   What this means is that we only update, and use, the amount of force that we've allowed for. This gives a lot of power to the programmer, in that the programmer not only can control which behavior is more important to the system (like the weights in the weighted sum method), but also makes higher-priority behaviors more *pure* by not including lower-priority behaviors at all if the max steering force has been used up. It also means that you can tune the amount of CPU time your AI system uses, by limiting the total force allowed so that at most only a few behaviors will be updated at a time.
- **Prioritized Dither.** This method was detailed by Craig Reynolds himself in one of his papers. Again, each behavior is stored in the manager in priority order. Each behavior is also assigned a probability value. When the manager goes to update the behavior collection, it first rolls the dice and tests against the behavior's probability value. If it passes, the behavior gets updated, and if the behavior does something (meaning, it sends back a steering vector), then the manager stops updating. Otherwise, the next behavior in the collection is tested.

In terms of CPU usage, prioritized dithering is very inexpensive. However, it is tough to tune the overall system to get what you want out of it. For behaviors that require very accurate results, a very high degree of probability must be assigned, otherwise that accuracy will be undermined by other behaviors firing and moving the agent in other directions. If you have more than one behavior that requires high accuracy, you might want to try one of the other combination methods.

Listing 20.2 shows the manager class header. The basics are here: update, reset, and draw. There are some secondary functions dealing with behaviors: You can add a behavior into the system (with `AddBehavior`), initialize a behavior in the system (with `SetupBehavior`), and disable a behavior that is currently in the system (with `DisableBehavior`). The rest of the class is the combination methods and an accessor for the final combined steering force.

LISTING 20.2   `SteeringBehaviorManager` header.

```
class SteeringBehaviorManager
{
public:
    //constructor/functions
    SteeringBehaviorManager(AIControl* parent = NULL);
    virtual void Update(float dt);
    virtual void AddBehavior(SteeringBehavior* behavior);
    virtual void DisableBehavior(int index)
                        {m_behaviors[index]->m_disable = true;}
    virtual void SetupBehavior(int behaviorIndex,
                               float weight,
                               float probability,
                               bool disable = false);
    virtual void Reset();
    virtual Point3f& GetFinalSteeringVector()
                        {return m_totalSteeringForce;}
    virtual void Draw();

    virtual bool CombineForceWeighted(Point3f& steeringForce,
                                      float weight);
    virtual bool CombineForcePrioritySum(Point3f& steeringForce,
                                         float weight);
    virtual bool CombineForcePriorityDithered(Point3f& steeringForce,
                                              float weight,
                                              float randChance);
```

```
protected:
    std::vector<SteeringBehavior*> m_behaviors;
    std::vector<SteeringBehavior*> m_active;
    std::vector<float> m_activeForce;
    int         m_numBehaviors;
    AIControl*   m_parent;
    Point3f     m_totalSteeringForce;
    float       m_maxSteeringForce;
}
```

The implementation of the combination methods is in Listing 20.3. The final part of the combination is done in the manager `Update()` function, shown in Listing 20.4. Notice how some methods require clamping after all summation is over, whereas others don't. Also, notice the *m_active* list. It stores all the behaviors that did something on any given update, so that you can use this info later. The draw function uses the active list to display the currently active behaviors on-screen.

LISTING 20.3   Implementations for the steering combination methods.

```
bool SteeringBehaviorManager::CombineForceWeighted(Point3f&
                                        steeringForce, float weight)
{
    m_totalSteeringForce += steeringForce * weight;
    return true;
}

//-----------------------------------------------------------
bool SteeringBehaviorManager::CombineForcePrioritySum(Point3f&
                                            steeringForce)
{
    bool retVal = false;

    float totalForce = m_totalSteeringForce.Length();
    float forceLeft      = m_maxSteeringForce - totalForce;
    if(forceLeft > 0.0f)
    {
            float newForce = steeringForce.Length();
            if(newForce < forceLeft)
                    m_totalSteeringForce += steeringForce;
            else
                    m_totalSteeringForce += steeringForce.Normalize()*
                                        forceLeft;
```

```
                    //if there's anything left over, say so
                    if((forceLeft - newForce) > 0)
                            retVal = true;
        }


        return retVal;
}


//-----------------------------------------------------------
bool SteeringBehaviorManager::CombineForcePriorityDithered(Point3f&
                                    steeringForce, float randChance)
{
        bool retVal = true;
        if(randflt() < randChance)
        {
                if(steeringForce.Length())
                {
                        m_totalSteeringForce = steeringForce;
                        retVal = false;
                }
        }


        return retVal;
}
```

LISTING 20.4 SteeringBehaviorManager's Update() function.

```
void SteeringBehaviorManager::Update(float dt)
{
        //don't do anything if you have no states
        if(m_behaviors.size() == 0 )
                return;

        //Clear out debug logs
        m_active.clear();
        m_activeForce.clear();

        //reset the steering vector
        m_totalSteeringForce.SetZero();

        //update all the behaviors
        bool needToClamp = false;
```

```
for(unsigned int i =0;i<m_behaviors.size();i++)
{
        Point3f steeringForce;
        steeringForce.SetZero();
        bool didSomething = m_behaviors[i]->Update(dt,steeringForce);

        if(didSomething)
        {
                //keep track of the behaviors that actually
            //did something this tick
                m_active.push_back(m_behaviors[i]);
                m_activeForce.push_back(steeringForce.Length());

                //now we want combine the behaviors into
            //the total steering force using
                //whatever method we decide upon
                bool keepGoing = false;

                //ONLY USE 'ONE' COMBINATION METHOD,
            //THEY'RE ONLY ALL HERE FOR THE DEMO CODE

                //This is for the "Simple weighted combination" method
//              keepGoing = CombineForceWeighted(steeringForce,
                                        m_behaviors[i].m_weight);
                //Now that we've taken all the behaviors into account
            //that we want to for each method, we
                //must "normalize" our results for the "Simple
            //Weighted Combination" method
//              needToClamp = true;

                //This is for the "Prioritized Sum" method
                keepGoing = CombineForcePrioritySum(steeringForce);

                //This is for the "Prioritized Dither" method
//              keepGoing =
                        CombineForcePriorityDithered(steeringForce,
                                        m_behaviors[i].m_weight);
//              needToClamp = true;

                //if we're done checking behaviors (for
            //whatever reason), exit out
                if(!keepGoing)
                        break;
        }
}
```

```
        if(needToClamp)
                CLAMPVECTORLENGTH(m_totalSteeringForce,
                                0.0f,m_maxSteeringForce);
    }
```

THE SteeringControl CLASS

The final part of the steering system (and also the beginning of the game-specific code) is the specific Control class, SteeringControl. This class sets up the behaviors to be used and contains some game specific functions. The header is shown below in Listing 20.5. The implementation code will be covered later when we show the full in-game system.

LISTING 20.5   SteeringControl header.

```
class SteeringControl: public AIControl
{
public:
    //constructor/functions
    SteeringControl(Ship* ship = NULL);
    void Update(float dt);
    void UpdatePerceptions(float dt);
    void Init();
    void Draw();
    void Reset();

    //perception data
    //(public so that states can share it)
    GameObj*      m_nearestAsteroid;
    float         m_safetyRadius;

protected:
    //data
    SteeringBehaviorManager* m_behaviorManager;
    int m_getPowerupIndex;
}
```

IMPLEMENTING A STEERING-CONTROLLED SHIP INTO OUR TEST BED

To get our AIsteroids program to use steering behaviors, we first need to determine the types of steering behaviors that we want to have exhibited by a ship during a game of asteroids. Although the list of behaviors *could* be large (if we really wanted to embellish), a short list of basics should suffice:

- **Approach.** (See Figure 20.2.) This method steers the agent directly towards an object. It uses the `Game.GetClosestGameObj()` function, so in essence we can use this behavior to approach any type of object. We set up the behavior with the types in which we're interested. The approach behavior will find the closest object and head to it.

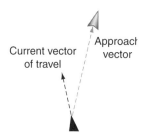

FIGURE 20.2   Depiction of the approach behavior.

- **Pursuit.** (See Figure 20.3.) This method is actually a child class of `approach`. It does essentially the same thing, it just heads towards the *future position* of the nearest object. This is useful for intercepting moving and/or unwilling objects (meaning, they're running away).

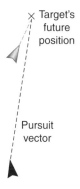

FIGURE 20.3   Depiction of the pursuit behavior.

- **Evade.** (See Figure 20.4.) The opposite of `pursuit`, this method heads away from an object. It also uses the future position of the object, to even more accurately slip away from the object in question.

Evade
vector

FIGURE 20.4   Depiction of the evade behavior.

■ **Arrive.** (See Figure 20.5.) This method is a child of pursuit. This behavior seeks towards an object's future position, but will slow down as it gets close, coming to a stop once it gets directly at the target.

FIGURE 20.5   Depiction of the arrive behavior.

■ **AvoidWall.** (See Figure 20.6.) Just as it says, this behavior tries to keep the ship from getting too near a "wall." A wall, in this case, is actually a data structure of a number of linked points, so this behavior can actually be used to avoid real walls, as well as any type of general obstacle that can be defined as a series of linked points.

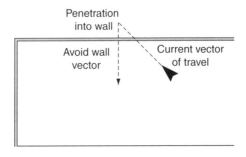

FIGURE 20.6   Depiction of the AvoidWall behavior.

- **AvoidBorder**. (See Figure 20.7.) This is a simplified AvoidWall-style behavior, optimized to work for our specific Asteroids game world. Since we know that the world is square, as such we can make the avoidance much simpler and less expensive for the CPU by using this behavior instead.

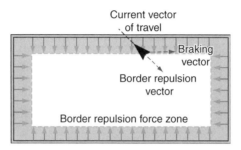

FIGURE 20.7   Depiction of the AvoidBorder behavior.

- **Wander**. (See Figure 20.8.) Although there are many ways to get an agent to wander around (like giving the agent random locations to go to, or giving the agent random velocities), many totally random methods give jerky, unnatural motion. Reynolds originally implemented this method, which uses an offset circle as a target. The exact spot the behavior steers towards is a position that randomly slides back and forth around the circumference of the circle. This indirect randomness gives the final behavior a smooth look.

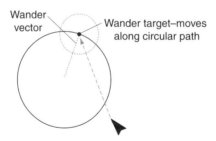

FIGURE 20.8   Depiction of the Wander behavior.

The next seven listings (20.6 through 20.12) will take us through the implementation for each of these basic behaviors.

`SteerApproach` (Listing 20.6) is performed with two main functions: `Update()` and `FindTarget()`. This class serves as a base for both the pursuit and (through inheritance) arrive behaviors. We'll be using this same two-step approach (find/update) for the whole family.

FindTarget uses the Game singleton's access to the global game object list to find the closest object of the particular type (or types) we're interested in. If it finds something, it saves it into the m_currentTarget variable and returns true.

Update calls FindTarget(), and then uses the SteerTowards() function inherited from SteeringBehavior. This gives a steering force that is directly towards the position of the found object. Since we're using the SteerTowards() call, we know that the force is the maximal allowed force in the direction we want to go.

LISTING 20.6 SteerApproach implementation.

```
bool SteerApproach::Update(float dt, Point3f& totalForce)
{
    bool adjustment = false;
    bool found = FindTarget();

    if(found)
    {
        Point3f steeringForce;
        steeringForce.SetZero();
        SteerTowards(m_currentTarget, steeringForce);
        totalForce += steeringForce;
        adjustment = true;
    }
    return adjustment;
}

//------------------------------------------------------------
bool SteerApproach::FindTarget()
{
    bool retVal = false;
    //turn and then thrust towards closest object that we care about
    SteeringControl* parent = (SteeringControl*)m_parent;
    GameObj* objToApproach =
        Game.GetClosestGameObj(parent->m_ship,m_objectsToConsider);

    if(objToApproach)
    {
        m_currentTarget = objToApproach->m_position;
        retVal = true;
    }

    return retVal;
}
```

SteerPursuit (Listing 20.7) builds upon SteerApproach. It overrides the implementation of FindTarget() to get the *future* position of the object being approached. The base class functions in SteerApproach do the rest.

LISTING 20.7   SteerPursuit implementation.

```
bool SteerPursuit::FindTarget()
{
    bool retVal = false;

    //if the guy you're pursuing is essentially
//in your path, then just approach,
    //otherwise we'll try and head him off using prediction
    SteeringControl* parent = (SteeringControl*)m_parent;
    GameObj* objToPursue    =
        Game.GetClosestGameObj(parent->m_ship,m_objectsToConsider);

    if(objToPursue)
    {
        Ship*    ship = parent->m_ship;

        //if the other guy is "to my front" and
        //we're moving towards each other...
        float dotVelocity = DOT(ship->UnitVectorVelocity(),
                              objToPursue->UnitVectorVelocity());
        Point3f deltaPos = objToPursue->m_position - ship->m_position;
        Point3f targetPos = objToPursue->m_position;
        if ((DOT(deltaPos,ship->UnitVectorVelocity()) < 0) ||
            (dotVelocity > -0.93))//magic number == about 21 degrees
        {
            Point3f shipVel = ship->m_velocity;
            shipVel = shipVel.Normalize() * ship->m_maxSpeed;
          float combinedSpeed        = (shipVel +
                            objToPursue->m_velocity).Length();
            float predictionTime  = deltaPos.Length() / combinedSpeed;
            targetPos = objToPursue->m_position +
                            (objToPursue->m_velocity*predictionTime);
        }
        m_currentTarget = targetPos;
        retVal = true;
    }

    return retVal;
}
```

SteerEvade (Listing 20.8) is the exact opposite of pursuit. It also overrides the implementation of FindTarget() to get the *future* position of the object being approached, but then uses SteerAway instead of SteerTowards.

LISTING 20.8 SteerEvade implementation.

```
bool SteerEvade::Update(float dt,Point3f& totalForce)
{
    bool adjustment = false;

    //move away from the nearest object that you're interested in
    SteeringControl* parent = (SteeringControl*)m_parent;
    GameObj* objToEvade =
                Game.GetClosestGameObj(parent->m_ship,m_objectsToEvade);
    Ship* ship = parent->m_ship;

    if(objToEvade)
    {
            //ensure minimum distance
            float minDist;
            if(m_evadedLastUpdate)
                    minDist  = 40.0f;
            else
                    minDist  = 20.0f;
            float speed  = ship->m_velocity.Length();
            float spdAdj = LERP(speed/ship->m_maxSpeed,0.0f,EV_SPEED_BUFFER);
            float adjSafetyRadius = minDist + spdAdj + objToEvade->m_size;

            Point3f steeringForce;
            steeringForce.SetZero();

            Point3f deltaPos = objToEvade->m_position - ship->m_position;

            //is the nearest guy too close?
            if(deltaPos.Length() < adjSafetyRadius)
            {
                    float dotVelocity = DOT(ship->UnitVectorVelocity(),
                                        objToEvade->UnitVectorVelocity());

                    //if the other guy is "to my front" and
                  //we're moving towards each other...
                    Point3f targetPos = objToEvade->m_position;
```

```
                        if ((DOT(deltaPos,ship->UnitVectorVelocity()) < 0) ||
                            (dotVelocity > -0.93))//magic number == about 21 degrees
                        {
                                Point3f shipVel = ship->m_velocity;
                                shipVel = shipVel.Normalize() * ship->m_maxSpeed;
                                float combinedSpeed = (shipVel +
                                                        objToEvade->m_velocity).Length();
                                float predictionTime  = deltaPos.Length() /
                                                        combinedSpeed;
                                targetPos = objToEvade->m_position +
                                            (objToEvade->m_velocity*predictionTime);
                                deltaPos  = targetPos - ship->m_position;
                        }
                        //opposite of pursuit
                        SteerAway(targetPos, steeringForce);
                        totalForce += steeringForce;
                        adjustment = true;
                }
        }

    m_evadedLastUpdate      = adjustment;
    return adjustment;
}
```

SteerArrive (Listing 20.9) builds upon SteerPursuit. It uses pursuit's
FindTarget() function to find the future position of its target. It has a new Update()
function, however, that gently slows the ship down the closer it gets to the target.
As you can see, it doesn't use the SteerTowards() call that the other approach-based
behaviors use. This is because SteerTowards() always returns a steering force with
max magnitude. The arrive behavior requires the force to become smaller and
smaller as the ship gets close. However, since we're not using SteerTowards(), we
have to remember to subtract off the ship's current velocity vector.

LISTING 20.9   SteerArrive implementation.

```
bool SteerArrive::Update(float dt, Point3f &totalForce)
{
    bool adjument = false;
    bool found = FindTarget();
    if(found)
    {
            Point3f targetDelta = m_currentTarget −
                                  m_parent->m_ship->m_position;
```

```
                    float distToTarget = targetDelta.Length();
                    if (distToTarget > 0)
                    {
                            //debugging info...shows the targeting X
                        //on the arrive target
    //                      m_parent->m_target->m_position = m_currentTarget;

                            float speed  = m_parent->m_ship->m_maxSpeed *
                                        (distToTarget/ AI_MAX_SPEED_TRY);
                            speed = MIN(speed, m_parent->m_ship->m_maxSpeed);
                            targetDelta.Normalize();
                            targetDelta *= speed;
                            totalForce  += targetDelta - m_parent->m_ship->m_velocity;
                            adjument       = true;
                    }
            }

        return adjument;
}
```

`SteerAvoidWall` (Listing 20.10) is actually a general case static obstacle avoidance behavior. It projects three sensors out from the "front" of the ship (in our case, since the saucer doesn't really turn, it uses the current velocity vector to determine the front). If any of these three sensors are penetrating a wall, we steer so that the sensor is freed by giving a force equal to the amount of penetration (scaled by a small factor to increase the behavior's effectiveness) in the direction of the wall normal.

Note that for large amounts of agents working with large numbers of walls, this can be a fairly CPU-expensive behavior. We can easily implement measures to help with this cost. For instance, a big savings could be had quickly by culling out walls that are outside of a cheap radius proximity check. The walls themselves are passed in by the `SteeringControl` class. More on that when we go over the implementation of `SteeringControl`.

LISTING 20.10 `SteerAvoidWall` implementation.

```
bool SteerAvoidWall::Update(float dt,Point3f& totalForce)
{
    bool adjustment = false;

    SteeringControl* parent = (SteeringControl*)m_parent;
    Ship*            ship = parent->m_ship;

    //set up sensors
    m_sensors.clear();
```

```
Point3f movingDir = ship->m_velocity;
movingDir.Normalize();

//we don't need to avoid anything if we're sitting still
if(ISZERO(movingDir.LengthSquared()))
        return adjustment;


//clamp this vector: make sure it has at least a 1 length,
//the upper bound is just a large number
CLAMPVECTORLENGTH(movingDir,1,80.0f);
Point3f sensorVec = movingDir;
//base sensor length partially on ship speed
//divide by 4 is a magic number, use smaller value
//if you want more speed influence
float sensorLength = (m_avoidedLastUpdate?50.0f :20.0f) +
                      (ship->m_velocity.Length()/4.0f);
//straight
m_sensors.push_back(Sensor(ship->m_position +
                            sensorVec*sensorLength,false));
//right
sensorVec = ROT2D(sensorVec, 45);
m_sensors.push_back(Sensor(ship->m_position +
                            sensorVec*(sensorLength/2.0f),false));
//left
sensorVec = movingDir;
sensorVec = ROT2D(sensorVec, -45);
m_sensors.push_back(Sensor(ship->m_position +
                            sensorVec*(sensorLength/2.0f),false));


//for each sensor, check for wall collision
Point3f temp;
Point3f intersectionPoint;
Point3f steeringForce;
steeringForce.SetZero();
int closestWallIndex  = -1;
float closestWallDist = 9999999.0f;
for (unsigned int i=0; i<m_sensors.size(); i++)
{
        bool collisionOccurred = false;
        //find closest collision
        for (unsigned int j=0; j<m_wall.size(); j++)
        {
                float lambda = 0.0f;
```

```
            LINEINTERSECT(ship->m_position,m_sensors[i].m_senseVector,
                        m_wall[j].m_point1,m_wall[j].m_point2, lambda,
                        temp);
        //if the intersection lambda was within the
    //line segments, we collided
        if (lambda >= 0.0f && lambda <= 1.0f)
        {
                //returns intersection point into temp
                float distToWall = (ship->m_position -
                                temp).Length();
                m_sensors[i].m_collision = true;

                if (distToWall < closestWallDist)
                {
                        collisionOccurred = true;
                        closestWallDist = distToWall;
                        closestWallIndex  = j;
                        intersectionPoint = temp;
                }
        }
    }
    //did the sensor hit a wall?
    if (collisionOccurred)
    {
        Point3f penetration = m_sensors[i].m_senseVector -
                            intersectionPoint;
        //create a force in the direction of the wall normal, with a
        //magnitude of the overshoot
        Point3f thisWallSegment = m_wall[closestWallIndex].m_point2-
                            m_wall[closestWallIndex].m_point1;
        steeringForce = thisWallSegment;
        steeringForce.Normalize();
        //force vector == normal to the wall
        float tempX       = steeringForce.x();
        steeringForce.x() = -steeringForce.y();
        steeringForce.y() = tempX;
        //use collision depth to
        //determine repel force magnitude
        //--we want to maximize repel at a depth of 20
        float collisionDepth = penetration.Length()/20.0f;
        steeringForce *=  (collisionDepth*ship->m_maxSpeed);
    }
}//do all sensors
```

```
        if (steeringForce.Length())
        {
                totalForce += steeringForce;
                adjustment = true;
        }

        m_avoidedLastUpdate = adjustment;
        return adjustment;
}
```

SteerAvoidBorder (Listing 20.11) is a simple behavior that takes advantage of the fact that our game world is square. It simply checks to see if you're near one of the borders, and gives the ship a slight braking force, as well as a force normal to the border they're close to. For a more general case obstacle avoidance behavior, see AvoidWall. But, for our square asteroids world, this simple behavior more than suffices.

LISTING 20.11   SteerAvoidBorder implementation.

```
bool SteerAvoidBorder::Update(float dt,Point3f& totalForce)
{
    bool adjustment = false;

    SteeringControl* parent = (SteeringControl*)m_parent;
    Ship*     ship                 = parent->m_ship;

    //ensure minimum distance
    float minDist;
    if(m_avoidedLastUpdate)
            minDist  = 30.0f;
    else
            minDist  = 15.0f;
    float speed  = ship->m_velocity.Length();
    float spdAdj = LERP(speed/ship->m_maxSpeed,0.0f,40.0f);
    float adjSafetyRadius = minDist + spdAdj;

    Point3f steeringForce;
    steeringForce.SetZero();

    //if you're near a border...
    int lowX,highX,lowY,highY;
    float borderProximityX = 0.0f;
    float borderProximityY = 0.0f;
```

```
if(adjSafetyRadius > ship->m_position.x())
{
        lowX = 1;
        borderProximityX = ship->m_position.x();
}
else
        lowX = 0;
if(adjSafetyRadius > Game.m_screenW-ship->m_position.x())
{
        highX = 1;
        borderProximityX = Game.m_screenW-ship->m_position.x();
}
else
        highX = 0;
if(adjSafetyRadius > ship->m_position.y())
{
        lowY = 1;
        borderProximityY = ship->m_position.y();
}
else
        lowY = 0;
if(adjSafetyRadius > Game.m_screenW-ship->m_position.y())
{
        highY = 1;
        borderProximityY = Game.m_screenW-ship->m_position.y();
}
else
        highY = 0;

if(lowX || highX || lowY || highY)
{
        //add a repulsion force to your current movement vector
        //plus a braking force
        steeringForce = ship->UnitVectorVelocity();
        steeringForce += (Point3f(1,0,0) + -steeringForce*0.5f)*lowX;
        steeringForce += (Point3f(-1,0,0)+ -steeringForce*0.5f)*highX;
        steeringForce += (Point3f(0,1,0) + -steeringForce*0.5f)*lowY;
        steeringForce += (Point3f(0,-1,0)+ -steeringForce*0.5f)*highY;
        //add in a braking vector the closer you're getting to a wall
        steeringForce += -ship->UnitVectorVelocity()*
            (MIN(borderProximityY,borderProximityX)/adjSafetyRadius);
        steeringForce *= ship->m_maxSpeed;
}
```

```
    if (steeringForce.Length())
    {
            totalForce += steeringForce;
            adjustment = true;
    }

    m_avoidedLastUpdate = adjustment;
    return adjustment;
}
```

SteerWander (Listing 20.12) is an implementation of Craig Reynolds's own version of the wander behavior. Instead of setting targets or directions directly, which could lead to very twitchy-looking wandering, Reynolds's version uses an indirect target method. The wander behavior keeps track of a "targeting circle," which is offset from the main agent. The actual target that the agent is steering towards is a spot that randomly slides back and forth on the targeting circle's diameter. In this way, the wandering agent seems to have a somewhat chaotic movement, but the overall motion is quite smooth.

LISTING 20.12   SteerWander implementation.

```
bool SteerWander::Update(float dt, Point3f& totalForce)
{
    bool adjustment = false;

    SteeringControl* parent = (SteeringControl*)m_parent;
    Ship*     ship          = parent->m_ship;
    Point3f steeringForce;
    steeringForce.SetZero();

    float delta = 0.15f;
    //theta represents "where" we are on the circle, perturbing
    //it is what causes the guy to wander
    //range on random is (-delta to delta)
    m_thetaValue += (randflt()*2*delta) - delta;

    // Calculate the point on the circle, and head there
    m_circlePosition = ship->m_velocity;
    m_circlePosition.Normalize();
    m_circlePosition *= m_wanderCircleDistance;
    m_circlePosition += ship->m_position;
    Point3f circleTarget = Point3f(m_wanderCircleRadius*cos(m_thetaValue),
                      m_wanderCircleRadius*sin(m_thetaValue),0.0f);
```

```
Point3f target = m_circlePosition + circleTarget;
SteerTowards(target,steeringForce);

float distanceToObject = steeringForce.Length();
if (distanceToObject)
{
        totalForce += steeringForce;
        adjustment  = true;
        m_targetPosition = target;
}

return adjustment;
}
```

CODING THE CONTROL CLASS

The SteeringControl class (see Listing 20.13 for the implementation of the important functions) is mostly just set up for the individual steering behaviors being used.
Almost all of the logic for the saucer is contained in the behaviors themselves, leaving
very little for the controller to do besides just getting the ball rolling initially.

The constructor for the class fills the SteeringBehaviorManager with the behaviors that we want to use in this implementation. You can see in the demo code
that several other behaviors have been commented out, giving you a head start
if you want to dive into the code and experiment with other behaviors and/or
combinations.

There's also a bit of code in the constructor dealing with "walls." The AvoidWall
behavior requires that you pass in a structure containing all the walls that it needs
to avoid during it's lifetime when you instantiate it. That's why we build the walls
list and include it in the parameters to AvoidWall. In this way, the definitions of
all the static obstacles within the game are centralized. It also means that the ship
can have more than one AvoidWall behavior, each of which has its own set of walls,
but with different priority values or weights. This feature can be very useful for
advanced behavioral setups, but also for getting AI CPU costs down by potentially
having simplified wall sets that run first, and then activate more complex wall sets
if required.

Lastly, the constructor sets up the individual steering behaviors with weights
and probability values. It can also optionally disable behaviors that you might want
to turn on later, when particular conditions are met. In the current demo setup, all
the behaviors are enabled by default, but notice that the controller makes record of
the steering behavior SteerPursuit that has been aimed at powerups. This will be
useful later when we want to disable powerup pursuit after the ship has reached it's
maximum powerup level.

The `Update()` method has two main parts. In the first part, the controller updates its `SteeringBehaviorManager` class, and then gets a final steering vector which it passes along to the ship. This is basic steering system code. The rest of the function is game specific: it fires the ship's gun when near an asteroid, and turns off the pursuit of powerups when it has achieved max powerup level.

This is the power of steering based systems. The base engine is very simple. Each steering behavior is very simple. The complex behavior we get out of the final ship is caused by the interplay of these simple chunks of code in reaction to the rest of the game world. In fact, the toughest part of using this technique is setting up the priorities and weights of the behaviors in the constructor of the controller.

LISTING 20.13   `SteeringControl` function implementations.

```
SteeringControl::SteeringControl(Ship* ship):
AIControl(ship)
{
    m_getPowerupIndex = -1;

    //make walls for avoidWall
    std::vector<WallSegment> walls;
    WallSegment temp;
    temp.Set(Point3f(30.0f,30.0f,0.0f),
                Point3f(Game.m_screenW-30.0f,30.0f,0.0f));
    walls.push_back(temp);
    temp.Set(Point3f(10.0f,Game.m_screenH-30.0f,0.0f),
                Point3f(30.0f,30.0f,0.0f));
    walls.push_back(temp);
    temp.Set(Point3f(Game.m_screenW-30.0f,30.0f,0.0f),
                Point3f(Game.m_screenW-30.0f,Game.m_screenH-30.0f,0.0f));
    walls.push_back(temp);
    temp.Set(Point3f(Game.m_screenW-30.0f,Game.m_screenH-30.0f,0.0f),
                Point3f(30.0f,Game.m_screenH-30.0f,0.0f));
    walls.push_back(temp);

    //construct the steering manager and add the necessary behaviors
    m_behaviorManager = new SteeringBehaviorManager(this);
//  m_behaviorManager->AddBehavior(new SteerSeparation(this,
                                GameObj::OBJ_ASTEROID));
    m_behaviorManager->AddBehavior(new SteerEvade(this,
                                GameObj::OBJ_ASTEROID));
    m_behaviorManager->AddBehavior(new SteerPursuit(this,
                                GameObj::OBJ_POWERUP));;m_getPowerupIndex = 1;
    m_behaviorManager->AddBehavior(new SteerAvoidBorder(this));
```

```
//   m_behaviorManager->AddBehavior(new SteerAvoidWall(this,walls));
//   m_behaviorManager->AddBehavior(new SteerWander(this));
     m_behaviorManager->AddBehavior(new SteerArrive(this,
                                    GameObj::OBJ_ASTEROID));
     m_behaviorManager->Reset();

     //this is where we'll initialize all the weights
     //and probability values for the behaviors
     m_behaviorManager->SetupBehavior(0,3.5f,1.0f);//evade asteroid
     m_behaviorManager->SetupBehavior(1,4.0f,1.0f);//pursue powerup
     m_behaviorManager->SetupBehavior(2,20.0f,1.0f);//avoid border
     m_behaviorManager->SetupBehavior(3,1.0f,1.0f);//arrive asteroid
}


//---------------------------------------------------------
void SteeringControl::Update(float dt)
{
    if(!m_ship)
    {
        m_behaviorManager->Reset();
        return;
    }

    UpdatePerceptions(dt);
    m_behaviorManager->Update(dt);
    Point3f totalSteeringForce = m_behaviorManager->GetFinalSteeringVector();

    //apply forces
    m_ship->SteeringThrustAccumulate(totalSteeringForce);

    //check to see if I should shoot
    bool checkForShooting = true;
    if(m_nearestAsteroid && checkForShooting)
    {
            Point3f astDelta  = m_nearestAsteroid->m_position -
                                m_ship->m_position;
            float astDistance = astDelta.Length();
            if(astDistance < 100.0f + m_nearestAsteroid->m_size)
            {
                    Point3f futureAstPosition = m_nearestAsteroid->m_position;
                    Point3f deltaPos = futureAstPosition - m_ship->m_position;
                    float dist  = deltaPos.Length();
                    Point3f bulletVec = deltaPos.Normalize()*BULLET_SPEED;
```

```
                bulletVec += m_ship->m_velocity + (totalSteeringForce*dt);
                float time = dist/bulletVec.Length();
                futureAstPosition += time*m_nearestAsteroid->m_velocity;
                Point3f deltaFPos = futureAstPosition - m_ship->m_position;

                float newDir = CALCDIR(deltaFPos);
                m_ship->Shoot(newDir);
            }
        }


    //if you have a behavior chasing powerups,
    //temporarily disable going after powerups if
    //you've reached your max limit
    if(m_getPowerupIndex != -1 && m_ship->GetShotLevel() >= MAX_SHOT_LEVEL)
            m_behaviorManager->DisableBehavior(m_getPowerupIndex);
    }
```

PERFORMANCE OF THE AI WITH THIS SYSTEM

The AI is essentially invincible with this system. I have come back after letting the game run and seen that the AI-controlled saucer has over 1200 extra lives, with a score in the tens of millions range. The steering behaviors provide the ship with all it needs to burrow its way to the powerups while still evading the asteroids long enough for the guns to dispatch anything nearby. So for the sheer performance of "winning the game," the system is nearly perfect. Yet it still does things that a human wouldn't do, and it could definitely use a few "stylistic" improvements:

- *Increased complexity of the math model.* The AI system still suffers the lack of ability in dealing with the world coordinates wrapping. Right now, the AI's primary weakness is that it loses focus when things wrap in the world, and considering borders while targeting and for collision avoidance would greatly increase the survivability of the AI ship.

    Also, the predictive math that the behaviors use is somewhat idealized and simple. Obviously, there is a "chicken and the egg" problem when dealing with future position prediction. The object I'm tracking is moving at a certain speed. We determine how long it would take our ship to get to the object by adding both agents' speeds together, and dividing that speed into the ship's distance to the target.

    We then change our target to where the object will be if it keeps on course for that length of time. But now the problem: Since the target has changed, the amount of time it will take the ship to get there has changed, and thus the prediction can never really be 100 percent on. This doesn't even take into account if the target object can potentially change its trajectory, or the ship has a turning radius, or obstacles are in the the ship's path. Increasing the accuracy of this prediction model would help the ship shoot down asteroids better, as well as pursue and evade more effectively.

- *Bullet management for the ship.* Same as in the other implementations, our ship would definitely benefit from being a bit more judicious with the allotment of in-air bullets that the ship has at any given time. Right now, the ship just points, and then starts firing. The firing rate on the guns is quite high, so it tends to fire clumps of shots toward targets. This is somewhat advantageous; when it fires a clump of shots into a large asteroid, the remaining shots will sometimes kill the pieces as the asteroid splits. But this can get the ship in trouble when it has fired its entire allocation of bullets and must wait for them to collide or expire before it can shoot again, leaving it temporarily defenseless.

- *Better evade behavior.* Even though our evade is much better than the state-based system (since we're using a saucer and can thrust in any direction), we still have some of the classic evasion issues. When humans evade incoming asteroids, they use preemptive positioning before an asteroid gets too close, or even braking to a stop to just slow down the action a bit. A bit of simple play-field analysis (using an influence map, or other such technique) would help the AI with some of these actions. By knowing which parts of the map had the lesser concentrations of asteroids, it could perform evasion tactics in the general direction of "more space," or even set itself up in low-concentration areas *preemptively* to give itself a better chance for survival.

PROS OF STEERING-BASED SYSTEMS

Steering behaviors are by definintion usually very simple algorithms. At their best, they are single-action systems (meaning, they only try to do *one* thing at a time; if you find that you're coding a behavior that has multiple states, think about splitting it into different behaviors). Single-action systems are usually very easy to design and implement, since they force you to focus on just the one problem to be solved.

Steering behaviors can be quite predictable. The rules they encode are straightforward enough that the name of the steering behavior is usually enough to explain what the behavior does. Even when combining behaviors, most people intuitively figure what's going to happen (at least until the number of behaviors being combined becomes large).

Steering behaviors can be quite easy on the CPU budget. Not only are individual behaviors usually very efficient, but the modular way in which steering systems are constructed allow even more performance to be squeezed out of the system. If you have a particular behavior that is costly, you can just increase the maximum force it can deliver, and then don't update it as often. You'll lose some accuracy with that behavior, but you will always have some tradeoff when looking for higher performance.

Cons of FSM-Based Systems

Since steering systems are almost always combinations of simple behaviors, combining becomes your number-one concern. Finding the best combination method is typically just a matter of knowing how many behaviors you have in your design, but also knowing just how "blended" you need your behavior to be (versus the dithered method that tends to behave more like a finite-state system with fuzzy perceptions). Instead, a lot of time seems to get spent on tuning the individual weights, priorities, and other parameters that control the overall behavioral blending.

Special care must be taken when tuning steering systems that have a lot of intermingled behaviors. Changing the parameters for a single behavior could upset a very careful balance between three others, and changing them could then snowball into a balance problem with even more problems.

In essence, combining steering behaviors represents a kind of "color-blending" artform. If you have too many colors, or too many of the same flavor, it is difficult to not blend them all into a sort of mud (as any kid trying to do too much with his giant set of Play-Doh will tell you). It's usually best to have orthogonal behaviors, that operate differently enough that they don't blend together into a final behavior that does nothing. However, if the behaviors are *too* different, they can potentially deadlock each other in a kind of agent-based tug-of-war. Hence, the aforementioned "artform." As a steering system programmer, finding the sweet spot between the push and pull of certain behaviors with the more subtle support offered by others can be challenging.

Steering behaviors tend to be single-minded, short-range tactics. They typically operate alone (without communication to other behaviors; not in the sense that there's only one behavior running at a time) and, as such, tend to have problems with *local traps*. These would be areas of the game world that can suck a steering-controlled agent in and are difficult to get out of. In fact, steering tends to work much better on open terrain environments. Dead ends and other architectural pitfalls can be navigated, but they typically take a special-case steering behavior to handle (you could run analysis on your environment, and generate special repulsion information tagged to game world features that a steering behavior could respond to, or just create special behaviors for handling dead ends specifically).

Large groups of agents all using steering behaviors can deadlock each other by getting mashed into a tight game area and find a trap in which their separation forces, the evade wall force, and whatever else they're running all mutually oppose one another, causing an entire cluster of agents to lock up. If the agents were using longer-range planning or were sharing information with their neighbors, they could do much better. In fact, in the clustering scenario, you could use what is known as the "follow the leader" behavior (have everybody target some offset from a chosen leader, as well as get out of the leader's way) and get much less deadlock since only one agent is in control of the pack. In a sense, "follow the leader" is a *group* steering behavior.

Since the behavior of steering systems is largely emergent, extra testing time must be allotted, since you'll need to try and get your agents into all the various combinations of situations they might encounter once in a consumer's hands. This is a general problem with emergent systems, however, and not really a specific downfall of steering behaviors.

Take care when using steering behaviors that you don't make your creatures robotic-looking. This can be caused by using a few, very specific or overpowering behaviors. Your agents will tend to look rigid and unthinking. Having more subtle behaviors that work well together (like the flocking set of cohesion, separation, and alignment) will give the overall agent behavior smooth, organic-looking movement.

Lastly, *idle* states can be difficult to achieve with steering systems. By definition, these behaviors primarily control the "steering" of the agents involved. They apply to *movement*. Hence, they tend to look best when the agent is constantly moving around, being directed by its behavior set. But getting a steering-controlled agent to stop (without specifically using a known end point, like the arrive behavior uses) means that you have to balance more than one behavior so that there will be "dead spots" in the world that the agent will be pushed to. These are areas where the sum of the agent's steering forces add up to zero, and thus the character will stop moving. Obviously, for a reasonably complex steering-controlled agent, this can be difficult to achieve. Instead, what many people do is create an arrive-style behavior that can be set to very high priority. If you need the character to stop somewhere, you use this behavior to essentially override the contributions of the rest of the behavior set.

EXTENSIONS TO THE PARADIGM

Steering behaviors have been around for a while, and many games have put them to good use in many different ways. In this section, we will go over some of the common extensions to the simple system discussed in this chapter.

LAYERED STEERING

Layered steering can actually mean a few different things. The game might include creatures that require more than one concurrent steering target. Consider a large multi-headed mythical hydra; its body movement is controlled by one steering target, and each head (and corresponding long neck) is focused on a potentially different target. True, the heads aren't "steering" anywhere per se, but they are turning and moving the head to face a particular target.

Another approach is to use a truly hierarchical layered steering system. In the setup, you are still heading to a number of different high-level targets (evade, pursuit, etc.). But each target is determined by running a steering system of its own. For any given high-level behavior, the combination of a number of sub-level steering behaviors is used to form the main target the agent will use.

In the case of evade, the list of sub-level behaviors would not only include "Evade Asteroids" (which is essentially the type of evade we've discussed in this chapter). In a more complex game, agents could also require more specialized behaviors like "Evade Incoming Gunfire" (used against enemy ships, this would use an entirely different algorithm, since you'd have to start evading fast projectiles much sooner and in smarter directions), "Evade Black Hole" (which might require special perception data), or "Evade Red Powerups" (perhaps the agent has been maxing out the *blue* powerups, and doesn't want to switch weapons to whatever is represented by the red powerups). All these sub-level evasion behaviors would be blended into one main evade target.

These high-level targets would then get blended again into the agents final steering target. In this way, you can really go into great depth with what it is for a given character to "evade" or "pursue," and give each of those behaviors real personality and nuance.

However, layered steering is probably more useful when dealing with creatures that don't require a great deal of high-level behaviors, since the high-level blend might deaden much of the subtle effects of the lower-level behaviors if there are too many. This is best used for simple minded, but very contextually deep creatures. An example would be an enemy that's always *chasing the player down* (simple minded; only one high-level behavior), but at the same time always chasing you *in the right manner* (contextually deep; the manner in which the enemy chases the player changes interactively and continuously).

LEARNING BEHAVIORS

As behaviors increase in complexity, or the direction that you want the agent to steer given the current environment gets more complex, it becomes increasingly difficult to write the code for the behavior by hand.

One way to counter this is to use learning techniques (genetic algorithms have been tried successfully in the past, but so have other techniques including various types of perceptrons, as well as neural nets) to have the agent learn the steering function necessary to perform the behavior.

In the 1990s, popular topics among AI researchers were not only steering behaviors (after Craig Raynolds published his steering papers) but the advent of genetic programming. Researchers used genetic algorithms to evolve steering solutions, especially co-evolving pairs of behaviors (predator/prey was a highly studied set). A casual Google search using the phrase "steering coevolution" will get you over 23,000 results, within fields ranging from chemistry to software design to papers written specifically about steering behaviors. In 1994, Reynolds himself published a few papers on this topic, "Competition, Coevolution, and the Game of Tag," and "Evolution of Corridor Following Behavior in a Noisy World." Both of these papers are great reading for programmers thinking of trying a scheme like this with steering behaviors. The papers also contained many hints to help you make your behaviors work well since many of the pitfalls of getting the genetic component to play nice with the steering paradigm have been addressed. They also provide insight into other ways of thinking about steering-based behavior systems, which might inspire you in completely new directions.

OTHER COMMON BEHAVIORS

The small number of behaviors covered in this chapter is by no means an exhaustive list. Some of the other commonly used behaviors include:

- **Pursuit With Offset.** This versatile behavior is just pursuit, except that you're not pursuing a target directly, but some offset from that target. This is useful for setting up formations (imagine whole groups of agents with column and row offsets from a commander agent; whenever the commander goes somewhere, the rest of his "army" follows in marching formation). This could also be used to make long "follow the leader" setups by linking an entire group of agents to this behavior with one leader, each one using an offset behind another in a daisy chain fashion ("A" is a leader. "B" is offset pursuing A, C offset pursues B, etc.).
- **Patrol.** This behavior would take a number of points in the game world and move the agent from one to the next in order. This is another highly versatile behavior. The target points passed to the behavior could be parameterized to control all aspects of patrolling. There could be targets that control the agent's locomotion type (does the agent run to this target, or walk, or swim, etc.). Targets can trigger special actions (a teleportation pad, or getting to the target simply makes the agent wait for one second, or just triggering a creaking door sound, for example). In our example code, you would use the same type of approach as `AvoidWall`, which is supplied with data from the `SteeringControl` class to define the walls. The controller class could instantiate all the patrol points and pass them to the steering behavior, or they could come from a data file, etc.

■ **Match Target Speed.** This behavior is a lot like alignment, except that the agent is conforming to a particular speed instead of a direction. Many times you just want to shadow the speed of another agent. You can include a scale factor, or some offset as well (agent A will always try to go half as fast as agent B, or agent A will always go just a touch faster than B).

■ **Hide.** This behavior tries to steer an agent such that it moves out of the view of some other agent. You would need to supply the behavior with the agent (or types of agents) that you want to hide from. The behavior would also require specification on the correct objects to hide behind. Can the agent hide behind any game wall, certain game walls, or even other types of agents? Should the character perform a particular function once it finds a hiding spot? Example actions might be ducking down, or turning on a cloaking device, or just playing a sound.

■ **Interpose.** This behavior steers the agent to be directly between two or more other agents. Another version might use future prediction on all the other agents, or other specific "lanes" between the target agents.

■ **Orbit.** Orbiting would entail circling around an agent in some fashion. The style of orbit could be standard elipsoidial, square, or any other looping manner. Other parameters could include speed, some kind of variance level (low-variance orbiters would always orbit the same path, high-variance agents could vary the path a lot, and/or randomize their speed).

■ **Flow Field Following.** This behavior responds to environmental data known as *flow fields*. Imagine if you overlaid a grid of uniformly spaced force vectors onto your game world. By adjusting these force vectors, you would have created a force "field" where your agent feels a steering effect from anywhere on the map, by summing up the effects of each vector within some proximity. An appropriate flow field could be used in our demo application to mimic the `AvoidBorder` behavior if we supplied a repulsive force along the entire outside of the game world. But with flow fields, we could make the shape of the game world non-rectangular, and the effect would be just as easy to achieve.

■ **Queueing.** When trying to get many fast-moving agents to pass through a narrow opening, basic algorithms tend to give very unintelligent-looking behavior. Real crowds of people slow down, keep somewhat spaced (although they do tend to give up personal space depending on the urgency of the current target), and if necessary will even create a single-file line (or a *queue*) in order to get through the bottleneck in a semi-orderly fashion. This steering behavior will mirror this: slow down, stay separated, and queue up at a bottleneck.

DATA-DRIVEN STEERING BEHAVIORS

Steering behaviors tend to build upon very simple algorithms. With some clever parameterization and a handful of base behaviors, you can create a data-driven steering system that would make for a truly rich agent creation experience. By designing the system to accept live updates, you could make things even better. Imagine a game designer sitting down with the game, and starting with nothing; the agent is standing still. With a single mouse click, the designer gives the agent a `wander` behavior instance. The agent begins to wander about the game world. The designer tunes some of the numbers, getting the `wander` behvior to perform in the wanted fashion. With another click, the agent is given an `avoid` behavior. The designer tweaks that behavior to avoid walls, and designates the walls that the agent should be concerned with. The designer adds a few more agents into the system, and assigns them all to follow the first agent's lead. After adding general flocking behaviors to the whole group (alignment, cohesion, and separation), the designer then tunes the weight values associated with the different interacting behaviors, and saves the resulting parameter file out to disk. Without touching code, or even talking to a programmer, the designer has created the exact creature movement the designer wants, and the cost to the game is a tiny text file that records which behaviors to instantiate for each agent, and the parameters to pass each.

OPTIMIZATIONS

Steering behaviors are naturally quite CPU friendly. They are generally simple algorithms. They are functionally focused, so they tend to not have the code overhead bloat associated with multi-stage or heavily orchestrated behavior. There is always room for optimization, however. Load balancing can always help, just as it does when used with other AI techniques. Another means to gaining some CPU power back is to adjust priorites and weights to put off expensive calculations until later on.

LOAD BALANCING

Steering behaviors can be load balanced in a few different ways. Agents' updates can be spread across multiple frames (so that only a certain number of agents will run each game loop). If you are building groups of flocking agents, this might lead to visually innappropriate behavior, since the vast majority of the organic look of the system is brought about by small, incremental reactive changes that flow smoothly. Spreading agent updates over multiple frames tends to lead to slightly jerkier behavior, because the steering vectors will tend to be larger since the behavior is having to compensate for a larger time period that the agent has potentially been moving in the wrong direction. It also introduces a small amount of lag to the overall group's behavior, because large direction changes or sudden reactions to external stimulus will also be spread across multiple frames. This technique would probably be fine, however, for agents that don't require a high level of reactivity, or where the amount of influences that need to be taken into account are lower.

Another load-balancing technique would be to use less costly combination methods for a certain percentage of the time, in order to partially bring down CPU cost without losing all the accuracy in your steering. So, if your system combines its behaviors with the simple weighted combination method but is using too many CPU cycles, the AI engine could instead use the prioritized dithering method on half the agents, and then every frame, switch which half of the agents you're downgrading. In this way, in every other frame, your agents are getting high-accuracy blended steering. In the other frame, those same agents are getting the most probable, high-priority behavior directly. Then the cycle repeats. As long as your maximum accelleration isn't very high, you shouldn't loose too much information on the low accuracy frames, and you have effectively shaved a lot of behavior updates out of your AI run. Of course, this method would require a bit of testing and tuning (as do all optimization methods) since you could have outlaying scenarios where this jostling of steering could cause unnecessary jitter. But jitter can be filtered out of the system with straightforward, inexpensive means.

Priority/Weight Adjustments

A more involved optimization step involves carefully considering the mix of steering behaviors within your agent design. Do you have a number of behaviors that are especially CPU-expensive, with most behaviors being relatively inexpensive? Then you could set up your priorities so that the least expensive behaviors are checked first, and then use a combination of methods that limit the number of behaviors that are updated on any given frame. Obviously, you can't do this if your expensive behavior is also the most critical as far as accuracy of steering goes. If the evasion behavior in your game is expensive, but it's the only thing keeping your agents from speedy death, you have to bite the bullet and find somewhere else to optimize. But for many systems, looking for ways to cut down on behavior update through priority exclusion and/or weighting can be a huge potential for savings.

Design Considerations

Remember, use the best tool for the job. Take stock in the game you are creating the AI engine for. You should consider all the design factors discussed in Chapter 2: types of solutions, agent reactivity, system realism, genre, content, platform, development limitations, and entertainment limitations. Make sure that the answer to at least some of those questions points to the use of steering.

TYPES OF SOLUTIONS

Steering behavior solutions are mostly tactical in nature. Because they're single-entity-based, as well as typically historyless (meaning, they recalculate their steering vector without the use of much historic data or state information) they usually make poor strategic decisions simply because they lack the depth of knowledge necessary to analyze strategic kinds of information and utilize that information.

However, this is not to say that they couldn't be adapted to some kinds of strategic decision making. If you're working on a real-time strategy game, you could write your city-building AI using an abstract form of steering. You would have a number of "steering behaviors" (building considerations) whose job it was to adjust the "movement vector" (which in this case is the direction that the AI is going to expand its base). These targets would be combined into a final vector which would give the AI a general direction in which it should expand its base, generated by blending a number of rich, focused targeting "behaviors" into a compound end target that would generally be better for the AI army.

AGENT REACTIVITY

Steering systems will work for any level of agent reactivity. But steering systems are really in a class by themselves when you're looking for *exceedingly* reactive systems. If the game you're building needs to show very subtle movements as game conditions change in small ways for every frame, then you should definitely experiment with steering. Steering provides smooth agent reactivity that ripples out from its source. Although steering does work well with individual unit reactivity, it is also uniquely suited to group dynamics, where the focus is more at the complex interactions of *groups* of agents over time, as opposed to the frame-by-frame movements of any one agent.

SYSTEM REALISM

Steering systems were initially created to try and model realistic, organic behavior, a category of computer modeling sometimes referred to as *artificial life*. Nature tends to use simple, instinctual rules for its inhabitants, and steering behaviors capture this very well.

Combinations of steering behaviors can sometimes lead to odd behavior, but this is more of a weighting/tuning issue than a systemic problem. Yes, it can become harder, as you add more behaviors into the mixture to maintain truly organic and flowing behavior, but just remember that:

1. No one AI technique should have to solve every problem; maybe you need to break up your steering across a simple state machine, so that any given

steering behavior mix is more simple and the agent just switches state to a different mix during certain considerations.

2. Life itself started out with pretty simple behavior combinations, and took a very long time to get the bugs out of the complex behavior combinations that drive human beings.

GENRE

Steering behaviors find their way into any genre that requires emergent, organic movement from its AI controlled agents. It has typically been used for groups of AI agents (like crowds or herds of animals) but it works just as well for games with singular agents as well.

Because of its emergent element, games that are very scripted, linear affairs usually don't find much use for it (unless it's a localized effect: the crowds of zombies in Capcom's *Dead Rising* are using steering behaviors to move around, even though the game itself is very story-driven when played in its primary mode).

One sub-note: some games that *look* like they're using steering behaviors actually aren't, and it's generally for a reason. Scrolling shooter games sometimes have waves of enemies that look like they're using steering behaviors as they swarm around and coalesce into formations and stylized movements. But these are typically the result of specifically scripted behaviors. These types of shooters tend to rely heavily on the fact that the enemies are *not* responsive to the player (except that some of the enemies will actually aim at the player when they shoot). The player is supposed to learn the patterns that the enemies take (so as to best position the player's ship and array of weapons), and emergent enemy reactions to other enemies and/or the player would definitely make recognizing a pattern harder to do.

CONTENT

Does your game contain a single, 30-foot robot as its enemy agent? Then maybe steering isn't the way to go. However, if you're making a game in which you're a shark, and you want to model realistic schools of fish that respond to your attacks and the environment in a realistic manner, there's really no other technique that will give you results as realistic as steering.

PLATFORM

Steering behaviors are basically platform independent because of their lightweight computation requirements. With today's fast CPUs, games can model large groups of realisticly moving creatures with moderate ease using simple steering behaviors.

DEVELOPMENT LIMITATIONS

Due to the emergent nature of steering systems, care must be taken that enough time is allotted to the tuning and tweaking phase of agent development. As said before in this chapter, as the number of steering behaviors being blended together in any one agent increases, the level of difficulty in getting exactly what you want out (or even in the neighborhood) gets harder and harder. It's simply a property of complexity theory: as the number of non-linear coupling rules increase within a system, the ability of an observer to truly predict the final outcome of that system rapidly falls to zero. It's like predicting the weather: No matter what the TV weatherperson says, they're really just guessing, since too many variables are interacting in too many non-linear processes to really make an accurate prediction.

ENTERTAINMENT LIMITATIONS

Entertainment concerns are another area to be watchful of with steering behaviors, or any emergent AI technique. Difficulty settings and game balancing can be tough when you're not really sure what the AI is going to be doing at any given moment. Obviously, for agents who are only using steering to avoid obstacles while getting around a game world, this is not the case. But for creatures who have entire decision structure that are just a conglomeration of steering behaviors, ensuring a particular player experience may be difficult without serious thought and tuning.

SUMMARY

Steering behaviors are a great way to infuse your AI creatures with realistic, organic, largely emergent group behaviors. They model subtle interplay between differing agent goals exceedingly well. They simplify certain kinds of group dynamics by making them emergent, meaning that you don't really have to code them at all; instead they come forth naturally from the combination of simpler parts that you did create.

- Steering behaviors were originally created by Craig Reynolds as an artificial life technique that attempted to model flocking behavior.
- The steering system in this book comprises three main classes: `SteeringBehavior`, `SteeringBehaviorManager`, and `SteeringControl`.
- The demo implementation of steering behaviors used in this chapter employ a saucer ship with four behaviors: `SteerEvade`, `SteerPursuit`, `SteerAvoidBorder`, and `SteerArrive`. Its performance is near optimal. It will play as long as you let it run.

- Extensions to the test bed for better and/or different performance include adding layered steering, employing automatically learned behaviors, using other common behaviors, or data driving the behaviors.
- The pros of steering systems are their ease of implementation, they are somewhat predictable, and they are inexpensive to execute on the CPU.
- The cons of steering systems are combinatorial complexity, their short-sightedness, deadlocking problems within an agent as well as with groups of agents, potentially large tuning-time requirements, they can look robotic if misused, and are not great at modeling idle states.
- Layered steering systems would allow for greater contextual depth of each steering behavior without muddying the overall agent behavior.
- Automatic learned behaviors could use a genetic algorithm approach (or some other learning method) to solve a particular steering system tuning/setup problem without requiring human interaction, saving programmer time.
- There are many more commonly useful steering behaviors than those covered in this chapter. Some of them include: pursuit with offset, patrol, match target speed, hide, interpose, orbit, follow flow field, and queue.
- Data-driving steering systems can be particularly easy and satisfying, especially because of the high tuning requirements of most complex steering behavior combinations.
- Load-balancing algorithms can be applied to steering systems, but care must be taken not to destroy the careful, subtle balance attained by the highly reactive steering method.
- Priority and weight adjustments can keep CPU-expensive behaviors from hogging resources, but again, care must be taken not to starve behaviors that require lots of updating to really look visually compelling.

21 Combination Systems

For every game AI problem, there is at least one solution. But most games have *many* problems. Most of these problems can be solved with general solutions, the kinds of nuts-and-bolts technology that can be used over and over within the game code. But some of the AI problems can be so fundamentally different from the rest that *wholly different AI systems* are required to solve them. In fact, creating almost any game will require knowing how to mold and combine the AI techniques within this book into parts of a larger problem-solving machine.

In this chapter, we will implement a combination system, using various methods from the rest of the book to flesh out a rounded AI engine that our demo application will use. Because of the simplicity of AIsteroids, the AI system built in this chapter will be vast overkill for the realities of the game. But the real demonstration is the ease at which more complex architectures are created, not the specific use of the techniques.

THE DEMO

The demo will use a much larger array of AI techniques than previous chapters, which were usually set up to showcase a single AI method per demo. In this chapter, the demo will include:

- Finite state machines (FSMs)
- A hierarchical FSM

- Steering behaviors
- An occupance tracking influence map
- A messaging system
- A simple script loader used for game parameter loading

A number of elements have been added to the demo. The system we'll be discussing in this chapter includes the following AI elements:

- An FSM will be used to control a ship. The ship will fly around, shoot asteroids, collect powerups, and engage in combat with another demo character: the saucer.
- The saucer character will use a steering behavior-based AI controller. This character will also shoot asteroids and collect powerups. However, the saucer is almost purely defensive; it will only attack the ship character if it gets too close.
- The approach state in the FSM for the ship will be a full-fledged FSM on its own, thus showing how hierarchical FSMs are used. Based on the circumstances, the approach FSM will cause the ship to approach the saucer, or an area of high asteroid concentration, as well as the nearest asteroid if need be.
- Within the ship's approach FSM, a modified ApproachState moves the saucer towards an area of high asteroid concentration. It uses an occupance-based influence map to make this determination.
- Also, the ship employs a new hunt state. This state makes better use of the wrapping world borders to find the best approach direction for the ship to use in stopping the saucer.
- The game now uses a script-loading system to set up key variables at load time. As in the earlier scripting chapters, the parsing system uses messaging to send parameter messages to any given game entity that wishes to respond to the script. There is also a keyboard shortcut to have the script reload during game play in order to increase the speed iterative tuning of the AI.
- There is now a small "planet" game object in the middle of the game world. This serves as an additional obstacle to both spacecrafts, but it also helps the saucer to evade the ship with a new steering behavior—UseCover.

We'll now begin to break down how all of the methods that have been layered into the demo. First, we'll cover the GameSession class. It requires a little work in order to handle all the new AI elements. In Listing 21.1, the important implementation changes within GameSession can be seen.

The GameSession class constructor is now instantiating two AI controllers, one for each of the AI characters: the ship and the saucer. This is also where the influence map is handled, giving any child controller access to the data analysis it provides.

The GameSession::Update() function no longer directly calls Update() for any particular AI controller. Instead, a few lines have been added so that *any* AI controller assigned to *any* game object will get an Update() call. Be alert to this simple refactoring. Now, specific controller Update() methods don't have a hardcoded call. To be sure, there are still other places in the code where specific AI controllers are referenced. But with a little organization and some structural changes, all of these could be eliminated.

Going through the code and eliminating as much hard coding as possible will go a long way towards ensuring that the AI engine being built will scale well as the number of AI controllers, game objects, and their level of interconnectedness grows. By making the Update() work in this way, we have effectively hidden more of the details of how each game object is operating from the GameSession code. This allows engine designers to create increasingly abstract systems.

A high level of abstraction is useful if a particular goal of the overall AI engine is to be data driven. In this case, scripts could be written that set up parameter lists for all the game objects. These scripts would drive generic factory methods that blindly create all the necessary game objects, as well as link them with all the optional resources they need to perform (these would include AI controllers, sets of perception variables, and any other data or code resources).

The rest of the differences within the GameSession.cpp file are small changes to operate the message pump, influence mapping, and handle spawning of additional game objects like the planet. In addition, a number of additional GetObject style functions have been included here. These functions are used by various behaviors and states discussed later in the chapter.

LISTING 21.1 Important GameSession implementation differences.

```
//----------------------------------------------------------
GameSession::GameSession()
{
  m_screenH            = 1024;
  m_screenW            = 1024;
  m_AIOn               = false;
  m_timeScale          = 1;
  m_humanControl    = new HumanControl();
  m_mainAIControl   = new FSMAIControl();
  m_enemyAIControl  = new SteeringControl();

  m_oInfluenceMap = NULL;
  m_oInfluenceMap = new OccupanceInfluenceMap();
  m_oInfluenceMap->Init(4,4,INITIAL_WORLD_SIZE,INITIAL_WORLD_SIZE);
  m_oInfluenceMap->DrawGrid();
  m_oInfluenceMap->DrawInfluence();

  m_cInfluenceMap = NULL;
```

```
// m_cInfluenceMap = new ControlInfluenceMap();
// m_cInfluenceMap->Init(32,32,INITIAL_WORLD_SIZE,INITIAL_WORLD_SIZE);
// m_cInfluenceMap->DrawGrid();
// m_cInfluenceMap->DrawInfluence();
}

//-----------------------------------------------------------
void GameSession::Update(float dt)
{
  //update the messge pump
  g_MessagePump.Update(dt);

  //update the influence map
  IMUpdate(dt);

  GameObjectList::iterator list1;
  for(list1=m_activeObj.begin();list1!=m_activeObj.end();++list1)
  {
    GameObj* temp = *list1;
    //update logic and positions
    if((*list1)->m_active)
    {
      //if you have an AI controller, and
      //the AI is turned on, update
      if((*list1)->m_control && m_AIOn)
        (*list1)->m_control->Update(dt);

      //actual object update
      (*list1)->Update(dt);

      //make sure position coordinates
      //are within the game world
      Clip((*list1)->m_position);
    }
    else continue;

    //check for collisions
    if((*list1)->m_collisionFlags != GameObj::OBJ_NONE)
    {
      GameObjectList::iterator list2;
      for(list2=m_activeObj.begin();
        list2!=m_activeObj.end();++list2)
      {
        //the first obj may have already collided
        //with something, making it inactive
```

```
        if(!(*list1)->m_active)
           continue;

        //don't collide with yourself
        if(list1 == list2)
           continue;

        if((*list2)->m_active          &&
           ((*list1)->m_collisionFlags & (*list2)->m_type) &&
           (*list1)->IsColliding(*list2))
        {
           (*list1)->DoCollision((*list2));
        }
     }
   }
   if(list1==m_activeObj.end()) break;
}

//get rid of inactive objects
GameObjectList::iterator end    = m_activeObj.end();
GameObjectList::iterator newEnd = remove_if(m_activeObj.begin(),
                                 m_activeObj.end(),RemoveNotActive);
if(newEnd != end)
   m_activeObj.erase(newEnd,end);

//check for no main ship, respawn
if(!m_mainShip)
{
   m_mainShip = new Ship;
     if(m_mainShip)
     {
        PostGameObj(m_mainShip);
        m_humanControl->SetShip(m_mainShip);
        m_mainAIControl->SetShip(m_mainShip);
        m_mainShip->m_control = m_mainAIControl;
     }
}
//occasionally spawn a powerup
m_powerupTimer-=dt;
if(m_powerupTimer <0.0f)
{

   m_powerupTimer = randflt()*6.0f + 4.0f;
   Powerup* pow = new Powerup;
```

```
      if(pow)
      {

        pow->m_position.x()= randflt()*m_screenW;
        pow->m_position.y()= randflt()*m_screenH;
        pow->m_position.z()= 0;
        pow->m_velocity.x()= randflt()*40 - 20;
        pow->m_velocity.y()= randflt()*40 - 20;
        pow->m_velocity.z()= 0;
        PostGameObj(pow);
      }
    }

    //occasionally spawn a saucer
    if(!m_enemyShip)
    {
      m_enemyShip = new Saucer;
      if(m_enemyShip)
      {
        PostGameObj(m_enemyShip);
        m_enemyAIControl->SetShip(m_enemyShip);
        m_mainShip->m_control = m_enemyAIControl;
      }
    }

    //check for finished wave
    if(!m_numAsteroids)
    {
      m_waveNumber++;
      WaveOver();
    }
    //check for finished game, and reset
    if(!m_numLives)
      GameOver();

    m_humanControl->Update(dt);
  }
```

FSM CHANGES

Next, we'll discuss the changes made to the finite state machine system we originally used in Chapter 15, starting with the FSMAIControl class. Listing 21.2 shows
the important implementation changes.

First notice that this class heavily uses the messaging system to get parameter
data from the script file. A large number of various settings on the AI-controlled

ship are all set using the initialization script. This file, named test.txt, can be edited, saved, and then reloaded while the game is running (by pushing the "r" key) to allow for quick turnaround while tuning the game parameters. Also in the GameSession constructor, notice that instead of using the ApproachState directly, the ship is now using a new class, MachineApproach. This is another sub FSM that controls all of the different states used by the ship when it wants to approach either the asteroids or the saucer.

The UpdatePerceptions() function is also radically different from before. The m_nearestPowerup and m_nearestEnemy variables are set using a special function that only returns nearby game objects that the ship can "reach". This takes into account the relative speeds of the two objects, and makes a calculation based on whether or not the system thinks the ship could catch it. This prevents the occasional endless chasing that has cropped up in the demo from time to time.

Also, the Update() function handles the determinations used by the new hunt behavior, which is the next thing we'll break down.

LISTING 21.2   Important FSMAIControl implementation differences.

```
//----------------------------------------------------------
FSMAIControl::FSMAIControl(Ship* ship):
AIControl(ship)
{
  //script parsing messages
// MessagePump::AddMessageToSystem(MESSAGE_TOKEN_PSCAN);
  g_MessagePump.AddMessageToSystem(MESSAGE_TOKEN_PSCAN);
  g_MessagePump.AddMessageToSystem(MESSAGE_TOKEN_MAXSPEED);
  g_MessagePump.AddMessageToSystem(MESSAGE_TOKEN_APDIST);
  g_MessagePump.AddMessageToSystem(MESSAGE_TOKEN_ATDIST);
  g_MessagePump.AddMessageToSystem(MESSAGE_TOKEN_SAFERAD);
  g_MessagePump.AddMessageToSystem(MESSAGE_TOKEN_POWSEEK);
  g_MessagePump.AddMessageToSystem(MESSAGE_TOKEN_SHIPAGG);
  g_MessagePump.AddMessageToSystem(MESSAGE_TOKEN_SHIPAGGCD);
  g_MessagePump.AddMessageToSystem(MESSAGE_TOKEN_SHIPAGGCS);
  g_MessagePump.AddMessageToSystem(MESSAGE_TOKEN_SHIPAGGPROX);
  g_MessagePump.AddMessageToSystem(MESSAGE_TOKEN_ENEMYSEEK);

  //must create the messageReceiver before you
  //register for any messages, since you have to
  //pass in the MessageID of the receiver
  m_messReceiver = new MessageReceiver;

  g_MessagePump.RegisterForMessage(MESSAGE_TOKEN_PSCAN,this,
              GetMessageID(),m_powerupScanDistCallback);
```

```
g_MessagePump.RegisterForMessage(MESSAGE_TOKEN_MAXSPEED,this,
                 GetMessageID(),m_maxSpeedCallback);
g_MessagePump.RegisterForMessage(MESSAGE_TOKEN_APDIST,this,
                 GetMessageID(),m_appDistCallback);
g_MessagePump.RegisterForMessage(MESSAGE_TOKEN_ATDIST,this,
                 GetMessageID(),m_attDistCallback);
g_MessagePump.RegisterForMessage(MESSAGE_TOKEN_SAFERAD,this,
                 GetMessageID(),m_safeRadiusCallback);
g_MessagePump.RegisterForMessage(MESSAGE_TOKEN_POWSEEK,this,
                 GetMessageID(),m_powerupSeekCallback);
g_MessagePump.RegisterForMessage(MESSAGE_TOKEN_SHIPAGG,this,
                 GetMessageID(),m_shipAggCallback);
g_MessagePump.RegisterForMessage(MESSAGE_TOKEN_SHIPAGGCD,this,
                 GetMessageID(),m_shipAggCDCallback);
g_MessagePump.RegisterForMessage(MESSAGE_TOKEN_SHIPAGGCS,this,
                 GetMessageID(),m_shipAggCSCallback);
g_MessagePump.RegisterForMessage(MESSAGE_TOKEN_SHIPAGGPROX,this,
                 GetMessageID(),m_shipAggProxCallback);
g_MessagePump.RegisterForMessage(MESSAGE_TOKEN_ENEMYSEEK,this,
                 GetMessageID(),m_enemySeekCallback);


//construct the state machine and add the necessary states
m_machine = new FSMMachine(FSM_MACH_MAINSHIP,FSM_STATE_NONE,this);
MachineApproach* mApproach =
           new MachineApproach(this);
// StateApproach* approach = new StateApproach(this);
// m_machine->AddState(approach);
m_machine->AddState(mApproach);
m_machine->AddState(new StateAttack(this));
m_machine->AddState(new StateEvade(this));
m_machine->AddState(new StateGetPowerup(this));
m_machine->AddState(new StateIdle(this));
m_machine->SetDefaultState(mApproach);


//setup for the script file parser
m_tokens.push_back(new TokenShipAggCD);
m_tokens.push_back(new TokenShipAggProx);
m_tokens.push_back(new TokenShipAgg);
m_tokens.push_back(new TokenShipAggCS);
m_tokens.push_back(new TokenEnemySeek);
m_tokens.push_back(new TokenPowerupSeek);
m_tokens.push_back(new TokenPowerupScanDist);
m_tokens.push_back(new TokenMaxSpeed);
m_tokens.push_back(new TokenApproachDist);
```

```
    m_tokens.push_back(new TokenAttackDist);
    m_tokens.push_back(new TokenSafeRadius);

    Reset();
}

//--------------------------------------------------------
void FSMAIControl::UpdatePerceptions(float dt)
{
    if(m_willCollide)
        m_safetyRadius = 2*m_safeRadius;
    else
        m_safetyRadius = m_safeRadius;

    //store closest asteroid and powerup
    m_nearestAsteroid = Game.GetClosestGameObj(m_ship,GameObj::OBJ_
            ASTEROID);
    m_nearestPowerup =
            Game.GetClosestGameObjICanReach(m_ship,GameObj::OBJ_POWERUP);
    m_nearestEnemy =
            Game.GetClosestGameObjICanReach(m_ship,GameObj::OBJ_SAUCER);

    //asteroid collision determination
    m_willCollide = false;
    if(m_nearestAsteroid)
    {
        float speed = m_ship->m_velocity.Length();
        m_nearestAsteroidDist =
                m_nearestAsteroid->m_position.Distance(m_ship->m_position);
        Point3f normDelta = m_nearestAsteroid->m_position -
                                m_ship->m_position;
        normDelta.Normalize();
        float astSpeed = m_nearestAsteroid->m_velocity.Length();
        float shpSpeedAdj = DOT(m_ship->UnitVectorVelocity(),normDelta)*speed;
        float astSpeedAdj = DOT(m_nearestAsteroid->UnitVectorVelocity(),
                                -normDelta)*astSpeed;
        speed = shpSpeedAdj+astSpeedAdj;
        float spdAdj = LERP(speed/m_maxSpeed,0.0f,90.0f);
        float adjSafetyRadius = m_safetyRadius+spdAdj +
                                m_nearestAsteroid->m_size;

        //if you're too close, and I'm heading somewhat towards you,
        //flag a collision
        if(m_nearestAsteroidDist <= adjSafetyRadius && speed > 0)
            m_willCollide = true;
    }
```

```
//enemy ship calculations
m_huntThresholdReached = false;
if(m_nearestEnemy && m_enemySeek)
{
  float distToEnemy =
      m_ship->m_position.Distance(m_nearestEnemy->m_position);
  if(!m_nearestAsteroid)//if there's no asteroids at all
      m_huntThresholdReached = true;
  else if(distToEnemy < m_shipAggressionCloseDistance)
  {
        )//if I'm really close anyways
      m_huntThresholdReached = true;
  }
  else if(m_nearestAsteroidDist - distToEnemy >
      m_shipAggressionProximity)
  {
  //if the saucer is much closer then any asteroid
      m_huntThresholdReached = true;
  }
  else
  {
    //if I just feel like attacking, roll dice between 0-99
    //ship has to roll positive "m_shipAggressionCountSetting"
    //number of times to trigger
    if(rand()*100 < m_shipAggression)
    {
      m_shipAggressionCount++;
      if(m_shipAggressionCount          >
        m_shipAggressionCountSetting)
            m_huntThresholdReached = true;
    }
    else
      m_shipAggressionCount = 0;
  }
}

  //powerup determinations
  m_powerupNear = false;
  if(m_nearestPowerup && m_powerupSeek)
  {
    m_nearestPowerupDist =
      m_nearestPowerup->m_position.Distance(m_ship->m_position);
```

```
        if(m_nearestPowerupDist <= m_powerupScanDist)
        {
            m_powerupNear      = true;
        }
    }
}
```

Listing 21.3 shows the `MachineApproach` implementation. This new state is actually another FSM. It has the initialization of a *state machine* (by allocating new state
members and adding each state to the machine structure), but also overrides a *state*
function, `CheckTransitions()`. This is because `MachineApproach` is used as a state
within the parent FSM inside of the `FSMAIController` class.

In this way, `MachineApproach` encapsulates the ship's goal to "approach" a potential target, be it a saucer or an asteroid. Targeting powerups may still be separate, but we could include the `GetPowerup` state within this FSM. However, getting a
powerup is really more of an episodic goal, as opposed to being a part of the overall
plan of positioning the ship in the best place to fire its gun, which is what `Machine-`
`Approach` is currently set up to do.

The reality is that there is no right answer; it all depends on how the engine
designer wants to organize the code in relation to the overall plan for the game
character's behavior. Grouping like states into sub-FSMs is a great way to keep a lot
of state transition checking out of the parent FSM (which can speed up the engine)
as well as making the AI code more structured and understandable. But poor or
inconsistent grouping of states can do the opposite, leading to confusing code and
inefficient CPU usage.

LISTING 21.3   `MachineApproach` implementation.

```
MachineApproach::MachineApproach(Control* parent):
FSMMachine(FSM_MACH_SHIPAPPROACH,FSM_STATE_MAPPR,parent)
{
    //make walls for hunt
    std::vector<WallSegment> walls;
    WallSegment temp;

    const int nside=18;
    for(int i=nside;i>0;i--)
    {
            Point3f start;
            Point3f end;
```

```
                          //the planet is centered at 512,512 and is PLANET_SIZE
                          start.Set(cos(float(i)*M_PI*2.0/nside)*PLANET_SIZE,
                              sin(float(i)*M_PI*2.0/nside)*PLANET_SIZE);
                          end.Set(cos(float(i-1)*M_PI*2.0/nside)*PLANET_SIZE,
                              sin(float(i-1)*M_PI*2.0/nside)*PLANET_SIZE);
                          start += Point3f(512,512,0);
                          end   += Point3f(512,512,0);
                          temp.Set(start,end);
                          walls.push_back(temp);
                }

        StateApproach* approach = new StateApproach(m_parent);
        AddState(approach);
        AddState(new StateHunt(m_parent,walls));
        AddState(new StateGotoBusySpot(m_parent));
        SetDefaultState(approach);
    }

    //----------------------------------------------------------
    int MachineApproach::CheckTransitions()
    {
        FSMAIControl* parent = (FSMAIControl*)m_parent;
        if(parent->m_willCollide)
                return FSM_STATE_EVADE;

        if(parent->m_powerupNear                                    &&
            (parent->m_nearestAsteroidDist > parent->m_nearestPowerupDist) &&
            parent->m_ship->GetShotLevel() < MAX_SHOT_LEVEL)
                return FSM_STATE_GETPOWERUP;

         if(!parent->m_nearestAsteroid ||
      parent->m_nearestAsteroidDist < APPROACH_DIST)
                return FSM_STATE_IDLE;

        return FSM_STATE_MAPPR;
    }
```

Next is Listing 21.4, which shows the StateHunt::Update() code. This state finds the *fastest unobstructed* route to the saucer, and will correctly use the world coordinate wrapping.

The *unobstructed* route goal is achieved by directly handing this state a list of all the walls within the game world, which in our case is only the planet. For larger game worlds, we would definitely not want to package up massive amounts of wall information and locally store it within the state. Instead, some kind of game world manager class should be constructed that each state could query when requiring information. But with only the single planetary wall, we can just pass in the small amount of data and have the state handle it directly.

In order to find the *fastest* route, the hunt state uses the `GameSession:` `:FindWrappedPoint()` function. What `FindWrappedPoint()` does is translate the point passed in to a *theoretical* game world that is offset from the current game world by the passed in parameters. This allows us to think about the game coordinate wrapping in a whole new way. In reality, when a game object passes the border of the game world, the code clips its position to the opposite side, which is what "wrapping" means.

But think of it another way: the ship has instead just left one game world and entered an identical game world (in fact, a perfect copy) stuck side by side with the first. Picture the "game universe" as a large, two-dimensional grid of repeating duplicate game worlds. How does this help? It allows the AI to make distance and angle checks across border boundaries. It allows the AI to steer towards targets that are beyond a warp point. In essence, the ship looks through a portal that allows it to see what is past the border, so that it can make intelligent decisions instead of blindly being affected by the border wrapping effect.

LISTING 21.4   `StateHunt::Update()` implementation.

```
//-----------------------------------------------------------
void StateHunt::Update(float dt)
{
   //turn and then thrust towards closest asteroid
   FSMAIControl* parent  = (FSMAIControl*)m_parent;
   GameObj* enemy        = parent->m_nearestEnemy;
   Ship* ship            = parent->m_ship;


   //find closest non-obstructed position (taking game world
   //wrapping into account)
   float bestDist = FLT_MAX;
   int bestX,bestY;
   Point3f enemyPosition = enemy->m_position;
   for(int i = -1; i < 2; i++)
   {
      for(int j = -1; j < 2; j++)
      {
         Point3f wrappedPosition = enemyPosition;
         Game.FindWrappedPoint(wrappedPosition,i,j);
```

```
        bool collision = false;
        for(int k = 0;k< m_walls.size(); k++)
        {
          //check for collisions first
          float lambda1 = 0.0f;
          float lambda2 = 0.0f;
          Point3f temp;
          LINEINTERSECT(ship->m_position,wrappedPosition,
            m_walls[k].m_point1,m_walls[k].m_point2,
            lambda1,lambda2, temp);
          //if the intersection was within the
      //line segments, we collided
          if ((lambda1 >= 0.0f && lambda1 <= 1.0f) &&
            (lambda2 >= 0.0f && lambda2 <= 1.0f))
          {
            collision = true;
            break;
          }
        }

        //don't use this direction if you run through a wall
        if(collision)
          continue;

        //find the closest direction of travel
        float thisDist = wrappedPosition.Distance(ship->m_position);
        if (thisDist < bestDist)
        {
          bestDist = thisDist;
          bestX = i;
          bestY = j;
        }
      }
    }
  }
  Game.FindWrappedPoint(enemyPosition,bestX,bestY);

  Point3f deltaPos = enemyPosition - ship->m_position;
  Point3f enemyVelocityNormalized = enemy->UnitVectorVelocity();

  //use braking vector if you're going too fast
  bool needToBrake = false;
  float speed  = ship->m_velocity.Length();
```

```
  if(speed > parent->m_maxSpeed)
  {
    needToBrake = true;
    deltaPos = -ship->m_velocity;
  }
  else
  {
    float dotVelocity = DOT(ship->UnitVectorVelocity(),
                           enemyVelocityNormalized);
    //if the other guy is "to my front"
//and we're moving towards each other...
    Point3f targetPos = enemyPosition;
    if ((DOT(deltaPos,ship->UnitVectorVelocity()) < 0) ||
      (dotVelocity > -0.93))//magic number == about 21 degrees
    {
      Point3f shipVel = ship->m_velocity;
      shipVel = shipVel.Normalize() * parent->m_maxSpeed;
      float combinedSpeed = (shipVel +
                           enemy->m_velocity).Length();
      float predictionTime = deltaPos.Length() / combinedSpeed;
      targetPos = enemyPosition +
                 (enemy->m_velocity*predictionTime);
      deltaPos = targetPos - ship->m_position;

      //don't clip in the hunt behavior, since we're more then
      //likely headed towards an offscreen coordinate
//    Game.Clip(deltaPos);
    }
  }
  //sub off our current velocity, to get direction of wanted velocity
  deltaPos -= ship->m_velocity;

  //find new direction, and head to it
  float newDir = CALCDIR(deltaPos);
  float angDelta = CLAMPDIR180(newDir - ship->m_angle);
  bool canApproachInReverse = needToBrake || ship->GetShotLevel()!=0;

  if(fabsf(angDelta) <3 || (fabst(angdelta) > 177 & canApproach
    InReverse))
  {

    //thrust
    ship->StopTurn();
```

```
        if(parent->m_nearestAsteroidDist >
        parent->m_nearestAsteroid->m_size + 20)
           fabsf(angDelta)<3? ship->ThrustOn() : ship->ThrustReverse();
        else
           ship->ThrustOff();
    }
    else if(fabsf(angDelta)<=90 || !canApproachInReverse)
    {
       //turn when facing forwards
         if(angDelta<0)
            ship->TurnRight();
         else if(angDelta>0)
            ship->TurnLeft();
    }
    else
    {
       //turn when facing rear
       if(angDelta>0)
          ship->TurnRight();
       else if(angDelta<0)
          ship->TurnLeft();
    }
    parent->m_target->m_position = enemy->m_position;
    parent->m_targetDir = newDir;
    parent->m_debugTxt = "Hunt";
}
```

Lastly, we come to the other new state created within the FSM portion of the code: `StateGotoBusySpot`. This state targets an asteroid in a nearby portion of the world that has an abundance of asteroids. An AI designer might want this behavior because ships heading towards high-concentration areas of asteroids will likely score more points faster. Imagine if the ship had limited fuel or time, and had to maximize its kills per unit of resources used. Other reasons to employ "busy spot style" behavior might include AI units in a real-time strategy game searching for the largest pile of gold to mine and bring back to the town, or AI-controlled ants that head in the direction of all their colleagues (hopefully, *one* of the ants is a more goal-directed leader, otherwise the ants might end up following each other in a big circle).

The actual workhorse of `StateGotoBusySpot` is a function within the `GameSession` class, `GetConcentricOccupanceGameObj()`. This function is shown in Listing 21.5. It uses an occupance tracking influence map to search for high concentrations of influence objects close to some other game object.

To utilize the function, it must be passed three values: the reference game object that we wish to find influence objects in proximity to, the minimum number of clustered influence objects to be considered "high concentration," and the max number of loops. This last parameter, maxLoops, is used by the function to determine how far out from the object to search within the influence map while trying to find an influence object. The function searches in a spiral pattern out from the position of the passed in object. A complete spiral around is one "loop." So, by taking into account the resolution of each influence cell, the AI programmer can limit the influence search by setting maxLoops to whatever value best suits his needs.

LISTING 21.5 GameSession:: GetConcentricOccupanceGameObj()implementation.

```
//-----------------------------------------------------------
GameObj* GameSession::GetConcentricOccupanceGameObj(GameObj* obj,
                        int thresholdValue,
                        int maxLoops)
{
  //go through the list, find the closest influence object
  //to the param "obj"
  float closeDist = 100000000.0f;
  GameObj* closeObj = NULL;

  Point3f objPos = obj->m_position;

  //first, find the nearby spot with the most influence objects
  int gridSizeX = m_oInfluenceMap->GetSizeX();
  int gridSizeY = m_oInfluenceMap->GetSizeY();
  int currentGridX,currentGridY;

  m_oInfluenceMap->ConvertPositionToGrid(objPos,currentGridX,
  currentGridY);

  //search variables
  int bestGridX, bestGridY, bestCount = -1;

  int numLoops = 0;
  bool goodEnough = false;
  do
  {

    //check spot immediately to my left
    currentGridX--;
```

```
int zoneCount =
  m_oInfluenceMap->GetInfluenceValue(currentGridX,currentGridY);
if(zoneCount)
{
   bestGridX = currentGridX;
   bestGridY = currentGridY;
   bestCount = zoneCount;
}
//now start the spiral around
//go up
for(int i = 0;i<numLoops*2+1; i++)
{
   currentGridY++;
   int zoneCount =
m_oInfluenceMap->GetInfluenceValue(currentGridX,currentGridY);
   if(zoneCount)
   {
      bestGridX = currentGridX;
      bestGridY = currentGridY;
      bestCount = zoneCount;
   }
}
//go right
for(int i = 0;i<numLoops*2; i++)
{
   currentGridX++;
   int zoneCount =
m_oInfluenceMap->GetInfluenceValue(currentGridX,currentGridY);
   if(zoneCount)
   {
      bestGridX = currentGridX;
      bestGridY = currentGridY;
      bestCount = zoneCount;
   }
}
//go down
for(int i = 0;i<numLoops*2; i++)
{
   currentGridY--;
   int zoneCount =
m_oInfluenceMap->GetInfluenceValue(currentGridX,currentGridY);
   if(zoneCount)
   {
      bestGridX = currentGridX;
```

```
        bestGridY = currentGridY;
        bestCount = zoneCount;
      }
    }
    //go left
    for(int i = 0;i<numLoops*2; i++)
    for(int i = 0;i
    {
      currentGridX--;
      int zoneCount =
m_oInfluenceMap->GetInfluenceValue(currentGridX,currentGridY);
      if(zoneCount)
      {
        bestGridX = currentGridX;
        bestGridY = currentGridY;
        bestCount = zoneCount;
      }
    }

  if(bestCount > thresholdValue)
      goodEnough = true;
}while (numLoops < maxLoops || goodEnough);

GameObjectList::iterator list1;
for(list1=m_activeObj.begin();list1!=m_activeObj.end();++list1)
{
  //watch out for yourself
  GameObj* gameObj = (*list1);
  if(gameObj == obj)
    continue;

  //only consider objects that are "influence" objects
  //that are in the closest busiest zone (as found above)
  if(gameObj->m_influence)
    continue;
  int gridX,gridY;
  m_oInfluenceMap->ConvertPositionToGrid(gameObj->m_position,
                    gridX,gridY);
  if(gridX != bestGridX || gridY != bestGridY)
    continue;

  //our "distance apart" should take into account our size
  float combindedSize = gameObj->m_size + obj->m_size;
  float dist = gameObj->m_position.Distance(obj->m_position) -
                    combindedSize;
```

```
    if(dist < closeDist)
    {
      closeDist = dist;
      closeObj = gameObj;
    }
  }
  return closeObj;

}
```

STEERING CHANGES

Now, we'll go over the major changes that were made to facilitate the implementation of a steering behavior-controlled saucer within the game demo. There were changes to the control class: we added a new behavior, and an overall modification of the saucer to make it more of a defense-based character instead of the ruthless killer that it was in earlier demos.

In Listing 21.6, we can see some of the key changes made in the SteeringControl class. The constructor sets up walls, which correspond to the outline of the planet; the saucer then uses the wall avoidance behavior to avoid running straight into the planet. The AvoidWalls function provides what is called *general object avoidance,* or GOA. GOA can be a difficult problem, and a full treatise on how to handle all forms of GOA could take up an entire book on its own. Needless to say, there are many other (much better and more optimized) methods to do GOA. Some of them include:

- Utilize a "contains walls" setting within each game object, and then define the bounding walls for a given object within its own code. This hides the inner details of the game object from the manager class, leading to greater abstraction and cleaner engine code. It also allows each game object to exactly define its shape using as many walls as necessary. Because this method isn't optimized for speed, however, the more walls the behavior uses to define its shape, the slower its behavior updates will become.
- If all the game objects involved in avoidance are regularly shaped, or can be surrounded by regularly-shaped collision surfaces (usually, people use cylinders that surround the game objects), a classical obstacle avoidance steering behavior will probably suffice. The obstacle avoidance behavior, created by Reynolds, uses a collision box projected out the front of the moving object. As this box collides with the collision cylinders of the obstacles, it deflects the ship. This isn't much different from the way that AvoidWalls works (it also works best with non-moving obstacles, just like AvoidWalls), but it is much

more optimized, since it's assuming cylinder-shaped obstacles and a collision box instead of the sensors that AvoidWalls uses. Another Reynolds behavior, unaligned collision avoidance, is more useful when the obstacles involved are moving.

■ If the game has many *static* obstacles, meaning ones that never move during the course of the game, a technique called *flow fields* (mentioned briefly in the steering chapter under *extensions*) can be used. A flow field is a data structure that stores the amount and direction of steering force that a steering-controlled object would have applied to it simply by residing at any given spot on the map. Think of flow fields as a topographic map, with each of the obstacles being mountain peaks and the space between the obstacles as valleys. Flow fields can be auto-generated by having a program mark a map with maximum repelling forces directly around each obstacle, slowly lowering the force in a radiating pattern as it marks the map farther away from the obstacle. Multiple obstacles within close proximity of each other would have an additive effect on the overall repulsion force. In this way, characters would be auto-repelled from obstacles, because the ground around each obstacle is covered with the strongest repulsion forces. This is also very low cost from a CPU perspective as an avoidance technique, since it involves simple addition of the flow-field vector to the player velocity wherever the player is on the game map, with no repulsion calculations necessary during runtime. This is what's called "offline AI data." All of this information is processed before the game ever runs. The cost is the memory necessary to store all the flow-field data.

LISTING 21.6   Important SteeringControl implementation differences.

```
//----------------------------------------------------------
SteeringControl::SteeringControl(Ship* ship):
AIControl(ship)
{
  m_getPowerupIndex = -1;

  //make walls for avoidWall
  std::vector<WallSegment> walls;
  WallSegment temp;

  const int nside=18;
  for(int i=nside;i>0;i--)
  {
    Point3f start;
    Point3f end;
```

```
        //the planet is centered at 512,512 and is PLANET_SIZE
        start.Set( cos(float(i)*M_PI*2.0/nside)*PLANET_SIZE,
                sin(float(i)*M_PI*2.0/nside)*PLANET_SIZE);
        end.Set( cos(float(i-1)*M_PI*2.0/nside)*PLANET_SIZE,
                sin(float(i-1)*M_PI*2.0/nside)*PLANET_SIZE);
        start += Point3f(512,512,0);
        end   += Point3f(512,512,0);
        temp.Set(start,end);
        walls.push_back(temp);
    }

    //construct the steering manager and add the necessary behaviors
    m_behaviorManager = new SteeringBehaviorManager(this);
    m_behaviorManager->AddBehavior(new SteerEvade(this,
                      GameObj::OBJ_ASTEROID));
    m_behaviorManager->AddBehavior(new SteerAvoidWall(this,walls));
    m_behaviorManager->AddBehavior(new SteerUseCover(this,GameObj::OBJ_
      PLANET,
                      GameObj::OBJ_SHIP));
    m_behaviorManager->AddBehavior(new SteerPursuit(this,
                      GameObj::OBJ_POWERUP));
    m_getPowerupIndex = 3;
    m_behaviorManager->AddBehavior(new SteerAvoidBorder(this));
    m_behaviorManager->AddBehavior(new SteerArrive(this,
                      GameObj::OBJ_ASTEROID));
    m_behaviorManager->Reset();

    //this is where we'll initialize all the weights
    //and probability values for the behaviors
    m_behaviorManager->SetupBehavior(0,3.5f,1.0f);//evade asteroid
    m_behaviorManager->SetupBehavior(1,3.0f,1.0f);//avoid wall
    m_behaviorManager->SetupBehavior(2,4.0f,1.0f);//use cover
    m_behaviorManager->SetupBehavior(3,3.0f,1.0f);//pursue powerup
    m_behaviorManager->SetupBehavior(4,5.0f,1.0f);//avoid border
    m_behaviorManager->SetupBehavior(5,1.0f,1.0f);//arrive asteroid
}
```

Also, note the radically different weights used by the saucer with this new mix of behaviors. Setting the weights for a complex steering-controlled character can be one of the most time consuming parts of using steering behaviors. In fact, the six behaviors the saucer is using are almost approaching the limit of what should be attempted within a straight steering-controlled character. While watching the demo run, it might appear that the saucer's behaviors aren't as purposeful or direct as in the straight steering demo from the steering chapter. This is because the saucer has more behaviors fighting for overall control of its travel direction, and the result can become muddied very quickly.

The saucer now employs a new `UseCover` behavior, which uses the planet as an interposed obstacle so that the ship can't directly attack. Notice that the `UseCover` behavior takes the type of object to use as cover. This allows the behavior to be much more reusable. If another type of game object was ever added to game that the saucer could also use as cover, simply adding this flag to the `AddBehavior` call for the `SteerUseCover` behavior would automatically use the new object for cover determination. Listing 21.7 shows the Update function for the `UseCover` behavior. Notice that the object types that the saucer considers for cover as well as enemies are both parameterized for further control of the behavior. By simply changing these parameters, an AI designer could use this behavior to create a character that moves around the world finding umbrellas to get shade from the sun (cover is the umbrellas, enemy is the sun), or remoras that cling to a shark while still watching out for nearby danger from other fish (cover is the shark, enemies are the other fish).

LISTING 21.7 `SteerUseCover::Update()` function.

```
//----------------------------------------------------------
bool SteerUseCover::Update(float dt,Point3f& totalForce)
{
  bool adjustment = false;

  SteeringControl* parent = (SteeringControl*)m_parent;
  Ship*            ship = parent->m_ship;

  GameObj* nearestEnemy = Game.GetClosestGameObj(ship,m_enemyTypes);
  GameObj* nearestCoverObject = Game.GetClosestGameObj
    (ship,m_coverTypes);
  if(nearestCoverObject && nearestEnemy)
  {

    float distanceToEnemy =
        nearestEnemy->m_position.Distance(ship->m_position);
    Point3f enemyVecToMe   = ship->m_position -
        nearestEnemy->m_position;
    Point3f enemyVecToCover = nearestCoverObject->m_position -
        nearestEnemy->m_position;
    float coverOffset = 55.0f;
    float distToCoverSpot = enemyVecToCover.Length() +
        nearestCoverObject->m_size +
        coverOffset;
    enemyVecToCover.Normalize();
```

```
      m_locationOfCover = enemyVecToCover*distToCoverSpot +
          nearestEnemy->m_position;
      float shipDistToCover =
          m_locationOfCover.Distance(ship->m_position);
      Point3f shipToCover = m_locationOfCover - ship->m_position;
      shipToCover.Normalize();

      if(shipDistToCover > 0 && distanceToEnemy < COVER_DIST)
      {
        float speed = m_parent->m_ship->m_maxSpeed *
          (shipDistToCover/ AI_MAX_SPEED_TRY);
        speed = MIN(speed, m_parent->m_ship->m_maxSpeed);
        shipToCover *= speed;

        //scale force as distance from enemy goes down,
        //will potentially double force if enemy is close
        float distScale = 2.0f - (distanceToEnemy/(COVER_DIST/2));
        shipToCover *= distScale;

        if (shipToCover.Length())
        {
          totalForce += shipToCover -
                    m_parent->m_ship->m_velocity;
          adjustment = true;
        }
      }
    }
    return adjustment;
  }
```

PERFORMANCE OF THE AI WITH THIS SYSTEM

In earlier chapters, the overall "performance" of the AI was mostly measured by how well the AI-controlled ship did at scoring points by shooting asteroids, as well as general survivability. But for this chapter, different rates of performance will be discussed.

1. How well does the AI engine perform in solving all the numerous challenges put to it?

   Combined AI engines, by definition, should be able to handle any AI problem that occurs. The reason for going with a combination AI system in the first place is to provide the flexibility to structure AI decision making in many different ways, such that any AI problem definition can be handled in stride by the best tool for the job.

Think of combination systems as having what a stock broker would call *portfolio diversification*. The engine isn't married to a single AI method so deeply that the AI programmer has to do back flips trying to fit an unusual special-case feature or an odd behavior requirement into a rigid, single decision-making structure. Rather, since the technology present in the game represents several ways of breaking down problems, as well as different ways of delivering answers, the programmer can be assured that if one method doesn't quite work for a particular issue that might come up late in the development schedule, another will.

If the scope of the game being developed is completely known up front, with all AI challenges known and accounted for, then system requirements can be accounted for directly, and will not require this kind of *hedging of bets* with the engine design. But within game programming, focus testing and overall "fun factor" issues generally don't lend themselves well to total pre-planning. After a new feature or AI behavior is created and in the game, actual people playing it almost always uncovers elements that could be tweaked or outright changed in order to make the game more entertaining. The AI engine should have enough wiggle room in the way it handles the decision structure of AI-controlled elements so that it can handle strange new features late in the development cycle. Otherwise, the game could be stuck with either a sub-par feature or the programmer could be stuck with a lengthy code-reworking scenario.

However, you shouldn't just "kitchen sink" the AI engine. Although the demo in this chapter *is* doing this by somewhat randomly including elements that aren't really necessary, this is a demo, not a real game. In real life, each AI method included within the game engine has a number of costs: initial implementation time, CPU time, maintenance time, potential memory requirements, and even some very esoteric things (like potentially making the code too large to fit into the main processor's program cache, for instance). Don't include technology just to include it. Rather, have a specific reason why the AI method needs to be there.

2. Was the creation of new AI elements within the asteroids game demo eased by having all of these additional AI methods within reach?

The creation of new AI solutions should be vastly eased by combination engines. If the right amount and types of AI technology has been included in the AI engine by a programmer who gave careful thought to the types of decisions that the game would require, the people that were going to be involved in it's creation, and all of the other host of factors, then actually implementing the game within the AI engine should technically be easy.

Of course, the length of the development cycle and/or the personnel available might not allow the engine programmer to have the best possible technology for the requirements, so this isn't always true. But one of the main reasons that an AI engine designer should pick a particular AI technique is because that technique represents the easiest way to create the code structure necessary to provide the AI characters with the types of intelligent decision making the game requires.

3. Finally, is the extra engine complexity costing more than it's worth?

Employing a combination of AI techniques should only be considered if it will buy the project significantly more than it will cost. If it turns out that the resource costs of any part of a combination engine (in any category: performance, memory, implementation time, or ease of creation/debugging) are too great, then the overall AI engine strategy needs to be adjusted. The only reason to bring additional technology into the AI system is if the game design has a specific need for it, or if using it could allow a vast improvement in both present and/or future development.

If the engine is working flawlessly, but switching to a data-driven model in certain areas would open the door for user-created content, then it might be a good idea. Just make sure the schedule allows for the time it would require to do the work, and that there are people out there that would *want* to add content to the game. An established game with a rabid following and plenty of community forums, where users are constantly asking for level editors and the like is one thing. The decision to add user content features would almost be obvious. But a new game franchise, with a very unique game play feel, should probably engage in plenty of focus testing with potential buyers to find out if there would be enough interest to warrant the extra work.

Also, be wary of new technology being added to the AI engine simply because it's new technology. There's plenty of marketing hype around things like "physics-driven animation" and "AI learning," but there are also good reasons why these things haven't been used in games yet. The technology behind both of these examples isn't new, and yet both are only used in the occasional game, and even then in mild, very controlled areas.

The reason behind both physics and learning not being ubiquitous to game development (as of 2008) is that both technologies require enormous quantities of time to develop, both in initial implementation as well as tuning and debugging. Yes, use of physics and learning are both ways that games could be made much more realistically responsive to interaction with the human player, but both are *highly* complex areas of analysis.

The physics of human physiology and the methods used to learn from outside stimulus couldn't be more different. But what *they do* have in common is this: both are orders of magnitude more complicated then people think. It is precisely this "illusion of simplicity" that makes systems like these attractive *and* dangerous. Game players see something happen in a video game and think "If only they'd use physics, the game would look so much better during these circumstances." Even professional game developers have been guilty of this. The problem is, almost nobody takes into account all the liberties that game programmers employ when creating game simulations in the first place.

Game characters sometimes perform impossible movements within the game purely because these movements *feel* right; they *feel* fun. Characters might move twice as fast as a real human, or turn around much faster than in real life. These are not the shortcuts taken to make up for missing animations or just bad programming. The elements discussed here are those liberties being taken by game characters *specifically because* of what they have positively added to the control, feel, and/or balance of the game play. But add in some real-life physics, and things can go awry in a hurry. Suddenly, those moves that used to make the game play fun break the physics simulations because of the super-human speeds, which can lead to some surprisingly bad reactions by the physics system. To try and remedy these bad physical reactions, the animations in question are reworked to play better with the vagaries of the physics engine. The question now is: has the game improved? Or did the programmers remove something that *was* fun, and replace it with a piece of technology that isn't fun, just better looking?

Don't get the wrong idea, some physics-based animation can help; animation transitions especially seem to be a promising area in which games have begun to make progress. The Madden NFL team has spent many years trying to use physics methods to help create more realistic player movement. Interviews with EA published in late 2008 tell of the monumental investment in animator time necessary to eke out even a small bit of help from physics-helped transitions. The old adage will always hold true: Hard work will create quality. The real winner in this case is not physics transitions, it is EA's realization of the care necessary to make animation transitions as smooth and responsive as possible.

Learning is also a developer "black hole." Many games have tried to include adaptive AI that react to the player over time. Almost every title to include even a modicum of learning has had strange results and plenty of community chatter concerning astronomically stupid behavior out of the AI system because of the strange ways that the AI "learned" to behave given a particular set of circumstances.

The reality is, most people assume that the only intelligent agent in the universe is the person they see in the mirror. If the game doesn't react *exactly* like the person would, it's dumb. Even if the game makes 10,000 good decisions in a row, but subtly blows number 10,001, it's stupid. Blurting out statements like "I can't believe the AI hasn't figured out what I'm doing yet," when the player is performing a twenty-three-step process to break down an AI learning system, is almost hilarious if it wasn't so tragically inevitable. Remember, too, that this is for a game in which the learning element is somewhat "working," like a sports game that determines where the player likes to score from and responds with more defense in that area. Games with more open-ended learning, like *Black & White*, have thousands of Web pages of personal experiences recanted by people who have witnessed the AI doing actions of such vastly inexplicable wrongness that some of these behaviors border on the insane.

An argument from the other side of these features is that although the features *seem* simple, most people don't realize *all* the costs associated with adding them. Simply saying "Let's add physics to our game" is a huge cost outlay. Yes, the person making that decision might be aware that there will have to be code created to simulate the physics, that the animation system will also need to be modified so that the characters can employ physics reactions, that new art will need to be created to back up this code, but how about the *second level* of costs? These would include things not directly accounted for. The code to run the physics might be large, taking up lots of memory, and potentially even more CPU time since physics calculations are typically complex and math heavy to perform. Debugging the way that physics affects the game might spiral into a never ending chore, as more and more special cases have to be added in order for the algorithmic physics system to allow for "fun factor" issues that require temporary breaking of the physics rules. Does your game have a number of different "modes" of play, in which the user could potentially change the game play environment enough (levels with "low gravity," or suspended normal game rules) that the physics might need to be separately tuned?

Combination systems are an invaluable, almost inevitable facet of AI programming. Very few games will have so few AI requirements that only state machines (or any other singular technique) will suffice to solve everything. Learning which methods work well together, and how to blend different AI tools into an overall engine is one of the things every AI programmer must learn well.

Learning how to combine AI methods into large-scale AI engines helps programmers learn one of the most important things to remember about AI engine programming: *Modularity* is a good thing. Suppose a single technique is used to solve every AI problem within a game. Later on, a particular feature comes up that calls for a behavior that can't be modeled by the current system. The base technique must be added to, or potentially changed. Even if the change is largely secondary, there is still a risk of causing changes to suddenly spring up in every area of the AI, since the whole system is using the same base code. With a more modular approach, this can be somewhat minimized, since the combination engine was most likely created with different AI classes working well together, and as such, creating a coding environment where feature changes only infect the smaller "module" of code that controls the features directly, not the entire game. Modularity also helps partition AI tasking amongst programmers, since it uncovers clear dividing lines in the code that are usually in line with features.

Now, if two features being implemented by separate programmers only require state machines, both programmers should use state machines. But maybe both of those tasks could be taken over by one of the programmers, and another AI task that involved a completely different system could be given to the second. This does two things: It keeps the two programmers from stepping on each other's toes as they implement the state-based behaviors (each programmer might have different ideas on how to use FSMs, or go off and extend the game's FSM code in similar, slightly different ways), and it also fosters code ownership by giving more clearly defined job duties to each programmer. Programmer One might start to get not only more comfortable with state-based behavior, but develop several extensions to the code base that wouldn't have occurred to the programmer if programming tasks were more varied. Plus, Programmer Two can potentially learn an entirely new AI technique and bring something wholly different to the game engine.

EXTENSIONS TO THE PARADIGM

The techniques used in the game demo were in no way exploited exhaustively. There are many ways in which even the simple demo could have taken advantage of the AI methods used. Below we will uncover some of the additional ways in which each technique might have been employed.

FSMS

Finite state machines are such a flexible technology that the list of things that could have been done is near limitless. A few of the more obvious include:

- *Game State.* The GameSession class currently handles the main "game state" very loosely. The class keeps an m_state variable, and anybody that cares about the specific game state accesses it directly to handle the behavior for each game state. This is mainly the GameSession::Draw() function, the HumanControl class, and the main loop inside of asteroids.cpp. Instead, the whole thing could be a formal FSM, run by the GameSession class or directly from the main AIsteroids application. Each game state would be encapsulated into its own state class, handling updates, drawing, and all the other state-specific behavior directly.
- *Behavior.* Currently the AI-controlled ships behave in a single, particular way. It could be said that the spacecraft are "single-minded," in that they'll never make sudden radical changes in behavior. If this was something the game design required, however, one technique used frequently with game characters is to have several "modes" of overall behavior for any given character, with the ability to switch modes as necessary. In this way, you can tune these modes in isolation

to each other, and not have to try and create one, overarching game entity that does everything. So, even for the saucer, which is currently being controlled by steering behaviors, we could define a number of "modes" (or states) where the mixture of weights for each of the individual steering behaviors could be radically different. In fact, individual states could include several steering behaviors in the mix that weren't used at all under other circumstances. The saucer would still be controlled by a parent `SteeringControl`. But the mixture of behaviors would be controlled by an FSM that would change out the particular `SteeringBehaviorManager` being used by the parent, and thus the different steering behaviors and their weights.

STEERING

Even within the simple arena of AIsteroids, we could have used steering behaviors to a greater degree. A couple of ideas would involve:

- *Indigenous Life.* The game world could include "indigenous life," like the animals walking around in *Age of Empires.* Since we have an open, outer space environment, steering would have been a lovely way to add some cheap swarms of flocking alien "bugs" that could roam around the map, maybe eating power-erups and scattering from ships and asteroids. Whole ecosystems of autonomous creatures could be created that prey off the objects in the game world, or even each other. These simple to create creatures would really make the simple asteroids world come alive, and give a much more organic feel to the demo than the fairly robotic behavior of the two ships.
- *Weapon Types.* New weapon types could be created, other than the simple `Bullet` objects currently being used. The bullets in the demo are simple physics objects; with have a velocity, a current direction, and a maximum life time. But a more complex weapon could be a type of smart missile that would seek out local targets using steering behaviors. These types of weapons could be used by anybody, even the FSM controlled ship, since the steering code would be used by the proposed `SmartMissle` class, not the ship itself.

INFLUENCE MAPPING

The game demo makes one use of influence mapping techniques, by employing an occupance map to make approach decisions. A few IM techniques could really make our demo shine:

- *IM Use.* Instead of the generic offense and defense behaviors exhibited by our current ship and saucer, the demo could start to look more like a real war if the behaviors used by the ship and saucer were to make heavy IM use. Both characters could rely on a control-based IM to make many decisions. The different craft would specifically look for asteroid targets within their own area of control, making it more difficult to be caught off guard while defending themselves from incoming asteroids. Evasion of the opposite craft could be made more intelligent by keeping track of "front lines" caused by two opposite character's control cancelling out and forming areas of zero control.

■   *IM Types*. New IM types could be created to give the AI characters even more battle intelligence. A special IM could track where each ship has made its kills, informing the enemy of where to lurk or set traps. If the saucer was using a flow-field behavior to avoid the planet (instead of the `AvoidWalls` behavior it's using currently) then another IM could track asteroid paths and use this data to affect the flow field for all the asteroids, giving the saucer general obstacle avoidance as well as wall avoidance.

SCRIPTING

Scripting is another completely open-ended AI technique. The demo barely scratches the surface of possible uses for scripting. Some additional uses would be:

■   *Story Elements*. Story elements could be added to the demo. Characters could be created that the player would interact with (through some kind of communication interface) for trade, or story progression. What these story characters say, as well as do, could be controlled directly by scripted behaviors. An FSM could be written that would take scripts as input and set up whole state machines based on the parameters in the script. The scripts could also contain dialogue for the characters, in the form of conversation-pair trees that a dialogue system could use (the first part of a conversation pair would be some comment to show the human player, the second would be a list of responses the player could choose. Each response would have its own resulting conversation pair, creating a conversation tree; see Figure 21.1).

■   *Space-bound Anomalies*. Since the game is set in outer space, we could allow for a number of simple space-bound anomalies that might drift through space, wander around, or some other simple behavior. These lightweight objects could be spawned by a game script that would give the number of each object, it's range of starting locations, speeds, and behaviors, as well as how often to appear. Even non-lightweight objects could be specified by these types of scripts, creating what amounts to level files for the asteroids demo. At key places or times in the game, the script would cause an instantiation of some game object that would then be controlled by some generic handler. In this way, Galaga-style scripted waves of enemies could be created and controlled.

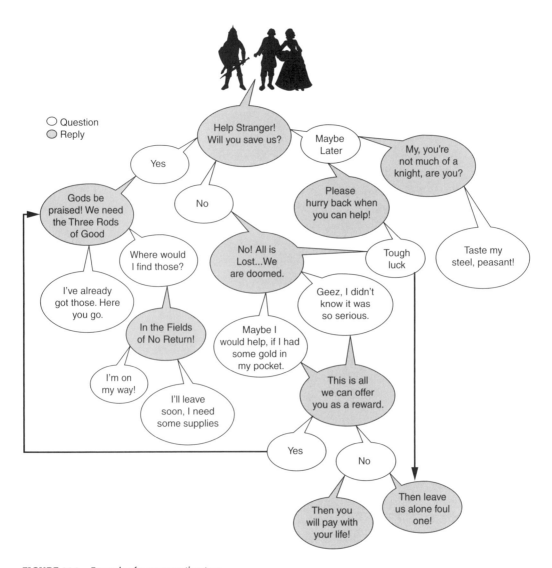

FIGURE 21.1   Example of a conversation tree.

MESSAGING

Another basic AI method, messaging could be used in a vast array of ways within the asteroids demo. A few key examples might be:

■ *Multiplayer Coding.* The great thing about messaging is that the objects involved generally don't know the origin of the message. Its job is to decouple chunks of code. So why not completely remove all connection? Since we have the messaging system within the game, we could easily set up a network layer, and start passing messages back and forth across a network, in effect creating a multiplayer version of the demo for people to play against each other on separate machines. Now, there's a lot more to multiplayer coding then just some messaging, but this is where to start. If the AI entities in the game are already sending and receiving a steady stream of messages, then the system is that much closer to being ready to try and make the full jump to networkable game objects.

- *Callback Handler.* Currently, the game has extensive polling within the `GameSession` class. It's checking to see if the ship and saucer have been killed off, and respawning each if so. It creates an occasional new powerup when a timer expires. It checks to see if the current wave of asteroids is over and updates the game state. Each of these small tasks could be handled much more efficiently with a callback handler and an correctly used message. When a ship dies, it could broadcast a death message that could be consumed by the `GameSession` class to handle respawning. The occasional powerups could be automatically done by a handler listening for a repeating message that has some set timer that expires every so often. When the final asteroid blows up, it could send a message that there weren't anymore. Even better, each exploding asteroid could broadcast a message of its death, and the `GameSession` object would update the number of asteroids left. In this way, additional data could be hidden to the individual asteroid game objects, instead of allowing access to all the `GameSession` data members as is currently the case.

SUMMARY

Combination systems are essentially the way that most game AI engines are written. Few and far between are the modern games that require only a single AI method for all their AI requirements. Recognizing that parts of the game being developed would be well aided by a carefully chosen piece of AI technology, and knowing how to wed that technology with the current system is the name of the game as far as large scale, complex AI engines are concerned. In this chapter, we showed that even within the microcosm of the AIsteroids demo, many different AI methods can be employed successfully and purposefully.

- The demo used in this chapter combined a number of AI methods into one large demo. These included a finite state machine, a hierarchical FSM, steering behaviors, an occupance-tracking influence map, a messaging system, and a simple script loader.
- The AI elements involved in the demo included an FSM-controlled ship, a steering controlled saucer, a new static Planet game element, and a number of

new state and steering behaviors. There is also an occupance-based IM running that is tracking the asteroids, and a scripting system that loads a number of game parameters on demand.

■ The `GameSession` class was augmented to make it more abstract in regards to AI controllers, as well as making allowances for the other demo codes it handles, like the message pump and the influence map.

■ The FSM used in the demo that controls the ship employs the script loader to initialize a number of parameters that it passes to its individual states.

■ The ship's approach behavior has been upgraded to a full FSM on its own, with a new border-aware hunt behavior, as well as an IM using `GotoBusySpot` state, in addition to the old `StateApproach` class.

■ The steering code has had changes made to it for the demo. The `AvoidWalls` behavior is being used to steer around the planet (there are other ways of doing this; a few were discussed). The overall mix of specific behaviors and their corresponding weights were adjusted so that the personality of the saucer allows it to attack only if approached by the ship; it will not seek out the ship. In fact, it consciously avoids the ship using a new steering behavior—`SteerUseCover`.

■ Combined AI engines, by definition, should be able to handle any AI problem that arises.

■ The creation of new AI solutions should be vastly eased by combination engines.

■ Employing a combination of AI techniques should only be considered if it will buy the project something significantly more than what it will cost.

■ FSMs could have been used within the demo to control the overall game state, as well as provide the saucer with an easy way to switch between radically different behavior sets.

■ Steering behaviors could have been employed to easily create indigenous life or new weapon types within the demo.

■ Use of other types of influence maps could have radically improved the behavior of both AI-controlled craft.

■ Scripting could control story elements and dialogue trees, as well as spawn game characters directly to make levels of patterned enemies.

■ The message system could be used as the start of a full multiplayer system within the game, as well as provide the game with a way to rid itself of much of the polling going on within the manager game objects by using messaging and callbacks instead.

22 Genetic Algorithms

In This Chapter

- Overview
- Basic Genetic Method
- Representing the Problem
- Implementing a Genetic Algorithm System into the AIsteroids Test Bed
- Performance Within the Test Bed
- Extensions to the Paradigm
- Design Considerations
- Summary

Sometimes, we face AI problems that defy solving, either because of computational difficulty, or simply because there isn't enough time. These problems have too many possible responses, or too many incoming variables to consider. It's always *possible* that a solution could be found, but only after many, perhaps hundreds or thousands, of programming iterations involving manually trying different avenues in a hunt for the best algorithm.

As an example, consider having to tune the performance parameters for the physics simulation used by each car in *Gran Turismo 4*. With more than five hundred vehicles and dozens of tweakable settings for each intricate piece of a car's handling system being simulated, this would truly be a daunting task for any company to accomplish (at least, within any reasonable time and monetary budget), especially if the goal was to accurately depict the real-life performance of each car.

OVERVIEW

In this chapter, we will cover a class of AI techniques called genetic algorithms (or GAs) that take lessons learned from evolutionary science to try and find novel solutions to these kinds of problems. We will cover the basic method by discussing the

513

natural model, and then show how the model can be applied to our game problems. A basic, general-case GA class will then be detailed and implemented into the AIsteroids test bed for illustration.

EVOLUTION IN NATURE

GA techniques try to use the principle of evolution, normally found in natural systems, to search for solutions to algorithmic problems. The process in nature works roughly like this:

- To survive as a species, all living creatures need to be able to reproduce. Reproduction is (heavily simplified) simply executing the encoded rules necessary to build an organism. These rules are stored in strings of DNA (made up of proteins) called *chromosomes*, which are found in every cell that makes up a living being.
- Chromosomes are in turn made up of small, modular protein sequences called *genes*, which are various permutations of the four basic proteins: thymine, adenine, cytosine, and guanine (or T, A, C, and G, respectively). Each gene holds information about the "settings," or *alleles*, of a particular trait (or number of traits, as each gene is usually linked to more than one trait within a body).
- In most complex organisms, when two parents reproduce, their DNA is split. Half the DNA of the child comes from one parent, and half from the other. This is called *crossover* or *genetic recombination*.
- Genetic crossover results in a new mixture of genetic traits that are passed on to the offspring. If this new mixture of traits is good, the offspring will have a full life and be able to reproduce as well, again passing on at least half of his or her traits to future generations. If, however, the child inherits weak or even bad traits, the offspring may not survive long, or even be able to reproduce at all (either because of biological reasons, such as infertility, or social reasons, in that it is not a desirable mate). Over many generations, the trend of organisms with a better mix of traits being more likely to reproduce, and creatures with bad gene mixes being starved out of the overall pool (and thus removing their genes), leads societies of creatures to evolve toward the genetically superior version of their species. The quality measure of any one creature's mix of traits is called its *fitness*, and the higher the fitness value, the better that creature is at applying its traits to the world, both in performance and reproductively.
- In human terms, a highly successful man might still lose out in the race because his all-encompassing drive to perform well in the working world might make him unavailable to have children and pass on his genes. Thus, both areas (performance and reproduction) need to be expressed for the traits to move forward.

- Occasionally, a flaw happens in this system (although whether this "flaw" process might be an integral component built into the system is often debated). A gene within a child organism is somehow different so that it is completely new and cannot be traced to one of its parents. The gene is replicated incorrectly, a chemical imbalance occurs during fertilization, or any number of things; we do not know all the causes at this time. When this happens, it is called a *mutation*, and the results are that the allele of the particular gene are now random, with random effects in the organism. In most cases, this results in negative traits. A bird is born with wings that are too short to fly, a tree sloth is born with a large brown spot on its head (and thus no other sloths will mate with it), or a monkey can hear very high wavelength sounds and goes insane from all the nighttime chatter.

- But sometimes, this mutation results in the offspring having traits that make it *better* at performing within its environment, which in some way makes it more likely to reproduce. When this happens, this mutated gene is more likely to be passed on to other generations through reproduction, and on and on.

- Thus, the "survival of the fittest" paradigm gradually changes the set of traits (called a *genome*) that the species contains on average toward the ideal set, which represents the most adapted genes for the particular creature in its current environment conditions.

EVOLUTION IN GAMES

So what does all this offer to our game AI? This evolutionary algorithm can be implemented within the confines of our game worlds and be used to tune behaviors, parameters, etc. for areas of gameplay that would take far too long to iteratively hand tune. The process can be thought of as "evolutionary search," in that we are still searching across the field of all the possible solutions to a given game problem, but we are going to use a method of searching that is likened to the process of evolution through genetic fitness.

The method is split into two unequal halves: evolving a solution, and using the solution. Typically, using the information gleaned from a genetic algorithm in the final game is a "black box" operation. This is a magic box that makes the particular problem behavior act in the best way possible (or in the best way possible you were able to find). The internals of how the black box works is most times not readily discernable to an outside observer. This isn't always the case, but the nature of complex problems and the abstracted solution found by the particular genetic algorithm are usually convoluted enough that they prevent dissection.

Evolving the solution is thus almost all the work, and this process is usually performed during the production of the game. Very few games actually go out the door with the evolving parts of their genetic algorithms still turned on. Some notable exceptions to this, where learning was one of the central tenets of the game, include the *Creatures* series, and *Black & White*. But the learning components of even these games are very closely monitored; the traits and behaviors that are being influenced by the learning elements are constructed in such a way that they constrain the learning or genetic elements, so that the learning or evolution is as tightly controlled as can be. The nature of these games also fosters unpredictability in the AI character's actions, so that the player will allow for some degree of leeway to be granted for stupid or inappropriate behavior by the AI.

GAs have tended to be computationally expensive (this process can take a good deal of time because you are forced to run many, many generations on a large population of possibilities), which made using them a costly choice in the past—one of the reasons that the evolutionary work is mostly done offline. Increasing performance of the average computer has allowed these methods to become more mainstream.

GAs belong to the class of *stochastic search* methods (others in this family include simulated annealing and threshold acceptance), which means they rely on an element of random chance or probability for directing the search. Hence, numerous search iterations are required (because you never know if the random element of the search has led you astray from the best solution path), but you are much less likely to get stuck around a particular "solution" (some applications may have many genomes that provide good results, but might not be the best possible; this is referred to as finding *local maximums* rather than *global maximums*, and having an element of randomness tends to "jump" the search out of the trap of local plateaus).

Unlike some searching systems, GAs separate their algorithm from the problem representation (the algorithm works for vastly different data structures), which allows them to easily find solutions in systems of mixed variable types (having both discrete, as well as continuous values). Although the most common technique for data representation is a string of bits, any data structure you want (including arrays, trees, etc.) can be used as long as each individual can encode a complete solution, and genetic operators can be constructed for your data structure.

One thing to consider about GAs is that they do not guarantee either performance, or success. In fact, a GA can, and sometimes will, perform in the worst possible ways. Such is the price for throwing an element of randomness into your algorithm; there's even a biological term for it—an "evolutionary dead-end." Your GA system will almost certainly spawn evolutionary dead-ends of its own. You will possibly need to tweak the structure of your genes, or even the GA's settings and operators if the system doesn't deliver the kind of behaviors that you were looking for. Even then, you might discover that GA methods just aren't suitable for your particular problem.

BASIC GENETIC METHOD

The basic algorithm for using GAs to find a solution to an AI problem can be broken down into three steps: initialize, evaluate, and generate.

INITIALIZE A STARTING POPULATION OF INDIVIDUALS

Genetic algorithms operate on a population of potential solutions. Each member of the population is an encoded blueprint for how to solve the problem. These "beings" can be generated randomly, or seeded with promising individuals given some specific knowledge concerning the problem domain. The size of the initial population is somewhat arbitrary and mostly depends on experimentation and resources, how much time you have to devote to the process, and what seems to work.

EVALUATE EACH INDIVIDUAL'S SUCCESS WITHIN THE PROBLEM SPACE

Each individual is then subjected to evaluation, by running a special fitness function, which returns a number value (or possibly a vector) representing the overall performance of this individual. GAs are so expensive because of the time necessary to calculate fitness. If you can look at an individual genome, and algorithmically calculate its fitness, then this process is quite fast.

But in the world of gaming, each being in the population must be run through the game loop for some period to determine its fitness score. A fitness test that requires each individual to play the game for 5 minutes, given a population of 100, would thus require 8.33 hours per generation, and a typical GA can take thousands, if not tens of thousands of generations to find any really useful solutions. Making your game simulation time scaleable can obviously speed up this process. But a sped-up world is not the same as the real game (for example, physics checks might miss collisions because of large deltas in time between frames), so your GA might learn things specific to a sped-up world, and not be as effective in real time.

Another technique involves using a GA to equate a specific part of the game decision-making process and have this particular part use a more straightforward algorithmic or time-scalable fitness function.

GENERATE NEW INDIVIDUALS USING REPRODUCTION

Once all members of the population have had their fitness calculated, a number of these individuals are selected for breeding. Selection style is another important part of the genetic process. If you only select the very best performers, you may converge on a local maximum too quickly because you have excluded too many genes from the pool. If you select too randomly, you may never find a good solution because you can cause too much random jumping. Several methods of selection will be covered later in this chapter.

Once all the parents have been selected, they are *bred* to create the next group of possible candidates. The next generation is spawned using three common methods: crossover (or sexual reproduction), mutation (or genetic variation), and elitism (which is taking the most fit, or elite, beings from the last generation and carrying them directly over into the next—which isn't exactly breeding, it's more like cloning). The specific mix of these three methods, as well as the exact operator with which to perform each method, is again up to experimentation and domain-specific knowledge. Many of these differing operators will be discussed in this chapter.

REPRESENTING THE PROBLEM

GAs are commonly written in the language of the thing being copied—evolution. We will design a way of representing our problem in a genetically compatible way and create iterative operators for dealing with this abstract representation.

THE GENE AND GENOME

First, determine the structure of the genes inherent in your problem. What, and how many specific traits are you seeking values for? Are the alleles of these traits binary (on/off), or are they real numbers, and if so, what are their ranges? Do any of these traits depend on each other?

The importance of these determinations cannot be overstressed. When you create a gene or genome structure for your GA problem, you are essentially defining the state space in which the GA will search, as well as formalizing the language in how you will receive your answer. Answers will be at the same resolution as the genes themselves. So, if you only encode the four cardinal directions as alleles for direction, your character will only move in those four directions in the solution. But fear not, GAs work just as well with analog allele states as they do with discrete values, at the cost of larger search spaces.

Herein lies the tradeoff. The larger the search space, the more likely your GA is going to find good, possibly surprisingly good, solutions. The larger search space creates two disadvantages, however: It is going to take longer to find that solution, and a greater chance exists that the GA might find an exploit in your logic. This means that you've set up your parameters in such a way that the GA finds a solution that maximizes your fitness function with behavior that doesn't follow the spirit of the game, or is inhuman enough that it is unwanted.

A (somewhat unconnected) example is the animation system used by the animators in the *Lord of the Rings* movies. In the massive battle scenes, which would have been cost prohibitive if each combatant was hand-animated, they used an AI system to control the warriors. The default settings of the AI system, however, were set up using commonsense values. When creating a massive battle between the humans and elves and the overwhelming forces of the orcs, all the AI-controlled humans and elves simply turned tail and ran into the woods when the battle started, because anything else was suicide. The default settings needed a bit of tweaking to reflect the unwavering morale and sense of duty that these soldiers felt in the book. GAs are notorious for finding loopholes in your calculations, and can find novel, yet unusable solutions to problems. Giving the GA too large of a search space to look within sometimes can exacerbate these kinds of issues.

One of the most common ways of encoding genes is as strings of bits. Consider the game world of *Pac-Man*. The main character has only four choices for his actions: Move Up, Move Down, Move Right, and Move Left. He can do any one action per game loop. He knows that the path in front of him in the direction he's currently moving has some "state" (defined as the containment of the path; does it contain regular ghosts, blue ghosts, dots to clear, or a wall). So, we could evolve a GA that would get *Pac-Man* to do the right thing when confronted with all the different permutations of world state that he encounters. Each gene would be two bits (representing the four actions he can perform). His genome would then be a string of genes that corresponded as proper responses to the different world states.

Another type of structure that is used often is an *order* or *content-sensitive* gene. An example of this is the classic Traveling Salesman Problem (TSP). Given a number of cities that the salesman has on his route (Figure 22.1 shows a typical setup), in which order should he visit them so that he goes to each city only once and also travels the shortest distance? The genome structure for this problem is obviously a list of cities. But unlike the string of actions in the earlier *Pac-Man* example, each gene would have to be unique for the genome to be valid because you can only visit each city once. We could technically define our *Pac-Man* genetic solution using a TSP-style structure, solving each board for optimal travel so that *Pac-Man* would clear the dots in the shortest distance. There's a problem, though. The ghosts are going to be in our way at some point, and *Pac-Man* might have to take a path (to escape) that he's already cleared. So, maybe we should leave *Pac-Man* with the first implementation type. *Pac-Man* isn't really a "shortest-path" type of problem. It requires dynamic reactivity to changing conditions, not an optimized route. If the ghosts in *Pac-Man* were on static paths, and in no way reacted to your presence, then you could use a shortest-path type of solution.

In fact, you should know that *Pac-Man* is really only being used in these examples because of the simplicity of the game world, as well as the almost universal

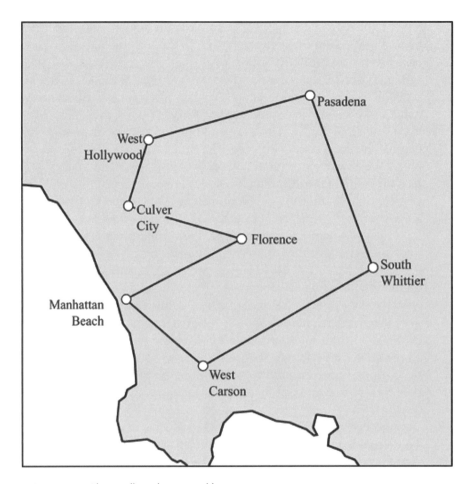

FIGURE 22.1   The traveling salesman problem.

familiarity that people have with the game. In reality, an AI system designed to play *Pac-Man* should probably use a more standard method, rather than GAs. In general, GAs are good for problem arenas in which you really just can't formulate a good way of determining solutions. The number of calculations that would need to be done to simulate the richness of the GA search method would leave a heuristic system either choking on the sheer number of computations, or mired in a sea of tunable values that require programmer time in which to balance. We will cover this more in the section on disadvantages of the system, later in the chapter.

Other types of structures that have been used as genomes within the general GA method include arrays and trees; both can easily be handled with the system, and both have had standard genetic operators written for them. All these examples can use genomes with both a fixed number of genes, and with a variable number of genes. The only real requirements of any genome representation are that it has the ability to encode a successful set of rules for the problem and that genetic operators can be written to manipulate the structure without breaking the system, or mangling the meaning of the genome, any individual gene, or allele.

THE FITNESS FUNCTION

Once we have determined the format of our genes and genomes, we then have to figure out how we're going to score each genome for performance within the world. This *fitness function* is very domain specific.

In *Pac-Man,* a fitness function might consider total score, speed of clearing the level, length of survival time, and the percentage of blue ghosts chomped. The function could take these elements into account with different bias coefficients (for example, so that survival is most important, then score, and then speed of level). The addition of "percentage of blue ghosts chomped" might be double dipping because you are already valuing score (you get points when you eat blue ghosts), as well as survival (chomping blue ghosts clears your way for easier survival). How you determine these coefficients would fundamentally mold the type of *Pac-Man* player you are trying to evolve: to what extent does your player value the best score, the fastest time, and sheer survival.

Your fitness function is really the essence of what your GA is trying to optimize its solution for, so you must carefully consider its design. Your fitness function is the heuristic that you use to direct evolution within your search space. Too many parameters, and the behavior of your GA is going to be diluted, as well as require many more generations of genetic manipulation to find a good solution. But too few parameters, and your GA is going to discard too much "unnecessary" genetic material from its population in favor of only those genes that maximize its limited fitness model.

Once a basic fitness equation has been designed, and we run our function on all the members of the current population, the fitness data must then usually be scaled, to prevent *premature convergence (PMC)* and/or *stagnation*. PMC occurs when exceptional individuals are born in an early generation, in a GA with a relatively small population, causing these early superbeing's genes to quickly spread to a large portion of the population as they dominate selection. Stagnation occurs more toward the end of the process, when many individuals have similar, high numerical fitness. In this case, the differences between individuals are minimized (at least to the selection process, which will be discussed during the reproduction section later in this chapter), which is not what we want because there is no longer very high selection pressure. In effect, scaling the fitness values brings out the various (and extremely small) advantages caused by the combinations of genes within the game entities. Some of the common ways of scaling the data include the following:

- **Sigma truncation.** The scaled fitness value (F`) is equated $F$` = F − (F^ − c * sigma). F^ is the average fitness, sigma is the population standard deviation, and c is a reasonable multiplier (usually between 1 and 3). Negative results are set to 0. You are basically scaling everyone's fitness using the standard deviation of the entire group, which means that there is more scaling when the group is composed of wildly different members (and hence, is usually more likely at the beginning of the simulation). The scaling will gradually take less effect as convergence gets underway and fitness scores start to become similar.
- **Rank scaling.** Rank scaling replaces the fitness score with its position in the sorted order of the fitness scores. So, whoever had the lowest score now becomes 1, the second-lowest score becomes 2, and the highest fitness scorer is the size of the population. Easily eliminating the chance of premature convergence, rank scaling does the opposite: It makes a GA take much longer to converge.
- **Sharing scaling.** A method that tries to encourage genetic variation, this scales down individual fitness scores that are very similar to each other. Essentially, the number of genes that different genomes share is recorded. Genomes are then grouped by how many shared genes they have (e.g., all those with five shared genes are in group 5). Finally, the fitness score of each genome is scaled by the number of other genomes in its sharing group.

REPRODUCTION

We have a population of individuals, and they have been evaluated by the fitness function. Now we must build an offspring generation, using the knowledge we've gained from this run. Two main types of reproductive cycles are common. The first is *generational* reproduction, referring to the process of using the last generation as a tool to create the next, either by copying directly or through genetic crossover and mutation, completely replacing the original generation. The second is called *steady-state* reproduction, wherein a few new individuals that are created through crossover or mutation replace specific individuals each generation, but the main body of the population remains unchanged. Who is replaced in steady-state implementations is another question (most common is to replace the worst, but other schemes involve replacing randomly, replacing the most similar, or replacing parents).

If we directly copy individuals from this generation to the next, this is called *elitism,* and it helps ensure that whatever selection routine we use doesn't accidentally miss the best beings in any given population. Elitism does the opposite of fitness scaling: It lessens genetic diversity and speeds up convergence, so care must be taken in its use. With too much elitism you will find local maximum solutions instead of global ones. Steady-state implementations do not require additional elitism because the method is *defined* by genetic carryover.

Other selection functions include the following:

- **Roulette wheel selection.** The random chance of a genome being selected is proportional to its fitness score. If a genome has the highest score, it also has the highest chance of being selected (it will have the largest slice of the roulette wheel). Notice that this selection doesn't take the genome out of the pool, so a highfitness individual may be selected multiple times. Notice, too, that it's still a random chance. Thus, the fittest individual is not *guaranteed* a place in the next generation, and this is the reason that elitism is a common practice in GA genome selection.
- **Stochastic universal selection.** This is a long-winded name for roulette wheel selection with a twist. The same roulette wheel is constructed, but now there's no need to spin. Take the number of individuals to select (n), and select the owner of the roulette slice at $1/n$ increments along the wheel. So, for 10 individuals, select the owner of the roulette slice pointed to each 1/10th of the wheel. This has the advantage over regular roulette wheel selection by keeping the spread of the fitness values chosen low and, thus, keeping genetic diversity high.
- **Tournament selection.** In this technique, a number of individuals are randomly drawn from the pool, and the highest scorer makes it to the next generation. Everybody goes back into the pool, and this is repeated for however many you need to make a new generation.

As individuals are being selected, you check each incoming pair for *crossover,* or sexual gene blending. The simulation keeps a crossover rate number, which is usually around $0.7f$ (your number may vary as you see fit). Generate a random number between 0 and 1. If the number is less than the crossover rate, you apply a crossover operator to the two individuals, creating two offspring. Otherwise, they become unaffected offspring. Which crossover operator you use depends on a number of things: the type of variables and structure your genomes are using, and a healthy dose of experimentation.

Some of the common binary variable crossover operators are the following (see Figure 22.2 for visual descriptions):

- **Single-point crossover.** A position is randomly chosen somewhere along the length of the genome. Swapping all the genes after this position among the parents forms the offspring.
- **Multipoint crossover.** Same as single point, except that two points are selected, and all the genes between the two points are swapped.

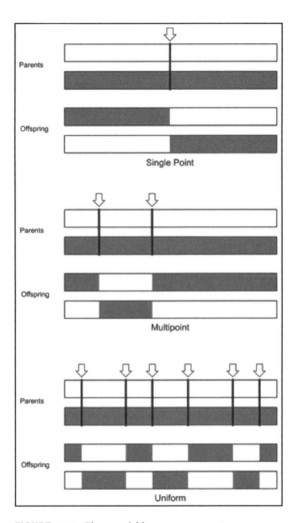

FIGURE 22.2 Binary variable crossover operators.

■ **Uniform crossover.** What could be called "every point" crossover; this method performs the mutation check with every gene, and swaps it with the other parent if it passes.

Common continuous value variable crossover operators are the following (see Figure 22.3):

■ **Discrete crossover.** Swaps the variable values between individuals.
■ **Intermediate crossover.** Determines the offspring's variable values as being around and between the parents' values. The offspring formula is `offspring = parent1 val + Scale*(parent2 val − parent1 val)`, where `Scale` is a scaling

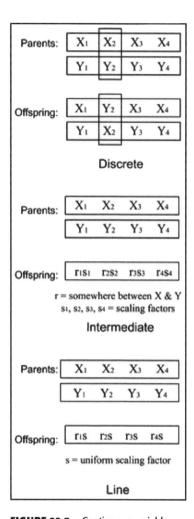

FIGURE 22.3   Continuous variable crossover operators.

factor chosen randomly for each value over the interval ($-d,1 + d$). Normal intermediate crossover uses $d = 0$, but if you want to extend the children outside the area of their parents, you can use a d>0.

■ **Line crossover.** The same as intermediate crossover, but all variables use the same Scale scaling factor.

Order-specific operators include the following (see Figure 22.4):

■ **Partially mapped crossover.** Sometimes called PMX, this operator selects two positions randomly within the Parent1 genome, defining a substring. For each gene in the substring, it is noted which gene corresponds positionally

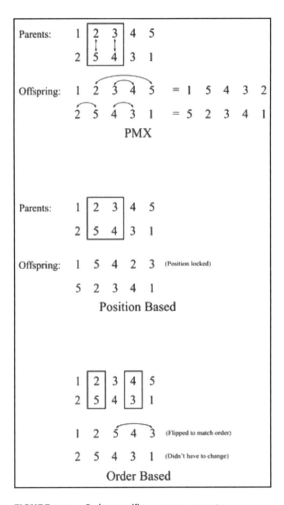

FIGURE 22.4 Order-specific crossover operators.

(or is *mapped*), in Parent2. Then, build the offspring by taking each parent, and copy the genes into the child, but every time you reach a mapped gene, swap the values.

- **Order-based crossover.** Choose several random genes from Parent1. Impose the same order they are found in the same genes within Parent2, by swapping values as needed.
- **Position-based crossover.** This is like order-based crossover, except we impose the position the randomly selected genes from Parent1 are found in to the Parent2 genome, and vice versa. Select some random genes in Parent1. Then, put these values into a new genome, in the same positions as you found them.

Then, fill the rest of the new genome with the values of Parent2, making sure not to use a gene that is already present in the array.

After everyone has been either copied or crossed over into the offspring population, the last step in reproduction can occur: mutation. Again, this is simply applying an operator to the genes in each offspring genome. The rate of mutation, or the chance that any one gene will be mutated, can vary wildly depending on the problem; various academic papers ([Bäck 93], [MSV 93]) have reported that 1/(number of variables in your GA) produces good results for a wide range of test functions. A typical number used in bit string style-genomes is around 0.0001f, whereas the rate when dealing with real numbers is usually much higher, more in the range of 0.05f to 0.2f. The specific type of mutation operator that you need to apply is related to the specific structure of the genomes you are using in your GA.

For order-specific genomes, common mutation operators include the following (see Figure 22.5):

- **Exchange mutation.** Swap two genes within the genome.
- **Displacement mutation.** Select two random positions within the genome, defining a substring. Then, remove this substring, and reinsert it into a random position.
- **Insertion mutation.** The same as displacement, except that the substring is only one gene. Tests have shown that for order-specific GAs, this operator performs consistently better than others do. Your results may vary, however.

Otherwise, non-order-specific operators include the following (see Figure 22.6):

- **Binary mutation.** Merely flip the bit with the genome.
- **Real-value mutation.** Offset the value of a gene by some delta. The size of the delta is somewhat difficult to choose; small steps are often successful, but may take much longer.

IMPLEMENTING A GENETIC ALGORITHM SYSTEM INTO THE AIsteroids TEST BED

Straightforward *Asteroids* (meaning without large extensions to the core gameplay) has very few problems that would actually require GA techniques to solve. Most of the determinations can be broken into simple math, with some breakup of individual states that might influence behavior. But, for illustration, one aspect of the AI's current behavior stands out as needing some help: the Evade state. For our sample implementation, the following will discuss a GA-designed solution to improve the evasion capabilities of our AI ship.

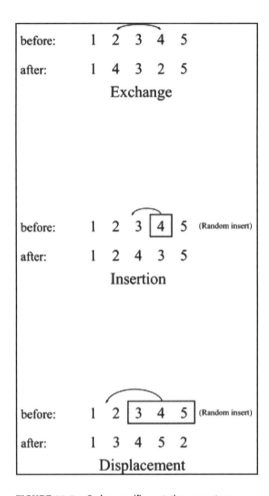

FIGURE 22.5   Order-specific mutation operators.

The gene design to be used is very simple, mostly because the ship's movement capabilities are so simple; at any given time, the ship can essentially only thrust or turn. So, a gene will be defined as a two chars, the first value meaning thrust type (forward, reverse, or no thrust), and the second representing an unsigned integer between 0 and 17 signifying the *sector* at which the AI wants the ship to point. A sector is defined as 20 degrees in our demonstration, meaning that there are 18 possible sectors. Given the range of these variables, this data could be compressed for size with no loss of resolution, if required.

The way that this gene's encoded information is used is as a solution to the question, "Given a certain game state, which direction should the ship turn to, and how should the ship use its thrusters?" The system will then create a means for defining the many possible current states of the game, such that the GA can solve a genome that

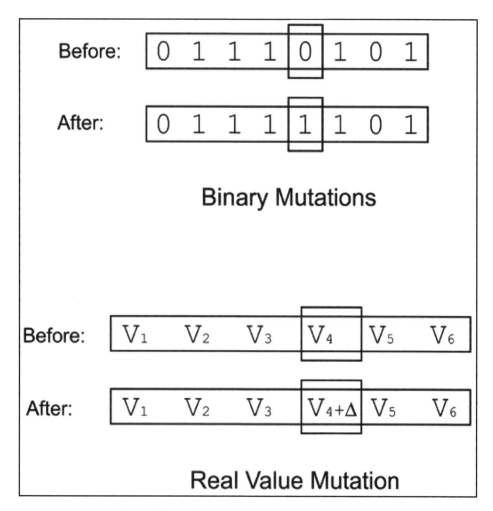

FIGURE 22.6   Non-order-specific mutation operators.

stores all the solutions for each game state. A simplified evasion-specific game state should consider three things (all concerning the ship, and the nearest asteroid):

1. **How fast is the ship moving toward the asteroid?** First, determine a normalized *delta* vector, defined as the sum of the normalized vectors of the ship's movement and the asteroid's. The speed at which the two are moving together is calculated by multiplying the ship's speed by the magnitude of this delta vector projected on its movement vector, plus the same calculation for the asteroid (see Figure 22.7). The higher this number is, the faster the two objects are moving together. Quantize this value into a manageable range, so scale it to the range 0–9, giving us 10 possible collision states.

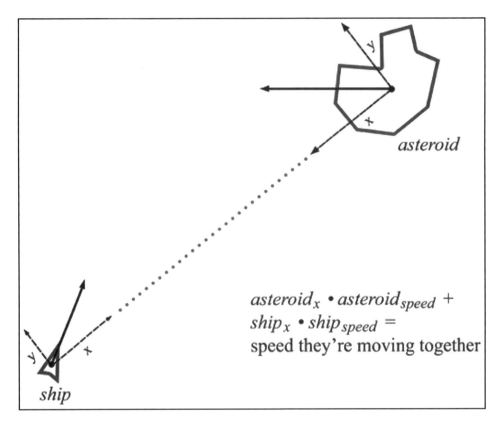

$$asteroid_x \bullet asteroid_{speed} +$$
$$ship_x \bullet ship_{speed} =$$
speed they're moving together

FIGURE 22.7   Diagram of the collision state calculation.

2. **What direction are the ship and asteroid moving in?** Again, quantize this value to limit the number of game states. Calculating this value will use the same normalized movement delta vector as the collision state. Simply calculate the angle that vector points in, and then scale it into 0–17 sector values, for 18 possible direction states.

3. **What is the separation distance?** Last, the ship needs to know how far away the asteroid is. The game really only cares when the two objects are pretty close, so quantize this value down into a few base distances that the game cares about. The way to do this is by metering the distance between the two objects in the units of "asteroid radii," referring to the asteroid the ship is trying to evade. Thus, if the asteroid is within one radius distance from the ship, its separation distance is one. Two radii is a separation distance of two, and so on, until four (or more) radii distance, which is used as the cap for the separation distance being considered, giving the game four distance states.

All told, this forms a defined theoretical set of rules, given the Collision state, Direction state, and Distance state of the ship and the nearest asteroid—520 given distinct evasion scenarios (10 * 8 * 4). If the ship knew how to react to all of these 520 possible game states, it would be pretty good at evading. Again, this implementation could definitely be done more simply using mathematical constructs; this will just demonstrate the technique.

So, this is the quest to set the GA towards solving. The genome is defined as the collection of rules that will most successfully solve all the necessary evasion rules, meaning the final genome will have 520 genes. Listing 22.1 shows the header for the gene and genome.

LISTING 22.1   Gene and Genome header information.

```
class Gene
{
public:
    //methods
    Gene() {m_thrust = randint(0,2);m_sector = randint(0,
NUM_SECTORS-1);}
    Gene(int a, int d):m_thrust(a), m_sector(d){}
    bool operator==(const Gene &rhs) const {return (m_thrust ==
                 rhs.m_thrust) && (m_sector == rhs.m_sector);}
    bool operator!=(const Gene &rhs) const {return (m_thrust !=
                 rhs.m_thrust) || (m_sector != rhs.m_sector);}

    enum
    {
        THRUST_OFF,
        THRUST_FORWARD,
        THRUST_REVERSE
    };

    //data
    char m_thrust;
    char m_sector;
};

class Genome
{
public:
    //methods
    Genome():m_fitness(0){}
    Genome(const int num_genes):m_fitness(0)
                    {for(int i=0; i<num_genes;++i)
                        m_genes.push_back(Gene());}
```

```
      bool operator<(const Genome& rhs){return (m_fitness <
                                             rhs.m_fitness);}

      //data
      vector<Gene> m_genes;
      float        m_fitness;
 };
```

Both classes shown are very simplistic. Gene stores the information that will be genetically modified, whereas a Genome is a collection of genes, as well as a fitness score. In our AIsteroids example, a "plan" for surviving a collision event will be stored, in the form of a thrust setting and a target direction sector. When used for a different game (or used within the same game), this is where you would define the set of genetic material you have to work with, whether it is bit strings, real variables like in our example, or complex data structures like trees. The Genome class can be used generically, but the Gene class is so basic to the particular implementation that you really have to address its design on a per-use basis.

Next is the implemention discussion of the *evolution application* (EA). This is the rule system that the real game code can use. The parts of this application will be a different GameSession class (called TestSession), a different set of keyboard controls (called HumanTestControl), a new AIControl class, GAAIControl, and most important, the GAMachine class, which houses the bulk of the GA functionality.

TestSession and HumanTestControl are mostly just the "game side" support code for the EA, meaning that they handle the inputs, drawing code, main game update loop, and so forth. The only controls that the tester application includes are the standard speed-up and slow-down buttons (. and , respectively), the "step" functionality still operates, and there is a Reset button (the *r* key). As for the session, it's basically the same application, except that it spawns a number of asteroids and ships, and when they collide, it just deactivates them, instead of killing them off. Then, at the end of a generation (when all the ships are deactivated), they are reset, reactivated, and start another round.

The real headquarters for the genetic algorithm code is in the GAMachine class. Listing 22.2 shows its header. The following code analysis is of the functional implementation, shown in Listings 22.3 to 22.11, with a brief discussion of each one in turn.

The first thing you should notice about the header is that there are more functions than are necessary for the test application. There are two types of selection, six crossover operators, and four mutation operators. These are implemented to provide you with additional tools to use in your AI programs, as well as to give you some things to tweak within the test bed, to see its affect on the quality of the evolution. Remember, GAs are all about experimentation, and finding out what operators to use, as well as how to tweak key values (the crossover rate, mutation rate, amount of elitism, etc.), is most of the difficulty in using the GA method.

LISTING 22.2   `GAMachine` header.

```
class GAMachine
{
public:
    GAMachine(GAAIControl* parent):m_parent(parent){}
    void SetupNextGeneration();
    void CreateStartPopulation();
    void Update(float dt);
    void UpdateFitness(int index);
    void Init();
    void Reset();
    void ApplyBehaviorRule(int index);
    bool WriteSolution();
    bool ReadSolution();

    //selection operators
    Genome& SelectRouletteWheel();
    Genome& SelectTournament();
    Genome& SelectRank();

    //crossover operators
    void CrossUniform(const vector<Gene> &parent1,
                      const vector<Gene> &parent2,
                      vector<Gene>&offspring1,
                      vector<Gene>&offspring2);
    void CrossSinglePoint(const vector<Gene> &parent1,
                          const vector<Gene> &parent2,
                          vector<Gene>&offspring1,
                          vector<Gene>&offspring2);
    void CrossMultiPoint(const vector<Gene> &parent1,
                         const vector<Gene> &parent2,
                         vector<Gene>&offspring1,
                         vector<Gene>&offspring2);
    //crossover operators - order based genes
    void CrossPMX(const vector<Gene> &parent1,
                  const vector<Gene> &parent2,
                  vector<Gene>&offspring1,
                  vector<Gene>&offspring2);
    void CrossOrderBased(const vector<Gene> &parent1,
                         const vector<Gene> &parent2,
```

```
                                    vector<Gene>&offspring1,
                                    vector<Gene>&offspring2);;
        void CrossPositionBased(const vector<Gene> &parent1,
                                const vector<Gene> &parent2,
                                vector<Gene>&offspring1,
                                vector<Gene>&offspring2);

        //mutation operators
        void MutateOffset(vector<Gene> &genes);
        //mutation operators - order based genes
        void MutateExchange(vector<Gene> &genes);
        void MutateDisplacement(vector<Gene> &genes);
        void MutateInsertion(vector<Gene> &genes);

        //elitism
        void CopyEliteInto(vector<Genome>&destination);

    protected:
        GAAIControl*    m_parent;
        //genetic data
        vector<Genome>  m_genomes;
        int             m_rankIndexLast;
        Genome          m_bestGenome;
        int             m_generation;
        float           m_crossoverRate;
        float           m_mutationRate;
        float           m_offsetSize;
        float           m_bestFitness;
        float           m_totalFitness;
        int             m_liveCount;
};
```

LISTING 22.3 GAMachine::Update() implementation.

```
//--------------------
void GAMachine::Update(float dt)
{
    //find best out of the maximum tries, then start over
    if(m_generation > NUM_MAX_GENERATIONS)
    {
        WriteSolution();
        //reset
        CreateStartPopulation();
        Reset();
    }
```

```
        m_liveCount = 0;
        for (int shpNum=0; shpNum<POPULATION_SIZE; ++shpNum)
        {
            if(!Game.m_ships[shpNum]->m_active)
                continue;
            m_liveCount++;
            m_parent->UpdatePerceptions(dt,shpNum);
            ApplyBehaviorRule(shpNum);
            UpdateFitness(shpNum);
        }

        //if the generation is over...
        if(!m_liveCount)
            SetupNextGeneration();
    }
```

The Update() function is the main loop of the GA. This function first checks
to see if you've run some maximum number of generations (thereby running an
entire *simulation*), and then writes out the best genome and starts it over. If you
want, you could write out the top-10 genomes, or the whole list. The reason for this
is that you will most likely be running this program overnight, or at the very least
unsupervised, to give it the time it needs to evolve fully into a working solution.
You could even set up the system to use slightly different GA parameters, or even
different genetic operators, for the different runs, and after an overnight session,
you would have a few different solutions to compare and contrast.

If the simulation isn't over, it updates each ship's perception values (take notice that the GAMachine is calling the GAAIControl::UpdatePerceptions() function;
usually the controller updates himself, but within our GA teaching program, more
than one ship is being controlled, so the GA machine has to update them separately), then applies the evasion rule for that ship (given those current perceptions),
and then scores the ship based on how well it is performing. If there are no active
ships left, it calls SetupNextGeneration(), the evolution function.

LISTING 22.4   GAMachine::ApplyBehaviorRule() implementations.

```
//--------------------
void GAMachine::ApplyBehaviorRule(int index)
{
    if(index < 0 || index > POPULATION_SIZE)
        return;

    Ship* ship = (Ship*)Game.m_ships[index];
```

```
    //not going to collide, just idle...
    if(m_parent->m_currentEvasionSituation == -1)
    {
        ship->ThrustOff();
        ship->StopTurn();
        return;
    }

    //thrust
    int thrustTp = m_genomes[index].
            m_genes[m_parent->m_currentEvasionSituation].m_thrust;
    ship->StopTurn();
    if(thrustTp == Gene::THRUST_FORWARD)
        ship->ThrustOn();
    else if(thrustTp == Gene::THRUST_REVERSE)
        ship->ThrustReverse();
    else
        ship->ThrustOff();

    //turn
    //-10 puts you in the middle of the sector
    float newDir = m_genomes[index].
                m_genes[m_parent->m_currentEvasionSituation].
                                    m_sector*20 -10;
    float angDelta = CLAMPDIR180(ship->m_angle - newDir);
    if(fabsf(angDelta)<=90)
    {
        if(angDelta >0)
            ship->TurnRight();
        else
            ship->TurnLeft();
    }
    else
    {
        if(angDelta<0)
            ship->TurnRight();
        else
            ship->TurnLeft();
    }
}
```

ApplyBehaviorRule() takes the particular ship's current Evasion state, m_currentEvasionSituation, and applies the correct rule coded within the ship's genome by setting the thrusters, and also possibly turning the ship toward some new goal direction. If the ship isn't currently in danger of a collision, the evasion state gets passed in as –1. When the ship registers this, it stops turning and thrusting.

LISTING 22.5   `GAMachine::UpdateFitness` **implementation.**

```
//-------------------
void GAMachine::UpdateFitness(int index)
{
    Ship* ship = (Ship*)Game.m_ships[index];
    if(ship && ship->m_active)
    {
        //if I'm currently surviving a collision situation,
            //incr fitness
        if(m_currentEvasionSituation != -1)
            m_genomes[index].m_fitness++;
        m_liveCount++;
    }
}
```

Fitness, for our test bed, is based on how often each ship was in an evasion situation and didn't die. The function does this by checking some perceptions (being active, and that the ship currently has something to evade), and if they are true, it increments the ship's fitness value. For our test bed, we aren't using any fitness scaling. Scaling the fitness scores would probably be done after all the individual genomes have been run through their update and fitness calculations. A very simple way to introduce scaling into the test bed is to implement rank scaling. Given that we already sort the genome list (for elitism, keeping fitness statistics, and roulette wheel selection), you could just make a post-sort pass through the list, changing each genome's fitness to be its position within the genome list. If you perform this exercise on the test bed, it should help keep the program from converging on a local maximum too early.

LISTING 22.6   `GAMachine::SetupNextGeneration()` **implementation.**

```
//-------------------
void GAMachine::SetupNextGeneration()
{
    //next Generation
    vector<Genome> offspring;

    //sort the population (for scaling and elitism)
    sort(m_genomes.begin(), m_genomes.end());
    m_rankIndexLast = POPULATION_SIZE-1;
```

```
//statistics
m_totalFitness = 0.0f;
for (int i=0; i<POPULATION_SIZE; ++i)
    m_totalFitness  += m_genomes[i].m_fitness;
m_bestFitness   = m_genomes[POPULATION_SIZE - 1].m_fitness;

CopyEliteInto(offspring);

while (offspring.size() < POPULATION_SIZE)
{
    //selection operator
    Genome parent1 = SelectRouletteWheel();
    Genome parent2 = SelectRouletteWheel();

    //crossover operator
    Genome offspring1, offspring2;
    CrossSinglePoint(parent1.m_genes,
        parent2.m_genes,
        offspring1.m_genes,
        offspring2.m_genes);

    //mutation operator
    MutateOffset(offspring1.m_genes);
    MutateOffset(offspring2.m_genes);

    //add to new population
    offspring.push_back(offspring1);
    offspring.push_back(offspring2);
}

//replace old generation with new
m_genomes = offspring;

for(i = 0;i<POPULATION_SIZE;i++)
    m_genomes[i].m_fitness = 0.0f;

++m_generation;

//reactivate the ships
for (int shpNum=0; shpNum<POPULATION_SIZE; ++shpNum)
{
    //reset test ships to startup state
    Ship* ship = (Ship*)Game.m_ships[shpNum];
```

```
      ship->m_active = true;
      ship->m_velocity.x() = 0;
      ship->m_velocity.y() = 0;
      ship->m_velocity.z() = 0;
      ship->MakeInvincible(3.0f);
   }


}
```

The `SetupNextGeneration()` function is where all the real genetic work happens. It sorts the genomes, tallies the statistics for the generation, uses the elitism function, and then creates the rest of the next generation by using roulette wheel selection, the single-point crossover operator, and the offset mutation operator. It also resets the ships for the next generation restart.

LISTING 22.7   `GAMachine::CopyEliteInto()` implementations.

```
//-------------------
#define NUM_ELITE             4
#define NUM_COPIES_ELITE      2
void GAMachine::CopyEliteInto(vector<Genome>&destination)
{
   int numberOfElite = NUM_ELITE;
   //copy the elite over to the supplied destination
   for (int i=numberOfElite; i>0; --i)
   {
      for(int j=0;j<NUM_COPIES_ELITE;++j)
         destination.push_back(m_genomes[(POPULATION_SIZE - 1) -
                                       numberOfElite]);
   }
}
```

The `CopyEliteInto()` function copies a set number of the top members of the population into the next generation. These are straight copies, with no crossover or mutation. You might want to introduce some mutation into these elements, possibly with lower probability, or with somewhat nonintrusive mutations (possibly offset mutation with a very small offset). Again, these types of experiments and tweaks are the requirement of working with a GA system.

LISTING 22.8 `GAMachine::SelectRouletteWheel()` implementations.

```
//--------------------
Genome& GAMachine::SelectRouletteWheel()
{
    float wedge = randflt() * m_totalFitness;
    float total = 0.0f;

    for (int i=0; i<POPULATION_SIZE; ++i)
    {
        total += m_genomes[i].m_fitness;
        if (total > wedge)
            return m_genomes[i];
    }
    return m_genomes[0];
}
```

`SelectRouletteWheel()` is a straightforward implementation of the roulette wheel algorithm. Also known as *fitness proportional selection,* it is built on the idea that the higher a genome's fitness, the better its chances of being chosen for reproduction. However, because this implementation relies completely on the random call at the top of the function, the real results of this selection process might not match your expectations. Indeed, it may completely miss the best individuals altogether, hence the reason that elitism is commonly used in conjunction with this type of selection. For certain problems, especially those with very small populations, stochastic universal sampling (SUS) or tournament selection are sometimes better for this reason.

LISTING 22.9 `GAMachine::CrossUniform()` implementation.

```
//--------------------
void GAMachine::CrossUniform( const vector<Gene> &parent1,
const vector<Gene> &parent2,

vector<Gene>&offspring1,vector<Gene>&offspring2)
{
    if ( (randflt() > m_crossoverRate) || (parent1 == parent2))
    {
        offspring1 = parent1;
        offspring2 = parent2;
        return;
    }
```

```
        for (int gene=0; gene<GENOME_SIZE; ++gene)
        {
            if (randflt() < m_crossoverRate)
            {
                //switch the genes at this point
                offspring1.push_back(parent2[gene]);
                offspring2.push_back(parent1[gene]);

            }
            else
            {
                //just copy into offspring
                offspring1.push_back(parent1[gene]);
                offspring2.push_back(parent2[gene]);
            }
        }
    }
}
```

The implementation of uniform crossover is simple. You pick a random location within the gene, swapping everything before that point, and straight copying
over everything after it. The operator checks (as does all the crossover operators) to
see if you've passed in identical parents, in which case it can skip the real algorithm.
Identical parents will have identical offspring, which is the reason that too much
convergence of your genetic material will lead toward a population with almost no
variation (this is fine only if you've found the solution to the problem).

LISTING 22.10   `GAMachine::MutateOffset()` implementation.

```
//--------------------
void GAMachine::MutateOffset(vector<Gene> &genes)
{

    for (int gene=0; gene<genes.size(); ++gene)
    {
        //check for thrust mutation
        if (randflt() < m_mutationRate)
        {
            genes[gene].m_thrust += (randint(0,1)?
                                    -m_offsetSize: m_offsetSize);
            //bounds check
            if(genes[gene].m_thrust > NUM_THRUST_STATES)
                genes[gene].m_thrust = 0;
```

```
            if(genes[gene].m_thrust < 0)
                genes[gene].m_thrust = NUM_THRUST_STATES;
        }

        //check for angle mutation
        if (randflt() < m_mutationRate)
        {
            genes[gene].m_sector += (randint(0,1)?
                                        -m_offsetSize: m_offsetSize);
            //bounds check
            if(genes[gene].m_sector > NUM_SECTORS)
                genes[gene].m_sector = 0;
            if(genes[gene].m_sector < 0)
                genes[gene].m_sector = NUM_SECTORS;
        }


    }
}
```

The offset mutation simply changes the real value of the variable by + or − the offset value. It also checks for wrapping of the value because we don't want the variables to hit a hard floor or ceiling. Instead, we want them to be able to move that little bit that might just find a better solution. The size of the offset is usually a tradeoff between being large enough to actually get the solution from the local maximum (without going right back in), without being so large that the algorithm might skip over solutions. Notice too, that smaller offsets are usually better, but your algorithm will take longer to find a solution.

The only function of note within the new GAAIControl class is its UpdatePerceptions() method, which is shown in Listing 22.11.

LISTING 22.11   GAAIControl::UpdatePerceptions() implementation.

```
//-------------------
void GAAIControl::UpdatePerceptions(float dt,int index)
{
    Ship* ship = (Ship*)Game.m_ships[index];
    if(!ship)
        return;

    //determine current game evasion state
    int collisionState = -1;
    int directionState = -1;
    int distanceState  = -1;
```

```
        //store closest asteroid
        m_nearestAsteroid = Game.GetClosestGameObj(ship,
                                        GameObj::OBJ_ASTEROID);

        //reset distance to a large bogus number
        m_nearestAsteroidDist = 100000.0f;

        if(m_nearestAsteroid)
        {
            Point3f normDelta = m_nearestAsteroid->m_position -
                                ship->m_position;
            normDelta.Normalize();

            //asteroid collision determination
            float speed = ship->m_velocity.Norm();
            m_nearestAsteroidDist = m_nearestAsteroid->
                            m_position.Distance(ship->m_position);
            float astSpeed = m_nearestAsteroid->m_velocity.Norm();
            float shpSpeedAdj = DOT(ship->
    UnitVectorVelocity(),normDelta)*speed;
            float astSpeedAdj = DOT(m_nearestAsteroid->
                            UnitVectorVelocity(),-normDelta)*astSpeed;
            speed = shpSpeedAdj+astSpeedAdj;
            speed = MIN(speed,m_maxSpeed);
            collisionState = (int)LERP(speed/m_maxSpeed,0.0f,9.0f);

            //direction determination
            directionState = GETSECTOR(normDelta);

            //distance determination
            distanceState  = MIN((int)(m_nearestAsteroidDist/
                                m_nearestAsteroid->m_size),4);
        }
        if(collisionState == -1)
            m_currentEvasionSituation = -1;
        else
            m_currentEvasionSituation=
            (collisionState*10)+(directionState*18)+distanceState;
    }
```

UpdatePerceptions() works just like it did in the previous controller classes: It computes the perception values that the decision-making portion of the program will use in making up its mind. In our case, its primary job for this demonstration is to compute the variable m_currentEvasionSituation, which the ship will use to employ the correct evasion rule. The reasoning behind this value's computation was covered earlier in this chapter.

PERFORMANCE WITHIN THE TEST BED

Even with the low level of genetic complexity being applied to our AIsteroids program, you can begin to see improvement in overall evasion behavior with only a few generations (50 or so), and letting the program run for thousands of generations leads to some very unusual, although still useful, behavior. Figure 22.8 shows

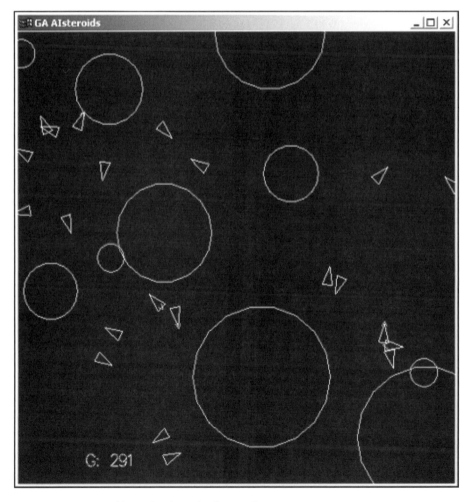

FIGURE 22.8   AIsteroids running the GA implementation.

a screenshot of the test bed running the GA solution. There are, however, some low points to the method as we have currently implemented it, and the performance of the GA could be improved in many ways. Some of them include the following:

- The system seems to converge too quickly on a few individuals; a different selection operator might improve on this, as would more individuals in the population, or slightly less elitism.
- We're trying to optimize a rule set with a substantially large number of rules. This means that to get a truly optimal set, we're going to have to let the system run for a very long time—hundreds of thousands of generations or more. Another way to encode the genes might be to use analog values that could be used as coefficients in a function that computes the best direction and thrust. Then, instead of trying to genetically search for the solutions to all the evasion states, we would only search for the necessary amount of coefficients within a sufficiently complex algorithm to represent our evasion calculations. A method like this would run somewhat close to being a simple neural net (albeit one that used a genetic algorithm to train), which will be discussed in the next chapter.
- The test application really needs to be fully time-independent, to allow the GA to run through generations at much higher speed. This would include small things like making sure that the `GameSession::m_timescale` variable is incorporated into all calculations dealing with time, and including speed determinations. Also, the collision detection would have to allow for collisions "within" a game tick. What this means is shown in Figure 22.9. What can happen is that the change in position that a game object might perform from one game loop to the next can become so large (when time is scaled very highly) that one game object could move straight through another, but because they were never touching during a collision check, one is never triggered. Solving this anomaly involves keeping track of the old position and actually performing a line-of-sight check to your new position, to check the entire path of motion along the delta. If another object resides along that path, then the object can't go all the way to its new position; the game should register a collision, and stop the object at the obstruction.

Pros of Genetic Algorithm-Based Systems

Although GAs are clearly not a universal tool in game AI construction, they do have a number of areas in which they work particularly well, including the following:

- *When you have a number of parameters that interact in highly nonlinear or surprising ways.* The more your parameters work in tune with each other, the easier it is to find a more traditional method for algorithmically solving your

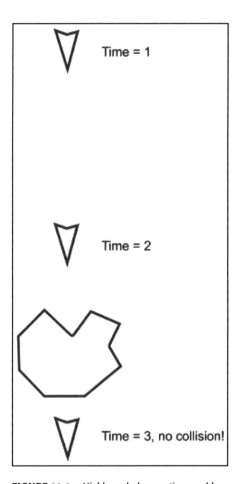

FIGURE 22.9 Highly scaled game-time problem.

problems. If this isn't the case, then GAs can help find the more "strange" interactions between inputs.

- *When you have many local maximums, and are searching for the* best *one.* An example might be the earlier stated case of tuning the physics parameters for the different cars and AI personalities in a driving game. Many different combinations will work, but the developers are looking for a particular feel; finding it will require more than just experimentation.
- *For solutions that involve discontinuous output.* Perfectly continuous output would be a simple mathematical function that always maps inputs to outputs with a simple function call. Semicontinuous output might be a state machine, where there are always actions in result of any given game state, but to encapsulate everything, it had to be broken up into separate, individual states that are islands of separate behavior. Discontinuous behavior is not smooth and

contains islands of action that are not connected to each other with any sort of relation.

- *When complementing traditional techniques.* GAs can be incredibly modular, fitting easily into the larger AI system when the need arises. Within a game, you might have an isolated state whose decision-making needs make it a good candidate for GA methods. If you can create a means within your game framework in which to allow a GA to evolve, and can come up with a suitable fitness function, then you're well on your way to evolving a solution instead of being stuck with trial and error methods.

- *When actual computation of a decision might be too costly.* Then, if you can find a suitable GA solution, you can probably save quite a bit of CPU time. GA solutions can be implemented as black box functions to replace complex mathematical constructs that algorithmically solve game problems, thus optimizing the AI. This is a bit like a neural net's ability to abstract mathematic constructs. You can, in essence, construct a nonlinear function, with some coefficients and extra parameters that become your genome. The fitness function then becomes the difference in output that your genetic function produces from your complex math function, and you can then set your GA on solving for the genome that minimizes that difference. Of course, you only win if the nonlinear function you've come up with is less CPU-costly than the one you're trying to outdo.

- GAs also have a number of *general* pros that are inherent to the method. They are very easy to set up, and start getting results, even if you don't know how to solve the problem otherwise. During evolution, you have an entire set of candidates to try out in your game, which could result in many of them being used to create variety or personality within your game AI characters. GAs are often very strong *optimization* algorithms, meaning that you can frequently find the optimal solution to a given situation. Finally, GAs tend to find global solutions rather than getting stuck in local ones precisely because they operate *in parallel*. In contrast with more traditional numerical or search-based techniques, which iteratively refine a single solution in hopes of coming up with an answer, GAs work by evaluating an entire population of candidate solutions simultaneously. In effect, more standard methods are asking the question "Do you know the time?" whereas GAs ask, "Does anybody in town know the time?"

CONS OF GENETIC ALGORITHM-BASED SYSTEMS

GAs are not a free lunch. Like any AI system, the more time you put into them, the better the results. Some of the shortcomings of GA systems include that they can be time-consuming, performance can be hit or miss, there are weak definitions of success and failure, there is no guaranteed optimal solution, and it is tough to tune and add functionality to GAs.

Time-Consuming Evolution

Often, evolution takes many generations, even with a good genome design and the right operators, to see results that are "game ready," meaning that they work well most of the time (a local maximum rather than a global maximum). Couple this with the fact that you might have to frequently change any one to all the component parts of the system while trying to increase performance (the gene makeup, one or more of the genetic operators, tweaks to the mutation or crossover rates, etc.), and then restart evolution, and you see the importance of ensuring that you have a considerable amount of time set aside for this portion of the method.

Again, this can be lessened if the system for which you are evolving a solution can be either arbitrarily sped up, or you can calculate an estimated fitness algorithmically from the genome, thus reducing each generation to be the act of running this function on each individual, instead of having to play through the game loop for some amount of time. Usually, however, this cannot be done. For game time, the algorithm as set up currently is quite slow to perform adequately. We couldn't allow the algorithm to run during real gameplay, evolving as it goes, because it would be dead long before it evolved a good evasion technique. Because of this, we perform the evolution offline, before the game is released, like most applications of the technique.

Hit-or-Miss Performance

With the myriad different ways you could encode a problem genetically, the vast array of different operators for selection, crossover, mutation, and fitness scaling, the large number of secondary parameters such as population size and mutation rate, as well as the highly subjective creation of a suitable fitness function, GAs are the absolute pinnacle of tweakability. Given your particular game problem, you may get very good performance with a certain crossover operator, but only if you use elitism, low crossover, a large population size, and real values for your genes. But figuring out that exact mix of usage might take a long time, experimenting with different combinations of these factors until you discover the right set of conditions necessary to find the solution. The only real way to become adept at knowing how to use the right factors with any given GA problem is through experimentation, especially because of the implementation-specific nature of GA solutions.

Weak Definition of Success and Failure

Your GA doesn't seem to be working, but you have no idea why. Is it that your mutation operator is scrambling things too much, so you're never converging on a solution, or have you converged on an inferior local maximum, and therefore need *additional* or more invasive mutations? Once more, you are left to the mercy of experimentation or gut feeling to divine these types of issues. In fact, the *reason* your GA might not be working or, working, may be a bug in your fitness function or genetic operators. Because of the nature of GA output, it's hard to tell the difference between buggy code and unevolved behavior. Real care must be taken in coding GA functions, so that this kind of problem doesn't come back to haunt you.

No Guaranteed Optimal Solution

GAs use stochastic techniques, and any time there's randomness, we have no guarantees. There are methods for ensuring a measure of safety (meaning, that you don't accidentally throw away winning solutions with bad selection operators or ill-timed mutations) while keeping the usefulness of GA methods, but it's all a gamble in the end. Another problem is that you most likely don't know the optimal solution (which is why you chose a GA in the first place), so you don't realize that if you'd just tweak a few things in your algorithm, you could get much better responses.

Tough to Tune, and Even Tougher to Add Functionality

Once you have a GA-developed solution to a problem, especially if that solution is hard won after a lengthy period of evolving and tweaking of the GA implementation, the tendency is to "leave well enough alone." Meaning that you don't want to muck with things very much, for fear of losing your hard-won system. Game developers rarely have the foresight to include everything into the up-front design of the games' AI requirements, however.

Most often, AI tuning is performed during the final period of the game, with many play testers and other personnel giving feedback. With code-based systems, these kinds of tuning issues or even the addition of small features (called *feature creep* by some, *polish* by others) can be accomplished relatively easily, especially if you've designed your AI system with this in mind (using a data-driven system, or some kind of extensible system). But with a GA-based system, these kinds of issues are much more difficult to approach. Basic tuning might still be capable, by slightly reevaluating how you interpret the GA solution data (as an example within in our test bed, we could point the ship toward a slightly different angle than originally planned).

Adding even small features, however, might involve completely starting over as far as the gene structure and GA evolution is concerned. This reason alone is the primary killer as far as games are concerned, and is the main reason why games are still using GAs for small parts of their games that *do* have locked-down designs and aren't subject to last-minute changes.

EXTENSIONS TO THE PARADIGM

Genetic algorithms are actually more of a methodology then a specific algorithm. There are many other ways in which GAs are being used then the simple system discussed in this chapter. Some of the common variations on common GA systems include so called "ant colony" algorithms, coevolution, self-adapting genetic algorithms, and genetic programming.

ANT COLONY ALGORITHMS

Individually, ants are not very good problem solvers. If you put a solitary ant in an environment, it's as good as dead. The ant will amble about in all directions, with no apparent plan or strategy. But this all changes when you have a large group of ants. If you put half a million ants into the same environment, they will centralize, build a colony, find food, defend themselves, and even conquer neighboring colonies.

This phenomenon is possible through what is known as *collective* (because it is brought about by a group) or even *emergent* (because it seems to come from nowhere) intelligence. One facet of this kind of intelligence that works well with GAs is the method by which ants find food. As ants walk around, they secrete a small amount of a special chemical, called a pheromone, onto the ground. The more they use a particular trail, the more pheromone is laid down. This chemical attracts other ants, and so the cycle continues until the ants have essentially built themselves a "freeway" to the nearest food source.

This all sounds remarkably like a kind of influence map, doesn't it? Actually, you could build an LBI system to encode the information necessary to help implement an ant colony algorithm, but it also involves (like GA methods in general) a hefty dosage of randomness and genetic recombination. In effect, we're using the notion of collective intelligence to help guide the genetic fitness of our GA populations. What this does for our GAs is to allow them to still start with the massive, random population that they do now while building toward solutions based on the successes of the entire population, rather than the success of an individual member with exceptional genes.

COEVOLUTION

Another fascinating area of GAs is the concept of cooperative and competitive evolution. If the fitness function of your GA can only be maximized when two or more creatures work together, you are encouraging cooperation. When you allow two elements within your game to evolve at the same time, and increasing the fitness of one decreases the fitness of the other, they are competing. In both cases, evolution by both creatures can be sped up dramatically because of the synergistic effect of the process between multiple entities [Hillis 91]. This idea has also been expanded to involve entire populations of entities, which in some ways model whole societies competing with each other. Sometimes referred to as *societal evolution,* this kind of GA evolution could be used to develop real-time strategic (RTS) civilizations that wage war on each other in the most efficient means given the specific groups, or could be used to build realistic animal communities within a game's ecosystem.

Self-Adapting GAs

The efficiency shown by our GAs depends heavily on how we use the various operators and parameters within the system. Often, it is hard to tune these systems manually. Several types of GA designs have been proposed that try to evolve the inner parameters of the GA as well as the problem-specific genetic material [Bäck 92]. So, during the evolution process, the crossover or mutation rates are influenced and changed. These types of GAs again sometimes work very well, and sometimes not at all for a particular GA problem. They sometimes have a tendency to converge too quickly, but various methods have been constructed to deal with this.

Genetic Programming

In this paradigm, the genetic material encoded in the genes is composed of actual program code itself. You are evolving the program that the individual will run to solve the problem, rather than coming up with a series of magic parameters that optimize a fitness function. Crossover and mutation of game code sequences is particularly difficult (at least, to do it and still have a legitimate program afterwards), so this type of GA system is rare. But with a data-driven game AI, in which your data is a series of small program instructions that represent behavior, the technique could be used to evolve AI character scripts instead of having to create them. Or, you could have the designers give you a series of working scripts as your initial population, and evolve several offshoots of these to give your AI agents some variation and personality.

Design Considerations

GAs are a brute force method that can find solutions in very difficult or computationally expensive areas of game AI, as well as come up with interesting solutions that may not have been found by a programmer. GAs are usually used offline because the evolutionary process is extremely slow in most cases. When designing your game, the question of whether to use GA methods should include the following reflections: types of solutions, agent reactivity, system realism, genre, platform, development limitations, and entertainment limitations.

Types of Solutions

Heavily strategic AI decision-making systems usually require numerous changes to their feature set during creation, as well as significant tuning for gameplay feel late in development, so they usually aren't a good match with GA methods. Tactical decisions are much more modular and can usually be split off into an evolutionary program more easily. Trying to evolve a diplomacy system within a large *civilization-style* game would require each member of a population to play the game for quite a long time to reach any sort of fitness determination, and would probably require optimizing an entire host of parameters. But a smaller, yet still difficult problem like city building could use a GA to evolve the best ways to optimally fit buildings into an area, while maximizing defense, utility, and the like.

AGENT REACTIVITY

The application of GA-spawned solutions are mostly black box, so they are exceptionally fast to use and usually represent somewhat optimal solutions. Therefore, reactivity of your game agents is up to you, and can be tuned to whatever you require.

SYSTEM REALISM

GA solutions are a mixed bag when it comes to realism. They can find solutions that are almost *too* optimized sometimes. Solutions could consider the effect of the randomness used in finding the solution, or combine all the elements of the AI character so well that the game no longer plays like a human player would (for example, in some first-person shooters/third-person shooters (FTPS) games you can use the blowback from your own weapons to blast yourself to places you couldn't normally get to; a GA derived deathmatch bot might perceive this and blast itself around the map continuously, never touching the ground). This kind of behavior can be constrained, however, because off-color activities like this merely represent exploits in your fitness function.

GENRE

Almost any genre can use GA techniques for some aspect of its game: RTS games could solve tough problems, such as building order determination or fending off a particular tactic such as rushing (a common human technique involving creating a mass of units early in the game and attacking quickly, hoping to finish off the AI opponent while it is in its buildup phase); FTPS or platform games could evolve better ways of dealing with map features; racing games can evolve more efficient racers; fighting games could coevolve whole characters.

PLATFORM

This is generally not a concern for GAs because the work is mostly done offline. In fact, the optimization effect of a GA black box might actually improve its chances of being a viable consideration on CPU-limited platforms.

DEVELOPMENT LIMITATIONS

For GAs, development matters are really the area of most concern. GAs are not debuggable in any real sense, so extra time must be allotted to tracking down small problems with the solutions. Will you also have enough time to actually evolve your solution, given that it might take a good amount of time to tune the GA (with different parameters, operators, and gene design) to get good results? Are the designers on your team going to require last-minute tweaks or changes that could endanger a proven GA solution? Do you want the evolutionary portion of the product to keep evolving in the field, or are you going to disable that part of the process and lock in a solution? Is your product set up so that testing and feedback of the GA results is built into the pipeline from the beginning, so that you can get fast turnaround on GA solutions within the game? All these types of questions will require that you consider the team you are working with in addition to the game you are working on.

ENTERTAINMENT LIMITATIONS

Game-specific concerns such as difficulty settings would probably best be handled by separate GAs for each level of difficulty, with a separately tuned fitness function. Tuning and game balance can be difficult. The real power of GAs is when your game design specifically calls for somewhat varied or surprising AI behavior, so that the anomalies that may be present within your GA solution can be accounted for within the game universe.

SUMMARY

Genetic algorithms are a fascinating way to solve or optimize difficult AI problems. They are easy to set up, but can be difficult to perfect, because of numerous settings and usages. GAs can find novel solutions to game situations, which is an important goal of today's games.

- Evolution in nature uses genes as encoded rule sets. Pairs of organisms are chosen, largely by their performance within the environment, to reproduce and pass on their genetic material to their offspring. But this new generation undergoes genetic crossover and mutation, which can further optimize its fitness.
- GAs are usually used offline because evolving solutions is time-consuming and requires many iterations before useful behavior begins to appear.
- GAs are stochastic methods and are considered a form of brute force search. They do not guarantee performance, or success.

- The basic algorithm can be stated as: (starting with a random initial population) run the population through a fitness function, then select favorable individuals to reproduce, apply a random mutation, and run this next generation. Keep doing this until the fitness of the individuals reaches some acceptable level.
- The gene and genome structure represent the solution to the problem you are trying to solve with the GA.
- The fitness function is the factor for which your GA is trying to optimize a solution. Its value can be used raw, or after some form of scaling to prevent or encourage data spread and clumping.
- Reproduction by the system culls out bad genes and helps promote good genes through selection. It also blends good individuals together through crossovers to help find optimal solutions, and mutates genes to keep solutions from being stalled in local maximum. There are many types of selection, crossover, and mutation operators.
- Implementing a GA into the test bed involved creating a new application that can be used for the evolving process, and creating the GAAIControl class, which handles the main algorithm.
- GAs are strong with problems that have many parameters related nonlinearly, have many local maxima, or involve heavily discontinuous output. They are well suited to complementing more traditional techniques and can be considered an optimization if replacing costly computational decision making.
- Evolution within GAs can be time-consuming and provide hit-or-miss performance. The reasons behind success or failure are somewhat hidden, so they are hard to tune and debug.
- Extensions to the paradigm involve ant colony algorithms, coevolution, self-adapting GAs, and genetic programming.

23 Neural Networks

In This Chapter

- Neural Nets in Nature
- Artificial Neural Nets Overview
- Using a Neural Net
- An Aside on Neural Network Activity
- Implementing a Neural Net Within the AIsteroids Test Bed
- Performance Within the Test Bed
- Optimization
- Pros of Neural Net-Based Systems
- Cons of Neural Net-Based Systems
- Extensions to the Paradigm
- Design Considerations
- Summary

Neural networks (NNs, sometimes called *artificial* neural nets, with the original neural nets being those in real brains) are an attempt by computer scientists to use lessons learned from biology in our AI solutions, somewhat similar to our work with genetic algorithms (GAs). But whereas GAs use survival of the fittest techniques to evolve a solution out of the possibilities, NNs strive to find solutions by using a method somewhat grounded in how the brain works, both organizationally and functionally. Although NNs don't do a very realistic job of modeling an actual brain, they do give us a very straightforward way of pattern matching and predicting trends in input data.

NEURAL NETS IN NATURE

Animals' brains are essentially a large cluster of interconnected nerve cells called *neurons*. The term "large cluster" is something of an understatement when dealing with some of the more intelligent creatures on the planet: human brains are

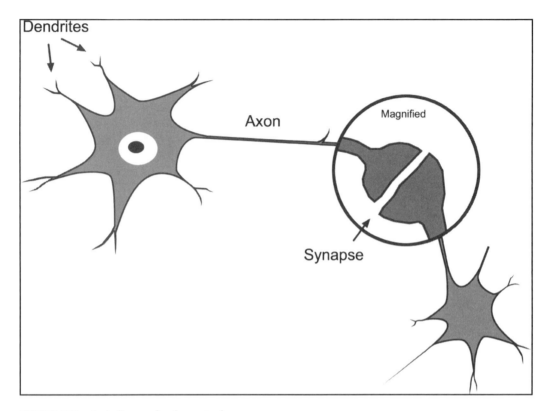

FIGURE 23.1 Basic diagram showing parts of a neuron.

composed of about 100 billion neurons; elephants have about 10 times that many. Each neuron has a large number of connections to other neurons (humans have about 10,000 connections *per* neuron), both coming in and going out. The incoming connections are called *dendrites*, and the outgoing connections are called *axons* (see Figure 23.1).

Although considered connections, neurons don't technically connect. Rather, the dendrites of one neuron come very close to the axons of other neurons (usually within about 0.01 micron), and the space between them is called a *synaptic gap*, or synapse. Neurons are essentially electrical (although their conductivity, overall charge, capacitance, and other factors are caused in some part by internal chemistry).

A simplified description of the behavior exhibited by a single neuron would be to liken it to the behavior of an electrical capacitor. Electricity is transmitted into the dendrites from nearby axons, gradually building up charge (like a capacitor) within the neuron. If this charge gets too large (above a certain *threshold*), it releases (the term typically used is *fires*) the collected energy down its axon, in what is called an *action potential*, where it may then be transmitted to the dendrites of other neurons.

If a particular neuron fires often enough, this will bring about small, biological changes within the neuron (such as a decrease in the electrical resistance along the dendrites and axon, an increased sensitivity to charge at the synapses, even changes in the size of the nerve fibers between various points), causing the electricity necessary to fire its potential to lessen. In effect, the neuron has "learned" that it usually requires firing with certain stimuli and will do so with less electrical resistance, rather than waiting for the entire charge to build up. The opposite effect can occur as well, where a particular neuron almost never fires and, thus, is subject to atrophy. Although this obviously offers a biological notion of learning through anticipation, it also establishes the concept of pattern recognition at a cellular level.

Another concept that occurs between neurons is that of exhibition and inhibition. A particular neuron could be said to be inhibitory to another if it deadens the electrical charge that reaches another neuron, or exhibitory for the opposite effect. This isn't the same as the synaptic changes within the cell, because it is not connection-specific. All connections coming into a particular neuron would be inhibited if the neuron in question were biased in such a way, whereas each individual synapse coming into the cell would have to atrophy for it to be inhibitive synaptically.

In essence, the brains of animals work by taking input, recognizing patterns within the input, and making decisions based on those patterns, which is precisely what we want to emulate with a NN in our software.

We are also trying to take advantage of the parallelism that the connectivity within the brain apparently gives our problem-solving ability. The human brain operates at roughly 100 Hz, a fraction of the speed of modern computers. But although computers are dealing with one instruction at a time (or possibly a few, given multiprocessor systems), the human brain can perform millions of instructions at once. Because of the symbolic way that our brains store knowledge and solve problems, we can mentally employ many levels of efficiency that allow us to use a tremendous amount of parallel processing. Obviously, unless you are using a parallel processing CPU, you will not be able to emulate actual human parallelism. But the hope is to employ the many parallel levels of correlation that can be encoded into a NN that would otherwise be difficult or impossible to find otherwise.

ARTIFICIAL NEURAL NETS OVERVIEW

Figure 23.2 shows the parts of an artificial neuron and a basic NN overview diagram. Note that the value associated with a neuron is the sum of all the input values multiplied by their connection weights, added to the neuron's bias value. Bias refers to the inhibitory or exhibitory effect the neuron has within the network. The "axon" on the neuron is represented by its output value, optionally filtered

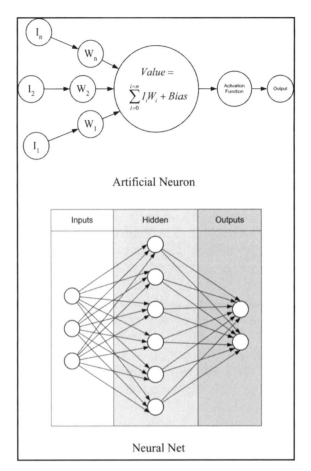

Artificial Neuron

Neural Net

FIGURE 23.2   An artificial neuron and a basic neural network diagram.

through an activation function, which will be discussed later, in the section "Using a Neural Net."

Within the overview diagram, the circles are the neurons (or *nodes,* as they are sometimes called when talking about artificial nets), and the lines between them represent connections between neurons.

The nodes in column one of the figure are parts of what is called the *input layer.* These nodes represent entry points into the network; places where outside inputs come in to be classified by the NN.

The second column encompasses a *hidden layer,* which represents internal data storage for the network. These nodes are useful in that they give the network room to grow, but also give the network greater ability to handle larger variation in patterns. The hidden layer may comprise one set of nodes, as shown, or multiple sets, to whatever complexity you are willing to work with. A special case is when you have no hidden layer at all, with the inputs directly mapping to the outputs, which is then called a *perceptron*. These are very low-functioning NNs, but they can still be used to do some linear pattern recognition.

The third column is called the *output layer*, and it corresponds to the actual categories that the network is trying to impose on its inputs. This is the answers that your net can give to any given set of inputs that you send it.

Also notice the connections themselves in the diagram. Each connection has an associated value, and a direction. The value represents the *weight* associated to the link, and is biologically equal to the strength of the connection between two neurons. As for direction, the NN shown in Figure 23.2 is an example of a feed-forward (FF) network because each layer only propagates forward into the network. Another type of NN, which doesn't have this restriction, is called a *recurrent* network.

In recurrent NNs, information can go from input to output, and back again, allowing for feedback within the system. To facilitate this, recurrent networks have a number of state variables associated with them and are thus a bit more complex than feed-forward NNs. In games, AI programmers almost universally deal with FF systems because they are easier to understand, more straightforward to tune, and less expensive to run (because the feedback phase requires data to be run through the network multiple times). Recurrent networks are technically more capable than FF systems, but you can generalize FF nets so easily that many of the benefits of recurrent systems can be gained by running multiple FF nets instead.

One last property of NNs is the amount of connectivity they exhibit. The diagram shows a fully connected NN, because each node is connected to every node in the next layer. If there were some nodes that weren't following this rule, for whatever reason, the NN would be called *sparsely* connected. Although building a sparsely connected node isn't much more difficult than the far more common fully connected version, they tend to slow down the performance of the system. A fully connected NN will automatically determine that a connection is unnecessary and adjust the weight of the connection accordingly. Thus, sparsely connected NNs are not commonly used.

In the business world, NNs have successfully infiltrated many different industries. One of the first large-scale successes with NNs was the United States Postal system, which uses a heavily trained NN for handwriting recognition when reading the addresses on mail. Other uses include trying to predict the weather, judging credit card fraud, voice recognition, diagnosis of diseases or other health problems, artificial vision techniques, and even filtering Internet sites against pornography or other graphic material.

Games have the same kinds of problems as the rest of the world, so NNs have been used for a number of the same sorts of issues dealing with pattern recognition or prediction. Any time you can identify a pattern within a system, it logically follows that you should be able to use that pattern to then help make decisions within the system, determine what kinds of decisions another is making within the system, or use previously stored data to try and predict what's going to happen in the future. All three of these are useful in the world of game AI.

At a basic level, NNs can be trained to become a black box for potentially expensive operations like animation selection (which dunk animation should the basketball player perform right now, given the state of the game, his skill, the surrounding players, the point spread, the difficulty level of the game, etc.), which is roughly analogous to using a pattern to directly make a decision.

The pattern recognition gleaned from a suitable NN could be used to form the basis of a player modeling system, to keep the AI on top of the human player by being able to predict what the human will do.

Finally, although uncommon in games, a NN could be used to "store" information, by allowing the learning element to continue to run during live gameplay, thus allowing the NN to potentially *learn* adaptive techniques. The reason this is uncommon is because of the unpredictable, as well as unstable, nature of the learning that NNs use. Some systems use this, but restrict the areas of learning severely to try to minimize the random element into the game world. *Black & White* would have suffered greatly if people's creatures suddenly exhibited what is called *catastrophic unlearning*, and couldn't perform any tasks at all after taking in a piece of knowledge that effectively unraveled the entirety of the relationships stored within their networks.

USING A NEURAL NET

The basic steps for implementing a NN system within your game is to set up your network, train it using specially prepared data that is treated as inputs, and then actually use it on live game inputs. The first step, designing the NN architecture for your game problem, requires that you consider several factors, including structure, learning, and training data.

STRUCTURE

Structure refers to both the type (feed forward, recurrent) and organization (how many nodes, how many hidden layers) of the NN to be constructed. Most people stick with feed-forward (FF) networks because some level of feedback can be built into an FF net, and they are much cheaper, performance-wise.

The number of variables you want the NN to categorize or pattern match on determines the number of input nodes in your NN. A NN might only have one input, in effect asking, "What is this, or What should I do with this?" But it might also have several pieces of information that it needs to make a decision. Try and minimize the number of inputs to the most essential because any additional elements you add here will translate to a much larger state space through which your NN must search. You are pretty much asking your system to find a pattern that links every one of your inputs together. So with two inputs, your NN only has to find a "line" that connects them, but with twelve inputs, your NN must find the nearest "dodecahedron" that fits nicely on your data points—not such an easy task. Note that abstract variables that represent combinations (or calculations) based on simpler variables tend to be better suited to NNs. So, in our test bed, a variable called "danger" might be better than many inputs about the closest few asteroids' positions, speeds, and so on.

There is only one basic rule about the number of nodes within the NN: the fewer you can get away with, the better. Again, the more nodes you include in a NN, the larger the search space becomes that the NN is slogging through to arrive at a suitable solution.

There are no real guidelines about how many hidden nodes you'll require (although one hidden *layer* seems to be fine for most of the problems that game AIs come up with). A common practice is to use a medium number of hidden nodes (two times the number of input nodes) and then go up or down a few and compare the performance until you see it tapering off. Many sources will state guidelines for the number of hidden nodes, or even give rules "that aren't to be broken." But like most hard-and-fast rules in life, this information is mostly useless, because these sources determine these rules based on the number of input and output nodes, and don't take into account essential factors like the number of training cases, the complexity of the function being solved, or the amount of noise (variance) in the outputs.

The number of output nodes is equal to the number of outputs that you require from the NN. Are you building a system that tells you whether or not you can see the game hero? Then your NN will only need two output nodes: Yes and No. Are you building a character-recognition system that can recognize all the numbers? Then you'll need 10 output nodes, one each for the numbers 0 to 9.

Each output doesn't have to be binary; it can have continuous values of activation. Thus, your output neurons could be "Turn Left" and "Turn Right," and the level of the neuron's activation would tell you how much to turn. Smooth activations are achieved by using a suitable *activation function*. Some of the common activation function types include the step function, the hyperbolic tangent and logistic sigmoid functions, and the Gaussian function.

Shaping the output is not the only reason for using an activation function on the final value of a given neuron. Using activation functions on the hidden nodes is also done for an entirely different reason. One of the most powerful capabilities of NNs is to encapsulate a nonlinear function that maps the inputs to the outputs. However, it can only do this if the NN itself can represent a nonlinear function.

Without a hidden layer, a perceptron is only capable of finding linear correlations between the inputs and outputs. But adding a hidden layer to a perceptron isn't enough; we must also use a nonlinear activation function on the nodes to give an element of nonlinearity to the network connections. Almost any nonlinear function will do, except polynomials. For backpropagation learning (which will be discussed later), the activation function must be differentiable, and it helps if the function is bounded, hence the choices for the common activation functions.

LEARNING MECHANISM

Once you have set up your NN, you need to determine how you want to train it. There are two main types of NN learning: the aptly named supervised and unsupervised methods.

Supervised learning involves using *training data* that consists of input-output pairs. You feed the input into the NN, and then adjust the weights of the network if there is a discrepancy between the output from the NN and the expected output given in the training data. Training continues until a certain level of accuracy is achieved. The name of this method is *backpropagation* because the way you adjust the network parameters is from the back to the front.

Another form of supervised learning is called *reinforcement* learning. In this system, desired outputs are not given to the algorithm, but the network is rewarded (or its behavior is reinforced) when it performs well. This would be an example of "positive" reinforcement. Some implementations also punish when the system performs poorly, which corresponds to "negative" reinforcement, but this is usually overkill.

Unsupervised learning involves having a program automate learning of the NN by statistically looking at the output and adjusting the weights accordingly. One technique for this is called *perturbation learning,* which is very similar to an academic AI technique called *simulated annealing.* In perturbation, your test program runs the NN, then adjusts some of the values a small amount, and runs it again. If the program gets better performance, it keeps going by repeating the process; otherwise, it goes back to its last best settings.

Another unsupervised technique that is quite common is to use a genetic algorithm to adjust the weight values of your NN. The relationship between the two methods really shows each technique's strengths: the NN is determining the pattern between inputs and outputs, whereas the GA is optimizing a set of numbers to maximize some fitness function.

CREATING TRAINING DATA

Now you have your network, and you know how to train it. If you have chosen to use supervised learning, your next job is to actually acquire the test data that you will use to train the NN. There are several ways to do this.

You could record a human performing the same kinds of tasks you are trying to teach your system, and then create test cases based on the human's behavior. This kind of training data is great because you can also use it to build human-level performance into the AI (you can also use data points when the human *didn't* do the right thing, or was subtly wrong), which will help your AI seem less robotic than it might if it were using finite states, or a script. But, this method is extremely time-consuming, and your AI's skill is then limited to the skill of the person being mimicked.

Another way is to write a separate program to generate reasonable input scenarios and have a human say which output should arise. This is fine (although again, very time-consuming) for binary or discrete output values, but is futile with real value or numerous outputs. You could generate random input and output pairs, and check them for validity, storing them only if you get winners. You could also use some kind of expert knowledge about the problem to try to generate some training data points. This might be hard, considering that the reason you're using a NN in the first place is because you might not have this kind of data.

The number of training cases required depends on the amount of noise in the targets and the complexity of the function you are trying to learn, but as a starting point, it's a good idea to have at least 10 times as many training cases as input units. This may not be enough for highly complex functions. For classification problems, the number of cases in the smallest class should be at least several times the number of input units. Optimally, you should strive for a training suite more along the lines of $10N$, where N is the number of inputs.

AN ASIDE ON NEURAL NETWORK ACTIVITY

The pattern recognition that NNs are capable of should really be understood in order to truly see why they do what they do. A good understanding of the process can also help in debugging or perfecting the performance of an NN that is acting up. The two primary (and somewhat similar) tasks that NNs are good at performing are *regression* and *classification*. Figure 23.3 displays an example of regression; Figure 23.4 shows a few classification cases.

Regression is defined as finding a function that fits all the data points within some tolerance. Say you're going to create an NN to help your AI enemy evade bullets shot by the player by sidestepping out of the way. You would input the enemy's facing direction, the position of the player, and the position of the enemy. Assuming that the bullets are going to head directly from the player to the enemy, the NN will determine a movement vector for the enemy. What is the NN really learning in this example? If you were to solve this problem algorithmically, you would calculate the vector between the two, and then take the dot product of that vector

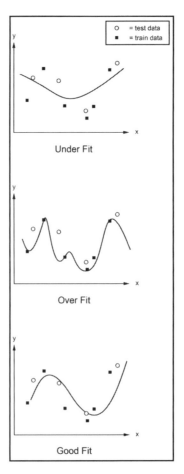

FIGURE 23.3 Examples of regression.

with a unit vector built from the enemy's facing angle, giving the player the angle needed to turn from their current facing direction. But would it turn left or right? Your program needs to perform the same operation again, but with a unit vector perpendicular to the enemy's facing direction. If you combine these mathematic operations into one large function, then you would have the exact function that the NN has to learn to solve this problem. The NN, in essence, is *learning* how to perform the right dot products and comparisons.

If you take this example a step further, it will give you a hint about the structure requirements of your nets. Imagine that all your NN's outputs are merely a *linear* function of your inputs. Say there was a smooth, ramplike hill in your game. An enemy on this hill knows how far he has traveled along the hill, but wants to know his current altitude. If you coded a NN to solve this conundrum, it would very quickly find the solution, and it could do so with no hidden nodes. That's

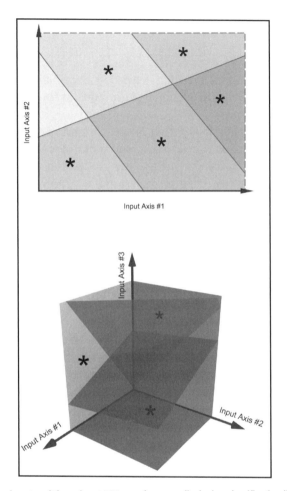

FIGURE 23.4   A two-input and three-input NN search space, displaying classification lines.

because the function it would be finding is the slope of the hill, a linear function of the input.

But, if your game hill was like a *real* hill, which had ever-changing slopes, valleys, plateaus, pits, and other features, then the NN would have to find a nonlinear equation (the equivalent of some form of complex Fourier transform, or the like) to approximate the "function" that the altitude is following. To do that, it would need plenty of hidden layers with nonlinear activation functions to store this kind of information.

Another benefit of visualizing your NN setup is in estimating or debugging the amount of training on your NNs. In the bottom graph of Figure 23.3, you can see how the line follows the trend of the data well. This NN has been trained correctly. It does a good job of determining the spirit of the data, without underfitting (the function would be too smooth, and miss key variation trends within the data) or overfitting (the regression function isn't smooth at all; it takes into account noise in the data, and thus has somewhat surprising results). Realizing what is occurring within your network is the first step toward being able to build NNs without having to spend large amounts of time experimenting to get them to operate smoothly.

The other, similar task that NNs thrive on is classification. If you are given a pile of buttons, and asked to separate them by color, you would push them into piles of each color represented in the group. You would *classify* them. When you give inputs to a NN, what you're asking it to do is categorize the inputs into the number of piles of output nodes.

But the NN is dealing with an entire search space instead of individual objects (by giving an NN two inputs, you're not giving it two distinct numbers, you're giving it two *axes* of inputs). It won't be dividing objects into piles. Instead, the output nodes represent lines of separation within the state space of input possibility. Visualizing a classification NN in this way is very powerful and useful. Think of each input as a theoretical axis in a graph, and each output as a line (or plane, or hyperplane, depending on the dimensionality of your system) separating distinct inputs into isolated categories. Figure 23.4 shows two examples, with two- and three-NN inputs.

When you think of your NN in this way, it becomes easy to see a number of aspects of NN behavior. Incorporating unnecessary input nodes makes it harder for the NN to solve the problem, by making the search space exponentially larger in dimensionality. Additional output nodes make for tighter categories, but also make the job of differentiation that much more complex. Although this is a simplified view of the internal workings of an NN, it helps you picture the effect.

IMPLEMENTING A NEURAL NET WITHIN THE AIsteroids Test Bed

First, we must determine what it is that we want an NN to do for our test-bed application. Although nothing in our simple game is screaming for an NN solution, we can definitely create a suitably difficult problem to see how well the NN handles solving the problem. For this chapter, we will once again attack the problem of asteroid avoidance. We'll strive to *teach* the ship how to avoid the asteroids. To do this, we can first create the necessary training data by recording a human player performing in the game. Then, we'll use this data to train the NN. Finally, we can start a fresh game, load in the trained NN data, and use it to perform the correct avoidance behaviors.

In our example, we'll be using a fairly simple NN, with one hidden layer that has eight neurons, four inputs, and three outputs.

The inputs we'll be using are the following:

- Two inputs, which will be the *X* and *Y* components of the vector between the ship and the nearest asteroid.
- The speed that the two objects are moving together, which is determined by taking the moving velocity of each object and finding the component of velocity that lies along the direct path to the other object.
- The ship's moving direction, which gives the NN a frame of reference with which to make correlations between the other inputs.

The outputs that the system will provide are simply Boolean values for the simple ship's controls. They will determine whether or not the ship should thrust, turn left, or turn right.

The NN system implementation will comprise four main parts:

- A `Neuron` is the basic element of an NN. A neuron structure stores several data fields, including the weights of each incoming connection to the neuron, the output value, and the error gradient computed from the expected outputs during training.
- The `NLayer` is a set of neurons that constitute a particular layer in the network. At this level, various operations can be performed on the inherent neurons, such as propagation (feeding the inputs forward through the network), back-propagation (calculating the error gradients at each neuron backward through the net), and steepest descent adjustment of the connection weights. The various kinds of activation functions are also found at this level.
- The `NeuralNet` class is the main interface for the network. All the functions are necessary to actually run and train the net are here.
- `NNAIControl` is the `Controller` class we'll be using for our networks. It provides a location for game-specific usage of an NN. Our controller will be set up to handle a few different "modes" of control, namely *training* of the network, versus actually *using* the network to perform AI tasks once it has been trained.

THE `NeuralNet` CLASS

To use an NN within a game, we will need to *construct* the actual network structure, *train* the network with a set of data, and then *use* the network to determine what to do with new data.

Listing 23.1 shows the header for the `NeuralNet` class.

LISTING 23.1   NeuralNet header.

```cpp
class NeuralNet
{

public:

    NeuralNet(int nIns,int nOuts,int nHiddenLays,int
nNodesinHiddenLays);
    void Init();

    //access methods
    void Use(vector<float> &inputs,vector<float> &outputs);
    void Train(vector<float> &inputs,vector<float> &outputs);
    float GetError()    {return m_error;}
    void WriteWeights();
    void ReadWeights();

protected:
    //internal functions
    void AddLayer(int nNeurons,int nInputs,int type);
    void SetInputs(vector<float>& inputs);
    void FindError(vector<float>& outputs);
    void Propagate();
    void BackPropagate();

    //data
    vector<NLayer>  m_layers;
    NLayer*         m_inputLayer;
    NLayer*         m_outputLayer;

    float           m_learningRate;
    float           m_momentum;
    float           m_error;

    int             m_nInputs;
    int             m_nOutputs;
    int             m_nLayers;
    int             m_nHiddenNodesperLayer;
    int             m_actType;
    int             m_outputActType;
};
```

Listing 23.2 shows the `NeuralNet` implementation. This listing might look somewhat mysterious but it's really fairly simple when broken down into its component parts:

- The *Init()* function is the primary set-up function for the network. It builds the internal structure of the net, by iteratively calling `AddLayer()` to instantiate each layer's neurons. The system is set up to handle simple nets with only an input and output layer (perceptrons) as well as general, multilayer NNs.
- *Propagate()* takes the inputs to the net and spreads their influence forward through the network. `BackPropagate()` effectively reverses this operation by taking the error of the final outputs and finding the correct error gradients throughout the network, from the last layer backward to the first.
- *Train()* and *Use()* are the two main functions for actually using the NN. During training, you call the `Train()` method with the input-output pair you want to train. It then propagates the inputs through the NN, finds the error from the expected outputs, and backpropagates that error. `Use()` assumes a trained net. It just takes the inputs and returns the network's outputs.
- *FindError()* determines the output error of the network from given outputs during training. Using the derivative of the activation function, it determines the error gradient for each output neuron, which will then be used to backpropagate the necessary changes to the connection weights within the network, to close in on the optimal weights to perform well.

LISTING 23.2   `NeuralNet` implementations.

```
//-------------------
void NeuralNet::Init()
{
    m_inputLayer    = NULL;
    m_outputLayer   = NULL;
    m_actType       = ACT_BIPOLAR;
    m_outputActType= ACT_LOGISTIC;
    m_momentum      = 0.9f;
    m_learningRate = 0.1f;

    //error check
    if(m_nLayers<2)
        return;

    //clear out the layers, incase you're restarting the net
    m_layers.clear();
```

```
    //input layer
    AddLayer(m_nInputs, 1, NLT_INPUT);

    if(m_nLayers > 2)//multilayer network
    {
        //first hidden layer connect back to inputs
        AddLayer(m_nHiddenNodesperLayer, m_nInputs, NLT_HIDDEN);

        //any other hidden layers connect to other hidden outputs
        //-3 since the first layer was the inputs,
        //the second (connected to inputs) was initialized above,
        //and the last one (connect to outputs) will be initialized
        //below
        for (int i=0; i<m_nLayers-3; ++i)
            AddLayer(m_nHiddenNodesperLayer, m_nHiddenNodesperLayer,
                    NLT_HIDDEN);

        //the output layer also connects to hidden outputs
        AddLayer(m_nOutputs, m_nHiddenNodesperLayer, NLT_OUTPUT);
    }
    else//perceptron
    {
        //output layer connects to inputs
        AddLayer(m_nOutputs, m_nInputs, NLT_OUTPUT);
    }
    m_inputLayer = &m_layers[0];
    m_outputLayer= &m_layers[m_nLayers-1];
}

//--------------------
void NeuralNet::Propagate()
{
    for (int i=0; i<m_nLayers-1; ++i)
    {
        int type = (m_layers[i+1].m_type == NLT_OUTPUT)?
                        m_outputActType : m_actType;
        m_layers[i].Propagate(type,m_layers[i+1]);
    }
}

//--------------------
void NeuralNet::BackPropagate()
{
    //backprop the error
```

```
    for (int i=m_nLayers-1; i>0; −i)
        m_layers[i].BackPropagate(m_actType,m_layers[i-1]);


    //adjust the weights
    for (i=1; i<m_nLayers; i++)
        m_layers[i].AdjustWeights(m_layers[i-1],
                             m_learningRate,m_momentum);
}


//--------------------
void NeuralNet::Train(vector<float> &inputs,vector<float> &outputs)
{
    SetInputs(inputs);
    Propagate();
    FindError(outputs);
    BackPropagate();
}


//--------------------
void NeuralNet::Use(vector<float> &inputs,vector<float> &outputs)
{
    SetInputs(inputs);
    Propagate();
    outputs.clear();
    //return the net outputs
    for(int i =0;i< m_outputLayer->m_neurons.size();++i)
        outputs.push_back(m_outputLayer->m_neurons[i]->m_output);
}


//--------------------
void NeuralNet::SetInputs(vector<float>& inputs)
{
    int numNeurons = m_inputLayer->m_neurons.size();
    for (int i = 0; i<numNeurons; ++i)
        m_inputLayer->m_neurons[i]->m_output = inputs[i];
}
//--------------------
void NeuralNet::FindError(vector<float>& outputs)
{
    m_error = 0;
    int numNeurons = m_outputLayer->m_neurons.size();
    for (int i=0; i<numNeurons; ++i)
    {
        float outputVal = m_outputLayer->m_neurons[i]->m_output;
```

```
            float error = outputs[i]-outputVal;
            switch(m_actType)
            {
            case ACT_TANH:
                m_outputLayer->m_neurons[i]->m_error = m_outputLayer->
                                           InvTanh(outputVal)*error;
                break;
                    case ACT_BIPOLAR:
                m_outputLayer->m_neurons[i]->m_error = m_outputLayer->
                                       InvBipolarSigmoid(outputVal)*error;
                break;

            case ACT_LOGISTIC:
            default:
                m_outputLayer->m_neurons[i]->m_error = m_outputLayer->
                                        InvLogistic(outputVal)*error;
                break;
            }
            //error calculation for the entire net
            m_error += 0.5*error*error;
        }
    }
```

THE NLayer CLASS

Because most operations on nets are on the connections from one layer to another, this is the real workhorse of the system. Listing 23.3 shows the header for the NLayer class, and Listing 23.4 shows the implementation.

LISTING 23.3   NLayer header.

```
class NLayer
{
public:
    NLayer(int nNeurons, int nInputs, int type = NLT_INPUT);
    void Propagate(int type, NLayer& nextLayer);
    void BackPropagate(int type, NLayer& nextLayer);
    void AdjustWeights(NLayer& inputs,float lrate = 0.1f,
                       float momentum = 0.9f);

    //activation functions
    float ActLogistic(float value);
    float ActStep(float value);
```

```
        float ActTanh(float value);
        float ActBipolarSigmoid(float value);
        void  ActSoftmax(NLayer& outputs);

        //derivative functions for backprop
        float DerLogistic(float value);
        float DerTanh(float value);
        float DerBipolarSigmoid(float value);

        //data
        vector<Neuron*> m_neurons;
        int             m_type;
        float           m_threshold;
    };
```

LISTING 23.4 Important `NLayer` implementations.

```
    //-------------------
    void NLayer::Propagate(int type, NLayer& nextLayer)
    {
        int weightIndex;
        int numNeurons = nextLayer.m_neurons.size();
        for (int i=0; i<numNeurons; ++i)
        {
            weightIndex = 0;
            float value = 0.0f;

            int numWeights = m_neurons.size();
            for (int j=0; j<numWeights; ++j)
            {
                //sum the (weights * inputs), the inputs
                //are the outputs of the prop layer
                value += nextLayer.m_neurons[i]->m_weights[j] *
                        m_neurons[j]->m_output;
            }

            //add in the bias (always has an input of -1)
            value+=nextLayer.m_neurons[i]->m_weights[numWeights]*-1.0f;

            //store the outputs, but run activation first
            switch(type)
            {
                case ACT_STEP:
                    nextLayer.m_neurons[i]->m_output = ActStep(value);
                    break;
```

```
                case ACT_TANH:
                    nextLayer.m_neurons[i]->m_output = ActTanh(value);
                    break;
                case ACT_LOGISTIC:
                nextLayer.m_neurons[i]->m_output = ActLogistic(value);
                    break;
                case ACT_BIPOLAR:
                    nextLayer.m_neurons[i]->m_output =
                                                ActBipolarSigmoid(value);
                    break;
                case ACT_LINEAR:
                default:
                    nextLayer.m_neurons[i]->m_output = value;
                    break;
            }
        }
        //if you wanted to run the Softmax activation function, you
        //would do it here, since it needs all the output values
        //if you pushed all the outputs into a vector, you could...
        //uncomment the following line to use SoftMax activation

        //outputs = ActSoftmax(outputs);
        //and then put the outputs back into the correct spots

        return;
    }


    //--------------------
    void NLayer::BackPropagate(int type, NLayer &nextLayer)
    {
        float outputVal, error;
        int numNeurons = nextLayer.m_neurons.size();
        for (int i=0; i<numNeurons; ++i)
        {
            outputVal = nextLayer.m_neurons[i]->m_output;
            error = 0;
            for (int j=0; j<m_neurons.size(); ++j)
                error+=m_neurons[j]->m_weights[i]*m_neurons[j]->m_error;
            switch(type)
            {
                case ACT_TANH:
                    nextLayer.m_neurons[i]->m_error =
                                            DerTanh(outputVal)*error;
                    break;
```

```
            case ACT_LOGISTIC:
                nextLayer.m_neurons[i]->m_error =
                                    DerLogistic(outputVal)*error;
                break;
            case ACT_BIPOLAR:
                nextLayer.m_neurons[i]->m_error =
                            DerBipolarSigmoid(outputVal)*error;
                break;
            case ACT_LINEAR:
            default:
                nextLayer.m_neurons[i]->m_error = outputVal*error;
                    break;
        }
    }
}


//--------------------
void NLayer::AdjustWeights(NLayer& inputs,float lrate,
                            float momentum)
{
    for (int i=0; i<m_neurons.size(); ++i)
    {
        int numWeights = m_neurons[i]->m_weights.size();
        for (int j=0; j<numWeights; ++j)
        {
            //bias weight always uses -1 output value
            float output = (j==numWeights-1)? -1 :
                                inputs.m_neurons[j]->m_output;
            float error  = m_neurons[i]->m_error;
            float delta  = momentum*m_neurons[i]->m_lastDelta[j] +
                        (1-momentum)*lrate * error * output;
            m_neurons[i]->m_weights[j]   += delta;
            m_neurons[i]->m_lastDelta[j]  = delta;
        }
    }
}
```

The class houses the activation functions and their derivatives. Also, each layer has a list of its constituent neurons, as well as an m_type field (is this an input, hidden, or output layer?), and a threshold value (which is normally set to 1.0*f*, this value represents the output value the neuron must accumulate to fire if using a simple step activation function, or the *gain* of the sigmoid function being used, which corresponds to the smoothness of the *s* shape in the output graph: very small values approach a flat line, and very large values approach a step function shape).

- *Propagate()* is the layer extension to the function with the same name at the net level. It cycles through all the neurons in the level and performs the standard NN formula: sum all the inputs to the neuron, multiply by the corresponding connection weights, and then run it through the specified activation function.
- *BackPropagate()* is also the layer-specific continuation of this operation. It sums the total weight on each neuron, and then calculates the gradient by multiplying it with the output value, after having run the output through the derivative of the activation function. Several activation functions have been supplied. The standard logistic function gives values between 0 and 1. Both the tanh and bipolar sigmoid functions give values from –1 to 1. The linear function is the equivalent of *no* activation function, meaning that the output isn't scaled at all.
- *AdjustWeights()* performs the steepest-descent adjustment method on the weights because we've computed a gradient of the delta we're looking for. Steepest descent is a greedy algorithm, meaning that it gets stuck in local minima very easily, so care must be taken with this method. Hence, we're using momentum within our weight adjustment, which means that adjustments have to come more frequently to make large changes because earlier changes have a much larger priority associated with them. This helps guard against the steepest descent method getting stuck, but it does make training slower, so you will want to adjust the momentum value.

THE NNAIControl CLASS

The NNAIControl class will serve as the AI controller for the neural network technique. This class houses the network itself and the technique-specific usage code that links it to the AIsteroids game proper. As you can see in the header (Listing 23.5; Listing 23.6 shows some of the important function implementations), this class stores all the usual controller information (perception data and update methods, as well as being inherited from the FSMAIControl class so that it can also deal with the states of the AI ship), but also contains all the data and functionality for training and using the NN.

LISTING 23.5 NNAIControl class header.

```
class NNAIControl: public FSMAIControl
{
public:
    //constructor/functions
    NNAIControl(Ship* ship = NULL);
```

```
        ~NNAIControl();
        void Update(float dt);
        void UpdatePerceptions(float dt);
        void Init();
        void Reset();
        void GetNetOutput();
        void TrainNetAndSave();
        void ReTrainNetAndSave();

        //perception data
        float      m_powerupScanDist;

        //network output variables
        bool       m_shouldThrust;
        bool       m_shouldTurnLeft;
        bool       m_shouldTurnRight;

private:
        int        m_numIterationsToTrain;
        int        m_numSavedTrainingSets;
        float      m_maximumAllowedError;

        //network input variables
        float      m_speedMovingTogether;
        Point3f    m_nearestAsteroidDelta;
        float      m_shipMovingDirection;

        //net, used for training and for actual usage in game
        NeuralNet* m_net;
        vector<float> m_inputs;
        vector<float> m_outputs;
        int m_numInputs;
        int m_numOutputs;
        int m_numHiddenLayers;
        int m_numHiddenNodes;
        int m_netMode;
};
```

The constructor for this class sets itself up to do what needs to be done based on whether we're instantiating the controller in training mode, retraining mode, or the regular "use" mode. During the training modes, the network is instantiated by the training functions themselves and closed down after execution. The regular game-use mode instantiates the network right away because the game will potentially be using it to avoid obstacles.

In regular training mode, there is no real AI running because the training uses real input from a human player. As you can see in the `Update()` function, the `NNAIControl` structure stores what will be the network input and output variables whenever the `m_willCollide` perception is true. When thousands of sets of data are collected, the `Update()` method then instantiates and trains a network using the data, and finally saves off the network weights so they can be reused later.

Retrain mode works by loading the saved input and output training data from a file and training the network, then exiting from the game. Retraining is useful when you want to try different network designs (such as adjusting the number of hidden layers or nodes, changing to different activation functions, using more or less training iterations, etc.). Of course, if you decide to change the number of inputs or outputs, you'll need to recapture new training data using the regular `NM_TRAIN` mode.

LISTING 23.6 `NNAIController` function implementations.

```
//--------------------
NNAIControl::NNAIControl(Ship* ship):
FSMAIControl(ship)
{
    m_net      = NULL;

    Init();

    if(m_netMode == NM_USE)
    {
        m_net = new NeuralNet(m_numInputs,m_numOutputs,
                              m_numHiddenLayers,m_numHiddenNodes);
        m_net->ReadWeights();
    }
    else if (m_netMode == NM_RETRAIN)
    {
        m_numSavedTrainingSets = 1000;
        ReTrainNetAndSave();
    }

}

//--------------------
void NNAIControl::Update(float dt)
{
    Ship* ship = Game.m_mainShip;
```

```
if(!ship)
{
    m_machine->Reset();
    return;
}

switch(m_netMode)
{
    case NM_TRAIN:
        UpdatePerceptions(dt);
        if(m_willCollide)
        {
            //write test data to file
            FILE* pFile;
            if ((pFile =fopen("NNtrainingdata.txt","a"))== NULL)
                return;

            fprintf(pFile,"%f %f %f %f ",
                    m_nearestAsteroidDelta.x(),
                    m_nearestAsteroidDelta.y(),
                    m_speedMovingTogether,
                    m_shipMovingDirection);
            fprintf(pFile,"%d %d %d ",ship->IsThrustOn(),
              ship->IsTurningRight(),ship->IsTurningLeft());

            m_numSavedTrainingSets++;
            m_inputs.push_back(m_nearestAsteroidDelta.x());
            m_inputs.push_back(m_nearestAsteroidDelta.y());
            m_inputs.push_back(m_speedMovingTogether);
            m_inputs.push_back(m_shipMovingDirection);
            m_outputs.push_back(ship->IsThrustOn());
            m_outputs.push_back(ship->IsTurningRight());
            m_outputs.push_back(ship->IsTurningLeft());

            fclose(pFile);
        }

        if(m_numSavedTrainingSets==NUM_TRAINING_SETS_TO_AQUIRE)
        {
            TrainNetAndSave();
            Game.GameOver();
        }
        break;
```

```
        case NM_RETRAIN:
            Game.GameOver();
            break;

        case NM_USE:
        default:
            UpdatePerceptions(dt);
            if(m_willCollide)
                GetNetOutput();
            m_machine->UpdateMachine(dt);
            break;
    }
}
//-------------------
void NNAIControl::TrainNetAndSave()
{
    m_net = new NeuralNet(m_numInputs, m_numOutputs,
                          m_numHiddenLayers, m_numHiddenNodes);

    vector<float> tempIns;
    vector<float> tempOuts;
    for(int i =0;i< m_numIterationsToTrain;++i)
    {
        for(int j = 0;j< m_numSavedTrainingSets; ++j)
        {
            tempIns.clear();
            tempOuts.clear();
            //get training set inputs
            for(int k = 0;k<numInputs;++k)
                tempIns.push_back(m_inputs[k+j*numInputs]);
            //get training set outputs
            for(k = 0;k<numOutputs;++k)
                tempOuts.push_back(m_outputs[k+j*numOutputs]);

            m_net->Train(tempIns,tempOuts);
        }
        float totalError = m_net->GetError();
        if(totalError < m_maximumAllowedError)
        {
            //save out net and exit
            m_net->WriteWeights();
            return;
        }
    }
}
```

```
//--------------------
void NNAIControl::ReTrainNetAndSave()
{
    FILE* pFile;
    if ((pFile = fopen("NNtrainingdata.txt","r")) == NULL)
        return;


    m_net = new NeuralNet(m_numInputs,m_numOutputs,
                            m_numHiddenLayers,m_numHiddenNodes);


    vector<float> tempIns;
    vector<float> tempOuts;
    for(int i =0;i< m_numIterationsToTrain;++i)
    {
        for(int j = 0;j< m_numSavedTrainingSets; ++j)
        {
            tempIns.clear();
            tempOuts.clear();
            //get training set inputs
            for(int k = 0;k<m_numInputs;++k)
            {
                float temp;
                fscanf(pFile,"%f ",&temp);
                tempIns.push_back(temp);
            }
            //get training set outputs
            for(k = 0;k<m_numOutputs;++k)
            {
                float temp;
                fscanf(pFile,"%f ",&temp);
                tempOuts.push_back(temp);
            }

            m_net->Train(tempIns,tempOuts);
        }
        float totalError = m_net->GetError();
        if(i> 100 && totalError < m_maximumAllowedError)
        {
            //save out net and exit
            m_net->WriteWeights();
            return;
        }
    }
}
```

```
//--------------------
void NNAIControl::GetNetOutput()
{
    //clear out temp storage
    m_inputs.clear();
    m_outputs.clear();

    //set up inputs
    m_inputs.push_back(m_nearestAsteroidDelta.x());
    m_inputs.push_back(m_nearestAsteroidDelta.y());
    m_inputs.push_back(m_speedMovingTogether);
    m_inputs.push_back(m_shipMovingDirection);

    //get output values
    m_net->Use(m_inputs,m_outputs);
    m_shouldThrust    = m_outputs[0] > BOOL_THRESHOLD;
    m_shouldTurnRight = m_outputs[1] > BOOL_THRESHOLD;
    m_shouldTurnLeft  = m_outputs[2] > BOOL_THRESHOLD;
}
```

Use mode actually operates a finite-state machine (FSM) to run the ship. A slightly adjusted Evade state the Update() function from the new class, StateNNEvade, is shown in Listing 23.7, then uses output from the controller's NN to determine what to do in the case of an imminent collision. The net's output is determined in the NNAIController::Update() function, which checks the collision perception and updates the net output if necessary. GetNetOutput() runs the values through the net to get the current outputs and converts those outputs back into Boolean values. You might be asking, why not just have the net output Booleans directly? Because using analog values makes it easier to determine error gradient information, which will help us train the network better and faster. Plus, we can then determine the amount of generalization we want from our net. If an output is 0.4f, you might have some systems where that would still be a positive output; the game could also set a secondary action to occur, or adjust the primary behavior to take into account the low level of net output given the current input data. The inverse would be that you want very high levels of output before you set off an action, but again; it is much easier to make these kinds of determinations if the values coming out of your network are analog instead of purely digital.

LISTING 23.7 StateNNEvade::Update() method.

```
//--------------------
void StateNNEvade::Update(float dt)
{
    NNAIControl* parent = (NNAIControl*)m_parent;
```

```
        Ship* ship = parent->m_ship;

        if(parent->m_shouldThrust)//thrust
            ship->ThrustOn();
        else
            ship->ThrustOff();

        if(parent->m_shouldTurnRight)
            ship->TurnRight();
        else if(parent->m_shouldTurnLeft)
            ship->TurnLeft();
        else
            ship->StopTurn();

        parent->m_debugTxt = "Evade";
    }
```

PERFORMANCE WITHIN THE TEST BED

Although relatively slow, training the network with these parameters and setup is fairly successful. Most of this success is based on capturing good evasion data, which is the issue with most NN systems. Given the right data, you can get the network to use many of the same techniques to evade collisions. In the game, the CPU hit of using the trained network is negligible, which is always a good thing.

Training the NN with the largest possible training data set will allow the best results, especially in this situation, where the net needs to learn a fairly complex task. However, if your training set (for whatever reason) simply can't be very large and varied, you might need to watch out for overfitting of the data. An overfit NN is one that doesn't generalize well because it has matched the patterns of the input *too* closely and is no longer flexible enough to accurately include errant data points.

One way to counter this involves what is called *early stopping* to keep the network from overfitting the data. The technique is simply to stop training at the point at which you have balanced the line between generalization and error. You want an accurate NN, which makes the right decisions most of the time, but you still want it to intelligently "guess" if the input variables are a bit off kilter. Finding the best point at which to stop training is another tricky problem, one that requires experience and experimentation to solve. Most systems monitor the error coming out of the network, and stop training when error starts to increase after a long period of decreasing. However, this is not a hard-and-fast rule: The net may be finding its way out of a local maxima, rather than degrading performance caused by overfitting.

OPTIMIZATION

Optimizing NNs generally involves optimizing the training phase, because most NNs are used offline; using an already trained network to make game decisions is very fast. To speed up training of the algorithm, try to remove any unnecessary inputs (or consolidate inputs into more complex calculations) or hidden nodes. Also, experiment with the amount of error you are willing to live with because even a small decrease in maximum error allowance can allow a savings of many thousands of training iterations.

The other level of optimization of using NN systems lies in lessening the time it takes to construct a viable network design and creating highly effective, relevant training data. For any NN task that is nontrivial, both of these tasks are difficult and can take up a lot of programmer time. Optimizing this step of the process, however, involves having an understanding of how NNs work and knowledge about the specific task at hand.

In short, the more knowledge you have up-front about the relationships you're trying to model with the net, the better you will be at picking the right net inputs and choosing the minimum needed outputs, and the better your training data will be. Some general things to think about if you're finding the process of training your NN taxing:

- If your network seems to be getting stuck too easily in local maxima, where the error becomes stable, but is still higher than you'd like it to be, then you might be using too few training sets, or your hidden layer might be too small (by not having enough neurons at the hidden level, you haven't given your network enough degrees of freedom in which to search for the best solution).
- If your training seems to be unstable (meaning that the error seems to jump all over the place, never seeming to settle down or lessen consistently), you might have too many hidden-layer neurons, and the network has essentially been given too much room to experiment within.
- Overfitting, as we have mentioned before, can happen when you have too few training sets because even a very simple net can store a lot of information about a limited amount of data. Another point is that overfitting might happen when you have too many training iterations with the data, and you have trained *too long*. Try reducing the amount of iterations for each training set.
- Underfitting could occur if you have a large amount of very noisy training sets, or you don't train for enough iterations. An underfit NN is all generalization, with almost no accuracy. If your data is very noisy, it can exacerbate the problem by making it hard for the net to filter the noise from the real data. Finding a way to scale these training sets, to bring out the differences between real data points and noise, can help this process.

- If errors seem to be oscillating between values, you may be using too large a learning rate, or your momentum might be too high.
- Gradient descent is a greedy algorithm and will perform poorly if the step size (in this case, the learning rate) is too high. Possible solutions might be to simply lessen the learning rate (which would help, but might also dramatically lengthen training times), to dynamically change the learning rate (if the network's error is going down, slowly increase the learning rate; decrease the rate if the error is going up), or even to use a more costly method like Newton's (which involves finding the second derivative of error for pinpointing the nearest minimum).

PROS OF NEURAL NET-BASED SYSTEMS

NNs are a great way to find abstract relationships between input conditions. They are great at storing esoteric knowledge in a very usable and optimized way. Some of the other benefits of the method include the following:

- NNs can extract very complex mathematical function solutions. These mathematic functions are essentially approximated into the weights of an NN, so that when you use the net in the game, you essentially save yourself the CPU cost of having to perform the actual math. It has been mathematically proven that an NN with at least one hidden layer and nonlinear activation functions can accurately depict almost *any* finite dimensional vector function on a compact state set.
- Nets have an excellent ability to derive meaning from nonlinear or imprecise data. They can generalize connections and relationships between data in ways that are unintuitive or even impossible to see for a human. A well-trained, well-designed NN can generalize better than a human expert.
- Training takes a fraction of the CPU time that trial-and-error methods take, once a suitable network design has been determined.
- Humans "make sense" of them. The way that NNs organize data and knowledge appeals to people in a way that we can get understand, and so they are easier to debug or experiment with than with a more esoteric approach, like fuzzy-logic systems.

CONS OF NEURAL NET-BASED SYSTEMS

NNs are a great way to solve some problems. Many people, upon hearing about and/or experimenting with NNs, tend to immediately start thinking of them as magic duct tape that can solve any and all problems. But they are not that simple.

Determining how to *train* a NN is usually the most costly aspect of using them. The problem has thus been shifted. Instead of figuring out how to solve the problem (which *may* be an exponentially hard problem) we have replaced our work with now figuring out how to teach the NN to solve the problem (which has *definitely* been shown to be an exponentially hard problem). Other points of contention are the following:

- NNs are not magical; garbage in = garbage out. If you use arbitrary, numerous, or even bogus inputs to the network, there's a good chance that the net will find *some* correlating factors between them. This does not mean that you're going to want the output of those correlations. In fact, NNs are *famous* for learning the wrong thing. Most of the difficulty in finding the correct inputs and training data is weeding out input and training set relationships that you *don't* want the network to learn. Usually these bad relationships are only found after a network has been trained and has learned the unwanted abstraction. Only then might you stumble on the realization why your network is behaving errantly. But the correlation might be so obtuse that it might never occur to you, and hence, you would be stuck with pure trial and error in getting around the problem.
- An NN is a mathematical black box, and thus, hard or even impossible to debug. Once trained, the weight data within an NN is incomprehensible. You can't look at them like you can the nodes of a decision-tree structure and determine what is going on within the net. The information in the network is distributed throughout the connections in highly parallel or multiply efficient means; not alphabetically, in some kind of hierarchical fashion, or even based on the order of training. Debugging an NN solution usually involves going back to the starting board to adjust the pretraining parameters or data, and then retraining.
- All input fields must be numeric. Fuzzy values, or inputs that might be represented better by an expression, cannot be modeled within an NN. It would be better to use a hierarchical system in this case, with the NN being used for the more straightforward elements, and a different overhead structure (like a decision tree, or simple FSM) handling the strange or less-defined cases.
- NNs are difficult to implement, because of the high number of factors that must be determined without guidelines or rules for the best way to approach it. These factors involve network structure, input and output choices, activation function, learning rate, training data issues, and so forth. Nets are also very sensitive to somewhat random factors like weight initialization or redundant inputs.
- Overfitting, or noise learning, ruins generalization power and must be countered with the techniques described earlier.

- NNs can sometimes suffer from a phenomenon known as *catastrophic unlearning*. This occurs when an almost fully trained network is given additional training data that completely undoes all previous learning. Late addition of NN functionality, possibly suggested because of feedback from testing or focus groups, should be handled with care, unless you have given yourself ample time to deal with problems from mucking with the network.
- Lots of training data and CPU time may be required for training, especially for complex learning scenarios within large search spaces. If bugs come up in quality testing because of the NN portion of your game AI, retraining the network might become prohibitive, so be sure to consider this when deciding to go with an NN system.
- NNs don't scale well. NNs larger than a thousand nodes are rare and not very stable. Although the reasons behind this aren't completely understood, it appears that the *curse of dimensionality* (as it is sometimes called) seems to cause the learning ability of these large nets to implode somewhat, where there is so much freedom of movement within the search space that the network can essentially cyclically vary its weightings forever, never getting closer to a solution. Luckily, the types of NNs you might use within games have almost no reason to get this large.

EXTENSIONS TO THE PARADIGM

The FF, backpropagated-trained NN used in this chapter is *far* from the only type of NN in the world today. The number of network types is large and each is specifically designed for unique performance within a particular area. Some of these models do not really apply to gaming use, but it is still important to know of their existence, so that future exploitation can occur. Most of these come from the academic or business world, where NNs have evolved during the almost forty years they have been around. Some of these other types or extensions to the method are listed here. Note that this is not an exhaustive list by any means.

OTHER TYPES OF NNS

The NNs we've described in this chapter are certainly not the only kind available to you. Below are several other types of NNs that can be found in use.

- **Simple recurrent networks.** These are basically a variation on regular multi-layer NNs. In this scheme, the hidden layer of the network is also connected back to the input layer, with each connection having a weight of 1. The fixed back connections result in basically maintaining a copy of the previous values of the hidden units (because the net propagates over the connections before the learning rule is applied). Thus, the network can maintain a sort of state, allowing it to perform such tasks as sequence-prediction, which are beyond the power of a standard multilayer networks.

- **Hopfield nets.** Designed to mimic *associative memory* within the brain, these networks allow entire "patterns" to be stored, and then recalled, by the system. Also like the brain, if some of the connections between various parts of the system fail or are severed, the recall still has a good chance of succeeding. These structures use a set of completely connected neurons, each of which can only store a Boolean value. There are no dedicated input and output neurons in this system. Rather, input is applied to *all* the neurons, and then allowed to propagate until a steady state is achieved, at which point the state of all the neurons is considered the output of the system.

  These are useful for pattern recognition, especially with recall of these patterns. If you store a number of images within a Hopfield network, and then input one of those images, but destroy or corrupt parts of it, the network will usually be able to determine which stored image you started with. One thing that Hopfield nets provide over normal NNs is that the number of nodes necessary to store information, as well as additional information, can be calculated directly. Unlike normal NNs, in which the number of nodes is somewhat mystical, the nodes within a Hopfield net are simply distributed storage for the array of patterns, and so their number is a function of how much information needs to be absorbed.

- **Committee of machines.** This is a technique in which multiple nets are trained on the same data, but each is initialized differently. Then, during usage, all the nets are run on the input data, and the collection of networks "votes" on the final output, by taking statistical notion of the output of all the separate networks. This has statistically been shown to smooth out the problems dealing with neural nets. It is, however, even more costly in initial time investment than normal nets.

- **Self-organizing maps (SOM).** Useful for classification tasks (or clustering, as SOM users call it), SOMs have two network layers: an input layer, and a *competition* layer. The sum of all the input connections to any one neuron in the competition layer is called a *reference vector* in the input space. In essence, the SOM consists of a number of input *vectors* that are represented by a set of neurons in the competition layer, which are usually laid out as a two-dimensional grid of neurons. SOMs use a form of unsupervised learning called *competition learning,* hence the layer's name. When a new input pattern is introduced to the net, the first step is to find the competition neuron whose reference vector is closest to the new pattern. The "winning" neuron is then singled out and becomes the focus of weight changes within the network. Not only does this neuron's weights change, however, but also those neurons within its *neighborhood* (defined as all the neurons within some grid distance from the winner), will change in proportion to their distance from the focus neuron.

The size of this neighborhood shrinks over time, so that when fully trained, the neighborhood size is zero. The effect of this method is that the organization of the input data becomes grouped within the net so that inputs that are the most similar will be located closer together. The chief usage of these kinds of maps is to visualize relationships and classes within large, highly dimensioned inputs. In games, it might be useful in player modeling, taking a number of dimensions of behavior into account and giving the AI system a better picture of the kind of player the human tends toward.

OTHER TYPES OF NN LEARNING

In addition to the methods of training NNs we discussed in this chapter, there are also several other commonly used ways.

- **Reinforcement.** The backpropagation technique used in this chapter is a form of supervised learning which some call *learning with a teacher,* because you are providing the network with output target values. Reinforcement learning also involves supervision, but only evaluative help. It has thus been called *learning with a critic.* When the network outputs some value because of the input information, the supervisor simply declares if the result was a good one. This can be done by a human expert or can be delivered to the network as an additional input signal broadcast from outside the network (the environment, or something else that the net has to interact with), which would allow the net to perform mostly unsupervised.

- **Unsupervised learning.** These techniques allow the network to train itself completely on its own. It does not require hand-fed training input data, or target outputs. Examples of unsupervised techniques include using a genetic algorithm to find the best set of NN connection weights (this technique becomes much like reinforcement learning, in which the GA fitness function becomes the critic), perturbation learning (in which the weights are iteratively and randomly adjusted and tested for improvement), or competitive techniques (which involve a number of neurons "competing" for the right to learn by having their weights adjusted within the net; the winner is usually based on the inputs being given to the net rather than a stated output). Another branch of unsupervised learning involves problems for which the output cannot be known ahead of time. In this case, the main job of the network is to classify, cluster, find relationships, and otherwise compress the input data in specific areas. SOMs are an example of this.

DESIGN CONSIDERATIONS

Neural networks are definitely not a "one size fits all" AI technique particularly in gaming, where their inflexibility toward debugging and extension make them hard to tune for gameplay concerns. Take careful note of the engine design considerations from Chapter 2, "An AI Engine: The Basic Components and Design": types of solutions, agent reactivity, system realism, genre, platform, development limitations, and entertainment limitations.

TYPES OF SOLUTIONS

NNs are great when you have simple, modular systems that map inputs to outputs in surprising, nonlinear, black box ways. Because of this, they tend to be much more *tactical* in nature, rather than high-level strategic solutions. You wouldn't want to train an NN to run the diplomacy campaign in your real-time strategy (RTS) game. That task is simply too large, too complex, and needs far too much tuning and tweaking. But you might use it to decide which animation you want to play to catch a baseball. Here we have a very atomic task, with specific inputs (the incoming ball, the player's position, and his skills), as well as specific outputs (each of the possible catch animations). The logic for mapping these together with more common techniques might be fairly CPU-intensive or complicated to construct. A small NN will be far less CPU-intensive, and the finished network wouldn't need changing unless additional catch animations are added to the game (in which case, traditional game logic might have to be added anyway).

AGENT REACTIVITY

NNs can actually optimize CPU-intensive calculations, so their use might actually contribute to faster reactivity by a game agent. Plus, they can be taught to actually employ more human reaction times.

SYSTEM REALISM

In many ways, NNs help make systems seem much more realistic, mostly because they are *general* pattern-matching systems, meaning that they are not special-case systems like FSMs or scripted entities that can react specifically to particular scenarios. Because of this, they might react wrongly to something, but still in a way that *seems right,* because the pattern still holds for whatever reason. People routinely run into the same problems, mostly because we're using the same sorts of general case pattern matching in our own minds. So you see people running into glass doors from time to time, or reaching out to where they *thought* the wall was to stop their fall. Whether or not this behavior translates into the video game world is up to the context of the action, the type of game you're creating, and the intended audience. A comedy adventure game primarily being played by more mature people might catch small details like this and perceive it as much more realistic and humorous. But a young child playing a serious, heavily action-based game might see such "mistakes" as "stupid AI."

GENRE AND PLATFORM

Genre and platform are not really a limiting factor for NNs. They are truly a modular technique, useful when you have a specific need for their categorization or predictive powers.

DEVELOPMENT LIMITATIONS

The primary concern for NN usage is development limitations. NNs require both an upfront investment in time and energy to design and collect training data. They also require a significant period to actually train, as well as deal with tuning issues later in development. Online learning (during live gameplay) in NNs requires an even larger commitment in time and design. If it is hard (or even impossible) for testers to restage crash events in your game because the adaptive NN in your AI system keeps dynamically changing behavior or game events, you are going to be hard pressed to completely debug the game. Plus, the sheer effort of trying to test a gameplay system that has large areas of adaptive or evolving elements is obviously much greater than static content that can be tested from A to Z.

ENTERTAINMENT LIMITATIONS

The difficulty in tuning, tweaking, and adding to an NN-driven system has been discussed throughout the chapter. For this reason, NNs should really only be used on areas within the game that require the kind of "do it once and leave it," black box sort of solution that NNs provide. Game developers often train an NN throughout the development cycle and then "freeze" it once the game ships to avoid support problems afterward.

SUMMARY

Neural nets are another AI technique that can help you solve difficult problems, especially if they are nonlinear or unintuitive in nature, and you can either come up with test data for training, or determine some way of using unsupervised methods to teach the system.

- Natural brains work by clusters of brain cells called neurons transmitting electrical impulses to each other over synapses crossing from axon to dendrite.

- Artificial neurons have a number of inputs (each with an assigned weight), an internal bias, and an output value with an optional activation function.
- Neural nets are connected systems of neurons in particular formations. The usual structure is a number of input nodes, followed by a number of hidden nodes, followed by a number of output nodes. Feed-forward networks are only connected in one direction. Recurrent networks are completely connected, in both directions. Other systems also exist.
- When using an NN, you must determine the NN structure, choose a learning type, and create training data. Then, you can implement your NN, and begin tuning the implementation to optimize your results.
- Pros of the method include the ability to extract and compress complex mathematic functions, their powers of generalization, fast usage in game, and the fact that their operation "makes sense" to most people.
- Cons of NNs involve their difficulty to implement and debug, their sensitivity to training, the time investment requirement to train and test them, and that they usually don't scale well to larger problems.
- Some extensions to NNs include recurrent networks, Hopfield nets, self-organizing maps, and the committee of machines usage. Other learning techniques besides supervised learning involve reinforcement and unsupervised learning.

24 Other Techniques of Note

In This Chapter

- Artificial Life
- Planning Algorithms
- Production Systems
- Decision Trees
- Fuzzy Logic
- Summary

This chapter will discuss a few of the remaining AI techniques that show promise in the game AI programming field. These techniques aren't widely used at present but have found their niches and may become important foundations for future AI engines. Each technique will be dissected with an overview of the method, some general usage notes, pros and cons, and design considerations.

ARTIFICIAL LIFE

Science, in general, has always been a search to find what some call "governing principles." That is, rules or truths so universal, so fundamental, that they cannot be broken down any further; rules that can be used without fail to understand aspects of nature and predict outcomes based on hard equations. Isaac Newton gave every other scientist of his time a collective warm fuzzy feeling when he "proved" Descartes' *clockwork universe* view of things (in which God set up everything like a clock; including the planets, plants, animals, and everything nonhuman), by providing the world with the equations necessary to boil down the movements of everything into neat, mathematical bundles.

We have since found entire *oceans* of circumstance where Newton's theories break down, and scientists are once again on the prowl for governing principles. Now that we are able to look closely at the behaviors of living organisms (or even at the behaviors of subatomic particles), we are increasingly astounded by the diversity and complexity that almost every system shows. With inanimate systems, we can break things down by deconstructing physical systems into components that can be isolated and studied and extract deeper knowledge. Living systems, however, do not typically yield to these methods. Life's very nature does not typically allow this kind of disassembly, and so we are usually at a loss.

Life scientists are also at a loss for examples of early "work." The earliest living system probably doesn't exist anymore; it was most likely replaced by more complex evolutions billions of years ago. An equivalent task would be for an alien race to try to determine how writing started on earth by studying *The New York Times,* and nothing older. The chances of finding any governing principles is very limited. A useful approach to learning more might be to construct our own, ultrasimplistic "life simulations" and, by doing so, find out more about how life in general operates.

Artificial life (or *alife*) is the field of studies that hopes to understand natural life better by attempting to recreate biological phenomena from within virtual computer environments, or other artificial means. It is actually the name for an entire *collection* of computer science and engineering disciplines, although they do share some ideas. One main tenet of the alife camp is that life is simply an emergent property of nature following some very simple rules over and over again. An emergent property refers to *a trait or behavior exhibited by a creature that reaches beyond the capabilities of its constituent parts.*

Within games, we search for emergent behaviors and gameplay situations as well. This has led many to investigate or try to employ alife principles in the search for new ways to have fun within the confines of a game environment.

ARTIFICIAL LIFE USAGE IN GAMES

Some popular games that are considered to be in the alife family include *Black & White* and the *Creatures* games, which were discussed in Chapter 14, "Miscellaneous Genres of Note" (and by popular, I mean critically popular; neither game was wildly *financially* popular). Both of these titles had beings that used very simple rules that combined in interesting ways to dynamically foster behaviors that hadn't been specifically programmed in by the game authors. The totem animals in *Black & White* were supposed to listen to the players' instruction and try to make the players happy while also catering to their own needs. *Creatures* actually modeled whole systems of chemistry and genetics to try to simulate "building" an entire being, which the game called Norns.

ARTIFICIAL LIFE DISCIPLINES

Some of the disciplines that are considered alife include Cellular Automata, self-organizing behavior and flocking, genetic algorithms, and robotics.

Cellular Automata (CA)

CAs are a group of algorithms that show a stunning amount of complex behavior with the very simplest of rules. One of the most famous CAs, *Conway's Game of Life,* is played using a two-dimensional (2D) collection of cells, each of which can be populated or empty, and each of which has eight neighbor cells. By then applying four simple rules to the cells of the playfield, a vast amount of complex behavior can be seen.

"The Rules" for a populated cell are:

- Each cell with one or no neighbors dies, due to loneliness.
- Each cell with four or more neighbors dies, because of overpopulation.
- Each cell with two or three neighbors survives.

"The Rule" for an empty cell:

- Each cell with three neighbors becomes populated, because of a birth.

Certain constructs in *Conway*'s CAs have even been shown to be able to perform mathematics. Others can reproduce various structures from nature with incredible detail, including plant structures, seashells, and coral reefs. The freeware program *MCell,* written by Mirek Wojtowicz, can display a vast amount of CA behavior. It has a general graphical interface for building and watching CAs in action. Some of its output can be seen in Figure 24.1.

CA behavior patterns can be found at the microscopic *and* macroscopic levels. At the microscopic level, these patterns can be used to simulate the growth of mold, or the spread of amoebae, and at the other end of the spectrum, they can be used to discover trends in traffic jams, or city building.

Genetic Algorithms

Genetic algorithms are sometimes lumped into alife, although many alife researchers would say that is a wrong classification. GAs are a fairly abstract system, and the one thing GAs try to model (evolution through genetic manipulation) is almost nothing like the simplified version used by the algorithm as we know it. Rather, think of GAs as an interesting tangent that computer science has devised by drawing on the *idea* of evolution.

Robotics

Although most of robotics deals with creating systems that can perform in places or ways that we cannot, it can be said that some roboticists are trying to create artificial beings, hence *physical* alife. They aren't trying to understand nature but,

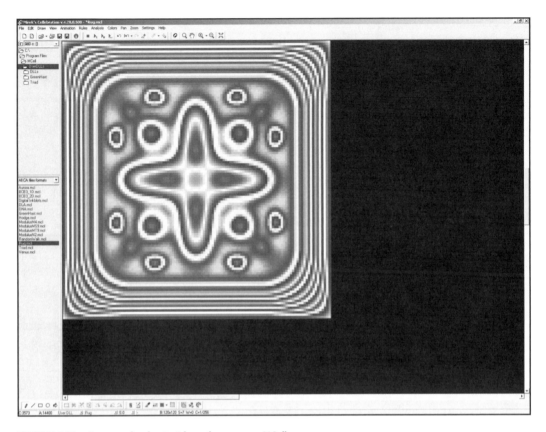

FIGURE 24.1 An example of output from the program *MCell*.

rather, are trying to create their own. In trying to emulate life, they end up with an understanding of how things are done in nature and the problems that nature is solving with its solutions, an example of very cyclical scientific thinking. Different researchers are going in opposite directions toward this end. Some are creating robots that are very simplistic, but can communicate with other simple robots to create hive-mind communities. Others develop robots that are being trained by humans to act like humans, including emotional response, a sense of personal space, and personality development.

PROS

As with any AI technique, there are reasons why its use is considered beneficial. For alife techniques, these include: emergent behavior and behavior reuse.

1. *Emergent behavior.* Alife is one of the best ways we currently have of creating emergent situations semiconsistently. The more scripted a behavior, or

sequences of behaviors are, the less emergence you are going to see, by definition. Conversely, emergent behavior will be most likely found in open games (meaning they allow the players and AI characters to perform many types of activities) with simple actions that can be combined in many different ways, leading to a wealth of different final behaviors.

2. *Behavior reuse.* Alife techniques force developers to build games out of building blocks, distilling down the gameplay until it can be expressed as simple rules that only have meaning over many iterations. In fact, most alife game creations are simple to code for, but take lengthy amounts of time to tune.

Cons

However, alife techniques also come with a couple of key costs: the unpredictability of emergent behavior, and tuning issues.

1. *Emergent behavior* is unpredictable. Emergence in the game industry is a huge double-edged sword. Alife *can* create solid, compelling gameplay situations out of thin air. But, that creation might never come, leaving you high and dry, with no real game of which to speak. The emergent behavior might not be that entertaining, or too subtle for most audiences. Any time you have free-form behavior, with no set outcome in mind, you open the door for both the magic *and* the mundane.

2. *Tuning issues.* What if tuning the game destroys the emergent behavior? Small changes to game parameters, or gameplay systems, could easily unravel the very thing that is the most compelling part of your game. In fact, fixing a bug sometimes sets in motion a chain of events that might subtly change gameplay for the worse. This situation can happen to any game, however, and sometimes (with some work) you can find out the reason behind the advantageous configuration of the buggy code and incorporate it into a bug-free version, minimizing this problem. However, there are no guarantees because several different factors are working in conjunction in obviously nonintuitive ways.

Areas for Exploitation Within Games

Game programmers could use alife techniques in a number of ways to enrich their games:

■ Further use of more sophisticated flocking techniques, for city crowds, and so forth.

■ Other types of movement can also be simulated using *Conway's Game of Life* rules. The exploratory creeping of single-cell organisms, or the spread of plant vines could be thus controlled algorithmically by suitable usage of Conway-style systems. In this way, the elements using these algorithms would move not in random or scripted ways, but in emergent, "life motivated" fashions that could be much deeper gameplay-wise in regard to gameplay than simpler setups.

■ MMORPGs could employ alife techniques with the indigenous creatures of their game worlds. This could lead to the creation of actual working ecologies within the world, instead of random spawn points with scripted monsters. A dragon living in an area might be surviving by predating a local herd of deer. If the player comes in and kills too many deer, it would anger the dragon, who's suddenly hungry because his food source has been cut off. The dragon might come after the player, start razing nearby towns, or have to migrate and find a new food source. Moving might invade another large predator's territory.

PLANNING ALGORITHMS

Planning is defined as *deciding upon a course of action before acting*, specifically by using knowledge of a larger scope, planners chain together actions that will lead them toward a more long-term solution to the problem at hand. A clear-cut example of this in real life is a creature that, although wildly successful, does no planning at all: the common housefly. Given its tiny brain, it can still fly rings around the typical human wannabe flykiller with almost comical efficiency. But a fly cannot, and will never, see a closed window and tell itself "Hmm. Better go around to the open door." This simple fact is the reason that more dead flies can usually be found in windowsills than anywhere else in the house. For flies, windows are the game-AI equivalent of badly connected pathfinding nodes, "If I just keep trying, I should be able to get out. . . ."

Conceptually, most planning algorithms follow a somewhat simple formula:

1. Break the abilities of the AI into distinct *operators*.
2. Design your AI character, as well as your game environment, so that it can be represented as being a member of a set of *states*.
3. Either *construct a tree* that shows the transition connections between states (listing the operators that will cause these transitions), or have rules embedded in each state that details which operators are available. The AI then forms plans within a local working memory by applying these transition operators on a copy of its current state, testing for the best action to get the AI to the behavior it wants.

Given the above setup, planning for a particular AI-controlled character involves knowing what state the character is in, what state the character wants to be in, and then finding the string of operators that will get the character from its current state to its wanted state.

In pathfinding, the operators are movement types (physically running or walking, as well as actions like taking the train, or using a teleporter, depending on the game type). The states in this case would be the pathnodes within the map that define the pathfinding network. This network is the tree that you would then use with your trusty A* algorithm to plan a path.

Taken a certain way, our standard decision-making paradigms, such as finite-state machines (FSMs) and all the rest, can all be considered a form of *preprocessed* planning, a sort of optimization on the planning process. Given a robust representation of the game, and a wide range of low-level operators, a planning algorithm should be able to find the best behaviors necessary to affect the game state in any legal way. But because planning algorithms can be costly, we have historically used "hardcoded" planning (in our case, a state machine, a script, etc.) that allows us to *usually* do the right behaviors. With more complex game environments, invariably our set patterns of behavior have areas in which they fail, and these are where exploits are born.

CURRENT USAGE IN GAMES

Most games use some form of planning algorithm already, in the form of the A* search they're using for pathfinding. The pathfinding system stores a wide scope of information about the game world and allows the AI-controlled creatures to make plans about how to travel from A to B.

Some games, especially real-time strategy (RTS) games, use the exact same system to also perform other planning tasks. Say an AI civilization in an RTS game sees a certain kind of enemy unit cruise by: the laser boat. It now knows that the enemy can build those units, and to defend its shoreline structures against this boat, this civilization will require its own laser boats, or a defensive structure called a tower of reflection. By having a technology tree, which describes the prerequisites necessary for researching any given skill or structure, the AI can effectively generate a "path" from where it is in the technology tree to where it needs to be to build one of the two units it requires. It can even determine which defense is "closer" (or cheaper, or whatever metric it might currently favor), and go there. Also, by noting that the enemy has a particular technology, the AI can update its tech-tree model for the enemy by checking off all the units that are prerequisites along the path to that technology.

Planning algorithms have just begun to be seriously used within games, mostly because of the advanced strategic thinking of RTS games. Some earlier genres, such as war games, had large quantities of advanced strategies. But most war games are historically based, and follow a semiscripted pattern that mimics the real historic battle; this usually works better than trying to model Napoleon, hoping that the game will fight the same way he did. In this way, these history-based games were actually more of an example of *expert systems*, sets of rules laid out by an expert (in this case, Napoleon) as opposed to modelled general intelligence. More on this later in the chapter.

Planning is finally being seen as a primary human skill, so advanced AI systems are increasingly turning to planning to seem more intelligent and humanlike. In an FTPS, for instance, endowing a bot with anticipation can make it seem much more lifelike. Anticipation is another form of planning. An AI bot sees a human player enter a room. The bot could run a planning algorithm that would try and conclude what the human is going to do in that room. If it's a dead-end room, with a nice powerup, then a planning run might come back that the plan is to get that powerup, and then come back out the same door. Not only does the AI have a good idea that the human will come back out the door, but because the bot has the action plan, it can even estimate about how long it will take for the human to appear in the door. The AI can set a very effective ambush.

Another planning scenario might involve seeing the human with an inferior weapon, and chasing the human down. But, the AI is also checking the human's potential "plan," and notices that in the direction the human is headed, a *much* better weapon is around the corner. If the AI is not very healthy, and was only pursuing because of a firepower advantage, the AI might be smarter to break off and head for a health powerup, knowing that it has some free time because the human is going to be busy getting the weapon.

This is serious AI behavior and needs to be used in gameplay situations when the human is expecting a serious opponent. You wouldn't want just any first-person shooters/third-person shooters (FTPS) enemy in a long, story-filled game firing a rocket into a door just as you got there; that would seem like cheating to the player, and neither fair nor fun. But in a deathmatch setting, on a high level of difficulty, the human player almost expects this kind of behavior (because the player also uses it), and would be disappointed by bots that don't use it.

The next level of this is to have the AI bot anticipate the human anticipating the bot. So if the bot runs into a room with no other exits, and had some notion that there was a human following it, it might fire a rocket toward the best ambush angle through the door, or simply wait in the room until the human gives up camping outside. This can get pretty expensive, but the concept is clear, and the benefit is that you have AI bots that cannot only exploit the players' moves, but can step out of their own routines if they sense players exploiting them, leading to advanced, humanlike performance.

Typically, even for planning that wasn't pathfinding, games have done this searching using A* (because most games have already implemented efficient, load-balanced versions of A* already). This is usually fine, especially because most computer games don't have large numbers of operators or agent states. However, if you find your planning algorithm slowing down your game, you should look into some of the more optimized planning search techniques, such as means-end analysis (MEA). MEA combines forward and backward searching of the decision tree, and tries to minimize unnecessary search specifically for planning algorithms.

Another common planning optimization is called patch recalculation, where a "broken" plan (one in which a step has been invalidated because of some game event) doesn't invalidate the entire plan but, rather, is sent to a function that will come up with planning steps that will work around the broken link, thus *patching* the hole in your plan. This method is only useful if the length of your entire plan is long enough to justify not just tossing the entire plan and starting over. But for long or computationally expensive plans, this method provides a way for keeping plans up-to-date without having to start from square one all the time.

Minimax is another planning algorithm, which considers that your opponent is going to be working against you every chance he can get. Although minimax has been mostly used in board games like *Chess* and the like, certain turn-based RPGs or civ games could (some already do) benefit from its use, by replacing the more scripted, repetitive combat sequences that are the norm of these games, and using a basic minimax to perform simple planning based on the abilities of the enemies and the humans. Specific battles could still be scripted, but most battles would not feel quite so monotonous and unchanging. The planner could also take into account some reinforcement learning, if you wanted to give the player a challenge by disallowing him (through effective defensive blocks) to get away with repeating similar, very effective combat maneuvers.

PROS

Planning provides a number of solid advantages. These include intelligent-looking behavior, data-independent solutions, and hierarchical implementation.

1. Planning algorithms provide *much* more intelligent-looking behavior. Very few decisions in life require no forethought whatsoever. In fact, it could be said that anything larger than basic reflexive actions require at least some plan. Even scratching your nose requires a plan if you're wearing a motorcycle helmet and mittens.

2. Planning is a generic algorithm and can provide data-independent solutions. So, the same pathfinding search algorithm in your RTS game can also help your AI research technology in the right order, set up the necessary orders to sequence a large-scale attack on an enemy, and set up its bases in such a way that it doesn't run out of room later in the game.

3. Like most generic algorithms, planning can be implemented hierarchically. You can layer your planning system, so that each layer has a much easier time creating its plan, thus optimizing the overall planning costs.

An example of this would be a high-level planner finding the plan "build large army, then attack next town." The next layer down would then make a lower-level plan for "build large army" and another for "attack next town." The process repeats until you've developed plans at a low enough level that the resultant plan involves giving behavioral orders to the individual characters involved. Each layer in the system can use just enough detail as is required to simplify a given *particular* layer of the planner but still give meaningful plans.

CONS

The costs associated with planners involve computation expense and can also affect AI reaction time.

1. Planning can be computationally expensive, if unnecessarily long plans are attempted. Most games (even strategic games) rarely require their AI to plan too far in advance. Lengthy plans are costly to create because human players are so unpredictable that a long plan rarely ever pans out. Plan depth is a careful balance between speed and flexibility of your plan versus having your plans be too short range to avoid gaffs. For long or expensive plans, some time can be regained by using patch recalculation.
2. Planning can make the AI seem sluggish or unreactive if plans are too monolithic, or take too long to adapt to new situations. Of course, this is within the confines of the game you are working on: large-scale civ games can require more planning than most, but they are also usually turn-based and, thus, will not be considered "sluggish."

AREAS FOR EXPLOITATION WITHIN GAMES

Games could use planning algorithms when creating strategic AI systems that require many steps to achieve goals. The previously mentioned RTS tasks are prime candidates. But action games could use some simple planning as well.

1. FTPS opponents can use anticipation to set ambushes and traps.
2. AI drivers can plan more complex racecar movements to pass an opponent in a more realistic way. Instead of strategic "speed-ups" that might actually cheat, AI drivers could feign on key corners, and then try to pass at critical times by planning maneuvers based on the other cars' positions, time left, and so forth.
3. Fighting games could plan combos like human boxers do: a boxer knows that if he strategically drops his guard and openly allows himself to take a

specific punch that his opponent will then be open for a much more damaging combination.

4. A football game could plan the order in which to perform plays to confuse the human, or to best take advantage of the time it has left on the clock.

PRODUCTION SYSTEMS

Production systems are sometimes referred to as *expert systems*—you might be using a primitive version in your game right now. This is because production systems are essentially *rule-based systems that strive to encompass expert knowledge within a specific area.* The simplest example is that of using hardcoded conditional if-then branches within your AI engine to make decisions. Back in the old days of AI, researchers tried very hard to create *general* computer intelligence; they believed that they could solve every problem with the suitable brute force application of logical rules.

The trend continued until 1969 when Alan Newell and Herbert Simon released their theory of the General Problem Solver (GPS) [Newell 61], which gave a basic set of rules for supposedly solving any problem, somewhat based on how they believed the human mind to operate, a process called means-end analysis. All that the algorithm needed was a statement of the goal to be achieved and a set of the problem's "rules." Although GPS was very versatile with the simple puzzles and chess problems that were defined well enough for its limitations, it didn't take long to discover that GPS definitely did not solve general problems. What it did do, however, was introduce the concept of using actions as operators to transform the current world state. Production systems are the field that grew out of GPS theory.

Ironically, production systems are used to perform the exact opposite of what GPS was intended for—generality. Instead, these systems are now used to store expert knowledge about a highly *specific* problem. The first expert system was used to interpret mass spectra, and since then expert systems have been diagnosing specific diseases and giving mortgage tax advice.

Games do this every day, with reams of code dedicated to the storage of expert rules necessary to play hockey, gobble power pellets, and rocket-jump. All of the code that traditionally detailed how to make decisions within games like this could be thought of as expert knowledge.

However, a full production algorithm is much more organized and is separated into four parts: a global database, production rules, a rule/situation matcher, and a conflict resolution function (for use with rule collisions). The global database represents all the current facts the system knows about its environment. The production rules are the actual if-then clauses that serve as operators to transform our environment. The matcher is the function for deciding which operator to use next upon the database to get closer to your goal. The simplest matcher can be as simple as a function that searches the database and compares rule "if" clauses to the current world state, but specialized algorithms are significantly faster than brute force, as they usually are. Conflict resolution happens when multiple rules are matched to the database simultaneously. Most resolution schemes are very simple, even random.

One thing to note is that traditionally, production systems have only used what is known as *forward-chaining inference* (meaning that they can only perform logical inference in the forward direction: if I AM ON FIRE, then I SHOULD JUMP IN THE LAKE), but modern extensions have allowed for *backward-chaining inference* to be used as well (I JUST JUMPED IN THE LAKE, therefore I MIGHT HAVE BEEN ON FIRE).

In practice, production systems can be used to code regular game logic, serve as a planning system (because they can solve order-of-operation problems in tasks that require more than one step), and can even be used as memory and learning devices (by allowing the addition and removal of data from the global database).

True rule production systems haven't *quite* made their appearance in mainstream gaming, but a forerunning academic project *is* making use of gaming to improve their production system. *Soar*, a project started by Alan Newell, John Laird, and Paul Rosenbloom (the same Newell from GPS) as a test bed for Newell's theories of cognition, have been used by the academic community since 1983.

Soar provides an open-source, ANSI C, general production system for cognitive scientists, and anybody else who wants to use it. See Figure 24.2 for a high-level *Soar* system overview. John Laird, after doing some *Soar* work with Defense Advanced Research Project Agency (DARPA) developing intelligent air combat agents, began experimenting with using *Soar* as a means for advancing AI performance within commercial video games. His team at the University of Michigan Artificial Intelligence Lab has successfully interfaced *Soar* with both *Decent 3*, and *Quake 2*, and created competent, nonscripted opponents for each game. Using a system of more than 700 rules, the team created a quake bot that could navigate arbitrary game levels, use all weapons and level elements (such as bounce pads and teleporters), and give good players a challenge. Also, the system performed planning, and so it could anticipate human actions, create custom-level routes of travel to maximize the amount of powerups it could collect, and perform intelligent ambushes and hunting behaviors.

PROS

Production systems are a good general algorithm. They have been heavily researched, are goal directed, and highly reactive.

1. *General algorithm.* Again, like planning algorithms, a production system's decisions are data independent, so separate areas of the game can use

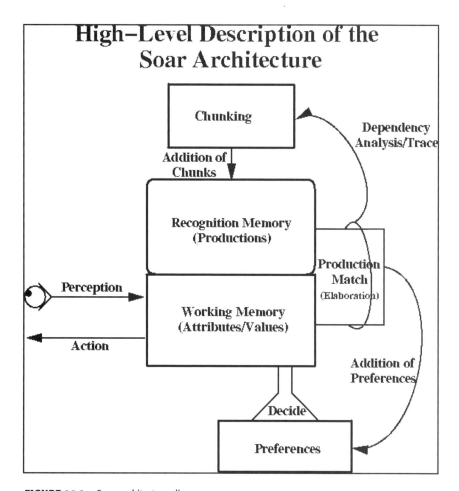

FIGURE 24.2   Soar architecture diagram.

production systems to provide disparate systems with rule-based decision making. This can be within separate databases, with different rule sets, or with any combination of sharing.

2. *Research.* Tons of research has been done on production systems. Fast-matching algorithms like RETE and TRETE (a stateless variation of RETE) have been created to dramatically speed up condition checking within a production system.

3. *Goal-directed.* Production systems are generally *goal-directed,* meaning they pick an overall goal and find a way to make it happen. This creates a much greater illusion of intelligence than purely reactive behavior does.

4. *Highly reactive.* These systems can be highly reactive and offer real similarity to human performance (with a good set of production rules).

Cons

Production systems also share planning systems' primary disadvantage.

1. Like planners, production systems can be computationally expensive, especially with games having a large rule set or nonarbitrary match collision-resolution. If the game has to *find* matches and must also perform heavy calculation to *arbitrate* matches, the cost of using the system can be high.

Areas for Exploitation Within Games

A production system could feasibly be written in a highly data-driven way, so that new rules, perceptions, and the like could be added to the game world by simply adding to the game's data files. The production system would just perform the same algorithm given the new set of production rules. A system like this would be highly extensible and infinitely reusable.

Decision Trees

Decision trees are another way in which commonly used code structures can be simply reorganized for greater flexibility and more functionality. Instead of having pages of if-then statements, you can implement each statement as a node on a tree and construct the tree such that you traverse the tree instead of a bunch of nested ifs. Figure 24.3 shows an example decision tree structure, representing the AI necessary to run a *Joust* opponent. The tree starts at a *root* node, which can also be labeled as the "question" node. What question is the tree answering? In this case, it is "What should I do now?" Note that our illustration diagram is a *binary decision tree* (BDT) because all of the answers to any given question nodes are Boolean, yes-or-no decisions. Special optimization algorithms, and even methods of reorganization after insertion and deletion are available to binary trees (because they are essentially red-black tree structures) that are not available to trees with arbitrary decision type.

There are two commonly used types of decision trees: *classification* trees, and *regression* trees, both of which are statistical methods that allow the construction of decision trees through algorithmic means by way of using a set of training data. Both methods can be considered a sort of "poor man's neural net," (NN) in that they try to generalize inputs to outputs. The differences between using decision trees and NNs is important to point out:

■ NNs are a black-box system; their internal weights cannot be meaningfully inspected and understood, whereas a fully "trained" decision tree can be very descriptive and easy to understand.

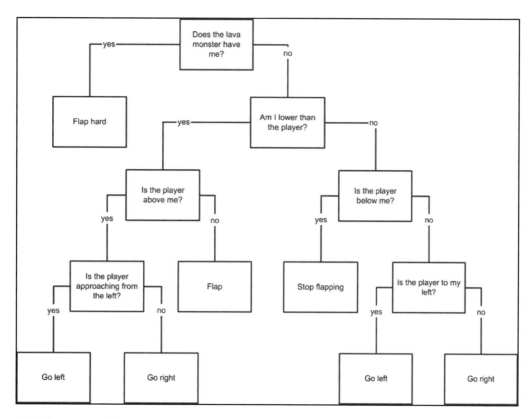

FIGURE 24.3   Decision-tree structure for *Joust.*

- Decision trees can only comprehend *hard* comparison limits within a (typically) binary outcome. Because of this, their predictive ability is somewhat limited and rigid. NNs are precisely the opposite in that they excel at gracefully handling very noisy data or data with gaps and strange jumps in behavior.
- Output from decision trees are always discrete values, whereas output from an NN can be a continuous value if using the right activation function.
- Decision trees consider a single variable at a time; this is referred to as a *monothetic* algorithm. It may miss the case when multiple variables are weakly influential separately, but are heavily influential on behavior in combination. NNs are considered *polythetic,* in that they consider multiple variables simultaneously. This is one of the things that make NNs hard to work with (in that an NN may find polythetic relations where you didn't expect them within test data, and this adversely affects its learning), but this trait is also precisely why they are so effective in areas that decision trees are not.

■ NNs are usually *much* more accurate than tree methods. A statistical examination of the relative error in a traditional example data set might be ten times or more for tree-based methods over a backpropagated NN.

Classification trees are BDTs that work on categorical input variables, whereas regression trees deal with continuous input variables. BDTs do allow a combination of variable types, but most game AI problems that would call for this method will usually be one or the other. A classification task might involve trying to determine what "type" of player the human is behaving like in an FTPS game (hunter, sniper, purely defensive, berserk, etc.) and setting the AI to a specific chunk of code tuned to deal with that type of player. A regression task would be more along the lines of a prediction task, in which the same AI system might try to predict the perceived difficulty that the human is encountering with the game, and then adjust its AI behaviors if this difficulty is too hard or too easy.

PROS

Using decision trees lead to plenty of pros. These include ease of use, tons of research, and they typically capture the level of detail and accuracy that games require.

1. Decision trees are easy to use and understand. This makes them perfect as a "rough pass" AI system; they can take example data and find logical connections where the programmers might not have seen it. It also provides this information in simple, logical rules. This readability also allows manual tuning, if necessary.
2. There is plenty of research on performance and ways of improving functionality. Decision trees are a huge part of the world of statistics, as well as its progeny, data mining. Because both of these fields are big business, decision trees have been dissected and reassembled by think tanks all over the globe. Many tried-and-true algorithms exist for designing, training, debugging, tuning, and optimizing decision trees.
3. Game AI problems are usually restrictive enough that decision trees actually make more sense than NNs do. The additional modeling power of NNs isn't usually necessary, and the readability of decision trees can be a huge boon to last-minute tweaking and improvements (both common game development tasks, which are almost impossible with NNs). Plus, additional complexity with trees can sometimes be attained with hierarchical decision trees. Any given node within a tree could be another whole tree, as long that the subtree evaluates to a yes/no decision.

Cons

When using decision-tree-based AI, consider the following method pitfalls:

1. BDTs tend to be brittle because they are dealing with distinct states and hardcoded boundaries between them. So, like large quantities of `if-then` statements in general, they don't scale forever and are difficult to maintain or extend once they get to a certain level of complexity.
2. There is a danger that if the tree isn't built to handle every possible game circumstance, the system will be left with what is sometimes referred to as "coverage holes," where a game case "falls through" the tree. A default rule must be defined that doesn't make the AI do something completely stupid. Doing nothing is generally just as stupid as doing the wrong action.
3. The size of your trees is a direct inverse correlation between accuracy and size, so if you need specific outputs, go with NNs (or some other method) instead because it will increase the size of your tree tremendously to provide high-resolution outputs.
4. Decision trees tend to lack the *finesse* that makes more emergent systems like NNs so desirable. But many games aren't looking for finesse; they're looking for quick ways of adding content.
5. In non-binary trees, there is no universal consensus that the additional complexity of multiple children in the tree will give you anything in the way of benefit when you consider the extra effort it is going to take to construct and use the tree. To solve specific cases within a particular game, you could set up exotic, non-binary structures, but for a more generic solution that can be used across the AI system for various tasks, the standard framework is much more desirable.

Areas for Exploitation Within Games

Decision trees are such a useful, intuitive way to construct small decision-making AI behaviors that a number of different game problems could be solved with their correct application. Player modelling, dynamic tree structures, and allowing non-programmers to use decision trees are all useful within game AI engines.

- A classification tree could be used to perform simple player modeling, where you would *want* the AI to have broad categories because your responses are going to be limited.
- By data driving the trees, you could potentially insert or remove nodes from the tree, as well as adjusting the binary check parameters, using it as a form of

memory or learning. *Black & White* used this to record the high-level "thinking" that a player's avatar did about its environment, given the avatar's experiences and training, and about which actions to take at any given time. The avatar's decision tree could change dramatically during the game.

■ Having a general BDT system in your game can give organization and structure to many binary decisions. By making these BDT definitions data driven, you allow designers to make these binary decisions in the way they see fit. You might have a tree that determines who wins a jump ball situation within a basketball game. The same system could also be used to provide custom results from binary decisions like "Can I get past my defender to get to the basket?," "Did the defender bite on the juke?," or even, "Did team X beat team Y in a simulated game?" Thus, designers could tweak a good part of a player's perception system, giving designers yet another vector with which to approach the game design.

FUZZY LOGIC

We covered fuzzy-state machines (FuSMs) in Chapter 16. However, true fuzzy logic is a far more advanced system, complete with its own logical proofs and methods. Fuzzy logic is a superset of Boolean logic that was introduced by Dr. Lotfi Zadeh of University of California—Berkeley in 1965 [Zadeh 65] to handle the concepts of partial truth: values somewhere between *totally true* and *totally false*. Zadeh originally used the concept to model the uncertainty he encountered when dealing with natural language.

There are very few examples of true fuzzy logic being used within non-game applications, much less games. Fuzzy logic has been slow to catch on, until recently. The Sony PalmTop is reported to use a decision-tree based on fuzzy logic to classify handwritten Kanji characters. Another implementation found its way into a prototype Mitsubishi car in 1993, which had an in-car safety system that studied the driver's normal driving habits. The car had a built-in radar system and could sense oncoming obstacles. The car would then try to decide whether or not the driver was responding to the threat, and if not, it would take over the controls to avoid a collision.

True fuzzy logic allows you to perform calculations on equations or rules using entirely fuzzy values, for example:

```
If Health is low AND WeaponStrength is lame OR Bravery is meek, then
Camping is high
```

In this formula, there are four fuzzy variables: `Health`, `WeaponStrength`, `Bravery`, and `Camping`. `Camping` is an *output* variable, the rest are inputs. There is also, associated with each variable, membership functions or *fuzzy subset methods* that determine relative fuzzy values: `low`, `lame`, `meek`, and `high`. These functions are specifically written to make quantitative measurements about the relative degree of membership in the variable's range. So, `low` can range from 0.0 to 1.0, depending on the value of `Health`. In determining the truth of this statement, each membership function is applied to its associated variable, to determine degree of truth. These truth values are then also subjected to the AND and OR operators defined in the rule, which in fuzzy terms are defined as:

```
Crisp: truth (x and y) = Fuzzy: minimum (truth(x), truth(y))
Crisp: truth (x or y)  = Fuzzy: maximum (truth(x), truth(y))
```

Because of the ability to conclude logical truth given these fuzzy parameters, these kinds of rules can be used within a fuzzy-logic production system, which follows all the rules of regular production systems, but performs all its inference using fuzzy logic instead. The general inference process proceeds in three (optionally four) steps [Kant 97]:

1. During *fuzzification,* the membership functions defined on the input variables are applied to their actual values, to determine the degree of truth for each rule premise.
2. Under inference, the truth value for the premise of each rule is computed, and applied to the conclusion part of each rule. This results in one fuzzy subset to be assigned to each output variable for each rule. Usually only MIN or PRODUCT are used as inference rules. In MIN inferencing, the output membership function is clipped off at a height corresponding to the rule premise's computed degree of truth (fuzzy logic AND). In product inferencing, the output membership function is scaled by the rule premise's computed degree of truth.
3. Under composition, all of the fuzzy subsets assigned to each output variable are combined together to form a single fuzzy subset for each output variable. Again, usually MAX or SUM are used. In MAX composition, the combined output fuzzy subset is constructed by taking the pointwise maximum over all of the fuzzy subsets assigned to a variable by the inference rule (fuzzy logic OR). In SUM composition, the combined output fuzzy subset is constructed by taking the pointwise sum over all of the fuzzy subsets assigned to the output variable by the inference rule.
4. Finally (optional) *defuzzification* is used when it is helpful to convert the fuzzy output set to a crisp number. There are more defuzzification methods than you can shake a stick at (at least 30). Two of the more common techniques are the *centroid* and *maximum* methods. In the centroid method, the crisp value of the output variable is computed by finding the variable value of the center of gravity of the membership function for the fuzzy value. In the maximum method, one of the variable values at which the fuzzy subset has its maximum truth value is chosen as the crisp value for the output variable.

These kinds of systems are in use within pattern recognition, financial systems, and other fields involving heavy data analysis. They are usually only implemented within systems that require a heavy amount of realism, since almost nothing in the real world is black and white, perfectly aligned, and exactly positioned. In games, on the other hand, these kinds of conditions *do* occur, and so the additional computation isn't really necessary for most games.

A common misstep in understanding fuzzy logic lies in thinking that fuzzy values constitute some other way of thinking about probabilities. But this is an untrue line of thinking. An example that contrasts the two ways of thinking involves a set of objects called "Drinkable," that is a subset of objects called "Liquids." If you come across two glasses, one labeled "90 Percent Drinkable Probability" and "90 Percent Drinkable Fuzzy Membership," which one do you drink? The answer is the 90 Percent Drinkable Fuzzy Membership. The 90 percent corresponds with it belonging to the drinkable set of liquids "almost completely," whereas the probability-based glass has a 1-in-10 shot of being *poisonous*. In fact, given the glass labeler's definition of drinkable, the fuzzy-labeled glass might contain cheap wine, or super tart fruit juice, or some other drink that he didn't consider fully "drinkable." Probability deals with statistical levels of chance that something *might be* true. Fuzzy set membership discusses to what extent something already *is* true.

PROS

Fuzzy systems primary advantage is that they extend normal Boolean logic to encompass more loosely-defined variables, so that arguments with these types of values can still be mathematically proven.

CONS

The primary disadvantage of using fuzzy systems are that they can be computationally expensive; systems that contain numerous fuzzy vectors can suffer from rule overload. Different methods have been created to combat this (like Combs method), but this remains an issue.

AREAS FOR EXPLOITATION WITHIN GAMES

Fuzzy systems do have a place within game AI engines, evidenced fully by their actual use in many commercial games. They handle player modelling well, and this player model could also be used in online games as well.

- Handling game problems dealing with a large amount of unknown or partially known information, like player modeling, is a great job for fuzzy logic usage. With heavily strategic games, like RTS, civ games, or even poker, player modeling is important if you are striving to really attack the problem intelligently. If your system isn't going to cheat by giving it omniscient access to all in-game data on the human player, then the AI system is going to have to rely on perception data to build a model of the human to react. This type of information will most likely be sketchy, uncovered in small pieces that might not be in sequence, and may even contain falsified elements (the human trying to fool the AI), so a fuzzy system could very well be the best way to approach this problem.

■ For online or multiplayer games, player modeling could actually be used by a game as a "helper" AI entity that could play the game for you temporarily, if you had to go to the restroom or answer the phone. This feature would be like pausing, except that you wouldn't interrupt the game for the rest of the players. The fuzzy system would try to model the way that you play the game and continue to use this style while you were away.

SUMMARY

As games continue to evolve, and game-AI engines have to respond to increasingly esoteric and/or complex game requirements, techniques might be required that most programmers haven't seen before in more run of the mill games. This chapter has covered a number of useful, but seldom seen AI techniques that might just help you as an AI programmer with a particularly tricky AI problem in need of solving.

■ Artificial life techniques try to use lessons learned in biology to create emergent behavior from simple rules.

■ Alife can create emergent, reusable behavior; it also suffers from unpredictability and brittleness.

■ Alife techniques pertaining to flocking, other types of organic movement, and ecology building are possible future game considerations.

■ Planning algorithms try to use additional information about a problem to decide what to do before you start, one hopes not making local mistakes.

■ Planning is already used in many games, in the form of pathfinding using the A* algorithm, or some variant.

■ Planning can provide AI systems with a large amount of additional intelligence, and are general enough to be used in different parts of the game engine. They can be CPU intensive and can make the AI sluggish if misused.

■ Uses for planning in games could be anticipation of human actions, and a greater degree of intentionality in AI actions leading to combinations of behaviors.

■ Production systems are generic methods of dealing with large amounts of expert knowledge about a specific subject.

- Production techniques are generic, heavily researched, goal directed, and highly reactive. They can be CPU intensive.
- Games could benefit from not only using production systems to organize their rule-based logic code, but could also be served by data driving the production system to maximize game extensibility.
- Decision trees are another way of organizing `if-then` structures using binary separation methods to optimize the structure and number of your variable checks.
- Both classification and regression trees are *similar* to neural nets, but have many important differences including readability, types of data they work well with, output types, variable consideration, and accuracy.
- They are easier to tune than some classifying systems, heavily researched, and very easy to implement. They can be brittle, don't scale well, and only provide discrete outputs.
- Games could use decision trees to perform simple player modeling, store memory like data, and provide a general, data-driven system for determining binary perception data.
- Fuzzy logic is a means of extending logic to encompass partial truth values.
- It allows games to use more loosely defined variables while relying on mathematically proven methods. Fuzzy logic can be CPU-expensive.
- Player modeling, and helper AI systems are ways that games might use fuzzy-logic systems.

25 Distributed AI Design

In This Chapter

- Basic Overview
- The Distributed Layers
- Summary

There are many individual goals within an AI engine no matter what type of game you're developing. Designing and creating an entire AI system is not a small undertaking. In this chapter, we will discuss a general design paradigm for approaching any type of large-scale AI engine design, called distributed AI design, that should help you break AI systems into manageable pieces. We will discuss the various parts to the method, and along the way, give plenty of examples. Finally, we will break down a classic game into different ways that it could be coded, given a modern-day AI engine.

BASIC OVERVIEW

In Chapter 2, "An AI Engine: The Basic Components and Design," we explored the various components of an AI engine (the main pieces being the decision-making system, the perception system, and navigation). Now that we have covered the main types of coding techniques that are used in games, we can discuss more properly the different AI methods that work well with each section of an AI engine, as well as determine which pieces work well together.

The first rule of *all* game programming (and most will also say the first rule of game design) is the old standby: Keep It Simple, Stupid (KISS). The design and creation of an entire AI engine is not an easy task, and over-engineering can stifle an already overwhelming experience. A game's AI has one major task—to provide interesting and challenging behavior whether as an opponent or for the player's "wingmen." The purpose of the distributed method is to simplify overall AI creation and maintenance by spreading out the AI tasks into modular, layered systems

615

that work with each other to create rich AI behaviors without overcomplicating any one area of the engine.

A REAL-LIFE EXAMPLE

To help describe the distributed design technique, we shall present a real-life (RL) example. Say that you are sitting at your desk. Suddenly, somebody from the next room calls your name. You rise, and go to where the voice came from to see who called you. Let's break down what happened exactly, except that we're going to assume that you are an AI character:

1. You are sitting and performing a behavior called DoingWork. You received an input, in the form of a game event (your name being called), or a changed perception variable (such as DistanceToNearestDisturbance, or BeingCalled, etc.) depending on how your perception system is set up.
2. Your decision-making system determined that the incoming perception was important enough to change your behavior in favor of a different, more applicable behavior.
3. The new behavior you have transitioned to (or been assigned), called Investigate, first gives you a new target location (which is approximately the location of the incoming sound that called you), which was created by either some algorithm for guessing sound locations, or by cheating and telling you the location of the call.
4. You run your pathfinding algorithm to determine how to get to the target. The pathfinder gives you a set of points to move to in sequence to get there.
5. Your movement code finally has a destination, and so it figures out which of your movement animations to play to look the best, and fit the motion closest.
6. You start moving to the nearest pathnode in the path list, but your desk is in the way. Your obstacle-avoidance system takes over, and moves you around the side of the desk. By heading toward the next pathnode, and using the avoidance system to navigate any dynamic objects in your way, you make it out the door and toward the sound.
7. As you leave the room, it occurs to you that the door is open, and you have your wallet out on your desk. You stop and close the door, and then continue.
8. Ten feet later, you see Bob and recognize that it was his voice you heard.
9. This new input perception (that it was Bob who called) changes your state from Investigate to ActCynical, and so you say, "What the heck do you want?"

And on and on it goes. The point is this: The first description we used was "I heard my name being called, and got up to see who it was," whereas the chain of determinations and levels of intelligent behavior that you used to do all of the above is much more involved than that initial sentence implies. Such is the plight of our AI systems. Every task is actually a dozen smaller tasks strung together in concert.

THE DISTRIBUTED LAYERS

Distributed AI design is the technique of fully embracing the multi-level quality of behavior in the real world and applying it to organizing and implementing an AI engine. We do this for a number of reasons:

1. It produces cleaner, more maintainable code that is also easier to understand and extend.
2. It spreads out the intelligence among a number of different systems, several of which will most likely be reusable by other elements within your game.
3. You don't end up with a huge AIPlayer.cpp file (or its equivalent), in which you store large amounts of special case code dealing with the AI characters. Instead, we will partition our intelligence into several layers:
    - **Perception/Event layer.** This layer filters incoming sense data for relevance and various other factors.
    - **Behavior layer.** This layer describes the specifics of how to perform a given action.
    - **Animation layer.** The animation layer determines which animation to play to fit the game state.
    - **Motion layer.** This layer handles aspects like pathfinding, collisions, and avoidance.
    - **Short-term decision making.** This is the narrow-view intelligence for the AI entity, primarily concerned with just the entity.
    - **Long-term decision making.** This layer handles wide-view intelligence issues, like planning, or team-based considerations.
    - **Location-based information layer.** This layer includes information transmitted to the entity from influence maps, smart terrain, or the like.

THE REAL-LIFE EXAMPLE REVISITED

We shall step through the RL example to introduce the main layers of the system, to dissect the tasks our systems must perform into more manageable, layered levels of intelligence.

1. The AI character's name is called. Let's assume this game is using an event system. Our AI entity thus receives a message from the game stating that his name is being called.

2. Let's also assume the game is using a hierarchical finite-state machine (FSM) (with a state stack, to use as a memory) for its primary decision-making scheme, as described in Chapter 15, "Finite-State Machines." The current state the entity is in at the start of the example, DoingWork, has registered for the MyNameIsCalled message. Getting the message sets up a state transition by pushing the state machine's current state onto the stack, and entering the Investigate state. This is an example of short-term intelligence because the interrupted behavior (DoingWork) wasn't being performed because of some personal perception, it was part of a larger (and within the HFSM, next level up) state, that of Afternoon.

3. Upon entering the Investigate state, the state calculates an investigation target for the character, based on the incoming sound data. The logic for this calculation is therefore within the action itself, and is thus part of the behavior layer.

4. The behavior then accesses the navigation layer by using the pathfinder to resolve movement toward its target.

5. With a valid direction to travel in, the movement layer is activated and starts the move. The first thing it does is use the animation layer to choose the right movement animation.

6. We start playing the movement animation, but immediately something happens: Another perception tips us to the fact that we're going to collide with a dynamic object in the environment (rather than a level element like a solid wall, which I would avoid using the pathfinder instead), and so the motion layer engages the avoidance system to steer us clear of it, as well any other objects on your way out.

7. When you go to leave, your wallet sends out a message that you've left it behind (through a smart object system, it is programmed to mention if you're more than a certain distance from it, and the Afternoon high-level state is listening for it because you don't want to lose your wallet while you're out during the day), and forces you to temporarily give up your current goal to take care of this problem first. The long-term decision system does some checking, and because your wallet is in your office, it will be safe to leave if you shut the door (computed with a simple planning algorithm). You shut the door using the behavior layer to set up the behavior, which in turn uses the animation layer to pick the right door-closing animation. You then return to your last state when this state is popped off the stack.

8. The perception system visually recognizes Bob (once you get within a certain distance, and you're both facing each other), and so sends out a message that the Investigate state is registered for "See Friend." The Investigate state intercepts the message, and checks to see if Bob's location is close to its investigation target. If so, it figures that it was Bob who

called. Again, this logic is part of the behavior system, embedded in the `Investigate` state.

9. The `Investigate` state then transitions to a new state, and makes a smart remark, by way of the familiar behavior-and-then-animation chain of layers necessary to set up the action as well as the animation to play.

Now that you can see the basic flow, let's break down each layer by discussing the reasons behind separating it, the decisions that we're going to delegate to each layer, the techniques that can be used to implement it, and some more examples of how each is used.

THE PERCEPTIONS AND EVENTS LAYER

The reason for splitting out perception calculation was primarily discussed in Chapter 2. Creating a central perception handler is a great way to optimize your AI calculations. It helps prevent game values from being recalculated in multiple places within a single game loop, and consolidation supports the development and debugging of important game values being tracked by your AI systems.

The intelligence being assigned to the perception layer is in the form of the reaction times and thresholds inherent in each individual perception. All these kinds of determinations can be separated from the act themselves by being tucked all the way down at this low level. Thus, all behaviors that incorporate a given perception, either for activation or transition conditions, benefits from the embedded "intelligence" in how the perception is updated.

Centralized perception systems work very well within message-based systems, so when a perception actuates, it can send out a message to a specific player, or your system can broadcast a more general event. The perception system encapsulates some additional AI computation by way of incorporating attribute data within the perceptions as well. So, if I swing a sword in the direction of two different characters, and one of them has very slow reflexes, he might be in for a nasty surprise, but the other character (who has superior reflexes) might have no problem dodging, parrying, or even shooting me, depending on the character. All simply because his perception system picked up on the incoming sword and the other did not.

THE BEHAVIOR LAYER

Within most games, each behavior is most likely considered a state that the character is in, with more complex actions being constructed out of a few states. As such, behavior layers are generally coded within whatever system of "state" or atomic actions you are going to use within your game. Even if you're writing a fighting game, in which the characters are in one game state the entire time (the equivalent of "Fight to the Death"), the final behaviors that you're going to be using with the characters (in this case, each fighting move) will still likely require special game logic to be embedded in them, even if it is only starting and stopping an animation.

The logic placed at this level usually involves transitions within the game's state machine (or whatever technique your game is using), as well as describing the series of actions necessary to perform the behavior from start to finish. In Listing 25.1, you can see some pseudocode for a fighting game behavior, in this case a large punch animation sequence, showing the series of events that are required:

LISTING 25.1 Pseudocode for a fighting game behavior called `BigPunch`.

```
Begin BigPunch
    ForInit
    {
        DoSound(GRUNT_BIG)
        UseAnim(rand(NUM_BIG_PUNCHES)+ANIM_BIG_PUNCH_FIRST)
    }
    ForFrames
    {
        1       AllowCombo(off)
        2..5    TimeScale(1.6)
        6       OffenseCollisionSphere(1,on)
        7..9    SpawnParticle(FORCE_LINES)
        10      DoSound(AIR_SNAO)
        11..16  TimeScale(0.8)
        17      OffenseCollisionSphere(1,off)
        18      TimeScale(1.0)
        19..25  AllowCombo(on)
    }
End BigPunch
```

Here you can see the behavior setting up things like sounds, animations, spawning particle effects, and turning on and off various game flags. Because this is a fighting game, each frame of the animation during the behavior may potentially have some code or an event associated with it, because the tuning and balance of fighting games needs to be just that precise. The behavior in Listing 25.1 includes several types of flags and events, like allowing other moves to interrupt (for combinations to occur), scaling the local time of the character (to fine-tune execution of animation data for dramatic effect), launching sound and particle effects, and toggling collision spheres (so that the attack will only "hit" the opponent during prescribed parts of the animation).

Notice that this example assumes that all the big punch animations have the same number of frames, this is somewhat important if you're going to try and balance gameplay with generic behaviors, but obviously isn't necessary if you're willing to create the code necessary to run fighting moves with any number of frames. Instead, the system could internally keep track of the number of frames in the animation, and also note the highest numbered frame the script refers to, and determine what percentage of the total time each frame should represent. In this way, frame counts would be relative, and as long as the "stages" of each animation were roughly the same (the first half is the windup, the third quarter is the hit, and the last quarter is the follow-through, or some equivalent determination), then the big punch moves could be whatever length the animator wanted.

In the RL example, when the code transitioned to the `Investigate` state, it called the `Enter()` method, where it then determined exactly what location the character was going to investigate, by calculating a target based on information attached to the original `MyNameIsCalled` message, namely the approximate angle and volume of the call. Like perceptions, the behavior layer should also be influenced by player attributes, to differentiate different characters when they perform the reusable behaviors. If you tell two very different characters to `Jump()`, they should check their attributes to determine how high, so to speak.

For many games, this layer is implemented in code, especially when they have a limited number of behaviors available to their AI characters. For the opposite case, however, this is a prime candidate for a data-driven solution. If you can use scripting to write the behavior code (as in the above fighting game example), or some other form of data-driven gameplay, this will prove to be a real boon to your system, as it represents a fairly major chunk of intelligence coding being directly in the hands of the designers. The more content they can put into this layer, the more virtually "calculation-free" personality and intelligence your characters will exhibit. Not that scripts cannot contain math, or be slower to run, but rather that scripting is a means of recording the common sense–style intelligence that the game characters' behaviors require to seem realistic into the game through the scripting language.

THE ANIMATION LAYER

In the old days, art resources came at a premium. The first *Super Mario Bros.* game for the NES had only 8K of sprite art for the entire game, including background tiles and all character animations. As games have become more complex, the amount of animation data associated with any given game character has risen dramatically. Main characters in modern action-heavy, third-person games can sometimes have animation data more than a thousand times the level of *Super Mario Bros.* entire art resources all to themselves.

The process of choosing the right animation to play at any given time has become a seriously non-trivial task in many games, especially in animation-heavy genres, like fighting and sports games. Fighting games might have dozens of unique moves for each character. Sports games, which generally rely heavily on motion-captured animations to retain the signature styles of the simulated players, might have a hundred or more different animations for a single action (dunks in a basketball game, batter warm-ups in baseball, end-zone celebrations in football, etc.).

Not only is the total number of animations high, but also, some of these determinations require expensive logic and mathematical calculations. Many of these might be simply randomized (with some checks to avoid possible repetition) like end-zone celebrations, for instance, which are simply fluff (defined as unnecessary for gameplay) animations that are numerous because they add entertainment value to the game.

But consider the determination, in the same game, for which animation to play when performing the behavior "Receive Pass." The code has to take a number of factors into account: the thrower's current direction of travel and speed, the amount and position of defensive coverage, the angle and direction of the incoming football, the kind of player the receiver is, as well as his skill level (he may not be skilled enough to perform certain catches, or rarely catches on his left side), and the direction he's going to want to travel after he gets the ball. Then, after the receive behavior generates a list of the available *possible* catches, the code has to run through each of these available animations to determine if one of them actually gets the player's actual catching hands within a certain distance of the future ball position (where the ball and the player will intersect), or at least close enough that your IK (inverse kinematics) system will be able to take over.

In addition, there are usually special considerations, like the fact that the receiver had to jump (to reach the catch before going out of bounds because someone could be diving at the receiver's feet), or that the receiver might want to catch the ball and then run straight out of bounds to stop the clock. Maybe the receiver collided with another player on the way to the ball, and now needs to recalculate everything in an attempt to recover from the hit. In another sport, like basketball, where almost every player on the court is constantly becoming an eligible receiver, this kind of calculation can cripple an AI system's performance if not done cleanly, and with a plan in mind before implementation.

In games with extensive animation resources, or heavy calculation requirements (thus meaning that these calculations are almost assuredly going to require plenty of tuning and balancing because of their complex nature), this is one of the places to start with a data-driven approach. Usually, animation selection systems are table-driven, like in Figure 25.1, where we see part of a database-style file describing a selection table for finding the correct layup animation in a basketball game.

In the table shown in Figure 25.1 (which, by the way, doesn't take into account other players in the way, or an entire host of other factors), we have a number of layup animations. Each animation has parameters which show how it fits into the overall decision structure description, or schema. The schema for this system

//Anim Name	//Angle of //Shot type	Approach	//Starting Speed	//Ball Quad
LayupUnder2ft	hard	efg	stand,walk	right
LayupBaseLtStand	norm	abc	stand,walk	front
LayupBaseRtStand	norm	fgh	stand,walk	front
LayupCtStand	norm	def	stand,walk	front
LayupCornerLtStand	norm	bcd	stand,walk	front
LayupCornerRtStand	norm	efg	stand,walk	front
LayupUnderStand	norm	efg	stand,walk	right
LayupBaseLtJump	norm	abc	all	left
LayupBaseRtJump	norm	fgh	all	right
LayupCtJump	norm	def	all	front
LayupCornerLtJump	flash	bcd	all	left
LayupCornerRtJump	flash	efg	all	right
LayupBaseLtRun	norm	abc	run	left
LayupBaseRtRun	norm	gh	run	right
LayupCtRun	norm	def	Run	front
LayupCornerLtRun	hard	bcd	Run	left
LayupCornerRtRun	hard	efg	Run	right
LayupUnder	norm	abc	Run	back
LayupRev	flash	abc	run	back
LayupRevTrick	flash	gh	run	back

FIGURE 25.1   Basketball layup animation selection table.

involves four parameters: shot type (the difficulty of the action; skill rating needs to be at certain levels to achieve hard or flash layups), angle of approach (the allowable angles of approach for the potential shooter; labeled as "a-h," each letter is a pie wedge in a circle radiating out of the basket, with "a" being straight left), the speeds the player is allowed to be in to use the layup, and the final quadrant that the ball will enter the basket from relative to the player.

The final parameter, ball quad, could probably have used the same angle system as approach, but the final behavior that used it needed quadrant values, so the data was preprocessed to save time during gameplay. The second reason the design uses a table is to save calculation time in determining these things when the game is running (the first reason is also to save time, but in hours of programming for the designer). Technically, you could actually run through each layup and determine all of these factors algorithmically, but it's an expensive process, and so we'll use a table instead. An algorithmic solution could generate the table, however. An "animation table tool" could be written to recognize schemas, and then it could be fed a large number of animations, which it then would crunch through to generate these tables. Any touch-ups or overrides could then be performed on the final file, but it would definitely save your designers (or you, if you end up entering the data) work.

Today, multiple animation channels are also very common. Two channels means that a character could be running one animation on its lower half (performing movement), while another on its upper half (aiming a gun, or throwing a football). Three or more channels could control whatever other parts or secondary objects your game design calls for (remember, we're talking about games here, so your main character might have three heads or four robotic arms). All of these additional channels would add to the complexity of your animation selection, but this really just translates to additional, or even nested tables if you choose to use that method of handling this problem.

Other implementations might include a scripted system like we described for the behavior layer, because in some games there are very little differences between animations and behaviors. The same kind of frame-by-frame control could be exercised, complete with launching of effects, events, and the like all from the animation's `Update()` function.

THE MOTION LAYER

As stated in Chapter 2, navigation tasks are another huge part of any game AI engine. Pathfinding (which is a form of planning, as we saw in Chapter 24, "Other Techniques of Note") and its younger brother, avoidance, are very influential factors when determining a character's behavior. Like the other layers in this system, they are separated because they need to be reused by other parts of the AI engine (specifically, any behavior that requires map movement), so it wouldn't make much sense to embed this kind of logic within the behaviors themselves.

Techniques for implementing the motion layer were discussed in Chapter 2. Because of its links to robotics, both pathfinding and avoidance have received a bounty of useful material and algorithms from the academic world. Even a casual search on the Internet for pathfinding methods useful within games will yield thousands of results.

But what other logic and functionality should we embed at this level? The answer, again, is to try and establish character personality and attribute level within this layer. By giving the basic pathfinding and avoidance systems attribute-based behavior patterns, you can get subtle (and not so subtle) classes of movement out of an otherwise totally utilitarian system. Maybe bigger characters don't dodge like smaller ones do; instead, they go around, or just pause and let the obstacle pass first. Different types of characters might traverse the level differently, meaning good jumpers might take precarious paths, wallclimbers might go places others might not, and smarter characters will know exactly which teleporter to use to get right to the player.

Another extension to this system might be additional means of obstacle avoidance that are game- or character-specific. If your creature is as strong as Superman, is your creature really going to go around that garbage can? Or is it going to pick it up and throw it into outer space? Or kick the can out of its way with a mad grunt as the character runs at another player? It makes an AI system look stupid when a character that can jump twenty feet through the air following a pathnode system has to go around six-foot-high crates to get at a player.

All of these kinds of things can be handled within the wrappings of the motion layer, and the rest of the system need not be bothered with it. Our overall goal with distributed AI is to have any layer be able to perform its job, and not have it negatively affect any of the other layers. Yes, avoidance technically detours a player from the path, which keeps the player from finishing their behavior of picking up the shiny powerup, but if it didn't, the player would be stuck mashing their face into the tree in front of them, and they would never get to the powerup in the first place.

SHORT-TERM DECISION MAKING (ST)

At the ST level, decisions involve matters that usually are associated with the specific character, either because of the character's attributes, its current perceptions, or its past experience. A character might be almost dead, and so has a very personal overriding goal to get a health powerup or run away. He might be dealing with the specifics of his weapon (he's out of ammo), or possibly his morale or bravery attribute is low, and is therefore grappling with the desire to run off into the woods to hide. We again split off this layer, to allow another branch for personality and attribute data to flavor reusable AI behavior.

The ST layer can be somewhat touchy to allocate behavior to: the more ST behavior you have, the more individual the character's movement is going to seem. But if you're trying to model a tightly regimented troop movement, and a third of the units have their girlfriend on their mind, things might get messy. Of course, your ST system could be state-based, to enforce group control during crucial periods, and allow for more varied behavior other times. In fact, given the more direct, situational nature of most ST decisions, they are usually created with a state-based system in mind.

LONG-TERM DECISION MAKING (LT)

LT decisions are likely to be outside of any one unit, because they involve many units, possibly even all the units in the game. At the LT level, we are usually concerned with strategic types of solutions, which take planning, coordination, and timing. Of course, not all games need these elements. But even a game as simple as single-player *Gauntlet* could be said to have a basic LT determination: the constant ticking down of a player's health as time passes. Whatever ST goals you have determined an AI *Gauntlet* player has set up for himself will all be set aside if the player's health gets too low, and he is forced to concentrate on trying to get more health to stay alive. Of course, multiplayer *Gauntlet* has even more LT usage, because players can more easily dispatch the enemies with teamwork than with completely independent actions.

LT systems can be constructed in roughly the same fashion as the ST layer. State-based systems work well, because games with a good amount of strategy can usually be broken into wide phases of strategy. Chess has its opening, midgame, and endgame; RTS games generally have a buildup phase, and then several cycles of exploration followed by conflict. Planning is usually important to some degree in LT systems—almost by definition the most LT decisions need to take a wide view of the problem, and make bigger decisions that involve the future.

Many times, an LT system will also make use of fuzziness as well, either with a fuzzy-state system (which works very well in RTS games; effectively allowing a player controllers for the separate yet parallel goals of offense, defense, resource gathering, research, etc.), or with a full fuzzy logic system. An RTS opponent controlled by a full fuzzy logic system would use the limited information it has collected through reconnaissance from the field to try and discern which actions are a "best guess" at to what to do next in order to win the game. This is much closer to how a human plays an RTS than a build script will ever be.

LOCATION-BASED INFORMATION LAYER (LBI)

Sometimes, too many things are going on in the environment to really make it feasible to have each object in the world keep scanning the nearby area for things that it is interested in. Instead, we turn the tables. LBI systems create a more centralized, decoupled means by which data about the world can be accessed by individual game characters. Smart terrain and objects broadcast their existence to game characters (and to each other) so that what looks like complex interaction with the environment can be simplified and optimized. Influence maps allow for a wealth of information to be stored, sorted, computed, and analyzed for a whole suite of AI systems.

LBI-layer information is a separate system that you can think of as a large blackboard architecture for creating AI engines. An LBI layer can help the LT decision-making layer with terrain analysis that can find weak points in the AI's defenses or identify key areas of military interest in the map (areas that have high enemy foot traffic, or where many individual units have died), and discover valuable ambush locations in an FTPS deathmatch map. Alerting units to high concentrations of nearby enemies (acting as a rough "sound" perception, perhaps) could affect the ST layer's decisions. Pathfinding can use influence map information to avoid potentially deadly portions of the map, either by design, or because of a human-laid trap.

One last way of using an LBI layer within your game is to embed triggers directly within your game world that are triggered by some game state, or merely by proximity. These triggers can set off events, messages, or entire game scripts that cause any number of things to occur. In this way, designers can tag specific areas of the world itself with "intelligence," which can help simplify other AI systems that might incur unnecessary baggage if they were to try to encapsulate these types of event data. Placement of these triggers is almost universally done within some kind of a level editor, although other systems have been used, like in game placement, or even simple text scripting of specific locations, although this last method isn't very friendly.

BROOKS SUBSUMPTION ARCHITECTURES

The distributed AI approach is somewhat close to Brooks subsumption architecture, referenced in chapter one. However, where Brooks designs are primarily directed toward modeling creatures with low intelligence (he hopes his robot designs to someday be as robust as natural insects: not that intelligent, but reliable in the face of sometimes an overwhelming number of adverse factors), the distributed method goes a few steps further upward in the chain, to bestow upon our AI systems a level of strategic planning and intelligence that goes above ant intelligence.

The subsumption goal, of being able to achieve all of your goals in the face of a dynamic number and type of impairments, is definitely our goal when building our game AI engine. We would like our systems, as well as the behavior of the AI-controlled characters within it, to competently handle whatever the human player does within the game, as well recovering (within context) from the adverse affects that might come up during any game situation.

Also, Brooks's notions of "reaching for insect intelligence first, and then on," is very poignant in the world of game AI. Our systems don't need to be super-intelligent. The intelligence of a housefly may just be enough to give the average gamer a run for his money in the twitch gaming world of the deathmatch arena. Ant colony-level mentality may be all that's required to impart an RTS AI system with all it needs to build up, defend itself, and occasionally conquer.

In the end, we're not trying to win; rather, we strive to engage the player. Most people feel a twinge of pride, and relief, after finally smacking the fly that has been harassing them for a half hour, rather than feeling stupid for not being able to kill something with a speck for a brain. The fly engaged the player, performed surprising and mostly useful behavior, which caused the human to focus his attention and energy, but in the end was not a match for the human; a nice lesson in perfect game AI behavior.

GAME BREAKDOWN GOALS

In this section, we will first break down a popular commercial game using the distributed method, and then giving several examples at the separate levels of how each AI layer could be implemented. Note, that this section is not describing how they *should* be implemented, for either efficiency or entertainment value. Rather, this is meant as an exercise into thinking about game AI problems from all possible angles, so that you can begin to truly understand the vast array of solutions that are available to any given game AI situation.

So, we'll strive for the "most effective" AI, meaning that it stops the player the most (or the most efficently), while confining ourselves to the spirit of the original game by not adding any additional animations or behaviors to the classic setup. Otherwise, we would just say, "And then the character whips out his rocket launcher, and fires. . . ."

Second, we will discuss how an AI-controlled main character might be created for each game. In this scenario, we are not trying to change the enemy behavior in any way, or affect gameplay. We are trying to create an AI system that plays the game well, and less importantly, like a human would. The examples given in this section are also not an indication as to the best way in which to implement the AI player, but are rather a broad spectrum view as to the types of solutions that are possible given the inputs and outputs.

DISTRIBUTED *SUPER MARIO BROS.*

Super Mario Bros. is a true classic, the first ever side-scrolling platformer (technically, other earlier games like *Pitfall* had many of the same elements, but didn't actually scroll).

It gave us the phrase "1-UP" (for a powerup that gives a player an extra life) and took hidden game elements to an entirely new level, by making it a cornerstone of the game. The game has 32 real levels, and about 20 hidden ones. The entire game is 32 K of code, and 8 K of graphics. Also, that 32 K of code isn't actually all code. A good-size chunk of that figure is utilized by the tile information necessary to construct the levels. Let's just say, when they designed this game, space was tight. Almost every element of the design is space-related. Mario wears a hat, to not have to animate his hair. He has a mustache so that we get the notion of a mouth, without having to display one.

Some familiarity with the game is required to make the discussion worthwhile. The basic mechanics that Mario employs are jumping and running. You can steer his jump to a certain extent. There are a few powerups in the game: a flower that makes Mario grow (he can break rocks by bumping them with his head, and can now touch an enemy without dying . . . instead he'll shrink back to normal size), a fire flower that allows him to throw fireballs, and a star that gives him a small period of invulnerability. The monster types that will be used for illustration later include:

- Regular creatures like the mushrooms (called Goombas), which can be squished by jumping on their head.
- The various kinds of turtles (or Koopas) can be disabled with one bounce, and then kicked, which sends them zooming along the ground as a projectile. In projectile form, they harm both Mario and other enemies, and bounce off walls to reverse direction. Some Koopas in later levels have wings, and can fly. These take three bounces to kill, the first takes their wings and turns them into a normal Koopa.
- The Hammer Brothers are special Koopas. They are taller than average, and always come in pairs. They try to jump to the same level of the screen as the player, all the while tossing dozens of harmful spinning hammers in a parabolic arc toward Mario.
- Lakitu is the name of a special enemy Koopa that actually rides on a small cloud along a line at the top of the screen during certain levels. He ducks if the player gets near him, and tries to hover around the player. If the player speeds up and tries to lose him, he speeds up as well. While he's around, he throws out special spiked turtles that the player can't bounce on to kill. Lakitu is actually one of the smarter enemies in the game, besides the Hammer Brothers.
- Bowser, the end boss of each level, is a huge Koopa that breathes out large blasts of fire, and jumps up and down. Occasionally, he also throws hammers like the brothers. Like every other creature in the game, he can be killed with a fireball from Fire-powered Mario, or by dropping Bowser into the lava by releasing the drawbridge he stands on.

AI ENEMIES IMPLEMENTATION

As released, the enemies in *Super Mario Bros.* use almost no AI at all. The enemies are essentially algorithmic (they travel in circles or patterns, or perform a set behavior every so often). The most common behavior used by the enemies is that they simply walk in the direction they are facing. An enemy of this type, placed in contained areas, will walk forward until they hit a wall, and will then turn around and walk the other way.

There are some uncommon elements that react to Mario's position (like the guy riding on the cloud, or the Hammer Brothers, and to some extent, Bowser the boss monster), but only to affect facing and movement. Overall, they are all but oblivious to Mario. They are merely well-placed moving obstacles to the advancing player as the player navigates each level.

Perception and Event Layer

Mario can't do much within the game. As for movement, he can go left or right, jump, and walk or run. There are also a few water-based levels where Mario uses the same controls (jump means "swim," but it is just an underwater jump), and the only thing that was different was the gravity on Mario. If Mario jumps in air (on land), gravity pulls him back down pretty quickly. Underwater, Mario sluggishly drifts back down to the bottom, allowing right or left movement to make it seem like he is swimming. Real running could only be accomplished when standing on the floor or a platform. Mario's status is one of four values: small, big, fired up, or invincible.

With this kind of limited action palette, the game's perception system can keep track of pretty much everything having to do with Mario, and do so quite frequently. Other perceptions that our AI might use include:

■   The location of the current left-side border of the screen. Since the game always scrolls to the right, and because you can't scroll backward, we'll know how far the human can see knowing this, as well as what the player can reach on the left side.
■   A calculation of how far away from Mario any given AI character is. By making this value signed, negative values mean Mario is to the character's left, positive distance means to the right.
■   The location of any other nearby creatures. Useful if your AI agents will perform any cooperative behaviors with other AI controlled characters, or use elements from within the game world against Mario.
■   Also, some additional complex calculations (like the distance from the platform an AI agent is on to the one before it in the level; given this value, the agent can predict where an incoming Mario might land or the path Mario might take).

The vast amount of applicable perception data is about Mario, rather than the individual AI character, so it makes a lot of sense to centralize these perceptions so that all the creatures in the game can share the calculations.

Behavior Layer

Mario's behaviors may be limited in *Super Mario Bros.,* but the average enemy's set of behaviors is even more so. The behaviors that any given enemy can perform are almost the simplest imaginable: they involve either playing an animation or performing some simple movement. A few enemies can throw a projectile.

An adequate behavior layer for this game would probably be to create three behaviors: `PlayAnimation` (taking parameters for the animation name, as well as starting frame, the time scale, etc.), `Move` (taking parameters for the speed, and a left/right direction), and `SpawnProjectile` (parameters would include projectile to use, speed, and path type of projectile: arc or straight line). There are only a few, so there's really no reason not to write them directly in code as a state that can be used within an FSM (which is probably what we'd use as our short-term decision-making solution).

Then, you could create inherited behaviors for the specific actions that game enemies use, like combination animations (the man-eating plants' only behavior is to first play "Rise out of pot," followed by "Chomp several times"), specific types of `Move` behaviors (straight line, circle, bouncing, etc.), and projectile attacks (hammer, breath of fire, bullets, etc.). These inherited behaviors could also be coded within the game, or written using a simple script system (the configuration script system from Chapter 18, "Scripting Systems," would work fine) to define sets of parameters that would be linked to a specific behavior.

Animation Layer

Super Mario Bros. doesn't have any animation issues with its enemies that could be made better by modern animation selection routines. At most, they have two frames, which they oscillate back and forth between. Many have only one frame, and repeatedly mirror the sprite to give the appearance of movement. So for this game, the animation layer of our AI engine will be non-existent if we're to stick true to the original game art. If the game were to be beefed up in that different enemy characters had a variety of animations to choose from for any given behavior, based on skill ratings or in response to player actions, then obviously the game would benefit from a more rigorous animation selection method using some AI technique like decision trees or the like.

Motion Layer

Behaviors for *Super Mario Bros.* creatures are pretty much just setting movements, so most of this layer will be sparse. We could do some limited pathfinding for enemies that are able to jump from platform to platform (as well as the flying creatures), so that they could hunt down Mario a bit better. Enemies are almost always localized (meaning tied to a particular area of a map world), so path networks could be local as well, not requiring connectivity throughout the level. Lakitu on his cloud could use a special "path" network that represented the line in the sky where his cloud could travel. Potential fields could be used to do the pathfinding, but the overall movement required from the system is digital, and potential field systems tend to give movement a more smooth, organic look and feel.

The levels aren't completely static (Mario can smash almost any brick within his jumping range when he's big), so any pathfinding data that linked blocks together for connectivity would need to be updated as Mario broke connected blocks, but only if you are using this same pathfinding information for enemies that can jump from block to block.

Short-Term (ST) Decision Making

Considering the limited number of behaviors and perceptions available to the enemies, the decisions required of individual characters are relatively simple.

Take the flowers that pop out of the flowerpots (which, in coding terms, means they play an animation). They can only come up if Mario isn't standing on the pot, and usually follow a set time schedule. If we relax the timed interval restrictions of certain enemies for our theoretical game, then the game could be made almost devilishly hard by setting off these creature's actions at the worst possible time: when Mario is in the wrong place, is vulnerable because of a bad jump, or has limited foot space to maneuver.

Because of the small action set that each AI enemy has (usually just `Walk`, and `TurnAround` if you collide with a wall; the most complex enemy has movement, jumping, and limited projectile attack capability), it's safe to say that we could use FSMs easily here. Most enemies would only have a couple of states, three or four at most.

Another method might be to use scripting to describe the simple actions that the enemies use. A few sample scripts (written in a pseudo C style) for this hypothetical system are shown in Listing 25.2.

LISTING 25.2 Sample behavior scripts for enemies in *Super Mario Bros.*

```
//Simple Guy
Update:
    WalkForward;
End;


OnWallCollision:
    TurnAround;
End;
//-------------------
//Hammer Brothers
Update:
    If(MarioHeight > MyHeight)
        JumpUp;
    Elseif(MarioHeight<MyHeight)
        JumpDown;
    FaceMario;
```

```
        SpawnThrownHammer;
End;


//-Advanced Script-------------------
//Simple Guy
Update:
        If(MarioIsJumping)
        {
            //returns if Mario will land to my left or right
            dir = CalcMarioLandingSpot;
            //FindBestOffset finds the best spot right next to
            //where he'll land, so that he won't squish me on
            //the way down
            dir = FindBestOffset(dir);
            If(dir != MyDir)
                TurnAround;
            //make sure enemies don't pile up, spread them out
            //so its harder to land safely
            WalkForwardNoCrowding;
    }
        else
        {
        if(!FireBallNear)
        {
            FaceMario;
                If(!NearEdge)
                WalkForwardNoCrowding;
            Else
                TurnAround;
        }
        else
            DodgeFireBall;
    }
End;
```

Since the scripts would be so simple, the script writing tool could even be implemented within a larger-level editing tool. The tool would allow you to construct the scripts, and then tag enemies placed within the maps with the scripts that they would use. You could allow the editor to run the game with your edited script, and immediately see the results of your changes. If your game had a console, you could even allow a designer to add or replace parts of an enemy behavior script from within the game.

The last script in the listing is an "advanced" version of the original, where we've tried to use more perception data to make it especially brutal on poor Mario. This script tries to dodge incoming Mario jumps and harmful fire-balls, and tries to keep the character from falling to his death by walking off ledges. It also tries not to clump up with other enemies, to create less space for Mario. Savage creatures indeed.

Long-Term (LT) Decision Making

Usually, the LT layer handles, by definition, long-term problems. But, because of the quick, fly-by nature of the game, an LT layer for this game would be concerned more with the other usage of LT systems, that of coordinating enemies toward a larger goal. The LT layer for *Super Mario Bros.* could be used to have multiple enemies work together to cut off all of Mario's methods of progressing.

The LT system could monitor which powerups and hidden blocks are within the current scene, and allocate particular enemies to guard them, while placing other enemies at strategic locations, in places where Mario needs to land to navigate the level. Implementation could be an FSM working either in parallel with the ST state machine, or as an "overseer" state machine that runs in sequence before the individual enemy AI state machines. In essence, the LT layer would assign tasks to particular enemies, and then each enemy's ST layer would decide the best way to perform their task.

We're going to assume that individual enemies are pawns of the system within the LT layer. Enemies will never decide to not perform their LT assigned task. The situation could come up in games in which you allow individual characters, be they soldiers in a war, or combatants in a fighting game like *Double Dragon,* to have morale or bravery statistics. If morale gets too low, or their assigned actions would lead to certain death, they might turn tail and run, instead of listening to the LT layer. But not here; in this game, everyone lives for the glory of the system, whose only goal is to stop Mario from getting the Princess.

Location-Based Information Layer

If we are creating an AI system for the game that learns over time, then an influence map could keep statistical track of the route that Mario takes through each level, which powerups he tries for, and the like, and this information could be used to position enemies for maximum detriment. Of course, this kind of information would only come after having Mario run through the level a few times.

The nice thing about a game that stored this information is that the AI system would then work on arbitrary maps. It would extract strategic information from Mario's movements rather than from level designer–placed cues, like jump connectivity points and lists of placed powerup blocks. The system would also adapt over time: as Mario responded to the enemies' placements by changing his methods to get through, the enemies' placements would change also.

AI PLAYER IMPLEMENTATION

For this part of the breakdown, we'll now assume that the enemies in the game are using the standard *Super Mario Bros.* behavior set. Now we want to make an AI-controlled Mario-like character that would perform all the things that a human player can do. A possible usage for this would be a game in which you have another player that is controlled by the CPU, running through the level at the same time as you, in a competition to see who can get the highest score, or collect the most powerups, in a sort of thematic race. Other uses might include cooperative or helper characters that would sidekick alongside of the human player, or AI-controlled "bots" in a multi-player game of some sort. The little character will be called "Tony."

Perception and Event Layer

The amount of input data that the character has is limited. As Tony sees enemies, the perception layer would add them to a list (`m_nearbyEnemies`, possibly), and track their type (for predicting their movement) and position. A list of nearby visible (and hidden but known) powerups would also be useful.

Behavior Layer

Tony has a few behaviors. He can walk, run, jump, and (if powered up) shoot a fireball. All of these behaviors can be constructed as very straightforward pieces of code except one: Jump. In *Super Mario Bros.*, as far as Mario is concerned, jumping IS the game. *Super Mario Bros.* is the game that introduced the concept of controllable jumps. You can hold down the jump button, for a higher jump (up to a certain max), but you can also *steer* your jump (using the direction pad) to a remarkably large degree. These simple additions make the jump behavior for AI Tony a large undertaking.

Jump steering is accomplished by using two things: in-air momentum, and the height of the jump. Figure 25.2 shows a diagram of the basic gameplay mechanic of Tony's steerable jump. When you push the jump button, the game takes into account your forward movement (initial momentum), and then starts adding to an accumulating value based on the direction you're pushing (positive value for forward direction, negative for reverse), and your height in the jump (the higher, the bigger the value), which is then used to affect the arc of the jump. To create a workable AI Tony, he needs to be taught how to jump within this game mechanic.

This can be done like any complex game behavior, invariably there are many different ways. You could find a series of joystick inputs that make Tony jump in useful ways, and use each jump specifically as a different behavior. So, you'd have a `LongestJumpPossible` behavior, and a `JumpToSingleBlockDirectlyAboveMe` behavior, as well as many more. You might even have specific jumps coded just for certain areas in the game. Certainly this method would work, because there are only so

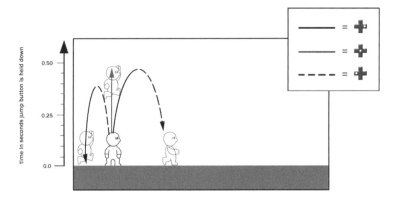

Jumping from a standing position

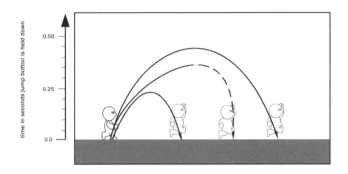

Jumping from a full run

FIGURE 25.2   The mechanics of Tony's jumping.

many constructs within the game that Tony needs to get past. You could create fifty different types of jumps (number chosen arbitrarily), and then create a system for determining which jump to use based on the delta vector between where you are and where you want to land. You could even train a NN or GA to determine the rules for when to use each type of jump.

Going further, you could also train a NN or GA to actually *find* the correct series of joystick inputs to navigate a specific jump vector. This might take a while, because you're talking about many rules (fifty in our example), with each rule possibly taking ten to thirty steps (assuming three things: thirty frames per second, that a jump animation is a full second long, and that you can steer the jump during the entire animation). Of course these numbers might be reducible; you would need to experiment to determine exactly how many rules and steps for each rule were necessary.

Animation Layer

Like the enemies, the number of animations that Mario has doesn't require the help of an animation selection system. The biggest variable in player movement is jumping, so different jumps could be animated for the numerous styles of jumps. But with the human controlling Mario, the game doesn't know when the player's going to let go of the jump button or quit steering a jump. With an AI Tony, however, we would know ahead of time the exact jump we are going to attempt, and trigger specific jump animations that will look cool for the different types of jumps. If Tony had twenty different jump animations (ten styles with two each) then a very simple animation system could compute which one to play based on the style of the jump, and then some random check to mix up which animation to play out of the two equivalent animations for each style. Other places for animation selection would include playing transition animations, so when you stop pushing forward suddenly, Tony would play the correct braking animation, or would react to repeated jumps with custom animations.

Motion Layer

Pathfinding would be necessary to give our Tony a sense of where to go, although the 2D nature of the game would drastically simplify the task. Paths would be mostly consistent of jump connectivity between platforms. We could even preprocess the necessary jump style to use to jump from one platform to another, and encode this data within the pathnodes themselves, to help optimize the game code from having to make these calculations during run time.

Pathfinding could even be performed in a sort of potential fields implementation, in which each platform location stored the force vector necessary to get to the next platform. If the platform was just a floor, connected to the next section, it would give a "walk" vector, otherwise it would give "jump" vectors. Sections that have both a walk and jump vector are near the edges of a platform, or have multiple successive places that can be reached. To find his way to a powerup block, or some higher-up platform, Tony would search backwards through the potential fields graph (from his target to his current location) to find a series of movement vectors that would get him there.

Obstacle avoidance could be done a number of different ways, depending on Tony's goals within the level. If he didn't mind skipping past some enemies, then the presence of enemies could invalidate certain paths, which would make him take alternate means to get through the screen. If he was a bit more bloodthirsty, we could note each opponent in turn, and if killable, he could plan a jump vector that would bounce him onto the nearest of them, and he could even try to compute bounces that would then daisy chain bounce him onto another enemy, giving him bonus points.

If Tony was using the potential fields method, then the enemies could also emit negative potential fields, making Tony jump automatically whenever he got too close to them. Tony usually has to jump *before* he gets to a given creature, so the potential field effect would have to be offset from the actual creature's position, or just large enough to affect Tony at a distance. A motion layer done this way wouldn't really have to be aware of the enemies of the level, because they would just affect how he traversed from one platform to another. Care would have to be taken, though, that Tony wouldn't automatically jump over an enemy and fall to his death into some pit.

Short-Term Decision Making

Short-term concerns might be things that only deal with the screen of space that Tony is currently on. Things like getting powerups, bouncing on enemies in a specific order so that he minimizes his danger, and making his way to the next screen can all be handled by the ST decision layer. A simple FSM (with a few states, like `EliminateCreatures` and `GetPowerups`, would probably suffice), especially if we've put a lot of intelligence within the other layers of the system.

Long-Term Decision Making

LT decisions might include time-based considerations (forcing Tony to take a pipe shortcut through a level, in order to finish the level before the time limit), or specifically taking a certain path to get a large cache of coins and the extra life that comes with them.

Tony has one area in which he needs somewhat advanced planning, that of determining the best way to break bricks to then get to certain well-hidden secrets. Consider this scenario: at a certain point in the game, Mario needs to break a brick, which gives him access to the one next to it as a step, and then break out three more that are up a level, followed by leaping across a small pit and breaking out one on that side, to *then* bump the secret block that sprouts a vine, taking him to the warp zone. That's quite a bit of planning for such a simple task. Although it could be done (as a classic planning algorithm, where you would have the state of the screen, and operators like `Jump`, `BreakBrick`, and so forth that would allow you to test different plans to find one that would work), this would be quite computationally expensive. Instead, because we don't have arbitrarily constructed levels, we can precompute how to achieve certain secret spots within the level, using small scripts of which blocks to break in what order, either written directly into Tony's script, or tagged to the areas of the map that they're required for.

Location-Based Information Layer

There are times when Tony pushes forward, and doesn't see any enemies. So, he jumps to the next platform, only to have the screen scroll, and land right next to an enemy that he didn't know was just off screen, which kills him. Now imagine that we implemented an influence map for all the floor space in the level, using occupance data that stored how many creatures, if any, had been on each patch of floor for some set time period. Thus, the occupance data would sort of *linger*, leaving a ghostly trail of occupance behind each creature that would gradually fade away. Having this kind of system, Tony would check where he was going to jump to, and note if anybody *had* been walking on the platform, but had just returned to the right of the screen. He could even, by watching the values decay over a few frames, determine the direction and speed of travel of the enemy. A system like this would virtually stop surprise run-ins like these, except for one-shot monsters that don't move until they get on screen.

Tony could definitely benefit from a smart terrain system. Powerups could tell him of their nearness, and even give him directions for how to get there. The different level elements (such as flower pipes, super jump pads, etc.) could also telegraph their location and use to Tony, so that he could use them "blind," as it were, simplifying his usage of level elements and also making it much easier to add new elements.

SUMMARY

Distributed AI design is a way of splitting up AI tasks into chunks that not only allow for a separation of functionality, but also as separate platforms for adding personality and individuality to AI-controlled characters. It helps AI systems add richness of behavior while providing reuse of code.

- Distributed AI design allows difficult AI problems to be broken into manageable chunks.
- The layers within the distributed method include perception, behavior, animation, motion, short-term decisions, long-term decisions, and location-based information layers.
- Distributed design adds to the Brooks's subsumption architecture with the inclusion of advanced strategic layers, as well as cooperation layers for dealing with multiple AI entities into a larger picture.
- The chapter fully dissected the game *Super Mario Bros.*, both from the perspective of trying to improve the enemy and boss AI, as well as in the creation of an AI-controlled "Tony" character.
- As you can see by their sheer number, not all of the techniques talked about during the classic game breakdown are simultaneously needed or even compatible. They demonstrate that the number of ways that we could code up the enemies and an AI player for *Super Mario Bros.* are quite diverse.

26 Common AI Development Concerns

In This Chapter

- Design Considerations
- Entertainment Considerations
- Production Concerns
- Summary

In this chapter, we will discuss many of the concerns that can arise in almost any AI engine development. Some of these are design considerations, others are entertainment related, and still others involve production issues. In general, this chapter hopes to provide insights into some of the issues that might flavor the implementation of your AI engine, as well as the AI-controlled entities themselves.

DESIGN CONSIDERATIONS

In this section, we'll look into a few areas of AI engine design and implementation that you should consider. These topics can not only shape the direction you might take in *designing* a particular game AI system, but also may affect the *details* of implemention:

Data-driven design considerations. Common snags to look out for if you're trying to decouple your game data or logic from your engine.

The one-track-mind (OTM) syndrome. This disorder affects some AI programmers, who think that they should find one AI method and stick with it, no matter what.

Level-of-detail (LOD) AI. Useful ideas for implementing an AI engine that allows for this optimization technique.

Support AI. Other uses for AI on a game project that you might not have thought of.

> **General AI design thinking.** Just some general ways of thinking that you should try when you're going about AI engine design.
>
> **General implementation ideas.** These are notions that are good to keep in mind during development, as well as general rules of thumb when coding AI systems.

CONCERNS WITH DATA-DRIVEN AI SYSTEMS

As the content level of games continues to rise, it becomes more and more of an imperative to get additional hands into the internals of the AI systems. Designers are increasingly requiring an immense amount of content from a behavior standpoint (meaning, the amount of *possible actions* that the AI can perform) and are thus also increasing the size and complexity of the game AI logic (or *when* to perform the actions).

Actual game behaviors are much more tightly coupled to game code (they might possibly have to access the animation system, deal with physics, spout particle and/or sound effects, and link into any in-game communication channels like a messaging system), so it is much harder to get the creation of behaviors into a system that a layperson can use. Generally, this means that data-driven design involves the *logic* side of AI development.

In a scripted AI engine, basic behaviors for the various characters are presented to the designers as keywords or functions that they can call from their scripts. In a visual system, you might have individual action nodes (that are representations of your game behaviors) that designers link into some sort of flow diagram.

One way to determine how to achieve the level of data-driven design within your system is to data drive the highest level of the system. Then monitor the usage of the tool, and if the designers are constantly bugging the programmers to add elements at the next level down, *then* data drive that layer, repeating this as necessary. This follows the same model as the most classically data-driven system within modern 3D games, the renderer.

A 3D renderer is a software system that knows how to draw a number of very low-level, completely reusable *primitives.* These primitives come in layers: the lowest would be *polygons,* which combine to make *models,* which then combine to form *scenes.*

At each level of the rendering pipeline, objects are completely constructed from objects of the level below it, and each level is pretty much independent of the others. Whenever making a system data-driven, the evolution from fully hard-coded to fully data-based is always from the highest-level primitive to the lowest-level.

To continue the analogy, some of the earliest 3D renderers were scene definition scripts. *POV-Ray,* a ray-tracing engine that was first created in the 1980s, is a prime example of this. *POV-Ray* had a number of primitives (toroids, spheres, heightfields, and many other shapes that can be defined using a mathematic equation). Rendering things with *POV-Ray* involved writing a little scene script, and then letting it run. Many young graphics experimenters got their first taste of making something visually impressive come out of their computers by using *POV-Ray*. But you can't define a model in *POV-Ray*, because it only renders mathematic constructs. A figure that looks like Crash Bandicoot would be somewhat tough to mathematically model.

So young experimenters had to find themselves a mesh modeler at some point. Mesh-based modelers use a different set of primitives (three-sided polygons called triangles or *tris,* and four-siders called *quads*) to define models, which could then be rendered using a different system, a mesh renderer, instead of mathematical rendering. This is where we currently are in 3D modeling. The reason that the polygons themselves don't require a data-driven design is that they're so low level, *so* primitive, that there really isn't any need to go further.

A game AI engine can be thought of as using analogous primitives: *animations,* which combine into *behaviors,* which combine into *strategies.* The first step in data driving the system, then, is to encode a system for designing the game strategies. Here's where current games mostly stop. Using (usually) either a script of some kind, or a table (depending on preference, really) we construct systems where designers can set up the game rules, the state machines, the fuzzy parameters for player attributes or the probability of behaviors, and the specific decisions to use for transitions, success or failure. But this is still all the first layer of data driving AI systems.

If you find that your designers are continually asking for additional behaviors, then the next step is to allow non-programmer authoring of behaviors. What this requires is coming up with a set of primitives from which all behaviors are built. Commonly, these primitives are thought of as translation within the world (movement), some sort of physical action (animation), and game events (to send information, or launch a sound or graphical effect). If your game uses translation data within the animations to move characters, then movement is also an animation.

Other games, like *The Legend of Zelda* and *Quake,* simply play a run animation, and then slide the model along the floor at a speed that tries to match the animation. Even if you are using the latter method, the movement speeds can be built into the animation that will be playing during the movement.

Thus, we can data drive the behaviors in the same way as the strategies, using *animations* and *events* as our primitives. You can define a state machine that moves from one animation to another, occasionally spawning a game event, either from a script or a table, just like the strategic AI layer.

If you're finding that this *still* isn't enough, and that your designers are requesting constant animation changes, you might have to go still further and give the designers the ability to build the animations themselves. While this isn't commonly done (because animation also includes art direction issues and the like), fighting games in particular have used this level of data-driven design. Animations are built out of the next primitive down, which is called a *frame* of animation. A frame represents a snapshot pose of the character's body position and movement for a very short slice of time. Not only do fighting game designers change parameters and send events keyed to specific frames, but they can actually construct combination animations by playing a few frames of one animation, then a few frames of another, blending between them if necessary.

Data-driven design is not a magic bullet; it won't universally improve any game or system. As you data drive lower and lower levels of your AI engine, the degree of organization with the creation pipeline needs to go up. Because the size of the data necessary to define all the possibilities goes up dramatically the lower in the system you are, data bloat and other issues come into play as well.

Make sure that you are not data driving areas of your game that could be done better with a code-based solution. If your animation system is completely data driven, but all the animations are using the same script except for one, then you are being pretty wasteful. You're probably going to be better off, in terms of both performance and data size, to use a code-based approach and just code a special case for that one exception to the system.

The lesson is, only support the amount of data-driven design that is required by your game, and even then, make sure that you're following the formula: create the reusable, simple primitives that allow users to build more complex objects. If creating those primitives becomes an issue, then go down a layer in complexity, and data drive that step as well.

THE ONE-TRACK-MIND SYNDROME

Another problem that affects some AI programmers is to focus on a particular technique and apply it by rote to every AI problem they come across, barely giving thought to its relevance. One of the central things to remember with AI techniques is that most are very context-sensitive; they only work for specific types of problems, given certain fields of input, and under particular game conditions. If your game is even moderately complex, there aren't really *any* game AI techniques that will be the one and only approach you'll need to get everything done in a clean, scalable, and manageable way.

One of the most common traps that AI programmers (especially new AI people, or even senior staff from other programming areas that start poking their heads into AI) fall into is the "state machines are all you need" trap. For good reason, a large swath of people find state machines easy to understand, and enjoy the way that they help break down problems. These sensible programmers then promptly lose their minds, buy a ring, and marry FSMs until death do them part.

FSMs can go a long way in the game industry. It's true, you probably *could* program 80 percent of games on the shelf with state machines. Especially with programmers who don't mind 100-hour crunch weeks, dredging through pages of nearly indecipherable state machine logic stuck in huge switch statements with somewhat arbitrary priority systems. All because they once again forgot that state machines don't scale very well, tending to get harder to maintain the more states added to them. FSMs are like a hammer. You can't build a house without your hammer. But trying to build a house with *just* a hammer can be a whole lot of extra work indeed.

An AI engine doesn't have to be all-encompassing. You can use an FSM for the basic state layout of your game (front end, introduction, gameplay, gameover), a FuSM for the main short-term decision layer, a simple planner to run your pathfinding and long-term decision layer, and a scripting system to data drive animation selection and run configuration scripts for the decision layers. Your perception system can be humming along in the background, sending out messages to all of these systems, and keeping the wheels turning. Sounds complex? As a whole it is, but it's a complexity born of relatively simple pieces working together.

Piece by piece, what you've really created is a straightforward, modular, scalable system that can be the basis for any number of game titles. It can handle all the problems thrown at it by the game, as well as last minute game ideas and tuning crises that might come up because of focus testing. If something comes up that is completely unplanned, something that it can't handle, it's flexible enough to incorporate another module, without breaking the "fragile, poorly balanced house of cards" that many large-scale complex FSM or rule-based AI systems become over time.

LEVEL-OF-DETAIL (LOD) AI

AI systems are generally strapped for resources. Polls at the Game Developer Conference over the years have seen a slow rise in CPU allocation for AI in games, from about 2 percent in the mid-1990s to around 10 percent currently. Certain genres, like turn-based games, obviously are outside this metric, but these numbers are considered averages.

Just like our graphics systems, one way in which to quickly tame rampant processor usage of AI systems involve using LOD levels within your AI. The different LODs are dependant, just like graphics, on the player not being able to see the shortcuts being used. A typical LOD list might entail:

- *Off-screen and faraway.* Characters in this category are completely nonexistent to the player.
- *Off-screen and close.* These AI characters cannot be seen, but the player might still hear them, notice doors closing from someone passing, etc. Many games

don't use this determination, in that they continue to treat the character as close by.

- *Very far-off.* A character in this LOD would be visible as a pixel or two.
- *Far-off.* Characters are now visible as solid colors, and possibly shapes, but no real detail yet. You can tell the difference between a monster and a humanoid, and tell a truck from a car.
- *Medium.* This distance would be your true area of sight, determined more by the camera angles used in your game, as well as where the depth fog starts to clear. A good distance might be somewhere between 40 and 70 yards.
- *Close.* Anything closer than Medium is considered close.
- *Interaction.* This distance implies that the character is actually interacting with the player in some way.

There are a few ways to handle the AI as it changes between the various levels. One is to actually run different AI routines. This is akin to the graphics practice of generating lower polygon models for LOD models that will only be seen from very far away. If you're scripting your AI, then you could just have different AI scripts for the LODs, or the functions buried *within* the AI engine that the scripts are running might perform LOD checking. A character will use full dynamic obstacle avoidance when the human is close by, but when the human is off screen or very far away, we can forget about this sometimes costly step. However, your engine must ensure that AI characters can recover from any sort of odd conditions that might come up by not using obstacle avoidance (like getting stuck inside large groups of obstacles), should the human player suddenly come back.

But from the character's AI system, it would always just be calling DoAvoidance(), and the avoidance function itself would query the LOD system to determine whether or not to perform real avoidance. The only real problem with this technique is also shared with its graphics analogy: You are usually required to write other versions of the script, or code, or database. In short, you multiply the amount of implementation and debugging work to create any behavior in a system using LODs, because you need to support the multiple routines.

Another way of handling LOD in AI systems involves varying the update frequency of the AI engine's Update() calls to specific areas. For characters within the human player's immediate area, AI decisions might be updated very frequently, upwards of ten to thirty times per second. For off-screen elements, this might fall to a figure more like two to five times per second, or even less. Nonessential behaviors (so called *window dressing*, because it serves no purpose other than looking pretty) can be reduced to not updating at all, if need be. When setting up these schedules, try to *load balance* your update calls so that you're not updating all of a specific type of unit at LOD level 3 every fifteen game loops. Rather, offset their starting update time, so that each individual unit still only updates every fifteen ticks, but only a *few* units of that type update each tick.

As an example, we'll discuss an NPC character in a 3D FTPS game. The NPC is a scientist and is running a small AI script that has him continuously moving between one of three workstations, playing a different animation at each one, to appear that he is working. Here we have a character that is adding nothing to game play other than contextual movement within the world. The ways that the different levels of detail would affect his behavior would be:

Off-Screen

When an enemy isn't visible, don't run its AI at all because it it's not influencing anything. You might want to continue playing the enemy's sounds occasionally if it's close to the player's location, but not if there's a nicely sealed lab door between the player and this character.

Very Far-Off

Stand still. The view distance is so far that even moving the character is unnecessary because it will likely only translate to a few pixels worth of movement anyway.

Far-Off

Slide the character (don't animate, pathfind, or avoid: just slide) occasionally back and forth in a straight line between his equipment. You'll still give the illusion of activity within the world, without all of the work. If the scientist were an acrobat instead, and was supposed to be performing cartwheels and huge aerial leaps, we couldn't just slide him, but all this means is that we'd just have to use a different technique for an acrobat at this LOD.

Medium Distance and Closer

For this distance, just run his regular AI because this particular guy isn't performing expensive calculations. Which brings up a good rule of thumb: try to get your designers to give nonessential game characters very few advanced AI tasks. Our scientist shouldn't need to use pathfinding to get between his equipment, and shouldn't be running any unnecessary perceptions.

As another example, let us consider an enemy civilization in an RTS game. These games are a bit different, in that the position of the player isn't really a set place, and *by design* the human player isn't going to be seeing the majority of AI units for large chunks of time because of the limited amount of world that can be seen at once, as well as the Fog of War. A sample breakdown for the different AI LODs in an RTS game might be:

Off-Screen and Faraway

All strategic AI continues to run (at all LOD levels), but at adjusted update rates. Another possible optimization might be that the AI has limited updates, but when a major event happens (for example, the AI reaches the next major upgrade in the technology tree), it gets a short time to perform major tasking during which the AI will update at a higher rate. However, tactical decisions and actions are dramatically simplified. Note that being under the Fog of War is equivalent to being off screen.

Movement can be done by just sliding the units along at some set speed in the direction of their target, and when within some range teleported to the exact final destination. Or they could be left idle until the travel time is up, and then teleported the entire distance. Unit-to-unit collision could be simplified, or even ignored during this LOD (although, you would have to ensure that two guys aren't sitting on each other before they become visible again).

Actions, especially combat, could be determined using statistics instead of actual fighting. Other actions, like building structures or mining resources, would also be statistically determined (so, the game wouldn't have to move peons back and forth between a gold mine and a resource center, but would instead determine the time it takes to get some amount of resource, and just apply a timer to a set-resource increment).

Off-Screen and Close

Because close likely means contact, this LOD should probably be close to full AI, except for the obvious visual elements. Tactical units might still play sounds, if not under the Fog of War. Animation selection is obviously ignored.

Very Far-Off to Close

These LODs would be roughly the same, in reference to an AI. What is "on screen" in an RTS game is usually much more localized than other genres, and the camera angle is almost always limited to a restricted, semioverhead view (*Myst* used a more general system). Because of these two facts you don't have the degree of perspective, where you see characters as specks far off in the distance, like you do in other games.

Interaction

At this level, everything is on, and the AI is updating at the highest frequency level that it needs to make intelligent decisions.

SUPPORT AI

Sometimes, you must design elements into your AI engine that don't have anything to do with the primary gameplay in the title you are developing. Other areas of the game can still benefit from AI techniques. Things to consider in terms of secondary AI systems include:

- *User interface.* Your game might have an intelligent inventory system, which stacks inventory items in such a way as to maximize space, or put crucial items into more accessible locations. Or, you might use mouse-based *gestures* (stylized movements that can be assigned a function; like side-to-side swipes, L shapes, or circles) to perform commands within the game. Both of these systems could be easily accomplished with a very simple offline trained neural net. Another big UI usage is "advisors" in a civ-style game (where you'd have a specific AI analysis, most likely the same one that an AI-controlled opponent would use, to look over the player's game and give personalized advice as to what options the player has within different areas of gameplay, like research or diplomacy).
- *Tuning game parameters.* Any time you find that an AI system has many parameters within a specific system, ask yourself these questions:
  1. Can I create a side program that can replicate this system in an atomic or single-purpose fashion, or at the very least run this system within my game over and over?
  2. Can I quantify the potential "goodness" of a set of parameters, within some normalized scale?
  3. Are there relations between my parameters that I haven't been able to find with just trial and error tuning?

     If you answered yes to these questions, then your system is a good candidate to try to use an AI method to tune the system for you. GAs are particularly good at tuning parameters, especially if the states of these variables can easily be translated to some kind of genetic representation.

     Because of the number of parameters that many games use to tune their gameplay settings, you might have to split up your game into special "states" (which may not be really any different other than the parameters are more related within these states, so you end up with a *number* of GA-tuned sets of parameters that you use based on which state your game is in), or you may have to try to GA-tune small portions of your parameter set, and hand-tune other parts. Games have used these methods for tuning parameters on physics simulations, or tuning the parameters on transitions within a state machine running deathmatch bots.
- *Automated testing.* As games increase in complexity, it becomes harder and harder to test every single possible combination of factors within the software to find potential crash bugs. One way of doing this is to use something that other software companies have used for years—an automated testing system. By constructing your software up front with this system in mind, you can have parts of your game be bug tested by an autonomous tool, giving you more time to spend on gameplay

tuning instead of bug identification and replication. Basically, the key to allowing for automated testing is to have a control system that is very generic, open, and spoofable (which means that you could have another program *spoof* this input without actually needing a person to create the input). Games are generally good candidates, because the interface to the game is the generic controller, keyboard, joystick, or mouse that the player uses, and it's usually an easy thing to generate this input, and feed it into the system instead of using actual input.

There are several types of testing along this line:

1. *Limits testing* is when you specifically use directed inputs that are around the limits of the system's capabilities, in combinations that might lead to bugs.
2. *Random testing* uses completely random input to the system.
3. *Smart testing* is a system that tries to employ real game-playing techniques to play the game, but might possibly then switch to one of the other methods at key points.

So, a smart system would play competently in a racing game; but when it finds itself surrounded by other cars on a bridge, it might start sending random input to test the robustness of the physics in handling cars on the bridge under collisions and different levels of control. Testing during development allows for specific testing scenarios to be run on smaller portions of the code, and also fixes bugs before other systems are implemented that might be affected by bad code behavior. All of these testing systems might use different AI systems to be implemented. You might use anything from GAs to random input to test a particular section of a game, or actually use the AI-controlled opponent of a game to test out the system (if the AI in your game has been executed by having it output controller data to interface with the game), and have it specifically test limits or sketchy moments within the game.

GENERAL AI DESIGN THINKING

When you're designing an AI engine, you're standing on the edge of a large sea of possibility. You're also at the near top of the development totem pole, as far as dependency issues are concerned. AI requires hooks into almost every other system of the game to make rational decisions, and make them quickly. When dealing with the sometimes daunting array of functionality that an AI system will require, you should take into account a few ideas:

■ During design, brainstorm like there's no tomorrow. Once your problem set has been laid out (meaning, you essentially know the scope of what the game is going to require from your AI engine), spend some quality time going over *as many ways as you can think of* for solving each of those problems. Don't think *about* them, however. Not yet. Just think them up, and write them down.

Brainstorming is about keeping as much electricity flowing through as many brain pathways as you can, for as long as you can. Coming up with outlandish ideas is not pointless or a waste of time because sometimes stupid ideas are just the seeds of really great ideas.

- Follow up your brainstorming sessions by having serious talks with the rest of the AI staff about each idea in your list. Again, don't throw away so-called stupid ideas just yet. Put things on the table, and cut them apart as a team. Dissect them, and find out if they're stupid to the core or if there's a golden egg buried in there. Getting additional brains involved in a large undertaking like AI engine design can help uncover ideas that were hazy or perhaps completely blank in even the best plan, and merely talking about the issues will get your brain in a state where it will be working things out in much more tangible ways, rather than the "I'm pretty sure how to do that" mentality that sometimes leads to giant holes in a design.

- If there's time in the schedule, try quick prototyping small-scale AI problems in a laboratory example, like the AIsteroids test bed that was used in this book. Advanced techniques can be worked up in a matter of hours or days, and given real-world testing without having to spend weeks only to find out that it's not suitable to your game. Moreover, implementation usually uncovers things you didn't think of in the design chair. Don't feel like you failed as a designer. There's *always* going to be too many variables to see everything. Don't try to predict the future. As soon as you have 80 percent of your solution, dive into the code, and *discover* the other 20 percent in a month of prototyping. Contrast this with spending months more in design, scratching and clawing to try and predict more of the "possible shortcomings and pitfalls," finding another 10 percent of your solution, having no code to show for it, and then *still* finding design holes when you start coding.

- Finally, just be open. Don't take other's ideas as attacks on your own ideas. Use a lesson from fuzzy logic when dealing with other people, especially programmers. If you are right, it doesn't mean that everyone else is wrong, and vice versa. You being 50 percent right, and the other guy being 50 percent right, still equals 100 percent right. Allow for fuzzy states of rationality in your dealings with others, and instead of arguing over semantics to prove that you're right, you'll instead be incorporating the factors of both ideas that are correct *together* into a better solution.

ENTERTAINMENT CONSIDERATIONS

Unlike some other software industries, our programs have two goals: to perform their stated functionality, *and* to give the player an entertaining experience. These two goals, while not exclusive, are rarely friendly, and how you create your game is almost always a careful balance between good programming and programming for the sake of goodness.

- *The all-important fun factor.* Points to consider when tap dancing around the one thing that we are *really* in the business for: to make fun games.
- *Perceived randomness.* The question of randomness, and it's perceived inequities on gameplay.
- *Difficulty concerns.* The level of difficulty that you create within your game is definitely an entertainment issue, and there are design and AI design considerations.
- *Some things that make an AI system look stupid.* These are things that mostly look bad, but are often used in games.

THE ALL-IMPORTANT FUN FACTOR

When you ask somebody about a new game, what do you really want to know? As an AI programmer, you might want to know how intelligent the AI systems seem, or maybe you're a jaded purist and really just want to know how the gameplay in *this* game is deviating from the norm for the genre.

But the typical Joe User wants to know one thing: Is it fun? What really makes a game fun? Psychology has several theories. One is that simple tasks, which combine quick visual identification skills with motor reflexes, awaken old, hunter-gatherer instincts within our brains. We are built by nature to discern movement, far more so than color or shape. Video games might provide these deeply seeded centers of the brain with the kind of stimulus that they haven't had since we left the African plains and started hiding in caves in France. Another theory lies in classical conditioning, which states that any sufficiently repeated task that is also given periodic positive reinforcement will cause physiological changes within our brains that will make us want to do it *more*. Still another theory talks about the fact that most people derive their deepest sense of "pleasure" when engaging in a task that they have a high degree of skill in and are also using to just shy of their limitations.

A fun game is one that gives the player rewards, but not too many, because it also needs to be challenging. How can we model our AI systems to best aid us in this endeavor? We need to maintain reaction speed of the system, to provide the right amount of drama and reactivity. We also need to make sure that the AI isn't too hard (because humans will give up easily if they feel like there's no chance of victory, to try and save face; "I didn't want to win anyways . . ."), but we must also strive to not be too easy, because the fun metric is for a game to be on the edge of your abilities. But, the "edge of your abilities" is different for every player, now isn't it? This is one of the driving forces behind *adaptive* AI difficulty determination. The system is supposed to monitor gameplay, and adjust the level of AI opponent difficulty based on the actions and performance of the human.

While this adaptive element is the Holy Grail of difficulty level problems, there are major hurdles to success with this method that have been discussed elsewhere in this book (most notable is purposefully poor human performance, to fool the adaptive system into lessening the difficulty of the game).

Malicious exploitation of adaptive systems may one day be overcome, however, then we will be able to deal with the question of difficulty level. One solution might be to model the player over time as to skill, and try to discern false negatives. Tuned correctly, the player should not be able to find a pattern of oscillating good and bad behavior that result in an overall *massive* advantage over the AI opponent. Again, the goal is for a slight advantage, to keep the player "at 40 percent health," meaning just on the verge of being in trouble, but still firmly in the game.

The other element of fun is novelty. Novelty allows us to try, and enjoy, experiences that might not be fun otherwise. We're willing to put up with the atrocious difficulty level of a game like *Defender* because it was new and unique. If somebody put out roughly the same game nowadays it probably wouldn't do well, mostly because the novelty is gone. Now all that's left is an unbalanced game with a difficult control scheme, nonexistent AI, and grainy graphics. Many people heralded the AI enemies in *Medal of Honor* as truly special, in many cases for one simple reason: that they would *pick up grenades you threw at them, and throw them back*. A simple addition to the AI scripts for an FTPS enemy, to be sure. But nobody had thought to put that element into a game before, and the *novelty* was instantly rewarded with praise.

Now, the AI exhibited by the entities in your game do not represent the total sum of either the difficulty level or the novelty within a game. Many other elements, including gameplay mechanics, control scheme, amount of powerups, time limits, etc., have plenty to do with this. So, there is room for all kinds of experimentation within the game AI world. But, if all else fails, the AI must be able to bend to the needs of the great fun meter. Because if it isn't fun, then you have essentially failed, no matter how smart it is.

PERCEIVED RANDOMNESS

Almost all games have an element of randomness inherent in their gameplay and AI. The reason is called *replayability,* which is the degree to which users want to play the game again even after they have either solved it, or have played it for a decently long period of time and have gained a level of proficiency. Two types of games have so far proved to be the most replayable: games with solid gameplay and multiplayer support (like *Quake,* or chess), and games with solid gameplay and *balanced* randomness (like *Tetris*, or poker). Note that in both cases, your success also depends on having a good, solid, game experience.

Balanced randomness means that an element of gameplay is random, but it doesn't grossly affect the game's outcome. Pretty much no matter what order the pieces fall in *Tetris*, if you can keep a level head and a good plan, you can survive very far in the game. Even in poker, where the luck really is in the draw, a good player can turn bad luck into a win. Unbalanced randomness is the opposite; randomness can have a large sway on the outcome of the game. Unbalanced randomness *feels* random. It makes the player feel like he's no longer in control of the game, and that at any second a string of dice rolls can undo any effort he might have achieved. A game that unknowingly uses too much unbalanced randomness in its primary gameplay systems or AI systems is surely doomed.

The way in which unbalanced randomness is introduced into games is deceptively simple: it is to use the normal `random()` call in your game code (which usually returns a random floating point number between 0.0*f* and 1.0*f*). When you let *actual* randomness dictate the behavior of your AI enemies, you typically get unbalanced randomness. The reason that this is wrong is simple. Human beings do not intuitively accept statistical random chance. If you ask someone the question "I've flipped this coin thirty times, and it's been heads *every time!* What do you think the next flip will be?" they will almost invariably say "Tails! It's due!" even though there isn't any more chance of it being tails than the last thirty. Probability is just about the most alien idea possible to the normal human brain; this is why the lottery people make so much money. If the average person realized they were actually about ten times more likely to get hit by lightning six hundred times than they are to win a typical state-run lottery, they might just ease up on the fifty dollars they spend every Friday.

So how do we allow for balanced randomness in our games? The answer is simple. Don't be random. Say you're coding an AI decision function that is only to respond true 70 percent of the time. If we were to use the expression "`random() 0.7f`," we've statistically solved the problem. Over the lifetime of this function, it will return true 70 percent of the time. But in the short run, say, a single game, it might actually always return false. Yes, the chances are small. But statistically it could happen. What does this mean for our game? Unbalanced randomness is what it means. Instead, we need to create a series of outputs that are balanced, to assure a closer approximation of what we consider a random series of results.

For this same function, a more balanced way would be to have it generate a string of numbers at game start, the length of which is approximately equal to the average number of times it gets called in a game. So, let's say that our little function gets called an average of twenty times per game. To create a balanced series of outputs, it would generate twenty Booleans, fourteen of which were true, and then apply a balancing function to spread out the negative and positive responses somewhat evenly, pushing the final array onto a stack for quick usage. Then, each time you called the function, it would return the next value popped from the stack.

Let's be clear: you're still going to get some variation in statistics. It might be that this run through the game the little function only gets called eighteen times, or maybe twenty-three times (if you do go long, just generate another ten-number sequence, or however many you feel is appropriate). You might even want to add in a little variance into the initial population creation (so that the function will actually return a random range of 65 to 75 percent, say). But what this buys you is a series of "random" results, in which you don't ever get too many failures in a row, and you basically ensure that the final statistics will always be fairly close to what you originally wanted: no reliance on "actual" randomness, and the result is that your players never feel cheated. Watch out so that you don't make your mixture too uniform; players would figure out real quick if every third shot went in. So there's still some randomness involved, it's just that we're making sure that in the *short run*, we won't be hit by large runs of positive or negative results.

SOME THINGS THAT MAKE AN AI SYSTEM LOOK STUPID

There are some behaviors that show up again and again in games, and yet almost universally make the game's AI controlled characters seem stupid. These are prime examples of behavior systems that we should, as AI programmers, be dilligent in ferreting out and eliminating. Some of the biggest cliché mistakes include standard machine gun enemy conventions, bad pathfinding, and non-contextual and oblivious enemies.

■ *The standard enemy with the machine gun "rules."* The rules are: miss the first shot, try not to shoot first, use tracer bullets to give away your position, and use a large cone of aim so that you miss a lot. These are good rules if used correctly. But if taken too literally, or abused, the opponent will look stupid, indeed. Sure, an AI enemy should miss quite frequently, but don't spray bullets like a fire hose. You can actually find targets that are decently close to the player, and still not hit him (amazing, isn't it?), which might even make the encounter more exciting for the player. You know the scene in the action movie where the hero runs across an open area and bullets cause little puffs of dust from the ground in a line trailing behind him as he runs? That's the kind of thing we should be shooting for. Obviously, in a first person game, we can't use the same trailing bullet trick (since the player won't see it), but we can use ricochet sparks off of nearby walls, railings, or other things in the environment. We *can* use the movie bullet trick with enemies shooting from the player's front.

■ *Bad pathfinding.* No one thing has contributed to the utterance of the phrase "stupid computer" than this problem. Bad pathnodes, characters without adequate dynamic obstacle avoidance, multiple friendly units piling up on a narrow bridge, a speedy unit orbiting around a spot because he hasn't gotten close enough to be "there" yet, a surrounded unit twitching wildly as it tries to move, and a fast unit repeatedly running into the back of a slow unit are all comically common examples of bad navigation gaffs. Other issues under this heading might be RTS peons that build a building from an angle that will trap them once built, units finding an alternate route that takes them right past the enemy's massive laser cannon array, units in formation that switch positions every time you click for them to move, and supersized creatures that can't fit through a doorway standing on the other side staring at you as you unload ammunition into them, without fear (instead of just running down the hall, out the large front door, around the side, and then punting the player into outer space).

■ *Non-contextual enemy animations and/or behaviors.* We've all played games in which enemies don't react realistically to game stimuli. Imagine a game scenario where you come around the corner and see an enemy in the distance; he also sees you. You duck back around the corner. The enemy, who knows that you're probably waiting with your chain gun ready, will look very stupid if he still walks calmly around the corner. Kamikaze tactics and zombies aside, intelligent enemies wouldn't do this. No, intelligent behavior would mean diving out from the corner toward another piece of cover, and possibly throwing a grenade in the player's direction. The game you are working on might go the extra mile and actually use intelligence with cover. But after awhile with no action, does the character then casually walk back out of cover and go back to his patrol? Again, not very intelligent. Behavior demontrating that the AI agent was unsure of your position, looking around from cover to investigate, calling for a buddy to come help, or using his radio to ask other guards if they've noticed and/or heard anything would be better.

■ *Oblivious enemies.* Another common problem is AI agents that are following a script and don't take any queues from the environment while running. Enemies that don't notice a pile of thirty-five dead bodies in one spot and think "Sniper?" or "Is there a Tower of death nearby?" but instead walk right over their friends to perform a patrol are just not intelligent enemies. A small amount of environmental consciousness can go a long way with enemies. Some of the stealth games make it a part of the gameplay mechanics to get the player to hide bodies so as to not alert other guards, but there's definitely an all-or-nothing consensus on this issue in most games.

PRODUCTION CONCERNS

There are also general concerns stemming from the actual production of the AI system itself. Games are being made bigger and more complex by larger teams on advanced hardware.

- *Coherent AI behavior.* Much like a lead artist needs to consider the look of the entire game when considering the quality and feel of each artist's contribution to the product, so too do separate AI programmers working on a single product need to think about the overall feel of the game AI.
- *Think about tuning ahead of time.* Creating your AI systems with tuning in mind from the very beginning will help the process to happily chug along from start to finish.
- *Idiot-proof your AI.* Assume unknown things are going to happen to your AI entities, and allow them ways out; you can help make your AI characters much smarter looking.
- *Consider designer used tools differently.* Designers are (generally) not programmers, and we shouldn't treat them as such. AI tools that will be given to designers to use have issues that need to be considered before implementation and release.

COHERENT AI BEHAVIOR

Everyone has played a game where levels 1 to 3 were fun, well paced, and gradually ramped in difficulty. Then they got to levels 4 and 5 to find radically different difficulty leveling, super-long levels that have only three spots of action spread thin through the levels, and were crippled by a frustrating gameplay mechanic that almost stopped you from playing the game. Most likely, this is because the game developer actually had multiple AI people working on the game, and these multiple people didn't really talk to each other to collaborate on technique or the feel of gameplay. While this problem has decreased dramatically in recent years because of the increasing importance of AI in our games, it still rears its ugly head from time to time. AI tasks are split among the available talent, and away they go to their separate rooms, coding away.

One way to fight this is to have the designers construct the game equivalent of a business mission statement. For any given game, they should have a fairly clear, simple description of what they're shooting for with the gameplay and AI systems for the game. A sports title might be "To provide a fun, fast basketball game that uses statistics to simulate signature moves, shooting ability, and play calling, but provides a quick, arcade-style movement system with over the top special moves and quick defensive opportunities." A fighting game might have the mission of "To create a karate simulation where the player will be able to quickly set off complex combinations of moves and counter moves and not have to worry about lining up his attacks."

Now, if you have different people implementing the different parts of your AI, they're still going to know what kind of game you want, and are going to be able to implement it with the designer's vision in mind. They're not going to have a strange notion as to which parts of the game you want to be a certain way, and which to code another.

THINKING ABOUT TUNING AHEAD OF TIME

Tuning game AI is quite possibly the *most* important part of the process. Take notice of Blizzard's games: *Warcraft, Starcraft,* and their current online foray, *Worlds of Warcraft.* Almost all of their games enter a beta-testing phase that generally ends up being almost as long as other companies spend on development in total. They routinely continue to polish games that *already* have achieved higher-than-current standards of gameplay, and will even continue to address gameplay balance issues after the game has been released. Why? Because they desire to put out the best product they can, partially because they know their fanbase demands it, but partially because they have extreme pride in their creation. Yes, they spend a lot of money to do this, but they also sell millions upon millions of games because they do. Other companies, like Square and Nintendo, follow this same formula. Tune, tune, and tune some more, until there's no more tuning to be done.

Facilitating this level of polish requires an upfront commitment to AI design that allows for quick turnaround of tweaking and balance issues. Data-driven AI is a huge step in the right direction for allowing the tuning process to be streamlined. Getting programmers out of the way of massive parameter tweaks, as well as other data-driven issues, like enemy placement within a level and specific enemy behavior in response to player location or condition, will go a long way in speeding up the process of tuning a content-heavy game. Plus, when tuning the game is fast and easy, the designers are more likely to do much more of it, and as such the process is self-reinforcing.

Another tip is to not put magic numbers in your AI decision-making systems. If your enemy has a line in one of its states that reads `if(m_nearestEnemy < 45)`, maybe you should change that 45 to some kind of variable, and expose that variable to whatever your game is using as a tuning system. Chapter 27, "Debugging," details a widget system that allows you to expose any game variable to a bank of tuning controls, where they can be adjusted in game. This kind of system is almost imperative for AI systems that rely on heavy game testing and tuning to get balance and gameplay to feel right.

IDIOT-PROOF YOUR AI

Always provide some measure of idiot-proofing. If you think there's any way that an AI behavior can screw up, it probably will. When there is doubt, there is no doubt. Software systems have a smirking way of finding the one open door you've accidentally left for them. Not to mention that dropping three human players into your game, each with their own notion of how to exploit the system, act as nothing short of a high-powered catalyst to AI decomposition.

Prepare for this by providing backdoors out of behaviors. Timers for behaviors that have gone on too long are the easiest to code, but simple exit conditions can really help stop an AI behavior that's making itself look stupid. Just get into the habit of giving your AI a way out.

Idiot-proofing extends to designer-provided data as well. A chunk of code that will save you tons of time in development is an ironclad "checker" that either runs on the data from a command line or at game load time (and can be removed from the project before release), and provides you with complete scanning of incoming AI data for inconsistencies, outright errors, overly complex or cyclical state diagrams, broken pathnode networks, missing elements, doubled elements, and the like.

This is throwaway code, but it's better than the weeks you'll spend debugging the pathfinder only to discover that a designer changed a file in an unexpected way, or that your version control corrupted a single byte in a script file that nobody has touched in four months, and it's causing odd behavior in a small wall switch on level 8 that, miraculously, no tester will check during quality control until twelve minutes before you go gold.

CONSIDER DESIGNER-USED TOOLS DIFFERENTLY

AI tools that will be used by designers need a special touch. If you're going to be exposing game logic to the designers, do so with some semblance of kid gloves. Don't put in every bit of functionality *you'd* want in an editor; put in just enough to get the job done while remaining straightforward, and simple. Are you going to be building logical expressions? Consider only allowing ANDs, and not ORs, XORs, etc. Logic gymnastics aren't the strong point of many programmers, much less people who may have started out in the industry testing games. This is not to be insulting to designers, they have one of the hardest jobs in the industry ("Great job on Game of the Year. Now get back to work on the *better* version for next year!"), and everybody thinks they're a designer. Sort of like everybody thinks they can sing.

Another don't includes command-line tools with lots of parameters to set (if possible, encapsulate this kind of thing as an Export button from within the editor, or at least make a batch file or six that they can run to do what you need of them). Provide lots of well-documented, functional examples with any tool or scripting system. Finally, be open to feedback from the designers on GUI issues and functionality problems or irritations.

SUMMARY

A modern-day game AI engine is a hugely complex software system, and there are many common things to consider when coding up one. This chapter looked at specific concerns dealing with design issues, entertainment issues, and production issues.

- Some of the concerns to think about during the design phase of the AI engine include data-driven problems, one-track mind syndrome, level of detail AI, support AI, and other general AI design ideas.
- Entertainment concerns include the fun factor, perceived randomness, difficulty settings, and general things that make AI systems seem stupid.
- Production concerns involve coherent AI feel, tuning the game, idiot-proofing your AI, and treating tools used by the designers differently.

27 Debugging

In This Chapter

- General Debugging of AI Systems
- Visual Debugging
- Widgets
- Summary

I n this section, we'll discuss a very important aspect of AI development: debugging your game from start to finish. We will cover common debugging issues, and bring up some ways in which to write your code to plan ahead for bugs. This chapter also includes a Windows MFC implementation of a useful runtime debugging and tuning tool called *widgets*.

GENERAL DEBUGGING OF AI SYSTEMS

Because of the nature of AI engines, debugging them can be cumbersome. AI invariably touches a number of game systems, bridging the gap between control, physics, sound, gameplay mechanics, and input/output systems. Many times bugs that appear to be AI-based end up being deep within one of the support system's code, but doesn't come out until the AI system starts taxing a particular chunk of game code. As a game designer, you will often have to not only show other people that they need to fix something in their part of the code, but also be ready to back it up by having either a test case set-up that can replicate the problem, or have them come over to your workspace and step them through it directly. You'll save a lot of time and energy this way, rather than sending off an e-mail saying "Fix your code," and then waiting for it to happen.

One benefit of using the distributed AI design from Chapter 25 is that it allows for setting breakpoints at multiple levels, and stratifies the functionality of each subsystem to the point of being easier to identify where a problem might be located in the code. Thus you debug specific systems, instead of having to trace through large combination systems or convoluted classes.

VISUAL DEBUGGING

Visual debugging means using viewable information from within the running game to see information about what the system is doing, in order to debug your programs. This can include having your AI characters display information while the game is running, including text about their current state, or graphical lines showing intent, direction of travel, and thought processing. You can also do so by watching influence map data change and move with the game to see problems. Game AI, more so than most systems, profits greatly from this kind of debugging information. The benefits are explored here.

A VARIETY OF INFORMATION

Visual debugging includes writing text to the game screen, as well as other visual aids. You might want to draw lines pointing toward the targets that each AI character is interested in, or even highlight pathfinding traces, to find bugs in your navigation system. A visual representation of the influence map data is especially useful for debugging the game (in fact, you might want to try turning off drawing of the regular game characters, to watch the influence data for anomalies), as is any abstract data organization method that can help you see a more simplified view of the game.

DEBUGGING AND TUNING

At each stage of your game, you should give yourself a good visual representation of what is going on, so that you can be sure that what is happening is expected. If you're coding up a specific perception that deals with line of sight, put a visual system in the game, so that you can either see all the traces the AI is doing to determine line of sight, or have it "signal" in some way, to let you know exactly when line of sight starts and stops. Then get in the game and actually stare down the barrel of the system, making sure that it's doing what you want, but also that you're getting the *feel* of the system that you're looking for. This is especially important with secondary characteristics, like reaction time. Put indicators in the game, and watch them happen a few hundred times. This kind of behavior will help you find strange math feedback bugs that create holes in behavior and perception, but it also helps you tune systems for proper gameplay feel *much* more quickly and easily.

TIMING INFORMATION

Frequently, it is hard to get events to happen within a debugger that only occur on one game loop, especially if your main game update loop is time-based (rather than frame-based) and you can't set it to use a constant delta during debugging. If your game timer is using the system clock of the processor that you're debugging in, stopping the code with a breakpoint. Then stepping through some code will give you a huge time delta because time continues passing when you're debugging. If you set your game to use a constant delta time for debug purposes, this problem can be minimized. If this is not possible, you can use visual debugging information to put up on-screen information while the game is running at full speed to try and determine the problem. Note that if you write too much text, you might slow down the game because of that, and again have problems getting your bug to repeat.

STATE OSCILLATION

When using a state-based decision structure, you can watch for odd state switching by allowing your AI system to display state information visually in the game. Have the game display this information directly on the character, or over its head, so that you can easily correlate the data with the character. Other useful state information might include hierarchy status, statistics like the time the character has been in the state, and transitional information.

CONSOLE DEBUGGING

On consoles, you typically develop in a Windows or Linux environment and then upload the executable in some way to a test console, while running a debugger on the PC. Because of the remote debugging issue, many common debugging tricks can't be done, and so drawing text or graphics on the console's screen becomes a big source of debugging aid.

DEBUGGING SCRIPTING LANGUAGES

Unless you've taken the time to completely write up a debugging system for your scripting language (and not many game schedules allow for this), you might be left high and dry with only in-game tactics in which to find bugs. One trick is to give your scripters specific debugging commands to put into their scripts; you can then set up on screen text from within an AI behavior script as well.

DOUBLE-DUTY INFLUENCE MAPPING

If your game has an influence map system, you can use it as a visual debugging tool as well. By either adding more space per influence cell (if you have room in memory), or taking over the system completely (if it's not something the part of your game you're debugging requires to run) to display additional, debug-specific information is a great and easy use of the technology. You could display terrain analysis happening on the fly, or avoidance code working on the various AI units in your game. Anything you can link to a specific location, that can be displayed by setting values in the map, can be shown visually by allowing the system to display the contents of the IM while the game is running.

WIDGETS

When coding specific behaviors or perception systems, you may come across in-game values that you wish you could not only see, but also change or tune while the game is running. Widgets are an implementation of this concept that you can easily add to your Windows games, or port over to non-MFC using applications and use anywhere.

Basically, widgets allow you to put a "control knob" on many types of variables within your game. While the game is running, a small window will appear, called a widget bank, that stores all the widgets you've created. Opening the bank allows you to change the values of the variables you've linked to each widget in real time, while the game runs.

IMPLEMENTATION

The code is pretty simple; it includes a few basic rules to get up and running. The entire system was written by Max Loeb, who, incidentally, also helped with most of the diagrams in this book. The basic system is as follows:

- `WidgetBank` is the highest level of the widget hierarchy. It is the "window" in which all the widget groups reside.
- `WidgetGroup` is the second level of organization. Each widget must be a part of a group; you cannot put widgets directly into a bank. Groups can include subgroups.
- The `Widget` class itself. A widget can be one of a few types: a `basic button` (for launching an event function of some kind), a `radio button` (for choosing between two labeled settings), an `OnOff button` (a special button for toggling Boolean values), a `Scrubber` (which allows you to *scroll* through values of a continuous variable), and a `Watcher` (which simply displays an ingame variable).
- The `EventHandler` class, which will allow us to use callback-like functionality within our widgets.

The Widget class is an empty base class that has two functions in it: Update and Draw. It merely provides a way for the other widgets to have common parenting, so that the widget bank and other classes can use any and all widgets.

The WidgetBank class (Listing 27.1 shows the header) is the main window for the system. It is the class that takes care of the MFC functionality for the windows.

LISTING 27.1   WidgetBank header file.

```
/***********************************************************************
* WidgetBank: This is the window that houses all the widget windows, ie.
*             camera widgets, bone widgets, light widgets, and so on.
*
***********************************************************************/
class WidgetBank : public CWnd
{
public:
    // constructors
    WidgetBank();
    virtual ~WidgetBank();

    // member methods
    BOOL Init();
    void RedrawWidgets();
    void UpdateWidgetBankSize();
    void Update();

    // widget creation methods
    int GetHeight();
    Group* AddGroup( char * label );
    afx_msg UINT OnNcHitTest(CPoint point);
    afx_msg void OnSize(UINT nType, int cx, int cy);
    afx_msg BOOL OnEraseBkgnd(CDC* pDC);

    // member variables
    Group * myWidgets[MAX_NUM_WIDGETS];

    int     m_numWidgets;
    int     m_totalWidgetHeight;
    CRect   m_ClientSize ;

    DECLARE_DYNCREATE(WidgetBank)

    DECLARE_MESSAGE_MAP()
```

```
private:
    int m_id;
public:
  afx_msg void OnNcDestroy();
  virtual BOOL CreateEx(DWORD dwExStyle, LPCTSTR lpszClassName, LPCTSTR
                        lpszWindowName, DWORD dwStyle,const RECT& rect,
                        CWnd* pParentWnd,UINT nID,LPVOID lpParam=NULL);
  afx_msg void OnVScroll(UINT nSBCode,UINT nPos,CScrollBar* pScrollBar);
};
```

A `Widget Group` is an organizational method for setting up your widgets to be displayed hierarchically. Upon startup, all the groups will be minimized. You can open a group by clicking on its label, which will *open* the bank for viewing of the individual widgets inside. By using groups, only those widgets you want to see at any one time have to have their groups open, which can help a lot if you've put widgets on a class that has a lot of instantiations in your game. The group class is a bit more involved because this is where the brunt of the widget organization functionality resides. Listing 27.2 shows the header; as you can see, most of the important functions deal with adding the various types of widgets to the bank, drawing them, and updating any window movement, resizing, and so on.

LISTING 27.2   Group header file.

```
/************************************************************************
 *    Group:     A Group represents an entry in the widget bank, and
 *               can house other groups or widgets. It contains a
 *               header which can be expanded/contracted to show/hide
 *               its child groups or child widgets, which are added with
 *               subsequent calls to AddScrubber, AddOnOff, etc.
 *
 ************************************************************************/
class Group : public CWnd {
public:
    // constructors
    Group( char * label, CWnd * pWin, int pos, int height, int width,
           const int level );
    virtual ~Group();

    // member methods
    virtual void Update();
    void OnClickHeader();
```

```
        bool IsExpanded(){ return m_status; }
        int  GetHeight();
        int  GetClientHeight();
        int  GetPrevPos(){ return m_prevPos; }
        void SetPrevPos( int prevPos ){ m_prevPos = prevPos; }
        void SetWidgetBank( WidgetBank * wb ){ m_widgetBank = wb; }

        Group * AddGroupWidget( char * label );

        ScrubberWidget<int> * AddScrubber( char * name, int & val );
        ScrubberWidget<float> * AddScrubber( char * name, float & val );
        ScrubberWidget<unsigned char> * AddScrubber( char * name, unsigned
                                                     char & val );

        OnOffButton * AddOnOff( char * name, bool & a, int ID1 = 0,
                            EventHandler * h = 0 );

        void AddWatcher( char * caption, float & val );
        void AddWatcher( char * caption, int & val );

        void AddText( char * caption );
        RadioButton * AddRadio( char * groupName, char * leftName, char *
                            rightName, int & val, int id1, int id2,
                            EventHandler * h = 0 );
        BasicButton * AddBasicButton( char * filename, int id,
                                EventHandler * h = NULL );

        int Draw( int y_pos );

        // MFC Overrides
        DECLARE_MESSAGE_MAP()
        afx_msg void OnNcDestroy();
        afx_msg BOOL OnEraseBkgnd(CDC* pDC);

        // member variables
    private:
        Group * m_childGroups[ MAX_CHILD_GROUPS ];
        Widget * m_childWidgets[ MAX_CHILD_WIDGETS ];
        WidgetBank * m_widgetBank;     // a pointer to the parent widgetbank

        CButton m_header;
        COLORREF m_color;              // the color of this widget
        int m_top;                     // position of the top of this widget
                                       // in widget bank
```

```
        int m_prevPos;                  // used for positioning groups when
                                        // drawing
        bool m_status;                  // is this widget currently
                                        //   expanded?
        unsigned int m_numChildGroups;  // number of subgroups contained in
                                        // this group
        unsigned int m_numChildWidgets; // number of child widgets in this
                                        //   group
        int m_level;                    // how many levels deep is this
                                        //   nested?
};
```

The `EventHandler` is a basic callback class, with a purely virtual function called `UIEvent()`. To use an event handler with a widget, you make a child class of `EventHandler` for the class that you need to use a callback from, instantiate a copy in your class, and then override the `UIEvent()` function to be your callback. Make sure you include a parent pointer back from your `EventHandler` child class, so the callback can have the access it needs. When you set up a widget button, you give it a button ID. When the button is pressed, it will call the `UIEvent()` function and pass in the button ID. Your overridden event function can then use the button ID to determine what it wants to do.

Moving right along, we come to the actual types of widgets themselves. Each one will be discussed in turn, and then a small sample file will be shown that then implements each type within a program.

BasicButton

The `basicbutton` is the simplest of widgets. It allows you to put a label on a button, and use it to set off a callback event. Listing 27.3 shows its header. As you can see, it's really just a wrapper for an MFC `CButton` that a widget can access.

LISTING 27.3   `BasicButton` header file.

```
class BasicButton : public Widget
{
public:
    BasicButton( EventHandler * eventHandler = 0 );
    ~BasicButton(void);
    void Create( char * label, int id, CWnd* pWin, int pos );
    void Draw();
    EventHandler * m_eventHandler;
```

```
        DECLARE_MESSAGE_MAP()
    protected:
        virtual BOOL OnCommand(WPARAM wParam, LPARAM lParam);

    private:
        CButton m_button;
    };
```

Watcher

A Watcher is a templated widget (although right now it's only implemented for int and float variable types) that just shows you the value of a variable; you can't change it from the widget itself. Wacthers are useful for constantly updating variables that wouldn't make sense to try and edit while the game is running since the game would immediately blow away your changes. Listing 27.4 shows the header file.

LISTING 27.4 Watcher header file.

```
template <class T>
class Watcher: public Widget
{
public:
    Watcher( int & watch);
    Watcher( float & watch);
    ~Watcher(void);
    void Create( CString label, CRect r, CWnd* pWin );
    void Draw();
    void Update();

private:
    CStatic m_label;
    CStatic m_watch;
    T & m_val;
    int m_frameCount;       // frame counter
    int m_updateInterval;   // update every this many frames
};
```

RadioButton

Radio buttons are standard Windows controls. They allow you to choose exclusively between items. The current implementation only supports two choices, but it could be easily extended to an arbitrary number of choices. The header is in Listing 27.5.

LISTING 27.5 `RadioButton` header file.

```
class RadioButton : public Widget
{
public:
    // constructors
    RadioButton( char * groupName, char * leftName,
        char * rightName, int & val,
        CWnd * pWin, int yPos,
        int id1, int id2,
        EventHandler * h );
    ~RadioButton(void);
    void Draw();

protected:
    virtual BOOL OnCommand(WPARAM wParam, LPARAM lParam);

private:
    // member variables
    CButton m_GroupButton;
    CButton m_LeftButton;
    CButton m_RightButton;

    int & m_val;

    EventHandler * m_eventHandler;
};
```

OnOffButton

The OnOff button widget is a special kind of button that toggles a Boolean value.
It's drawn using the check box type of Windows control, or the standard push button, depending on which style is set. Listing 27.6 shows its header information.

LISTING 27.6 `OnOffButton` header file.

```
class OnOffButton : public Widget {
public:
    // constructors
    OnOffButton( bool & state, EventHandler * eventHandler = 0 );

    // member methods
    void SetStyle( int style );
    void SetCheck( bool checked );
```

```
        int GetCheck();
        void Draw();
        CButton m_button;

        DECLARE_MESSAGE_MAP()
protected:
        virtual BOOL OnCommand(WPARAM wParam, LPARAM lParam);

private:
        // member variables
        bool & myState;

        EventHandler * m_eventHandler;
};
```

ScrubberWidget

A Scrubber is one of the more useful widgets. It allows you to reference a float, int, or char type variable, the value of which is shown in the widget. However, if you click and hold the mouse cursor on the widget, you can drag the values left and right between minimum and maximum values that you set. You can also set the speed of the scrubbing (between slow, regular, and really slow). Listing 27.7 is the header.

LISTING 27.7   ScrubberWidget header file.

```
template <class T>
class ScrubberWidget : public Widget {
public:
        // constructors
        ScrubberWidget(T & var );
        ~ScrubberWidget();

        // member methods
        void Refresh();
        void Draw();
        void OnEditKillFocus();
        void Create( char * label, CWnd* pWin, int pos, SCRUB_SPEED speed =
                     REGULAR_SPEED );
        void SetMin( T min ){ myHoverButton->m_minValue = min; }
        void SetMax( T max ){ myHoverButton->m_maxValue = max; }
        void SetMinMax( T min, T max ){myHoverButton->SetMinMax( min, max );}
```

```
            // Overrides
            afx_msg BOOL OnEraseBkgnd(CDC* pDC);

            // member variables
            CEdit myEdit;
            HoverButton@T: * myHoverButton;

            T &scrubVar;                    // the value being changed

            DECLARE_MESSAGE_MAP()
            afx_msg void OnNcDestroy();
        };
```

Integration Within a Program

To use widgets in your program, follow these simple steps:

1. Include the `WidgetBank.h` file in any class that you want to put widgets onto.
2. Add a function, called `AddWidgets()` to the class. If the class is to be a main class, which will spawn groups as well as widgets, then the function should take a `WidgetBank` pointer. If the class is a "secondary" class, which will instead only have values that you want to use widgets upon, then the function should take a `Group` pointer.
3. Override the `AddWidgets()` call in your class to add whatever bank, groups, or widgets you want, using the examples in Listing 27.8 as guidelines.
4. Figure out how you want to update the `WidgetBank`; it has an `Update()` function that you should call every frame if you want completely updated widgets.

LISTING 27.8   Widget use guideline example.

```
// Our car's EventHandler class. Note that it must
// be created with a pointer to the car so that
// we can interact with it in our UIEvent's switch
// statement. Alternatively, we could also
// simply derive our car class directly from
// an EventHandler, and remove the need for
// a Car pointer.
class CarEventHandler : public EventHandler
{
public:
    CarEventHandler( Car * car ){ m_car = car; }
    virtual void UIEvent ( WPARAM id );
```

```cpp
private:
    Car * m_car;
};


void CarEventHandler::UIEvent(WPARAM id )
{
    switch (id)
    {
    case Car::IGNITION_KEY:
        m_car->StartCar();
        break;
    case Car::WIPERS_CONTROL:
        m_car->StartWipers();
        break;
    case Car::AIR_COND:
        m_car->ToggleAirCond();
        break;
    }
}


class RacingGame
{
public:
    RacingGame(){};
    void AddWidgets( WidgetBank wb );

private:
    Car     m_car;
    Track   m_track;
};


class Car
{
public:
    enum {
        IGNITION_KEY,
        WIPERS_CONTROL,
        AIR_COND
    };
    void AddWidgets( Group * g );
    void StartCar(){ m_engine.Start() }
    void StartWipers(){ m_wipersOnOff = true; }
    void ToggleAirCond( m_air ? m_air = FALSE : m_air = TRUE );
```

```
private:
    Engine  m_engine;
    bool    m_lightsOnOff;
    bool    m_transmission;
    bool    m_air;
    bool    m_wipersOnOff;

    CarEventHandler m_eventHandler;
};

/***********************************************************************
 *    Name:     AddWidgets
 *
 *    Info:     A typical AddWidgets function for a fictitious racing
 *              game. Because the RacingGame object is high level, it
 *              will be adding Groups directly to the widget bank. Actual
 *              Widgets will be added to these groups by the AddWidget
 *              functions of lesser, individual components of the game.
 *
 *    Args:     wb - A pointer to the WidgetBank, which is the top-level
 *              parent of all Widgets and Groups. Again, you don't add
 *              widgets
 *              directly to the widget bank—you only add Groups.
 *
 ***********************************************************************/
void RacingGame::AddWidgets( WidgetBank * wb )
{
    Group * g;

    // Add our first group to the widget bank. AddGroup() returns a
    // pointer to the group it created. You can either use this pointer
    // to add widgets now, or, preferably, pass it to the AddWidgets()
    // function of a lower-level contained class.
    g = wb->AddGroup("Car Properties");

    // Now that we have our group, we'll pass it to the AddWidgets
    // function of our car class object, which is a member of a
    // RacingGame object.
    m_car.AddWidgets( g );

    // That takes care of the car's widgets, so let's add widgets for
    // the race track. We'll make another group, and reassign our
    // group pointer to it
```

```
    g = wb->AddGroup("Track Properties");

    // Again, we pass the newly assigned pointer to the AddWidget()
    // function of a lower level class, this time a RaceTrack object.
    m_track.AddWidgets( g );
}



/*********************************************************************
 *  Name:    AddWidgets
 *
 *  Info:    A typical AddWidgets function for a fictitious car class
 *           to demonstrate the use of widgets. This example only
 *           covers a Car object, but remember that you have to write
 *           an AddWidgets function for any class that you want
 *           to have widgets. From here you might write AddWidgets
 *           functions for your racetrack class, your environmental
 *           class, your AI classes, etc.
 *
 *  Args:    wb - A pointer to a Group. We use a Group pointer
 *           to add the actual Widgets to our application.
 *
 ********************************************************************/
void Car::AddWidgets( Group * g )
{
    // We'll need a pointer to a group. We'll call it pg, for "parent
    // group"—be careful not to confuse it with the group pointer
    // that is being passed into this function.
    Group * pg;

    // Our car class contains an engine object. Let's give it its own
    // widget group. Groups can contain other groups, which gives
    // you a lot of flexibility to organize your widgets.
    pg = AddGroup("Engine Properties");

    // Our engine class has its own AddWidgets function, so we'll
    // pass it our new group pointer

    m_engine.AddWidgets( pg );

    // Our car class has some member variables that would
    // be fun to control while the game runs. We'll hook up
    // some widgets to them now, using the group pointer
```

```
        // that was passed in

        // let's start by adding a widget to control the on/off state
        // of the car's headlights
        g->AddOnOff( "Headlights", m_lightsOnOff );

        // it would be nice to monitor the car's fuel gauge—we'll
        // add a Watcher widget.
        g->AddWatcher( "Fuel Level", m_fuel);

        // We want to tune the car's mass as it drives around, so
        // we'll attach a ScrubberWidget. We're going to catch the
        // ScrubberWidget pointer that this function returns, so that
        // we can change a setting
        ScrubberWidget * sw;
        sw = g->AddScrubber( "Mass", m_mass );

        // We don't want negative or absurdly huge values for the mass of
        // this car during scrubbing, so we'll set some limits on the value
        // using the pointer we got back from the AddScrubber function
        sw->SetMinMax( 0, 10000);

    // Car objects can have automatic or manual transmissions. We'll use
    // a radio button, which allows you to have a caption for the overall
    // control, as well as each actual button.
    g->AddRadio( "Transmission:", "Automatic", "Manual", m_transmission );

    // For our final widget, we'll add a button that starts the car's
    // engine and other systems. Because we want to attach some
    // functionality to this button(it won't do anything if we don't), we
    // pass in an EventHandler object that we've written for Car Objects.
    // We also pass in an enum name for the button. This enum value will
    // become the id number of the widget. When the button is actually
    // pressed by a user, its id number is passed to the EventHandler's
    // UIEvent function, and is used in a switch statement to call that
    // widget's particular code.
    g->AddBasicButton("Start Car", IGNITION_KEY, m_eventHandler );

    // We'll add a few more widgets that use the same EventHandler.
    g->AddBasicButton("Windshield Wipers", WIPERS_CONTROL,
                      m_eventHandler);
    g->AddOnOff("Air Conditioning", m_air, AIR_COND, m_eventHandler );

}
```

Now go forth and populate your game with widgets. You'll quickly find that they'll speed up both debugging and tuning of your game. Some ways that you might extend the widget system, to get even more out of them:

- Wrap all your `AddWidgets()` functions with `#ifdef DEBUG`, or whatever you are using for conditionally compiled code in your project, and then use the preprocessor to conditionally remove all of your widget stuff when you go to release the game.
- Use a `BasicButton` to save or write a text file containing all your widget values. You could serialize all your widget values within a file, and when the game starts back up, it could then initialize all of your variables with the values from the file. In this way, you wouldn't spend an hour tuning a value, and then have to write them all down on paper to adjust your initialization values in game. Before you release the game, however, you would have to transfer all the initial values out of the file (or actually use the file as a configuration script).

SUMMARY

Debugging AI systems can be quite a chore, because they interface with a majority of other game systems, can be filled with specific case code or data, and require complex setups to replicate bugs within. This chapter discussed many issues for AI developers to watch for when debugging game AI engines.

- General AI debugging problems might appear in other people's code, and many concerns can be alleviated by using the distributed AI method.
- Visual debugging provides a variety of information, helps also with game tuning, can provide timing information, can help watch for state oscillation, is especially useful for console development, is useful when debugging scripting languages, and can dovetail nicely into influence mapping systems already in use within a game.
- The widgets library introduced in this chapter provide the user with a general platform for exposing variables to a simple user interface that allows monitoring, as well as changing of a variable's values while the game is running.

28 Conclusions, and the Future

In This Chapter

- What Game AI Will Be in the Future

W e've covered a lot of ground in this book, and the hope is that enough of these techniques have stuck that you're already brimming with ideas that you are going to implement, using a little skeletal code from the CD-ROM, as well as a serious amount of your own hard work and creativity. We've covered everything from the simple to the very complex, both in theory and practice, and along the way discussed an entire paradigm for approaching AI engine design.

During engine design, split up your AI engine tasks into a distributed, layer-based system, using any of the applicable layers:

Perception/Event layer

Behavior layer

Animation layer

Motion layer

Short-term decision making

Long-term decision making

Location-based information layer

For each layer you intend on implementing, consider these eight areas when choosing the type of decision-making techniques:

1. Types of solutions
2. Agent reactivity
3. System realism
4. Genre

5. Content-specific requirements
6. Platform
7. Development limitations
8. Entertainment limitations

WHAT GAME AI WILL BE IN THE FUTURE

The push for better AI opponents will continue. Although online play allows more and more humans to play each other, many people still play only single-person games, lack the time for larger multi-player games, or simply do not go online to search for opponents. These people are still the majority of game players, and they demand increasingly complex and compelling game agents to play against.

AI has, and will continue to become increasingly important to the public opinion of any particular game. Game reviews spend most of their time on the pros and cons of the AI exhibited by the game. The last ten years were almost completely focused on the realm of game graphics, and we can now see the fruition of that effort: huge polygon counts, texturing and lighting that is approaching photographic levels, and overall movie-quality visuals are almost the norm. An equivalent push is now coming into play for the AI systems in games. We will see increasingly complex and creative AI in games, from enemies that learn the human player's style and react accordingly (learning, and opponent modeling), AI opponents that come up with novel solutions to gameplay problems (inference, emergent behavior, or even creativity), even opponents with humanlike moods (emotion).

Another thing that games have suffered from in the past is lack of personality. There are very few differences between opponents. Minor differences that are purely from a statistical point of view (like enemy A being slightly stronger than B, and B being faster). The reason, of course, is that enemies of the past have been more hard-coded (written in a very specific and code-based way), for balancing concerns as well as coding time.

In stark contrast are the enemies in a game written mostly around a learning system with very basic knowledge of the game world, and who would make decisions based more on the game situations that they have been involved with over their lifetimes. *Black & White* uses a system somewhat like this (although the description is overly simplified), and almost no two totem creatures turn out the same, even if played by the same person. The personality of the creatures is determined by such a large number of factors that emergent behaviors and personality traits are inevitable. Implementing enemies using this more "experiential" method leads to a much more personal view of the game's creatures, and an overall more satisfying outlook on the intelligence of the system.

This is analogous to an experience of playing a pen-and-paper role-playing game being much more personal and intelligent than the experience of reading a book about the same game world. Playing the game is interactive, and thus awakens instinctual perceptions within ourselves that give life to the characters and elements that we come across, simply because we are a part of the process. We can interface with the world, change the world, and become a part of the world. Reading the book is merely taking in a story, and although it can seem compelling and to some lesser degree real, it will never be able to answer all the questions we have, or give us a look from another angle.

There is a distancing from the material that is created by the author's mode of writing, as well as his overall storytelling ability. Which is why wholly-scripted AI systems will not completely satisfy us. These are again limited by the scripter, and while adding richness to the gaming experience, will never be equal to the experience of dealing with another intelligent *person.*

AI will also incur the changes to gaming in general, and need to make strides to accommodate them. In the short run, a number of these changes might be in the area of human interfaces. A large number of games are beginning to incorporate voice commands from a headset or microphone. Games may one day offer full speech recognition, as well as translation-type abilities. Also, many games are becoming online, persistent world endeavors. The AI associated with enemies or NPCs in these games might have opportunities for long-view learning and personality building, simply because the game doesn't ever stop.

In the far-flung future of our games, we may one day have full-featured intelligent systems that competently play our games with us, at the difficulty level chosen specifically for each player, with style, creativity, personality, and a degree of *humanity.* Oh, what fun we'll have.

APPENDIX
A

About the CD

The CD-ROM included with this book contains all the source and demonstration programs referenced within the book, as well as some other useful materials. Also, you can refer to the main Charles River Web site (*www.charlesriver.com*) for updates and additional support information.

CONTENTS

Source Code. All the source for the various topics is arranged in subdirectories by chapter of introduction. Each demonstration is compiled using Microsoft Visual C++ 6.0, as well as Visual C++ 2005. Both the "old" and "new" VC++ style of project files are included (the newer Visual Studio uses solutions, the older, used projects). The compiled binaries can be found in the specific output directories.

Figures. All of the figures from the book are included in this directory. They are named the same as they are in the chapters.

Useful Web Bookmarks. Here are a few pages of links to various Web resources, from general to very specific. The links are divided up into categories: ALife, fuzzy logic, general AI Web sites, genetic algorithms, location-based information, neural nets, scripting, various AI links, game source code, and various game AI issues.

Libraries. The CD contains the newest available download of the two libraries used by the demonstration code: the GLUT wrapper for OpenGL, and the Lua language. Of course, you would want to check the Internet for newer versions, but the demos in this book have only been tested with these versions.

SYSTEM REQUIREMENTS

All the demonstration programs on this CD-ROM are minimally taxing on any modern computer. GLUT works on pretty much all versions of Windows (ME, 2000,

XP, Vista), so the demos should compile and run on almost any Windows machine available within the last nine years or so. All the code was written and compiled using Microsoft Windows Visual C++ 6.0 and 2005; GLUT and OpenGL was installed on the machines.

APPENDIX B

References

CHAPTER 1

[Brooks 86] Brooks, R. A robust layered control system for a mobile robot. *IEEE J. Rob. Automation* 2 (1986), pp. 14–23.

[Brooks 98] Brooks, R. A., Breazeal, C. Irie, R., Kemp, C. C., Marjanovic, M., Scassellati, B., Williamson, M. M. *Alternative Essences of Intelligence*. AAAI/IAAI 1998: 961–968.

[Premack 78] Premack, D. G. & Woodruff, G. (1978). Does the chimpanzee have a theory of mind? *Behavioral and Brain Sciences*. 1:515–526.

[Russel 95] Russel, S., Norvig, P., 1995, *Artificial Intelligence: A Modern Approach*, Prentice-Hall, Inc.

[Wimmer 83] Wimmer, H. & Perner, J. (1983). Beliefs about beliefs: Representation and constraining function of wrong beliefs in young children's understanding of deception. *Cognition*, 12, 103–128.

[Woodcock 01] Woodcock, S., Game AI: The state of the industry 2000–2001: It's not just art, it's engineering, *Game Developer*, August 2001: pp. 24–32.

CHAPTER 2

[Reynolds 87] C. Reynolds. Flocks, Herds and Schools: A Distributed Behavioral Model. *Computer Graphics*, 21(4), 1987, pp. 25–34.

[Reynolds 99] Reynolds, C. W. (1999). Steering Behaviors for Autonomous Characters, in the proceedings of Game Developers Conference 1999 held in San Jose, California. Miller Freeman Game Group, San Francisco, California. pp. 763–782.

CHAPTER 22

[Back 93] Back, T., Hoffneister, F., Schwefel, H., *Applications of Evolutionary Algorithms, extended edition*. University of Dortmund. August 1993.

[MSV 93] Mühlenbein, H. & Schlierkamp-Voosen, D. Predictive models for the breeder genetic algorithm. *Evol. Comput.*, 1:25–49, 1993.

[Hillis 91] Hillis, W. D. Co-evolving parasites improve simulated evolution as an optimization procedure, *Emergent Computation*, pp. 228–234. The MIT Press (1991).

[Back 92] Back, T., (1992). The interaction of mutation rate, selection, and self-adaptation within a genetic algorithm. In R. Manner and B. Manderick (Eds.), *Parallel Problem Solving from Nature* (pp. 85–94). Amsterdam: Elsevier.

CHAPTER 24

[Reynolds 87] C. Reynolds. Flocks, Herds and Schools: A Distributed Behavioral Model. *Computer Graphics,* 21(4), 1987, pp. 25–34.

[Newell 61] Newell, A. & Simon, H. (1961), GPS, a program that simulates thought, *in* H. Billing, ed., *Lernende Automaten,* R. Oldenbourg, Munich, Germany, pp. 109–124.

[Zadeh 65] L. A. Zadeh, *Fuzzy sets,* Information and Control, Volume 8: pp. 338–353, 1965.

[Kant 97] Kantrowitz, M., Horstkotte, E., Joslyn, C., "Answers to Frequently Asked Questions about Fuzzy Logic and Fuzzy Expert Systems," comp.ai.fuzzy, 1997.

Index

UNIVERSITY OF WOLVERHAMPTON
LEARNING & INFORMATION SERVICES